# The Germans and the East

Central European Studies

Charles W. Ingrao, senior editor
Gary B. Cohen, editor

# The Germans and the East

Edited by Charles Ingrao and Franz A. J. Szabo

Purdue University Press
West Lafayette, Indiana

**Library of Congress Cataloging-in-Publication Data**
The Germans and the East / edited by Charles Ingrao and Franz A.J. Szabo.
    p. cm. -- (Central European studies)
  Chiefly papers presented at a conference held Sept. 17-20, 2002, at the
University of Alberta.
  Includes bibliographical references and index.
  ISBN-13: 978-1-55753-443-9 (alk. paper)
  ISBN-10: 1-55753-443-8 (alk. paper)
  1. Germans--Europe, Eastern--History. 2. Germans--Europe, Central--
History. 3. Europe, Eastern--History. 4. Europe, Central--History. I. Ingrao,
Charles W. II. Szabo, Franz A. J.
  DJK28.G4G468 2007
  947'.000431--dc22

                                                         2007001055

# Contents

# Introduction

## ❖ Franz A. J. Szabo and Charles Ingrao ❖

The title of this volume, "The Germans and the East," masks numerous analytical difficulties and requires some qualification, which even the addition of an elaborate subtitle would not solve. When we speak of "Germans" do we speak of German-speakers or of the citizens of a state that calls itself "Germany"? For that matter, even when speaking of "Germany" we must bear in mind that there is a considerable difference between what was colloquially referred to as "Germany" in medieval and early modern times (The Holy Roman Empire of the German Nation) and the state of "Germany" (or the German Reich) that emerged in the 1866–1871 period, and which continues to exist to this day in modified form as the Federal Republic of Germany. In 1910, for example, nearly 10 percent of the population of the German Reich was not German-speaking, while nearly a quarter of all German-speakers in Europe lived outside the boundaries of that Reich.[1] To this day nearly 15 percent of all German-speakers in Europe live in states other than the one that calls itself "Germany." Indeed, even an "imagined community of German speakers" poses difficulties as the argument has been well made that despite all international standardization efforts German remains a polycentric language, not merely in dialect but in structure and vocabulary as well.[2] To speak of "Germans" and "Germany," in short, means to enter into the debate on German identity.

That debate is complicated by the general tendency of the historical literature to use the word "German" to describe both citizens of the post-1871 German state and people who spoke various forms of German. It is indeed lamentable, as has been rightly pointed out, that the word "Germanophone" has not taken hold in the same way "Francophone" and "Anglophone" have, for the use of the word "German" in contemporary usage "still bears unmistakable traces of its origins in a particular definition of German nationalism."[3] That nationalist narrative, particularly in its post-1871 incarnation, has always sought to obfuscate the fact that what was proclaimed in the Palace of Versailles in January 1871 was merely *a* German Empire,

1

not *the* German Empire. In the lengthy and acrimonious debates on the title the new emperor was to adopt there was still a clear sense of the difference between the "Emperor of Germany" and a "German Emperor"[4] (which was the title chosen), and this uncertainty about the identity of the new state was well reflected in its national symbols.

The rejection by Crown Prince and later Emperor Frederick of the double-headed eagle of the Holy Roman Empire for the coat of arms of the new German Empire and the adoption of a one-headed eagle with a Prussian eagle on its breast shield surrounded by the Prussian Order of the Black Eagle was only the first sign. The "German Reich" did not adopt a national flag until some twenty years after its proclamation, and when it did so, it deliberately retreated to the ambiguity of adding a red parallel bar to the Prussian black-and-white rather than opt for the pan-German colors of black-red-gold of the *Burschenschaften* and of the revolutionaries of 1848.[5] The national anthem remained the Prussian "Heil Dir im Siegerskranz" sung to the tune of Britain's "God Save the King," and a unified postal system with all the symbolism of "national" stamps was never adopted.

That "the conquest of Germany by Prussia"—or at least the conquest of part of the German Confederation by Prussia—was followed, in the late A.J.P. Taylor's felicitous phrase, by "the conquest of Prussia by Germany,"[6] was well reflected not only by the new destabilizing dynamism of Wilhelmine Germany but by the Weimar Republic as well. The latter did not shy away from the pan-German symbolism of the revolutionary colors of 1848, or even the appropriated Austrian imperial anthem with its revised revolutionary pan-German text by Hoffmann von Fallersleben. Curiously even a chastened Federal Republic of Germany, both in its "West German" and current incarnations, could not bring itself to do without these suggestive and misleading symbols that effectively conflate notions of "German" and "Germany" and appropriate many of the assumptions of the pan-German nationalist narrative. That this is frequently done innocently and thoughtlessly—often much to the consternation of Germany's German-speaking neighbors[7]—only illustrates the difficulties of terminology faced by this volume.

The problems and issues addressed by the essays that follow, therefore, proceed from different understandings of "German" and "Germany" through the ages: from the Germanic tribes and German "stem-duchies" of the Middle Ages through the highly decentralized and multiethnic Holy Roman Empire of late medieval and early modern times and the German Confederation of the 1815–1866 period to the various forms of the German state from 1871 to the present. It thus encompasses both the relationship of German-speakers to their eastern non-German speaking neighbors, as well as that of "Germany" both to those neighbors and to German-speakers living beyond the borders of the modern German state. In addition, some attention is also paid to the German perception of the "East" during this unfolding relationship.

The traditional description of Germans living within the post-1871 German Reich was *"Reichsdeutsche,"* while those that belonged to the Germanophonie beyond the borders were deemed members not of the *"Reich"* but of the *"Volk"* (people) and thus called *"Volksdeutsche."* The latter included all German-speakers living within the ethno-linguistic continuum adjoining Germany—viz., the Austrian Empire and Switzerland—as well as those that lived in various German-language speech islands dispersed throughout Central and Eastern Europe. Germanophones in these speech islands were often referred to by regional names: Baltic Germans, Volhynian Germans, Transylvanian Saxons, Danube Swabians, Dobruja Germans, Bessarabian Germans, Volga Germans, and so on. To complicate matters, the German national-ist narrative not only looked at all *"Volksdeutsche"* as inhabiting a so-called "German linguistic ground (*Deutscher Sprachboden*)" but at much of the non-German speaking surrounding countryside as "German cultural ground (*Deutscher Kulturboden*)." The latter effectively subsumed all Czechs, Slovenes, Latvians and Estonians as well as substantial chunks of Hungary in the German cultural orbit.

This complex reality as it stood before the brutal mass murders, ethnic cleans-ing and "population transfers" of the Second World War and its aftermath (roughly 1939–1949) was centuries in the making. Though Germanic tribes had inhabited lands as far east as the Vistula valley in antiquity, the dramatic migration period in the fourth and fifth centuries (known in German as the *Völkerwanderung*) brought them ever westward until they had overrun the entire western half of the former Ro-man Empire. In the process lands in the east were abandoned, so that by the early sixth century the Germanic linguistic frontier had retreated west of the Elbe River and the Bohemian mountains. With the emergence of the Franks as the dominant tribe of the West and the establishment of a Frankish empire under the Merovingians and Carolingians from the fifth to the ninth centuries, Germanic Western Europe was stabilized. Under the greatest of its monarchs, Charles the Great, Frankish policy gradually oriented itself to the east. The conquest of the Saxons brought the Frankish empire to the Elbe frontier, and the integration of Bavaria and a long confrontation with the Avars in the Danube valley pushed the empire into present-day Austria and Hungary. Slavic tribes between the Elbe and the Oder as well as the Czechs in Bohe-mia and Moravia and Croats to the south hastened to recognize Frankish suzerainty and became dependencies of the empire.

The decline of the Carolingian Empire in the ninth and tenth centuries as well as the emergence of new threats in the form of Norsemen and Magyars saw a reverse of many of Charles's gains, but under the new Saxon dynasty these threats were subdued and a new eastward momentum began. Already under Henry I Bohemia again acknowledged the overlordship of the East Frankish Kingdom. Under Otto I a series of marches and bishoprics were established between the Elbe and the Oder, and in the southeast establishment of the Duchy of Carinthia and the strengthening and expansion of the Eastern March laid the foundations for the future Austria. The pillaging that accompanied the forcible conversion of the Slavs between the Elbe and the Oder, however, led to fierce uprisings that forced a Germanic retreat to the Elbe for well over a generation. Gradually the ground was reconquered, and by the twelfth century expansion and colonization in the northeast was vigorously resumed by some of the powerful princes of northern Germany. Motivated by a mixture of defensive anxiety, confessional zeal and a thirst for new arable land, German settlers penetrated to the lower Oder valley and along the Baltic coast of Pomerania. Crusading orders, such as the Knights of the Sword and the Teutonic Knights, began to operate in the Baltic lands in support of missionaries and colonists, and despite some serious setbacks, by the end of the thirteenth century they had conquered and colonized Prussia, and established strong positions in Courland, Livonia and Estonia. The German grip in the Baltic was strengthened by the commercial activities of the Hanseatic League, a cooperative association of port cities that controlled the mouths of most important rivers and monopolized all Baltic trade.

From the late twelfth century a new trend encouraging German settlement eastward began to manifest itself: now the medieval rulers of Bohemia, Poland and Hungary increasingly began to invite German settlers to their lands to exploit new agricultural areas, establish mining operations and develop new cities. In the subsequent two centuries important German-language enclaves were created in Transylvania (Transylvanian Saxons) and in Szepes County in northern Hungary (Zipser Germans), the upper Oder valley became Germanized, and the kings of Bohemia (particularly Otakar II Přemysl [1253–1278] and Charles IV of Luxembourg [1346–1378]) strongly encouraged German settlement in their domains. Many towns in Bohemia, Hungary and Poland saw a growth of the German component in their population, the most striking symptom of which was the dramatic spread of so-called "German Law," which enshrined municipal privileges, throughout the cities of Central Europe. A combination of nativist resentment (particularly the Hussite uprising in Bohemia) and a dramatic drop of the population due to the Black Death halted this momentum, and the medieval German colonization of lands to the east (*Ostkolonisation*) gradually drew to a halt by 1400.

Though the Reformation period can be said to have contributed a small dimension to German eastward migration in the form of confessional dissidents (mostly Anabaptists of various denominations) who fled the Holy Roman Empire and found refuge in Eastern Europe (frequently retaining archaic regional dialects for centuries[8]), the next conscious colonization phase came in the eighteenth century. This phase was decidedly state-directed by several generations of Austrian Habsburgs and by Catherine II of Russia. Habsburg colonization efforts came in the first instance in the wake of the reconquest of Hungary from the Ottoman Turks at the end of the seventeenth and early eighteenth century. Large swaths of southern Hungary had been left depopulated by the conflict and successive Habsburg monarchs began an aggressive programme of resettling these areas, sometimes with South Slav refugees from the Balkans, but even more frequently with German colonists, largely from southwest Germany, who subsequently came to be known as "Danube Swabians." Counter-Reformation policies of banning Austrian "Crypto-Protestants" to remote regions of the Habsburg Empire (largely Transylvania) also continued well into the 1770s, and after the first partition of Poland an additional wave of German settlers was lured to the new Habsburg provinces of Galicia and Bukovina. At the same time Catherine II of Russia began an aggressive campaign to bring German colonists to Russia, initially to the lower Volga region and to the Ukraine and eventually also to Bessarabia. A final German colonization burst came in the 1860s, when German settlers bought out financially hard-pressed Polish landowners in the Volhynia region of Russian Poland.

This centuries-long development created a "Germany" that did not cover the Germanophone linguistic continuum in Central Europe and that left a checkerboard of German speech islands throughout Central and Eastern Europe by the later nineteenth century. In the era of mounting nationalist passions in the nineteenth and twentieth centuries these realities were to form a fundamental element not only in the relationship of German-speakers with their eastern neighbors but also in the relationship of the post-1871 German state first with the Habsburg Monarchy and then with the successor states of Central Europe. The two issues, though separate, tended to become conflated in the era of the world wars, particularly when Nazi-German imperialism began to exploit the "*Volksdeutsche*" card in the pursuit of its territorial ambitions. The slogan "Home to the Reich (*Heim ins Reich*)" was applied to the contiguous linguistic language area for public consumption, but as the destruction of rump Czechoslovakia in March 1939 demonstrated, the real agenda was the full annexation of the so-called "*Deutscher Kulturboden.*" What is more, school atlases now no longer simply referred to "*Deutscher Sprachboden*" or "*Deutscher Kulturboden*" but to a "zone of German-language communication in Eastern Europe (*Gebiet der deutschen Verkehrsprache im Osten*),"[9] which covered territory well into Russia proper and presaged Nazi ideas of a "Greater German Empire." The racial premises that underlay this ambition, combined with a ruthless disposition for social engineering, led to policies of extermination and population transfer of such brutality that it is small wonder that in the immediate postwar environment a similar fate would be visited upon German-speakers outside the boundaries of the two new Germanies, Austria and Switzerland.

The historical burden of the Nazi past and the expulsion of German-speakers from Central and Eastern Europe, of course, left a bitter legacy and fundamentally affected the nature of the relationship of the two Germanies and Austria with their eastern neighbors. That these realities would affect historical perspectives of both

German-speakers and non-German speakers about the thousand-year history of "the Germans and the East" is therefore hardly surprising. However, it is precisely for this reason that the subject bears scholarly revisiting at regular intervals, particularly as Europe attempts to move to greater integration and to overcoming the burdens of its past.

This volume analyzes and examines in detail critical aspects of this long historical development. It is a product of an ongoing international colloquium series of European and North American historians, which originated in a suggestion by the late Karl Otmar Freiherr von Aretin to Charles Ingrao in 1980 to bring together North American and German scholars of the Holy Roman Empire for a conference. That initial meeting, held in Chicago in 1984, was sponsored by the *Journal of Modern History*. Entitled "Politics and Society in the Holy Roman Empire, 1500–1806," it resulted in a special supplementary volume of the journal shortly thereafter.[10] The second conference, sponsored by the Institut für Europäische Geschichte of Mainz, West Germany, in September 1986 focused on Estates and Society in the Holy Roman Empire.[11] Subsequent conferences alternated between Germany and North America, and gradually evolved to include scholars from other countries as well. To date over 100 scholars from eight European countries, Canada and the United States have taken part, and the focus has enlarged to include the Habsburg Monarchy. The third conference's theme, "State and Society in Early Modern Austria," also saw this enlarged dimension embodied in the institutional sponsors: The Center for Austrian Studies and the Center for Early Modern History of the University of Minnesota. The subsequent volume was the first to be published by Purdue University Press[12]—a tradition continued in the present volume. A 1996 conference, "Reich oder Nation: Mitteleuropa, 1780–1815," was jointly sponsored by the Institut für Europäische Geschichte in Mainz under its new head, Heinz Duchhardt, and the University of Halle in September 1996 and its proceedings published in 1998.[13]

In 1998 a new Canadian Centre for Austrian and Central European Studies (recently renamed the Wirth Institute for Austrian and Central European Studies) was established at the University of Alberta in Edmonton, Canada, which soon agreed to become a partner in the colloquium series and to engage other Canadian institutions in the process. With the cooperation of the University of Toronto-DAAD Joint Initiative in German Studies the "Germans and the East" project was mapped out in a series of roundtable discussions at the University of Toronto in April 2001, while the conference itself was held at the University of Alberta on 17–20 September 2002. We want to express our gratitude in particular to Heinz Duchhardt, head of Mainz's Institute für Europäische Geschichte, and Scott Eddie, former director of the UofT-DAAD Joint Initiative, for their labors in helping to organize both the roundtable and the subsequent colloquium, and we also want to thank the sponsors of both events, particularly the University of Alberta's Wirth Endowment, the Deutsche

Forschungsgemeinschaft, the UofT-DAAD Joint Initiative and the Canadian Centre for German and European Studies at York University in Toronto. A glance at the table of contents of this volume will reveal that the theme under consideration is arranged into subsections, each of which was organized by section leaders specifically responsible for recruiting appropriate contributors. These included Klaus Zernack for the medieval period, Charles Ingrao for the early modern period, Horst Haselsteiner for the nineteenth century,[14] Ronald Smelser for the era of the two world wars and Günter Bischof for the postwar period. We are grateful to them for hard work in assembling contributors and preparing introductions for each section, as we are to Béla Bardo, Martin David, Robert Forrest, Pieter Judson, David Pickus, Karl Roider and John Swanson, each of whom subsequently provided important coverage for key subjects that had not been covered in the original conference.

# Notes

1. Out of the German Reich's population of 64.6 million in 1910, approximately 60 million were German-speakers, while the rest had Polish, French, Danish or Sorb as their mother tongue. Another 16.5 million German-speakers were to be found outside of the German Empire (not counting emigrants to North and South America, Australia, and other parts of the world). These included 12,010,669 in Austria-Hungary, 2,599,154 in Switzerland, 1,813,717 in the Russian Empire, and over 50,000 in the Balkans and Italy.
2. Hans Moser, "Deutsch als plurizentrische Sprache—das österreichische Deutsch," in Ingeborg Ohnheiser, Manfred Kienpointer and Helmut Kalb, eds., *Sprachen in Europa: Sprachsituation und Sprachpolitik in europäischen Ländern* (Innsbruck, 1999), pp. 13–31.
3. Katherine Arens, "For Want of a Word…: The Case for *Germanophone*," *Die Unterrichtspraxis* 32, 2 (1999), 130–142 (quote on p. 130).
4. Otto Pflanze, *Bismarck and the Development of Germany*, Vol. 1: *The Period of Unification, 1815–1871* (Princeton, NJ, 1963), pp. 490–497.
5. Cf. Harold James, *A German Identity, 1770 to the Present* (London, 1989, pb. edition cited here, 2000), p. 89.
6. A.J.P. Taylor, *The Course of German History: A Survey of the Development of Germany since 1815* (London, 1946) (pb. edition with a new preface, New York, 1962). The phrases are used in the chapter headings of chapters 6 and 8 respectively.
7. A catalogue of such tendencies was compiled by Gabriele Holzer, in *Verfreundete Nachbarn: Österreich—Deutschland, Ein Verhältnis* (Vienna, 1995).
8. The Hutterites form a classic example, retaining their Tyrolese dialect through a centuries-long peripatetic migration from Tyrol to Moravia, Hungary, Ukraine and eventually North America. Cf. Herefried Scheer, "The Largest Austrian Dialect Speech-island in North America," in Franz A.J. Szabo, ed., *Austrian Immigration to Canada: Select Essays* (Ottawa, 1996), pp. 93–102.
9. Max Pehle, Hans Silberborth and Martin Iskraut, eds., *F.W. Putzgers Historischer Schul-Atlas*, 52nd edition (Bielefeld and Leipzig, 1935), p. 140.
10. *Journal of Modern History* 58 (1986) Supplement, ed. Charles Ingrao.
11. The colloquium proceedings were published in Georg Schmidt, ed., *Stände und Gesellschaft im alten Reich* (Stuttgart, 1989).

12. Charles W. Ingrao. ed., *State and Society in Early Modern Austria* (West Lafayette, IN, 1994).
13. Heinz Duchardt and Andreas Kunz, eds., *Reich oder Nation? Mitteleuropa 1780–1815* (Mainz, 1998).
14. After the conference the task of completing this section was taken over by Charles Ingrao and Lothar Höbelt, who authored the introduction.

# The Middle Ages

## ❖ Klaus Zernack ❖

Ever since the Carolingian period people the locals called "Niemcy" have migrated into the Slavic world, and during their thousand-year history in Eastern Europe they have not always met with rejection. On the contrary, they were mostly able to settle and assimilate in the East. What we call "German history" is therefore the result of a cultural development that ran from West to East and that was a characteristic trend in Europe in general. To a great extent this led to a demographic intermixing and a structural permeation of the "Niemcy" in the Slavic, Baltic, and Magyar populations living along the western border of Eastern Europe. In other words, one could say that "Germany" grew out of the Carolingian East Frankish Kingdom between the Rhine and the Elbe by producing its eastern half on colonized Slavic and to some extent Baltic land. Thus the genesis of the German Empire took place within the perimeters of Europe's "eastward expansion" (*Osterweiterung*). It consisted, on the one hand, of Christian state-building in the Slavic-Hungarian East in the ninth and tenth centuries, and on the other—beginning in the twelfth century—of the migration and resettlement of the population from the older colonized areas west of the Elbe, the Bohemian Forest and the Enns. With a more developed legal framework and new economic methods these emigrants advanced the medieval development of the land in the East. In general, one can regard this as a process of cultural Westernization. This trend was certainly tied to the territorial expansion of German rule, but it was not limited to the eastward expanding borders of the Holy Roman Empire. Rather, continuous new waves of German miners, peasants, craftsmen and merchants, as well as knights and clergymen, emigrated and permanently settled in countries neighboring Germany in the East and Southeast. Jewish emigrants from the West also took part in this migration process.

Until well past the middle of the nineteenth century Germans were still coming to Eastern Europe—until the creation of a German Empire in 1871 brought about a turning point and the industrial West became a demographic magnet. It was only in the twentieth century that the flow of populations from West to East was totally reversed, no longer following structural demands but instead political opportunism—and this with a rate of acceleration, brutality and totality that were particular to the twentieth century. The experience of two world wars drastically changed the image of the Germans into one of horror; for the people of Eastern Europe they were the "Huns" of modern history. In German-occupied Eastern Europe during the Second World War, the entire Jewish population fell victim to the incomparable crimes of the Holocaust.

Following Germany's war of annihilation, in a terrible act of expulsion German descendants who had settled in Eastern Europe over the course of almost a thousand years were forced back over the same border along which migration had begun in the Middle Ages. Only very few of them remained in the land their forefathers had settled—for the most part Germans in Romania and a smaller number of them in Silesia. The Germans living in Russia were forced out of their eastern Slavic home and resettled further east within the Soviet Union.

This undoing of Jewish and German settlement in the East was the result of modern nationalism and its ethnic radicalism that climaxed with the racist delusions of German National Socialism. On the other hand, the emigration and settlement of "Niemcy" in Eastern Europe in the Middle Ages and in the early modern period were elements of a developmental process and are related to the phenomenon of *Ostkolonisation* ("colonization of the East"), which can only be understood in its larger historical perspective. From this perspective "colonization" refers to an essential element in the construction of Europe itself, as well as Europe's historical influence on northern Asia—that is, in the expansion of the Eurasian empire of Russia.[1] *Ostkolonisation* thus refers to the cultural development that spread eastward beginning in the Carolingian period, and in general it can be said that, compared to the ancient cultural world, all countries outside this model of civilization were in need of colonization. Their historical need to catch up brought them into the dynamic of a universal spreading of culture. What the Western European countries in the land of the former Roman Empire had gained through cultural continuity, the eastern regions of Europe attained through the process of colonization and development. Thus European history after antiquity is characterized by a colonization process from west to east, and the so-called *deutsche Ostsiedlung* (Germans settling in the East) constitutes only one aspect of this process in the High Middles Ages and the early modern period.[2] After World War I, it was Polish historians[3] who drew attention to the universal historical relevance of European east-west relations. The history of the eastern half of Europe was seen as the history of its cultural Europeanization. Understood in this broader context, *Ostkolonisation*—that is, Europe's coming into being from west to east—could in their view not be construed as a "great deed of the German people,"[4] as had been the tradition of German "*Ostforschung*."[5] This interpretation, which puts the history of the

European-north Asian region into a different context, yields a better understanding of the fact that, in the cultural process of colonization, European nations are mutually constituted. It is thus not the cultural championing of any putative "great German deed" that is important, but rather the process of cultural transfer, reception, and transmission. In this way the zones in which culture is transformed and transferred become interesting objects of research in colonization studies.[6]

In connection with the emigration and settlement of Germans in the East Central European and Eastern European world, the following zones of transformation and transfer can be posited as a starting point:

1. During the eighth century in the southeastern border region of the Carolingian Empire, various forms of organization and administration of the *Ostland* could be observed in conjunction with Bavarian emigration following the defeat of the Avar Kingdom. The area between the Enns River and the Vienna Woods, which later became *Ostarrichi* (as the Bavarian Eastern March was known after 996)—became an important field for the Frankish strategy of frontier marches and the Bavarian settlement promoted by it.[7]

2. The area farther north between the Elbe and the Oder Rivers, between the Saale and the Bober and between the Baltic Sea and the Sudeten Ridge was also an important zone that was included early on in the political reach of the East Frankish-German Empire. Here the Elbe Marches of the Ottonian period were transformed after Christianization in the twelfth century into eastern German territorial states such as Mecklenburg, Brandenburg, Meißen, etc. These territories should be regarded as the first zone of *Germania Slavica*.[8]

3. While the political expansion of German territorial power soon ran up against the borders of established states such as Poland, Bohemia, and Hungary, the emigration of settlers continued and led to a sharp increase in population in the previously colonized lands. The population for the whole of Europe is estimated to have grown from 42 million in the year 1000 to 73 million in 1300.[9] The monarchs in East Central Europe were interested in the further development of their land and recruited foreign settlers to cultivate it. In the western regions of Poland that embraced Silesia, the middle Oder Valley, and Pomerania emigration was so heavy that the Slavic population mixed with the emigrants and gave rise toward the end of the Middle Ages to new, ethni-

cally mixed German-speaking peoples referred to as "*Neustämme.*" Thus an "East Germany" was created along and east of the Oder, which we can regard as the second zone of a *Germania Slavica*. In the area of East Prussia, the colonial state-building of the Teutonic Knights led to an analogous result, the creation of a new German-Baltic people, the Prussians.[10]

4. German peasants and townspeople had also emigrated to areas east of these two zones of *Germania Slavica,* though not in strong enough numbers to have constituted new peoples. Instead, these settlers inserted themselves into the states of East Central Europe in the form of isolated German settlements with a discrete legal status.[11]

5. Regardless of whether they were instigated by German emigrants or not, the innovative institutions of medieval land development *iure theutonico* continued to spread. The Hanseatic League must be seen as one particular product of this process of colonization, which contributed to the special regional character of the Baltic Sea area.[12]

It was within the boundaries of the Polish-Lithuanian Commonwealth that the colonial model of structural improvement via colonization was carried further east into the old Lithuanian-East Slavic principalities. This began in the fifteenth century and was completed with the judicial and legislative system of the so-called "Golden Age" of the Polish-Lithuanian aristocratic republic in the sixteenth century. In this context one thinks of Zygmund August's *Hufenreform* of 1558, and the Lublin Act of Union of 1569. A colonizing Polish-Lithuanian-Ruthenian Commonwealth, influenced by the political culture of Poland, thus emerged through which wide segments of East-Slavic Orthodox Eastern Europe were included in the course of this west-east cultural development. That is why Kiev, Smolensk, and Vitebsk were endowed with Magdeburg city law, but not Moscow and Novgorod.[13]

All the other zones were influenced by *jus theutonicum* in the course of their civilization. Structural improvement was achieved through the creation of a uniform class of peasants who labored for landowners, but who, within these parameters, had a constitution granting them property rights. This type of East Central European agrarian constitution has been characterized as the most advanced stage of feudalism. In the context of constitutional history, establishment of the so-called *sunder dorfrecht*[14] helped create the elements of mature feudalism, which Otto Hintze characterized as a work-free pension for knights as well as their order's participation at the level of local governance.[15] This was the basis for aristocratic society's expansion under the banner of advanced freedoms for its class, which found particular expression in East Central Europe during the late Middles Ages and the early modern period.[16]

In a different way, the consciousness of belonging to a township, though not nationalist in nature, provoked a more emphatic articulation of national sentiments among the aristocracy and, eventually, the clergy.[17] This can be explained in two ways. On the one hand, the first urban communities were recruited almost exclusively from German immigrants, who adapted to close quarters in the towns by forming a community with special rights. On the other hand, belonging to a network of simultaneously and uniformly founded towns allowed the inhabitants to develop a consciousness of being part of a greater state oriented around the crown, or even a consciousness of something beyond the level of the state. This was not really a national feeling, which was more clearly articulated in East Central Europe in the fourteenth and fifteenth centuries by the newly arrived Slavic-speaking citizens. But the German townspeople's consciousness of belonging to an empire stood in stark contrast to the rural patriotism of the aristocracy, who were pushed further and further towards a politicization of their class as well as an ideological solidification of their position as the only representative of a *gens Polonica* in opposition to the rulers and the towns. Xenophobia was thus a correlative to the formation of the aristocratic concept of the nation (i.e., the political nation). The Polish clergy likewise emphasized the national differences between the *gens Polonica* and the *gens Teutonica*, who had immigrated into the country. The language of their sermons shows clear evidence of this.

Burghers first became truly nationalized in the sixteenth century following their Polinization. Prior to this period, towns with a primarily German and Jewish population saw in the king a protection against the magnates and, thus, were a stabilizing factor for the monarchy. Their far-reaching contacts and their wide horizon—one needs only think of the rebellion of the Prussian towns against the German Order in 1454—contributed to their successful political expansion.

In Bohemia in the first half of the fifteenth century, a demonstration of medieval xenophobia found its way into literary expression: the chronicle of Dalimil exhibited an aristocratic nationalism in the form of an unrestrained hatred of Germans. Around the same time, a language-based nationalism grounded in early humanism appeared among the Hussites in the form of praise for the beauty, literariness, and dignity of the Czech language. Both these expressions of nationalism prevailed in the developed townships spreading across Bohemia. The close quarters of the cities and towns and their particular social dynamics, combined with the proximity of two language groups, led to a systematic or systems-theory confirmation of the thesis that the horizon of a "secondary nation" was being established. In contrast to the "primary nation" of the political elites, this secondary nation is a socially more open "system" determined by the conditions of urban societies. In the search for an identity, the difference between self and other—the foreign other—became relevant again. Occasionally in Bohemian literature a sharp anti-German sentiment flared up, such as in Dalimil's *Dictamen*.[18]

But after the populist-nationalistic Hussite Wars, Bohemia experienced quieter times during the Utraquist era. This was also true for Bohemia during the Reformation. Now the building of a political nation of two peoples in the sense of a republic organized by social order and bound together by the *natio-gens* structure (similar to the aristocratic republics of Poland-Lithuania and Hungary) once again gained the upper hand until the Bohemian uprising of 1618. These universalistic republican movements oriented around social orders always coincided with a decline in the political significance of cities and towns.

The *Rzeczpospolita obojga narodów* of Poland-Lithuania was in fact already a republic of many peoples, one with the structure of *natio-gens: Natione Polonus-gente Prussicus.* This could be applied, for example, to Copernicus as well as to many people of Danzig. The assertion of the citizens of Danzig in their tariff dispute with King Wladyslaw IV in the mid-seventeenth century that they were not Poles but Germans in Prussia (*non sumus Poloni, sed Germani in Borussia*),[19] can be understood in this context. What this meant was that one felt at home in the old Poland, a quality expressed from the sixteenth to eighteenth centuries in the positive stereotype of the *heimatlicher Ausländer* (a foreigner who feels at home). It is a concept that can be applied to all of East Central Europe, where speaking a different language in the fully formed aristocratic state was no longer cause for discrimination. As Benedykt Zientara has argued in his reflections on the problem of language, nation-building and foreigners, a common language

> plays a role in different stages of the formation of a national community. This is certainly true for the initial stages, as language helps to differentiate self from other, often in conflicts with foreign-language-speaking external enemies. But language can be replaced in later stages of nation-building by other ties, if these ties constitute a sufficient basis for common interests in a multi-lingual population. The multi-lingual national communities of medieval Holland, contemporary Belgium and Switzerland came into being in this way. In the Polish aristocratic republic and the old Hungarian monarchy, the language differences did not hinder the formation of a strong national consciousness—which was, of course, limited to the *Szlachta*. But multi-lingual nations are less closed and more subject to centrifugal forces than mono-lingual nations; this explains the aspiration toward a unified language in nation-states.[20]

The introduction of the notion of the nation-state as the "highest value" turned everything upside-down, though some of what it brought forth in terms of the "re-foreignization" of the "Niemcy" who had made Eastern Europe their home had already begun to announce itself earlier, such as in the intolerance toward "foreign" confessions during the Counter-Reformation. East Central Europe was initially exempted from this, but the effects of the Warsaw Tolerance Act of 1573 were significant. Western Europeans fleeing religious intolerance found refuge en masse in the aristocratic republic, particularly in royal Prussia. It was only in the seventeenth and eighteenth centuries that Poland became intolerant toward non-Catholic Christians and Jews. But when colonization began again as a means of populating and developing the land, there was little resistance to the renewed influx of foreigners. With this, however, we have already reached the Early Modern period, which is the subject of the next section of this volume.

# Notes

1. Klaus Zernack, "'Ostkolonisation' in universalgeschichtlicher Perspektive," in *Universalgeschichte und Nationalgeschichten*, ed. Gangolf Hübinger, Jürgen Osterhammel, and Erich Pelzer (Freiburg, 1994), pp. 105–116.
2. *Die deutsche Ostsiedlung des Mittelalters als Problem der europäischen Geschichte: Reichenau-Vorträge 1970–1972* (Sigmaringen, 1975).
3. Oskar Halecki, "L'histoire de l'Europe Orientale. Sa division en époques, son milieu géographique et ses problèmes fondamenteaux," in: *La Pologne au V^e Congrès International des Sciences Historiques a Bruxelles 1923* (Warsaw, 1924), pp. 73–94; Marceli Handelsman, "Monde slave ou l'Europe Orientale?" *Bulletin d'Information des Sciences Historiques en Europe Orientale* 3 (1930): 124–131.
4. Karl Hampe, *Der Zug nach dem Osten. Die kolonisatorische Großtat des deutschen Volkes im Mittelalter* (Leipzig, 1921).
5. The best criticism of this tradition is still Walter Schlesinger, "Die mittelalterliche deutsche Ostbewegung und die deutsche Ostforschung," *Zeitschrift für Ostmitteleuropaforschung* 46 (1977): 427–457.
6. Robert Bartlett, *The Making of Europe: Conquest, Colonisation and Cultural Change, 950–1350* (London, 1993).
7. Erwin Herrmann, *Slawisch-germanische Beziehungen im südostdeutschen Raum von der Spätantike bis zum Ungarnsturm. Ein Quellenbuch mit Erläuterungen* (Munich, 1965).
8. Christian Lübke, *Regesten zur Geschichte der Slaven an Elbe und Oder (vom Jahr 900 an)*, parts 1–5 (Berlin, 1984–1988); Christian Lübke, ed., *Struktur und Wandel im Früh- und Hochmittelalter. Eine Bestandsaufnahme aktueller Forschungen zur Germania Slavica* (Stuttgart, 1998), pp. 9–30.
9. See Benedykt Zientara, *Henryk Brodaty i jego czasy* (Warsaw, 1975), pp. 15, 343.
10. Marian Biskup, "Das Problem der ethnischen Zugehörigkeit im mittelalterlichen Landesausbau in Preußen. Zum Stand der Forschung," *Jahrbuch für die Geschichte Mittel- und Ostdeutschlands* 40 (1991): 3–25.
11. *Die deutsche Ostsiedlung* (as in note 2); a good summary is Werner Conze, *Ostmitteleuropa. Von der Spätantike bis zum 18. Jahrhundert* (Munich, 1991), pp. 62–92; Cf. *Quaestiones medii aevi novae*, vol. 3 (Warsaw, 1998). The whole volume is dedicated to the problem of foreign experts in East Central Europe.
12. For the current discussions about this regional conception, see Ralf Tuchtenhagen, "Nordosteuropa," in *Studienhandbuch östliches Europa*, vol. 1 of *Geschichte Ostmittel- und Südosteuropas*, ed. Harald Roth (Cologne, 1999), pp. 73–80.
13. Rudolf Mumenthaler, "Spätmittelalterliche Städte West- und Osteuropas im Vergleich. Versuch einer verfassungsgeschichtlichen Typologie," *Jahrbücher für Geschichte Osteuropas* N.S., 46 (1998): 39–68.
14. Eike von Repgow, *Sachsenspiegel (Landrecht)*, ed. J. Weiske, 11th edition (1929) III, 79, 2.
15. Otto Hintze, "Wesen und Verbreitung des Feudalismus," in *Otto Hintze, Feudalismus—Kapitalismus*, ed. Gerhard Oestreich (Göttingen, 1970), pp. 12–47.

16. Hugo Weczerka, ed., *Stände und Landesherrschaft in Ostmitteleuropa in der frühen Neuzeit* (Marburg, 1995); Joachim Bahlke, Hans-Jürgen Bömelburg, and Norbert Kersken, eds., *Ständefreiheit und Staatsgestaltung in Ostmitteleuropa. Übernationale Gemeinsamkeiten in der politischen Kultur vom 16.–18. Jahrhundert* (Leipzig, 1996).

17. Slawomir Gawlas, "Spoleczny zasieg polskiej swiadomosci narodowej w póznym sredniowieczu. Analyza mechanizmów zjawiska," *Przeglad Historyczny* 77 (1981): 637–660; see also Michael Ludwig, *Tendenzen und Erträge der modernen polnischen Spätmittelalterforschung unter besonderer Berücksichtigung der Stadtgeschichte* (Berlin, 1983).

18. Rainer Christorph Schwinges, "'Primäre' und 'sekundäre' Nation—Nationalbewußtsein und sozialer Wandel im mittelalterlichen Böhmen," in *Europa Slavica—Europa Orientalis. Festschrift Herbert Ludat*, ed. Klaus-Detlev Grothusen and Klaus Zernack (Berlin, 1980), pp. 490–532.

19. See Herbert Ludat, *Polen und Deutschland. Wissenschaftliche Konferenz polnischer Historiker über die deutsch-polnischen Beziehungen in der Vergangenheit* (Köln, Graz, 1963), p. 77.

20. Benedykt Zientara, *Swit narodów europejskich. Powstanie swiadomosci narodowej na obszarze Europy pokarolinskiej* (Warsaw, 1985), p. 13.

# Before Colonization

## Christendom at the Slav Frontier
## and Pagan Resistance

### ❖ Christian Lübke ❖

Relations between Germans and Slavs have mostly been made a subject of discussion related to the expansion of Germany in the high and late medieval periods, when Slavs were superseded by German colonists immigrating to the eastern parts of the European continent. In recent decades modern research in Germany has overcome the idea that this historical process rested upon a cultural superiority of immigrants who completely replaced the inferior Slavs. In modern German historiography the term *Germania Slavica* has come to signify the interaction of German- and Slavonic-speaking peoples during the colonization period[1] when a process of linguistic unification and ethnic intermixture produced, in the words of Walter Schlesinger, the German *Neustämme*[2] (unlike the *Altstämme* to the west of the rivers Elbe, Saale and Enns) and by this means the German people itself. In this way *Germania Slavica* conceptualizes the Slavonic share in German history that up to the present is evident in the existence of special place and personal names in the German-Slavonic contact zone. The Slavonic place names and especially the mixed Slavonic-German names reflect the collaboration between Germans and Slavs in the settlement process of the High Middle Ages (*aedificatio terrae*, or *Landesausbau*).[3] Naturally, a fair estimation of these interactions must take into consideration the German-Slavonic contacts in the centuries prior to this process and, above all, the originally prevailing Slavonic conditions.

Leaving out the discussions on the chronology of the settlement of the Slavs in the eastern parts of Central Europe and on the possible contacts between Germanic remnants and the Slavs in the region between the Elbe and the Oder Rivers,[4] the starting point of such a discussion might be the conceptualization of the vast regions between the Western Roman (Frankish, and especially East-Frankish) and Eastern Roman (Byzantine) Empires as a political and cultural "gray area," as it was characterized by the Polish historian Alexander Gieysztor.[5] This estimation is based on the observation that there were only few impulses for exchange between the Slavonic groups which scarcely differed among each other in their ways of life and in their material culture and which produced merely regional structures in their political organization. But stimuli came from the periphery since the ninth century and were transmitted by transit trade that provided regional rulers the means to maintain strong armed retinues (*družiny*) by employing silver coins, weapons and luxury goods from the Muslim world.[6] Such export commodities that were introduced to long-distance trade originated from tributes and taxes paid in food (grain) and forest products (honey, wax, furs), but the biggest profit was earned from the sale of slaves, principally war hostages. These were the economic structures that allowed the rise of the first Slavonic empire on the periphery of the East Frankish Empire in the ninth century, Greater Moravia. It was followed by the realms of the East European native princely dynasties after the tenth century, the Rjurikids in Old Russia (i.e. Kievan Rus), the Piasts in Poland, the Premyslids in Bohemia and the Árpads in Hungary.[7] But such powerful princes did penetrate into the Elbe region, i.e. into the immediate neighborhood of the East Frankish Empire and its successor kingdom ruled by the Saxon Ottonians in the tenth century, who for a time participated in this system. Quite the contrary, the map of the Polabian Slavs[8] shows a variety of autonomous tribes that only partly formed federations or were bound together by temporarily ruling princes.[9] It seems as if this part of the Slavonic world in particular preserved archaic forms of life and political organization,[10] as these acephalous and "segmental" societies kept their traditional creeds and freedom from princely domination more successfully and longer than any others.

The beginning of a real, planned "eastern policy"[11] by Germany's rulers toward their Slavonic neighbors becomes evident during the reign of King Henry I "The Fowler" (919–936). Yet the West had already begun to exert its influence on the Slavonic societies at the end of the eighth century when Charlemagne decided to control the approaches to his empire in the East by making war on the tribes of the Abodrites and Wilzes in the North, as well as on the Sorbs (east of Thuringia) and Czech tribal princes. The interest in and knowledge of Eastern European regions are shown by the detailed listing of the tribes and peoples living between the Danube and the Volga Rivers, and between the Baltic and the Black Sea in the so-called *Geographus Bavarus*.[12] In the first instance, the Franks aimed at the protection of the empire's borders along the Elbe and Saale Rivers, which did not, however, produce an ethnic or linguistic partition between Germans and Slavs. As shown by the Slavonic place names, Slavs settled up to dozens of miles west of both rivers, especially in Thuringia and northern Bavaria and, in some cases, individual Slavs reached the Rhine basin.

The area east of the Frankish Empire should therefore be seen as a bi-lingual and bi-ethnic frontier area or *Mark* (march). Slavs living in this region became a part of the feudal system of the Franks and settled in the manorial lands of various lay and ecclesiastical lords. A political organization of these Slavs living under the domination of the Franks may have existed at the local level.[13]

Although there were some violent encounters, conditions in the marches were relatively stable and peaceful until the Hungarians crossed the Carpathians, occupied the Danube lowlands, defeating the Moravians and Bavarians and launching raids into Italy, France and Germany. The land of the Daleminci, a Slavonic tribe on the middle Elbe, became a base for Hungarian attacks on Thuringia and Saxony, which hit the possessions of the Saxon Duke Otto and his son (and, later, king) Henry.[14] In this situation one can find the starting point for strategic plans to control the Polabian regions east of the Elbe and Saale Rivers and even in Bohemia, which came to pass in the nine years' truce between King Henry and the Hungarians (924–933).[15] But after Henry had subdued all Slavonic regions in his eastern dominions and even defeated the Hungarians on the Unstrut in 933, a coup d'état in Bohemia supplied the foundation for the further autonomous development of the Premyslid state. Vaclav of Prague, who had submitted to Saxon supremacy, fell victim to his brother's ambush, and when Boleslav I seized power he succeeded in uniting the Czech tribes under the leadership of Prague.[16] While it is true that the Premyslid princes were later regularly obliged to take an oath of fealty to the Holy Roman emperor,[17] they kept their right of self-government within Bohemia. The cult of the Christian martyr Vaclav soon played an important role in developing an ideology for the new state that was based mainly on the power of the dynasty, on the existence of a national church under the bishop of Prague, on the efficiency of a military retinue, and on the profits received from trade.[18] Later on, the organization of the services of all rural inhabitants formed the economic basis of ducal power. Parallel systems existed in the organization and administration of the Polish Piast and the Hungarian Árpad kingdoms.[19]

The further development of the Slavonic tribes in the north of the Ore Mountains was completely different. Henry I and even more so his son and successor, Otto I "the Great," broke the resistance of the Polabians, after which they placed power in the conquered regions in the hands of their secular and ecclesiastical representatives, while donating estates to loyal nobles and the church.[20] The bonds connecting Thuringia and eastern parts of Saxony (particularly the Harz) with the lands east of the Saale gradually grew, and the new landowners in some cases undertook colonizing measures.[21] In this region the former elite of the Slavonic tribes was set aside, if not killed. The note of the Saxon chronicler Widukind from the late thirties of the tenth century that Margrave Gero had killed almost thirty Slavonic *principes barbarorum* is often seen as evidence of hostility between Germans and Slavs and of plans for eliminating the Slavonic elites.[22] But at the same time Slavonic rulers collaborated with Saxon authorities and may have been integrated in the Saxon society.[23] And in the north of Polabia along the Baltic, the Abodrite dynasty of the Nakonides sometimes worked together with the dukes of Saxony and ruled, with some interruptions caused by pagan uprisings, for a considerable period of time.[24] One of the Abodrite princes, Gottschalk, whose name reflects his Christian education in Lüneburg, lived as an adventurer who fought against the Saxons, then belonged to the followers of the Anglo-Danish King Knut the Great, came back to his homeland, defeated a pagan uprising, promoted Christian missions, and built a principality that was on the way to becoming an autonomous state before he lost his life in another pagan war. One of his successors, Heinrich, ruled as a Christian prince over a pagan society.[25] Later on, in the last decades of the twelfth century, the Abodrite princes were partly integrated into the feudal system of Germany and became dukes of Mecklenburg.[26]

In the tenth century King Otto established his most important strongholds at Brandenburg on the Havel River and at Meißen on the Elbe,[27] winning victories over the pagan Hungarians and Slavs that were a decisive factor in his coronation as Holy Roman Emperor in 961 and in the foundation of the archbishopric in Magdeburg in 968.[28] Actually the new emperor and his Saxon followers were much more interested in dominion and tributes than in the conversion of the pagan Slavs to Christianity. Prospective Saxon nobles like the Margraves Dietrich (Haldensleben family) and Ekkehard (the first of the Ekkehardiner family) got deeply engaged in the Slavonic regions, coming into contact with the Polish Piasts. Marriage contracts strengthened their positions in the East.[29] This was the basis of Margrave Ekkehard's candidacy as king after Otto III's death in 1002, until he himself was killed by personal enemies.

With the succession of Otto the Great's son, Otto II, the entire region up to the Oder River was already integrated ecclesiastically into the German Church and administratively into the organization of the marches. "Burgwards," in the center of which Saxon military forces may have been stationed, began to spread from the south to the north, and churches and monasteries may have been built in the diocese of Starigard/Oldenburg.[30] *Germania Slavica* thus reached a territorial extent that it only surpassed in the second half of the twelfth century. For a time, however, it was reduced in size after 983, when an uprising of the Slavs in the north completely surprised the Saxon authorities and destroyed the signs of imperial and Christian church power.[31] Margraves and bishops had to flee from the sees in Starigard/Oldenburg, Brandenburg and Havelberg, to which they could only return in the middle of the twelfth century. Although Bishop Thietmar of Merseburg, who was a prime eyewitness and chronicler of the events around the year 1000, gives a description of the revolt's center[32] at the pagan temple and stronghold of Riedegost (better known as "Rethra") in the region of the Redarians (in the east of today's federal state of Mecklenburg-Hither Pomerania[33]), we do not have any concrete information about what went on in the lands where the revolt was successful. But it seems to be very clear that, in subsequent years, in the eyes of their Saxon neighbors the Polabians in the North turned from a bundle of tribes into a strong and well-organized federation that assumed a new identity as "Luticians." It was undoubtedly paganism and hatred for the authorities of the Christian church and of the empire that drove the revolt; and it was a political organization that was grounded on public meetings in a pagan temple that united the different tribes.[34] Although Lutician political and social structures were archaic compared to the newly forming Christian states in Poland, Bohemia, Hungary and Russia, they helped to preserve their ethnic identity and independence for more than 150 years. And, contrary to the sometimes horrific reports of the Saxon chroniclers, the pagans promoted the coming of Christian traders. Archaeological findings show that their country's culture and economy never atrophied, as did those of their neighbors.[35]

It was the crisis caused by the Lutician uprising that intensified the military and strategic collaboration between the empire and another power located in the Luticians' rear, namely the Polish Piasts. Prince Mieszko, who died in 992, repeatedly helped the German armies against the pagan Slavs, and his son Boleslaw the Brave hosted a magnificent reception for Emperor Otto III in his capital of Gniezno at Easter of the year 1000.[36] Otto dubbed him *cooperator imperii,* became the godfather of his youngest son, and arranged the marriage of his successor Mieszko II with an imperial princess, Richeza. As the Piasts had engaged themselves in the central and southern parts of Polabia and were in close contact with the families of the margraves of Brandenburg and Meißen, it seemed as if the Saxons and the Poles would share control over the Polabian lands in the future, once the pagan reaction had been defeated. But history took a different course when Otto, at the age of twenty-one, died in 1002, and his successor Henry II turned back sharply, entering into a league with the pagan Luticians and initiating a war against Poland.[37] In the longer perspective this decision determined his successors' policies toward the new states, including their insistence on imperial supremacy.[38] With this objective the German kings (and Holy Roman emperors) undertook military expeditions against Poland until the late twelfth century, albeit without much success. Wars against Poland that affected the southern marches only came to an end in the fourth decade of the eleventh century. This was one, but not the only, reason why these areas experienced very little economic development. It also appears as if the Saxon masters aimed mostly at profitable plundering of their lands and that the Slavonic inhabitants lived in continuous danger of being sold as slaves. This was the normal sentence for punishable Slavic dependants[39] and the normal fate of war prisoners, while the Saxons often interdicted the sale of Christian slaves to infidels, especially Jews.[40] Compared to the neighbors in the West, Slavonic inhabitants east of the Saale River did not grow to be very old.

Conditions changed slowly after the closing decades of the eleventh century, perhaps reflecting the general upturn in the European economy. The rise of towns and the growing division of labor promised profits from agriculture, which may explain the career of Wiprecht of Groitzsch.[41] Born of Slavic descent around 1050, he had been a ward of the sometime margrave of Meißen, Udo von Stade. Wiprecht's fortunes rose after he exchanged his lands in Belcsem on the Elbe left bank for Groitzsch (south of Leipzig), where he came into conflict with other German noble landowners. Supported by King Henry IV and the Bohemian King Vratislav, whom he had served and whose daughter he had married, he successfully enforced his claims in bloody duels with his rivals. At the time of the Saxon wars he acquired new fiefs from both kings and assorted ecclesiastical lords. Although he was never invested as margrave and never ruled as a territorial sovereign, his dominions ultimately reached from Thuringia to Upper Lusatia, where his wife had her residence in Bautzen.[42]

Thus Wiprecht was, in many respects, equal to the first generation of German lords in *Germania Slavica*, especially to Ekkehard of Meißen. What distinguished him was his promotion of planned settlement. As a penance for his bloody deeds he founded the first monastery east of the Saale in Pegau (1096), called in new settlers from Franconia and promoted urban development. Thus his efforts anticipated the later heyday of *aedificatio terrae*, which may have already been practiced to some extent as early as the tenth century.[43] In any event missionary aims were linked with the idea of colonization for the first time in 1108 when the archbishop of Magdeburg and other magnates invited Saxons, Flemings, Franks and Lotharingians to take possession of the pagan land.[44] At the same time the Polish prince Boleslaw III Wrymouth successfully made war against the Pomeranians as part of a planned westward extension of his power to the Oder. For this purpose he favored the missionary activities of Bishop Otto of Bamberg near the Oder's mouth. But Boleslaw came into conflict with the Danish king and with the German lords, whose protection the Pomeranian prince Wartislav sought. In 1135 Boleslaw had to take the island of Rügen and Pomerania as fiefs from Emperor Lothar, thus acknowledging the imperial authority over Slavonic lands that had not yet been conquered.[45]

But there was growing pressure on the last pagan lands in the heart of Europe, where the Lutricians had already lost their power in the second half of the eleventh century. They were followed partly by already baptized regional princes who ruled over pagan societies. The appeal of 1108 already contained the idea of a crusade that was ultimately carried out in 1147.[46] By then, however, the lords of Saxony, accompanied by the Danish king, wanted above all to prevent their rivals from subjecting and converting the pagans. Margrave Albrecht the Bear soon won control over the Havel region by a contract of inheritance with the last Slavonic prince of Brandenburg, Pribislav, while Duke Henry the Lion of Saxony subjugated the Abodrites after 1155. Finally the Danes conquered the island of Rügen and destroyed the last pagan temple at Cap Arkona in 1168. Soon the new German, Danish and eastern Slavonic rulers and their vassals took suitable actions to transform and colonize the conquered land with the help of monasteries (mainly founded by the Cistercians) and settlers from the west. The eyewitness of these deep changes, the chronicler Helmold of Bosau, could then conclude that, by the grace of God, "the whole Slavonic region between the Baltic Sea and the Elbe River has been transformed into a settlement region of the Saxons."[47]

# Notes

1. Wolfgang H. Fritze, "Germania Slavica. Zielsetzung und Arbeitsprogramm einer interdisziplinären Arbeitsgruppe," in Wolfgang H. Fritze, ed., *Germania Slavica* I, (Berlin, 1980), pp. 11–40; idem, "Der slawische Aufstand von 983—eine Schicksalswende in der Geschichte Mitteleuropas," in E. Henning and W. Vogel, eds., *Festschrift der Landesgeschichtlichen Vereinigung für die Mark Brandenburg zu ihrem hundertjährigen Bestehen* (Berlin, 1984), pp. 9–55; Christian Lübke, " Germania-Slavica-Forschung im Geisteswissenschaftlichen Zentrum Geschichte und Kultur Ostmitteleuropas e.V.: Die Germania Slavica als Bestandteil Ostmitteleuropas," in Christian Lübke, ed., *Struktur und Wandel im Früh- und Hochmittelalter. Eine Bestandsaufnahme aktueller Forschungen zur Germania Slavica* (Stuttgart, 1998), pp. 9–16.
2. Walter Schlesinger, "Die geschichtliche Stellung der mittelalterlichen deutschen Ostbewegung," *Historische Zeitschrift* 183 (1957), 517–542. Cf. Fritz Backhaus, "Das größte Siedelwerk des deutschen Volkes. Zur Erforschung der Germania Slavica in Deutschland," in Lübke, ed., *Struktur und Wandel*, pp. 17–30.
3. Wolfgang Irgang, "Landesausbau und Kolonisation—Ostmitteleuropa und Ungarn," in *Lexikon des Mittelalters*, vol. 5 (Munich, 1991), pp. 1649–1663.
4. This is related to the question for the "Urheimat" and the ethnogenesis of the Slavs and to the discussion on possible contacts between remnants of Germanic tribes and the Slavic newcomers. Cf. K. W. Struve, "Die Ethnogenese der Slawen aus der Sicht der Vor- und Frühgeschichte," in W. Bernhard and A. Kandler-Palsson, eds., *Ethnogenese europäischer Völker* (Stuttgart and New York, 1986), pp. 297–319; Sebastian Brather, *Archäologie der westlichen Slawen: Siedlung, Wirtschaft und Gesellschaft im früh- und hochmittelalterlichen Ostmitteleuropa* (Berlin, 2001).
5. Aleksander Gieysztor, *L'Europe nouvelle autour de l'an mil. La papauté, l'empire et les "nouveaux venus"* (Rome, 1997); idem, "L'Europe chrétienne autour de l'an mille et ses nouveaux adhérents," in Przemysław Urbańczyk, ed., *Early Christianity in Central and East Europe* (Warsaw, 1997), pp. 13–19.
6. Michael Müller-Wille, ed., *Oldenburg - Wolin - Staraja Ladoga - Novgorod - Kiev. Handel und Handelsbeziehungen im südlichen und östlichen Ostseeraum während des frühen Mittelalters* (Berichte der Römisch-Germanischen Kommission, vol. 69, 1988).
7. Related to East Central Europe see the contributions to the voluminous catalogue of the exhibition "Europas Mitte um 1000" Alfred Wieczorek and Hans-Martin Hinz, eds., *2000: Europas Mitte um 1000. Katalog und Handbuch* (Stuttgart, 2000); on Slavic societies in general, Joachim Herrmann, ed., *Die Welt der Slawen* (Leipzig, 1986), and Bohuslav Chropovský, *Historický, politický a kulturní vývoj a význam* (Prague, 1989); on the East Slavs and Rus' principalities, Carsten Goehrke, *Frühzeit des Ostslaventums* (Darmstadt, 1994).
8. There is no historical collective name for all the Slavs between the Holy Roman Empire on the one hand and the rising states of Bohemia and Poland on the other. I prefer "Elbslaven" = "Polabians" (derived from the Slavic name of the Elbe: Laba), which was already used by Czechs (Polabí) and Poles (Polabianie) in the nineteenth century in place of "Nordwestslaven." There was also a single small tribe of "Polabians" living on the Elbe

near Ratzeburg. Cf. Christian Lübke, "Slaven zwischen Elbe/Saale und Oder: Wenden - Polaben - Elbslaven? Beobachtungen zur Namenwahl," *Jahrbuch für die Geschichte Mittel- und Ostdeutschlands* 41 (1993), 17–43.

9. Joachim Herrmann, ed., *Die Slawen in Deutschland* (Berlin, 1985), Table 1.

10. Wolfgang H. Fritze, "Probleme der abodritischen Stammes- und Reichsverfassung und ihrer Entwicklung vom Stammesstaat zum Herrschaftsstaat," in Herbert Ludat, ed., *Siedlung und Verfassung der Slawen zwischen Elbe, Saale und Oder* (Gießen, 1960), pp. 141–219; Christian Lübke, "Forms of Political Organisation of the Polabian Slavs (until the 10th Century)," in Przemysław Urbańczyk, ed., *Origins of Central Europe* (Warsaw, 1997), pp. 115–124.

11. Lothar Dralle, "Zur Vorgeschichte und Hintergründen der Ostpolitik Heinrichs I.," in Karl-Detlev Grothusen and Klaus Zernack, eds., *Europa Slavica - Europa orientalis, Festschrift für Herbert Ludat zum 70. Geburtstag* (Berlin, 1980), pp. 99–126.

12. Aleksandr V. Nazarenko, ed., *Nemeckie latinojazyčnye istočniki IX–XI vekov. Teksty, perevody, kommentarij* (Moskow, 1993), pp. 7–51.

13. Herrmann, *Slawen in Deutschland*, pp. 354ff.; Christian Lübke, "Die Erweiterung des östlichen Horizonts: Der Eintritt der Slaven in die europäische Geschichte im 10. Jahrhundert," in Bernd Schneidmüller and Stefan Weinfurter, eds., *Ottonische Neuanfänge. Symposium zur Ausstellung "Otto der Große, Magdeburg und Europa"* (Mainz, 2001), pp. 113–126.

14. Christian Lübke, ed., *Regesten zur Geschichte der Slaven an Elbe und Oder (vom Jahr 900 an)*, part 2, (Berlin, 1984), nos. 5, 6, 8, 11, 12, 14, 17 and 21.

15. Paul Hirsch, et al., eds., *Widukindi monachi Corbeiensis rerum gestarum Saxonicarum libri tres* (Hannover, 1935) I/32; Lübke, *Regesten* II, nos. 25–39.

16. Dušan Třeštik, "Von Svatopluk zu Bolesław Chrobry. Die Entstehung Mitteleuropas aus der Kraft des Tatsächlichen und aus einer Idee," in Premysław Urbańczyk, *The Neighbours of Poland in the 10th Century* (Warsaw, 2000), pp. 125–145.

17. Wolfgang Wegener, *Böhmen/Mähren und das Reich im Hochmittelalter. Untersuchungen zur staatsrechtlichen Stellung Böhmens und Mährens im Deutschen Reich des Mittelalters* (Cologne and Graz, 1959), pp. 919–1253.

18. František Graus, *Die Nationenbildung der Westslawen im Mittelalter* (Sigmaringen, 1980).

19. Lübke, "Germania-Slavica-Forschung . . . ," passim.

20. Lübke, *Regesten* II; idem, "Die Ausdehnung ottonischer Herrschaft über slawische Bevölkerung zwischen Elbe/Saale und Oder," in Matthias Puhle, ed., *Otto der Große, Magdeburg und Europa* (Sigmaringen, 2001), pp. 65–75.

21. Gertraud Schrage, "Zur Siedlungspolitik der Ottonen. Untersuchungen zur Integration der Gebiete östlich der Saale im 10. Jahrhundert," *Blätter für Deutsche Landesgeschichte* 35 (1999), 189–268.

22. *Widukind*, I/20.

23. So the later king Otto I had a love affair with a Slavonic princess, probably from Brandenburg, who gave birth to Otto's son Wilhelm, the later archbishop of Moguntia; Prince Tugumir from Brandenburg helped Otto occupy this important stronghold and to dominate the land up to the Oder River. The fusion of the Saxons and the Slavonic dynasty of Brandenburg was shown by Herbert Ludat, "An Elbe und Oder um das Jahr 1000. Skizzen zur Politik des Ottonenreiches und der slawischen Mächte," in Mitteleuropa (Cologne, 1971); for more examples of Saxon-Slavic cooperation in tenth century, see Christian Lübke, "Slaven und Deutsche um das Jahr 1000," *Mediaevalia Historica Bohemica* 3 (1994), 59–90.

24. Bernhard Friedmann, *Untersuchungen zur Geschichte des abodritischen Fürstentums bis zum Ende des 10. Jahrhunderts* (Berlin, 1986).
25. Walter Lammers, "Die Slawen," *Geschichte Schleswig-Holsteins* 4 (1981), 93–152.
26. Manfred Hamann, *Mecklenburgische Geschichte* (Cologne and Graz, 1968), pp. 85–92.
27. Wolfgang Ribbe, ed., *Das Havelland im Mittelalter. Untersuchungen zur Strukturgeschichte einer ostelbischen Landschaft in slawischer und deutscher Zeit* (Berlin, 1987). The region of the Slavonic Daleminci and Meißen as the place of a margrave and a German bishop (since 968) is a subject of research in a "Germania Slavica" group of scholars at the Geisteswissenschaftliches Zentrum Geschichte und Kultur Ostmitteleuropas. Monographic studies on the archaeology of Meißen (by Arne Schmid-Hecklau and Gertraud Schrage) on the aspects of settlement in the possessions of the chapter of Meißen will be published shortly. Cf. Schrage and Arne Schmid-Hecklau, "Die archäologischen Untersuchungen auf der Burg Meißen," in Alfried Wieczorek and Hans-Martin Hinz, eds., *Europas Mitte um 1000. Handbuch*, vol. 2 (Stuttgart, 2000), pp. 703 ff.
28. Otto the Great has been valued in a big exposition in Magdeburg recently; cf. Schneidmüller/Weinfurter 2001; Puhle 2001.
29. Herbert Ludat, *An Elbe und Oder um das Jahr 1000. Skizzen zur Politik des Ottonenreiches und der slawischen Mächte in Mitteleuropa* (Cologne, 1971); Lübke, *Regesten* II, nos. 194 and 216; III, nos. 227, 246 and 357.
30. Gerhard Billig, *Die Burgwardorganisation im obersächsisch-meißnischen Raum. Achäologisch-archivalisch vergleichende Untersuchungen* (Berlin, 1989); Michael Müller-Wille, ed., *Starigard/Oldenburg. Ein slawischer Herrschersitz des frühen Mittelalters in Ostholstein* (Neumünster, 1991).
31. Wolfgang H. Fritze, "Der slawische Aufstand von 983—eine Schicksalswende in der Geschichte Mitteleuropas," in E. Henning and W. Vogel, eds., *Festschrift der Landesgeschichtlichen Vereinigung für die Mark Brandenburg zu ihrem hundertjährigen Bestehen* (Berlin, 1984), pp. 9–55; Lübke, *Regesten* III, No. 220.
32. Robert Holtzmann, ed., *Thietmari Merseburgensis episcopi chronicon* (Berlin, 1955), IV/23.
33. The identification of the place has been disputed for some time. The most recent suggestion of Volker Schmidt ("Rethra - Lieps am Südende des Tollensesees," *Studia Mythologica Slavica* 2 [1999], 33–47), who believed to have found the traces of Riedegost at the Tollensesee, has largely been rejected. For more information about Rethra and other cult-places of the Polabians, cf. Leszek Paweł Słupecki, *Slavonic Pagan Sanctuaries* (Warsaw 1994), pp. 51–69.
34. Lübke, "Forms of Political Organisation . . . "; idem, "Religion und ethnisches Bewußtsein . . ."
35. Thorsten Kempke and Christian Lübke recently attempted to summarize available information about the northern lands of Polabia in the eleventh century. The article ("Polens Nachbarn im Nordwesten: Das Land zwischen Niederelbe und Oder im 11. Jahrhundert") will be published shortly.
36. Michael Borgolte, ed., *Polen und Deutschland vor 1000 Jahren. Die Berliner Tagung über den "Akt von Gnesen"* (Berlin, 2002).
37. Knut Görich, "Eine Wende im Osten: Heinrich II. und Boleslaw Chrobry," in Bernd Schneidmüller and Stefan Weinfurter, eds., *Otto III. - Heinrich II. Eine Wende?* (Sigmaringen, 1997), pp. 95–167.
38. Herwig Wolfram, *Konrad II., Kaiser dreier Reiche* (Munich, 2000), pp. 215–256.
39. This is shown by a decree of Bishop Thietmar (Thietmar III/16), that his bishopric, when it was dissolved in 981, had been distributed like a Slavonic family that had been sold; cf.

Walter Schlesinger, "Die Verfassung der Sorben," in Ludat, *Siedlung und Verfassung,* pp. 97–102.

40. Thietmar VI/28, IV/54; Lübke, *Regesten* III, nos. 401, 420.
41. The desription of his life is a part of the *Annales Pegavienses,* written by a monk of the monastery in Pegau. Cf. Hans Patze, "Die Pegauer Annalen, die Königserhebung Wratislaws von Böhmen und die Anfänge der Stadt Pegau," *Jahrbuch für Geschichte Mittel- und Ostdeutschlands* 12 (1963), 1–62.
42. Rudolf Kötzschke and Hellmut Kretzschmar, *Sächsische Geschichte* (Frankfurt, 1965), pp. 65ff.
43. Schrage, passim.
44. The charter was published in Friedrich Israel and Walter Möllenberg, eds., *Urkundenbuch des Erzstiftes Magdeburg,* vol. 1 (Magdeburg 1939), no. 1393; the last analysis of the document's content by Peter Neumeister, " Die slawische Ostseeküste im Spannungsfeld der Nachbarmächte (bis 1227/39)," in Ole Harck and Christian Lübke, eds., *Zwischen Reric und Bornhöved. Die Beziehungen zwischen den Dänen und ihren slawischen Nachbarn vom 9. bis zum 13. Jahrhundert* (Stuttgart, 2001), pp. 37–55.
45. Jürgen Petersohn, *Der südliche Ostseeraum im kirchlich-politischen Kräftespiel des Reichs, Polens und Dänemarks vom 10. bis 13. Jahrhundert* (Cologne and Vienna, 1979).
46. Friedrich Lotter, *Die Konzeption des Wendenkreuzuges: Ideengeschichtliche, kirchenrechtliche und historisch-politische Voraussetzungen der Missionierung von Elb- und Ostseeslawen um die Mitte des 12. Jahrhunderts* (Sigmaringen, 1979).
47. Bernhard Schmeidler, ed., *Helmoldi Bozoviensis presbyteri chronica Slavorum* (Hannover, 1937), chapter 110.

# Medieval Colonization in East Central Europe

## ❖ Jan M. Piskorski ❖

The French historian Marc Ferro has stated that the phenomenon of colonization emerged in ancient Greece. He understood "colonization" to be the occupation of foreign territories and their later settlement. Between the Roman period and the era of great transoceanic expansion of modern Europe there were not supposed to have been any colonization processes in progress, and the terms "colonizer" and "colonization" allegedly vanished from the sources. One sort of exception was—according to Ferro—the medieval trade factories of Genoa and Venice, and also perhaps Russian eastward expansion toward the Urals and, in time, to Siberia.[1]

It is not surprising that the above opinion is rather widely held in the field, although it is usually accompanied by various—although, in my view, inadequately formulated—qualifications. It is, indeed, the case that from the perspective of global events the conquest and colonization of the Americas was of utterly transformative significance.[2] However, the modern expansion of Europe would be unthinkable without earlier experiences of colonization related to the extension of Europe's frontiers, whether southwest over the Pyrenees, southeast to the Levant of the Crusaders, across the Black Sea and Mediterranean by the Italian cities. One might also mention the English colonization of Wales, Scotland and Ireland. Finally, from the lower Rhine to the Elbe and beyond, we are faced with the so-called "colonization of the East."[3] Nor should we forget the great expansion of Russia towards the east, undertaken primarily in the late fifteenth and sixteenth centuries.[4]

Historical research on the Middle Ages has shown that in the long period between the fall of the *Imperium Romanum* and the discovery of America (1492) and road to India (1497), colonization processes not only took place, but intensified. Although they took the form of pure *melioratio terrae* ("reclamation of land")[5] on some occasions and were motivated by expansionism on others, they most often embodied a mixture of the two. An illustrative example of medieval colonization is the English conquest and settlement of Ireland in the second half of the twelfth century, especially as we are dealing with overseas colonization here.[6] It also is impossible to overlook the so-called *reconquista* on the Iberian Peninsula.[7] Many characteristics of colonial conquest and settlement are also to be found in Livonia (today's Latvia and Estonia), reached by sea in the twelfth century by a modest group of German clergy, knights and burghers.[8] The terms mentioned by Ferro also did not vanish from the sources. It is enough to recall the formulation by Helmold of Bosau from the mid-twelfth century on the subject of the transformation of Slavonic western Mecklenburg *in unam Saxonum coloniam*.[9] Sources from the British Isles also speak of colonization. At the end of the tenth century Aelfric of Eynsham explained the term *colonia* as a *peregrinorum cultura*, which could only mean "the settlement of foreigners." Gerald of Wales reflected at the turn of the twelfth and thirteenth centuries on how the English king could rule a conquered Wales. After the expulsion of the old population, he should—according to Gerald—transform Wales into a colony (*coloniam*).[10]

Thus when considering the phenomenon of colonization it is clearly not possible to ignore the Middle Ages, and not only in Europe.[11] Rather, it is necessary to conduct new and very thorough research into the similarities and differences between colonization processes in the ancient, medieval and modern periods. The opinion widely held among modern and contemporary historians that these processes greatly differed appears somewhat artificial and unfounded, if, of course, we consider these processes qualitatively rather than quantitatively.[12]

Medievalists tend to distinguish two main colonization waves in the history of medieval Europe. The first embraced Carolingian Europe and occurred in the eighth and ninth centuries. The second, which covered almost the entire continent, began in the eleventh century and gained momentum in the following two or three centuries. Without ruling out the matter of a possible relationship between these two waves it is worth noting that the first had a military character, though not exclusively so, as it usually took the form of *Landnahme*, that is, the gain and occupation of conquered territories. The second wave was rather based—though again not exclusively—on economic causes. One of the most important features within the framework of the second wave of medieval colonization processes was medieval eastern colonization. This was a settlement movement which began in the eleventh century in Holland and Flanders and reached the lower Elbe at the beginning of the twelfth century—strengthened by German settlers—to embrace the Elbe territories, then the Polish, Czech and Hungarian lands. Finally Lithuania, Prussia, Livonia and West Russia, parts of Scandinavia, Finland, Romania and the Balkans were also affected.

Until recently eastern colonization was equated with the migration of Germans. However, it is now known that handfuls, rather than crowds, of people went east in

search of bread, freedom and adventure—in a word, a better life, as the Flemish settlers sang. These few were still the most industrious and mobile, the most dissatisfied
with their social and economic status so far and, in a word, a sort of elite of the elite
(indeed not only in the positive sense). According to the rather courageous estimates
of Walter Kuhn, in the twelfth and thirteenth centuries we can count on an annual
German emigration of around 2,000 to 2,500 people.[13] Certainly on the territories
of East Central Europe, where the influx of many peoples have resulted in millennia
of mixing, it is never possible to state precisely—even in percentages—how many
immigrants arrived in the course of medieval colonization.[14] The British example,
however, is instructive and not at all surprising. Research conducted there on the
Y chromosome has shown that the majority of the inhabitants of the British Isles,
despite the Anglo-Saxon and Norman invasions, is of Celtic origin, although many
expected—on the basis of poor analysis of the written sources—a completely different
result.[15] They had forgotten that the incoming population always pays more attention
to itself, which by no means suggests a numerical dominance. Indeed it is still the case
today—particularly in the mass media—that anomalies are spoken of, rather than of
ordinary everyday events that are too banal to arouse any interest.

The new settlers, probably due to their generally young age, augmented the
numerous offspring of the countries to which they emigrated, though demographers
are still debating the results of long-term migration processes. Many of them are
of the opinion that *pro summa*, migrants did not cause a significant increase in the
demographic potential of their target areas, nor—most importantly—a reduction
of population size in the territories from which they came. The biological answer to
migration is to be found in the increased birth rate and decreased death rate of the
remaining population, while the growing numbers of migrants in the colonized areas
appears to have caused a declining birth rate among the local population.[16]

Insofar as it is possible to draw conclusions from the less than rich medieval
source material, it appears that at least in some East Central European territories the
population increased significantly. It is however possible to contest to what extent
this was a direct result of migration and how far it was due to increased agricultural
productivity and the gathering pace of urbanization. Yet these would not have been
possible, at least not at such a pace and on such a scale, without a fundamental change
in the model of social organization. This required a more attractive law, modern—by
contemporary standards—production techniques and technologies, a more rational-
ized and normalized tax system and, finally, a climate of social ferment. The latter
occurred particularly through the growing mobility of almost all social strata and
the increasing creativity of individuals who believed that colonization was a chance
for them to significantly increase their quality of life, both materially and in their
social status. It is not important here how realistic these dreams were, although it is
possible to suppose that the majority of immigrants, at least in the first generation,

did not see them realized. German proverbs from the beginning of the thirteenth century leave no doubt: *"Tod—Not—Brot,"* that is, the first generation of colonists, not only as a result of relations with the indigenous, were to be faced with death, the second with poverty and only the third with bread.[17] Similar disappointments awaited many new settlers in California in the mid-nineteenth century. The unful-filled hopes of striking gold led immigrants to coin the description of California as a "God forsaken land."[18]

The two most fundamental changes to be mentioned related to real Dutch, Flemish or German colonization and the so-called colonization of Dutch, Flemish or German law in Central and East Central Europe are the contract between the land-owner and the settlers holding it by lease, and urbanization. The contract included, above all, decisions relating to the size of plots of land, inheritance rights, the level of rent and tithes. It also included the settlers' liberties (for example the right to leave the place of residence, choice of the legal bench, autonomous administration and so on) and their responsibilities (for example in relation to military service and services for the landowner).

In the same way new towns were founded and old ones reformed. Their numbers increased rapidly in East Central Europe beginning in the twelfth and thirteenth centuries. These were towns of a new type, so-called free towns, which enjoyed a great degree of internal autonomy. Furthermore, the influx of foreign immigrants concen-trated in and around the towns—Jews, Walloons, Dutch, Flemish and Germans, who undoubtedly dominated in Central and East Central Europe. There were also Italians (particularly in Hungary) and later also Poles (above all in Lithuania and Kiev-Rus, today's Ukraine, but also in Hungary, including present-day Slovakia), Armenians, Tartars and other Muslim population groups (especially on the territory of historical eastern Poland, above all in Lviv). The towns became "melting pots" in which the languages and customs of various groups of immigrants and existing inhabitants mixed. Together with the immediate rural hinterland, they played the role of what are known as islands of intensity, where production increased most swiftly and from where new organizational, technical and technological advancements spread.[19]

The sources leave no doubt that rather numerous German settlers arrived into many areas of East Central Europe and that especially in the earliest period of eastern colonization the so-called German law was introduced above all by immigrants from the German lands. This particularly affected the territory between the Elbe and the Oder, Western Pomerania, Prussia, western Poland, the Czech lands (and especially Moravia), Carinthia and Transylvania.

Depending on the circumstances in which colonization occurred, relations between the immigrants and local population varied. In the Czech lands, Poland and Hungary the settlers were invited by local dynasties, who counted on their help to achieve the more rapid modernization of their countries. The situation was different in most of the lands between the Elbe and the Oder, in Prussia and Livonia, which were conquered and served as points of departure for the construction of new states by the eastern German princes and German knightly orders. It appears however that it is never possible to fundamentally equate colonization with Germanization, as earlier historiography has done. Colonization was a rather rapid process and on the scale of one province, it never lasted more than one or two generations. On the contrary assimilation and acculturation processes were drawn out over many generations. Following the influx of Germans to key Polish cities such as Cracow and Poznań in the mid-thirteenth century, their assimilation into the Polish nation and society took no less than two centuries. It also took a few centuries before the German influx into Western Pomerania resulted in the Germanization of the Slav population there. Their remnants—the so-called Slavonians (Słowińcy)—still existed in the interwar period. The Lausatian Sorbs survive to this day.

All this does not mean that there was no conflict between the native population and immigrants, nor that there were not expulsions of natives on a regional scale, as Helmold has written in relation to eastern Holstein. It is known that these anti-foreign confrontations were sometimes bloody, particularly in towns. Everywhere the sources indicate that hatred was basically directed against those newcomers who had no command of the local language. In Cracow at the dawn of the sixteenth century, during the successive Polish wars with the Teutonic Knights, it appears that Polonized burghers of German origin in particular expressed their antipathy towards the Germans.[20]

Historians are generally in agreement that medieval German colonization and colonization of so-called German law were the second great step after Christianity in the development of East Central Europe at the turn of the first and second millennia. There also appears to be no doubt that without the great modernization of these societies and their economies the increased role of Poland, Bohemia and Hungary, and certainly to some extent Austria, in the late Middle Ages, would have been unthinkable. Ferdinand Seibt has called this the age of great kings, with reference to the "eastern periphery" of Western Europe, including East Central Europe.[21]

Evaluations of the long-term influence of eastern colonization on the development of East Central Europe are however not so unified, even excluding Russian, Soviet and most Pan-Slav historians, for whom medieval colonization by Germans and of German law was always a violation of Slavonic Europe. Among the fathers of Czech and Polish historiography—František Palacký and Joachim Lelewel—the picture painted of medieval colonization is also far from rosy. While they did recognize its advantages, particularly urbanization, they wrote mainly of its disadvantages. Recently Sławomir Gawlas, referring to Marian Friedberg's suggestion, wondered whether the accelerated social and economic transformation imposed on society from above from the twelfth to the fourteenth centuries, which changed the course and mechanism of indigenous processes, was not the basis for the later developmental anomalies of East Central Europe.[22]

This question is undoubtedly interesting and worth developing. However, it is above all necessary to ask whether Bohemia, Poland and Hungary could have followed any alternative, indigenous routes. Declared occidentalists answered briefly—no. Karol Potkański, one of the most interesting Polish historians of the turn of the nineteenth and twentieth centuries, gave a different response, though he reached similar final conclusions. In his opinion, an alternative did exist and it would have been at least theoretically possible to solve the problem of transition from an economy in kind to a money economy in East Central Europe by indigenous means. This would admittedly have taken longer and it is not stated whether this whole process would have ended more successfully. Potkański immediately added that there was no third way of isolation from the economic and social changes taking place in Europe, as this would have meant suicide. "A nation cut off from all external influences, which faced similar economic pressures [to Poland and East Central Europe] would have to manage and create new forms of economic and social life alone. This isolation is nevertheless something exceptional—usually the course of events is different: the nation negotiates a kind of loan, subject to influences from neighboring nations which are higher up the economic ladder, adopting these forms, altering and transforming them according to its needs. The further existence and development of the nation is dependent of this adoption and adaptation. If, however, it is not in a fit state to adopt these higher forms, it is threatened with the usual danger of absorption by the more developed nation." Potkański emphasized that—from a national point of view—the "plough" can sometimes be more dangerous than the "sword"; in this sense, the transformation process could have ended much more badly for Poland and other countries of the region. However these societies proved to be generally well prepared for adapting imported organizations and production techniques, integrating them into the very process of transformation, which certainly grew above the heads of those who initiated it, completely and permanently changing the organization of society, economy and the state.[23]

The question posed by Friedberg and Gawlas influenced many scholars working on modern colonization processes. It is stressed that in many cases European colonization stifled the evolutionary development of the indigenous societies, which caused what is known as involution. In fact, in other cases "European penetration revived indigenous modernization processes which had become bogged down."[24] And if one can at all compare the colonization processes in medieval East Central Europe with modern European penetration of the so-called New World, we would be dealing with the second case here. It is worth remembering however that in Europe—unlike in the New World—really very similar societies encountered each other. With minor exceptions they were already members of the Christian family, which was not without impact on their social and economic organization. Before the so-called German law began to affect Bohemia, Hungary and Poland, the local elite and the Church had begun to seek new forms of managing their estates, to which the rather substantial information about colonization on so-called indigenous law (*mos gentis nostre, ius Slavicale*) from the mid-twelfth century is related. Within this context, local *"hospites,"* an institution undoubtedly borrowed from the West via the Church, cleared forests and farmed fallow land, while retaining their personal freedom. In time, due to the lack of settlers, the institution of the *hospites* was opened up even to the unfree, in order to increase the productivity of their work.

Potkański was right to underline so firmly the preparation of East Central European societies for a new phase of occidentalization. If this had not been the case, these states would certainly have vanished from the map of Europe. This time the exact opposite occurred—colonization strengthened and, in sum, allowed them to sign up permanently to the family of European states and nations. Only the pagan Slavonic tribes between the lower Elbe and lower Oder and the pagan Prussians paid the "price" for their conservatism and sluggishness in reforming. Whether they needed to pay this price and what factors combined to cause the ossification of their social organization and their inability to adapt to their surroundings are completely different, though no less important questions.[25]

Not only the example of ancient Sardinia, which borrowed from Phoenician metallurgy, as Fernand Braudel so beautifully demonstrated, proves that cultures which are open and independent are not afraid of borrowings and foreign inspiration, and they are well able to take advantage of these.[26] After all, imitation on no account means simple copying, and even a good copy is not bad in itself. In ancient southern Italy, Greek colonial ceramic appears at the same time as local imitations. It would therefore be difficult to define Italy in that period as a backward region.[27] Another example of the success of an open cultural model may be the migration of the Slavs in the second half of the first millennium. We are still not able to understand their pace, range and results; they occupied half of Europe from Greece to Denmark. Yet among archaeologists the opinion is widely held that the basis of this success was the Slav ability to adapt and openness to foreign influences.[28] East Central Europe from the twelfth to the fourteenth centuries, the "younger Europe," is another example of civilizational progress through the skilled usage of neighbors' advances. The region adopted so-called German law and through this, the organizational and economic gains of the "old" southern and western Europe, adapting them to its own advantage and according to its capabilities. The history of so-called German law which, the further east it went, had less and less in common with its origins from the region between the Elbe and the Oder, is perhaps the most visible example of this, but far from the only one. Furthermore, as the example of land division into "spear measures" (*łany*) in Lithuania illustrates, their early Christianization and modernization meant that the countries of East Central Europe were able to pass on all these achievements to successive societies situated even further away from the Mediterranean cradle of European civilization.

# Notes

1. Marc Ferro, *Histoire des colonisations. Des conquêtes aux indépendances. XIII<sup>e</sup>–XX<sup>e</sup> siècles* (Paris, 1994).

2. Cf. Fernand Braudel, "The Expansion of Europe and the 'longue durée'," in H.L. Wesseling, ed., *Expansion and Reaction: Essays on European Expansion and Reaction in Asia and Africa* (Leiden, 1978), pp. 17–27, esp. pp. 18 f., 19, 22, 27.

3. Robert Bartlett and Angus MacKay, eds., *Medieval Frontier Societies* (Oxford, 1992); Robert Bartlett, *The Making of Europe: Conquest, Colonization and Cultural Change, 950–1350* (Princeton, 1994); John Elliott, *Britain and Spain in America: Colonists and Colonized* (Reading, 1994); Klaus Zernack, "'Ostkolonisation' in universalgeschichtlicher Perspektive," in Gangolf Hübinger et al., eds., *Universalgeschichte und Nationalgeschichten* (Freiburg im Breisgau: Rombach Verlag, 1994), pp. 105–116; and Jan M. Piskorski, "The Historiography of the So-called 'East Colonisation' and the Current State of Research," in Balazs Nagy and Marcell Sebok, eds., *The Man of Many Devices, Who Wandered Full Many Ways: Festschrift in Honor of Janos Bak* (Budapest, 1999), pp. 654–667.

4. Gotthold Rhode, "Die Ostbewegung des deutschen, polnischen und russischen Volkes im Mittelalter. Versuch eines Vergleichs," in *Europa Slavica—Europa Orientalis: Festschrift Herbert Ludat* (Berlin, 1980), pp. 178–204; Zernack, "Ostkolonisation . . . ," pp. 115 f.; Jan M. Piskorski, "The Colonisation of Central Europe as the Problem of World History and Historiography," *German History* 22 (2004), pp. 323–343.

5. William H. TeBrake, "Reclamation of Land," in Joseph R. Strayer, ed., *Dictionary of the Middle Ages* (New York 1989), vol. 10, 272–279.

6. John A. Watt, "Approaches to the History of Fourteenth-century Ireland," in Art Cosgrove, ed., *A New History of Ireland,* vol. 2: *Medieval Ireland: 1169–1534* (Oxford, 1993), pp. 303–313, esp. p. 313.

7. Dietrich Claude, "Die Anfänge der Wiederbesiedlung Innerspaniens," in Walter Schlesinger, ed., *Die deutsche Ostsiedlung des Mittelalters als Problem der europäischen Geschichte* (Sigmaringen, 1975), pp. 607–656; Manuel González Jiménez, "Frontier and Settlement in the Kingdom of Castile (1085–1350)," in Bartlett & MacKay, *Medieval Frontier Societies,* pp. 49–74; John V. Tolan, "Using the Middle Ages to Construct Spanish Identity: Nineteenth and Twentieth-century Spanish Historiography of Reconquest," in Jan M. Piskorski, ed., *Historiographical Approaches to Medieval Colonization of East Central Europe: A Comparative Analysis against the Background of Other European Inter-ethnic Colonization Processes in the Middle Ages* (Boulder and New York, 2002), pp. 329–347.

8. Manfred Hellmann, *Das Lettenland im Mittelalter: Studien zur ostbaltischen Frühzeit und lettischen Stammesgeschichte, insbesondere Lettgallens* (Münster, 1954); Charles Higounet, *Les Allemands en Europe Centrale et Orientale au Moyen Age* (Paris: Éditions Aubier, 1989), pp. 225 ff.; Jan M. Piskorski, "Die deutsche Ostsiedlung des Mittelalters in der Entwicklung des östlichen Europa," *Jahrbuch für die Geschichte Mittel- und Ostdeutschlands* 40 (1991), 3 f.; Bartlett, *The Making of Europe,* pp. 31 ff., 111 ff.

9. Helmold von Bosau, *Slawenchronik,* ed. Heinz Stoob (Darmstadt, 1973), lib. II, cap. 110, 382.

10. Giraldus, *Itinerarium Kambriae et descriptio Kambriae,* ed. James F. Dimock (= Giraldi Cambrensi opera, vol. 6) (London, 1868), lib. II, cap. 9, p. 225, note 4. Prof. John Gill-

ingham (London) directed me towards the British examples. Cf. his *The English in the Twelfth Century: Imperialism, National Identity and Political Values* (Woodbridge, Suffolk: Boydell Press, 2000); idem, "The Second Tidal Wave? The Historiography of English Colonization of Irland, Scotland and Wales in the Twelfth and Thirteenth Centuries," in Piskorski, *Historiographical Approaches*, pp. 303–327.

11. Felipe Fernández-Armesto, *Millennium: A History of the Last Thousand Years* (London: Black Swan, 1996), pp. 36 f.; Wang Gungwu, *The Chinese Overseas: From Earthbound China to the Quest for Autonomy* (Cambridge, MA, 2000).

12. Interesting but very traditional on this subject is Jan Kieniewicz, *Od ekspansji do dominacji: Próba teorii kolonializmu* (Czytelnik, 1986), esp. p. 15.

13. Walter Kuhn, "Die Siedlerzahlen der deutschen Ostsiedlung," in idem, *Vergleichende Untersuchungen zur mittelalterlichen Ostsiedlung* (Cologne, 1973), p. 229; Lothar Dralle, *Die Deutschen in Ostmittel- und Osteuropa* (Darmstadt: Wissenschaftliche Buchgesellschaft, 1991), pp. 43–102.

14. Lista przodków zapisana w DNA, Rzeczpospolita 31.12.2002/1.01.2003 (from the journal *Science*).

15. "Surprising lack of Anglo-Saxon DNA," *The Guardian* 26 June 2003 (from the journal *Nature*).

16. Dennis Hume Wrong, *Population and Society*, 2d rev. and enl. ed. (New York., 1963), pp. 82–99.

17. Erwin Assmann, ed., *Godeschalcus und Visio Godeschalci* (Neumünster, 1979). Compare Jerzy Strzelczyk, "Eschatologia na pograniczu niemiecko-słowiańskim w końcu XII wieku," *Roczniki Historyczne* 50 (1985), 141 ff.

18. Sarah Royce, *A Frontier Lady: Recollections of the Gold Rush and Early California*, ed. Ralph Henry Gabriel, 2d ed. (Lincoln: University of Nebraska Press, 1977), pp. 86 f. Cf. also the case of Siberia in the late nineteenth century: Donald W. Treadgold, "Russian Expansion in the Light of Turner's Study of the American Frontier," *Agricultural History* 26 (1952), 150.

19. Jan M. Piskorski, *Kolonizacja wiejska Pomorza Zachodniego w XIII i w poczatkach XIV w. na tle procesów osadniczych w sredniowiecznej Europie* (Poznańskie Towarzystwo Przyjaciół Nauk, 1990), p. 247 f., where the additional literature is cited.

20. Raimund Friedrich Kaindl, *Geschichte der Deutschen in den Karpathenländern*, vol. 1 (Gotha, 1907), pp. 143 ff. Cf. Jan M. Piskorski, "After Occidentalism: The Third Europe Writes Its Own History," in Piskorski, *Historical Approaches*, pp. 10 f.

21. Ferdinand Seibt, *Karol IV*, tr. Czeslaw Tarnogórski (Powszechny Instytut Wydawniczy, 1996), p. 10.

22. Marian Friedberg, *Kultura polska a niemiecka: Elementy rodzime a wpływy niemieckie w ustroju i kulturze Polski średniowiecznej*, vol. 1 (Poznań, 1946), p. 229; Sławomir Gawlas, *O kształt zjednoczonego Królestwa. Niemieckie władztwo terytorialne a geneza spolecznoustrojowej odrębności Polski* (Wydawnictwo DIG, 1996), esp. p. 95.

23. Karol Potkański, "O pochodzeniu wsi polskiej," in idem, *Pisma posmiertne*, vol. 2 (Polska Akademia Umiejętności, 1924), pp. 346–387, esp. pp. 352 (cited here) and 373. Cf. also Jan M. Piskorski, "The Medieval 'Colonization of the East' in Polish Historiography," in idem, *Historiographical Approaches*, pp. 97–105.

24. H.L. Wesseling, "Expansion and Reaction: Some Reflections on a Symposium and a Theme," in idem, ed., *Expansion and Reaction*, p. 3. Cf. Clifford Geertz, *Agricultural Involution: The Process of Ecological Change in Indonesia* (Berkeley, 1963).

25. Cf. the short summary on this subject: Jan M. Piskorski, *Pomorze plemienne. Historia—archeologia—językoznawstwo* (Sorus, 2002), p. 80.

26. Fernand Braudel, et al., *Morze Śródziemne. Region i dzieje*, trans. Maria Boduszyńska-Borowikowa (Wydawnictwo Morskie, 1982), p. 79.

27. Adam Ziolkowski, *Storia di Roma* (Mondadori, 2000).

28. Herwig Wolfram, "The Ethno-Political Entities in the Region of the Upper and Middle Danube in the 6th–9th Centuries A.D.," in Przemyslaw Urbańczyk, ed., *Origins of Central Europe* (Warsaw, 1997), p. 52; Przemysław Urbanczyk, *Władza i polityka we wczesnym średniowieczu* (Wroclaw, 2000), p. 137.

# The Most Unique Crusader State

## The Teutonic Order in the Development of the Political Culture of Northeastern Europe during the Middle Ages

### ❖ Paul W. Knoll ❖

For the most part, the German presence in the region of East Central Europe in the Middle Ages and after was the product of expansion from established territories and of the rather more peaceful process of immigration in what has come to be known as *melioratio terrae*.[1] There is, however, one important exception, and that is the establishment of a unique crusader state on the Baltic littoral by the Knights of the Teutonic Order. Their regional presence shaped a political culture that was to have long-term implications, but at the same time they, too, were responsible for immigration and settlement policies that reshaped economy and society in what came to be known as Prussia.

The military-religious corporation known most conveniently in English as the "Teutonic Order" or the "Teutonic Knights"[2] was founded during the crusading era to defend a pilgrim hospital in Jerusalem, St. Mary's of the Germans. With the loss of Christian territory in the Levant, the Order had returned to Europe, briefly serving King Andrew II of Hungary against the pagan Cumans in the early thirteenth century.[3] The Order's energetic activity and aggressive colonization policy foreshadowed later developments in Prussia. Their ambitions and growing independence evoked a reaction from Andrew, and he successfully expelled them from Hungary in 1225.

Shortly thereafter, they were invited, under circumstances that have been controversial to the present,[4] to assist Duke Conrad of Mazovia in Poland in defending Christian territory and to undertake the conversion and conquest of the still pagan Prussians. Subsequently pagan Lithuania was added as a focus of the Knights' crusading campaigns. Originally small in numbers, by the 1230s substantial reinforcements had arrived and begun the arduous and dangerous task of the forcible conversion and conquest of the Prussians. Their task was complicated in 1237 when the Order subsumed the remnants of another military religious crusading order in the region, that of the Sword Brothers, created in 1202 by the Bishop of Riga to protect German merchants in Livonia. Henceforth the Teutonic Knights were engaged in the double task of defending Livonia against, among others, the Lithuanians and of extending their control of Prussia. In addition to members of their own Order, the Knights relied upon Poles, Pomeranians, as well as pilgrim-knights from the Empire that were to foreshadow the *Reisen* of later generations.[5] The campaigns in Prussia and against the Lithuanians were of such intensity that one recent scholar has remarked that "the crusades in Prussia concentrated piety and war in a way experienced nowhere else in Europe save perhaps Spain."[6] By the 1280s, the Order had been successful in conquering the Prussians and establishing a territorial base, a distinctive kind of ecclesiastical state, an *Ordensstaat*, creating in the meantime an image of military power and invincibility that was greatly admired in Europe. In doing so, however, it is important to recognize that the previous population in Prussia was by no means destroyed or even, in some instances, suppressed. Where conversion took place, the local population became integrated into the new Prussian society created by the Teutonic Knights.[7] Eventually the residence of the Grand Master of the Order, which continued to have branches elsewhere in Europe, was moved to Marienburg in Prussia.[8]

At the same time the military mission was pursued, the Teutonic Order promoted very substantial colonization. In the first six decades of what has become known as "the Prussian Crusade,"[9] the Order issued about 500 grants of lands and privilege to immigrants, chiefly (thought not exclusively) from Westphalia to come settle in Prussia.[10] These individuals, while they were often called upon to provide a degree of military service or provisioning, were the northern example of the *melioratio terrae* taking place elsewhere in the East Elbian lands.

For most of the thirteenth century, the Order had lived in relative peace with its neighbors, except, of course, for those pagan tribes and peoples against whom its mission was directed. At the beginning of the fourteenth century, however, this changed. An uprising in Danzig against the rule of the Duke Władysław Łokietek of Little Poland (*Polonia minor/Małopolska*), who aspired to the crown of Poland, resulted in the Teutonic Knights being called in to restore order. They did so, but subsequently refused to restore control to Łokietek. They incorporated the city into their *Ordenstaat* and subsequently conquered the region of Gdańsk Pomorze (Danzig Pomerania), which was claimed by Poland.[11] This initiated an extended period of conflict between the two that was to endure for more than a century. During the late 1320s and early 1330s open conflict between the Order and Poland resulted in almost annual campaigns.[12] The exclusive focus of the Knights' mission against pagans was compromised to a degree as a result of their involvement in a more straightforward *Machtkampf*. Eventually the Knights were able to sign a peace treaty at Kalisz in 1343 with Łokietek's son and successor, Casimir the Great. Until his death in 1370, there was, for the most part, peace between Poland and the Teutonic Order.

The Knights were able to turn their attention in these decades to Lithuania and the region of Samogitia, which they hoped to conquer and conjoin with their territory in Livonia. With continuing reinforcements from the chivalric society of Central and Western Europe,[13] they were successfully able to sustain their mission and even to enhance their international reputation. These were the years when the Teutonic Order reached the height of its medieval power. Later generations remembered this as its golden era (*goldene Blütezeit*), a time—as a contemporary remarked—when "under Grand Master Winrich [von Kniprode, 1352–1382] Prussia stood amid great honor and praise."[14] At least once yearly campaigns were mounted into Samogitia and Lithuania, and these *Reisen* reflected the epitome of the Order's triumphs, public acclaim, and international popularity. This was the period when Chaucer's "parfit gentil knyght" found that he could follow "chivalrie, trouthe and honour, fredom and curtesie," and had been given the place of honor "above alle nacions in Pruce," for "in Lettow hadde he reysed and in ruce, no cristen man so ofte of his degree."[15]

At the same time that it prosecuted the crusade aggressively, the Teutonic Order did not neglect colonization. Between 1321 and 1410 the Order issued 508 settlement privileges for the area of Danzig alone (258 of them under Winrich von Kniprode), and the population there grew to over 20,000, making it the largest city in East Central Europe. The commerce of Danzig grew accordingly, making it an international entrepôt of the first order. Elsewhere within Prussia, other settlements were established. Although the population was predominantly German in origin, there were numerous Polish colonists, and more than 80 of the nearly 500 villages founded in the fourteenth century were established under various forms of Polish law. All together, by 1410, 94 towns had been founded *de novo* or re-founded and expanded.[16]

The political culture and the position of the Teutonic Order in the region were profoundly altered by events in the late fourteenth century. Following the death of Grand Prince Gediminas of Lithuania in 1341/42, his son and successor Algirdas had tended to focus upon the eastward expansion of the Grand Duchy, eventually occupying Kiev and reaching Moscow in 1368 and again in 1370. His brother Kestutis had concentrated upon the frontiers with Poland (which after 1340 had sought control of the Ruthenian lands[17]) and the Teutonic Order. Throughout the 1360s and 1370s the Order had been able to sustain its crusading offensive against the Lithuanians. When Algirdas died in 1377, Kiestutis was challenged for leadership in the Grand Duchy by Jogaila, Algirdas's son, who was unwilling to limit his sphere of influence in the Grand Duchy to the eastern lands. In the resultant civil war, Jogaila played Kiestutis's son Vytautas off against his father, skillfully manipulated the issue of religion in secret negotiations with the Teutonic Knights, implying he would consider conversion. By the mid-1380s he had arranged the murder of Kiestutis, successfully outmaneuvered his cousin Vytautas, and effectively consolidated his rule in the Grand Duchy without following through on his implied promises to the Teutonic Order.[18] At this point he was faced with the option of trying to sustain reasonably peaceful relations with the Order or to work out a different solution. His conclusion was a practical one. To protect the Duchy against the mission of the Knights, he decided to ally with what was by now another traditional opponent of the Order, the Kingdom of Poland.[19]

Lithuanian representatives met with the Polish nobility in Cracow in January 1385 and presented their proposal, which was to be sealed by the Grand Duke's marriage to the Polish ruler, Jadwiga of Anjou. In August 1385, Polish and Lithuanian representatives met in Krivias (Krewo in Polish) near Vilnius and there worked out final details. The Grand Duke promised to recover all lands that Poland had lost to the Teutonic Order at his own effort and expense, to baptize all pagan inhabitants of his realm into the Catholic faith, and to join the lands of Lithuania and Ruthenia to the Polish crown in perpetuity (*perpetuo applicare*). In February 1386, he formally converted to Christianity, taking the name Władysław (thus identifying himself with the royal tradition of Władysław Łokietek; he is also known as Jagiełło, the Polonized form of his pagan name) and married Jadwiga, thus creating a personal union between the two states.

With the conversion of pagan Lithuania, the Teutonic Order was faced with the theoretical possibility that its mission in the region had come to an end and its very rationale undermined. The political reality of the existence of an *Ordensstaat*, carrying with it not only crusading obligations but also political rule over a subject population and economic responsibilities for a settled urban and rural society in Prussia, mitigated against the Knights' accepting such a conclusion. Instead the Order adopted the position that Jogaila's conversion had been a sham and that beneath a thin artificial veneer of Christianity, paganism remained the religious reality in the Grand Duchy. Thus crusades continued, supported by the on-going presence of knights from the west (including in 1390 Henry Bolinbroke, the future King Henry IV of England).[20] The decade of the 1390s saw an intensity in the brutality of warfare that outstripped even the conquests of the thirteenth and campaigns of the earlier fourteenth century. The Knights aimed not only at the subjection of Lithuania, but also increasingly at the conquest of Samogitia, which still separated the Prussian and Livonian holdings of the Order. On the diplomatic front the leadership of the Order sought to create antagonism between Jagiełło and Vytautas (Witold in Polish historiography), who had succeeded him as Grand Duke. This policy was ultimately not successful—though it did bring momentary advantages, such as in 1398 when, in return for the Order's support for his campaigns into the steppes to the southeast,

Vytautas ceded Samogitia to them.[21] This proved to be, however, a short-term gain. In 1409 the Samogitians revolted, perhaps at the instigation of Vytautas himself, who proved to be an unreliable ally for the Order. By the early years of the fifteenth century, he and Jogaila had reconciled, and the campaign of diplomacy and political propaganda undertaken by the Order had resolved nothing. Relations between the Knights and Poland-Lithuania worsened under a new, more aggressive Grand Master, Ulrich von Jungingen, after 1408.

In 1409 war broke out, and in July 1410 a combined Polish-Lithuanian force of 30,000 cavalry and infantry (including Ruthenians, Tatars, Bohemian mercenaries, and troops from other areas) met the army of the Teutonic Knights, which may have numbered 20,000 at the battle of Tannenberg/Grunwald/Żalgris (as it is knows to Germans, Poles, and Lithuanians respectively). The Order was decisively defeated militarily, losing according to the earliest and most conservative estimate some 8,000 men, with many others captured. Among the dead were the Grand Master and scores of Commanders.[22] Despite the crushing military defeat, the Order was able subsequently to exploit Polish-Lithuanian weaknesses and recover. By the terms of the First Peace of Thorn (Toruń) in 1411, which ended the war, the Order lost no territory even though it had to pay significant indemnities to Jagiełło.

The years after this peace was the period when the Teutonic Order lost its aura of military invincibility. It also was put on the diplomatic defensive at the Council of Constance (1414–1418), when Polish representatives attacked it effectively.[23] Support from elsewhere in Europe began to diminish, the economic resources of the Order in Prussia were weakened, and in general the Order became, as one modern scholar has called it, "an aristocratic corporation in crisis."[24] Continued intermittent military conflict with Poland during the 1420s brought no resolution to either side, but even with consistent support from the emperor of the Holy Roman Empire and the papacy, the Order struggled. The subjects of the Order in Prussia sought to extend their urban and social privileges, and gradually during the first half of the fifteenth century, the Prussian Estates became well established as a counterbalance to the Order's authority. These represented a mixed population of immigrant descendants from the German lands and elsewhere, including Poland, along with the descendents of the indigenous population who had converted and become part of Christian Prussian society. Whatever their origins, the local nobility came increasingly to be conscious of itself as a community separate and distinct from the Order. Increasingly the Knights of the Teutonic Order were isolated from the rest of Europe and pitted against their own subjects.

In the meantime, the social character of the Teutonic Order itself had been undergoing change. New recruits came more and more from the upper and middle ranks of patrician families in selected parts of the German lands, and as administrators of territorial units in Prussia, these individuals were ill-equipped to respond to the needs of their subjects and of the cities. Such issues as inheritance customs and the terms of land tenure widened the gap between the Order and its subjects—both rural and urban.[25] Moreover, there were a number of concomitant problems that plagued the Order. These included factionalism in the leadership cadre of the Knights, issues of religious reform that made demands upon the very nature of the monastic dimensions of the Order, increasingly oppressive governance and taxation (driven in some measure, to be sure, by economic considerations), and a declining number of those who wished to enter the Order.[26] The organization in 1440 of the Prussian Union, composed of local nobles and cities, was designed to protest the policy of the Teutonic Order in matters of taxation, economic policy, and political rights. When the Order resisted, the Union revolted, withdrew allegiance to the Knights, and recognized the lordship of the King of Poland, Casimir the Jagiellonian.

War broke out between the Order and Poland-Lithuania in 1454.[27] The ensuring thirteen-year conflict was costly to both sides, but the economic and financial drain upon the Order was particularly heavy.[28] To support its military efforts, the Order granted large landed estates with legal rights over peasants to some of its mercenary leaders and to local nobles. Other supporters of the Order were war-profiteers who bought or seized great estates and properties. In the process, the social class known as "Junkers" that was to dominate the region for generations gradually came into being. This stratum felt little allegiance to the Teutonic Order or later, after the partition of Prussia, to Poland.

Hostilities between Poland and its allies in Prussia and the Teutonic Order were ended by the Second Peace of Thorn (Toruń) in 1466, and it cost the Order dearly. It lost significant territories, especially in the west of the *Ordensstaat*, constituting the more urbanized and economically developed parts of Prussia. These lands were incorporated into the Kingdom of Poland, becoming known as Royal Prussia. The lands that the Order retained were less prosperous and economically valuable, and the terms of the treaty required the Grand Master to recognize the Polish king as his overlord.

For the next three-quarters of a century, the Teutonic Order struggled to adapt to these changed circumstances in the political culture of the region. The capital was moved to Königsberg, and the Grand Masters increasingly appeared to be territorial princes presiding over the devastated and economically depressed lands of eastern Prussia. In many ways, however, the central issue for them was the actual nature of their relationship to the Polish king.[29] Supported by the emperor and the pope (to whom the Order was theoretically subject), they refused to recognize the legality of the Second Treaty of Thorn, rejecting thereby their ostensible feudal subjugation to the King of Poland. Maneuvers in both political and ecclesiastical matters turned on this issue, and in some instances brought the Order into alliance with states, such as the Grand Duchy of Moscow, that sought to enhance themselves at Poland-Lithuania's expense.[30] In addition, the Grand Masters had to struggle with the continuing political challenge from the Prussian estates. During these years, there were efforts to reform the Order, but, for the most part, they came to naught.[31]

A significant turning point in the history of the Order came in 1474, when, with the agreement of the Polish king, Duke Frederick of Saxony-Meissen was elected Grand Master. He had not previously been a member of the Order, and his choice was a crucial signal that the character and status of the Order was in transition. It was clearly no longer a religiously oriented *ordo* with a crusading mission but had become a territorial state that worked out its political destiny within a regional context. As William Urban has recently noted, the Order's status reflected a basic flaw: "its awkward mixture of secular and clerical duties that made it something more than a religious order and something less than a sovereign state."[32] Frederick strove successfully during his rule to resist accepting formally the overlordship of Poland for the lands of the Order. At times his relationship with Casmir the Jagiellonian and the three sons who succeeded him one after another was so strained as to bring the two states near to conflict. Both popes and emperors, especially Maximilian I, supported Frederick, but used diplomacy to prevent the outbreak of hostilities.[33] Frederick's successor as Grand Master in 1511 was Margrave Albrecht of Hohenzollern, Elector of Brandenburg, who was the nephew of King Sigismund the Old of Poland. Albrecht, too, sought to avoid swearing formal allegiance to Sigismund (he was forbidden to do so by his imperial and papal supporters), and in so doing was brought into the maelstrom of East Central European affairs: conflict between Poland-Lithuania and Moscow, Poland's support in opposition to the Habsburgs in Hungary, and the growing Ottoman threat to the south. Eventually war broke out between Poland and the Order in 1520, to be resolved a year later by a compromise peace that opened all issues to mediation.[34]

Against this backdrop, there was the issue of the Protestant Reformation. By the early 1520s Lutheran support was growing in Brandenburg, where Albrecht was not only margrave but also an elector of the Holy Roman Empire. He became familiar with and attracted to Luther's teachings in a visit to Nuremberg in 1522. Luther eventually counseled Albrecht to follow the example of some German bishops who were turning Protestant and secularizing their lands.[35] This is what he did in 1525. In Prussia, he transformed his ecclesiastical state into a secular one, becoming thereby a territorial prince, eventually duke. As a Protestant, he could now count on neither pope nor emperor for support and clearly needed to legitimate his status. Thus he concluded an agreement with Sigismund, and on 8 April 1525 came to Cracow formally to recognize Polish suzerainty over what now became Ducal Prussia.[36] Unlike Royal Prussia, these lands were not incorporated into the Polish crown, with large implications for later history. Less than four decades later, as the Protestant Reformation continued its progress in the Baltic, the Livonian lands of the Order were also secularized.

By these developments, the history of the Teutonic Order in northeastern Europe effectively came to an end. (The Order itself survived by returning to German lands in the west, eventually settling in Vienna, where it has continued to be active to this day as a religious and charitable institution.[37]) The richness of its history there, however, and the impact it made upon the land and the peoples of the region have ensured that despite the vicissitudes of subsequent centuries its regional importance must be the subject of serious scholarly study. The roles that the Order and Prussian society played were substantial. Arriving as an extension of the military-religious mission that Robert Bartlett has seen as part of the "making of Europe,"[38] they were transformed into a distinctive society whose character constituted a rich amalgam of the immigrant and of the culturally transmuted local. For much of the nineteenth and twentieth centuries, the focus of the study of this history was driven by intense nationalism.[39] In the last decades, however, a more balanced scholarly approach has been evident.[40]

## Notes

1. See, for the first, Robert Bartlett, "Colonial Aristocracies of the High Middle Ages," and Friedrich Lotter, "The Crusading Idea and the Conquest of the Region East of the Elbe," both in Bartlett and Angus MacKay, eds., *Medieval Frontier Societies* (Oxford, 1989), pp. 23–47 (esp. 41–44) and 267–306 respectively. For the second, see the important collection *Die Deutsche Ostsiedlung des Mittelalters als Problem der europäischen Geschichte*, ed. Walter Schlesinger (Sigmaringen, 1975). I have treated both developments in "Economic and Political Institutions on the Polish-German Frontier in the Middle Ages: Action, Reaction, Interaction," in Bartlett and MacKay, *Medieval Frontier Societies*, pp. 151–174.

2. The official title of the corporation in Latin is "Ordo Hospitalis S. Mariae Domus Theutonicorum Ierosolimitani." The common German name is *der Deutsche Orden* (The German Order), while in Polish they are most frequently designated *Zakon Krzyżacki* (the Order of the Knights of the Cross), for the black cross on the white tunic the knights wore.

3. In English the most convenient brief treatment is now Pál Engel, *The Realm of St. Stephen: A History of Medieval Hungary, 895–1526* (London and New York, 2001), p. 90. For more detail, see William Urban, *The Teutonic Knights: A Military History* (London, 2003), pp. 31–40, who presents a rather more sympathetic picture than Engel. The short assessment of this episode in the Order's history by Hartmut Boockmann, *Der Deutsche Orden. Zwölf Kapitel aus seiner Geschichte*, 2nd ed. (Munich, 1982), pp. 68–70 is characteristically full of balanced insight.

4. The issues connected with these problems have been analyzed by, among others, Gerard Labuda, "Die Urkunden über die Anfänge des Deutschen Ordens im Kulmerland und in Preußen in den Jahren 1226–1235," in *Die Geistliche Ritterorden Europas*, ed. Joseph Fleckenstein and Manfred Hellmann (Sigmaringen, 1980), pp. 299–316; see also Labuda's treatment of these matters in Marian Biskup and Gerard Labuda, *Dzieje Zakonu Krzyżackiego w Prusach. Gospodarka—Społeczeństwo—Państwo—Ideologia* (Gdańsk, 1988), pp. 118–121, esp. n. 95. (This latter work is available in a German translation, *Die Geschichte des Deutschen Ordens in Preußen. Wirtschaft—Gesellschaft—Staat—Ideologie*, Klio in Polen, 6 (Osnabrück, 2000).

5. For example, in the summer campaign of 1233 some estimates are that as many as 10,000 men took the Cross, enabling the knights to build the fortress of Marienwerder; see William Urban, *The Prussian Crusade* (Lanham, MD, 1980), pp. 119–121, with references to sources. On the general question of the size and composition of the Order and its crusading forces at this time, see the older work by A. L. Ewald, *Die Eroberung Preussens durch die Deutschen*, esp. vol. 1 (Halle, 1872), which is still unmatched for its thoroughness.

6. S.C. Rowell, "Baltic Europe," in *The New Cambridge Medieval History*, vol. 6: ca. 1300–1415, ed. Michael Jones (Cambridge, 2000), p. 729.

7. This is particularly clear from the study of Reinhard Wenskus, "Der Deutsche Orden und die nichtdeutsche Bevölkerung des Preußenlandes mit besonderer Berücksichtigung der Siedlung," in *Der Deutsche Ostsiedlung des Mittelalters*, pp. 417–438.

8. The details of this extended process, which the fourteenth-century chronicler of the Order, Peter of Duisburg, subsumed under the rubric of the "bellum Lithuanicum," are best traced in the following: Boockmann, *Der Deutsche Orden*, pp. 66–114; and Biskup and Labuda, *Dzieje Zakonu Krzyżackiego*, pp. 118–161, 178–188. The period is also treated effectively by Karol Górski, whose *Zakon Krzyżacki a powstanie państwa pruskiego* (Wrocław, 1977) is available in an Italian translation, *L'ordine teutonico. Alla origini della stato prussiano* (Turin, 1977). The treatment by Urban, *The Teutonic Knights*, pp. 41–108, is rich with detail and based on sound scholarship, though the text is directed at a popular audience. See also Eric Christiansen, *The Northern Crusades: The Baltic and the Catholic Frontier, 1100–1525* (Minneapolis, MN, 1980), pp. 89–108.

9. This is the title of William Urban's study of this process (see above, note 5), but in its earliest stages, whether the Order's activity was in fact a crusade in a narrow, technical sense is a question to which the answer is ambiguous. By the fourteenth century, however, the campaigns against the pagans were waged as crusades. Thus Boockmann, *Der Deutsche Orden*, pp. 101–108, following Peter of Duisburg, speaks about the conquest of Prussia as being a *Heidenkrieg;* for the later campaigns against the Lithuanians, however, the characterization is explicitly *Kreuzzüge* (pp. 151–169).

10. From the older literature on this topic, see K. Kasiske, *Die Siedlungstätigkeit des Deutschen Ordens im östlichen Preussen bis zum Jahre 1410* (Königsberg, 1934); and Henryk Łowmiański, *Polityka ludnościowa zakonu niemieckiego w Prusach i na Pomorzu* (Gdańsk, 1947). More recently, and more balanced, see Biskup and Labuda, *Dzieje Zakonu Krzyżackiego*, pp. 189–198; and Boockmann, *Der Deutsche Orden*, pp. 121–130.

11. I have treated this in my *The Rise of the Polish Monarchy: Piast Poland in East Central Europe, 1320–1370* (Chicago, 1972), pp. 28–31. See also Kazimierz Jasiński, "Zajęcie Pomorza Gdańskiego przez Krzyżaków w 1300–1309 roku," *Zapiski Historyczne* 31, 3 (1966): 7–61. Boockmann, *Der Deutsche Orden*, pp. 140–150, is particularly successful at teasing out the implications for future Polish-German relations in these events.

12. On one of these, the Polish army decisively defeated the forces of the Order at the Battle of Płowce in September 1331. In retrospect, this victory came in Polish eyes to have considerable propaganda significance; see Marian Biskup, "Analiza bitwy pod Płowcami i jej dziejowego znaczenia," *Ziemia Kujawska* 1 (1963): 73–104, esp. 101; and Knoll, "National Consciousness in Medieval Poland," *Ethnic Studies* 10 (1993): 70.

13. See the superb treatment of this aspect of the Order's history by Werner Paravicini, *Die Preußenreisen des europäischen Adels*, 2 vols. so far (Sigmaringen, 1989–1995).

14. Cited by Marian Tumler, *Der Deutsche Orden im Werden, Waschen und Wirken bis 1400* (Vienna, 1955), p. 350, from *Codex epistolaris Vitoldi*.

15. All quotations from Geoffrey Chaucer, *The Canterbury Tales*, "General Prologue," in *The Works of Geoffrey Chaucer*, ed. F. N. Robinson, 2d ed. (Boston, 1957), pp. 17–18.

16. Rowell, "Baltic Europe," pp. 713–715. For the development of Danzig in greater depth, see Henryk Samsonwicz, Gdańsk jako ośrodek handlowy," in *Historia Gdańska*, ed. Edward Cieślak (Gdańsk, 1982), II, 260–329. See also his "Der Deutsche Orden als Wirtschaftsmacht des Ostseeraumes," in *Zur Wirtschaftentwicklung des Deutschen Ordens im Mittelalter*, Udo Arnold, ed. (Marburg, 1989), pp. 103–112.

17. See Knoll, *Rise of the Polish Monarchy*, pp. 121–177.

18. These complicated details are now best traced in English in Rowell, "Baltic Europe," pp. 709–710. See also Rasa Mažeika, "The Relations of Grand Prince Algirdas with Eastern and Western Christians," in *La Cristianizzazione della Lituania* (Vatican City, 1989), pp. 63–85.

19. The various options open to Jogaila are analyzed by Michał Giedroyć, "Lithuanian Options Prior to Kreva (1385)," in *La Cristianizzazione della Lituania*, pp. 87–105. The stance of the Teutonic Order in the crucial months of 1384/1385 is discussed by Urban, "The Teutonic Order and the Christianization of Lithuania," in *La Cristianizzazione della Lituania*, pp. 128–130.

20. These developments are treated by H. Gersdorf, *Der Deutsche Orden im Zeitalter der polnisch-litauische Union. Die Amtszeit des Hochmeisters Konrad Zöllner von Rotenstein (1382–1390)* (Marburg, 1957).

21. The Treaty of Sallinwerder in that year actually came against a more complicated diplomatic backdrop, for it brought temporary peace between Poland-Lithuania and the Order so that they, in unusual combination with the Tatars, could take action against the threat posed on the steppes by the Turkish advance of Timur (Tamerlane).

22. The war of 1409–1411 and its chief battle have been treated extensively. German scholarship is analyzed in Sven Ekdahl, *Die Schlacht bei Tannenberg 1410. Quellenkritische Untersuchungen*, vol. 1: *Einführung und Quellenlage* (Berlin, 1982). The standard Polish treatment is by Stefan Kuczyński, *Wielka wojna z Zakonem Krzyżackim w latach 1409–1411*, 5th ed. (little changed from the 3rd edition of 1966) (Warsaw, 1987), though scholars from Poland, Germany, and elsewhere have disputed many of his views. See the treatment of these years in Biskup and Labuda, *Dzieje Zakonu Krzyżackiego*, pp. 353–368, and the brief—but balanced—coverage in Boockmann, *Der Deutsche Orden*, pp. 178–180. Lithuanian interpretations are presented by C. R. Jurgela, *Tannenberg* (1961). Urban's *The Teutonic Knights*, pp. 195–229, is solid and even-handed. The best study of the banners of the Order captured on the field of battle is Ekdahl, *Die "Banderia Prutenorum" des Jan Długosz—eine Quelle zur Schlacht bei Tannenberg* (Göttingen, 1948).

23. The diplomacy of the Order in these years is best analyzed by Boockmann, *Johannes Falkenberg, der Deutsche Orden und die polnische Politik* (Göttingen, 1975). The leading Polish spokesman who led the attack on the Order at Constance was Paulus Vladimiri of Brudzeń. The most comprehensive analysis of his works is the magisterial study, including the texts of many of Paulus's treatises, by Stanislaus F. Belch, *Paulus Vladimiri and His Doctrine Concerning International Law and Politics*, 2 vols. (The Hague, 1965). See also Krzysztof Ożóg, "Udział Andrzeja Łaskarzyca w sprawach i sporach Polsko-Krzyżackich do soboru w Konstancji," in *Polska i jej sąsiedzi w późnym średniowieczu*, K. Ożóg and Stanisław Szczur, eds. (Kraków, 2000), pp. 159–186. In English, see my "The University of Cracow in the Conciliar Movement," in James M. Kittelson and Pamela J. Transue, eds., *Rebirth, Reform and Resilience: Universities in Transition, 1300–1700* (Columbus, OH, 1984), pp. 194–198. A recent, very balanced account of these controversial confrontations is Stefan Kwiatkowski, *Der Deutsche Orden im Streit mit Polen-Litauen. Eine theologische Kontroverse über Krieg und Frieden auf dem Konzil von Konstanz (1414–1418)* (Stuttgart, 2000).

24. The phrase is Michael Burleigh's; see *Prussian Society and the German Order: An Aristocratic Corporation in Crisis c. 1410–1466* (Cambridge, 1984), to which my analysis in the text owes much.
25. Some of these developments were treated by F. L. Carsten in his classic study, *The Origins of Prussia* (Oxford, 1954); see also his "The Origins of the Junkers," *English Historical Review* 62 (1947): 145–178, esp. 157–160. Boockmann has dealt with other aspects in "Zu den politischen Zielen des Deutschen Ordens in seiner Auseinandersetzung mit den preussischen Ständen," *Jahrbuch für Geschichte Mittel- und Ostdeutschlands* 15 (1966): 57–104. More recently on these issues in comparative context, see Henryk Samsonowicz, "Miasta pruskie w XV wieku na tle porównawczym miast Europy," in *Prusy—Polska—Europa. Studia z dziejów średniowiecza i czasów wczesnonowożytnych*, Andrzej Radzimiński and Janusz Tandecki, eds. (Toruń, 1999), pp. 303–311.
26. Boockmann, *Der Deutsche Orden*, pp. 181–207; Burleigh, *Prussian Society and the German Order*, pp. 70–126; and Urban, *The Teutonic Knights*, pp. 230–235.
27. The course of the war has now been classically treated by Marjan Biskup, *Trzynstoletnia wojna z Zakonem Krzyżackim 1454–1466* (Warsaw, 1967).
28. See the fine study of Lothar Dralle, *Der Staat des Deutschen Ordens in Preußen nach dem 2. Thorner Frieden. Untersuchungen zur ökonomischen und ständepolitischen Geschichte Altpreußens zwischen 1466 und 1497* (Wiesbaden, 1975).
29. The scholarly debate over this issue is reflected in Erich Weise, "Die staatsrechtlichen Grundlagen des Zweiten Thorner Friedens und die Grenzen seiner Rechtmäßigkeit," *Zeitschrift für Ostforschung* 3 (1954): 1–25; Weise, "Die Beurteilung des Zweiten Thorner Vertrages von 1466 durch die Zeitgenossen bis zum Ende seiner Rechtswirksamkeit im Jahre 1497," *Zeitschrift für Ostforschung* 15 (1966): 601–621; Biskup, "Zagadnenie ważności i interpretacji traktatu toruńskiego 1466 r.," *Kwartalnik Historyczne* 69 (1962): 295–334; Wojciech Hejnosz, "Der Friedensvertrag von Thorn (Toruń) 1466 und seine staatsrechtliche Bedeutung," *Acta Poloniae Historica* 17 (1968): 105–122; Biskup, "Das Ende des Deutschordensstaates Preußen im Jahre 1525," in *Die geistlichen Ritterorden Europas* [as above, note 4], pp. 403–416, esp. 408.
30. See, most recently, the excellent diplomatic study by Maike Sach, *Hochmeister und Großfürst. Die Beziehungen zwischen dem Deutschen Orden in Preußen und dem Moskauer Staat um die Wende zur Neuzeit* (Stuttgart, 2002).
31. For examples, see Biskup, "Plany reformy Zakony Krzyżackiego w Prusach z 1492 roku," in *Prusy—Polska—Europa*, pp. 277–285.
32. Urban, *The Teutonic Knights*, p. 255.
33. These developments are effectively analyzed by Kurt Forstreuter, *Vom Ordensstaat zum Fürstentum. Geistige und politische Wandlungen im Deutschordensstaate Preußen unter den Hochmeistern Friedrich und Albrecht (1498–1525)* (Kitzingen, 1951).
34. Jan Tyszkiewicz, *Ostatnia wojna a Zakonem Krzyżackim 1519–1521* (Warsaw, 1991). See also Sach, *Hochmeister und Großfürst*, pp. 239–434.
35. See the discussion of Boockmann, *Der Deutsche Orden*, pp. 218–220.
36. German scholars of the Teutonic Order have traditionally minimized these developments; Polish scholars, however, have seen these events as central to some of the most important issues of the history of Poland-Lithuania. See particularly the bibliography in Biskup and Labuda, *Dzieje Zakonu Krzyżackiego*, pp. 548–550, as well as Biskup's own treatment in this volume, pp. 462–497, which develops in more depth his earlier and briefer "Das Ende des Deutschordensstaates" [above, n. 29].
37. Boockmann, *Der Deutsche Orden*, pp. 221–224.
38. Robert Bartlett, *The Making of Europe: Conquest, Colonization and Cultural Change, 950–1350* (Princeton, 1993).

39. The overview provided by Boockmann, *Der Deutsche Orden*, pp. 234–254, is characteristically full of insight. See also R. D. Kluge, "Darstellung und Bewertung des Deutschen Ordens in der deutschen und polnischen Literatur," *Zeitschrift für Ostforschung* 18 (1969): 15–53. For a case study of the way in which events and places in the history of the Order have been used for nonhistorical purposes, see Eckdahl, *Die Schlacht bei Tannenberg*, pp. 14–64, and Boockmann, "Das ehemalige Deutschordensschloss Marienburg 1772–1945. Die Geschichte eines politischen Denkmals," in *Geschichtswissenschaft und Vereinswesen im 19. Jahrhundert. Beiträge zur Geschichte historischer Forschung in Deutschland* (Göttingen, 1972), pp. 99–162.

40. In addition to the often cited work of Boockmann, see also Udo Arnold, ed., *Zur Wirtschaftsentwicklung des Deutschen Ordens im Mittelalter* (Marburg, 1989) and his catalogue for the extensive 1990 exhibition devoted to the Teutonic Order in Nuremberg, *800 Jahre Deutscher Orden* (Gütersloh and Munich, 1990). From the Polish side, few individuals have done more in recent years to take up the tradition of Labuda and Biskup than the prematurely deceased Zenon Hubert Nowak, who presided over a continuing series of conferences in Toruń and the resulting conference volumes (*Ordines Militares—Colloquia Torunensia Historica*). These have done much to bring comparative scholarship of the highest quality on the Teutonic Order; see especially no. 10: *Der Deutsche Orden in der Zeit der Kalmarer Union 1397–1521* (Toruń, 1999). Nowak also edited a very useful volume, *Państwo Zakonu Krzyżackiego w Prusach. Podziały administracyjne i kościelne od XIII do XVI wieku* (Toruń, 2000), which appeared posthumously. Nowak's place has been ably taken by Roman Czaja.

# An Amicable Enmity

## Some Peculiarities in Teutonic-Balt Relations in the Chronicles of the Baltic Crusades

### ❖ Raisa Mazeika ❖

German expansion into the northeastern frontiers of Europe—the lands on the south and east shore of the Baltic Sea—occurred through the Baltic Crusades conducted by the Teutonic Order.[1] This order of fighting monks, having conquered present-day Estonia, Latvia and Prussia after fierce resistance, met its match in a century of unsuccessful warfare against the pagan Lithuanians. United into a state that became the Grand Duchy of Lithuania, the Lithuanians drew on the financial and military resources of allied and subject Ruthenian lands in modern-day Belarus and Ukraine,[2] and were able to use European technology and cultural norms to fight against the flower of European knighthood.

Yet interchanges between German and non-German on the Baltic frontier did not take place only on the battlefield. Even with pagans there was a steady interaction, often overlooked by earlier historians, in the areas of trade,[3] diplomacy,[4] military weaponry and tactics,[5] architecture,[6] customs,[7] and for that matter, the seeming adoption of some pagan religious beliefs by the crusaders.[8] This chapter will glance only at one surprising aspect—the mutual respect and even friendly interchanges that sometimes developed between pagan and crusader nobles.

The brutality of warfare in the Baltic Crusade cannot be denied.[9] Yet brutal wars in Europe were by the later Middle Ages modified by some chivalrous customs or by a shared warrior code. At least occasionally, such common European practices as well as a personal relationship between Christian and pagan and a shared sense of noble privilege nuanced the war against Europe's last pagans, the Balt tribes of present-day Prussia and Lithuania. This places the Baltic Crusade wars and especially the princes of pagan Lithuania more squarely in the European tradition.[10] As Robert Bartlett wrote, the people and wealth of "remote pagan parts" were being drawn "into the central programmes of Latin Christendom."[11] More broadly, it reminds historians of any field that shared cultural elements, respect and peaceful interchange can co-exist with eagerly and brutally pursued warfare. Respect, even friendship, need not mean the end of warfare—in fact, one can greatly appreciate an enemy who puts up a good fight, presenting one with a chance to display skill and win more glory in this world and the next.

Lithuanian historians have already noted the growth of what they termed an "orientation to the model of the European knight" as shown by occasional acts of the Lithuanian higher nobility.[12] But those raise the problem of differentiating age-old Indo-European warrior customs from specifically medieval chivalry, a problem that is probably insoluble in the fragmentary Baltic sources. There can be little doubt that Balt nobles and the Teutonic Order's crusading monks who fought them tried their best to possess some qualities which form the traditional attributes of the textbook chivalrous knight: skill at arms, physical strength, bravery, loyalty to one's lord, prob-ably a generosity with booty, and above all a thirst for glory or honor.[13] Many warrior societies value these attributes, however, and for very practical reasons. Certainly the one new factor which European chivalry introduced, "courtesie" and romantic love of women, is only very occasionally attributed to Teutonic Order brothers in their service to the Virgin Mary, and is completely absent in any description of pagan Balts. The two new customs that the pagan Lithuanians clearly learned from their enemies, ransoming of prisoners and the occasional formal duel, have been discussed by other historians.[14] Therefore, this chapter focuses not on customs but on attitudes—i.e., some hints of personal relationships based on personal respect between the enemies.

What did the chroniclers think of their enemies? Peter von Dusburg, a priest of the Teutonic Order whose chronicle was written in 1326,[15] names the various Prus-sian tribes and notes that they were all militarily strong in the thirteenth century, when the Teutonic Order first moved into the Baltic area. Praise of pagan prowess in the Teutonic Order's chronicles is suspect because of the need to glorify the Order's knights by showing that they fought a formidable enemy. Indeed, Dusburg draws exactly that moral in this passage. Yet he does mention one tribe, the Sudovians or Jotvingians, as outstanding: "The Sudovian nobles," he writes, "just as they surpass the other [tribes] in nobility of their manner [i.e., customs], so they surpass them in riches and in power."[16] Conquering them, says Dusburg, shows how incredible was the achievement of the Teutonic Order, and demonstrates God's power—"signa dei magna et mirabilia forcia." Dusburg also writes that the Prussians who attack Königsberg are "viri experti et subtiles in bello" (men expert and cunning in war), and they almost defeat the garrison of a fort by interrupting its food supply.[17] Here the chronicler is emphasizing qualities—cunning and intelligence—which are important in Germanic heroic literature and also in the real wars of the Baltic Crusade, where one of the most frequent forms of battle was the ambush.

Still, sheer bravery won even more respect from enemies. Dusburg describes Lithuanian nobles who, "seeing his bold audacity," "greatly admire" the leader of a Teutonic Order army and ask who he is, because he dares to attack the Lithuanians even though he knows they have been forewarned.[18] Philippe de Mézières, who accompanied crusaders to Prussia in 1364, writes of the Lithuanians that they are "sons ydolatres" yet adds they are *"Une gens sans lectre et sans clergie, mais assez bien combatant, testmoings las vaillans croisiez de Prusse."*[19] Heroic pagans are also presented in the Rhymed Chronicle of Livonia, written soon after 1290.[20] Peter von Dusburg relates admiringly about Teutonic Order knight Ludwig von Libencele:

> When he was captured, he was presented to [the Prus noble] Scumandus, who, because [Ludwig] was like unto him in bravery (*audacia*), loved him greatly. Whence it happened, that [Scumandus] took him, while yet in captivity, to a place where the powerful men of Sudovia had gathered to a banquet. At this drinking bout one powerful and noble man provoked brother Ludwig to tumult of spirit by insults and quarrels. Whence he said to Scumandus, "Have you brought me here, so that my heart could so painfully be afflicted by his words?" To which Scumandus answered, "I grieve for your trouble, and if you dare, avenge the injury done to you and I will help you." Hearing this brother Ludwig bestirred himself and killed the envious one with a sword.[21]

Later Ludwig escaped or was released, probably after payment of ransom. Scumandus himself later surrendered to the Order and became a Christian, but the shared values, which may have made this move more palatable, were more military than religious. Recognition of shared noble status probably created much of the bond between Christian and pagan, German and Balt warriors. The nobility of the Balt chieftains seems to have been recognized and appreciated by the crusaders. According to chronicler Jean des Preis (Jean d'Outremeuse), Margiris, commander of the Lithuanian fort of Pilènai, was of such noble birth that even King John of Luxembourg was willing to fight a duel with him.[22]

Yet personal relationships could also depend on mutual obligations, even to a non-noble. In Dusburg's chronicle, the Prus leader Herkus Mantus, who had spent his youth as a captive hostage of the Teutonic Order, shows friendship to Hirtzel, a burgher of Magdeburg fighting in the Teutonic Order's army who is captured by the Prus. Herkus tries to save him from being sacrificed to the pagan gods, because the burgher appeals to him to remember favors he has done for Herkus in Magdeburg. Two times in casting the lots Hirtzel is chosen from among the captives to be sacrificed, and two times Herkus intervenes. The third time the lots are cast and give the same result, the pagans and the crusader himself accept his grisly fate as divine will, and he is burned alive.[23] Here the Prus leader is portrayed as interfering in a sacred pagan rite for the sake of a sense of personal obligation. In the end, however, personal considerations were sacrificed by both Christian and pagan to their religious ideals.

By the beginning of the fourteenth century the Prus were conquered, only the Lithuanians remained as un-subdued pagans, and they seem to have won the respect afforded to a worthy foe. In the later chronicles of the Teutonic Order the princes of the Lithuanians are sometimes presented as evil but not alien, able to parlay and even joke with the Christians whose mission it is to fight them. Wigand von Marburg tells how Grand Duke Vytenis and Heinrich Dusemer, later Grand Master of the Teutonic Order, joke after fighting: Vytenis has been wounded, a truce is being concluded, and Vytenis says, "One of you, whose head was helmeted [i.e. his face was hidden], wounded me. I would like to see him." Dusemer is presented, and Vytenis says to him, "You with your sharp sword almost killed me!" The Teutonic Knight replies, "So I would have, if you had waited for me!"[24] Here the joke is at the pagan's expense—the implication is that he ducked the blow, or rode out of the way, yet the humor lies in the improbability of any fighter simply waiting for a blow to fall, so that Dusemer's remark is in a sense self-deprecating and a compliment to Vytenis's skill. Paradoxically, this immediately follows a passage in Wigand's chronicle where Vytenis tramples the Communion host and mocks God, thus we might expect him to be presented as the incarnation of evil, not as a knight joking among other knights.

Interestingly, Vytenis (ruled c. 1295–1316) was the first Lithuanian pagan ruler to build Christian churches in his realm and to invite Franciscan monks to serve them.[25] Lithuania's rulers were learning to make use of European culture and to negotiate with Christians for what they needed. This was much resented by the Teutonic Order's chroniclers, who accused Vytenis's brother and successor Gediminas (ruled c.1316–1341) of lying because he began negotiations for baptism, which he canceled after achieving a peace treaty.[26] There are no indications of personal relationships between crusaders and Gediminas, perhaps because this ruler seems not to be personally in the battlefield so much as other Lithuanian rulers, or because Gediminas was a close ally of the Order's enemy, the city of Riga.

Gediminas was succeeded by his son Algirdas, who ruled from 1345 to 1377 with the support of his brother Kęstutis and other family members. Prince Kęstutis led many armies against the Teutonic Knights and became well known to them. The "ältere Hochmeisterchronik" describes him thus: "Kęstutis was indeed a valiant man and true. If he wished to raid in Prussia [i.e. the territory ruled by the Teutonic Order], he told that to the marshal beforehand, and would indeed come. Also if he made a peace with the Master [of the Order], he would hold fast to it. Whichever brother of the Order he considered bold and manly he would love, and would show him great honor."[27] We might mistrust this chronicle, written after 1433 (long after Kęstutis's death and when the Baltic Crusade is in fact over). Yet we see an episode in the earlier chronicle of Wigand of Marburg in which Kęstutis is indeed portrayed as valiant, truthful, warns of an attack, and keeps his agreements. In 1369 the Teutonic Order began to build the fort of Gotteswerder beside the Memel River. Kęstutis immediately warned that he would try to prevent this if he could. The fort was completed and garrisoned, then Grand Duke Algirdas and his brother Kęstutis arrived with a huge army and besieged it so vigorously with siege engines, that the Master was forced to negotiate the release of prisoners. The Teutonic Knights took advantage of the negotiations, protracting them until help could arrive, but Kęstutis, although angry, did not break the truce until he had notified the marshal.[28]

As for loving and honoring some brothers of the Teutonic Order, Kęstutis saved a komtur or fort commander, John Surbach, from being sacrificed to the pagan gods by the Lithuanians.[29] Perhaps the pagan leader was motivated by a hope of ransom.[30] Another likely practical motivation would be adherence to the rules of taking captives, from which Kęstutis himself had benefited several years before this episode, being taken prisoner and then managing to escape. There were frequent parlays between Kęstutis and the crusaders, for example in 1362 outside Kaunas as this important Lithuanian fort was being taken and Kęstutis arrived with an army too late to succor it. Despite his anguish over the destruction of Kaunas castle, where his son perished, Kęstutis continued formal negotiations. According to Wigand of Marburg, he and Algirdas asked for a list of prisoners in writing, which must mean they had gone to the trouble of bringing literate clerks with them. The Teutonic Order's marshal had his notaries prepare formal lists.[31]

Orderly exchanges in the midst of war on the Baltic front did not mean that the rules were not sometimes broken and prisoners killed by both sides. As we have seen, Kęstutis had to save John Surbach, while the marshals of the Teutonic Order's armies could not always guarantee the safety of prisoners. Wigand of Marburg writes that the Lithuanian noble Goštautas, commander of the fort of Veliuona, as the fort is burning called out to the marshal that he wished to surrender. The marshal agreed but warned, "I do not wish to be blamed if when you descend from the fort you are cut down." Goštautas was taken to the marshal's tent, but a soldier killed him there, to the great displeasure of the marshal, who initiated a formal complaint.[32] Nevertheless, this shows that an acknowledged procedure for surrender existed in the Baltic Crusade wars even if it did not always work.

Prisoner exchanges must have had a strong practical motivation, as did the many treaties that Lithuanians are known to have made with their enemies. Yet there was a personal element, which was not so much practical as social, growing out of the shared values of the opposing sides—bravery, as we have seen, and also liberal hospitality. In Wigand of Marburg's chronicle, a Lithuanian prince [this may be either Algirdas or Kęstutis] not only talked with the enemy but wined and dined some with whom he had a personal relationship.[33] After an attack by the Teutonic Order's forces on Vilnius in 1377,

> The King spoke with the Marshal on certain matters, until the Marshal gave him his hand and suddenly ascended the drawbridge, all the commanders with the Germans pressing after him. And the King indignantly said to the Marshal "I gave my hand to you alone, and the others conveniently came!" and he added, 'I would like to see one commander, namely von Hohenstein'. The Marshal: "He is in his tent." The King: "I wish him to dine with me." The Marshal: "I will order this under safe conduct" . . . [Gottfried von Hohenstein came to Vilnius castle] where he was received with honor by the King, and he was merry with him. In the evening he returned to the army. At sunrise, with flags aloft and much noise, they [the crusaders] besieged Vilnius castle, and this seemed to the pagans a dishonest action. At the hour of vespers the King talked with the Marshal and they made peace. The King indeed invited the commanders to dine, especially counts Eberhard and Theodoric von Katzenelbogen. Above and beyond this, the King gave the commanders much mead with bread. And the truce lasted the night. For the King petitioned that they spare the center of the city, in which matter they were able to agree. However, [this agreement] was neglected, since the Christians burnt the city center; whence the Marshal was most grieved.[34]

We see that the pagan ruler of Lithuania had special friendships with some, but not all, of the Teutonic Order's commanders, and a dinner between friends could happen during lulls in the fighting. Nevertheless, agreements between the upper nobility did not always work to control the ravages of a looting crowd. Through such social interchanges as well as through capture of men and weapons, pagan nobles came to know the German enemy's customs. Prince Kęstutis, according to Wigand, even impersonated the Grand Master of the Teutonic Order when escaping from captivity, riding his horse and wearing his habit.[35] Lithuanians also learned some military tactics from the crusaders, and quickly adopted their weapons.[36] In the words of Robert Bartlett, Lithuania's "gods were old, but its guns were new."[37]

As the other side became less alien, it is no wonder that warriors sometimes fled to serve in the enemy forces. Prus, Letts and later Lithuanians had done this from first contact, but one could argue this was only because the fight seemed hopeless. Later defections seem to have been more political. Kęstutis's own son fled to the Teutonic Order, was baptized and then invaded Lithuania in an unsuccessful attempt to seize the throne.[38] More surprising, in the fourteenth century there were several episodes of Teutonic Order knights fleeing to the Lithuanians, for example Johannes Vlowere in 1376, and John Lanzeberg and Frederick de Missen with all their followers in 1374.[39] Stranger still, Lanzeberg was able to return to the Order a year later.[40] St. Paul asked rhetorically, "What concord hath Christ with Belial, or what part hath he that believeth with an infidel?" (2 Cor. 6:15), and this was approvingly quoted by an early chronicler of the Baltic crusade, Henry of Livonia.[41] But in fact Christians and infidels, Germans and Balts, could interact quite amiably during the Baltic wars while sharpening their swords for the next round of fighting.

# Notes

Due to space limitations, bibliographical references have been kept to a minimum and works in English given preference. Readers should consult the works cited for further references.

1. The classic works in German on these Crusades are too numerous to list; see Marian Tumler, *Der Deutsche Orden im Werden, Wachsen und Wirken bis 1400* (Vienna, 1955); Helmut Beumann, *Heidenmission und Kreuzzugsgedanke in der Deutschen Ostpolitik des Mittelalters* (Bad Homburg, 1963); and especially Werner Paravicini, *Die Preussenreisen des Europäischen Adels,* parts 1 and 2 (Sigmaringen, 1989 and 1995). For an overview of the historiography, see Alvydas Nikžentaitis, "Litauisch-preussische Beziehungen im Mittelalter. Der litauische Forschungsstand," and Sven Ekdahl, "Die preussisch-litauischen Beziehungen des Mittelalters. Stand und Aufgaben der Forschung in Deutschland," both in *Deutschland und Litauen. Bestandsaufnahmen und Aufgaben der historischen Forschung,* Norbert Angermann and Joachim Tauber, eds. (Lüneburg, 1995), pp. 21–30 and 31–44. There are many studies in Polish and Lithuanian, e.g., Marian Biskup, ed., *Ekspansja Niemieckich Zakonów Rycerskich w strefie Bałtyku od XIII do połowy XVI wieku* (Toruń, 1990), and Juozas Jurginis, ed., *Lietuvių karas su kryžiuočiais* (Vilnius, 1964). Good introductions to this Crusade in English are Eric Christiansen, *The Northern Crusades* (London & Minneapolis, 1980; new ed., New York, 1997); Norman Housley, *The Later Crusades, 1274–1580* (Oxford, 1992), 322–375; Jonathan Riley-Smith, *The Crusades, A Short History* (London, 1987),161–165, 212–215; Marie-Luise Favreau-Lilie, "Mission to the Heathen in Prussia and Livonia: The Attitudes of the Religious Military Orders toward Christianization," in *Christianizing Peoples and Converting Individuals,* ed. Guyda Armstrong and Ian Wood (Turnhout, 2000), pp. 147–154.

2. For an overview in English, see Stephen C. Rowell, *Lithuania Ascending: A Pagan Empire within East-Central Europe 1295–1345* (Cambridge, 1994); in German, Kurt Forstreuter, *Deutschland und Litauen im Mittelalter* (Köln/Graz, 1962). On Rus participation, Henadz Sahanovich, "'Rus' u vaine z Niametskim ordenam," *Belaruski Histarychny Ahliad* 8 (2001): 3–24.

3. Rasa Mažeika, "Of Cabbages and Knights: Trade and Trade Treaties with the Infidel on the Northern Frontier, 1200–1390," *Journal of Medieval History* 20 (1994): 63–76.

4. In English: Rasa Mažeika, "Bargaining for Baptism: Lithuanian Negotiations for Conversion, 1250–1358," in *Varieties of Religious Conversion in the Middle Ages,* ed. James Muldoon (Gainesville, 1997), pp. 131–145; Stephen C. Rowell, "A Pagan's Word: Lithuanian Diplomatic Procedure 1200–1385," *Journal of Medieval History* 18 (1992): 145–160.

5. Werner Paravicini, *Preussenreisen,* part 2, pp. 47–49, documents the up-to-date weaponry of the Lithuanians. Cf. Alvydas Nikžentaitis, "XIII–XV a. lietuvių kariuomenės bruožai (organizacija, taktika, papročiai)," in *Karo archyvas* XIII (Vilnius, 1992), pp. 3–33.

6. Probable German architecture of a thirteenth-century church found under the present cathedral in Vilnius, Lithuania: Napalys Kitkauskas and Albertas Lisanka, "Nauji duomenys apie viduramžių Vilniaus katedrą," *Kultūros Barai* (1986, nos. 4, 5, 6), 59–63, 56–61, 47–51; Vytautas Urbanavičius, "Pałac władców Litwy na Zamku Dolnym w Wilnie," *Konteksty: Antropologia, Kultury, Etnografia, Sztuka* 47, nos. 3–4 (1993): 30–33; in

English: Algimantas Kajackas, "History and Recent Investigations of Vilnius Cathedral," *La Christianizzazione della Lituania* (Vatican City, 1989), pp. 263–284.

7. On cremation of their dead by the Teutonic Order, despite express prohibitions by the Church: Herman de Wartberge, "Chronicon Livoniae," in *Scriptores Rerum Prussicarum,* vol. 2, ed. T. Hirsch, M. Töppen, and E. Strehlke (Leipzig, 1863), p. 109.

8. Rasa Mažeika, "Granting Power to Enemy Gods in the Chronicles of the Baltic Crusades," in *Medieval Frontiers: Concepts and Practices,* ed. David Abulafia and Nora Berend (Aldershot, 2002), pp. 153–171.

9. William Urban, "Victims of the Baltic Crusade," *Journal of Baltic Studies* 29 (1998): 195–212.

10. But this sort of relationship also applied to Muslims outside that tradition: Catherine Wendy Bracewell, *The Uskoks of Senj: Piracy, Banditry and Holy War in the Sixteenth-century Adriatic* (Ithaca, 1992), pp. 180–187, on respect and even blood brotherhood between Christian and Muslim, yet "the inevitability of warfare between Christian and Muslim remained an unquestioned assumption" (p. 187).

11. Robert Bartlett, *The Making of Europe: Conquest, Colonization and Cultural Change, 950–1350* (Princeton, 1993), p. 268.

12. Nikžentaitis, "XIII–XV a. lietuvių kariuomenės bruožai," pp. 29–31; Kastytis Antanaitis, "Riterijos apraiškos Lietuvoje XIV–XVI amžiais," *Darbai ir Dienos* 5/14 (1997): 125–142.

13. Space limitations preclude quoting here the many works on this topic; for a succinct overview of courtly culture, see Werner Paravicini, *Die ritterlich-höfische Kultur des Mittelalters* (Munich, 1994). See pp. 7–9 for desirable qualities in a warrior society.

14. See works cited in note 12 above, also Sven Ekdahl, "The Treatment of Prisoners of War during the Fighting between the Teutonic Order and Lithuania," in *The Military Orders: Fighting for the Faith and Caring for the Sick,* ed. Malcolm Barber (Aldershot, 1994), pp. 263–269; Paravicini, *Preussenreisen,* part 2, p. 101; Stephen C. Rowell, "Unexpected Contacts: Lithuanians at Western Courts, c. 1316–c. 1400," *The English Historical Review* 111 (1996): 557–577, here pp. 561–562.

15. On Peter Dusburg, see *Geschichtsschreibung und Geschichtsbewußtsein im späten Mittelalter,* ed. Hans Patze (Sigmaringen, 1987), pp. 449–454; Marzena Pollakówna, *Kronika Piotra z Dusburga* (Wrocław, 1968).

16. Peter von Dusburg, "Chronicon Terrae Prussie" III (3), *Scriptores Rerum Prussicarum* [henceforth SRP] vol. 1, ed. T. Hirsch, M. Töppen, E. Strehlke (Leipzig, 1861; reprint, Frankfurt-am-Main, 1965) p. 52, "Sudowite generosi, sicut nobilitate morum alios precedebant, ita diviciis et potencia excedebant."

17. Dusburg III (102), SRP I, 106.

18. Dusburg, III (311), SRP I, 177: "Gevehardus de Mansfelt commendator de Brandenburgk et multi fratres cum mille et quingentis viriis equitaverunt ad territorium Pograude, et licet scirent Lethowinos premunitos et paratos . . . audacter intrantes dictum territorium, interfecerunt multos homines et ceperunt, incendio et rapina multipliciter devastantes . . . . Masio et Sudargus et alii nobiles, videntes eorum presumptuosam audaciam, ammirati sunt ultra modum . . . Postea Lethowini quesiverunt, quis fuerit capitaneus dicti exercitus. Quibus responsum fuit, quod commendator de Brandenburgk homo juvenis et virilis. At illi: dicatis ergo ei, quod nunquam veniet ad etatem debitam, si sic presmptose nobis presentibus cum tam paucis pugnatoribus nostras terras voluerit depredare."

19. Philippe de Mézières, *Le Songe du Vieil Pèlerin,* ed. G. W. Coopland, 2 vols. (Cambridge, 1969), p. 235.

20. Alan Murray, "The Structure, Genre and Intended Audience of the Livonian Rhymed Chronicle," in *Crusade and Conversion on the Baltic Frontier, 1150–1500,* ed. Alan V.

Murray (Aldershot, 2001), pp. 235–251, here p. 245; Leo Meyer, ed., *Livländische Reim-chronik* (Hildesheim, 1963), p. 233, lines 10171–10176:

wen die Semegallen dar
quamen kein der bruder schar,
sie liefen so einander an:
hette ez er Ecke hie vor getan,
und von Berne er Ditterich,
sie weren von rechte lobes rich.

21. Dusburg III (210), SRP I, 142: "Frater Lodewicus de Libencele, vir nobilis et in rebus bellicis ab adolescencia exercitatus , mira gesta fecit in vita sua, que inferius apparebunt. Hic dum captus esset, presentatus fuit Scumando, qui, quia similis ei fuit in audacia, multum dilexit eum, unde accidit, quod ipsum adhuc in captivitate positum duxit se-cum ad locum, ubi pociores terre Sudowie convenerant ad potandum. In hac potacione quidam vir nobilis et potens fratrem Lodewicum contumeliis et jurgiis ad turbacionem animi provocavit. Unde ait ad Scumandum: duxisti me huc, ut iste cor meum injurio-sis affligeret verbis suis? Cui respondit Scumandus: doleo de turbacione tua, et si audes, vindica injuriam tibi factam, ego te juvabo. Hoc audito frater Lodewicus animatus fuit, et emulum suum gladio interfecit. Postea frater Lodewicus per quendam famulum dicti Scumandi liberatus fuit a captivitate et ad fratres reductus."
     Such episodes belie assertions that in Dusburg's chronicle there is "eine manichäist-ische Einstellung" where "Das absolut Gute, verkörpert durch den Orden, kämpft gegen das absolut Böse in der Gestalt der Heiden": Wolfgang Wippermann, *Der Ordenstaat als Ideologie* (Berlin, 1979), p. 43. For Dusburg God or the Devil can be at work in both camps; thus he can speak of sinning brothers of the Order and pagans who do good deeds.
22. Alvydas Nikžentaitis, *Gediminas* (Vilnius, 1989), pp. 10–11, citing the chronicle of Jean des Preis and other sources. For Lithuanian nobles challenging crusaders to duels, see Rowell, "Unexpected Contacts," p. 561, note 4, citing SRP I, 286.
23. Dusburg III (91), SRP I, 101.
24. Wigand von Marburg, SRP, vol. II, ed. T. Hirsch, M. Töppen, and E. Strehlke (Leipzig, 1863; reprinted Frankfurt-am-Main, 1965), pp. 456–457: "Post breve intervallum facte sunt treuge, et rex [Vytenis] ait preceptoribus, unus e vobis, cuius caput ferreum fuit, molestavit me, quem libens adhuc viderem. Magister quoque destinavit ei eum Tusemer dictum, cui rex: tuo acuto gladio me quasi interfecisses; et ait: sic factum fuisset, si mei expectassetis."
25. According to his brother Gediminas: *Liv-, Est- und Kurländisches Urkundenbuch,* part 1, vol. 2 (Reval, 1855; reprint, Aalen, 1968), no. 687, col. 140.
26. S. C. Rowell, "The Letters of Gediminas: 'Gemachte Luge'? Notes on a Controversy," *Jahrbücher für Geschichte Osteuropas* 41 (1993): 321–360.
27. *Die Altere Hochmeisterchronik* SRP, vol. III (Leipzig, 1866; reprinted Frankfurt-am-Main, 1965), pp. 593–594: "Der selbe Kynstutte was gar eyn streithafftig man und worhaftig. Wen her wolde reisen zcu Prewsen ins land, das entpot her czuvor dem marschalke, und quam ouch gewisse. Ouch so her mit dem meister eynen frede machte, den hilt her gar veste. Welchen bruder des ordens her ouch irkante kune unde manhaftig, den libete her un irczeigete em vil ere."
28. Wigand von Marburg, SRP II, 561–562.
29. Wigand von Marburg, SRP II, 596.
30. For examples of ransom exchanges between Lithuanians and crusaders, see Paravicini, *Preussenreisen,* part 2, p. 101, note 444.
31. Wigand von Marburg, SRP II, 537.

32. "cepit querulari de occisione eius." Wigand of Marburg, SRP II, 540, 547 (the episode is related twice).

33. On the importance of banquets to the Teutonic Order, see Paravicini, *Preussenreisen,* part 2, pp. 127–128.

34. Wigand von Marburg, SRP II, 589: "Rex loquitur cum marschalko in certis casibus, donec marschalkus ei manum daret et statim ascendit pontem, preceptores comprimunt post eum cum Teutonis, et rex indignanter ait marschalko: tibi soli prebui manum, et alii eciam convenienter veniunt, et addidit: unum preceptorem libenter viderem sc. de Hoensteyn. Et marschalkus: est aput tugurium suum. Rex vero: volo ut mecum commedat; et marschalkus: ordinabo hoc sub salvo conductu. Transiitque ad exercitum juxta aquam vulgariter Woke, ubi pernoctabant, vocatque fratrem de Hoenstein, qui ad votum regis venit in castrum, ubi a rege honorifice est susceptus, et letatur cum eo. Nocte rediit ad exercitum. Orto sole erectis vexillis cum clamore castrum Wille obsident, visumque fuit paganis inhoneste actum. Hora vesperarum rex cum marschalko loquitur, faciunt pacem. Rex vero preceptores vocat ad prandium, comitem Eberhardum et Theodericum de Katzenelbogen singulariter. Ultra hec rex dedit preceptoribus medonem cum pane sufficienter. Paxque stetit per noctem. Petiit tamen rex, quod dimitterent medietatem civitatis, in qua sibi complacere possent. Neglectum tamen fuit, quum medietatem christiani exurebant; unde doluit marshalkus . . ."

35. Wigand von Marburg, SRP II, 528.

36. See note 5 above.

37. *The Making of Europe,* p. 312.

38. Wigand von Marburg, II, 551–553; Paravicini, *Preussenreisen,* part 2, p. 108.

39. Herman von Wartberg, "Chronicon Livoniae," SRP II, 111 and 105.

40. Ibid., II, 116.

41. *Heinrici Chronicon Livoniae,* XXX (1), Leonid Arbusow and Albert Bauer, eds., *Heinrichs Livländische Chronik, MGH Scriptores rerum Germanicarum* (Hannover, 1955), p. 216: "cum non sit coniunctio conveniens Christi cum Belial nec pagani copula congrua cum christiana."

# The Early Modern Period

## ◆ Charles Ingrao ◆

In recent years it has become fashionable to speak of "Old" and "New" Europe. To the extent that it is true, the conceit behind this dichotomy owes much more to Peter the Great and the early modern period than it does to the geopolitics of the post-Communist age. After all, it was the Russian tsar who first commissioned maps delineating the Urals as the continent's eastern edge. With the stroke of a draftsman's quill, he gave Europe an artificial unity that it may not have merited then and that may still be incomplete today, depending on the criteria employed. Nonetheless, the early modern period bound East and West together in a single continent in many ways, none more than by the *perception* that it represented a single entity.

And most of the progress was made during the eighteenth century. Thanks in large part to the Mongol and Ottoman invasions, the disparate peoples of Russia and the Ottoman Balkans had much less contact with Germany and the rest of the continent's western half during the sixteenth and seventeenth centuries. Although Russia eventually emerged from the Mongol yoke, the Time of Troubles and its residue assured that the seventeenth century would pass before it would look farther west than Poland-Lithuania for substantive commercial, political and cultural relations. Admittedly, Poland was much more engaged with Germany and the West, whether as an exporter of grain or as an end station for the spread of Renaissance culture and Protestantism. But here too, the seventeenth century represented the end of an age of limited contact, rather than one of continuity with the dramatic developments of the eighteenth century.

Certainly, Germany did not contribute much to expanding these ties before then. The Reformation encouraged its nascent Lutheran majority to look inward. Although Protestantism spread to Hungary, Poland and the Baltic Littoral, adoption of the Augsburg Confession was largely limited to the German diaspora. Meanwhile, large-scale German migration remained a thing of the past, although there was some movement in the other direction as Hungarians and South Slavs fled west and north before the Ottoman advance. Indeed, aside from localized commerce and freeboot-ing, the Ottoman-Habsburg frontier became in all other respects the early modern equivalent of the Iron Curtain.

Yet, even as it closed the Balkans off to the West, the Turkish onslaught reengaged Germany in the East through the medium of dynastic politics. Following the great Ottoman victory of Mohács, the Habsburgs became the first of Germany's dynastic "westernizers," a mantle that they accepted with their election as kings of Bohemia and Hungary in 1526/27. Over the next two centuries, the Habsburgs introduced a wide array of administrative structures and practices to both kingdoms that included a chancery (*Hofkanzlei*) for each kingdom, as well as a central treasury (*Hofkam-mer*) and war council (*Hofkriegsrat*) in Vienna, and extended down to the local level through German military garrisons and tax collectors. This process intensified in the Bohemian lands following the Battle of White Mountain (1620), after which Czech social elites increasingly affected high culture through the German language and Austrian Baroque style.

Yet the Habsburgs' dynastic advance had little immediate effect beyond Bohemia and Hungary. Through the middle of the seventeenth century, high politics in the East was performed on a narrow stage on which Russia, Poland and Sweden were the only actors, while the western powers served as little more than a diffident audience. Soon afterward, the broader imperial interests of Sweden and the Ottomans helped to expand the theater of operations, first by drawing Brandenburg and Austria into the Great Deluge (1655–60), then by bringing the tsar and emperor together in the Holy League (1684). Thereafter, the Habsburgs and Hohenzollerns felt obliged to face both east and west in advancing their dynastic interests.

As Michael Müller's contribution ably demonstrates, a new era of integration began in 1697 with the conversion and election of Saxon Elector Friedrich August I to the Polish throne, which he and his son held until 1764. Even as he traveled to Warsaw for his coronation as Augustus II, Tsar Peter was traveling in the opposite direction on a momentous two-year odyssey to the Netherlands and England that, nonetheless, began in Königsberg and ended in Vienna. One of the many ramifications of that trip was Peter's initiation of the practice of wedding Romanov heirs to German princelings. By 1761 both the tsar and tsarina were themselves pedigreed offspring of lesser German royalty. Thereafter, six successive tsars chose German consorts until the string ended in 1917 in a basement in Ekaterinburg. By then Germany had also provided royal dynasties for Greece (1832), Romania (1866), Bulgaria (1879), and Albania (1913).

A critical ingredient in Peter's interest in Germany was the Habsburg alliance that was initially formed against the Ottomans, but which his immediate successors readily expanded to include close collaboration vis-à-vis Poland. By mid-century, however, Frederick the Great had inspired a new generation of German princelings, including Peter of Holstein-Gottorp and, more significantly, the young Catherine of Anhalt-Zerbst, for whom Prussia became the Russian ally of first resort. By the second half of the eighteenth century, the offensive tandem of Frederick and Catherine had progressively eliminated the expanses of Polish and Ottoman territory that had heretofore blocked Russia's full admission to the European stage, much as it recast international relations into a vehicle for expansionist *Realpolitik.*[1]

Russia could not have become such an engine of conquest without domestic restructuring, for which it turned once again to Germany for inspiration. Although it is fashionable to extol the worldwide impact of English constitutionalism and French absolutism, we cannot overlook the far more pervasive role played by models of feudal intermediation and bureaucratization espoused by the German political and economic theorists. Aside from adopting the medieval Magdeburg Law for self-governing municipalities,[2] Peter the Great became a ready convert to the cameral sciences, which he may have adopted from Swedish institutions, but which was the love child of Protestant Germany's princes and universities. Even before his death, large numbers of Petrine officials trooped to the University of Königsberg to learn cameralist theory and administrative practice. Russia's engagement with Germany and the West was further cemented by a plethora of German civil and military officials on whom Peter and his successors relied for their expertise on government, administration and military science. From Münnich to Münchhausen Russia offered employment, adventure and fame to German soldiers willing to push the Ottomans back to the fringes of the Black Sea, the Balkans, and beyond. Back in Moscow and St. Petersburg, Petrine absolutism was molded by key German officials like the Old-enburger Münnich, whose ambitious restructuring of the Russian army was cut short by Andrej Ivanovic Ostermann (1686–1747), the Westphalian-born, Jena-educated son of a Lutheran pastor, who dominated the country's domestic and foreign affairs for two decades under Peter and his three immediate successors. Yet the rigorous implementation of the cameral sciences did not peak until the reign of Catherine the Great, who may have given a public nod to Montesquieu's *Esprit de Lois,* but whose advocacy of feudal intermediary bodies reflected her native Germany's confidence in *Zwischengewälte* for solutions to the daunting problems of imperial governance.[3] By the end of the eighteenth century, Russian administration clearly bore the mark of its German reformers, both in substance and appearance, given the proliferation of German cognates like *ober-fiskal* and *ober-politseimeister.* Although native Russians held an ever-increasing share of such offices, some key posts continued to be entrusted to Germans, including the Silesian and Holstein officials who shaped Catherine's system of *Collegia,* together with the disproportionately large percentage of Baltic Germans who staffed them.[4]

Admittedly, German ideas and officials left a somewhat smaller imprint on eighteenth-century Poland, largely because of the impermanence of Wettin rule and the two kings' minimal success in implementing political and institutional change. Their influence on high culture was more profound, as governmental and academic elites alike looked primarily to German universities for inspiration, a choice that owed a great deal to the role played by Royal Prussia as a mediating agent for the early German enlightenment.[5] Indeed, the single most influential proponent of Enlightenment rationalism in Poland—and even among the French-speaking courtiers of Catherine the Great—was not Voltaire or Locke, but the *Aufklärer* Christian Wolff.[6] It was only in the second half of the century, on the eve of Poland's disappearance at the hands of its neighbors, that its intelligentsia turned toward France.

Ironically, the appetite with which Polish, Russian and even Balkan elites embraced French culture may have been sharpened by the perceptual barriers that that country's Republic of Letters had helped erect between East and West during the Age of Reason. After centuries of commerce, colonization, and conquest, early modern Latin Christendom had already developed a sense of what constituted the "East." In his path-breaking study, *Inventing Eastern Europe*, Larry Wolff showed how visitors from as far away as the continent's Atlantic littoral envisioned the continent's eastern (and largely Slavic) marches as a frontier across which the positive attributes of "western" civilization steadily dissipated as Europe converged with Asia.[7] The eastward passage through Poland into Muscovy, and through Hungary into the Balkans, reaffirmed what the "West" was all about—and what the "East" needed to acquire if it was to narrow the gap. There was no question where Germany and its cultural mediators stood in this world of haves and have-nots. Despite their diversity and the highly articulated gradations of Anglo-French conceit, Germany, Scandinavia, and even Spain were inextricably linked with Britain, France, the Low Countries and Italy. David Pickus's contribution shows the parameters of this divide: subscription to an Enlightenment mindset.

At the same time, Germany's relative proximity to Bohemia, Poland, and Hungary afforded its elites an opportunity to help bridge the divide, blurring the distinctions that so captivated the readers of early modern travel literature. In fact, one of the remarkable features of German-Slav interaction during the early modern period was the relative absence of group conflict, which has so dominated the perception of ethnic relations in the next two centuries. There was certainly some resentment of the prominent role played by expatriate German elites in Hungary, Poland and Russia, particularly among indigenous nobles whose own mobility and status they may have arrested. What is indisputable, however, is that the German communities readily accepted and identified with their adopted homelands; thus the towns of Royal Prussia were proud constituents of the Polish commonwealth, while the landed nobility of the Baltic littoral loyally served generations of Swedish and Russian monarchs. Even in rebellion the Protestant German communities of the Bohemian and Hungarian crownlands had no difficulty in joining their Czech and Magyar coreligionists against the confessional absolutism of the German Habsburgs, just as many of Bohemia's Czechs and virtually all of Hungary's Catholic and Orthodox Slavs remained steadfastly loyal to the dynasty. Coexistence characterized relations throughout the Habsburg and Russian empires well into the nineteenth century. As Karl Roider and Robert Forrest show in their contribution, the German colonists who settled the Banat and Vojvodina struggled mightily against disease and famine, not the indigenous population. Indeed, the western—or at least German—attributes of hard work, parsimony, discipline, and reliability were more likely to incite admiration and imitation than jealousy and resentment among indigenous peoples, such as the Romanian peasants of contemporary Transylvania, who still employ clichés that mark their appreciation of the German contribution to the region they colonized.[8]

# Notes

1.  Paul Schroeder, *The Transformation of European Politics, 1763–1848* (Oxford, 1999) provides an excellent narrative of the process, though without quite appreciating its disruptive effects on classical diplomacy. Cf. Charles Ingrao, "Paul Schroeder's Eighteenth-century Balance of Power: A Critique," *The International History Review* 16 (1994), 661–80.
2.  J. Michael Hittle, *The Service City: State and Townsmen in Russia, 1600–1800* (Cambridge, MA, 1979), 78–79.
3.  Marc Raeff, "The Well-Ordered Police State," *American Historical Review* 80 (1975); Rudolf Vierhaus, "Montesquieu in Deutschland," in *Deutschland im 18. Jahrhundert: Politische Verfassung, soziales Gefüge, geistige Bewegungen* (Göttingen, 1987).
4.  Paul Dukes, *The Making of Russian Absolutism, 1613–1801* (London and New York, 1990), 75–77.
5.  Ibid., 100; Daniel Stone, *The Polish-Lithuanian Commonwealth, 1386–1795* (Seattle, 2001), 309–12.
6.  Eduard Winter, *Frühaufklärung: Der Kampf gegen den Konfessionalismus in Mittel- und Osteuropa und die deutsch-slawische Begegnung* (Berlin, 1966).
7.  Larry Wolff, *Inventing Eastern Europe: The Map of Civilization on the Mind of the Enlightenment* (Stanford, 1994).
8.  Katherine Verdery, *Transylvanian Villagers: Three Centuries of . . . Change* (Berkeley, 1983), 65, 230–42, 256–69.

# Absolutism and Reform in Eighteenth-Century Central and Eastern Europe

## ◆ Michael G. Müller ◆

A history of the Germans in Central and Eastern Europe in the eighteenth century would have to cover a wide, and in fact rapidly extending, range of phenomena. This seems to be true in particular when one conceptualizes the notion of "German" in a way as to not merely refer to the history of German-speakers, groups and individuals in Central and Eastern Europe, but to cover the much wider field of *Beziehungsgeschichte*—including the transfer of goods and technologies, ideas and cultural practices, the interaction between states in politics and war, or the complex processes of the shaping and renegotiating of collective identities against the background of changing perceptions of "the other."[1] Since only some of the relevant issues can be highlighted in this outline article, certain selection criteria have to apply. The present text largely excludes such aspects that in one way or the other may be understood as a continuation of medieval or early modern patterns of German migration to, or performance in, the region. Instead, it aims at identifying those fields of interaction between Germans or Germany and the Central and East European states and societies in which the century witnessed the emergence of specifically new contexts of *Beziehungsgeschichte*, and to discuss some of them in more detail.

Under such criteria, the history of German settlement in the regions under consideration can thus—although having always attracted German scholarly interest[2]—largely be neglected. It is true, of course, that colonization processes and, in this context, the immigration of Germans from the Holy Roman Empire, the western lands of Poland or the Baltic territories continued; the settlement of the "Bamberger" in the Poznan region since 1719, the continuing participation of German settlers in establishing further *Holländereien* in central Poland, and the arrival of German

64

colonists in the Volga region or New Russia could be stated as examples. Moreover, the idea that "apt and industrious people" constituted the true wealth of a nation, and that recruiting rural and urban settlers from the economically more developed countries of the West could remedy Eastern Europe's lack of economic and demographic potential, became probably more popular than ever: Russian rhetoric of enlightened reform ever since Peter the Great strongly emphasized the importance of attracting foreign settlers to the empire.[3] Both the Habsburg Empire and, since the partitions of Poland, Prussia sought to strengthen the economic structure of their eastern provinces (but also to tighten their administrative grip on their non-German possessions) by channeling migration flows to their own "colonial East."

In quantitative terms, however, old-style colonization with German participation played a clearly less significant role in transforming economies and shaping societies than in preceding centuries. Not only did the overall figures of incoming foreign settlers—and the immediate benefits that colonization actually rendered—hardly meet the expectations associated with the Enlightenment projects for *Peuplirung*. But also the share of German colonists in the processes of rural and urban colonization in Central and Eastern Europe was in steady decline, and at the same time outward migration of Germans in a western direction became a statistically significant phenomenon. With an estimated 40,000 colonists of German origin arriving in central Poland in the course of the century,[4] or just over 30,000 Germans responding to the first Catherinian settlement program for New Russia,[5] even the quantitatively most significant individual settlement schemes involving Germans did not have structural effects in any way comparable to the social and cultural transformations of the Middle Ages.

In at least three ways the presence of Germans in Central and Eastern Europe indeed acquired new meanings, and the relations between Germany or the Germans with the societies and states in the region underwent major changes in the eighteenth century:

1   As military reform and modern state- and society-building created
    a new demand for "human capital," immigrants from German
    and Baltic territories were to play an increasingly significant role
    among the functional elites of the modernizing states and societ-
    ies, be it in state bureaucracies and new-style armies, as entrepre-
    neurs and technical experts, or in the academic and intellectual
    fields. To some extent, and in some contexts, the recruitment of
    *gens de mérité*[6] from Germany had as a background—and also as a
    side-effect—the emergence of specific images of "German" educa-
    tion, "German" philosophy—but also of "German *policey*" etc.

2   Great power politics fundamentally changed the general frame-
    work for Central and Eastern European encounters with Ger-

many and the Germans. On the one hand, they brought to bear
increasing diplomatic and military presence of German powers
in the East, and, since 1772, straightforward territorial expansion
across the century-long stable border with the Lithuanian Commonwealth, resulting in direct German rule over large parts of
the Polish lands. On the other hand, Russia moved closer to, and
became more directly involved in, "German" politics (or rather
the *querelles allemandes*), ultimately to acquire the position of an
*arbiter Germaniae* with the Teschen peace of 1779.

3    The transformation of premodern, largely elite-related, self-
perceptions of cultural identity in the region introduced new
concepts and practices of demarcation between the respective
majorities and "foreigners." While the highly diversified German-
speaking communities in Central and Eastern Europe hardly
communicated among themselves, let alone developed a sense of
common "national" belonging, their Slavic and Baltic neighbors
in the region started to identify the "Germans" (in particular the
German-speaking Protestants) as a "national" minority.

Clearly, the dramatic shifts in great-power relations since the turn from the seventeenth
to the eighteenth century represented the most conspicuous change of context. Already
in 1697, the election of Frederick Augustus I of Saxony to the Polish throne brought to
bear new perspectives for an eastward expansion of the Holy Roman Empire's political
presence in Central Europe. The Saxon elector's candidature for the succession to Jan
Sobieski as king of Poland and Lithuania (thoroughly coordinated with the Imperial
Court in Vienna and prepared by the well-timed religious conversion of the elector
to Catholicism) had its roots in ambitious plans for the Wettin dynasty. The position
as elective king to the Commonwealth entitled Augustus II to continue the struggle
against the Ottomans along the lines of the Holy League and to actively pursue the
reconquest of formerly Polish Livonia; prospective military success promised to be
rewarded by the opportunity for the Saxon dynasty to establish hereditary rule over
conquered territories—be it in Moldavia or Livonia. Moreover, given the geographical
and strategic closeness of the two Wettin lands, the dynastic union between Saxony
and Poland-Lithuania had the potential of being transformed into a *Realunion, i.e.,*
a construct of Saxon-Polish statehood that would allow the Wettins to export their
model of direct government to the Polish-Lithuanian Republic.[7] The Great Northern War (1700–1721), of course, frustrated such expectations. Although, after the
interlude of Swedish occupation, Augustus II returned to the Polish throne, Saxony
was no longer among the major political actors in the region. Instead, the postwar
decades witnessed the emergence of a so-called *"Entente cordiale* of the Three Black
Eagles"* as the dominant structure in Central European power relations. Russia,

Austria, and Prussia joined forces in maintaining the Polish-Lithuanian Republic in a state of weakness and political isolation and, eventually, in entirely eliminating the Commonwealth from the political map of Europe in the course of an unprecedented act of arbitrary occupation and dismemberment.[8]

It was not without reason that many contemporary observers indeed perceived the partitions of Poland very much in such a way. The fact that a given territory, even an important one, fell victim to secret arrangements between its more powerful neighbors could, of course, hardly be considered an exception, let alone a novelty to early modern great power politics. But in several respects, the dismemberment of Poland represented much more than just another case of monarchic bargaining about territorial wealth (*Länderschacher*). It was effected, as Edmund Burke claimed, "without even the pretence of right," i.e. without even an attempt by the powers involved to justify their action on the basis of accepted principles—either legal claims deducted from succession rights and hereditary contracts or the right and vocation of legitimate powers to intervene for the sake of maintaining the contractual system of European peace and stability as established by the Peace of Westphalia. Moreover, unlike the Wettins' plans for a Polish-Saxon *Realunion* (and in fact most of the other schemes of territorial expansion pursued in the century—in the case of Silesia, Bavaria, or Courland), the politics of partition that came to bear since 1772 did not aim at placing an existing territorial entity and its institutional structures under a new dynastic regime, but instead at physically dismembering the Polish-Lithuanian Commonwealth and ultimately eliminating its statehood altogether. Not least, and quite importantly in our context, the Prussian politics of partition in particular were rooted in a thoroughly elaborated scheme of eastern territorial expansion that, well before 1772, had explicitly specified the desired objects of annexation and premeditated a thorough "Prussification" of the lands to be the annexed: In all three cases (1772, 1793, and 1795), the full-scale administrative, and symbolic, *Inbesitznahme* of the respective Polish territories by the Prussian authorities was underway within days; and well ahead of nineteenth-century politics of anti-Polonism the representatives of Prussian rule in Poland advocated and pursued a course of de facto Germanization as, allegedly, a prerequisite for the successful integration of the new provinces into the Hohenzollern monarchy.

Of course, the prehistorychris bell [tooferbell@yahoo.com] of the partitions of Poland cannot be reduced to the story of a Prussian, let alone German, "urge to the East" in the eighteenth century. The motivations behind individual political acts in the course of events were far more complex, and even more so the circumstances that ultimately provided Prussia with the opportunity to implement its program of expansion at the expense of Poland-Lithuania. At the outset, after the Great Northern War, the interests of the future partitioning powers seemed in fact wide apart. While Russia's primary preoccupation seemed to be to neutralize Poland-Lithuania as a potential threat to post-1721 Russian hegemony in the European north, the Hohenzollern monarchy had, for the time being, to cope with Saxony as its major political competitor, and the emperor at Vienna sought for a new equilibrium between his traditional adversaries in the West and the newly emerged "arbiter of the North." "Controlling" Poland-Lithuania, i.e. perpetuating (through active political interference) the state of political "anarchy" in the Polish Republic of Nobles, was therefore a common objective without specific further implications—until the Prussian conquest of Silesia in 1740 triggered the secular conflict between the leading powers in the Holy Roman Empire that was to determine the relations between Austria, Prussia, and Russia until the end of the century.[9] From now on, two competing sets of interests dominated the development of diplomatic relations between the leading East European powers in view of Poland-Lithuania. While Russia was to grow more confident, in particular after the Seven Years' War, to be able to "govern Poland on her own," the two German powers departed on "gambling" over Poland in view of settling their dispute over Silesia. The well known outcome of that great-power game—the first partitioning treaties between the three powers, signed in 1772—however, still remains somewhat of a miracle to historians: Although Russia hardly had substantial reasons to resign, in 1770/71, from its claim to decide one-sidedly about the fate of Poland, St. Petersburg ultimately committed itself to the proposal of resolving the current international crisis of civil war in Poland and great-power dispute over Russian conquests at the expense of the Ottoman Empire by accepting a Prussian-inspired plan for the joint dismemberment of Poland to ease the international tension.[10] With each power annexing neighboring Polish provinces, it was agreed that the respective annexations would be considered as an adequate compensation for the claims made in the course of the crisis. However, the partition of 1772 provided only a feeble basis for balancing the competing interests of the powers involved. Since Russian interests in Poland had not been met, nor was the Habsburg-Hohenzollern conflict actually resolved, the dismemberment of Poland was bound to be continued; for Prussia, it was now only a matter of time and of convenient circumstances to try and push forward the partitioning process until its conclusion in 1795.

As a result of the three partitions of Poland, the two German powers in the partitioning alliance established territorial rule over the whole of Poland proper and much of the Ukraine. Moreover, eighteenth-century absolutism provided for a much more direct presence of the center's culture of government in their respective eastern provinces: While the Wettins' rule as elective kings in Poland-Lithuania had left the structures of regional government and the hierarchy of domestic power relations largely intact, the agencies of both Habsburgian and Prussian statehood in Poland immediately started to implement their own regime of direct bureaucratic rule. More or less at the same time, the Vienna-style and, through its personnel, essentially German manner of administering provincial rule was to reach Bohemia and Hungary. By the end of the century, a "German" model of absolutist rule was firmly established in Central Europe, and the domestic elites started to conceptualize the crisis of the *ancien régime* as a problem of conflict between "national" traditions, and elites of government, and "foreign" German rule.[11]

From a Russian perspective, the de facto expansion of German political influence on, and presence in, Central and Eastern Europe had a somewhat different dimension.[12] For Peter the Great, relations with the German powers had primarily been about winning allies among the "distant" Western powers for Russia's decisive confrontation with Sweden and Poland, as well as about narrowing the gap that still seemed to separate his empire from the more "civilized" parts of Europe. His successors instead were to become increasingly aware of, and concerned about, Russia's entanglement in what, since 1721 at the latest, appeared to be an all-European power game, and about the fact that the politics of the Germanic world were moving ever closer to the Russian Empire. This was dramatically the case since the onset of the Prussian-Austrian conflict in 1740, which was to upset for decades not only the balance of power in the Holy Roman Empire but also Russia's thoroughly constructed security system in Central and Northern Europe. Russia's response was intervention:[13] In the Seven Years' War, Empress Elizabeth undertook to actively contribute to the containment of Prussia as an expansionist power, and although her sudden death saved the Hohenzollern king from ultimate military defeat, the political aims of Russian intervention were at least partly achieved. Catherine II could count once more on Prussian compliance with Russia's security interests in Central and Northern Europe, and she was in a position to actively shape the balance of power in the Holy Roman Empire as well as, in the long run, to grow into the role of a new "arbiter Germaniae." Her "German" politics were ultimately rewarded by the formal acknowledgment, in the Peace of Teschen, of Russia's status as one of the powers guaranteeing the constitution of the Holy Roman Empire. And even more importantly perhaps, the development of international relations in Central Europe, and the partitions of Poland in particular, established a mutual dependence between Russian and German politics of unprecedented intensity. Not only did Russia's European position at the end of the century firmly rely on the political links established with the two leading German powers, but since 1795, the empire also immediately bordered with them territorially.[14]

On a quite different level, German relations with Central and Eastern Europe intensified in the eighteenth century through a massive transfer of "human capital" in the context of enlightened reform and modern state-building: the recruitment of skilled diplomats, administrators, entrepreneurs, scholars, and artists from German and Baltic territories to join the modern *functional elites*. As the abundant scholarly literature on that topic suggests,[15] the contribution of Germans to modernizing Eastern Europe in the Age of Enlightenment can be considered indeed significant. On the other hand, the transfer of ideas and human capital over the course of the century of "westernization" was not, as Günther Stökl has rightly stressed, the work of an individual nation but always that of Europe.[16] Alongside with Germans, also Scots, Italians, French, and Swiss figured among the foreign personnel of diplomatic corps and armies or administrations and academies. Moreover, with the exception of the few who, like Ernst Johann Biron (von Bühren) and Heinrich Graf Brühl, owed their political careers in Central and Eastern Europe to dynastic links with German territories, the German "experts" did not come to their host countries as representatives of their home territories, let alone of Germany as a political or cultural entity; many among them, like the migrants from the Baltic territories, are not even likely to have shared a sense of belonging to Germany other than in terms of language, certain educational traditions, and, perhaps, religious confession. Not least should one take into account that elite migrants to Central and Eastern Europe developed specifically new migration patterns of their own that, in many cases, involved alienation from both their homelands and the host societies. Neither was the eventual return to their places of origin in Germany, even if desired, a valid option for the majority, nor did their respective positions in the host country necessarily open up an opportunity for long-term integration beyond the individual professional career. Obviously, such characteristics of German elite migration to Central and Eastern Europe do not only apply to the eighteenth century. But neither before nor after did that specific segment of migrant population have such a decisive impact on the transformation of Eastern European societies and on the shaping of German-East European relations as in the Age of Enlightenment.

The contribution of Germans to the development of state and society in Russia since Peter the Great certainly represents the most spectacular, and best researched, case to prove that point. Germans were among the first foreign advisors and collaborators of the "reformer tsar" himself—like the educationist and tsarevich's tutor, Heinrich Huyssen, the expert bureaucrats Fick and von Lüben, or the diplomat and future vice-chancellor Heinrich Graf Ostermann. It was also Peter I who gave the initial impulse for the rapid development of German-Russian collaboration in the academic field when he involved Leibniz and Christian Wolff in his plans to establish a Russian Academy of Sciences. Not least were the early careers of several influential German statesmen and military leaders in Russian service associated with Petrine recruitment; an example is the military engineer Burchard Christoph Münnich, who started as Peter's supervisor for the Ladoga canal project and, under the rule of Empress Anna Ivanovna, rose to the honors of Russian field marshall, cabinet minister, and president of the War College.

The major fields of activity for the German newcomers to the empire's functional elites had thus been demarcated already by 1725. The patterns and purposes of recruitment as well as functions in which Germans performed within the modernizing state and society were to change, however, in subsequent decades. This had to do, on the one hand, with the changing political climate in Russia under Peter's successors. As Anna Ivanovna's reign seemed to open for the "German" collaborators in her entourage, in particular Johann Ernst Biron, almost unlimited opportunities in the highest ranks of Russian politics, internal animosities against the German "intruders" to the highest circles of power grew steadily, and after the liquidation of the "Bironovshchina" under Empress Elizabeth, the access of Germans to careers like Münnich's and even Ostermann's was to become much more restricted. More importantly however, the requirements of recruitment and, as a consequence, the opportunity patterns were to change substantially as, in the second half of the century, the development of modern statehood in Russia rapidly progressed, and indigenous functional elites consolidated.

The role and position of the German state functionaries and other *gens de mérite* from Germany were therefore a quite different one in the time of Catherine II. On the one hand, the influx of academically trained professionals from Germany constantly increased, and the empress's knowledge of, and commitment to, "German philosophy" or German models of "good government" (*gute policey*) in fact created most favorable conditions for ever growing numbers of German volunteers. On the other hand, however, the newcomers now met with fully developed institutional structures in the administration, the army, or academia of the Russian Empire, and they had to perform in cooperation, and at times in marked competition, with equally skilled Russian coprofessionals. As the famous dispute between Michail W. Lomonosov and his German colleagues Gottfried Siegfried Bayer and Gerhard Friedrich Müller in the 1760s and 70s demonstrated,[17] Russian scholarship was, by now, prepared to not only take over the task of defining the parameters for a "patriotic" perspective on Russian history, but also to critically reinterpret the contribution of foreign (German) scholarship of the past to the development of enlightened academic discourse in the empire. By the end of the century, the German representatives of Western expertise—although still valuable if not indispensable for Russia—had clearly lost their monopoly position: Catherinian Russia made her choices in a European market of ideas and selected from a European market of academically skilled labor among those who were apt and ready to perform in the empire's existing institutional and conceptual framework.

How can the "German" contribution to the modernization of Russia along the lines of Enlightened absolutism in the century be qualified? Quite obviously, it did not consist of a *Kulturträgerrolle* in the sense that a given Western (German) milieu transferred its collective knowledge as well as the personnel necessary for its implementation to a region of "colonization." Of course, there might have been a certain "natural" Russian affinity to German experiences and concepts of modernisation rather than to others, since Russia and the majority of the German territories in fact shared the fate of late-comers to enlightened reform in Europe; German projects of modernization may have appeared closer to Eastern European realities than, for example, British or French. Furthermore, the German territories, more than other European regions, provided a substantial surplus of skilled personnel ready to commit themselves to a career in foreign service. In any case, the activities of German, or German-speaking, *gens de mérite* in the various sectors of governmental and societal modernization in the Russian Empire should be understood against the background of specific negotiating processes: the concepts of military, educational, bureaucratic, or scholarly modernization developed in the leading German territories were adopted and modified according to local requirements, and the Russian Empire selected the available human capital in the German and Baltic lands in view of such specific requirements. In fact, absolutist modernization in the Russian Empire was very much the result of a process of adaptation with rather unique solutions to the problem of accommodating foreign models as well as integrating foreign personnel. The formidable results of Russian modernization with the support of German experts belong at least as much to Russian history as to that of German-Russian *Beziehungsgeschichte*.

"German" presence among the elites in Central and Eastern Europe in the eighteenth century was, however, not restricted to Russia and to the milieu of absolutist modernization. Poland-Lithuania in the "Saxon period" represents an interesting case of elite transformation with German participation in another, "republican" climate. Although the project of a Polish-Saxon *Realunion* under the common roof of the Wettin dynasty ultimately failed, the activities of Saxon politicians, bureaucrats, entrepreneurs and artists in Poland proved as influential on the further development of Polish civilization as did the encounters of Polish elites with the culture of the Wettin court and government, and the political and cultural life of the Saxon capital.

This may not seem obvious at first sight, since, in Polish collective memory, and by the majority of the historians, at least the prominent protagonists of Saxon rule like Christoph August Wackerbarth, Jakob Heinrich Flemming or Heinrich Count Brühl are associated almost exclusively with arbitrary "foreign" rule, and the disastrous results of Wettin Polish politics in general. In fact, the Commonwealth's political experience with the Saxon regime under both Wettin kings justified such views to some extent. Augustus II not only used Saxon troops to pursue his military aims in Poland and, in 1714, to challenge his political opponents in the Republic, but he also employed his confidants in the Saxon *Geheimes Kabinett* (such as Ernst Manteuffel and Jakob Flemming) to prepare and implement a coup d'état in order to establish direct Saxon rule in Warsaw. That the latter plans implied the coming to power in Poland of a Saxon Protestant government was obvious, and provided the "Republican" Polish opposition with the reason to try, when the civil war between the king and the Tarnogród confederates was ended in 1716, to constitutionally exclude the foreign "agents of absolutism" from the Republic for good. The exclusion by law of Protestants from offices and honors in the Republic as stipulated by the "Mute

Diet" of 1717, and confirmed by subsequent *Sejmy*, was a political measure against an "invasion" by the personnel of Saxon absolutism rather than a religious option.[18] Augustus III, in turn, proceeded more cautiously in this respect, but could nevertheless not avoid a similar conflict between king and nation. The attempts since the late 1730s at establishing a ministerial system of government in Poland under the supervision of Chancellor Brühl provoked as much public aversion as did the very fact that Saxon dignitaries like Brühl, Flemming or Karl von Heinicken accumulated public functions in the Polish governmental apparatus and allegedly drew enormous wealth from them.[19] To ultimately stigmatize the Germans in the service of the Polish king was to contribute, however, also the propaganda of the last Polish king, Stanislas Augustus Poniatowski, for whom the radical critique of the Wettin kings and the protagonists of their rule was part and parcel of a strategy to highlight his own government as the unique source of progress, and his accession to the throne as the historical watershed between Sarmate anarchy and enlightened reform.

The fact that Wettin rule over the Commonwealth and the presence of Saxons in the country also had more lasting, positive effects on Poland has therefore been largely overlooked. As recent research suggests, the "Saxon period" was in fact critical for the formation of a new, "post-Sarmate" political class in Poland-Lithuania from which the reformer king Stanislas Augustus Poniatowski was to recruit his followers in the "age of reform" after 1764. Not only the leaders of the pro-reform magnate families, including the Mniszech or the Czartoryski as well as young Poniatowski himself, went through the school of Saxon *"Staatskunst,"* but also hundreds of *szlachta* members who were trained as an elitist service class at the Dresden cadet corps or the court's pages corps—in order to subsequently benefit from such qualification in privileged military and civil careers at home.[20] Not least, the role of the Polish capital as a forum of cultural interaction and transfer has to be taken into account. While, due to a progressing decentralization of power in the Republic as well as result of widespread political resentment against monarchical rule and representation, Warsaw's importance as the political center of the Republic actually declined in the "Saxon period," the opposite was true for its role as an internationally acknowledged royal residence and a cultural and intellectual metropolis.[21] Several waves of migration from Saxony to Poland—the most important one after the Prussian invasion of Saxony at the beginning of the Seven Years' War—brought skilled artisans, artists and scholars to Warsaw by the thousands, not to mention the whole entourage of the Dresden court or the international diplomatic corps together with their Saxon personnel. The effects showed in the capital's architectural transformation, the revival of educational activities (in the *kolegium jezuickie,* the *kolegium pijarskie,* the *Collegium Nobilium* or the Zaluski library founded in 1747), and the rapid development of public cultural life and elite sociability, but also in Warsaw's acquiring the function of a transnational marketplace for the exchange of ideas. Not only Germans, of course, were the actors in this cultural revival, but a larger European community of artists and intellectuals that had been attracted to Wettin Dresden first, and followed the court to Poland—among them the most prominent Italian artists in Poland, Marcello Bacciarelli and Bernardo Bellotto (known as Canaletto).

After well over sixty years of Saxon rule, the cohabitation of German newcomers with Poles and Lithuanians had thus influenced Polish society and civilization not only negatively. The reformer king Stanislas Augustus owed in fact much more to Saxon rule and its German protagonists than he was ready to admit.

The emergence or transformation of "German" identity in Central and Eastern Europe in the eighteenth century was a most complex, even contradictory process. It involved at least two different issues that have to be discussed separately: the development of the self-perception of German-speaking groups and their concepts of loyalty on the one hand, and the changing usages of "German" as a marker of otherness by the (majoritarian) non-German societies on the other hand. The self-identification and hetero-perception of "ethnic" Germans in the region still remained wide apart; they influenced each other only partly and developed on the basis of different dynamics and chronologies.

In terms of self-perception, the German-speaking groups maintained, in their majority, a local or regional sense of belonging that excluded much rather than supported identification with other German-speaking communities—whether in the region or in the *Reich*. This was true in particular for those German speakers who, like the urban elites in Royal Prussia, had not only been in the region for centuries but also benefited from established traditions of self-determination that they were anxious to defend against any kind of "foreigners," German-speaking or not. For the Danzig burghers, the notion of fatherland was primarily associated with self-government within the boundaries of the urban territory, with a semi-aristocratic lifestyle and culture of the patricians, and with Protestant faith. It furthermore implied political loyalty towards the Crown and the republican institutions of the Prussian province and the Commonwealth as a whole. There was a consciousness of belonging to the linguistic community of the "German tongue" too—however with the understanding that linguistic specificity marked the social and political distance between full burghers and "foreigners" in the urban context itself, but this did not imply the commitment to "German" lands, groups, or institutions outside.[22] It was therefore very much in line with the urban project of identity that Danzig vehemently fought against the Wettins' politics of extending the central state's power to the royal towns and refused to surrender to the authority of partitioning Prussia until the last minute. The agents of both Saxon and Prussian statehood, although "fellow nationals" in ethnic terms, represented to the Danzigers "the other" as much as the Swedish, Russian or French occupants in the past.[23]

But even newcomers to Central and Eastern Europe, like the Saxon personnel of Wettin rule in Poland or the German civilian and military personnel in Russian service, shared such self-perceptions and commitment to territorial or local loyalty, in at least some respects. As a linguistic and confessional minority in Warsaw or St. Petersburg they were inevitably identified by the host society as Germans—and probably adopted such classification for themselves to some extent (like Germans and other European nationals develop a sense of being European in the specific context of encounters with non-Europeans). Nevertheless, other factors and levels of identification remained salient, and probably prevailed until the end of the century: the loyalty towards the dynasty and territorial patriotism, religious adherence to one of the competing German confessional churches, but also the identification with transnational communities such as the European aristocracy, or religious, academic and professional groupings.

For the perception of the Germans by non-German groups and societies, on the other hand, the latter's self-identification was of limited relevance. Rather the way in which societies or specific groups conceptualized the "otherness" of the German speakers depended on the parameters of one's self-representation. Already the seventeenth century witnessed, for example, the emergence of an anti-German ethnic (Sarmate) discourse of Polishness addressed to the Protestant part of the German-speaking elites in the Republic's own provinces. Confronted with the shock of the *potop,* the majority of the political nation was ready to accept the narrative of German/Protestant "collaboration" with the Swedish invaders as an explanation for the catastrophe—and also as an appeal to the Poles and Lithuanians to "close their ranks" as a Catholic and Polish-speaking nation of nobles against their "foreign" enemies. The fact that the German burghers in Royal Prussia had delivered no reason at all to justify the allegations, and that they affirmed, in practice and in propaganda, their singular relationship of loyalty to king and Republic, had no impact on public opinion at all.[24]

Examples from the eighteenth century confirm that pattern. In the Polish case, the conflict *inter maiestatis ac libertatis* between the Wettin dynasty and noble opposition brought a revival of the *potop* discourse—with the difference that anti-Saxon propaganda stressed the anti-Protestant aspect more than that of ethnic otherness, although the combination of social, linguistic and confessional markers identifying the other persisted. In Russia, "Germanness" seems to have been conceptualized in contradictory ways, depending on the specific context: negatively in the context of an allegedly excessive influence of "Germans" in the empire's politics under the rule of the successors to Peter the Great, and positively in view of the merits of "German" science and political philosophy, or the contribution of "talented" German migrants to the empire. In every instance, however, the emergence of specific images of Germany and the Germans preceded the development of a "German" identity among the German actors in the region quite significantly; it was primarily in confrontation with external definitions of Germanness, and context-bound processes of exclusion, that individual groups or communities of German speakers were put into the position of opting for or against a cultural German identity—and not always did such contextual options develop into persistent concepts of "national" self-representation.

Studying the eighteenth century, one becomes, once again, aware of the methodological problematic behind this volume's topic, and of the conceptual choices involved. A comprehensive overview of the role, status, identity and hetero-perception of Germans in Central and Eastern Europe would have to cover an extremely wide range of phenomena that were, if at all, only loosely interlinked. Methodologically valid proposals in this perspective were made in recent research, although they have not yet produced any comprehensive study of the matter. Instead, hardly any of the issues raised in this paper could be adequately discussed in the context of a narrative of "German history in the European East," since for most of the relevant phenomena one could hardly argue that the actors, or agencies involved were German in a specific sense. The very idea of writing a history of the Germans in Central and Eastern Europe appears to remain incompatible with the methodological requirement of a multilateral perspective as implied in the competing concept of *Beziehungsgeschichte*.

# Notes

1.  For the methodological concept of *Beziehungsgeschichte,* see Klaus Zernack, Das Jahrtausend deutsch-polnischer Beziehungsgeschichte als geschichtswissenschaftliches Problemfeld und Forschungsaufgabe", in Wolfgang H. Fritze, ed., Grundfragen der geschichtlichen Beziehungen zwischen Deutschen, Polaben und Polen. Referate und Diskussionsbeiträgen aus zwei wissenschaftlichen Tagungen (Berlin 1976), 3-46. An early example for such an approach to interpreting the history of Germans in Central and Eastern Europe is Günther Stökl, *Osteuropa und die Deutschen*, 1st ed. (Stuttgart, 1967); exemplary recent studies are Claus Scharf, *Katharina II., Deutschland und die Deutschen* (Mainz, 1995); and Karin Friedrich, *The Other Prussia. Royal Prussia, Poland and Liberty, 1569–1772* (Cambridge, 2000).
2.  Not only traditional German *Ostforschung* but also more recent German scholarship has clearly privileged the topic of "German colonization" in Central and Eastern Europe through the centuries; see Oskar Kossmann, *Die Deutschen in Polen seit der Reformation. Historisch-geographische Skizzen* (Marburg, 1978); Joachim Rogall, *Die Deutschen im Posener Land und in Mittelpolen* (Munich, 1993); Detlef Brandes, "Die Ansiedlung von Ausländern im Zarenreich unter Katharina II., Paul I. und Alexander I.," *Jahrbücher für Geschichte Osteuropas* (*JGO*) 34 (1986): 161–87.
3.  Roger P. Bartlett, *The Settlement of Foreigners in Russia 1762–1804* (Cambridge, 1979).
4.  The figures established by Jerzy Topolski, "Gospodarka", in Bogusław Leśnodorski, ed., Polska w epoce Oświecenia (Warsaw 1971), 171-211, seem to give, although disputed by Kossmann, a valid orientation.
5.  Roger P. Bartlett, *Human Capital: The Settlement of Foreigners in Russia, 1762–1804* (Cambridge, 1979), 109–42.
6.  The expression used by Catherine II in a letter to Grimm of 5 April 1784, cited by Scharf, *Katharina II.,* 148.
7.  The most comprehensive study of Saxon politics in Poland in the era of Augustus II is Jacek Staszewski, *August II Mocny* (Wrocław, 1998).
8.  For the debate over the Great Northern War and its lasting effects on great-power rela-

tions in Eastern Europe until the end of the eighteenth century, see the classical studies by Klaus Zernack, among others, "Das Zeitalter der nordischen Kriege von 1558 bis 1809 als frühneuzeitliche Geschichtsepoche," *Zeitschrift für historische Forschung (ZHF)* 1 (1974): 55–79; "Negative Polenpolitik als Grundlage deutsch-russischer Diplomatie in der Mächtepolitik des 18. Jahrhunderts," in idem., *Preußen-Deutschland-Polen. Aufsätze zur Geschichte der deutsch-polnischen Beziehungen* (Berlin, 1991). For an overview of the history of the Polish partitions, see Michael G. Müller, *Die Teilungen 1772–1793–1795* (Munich, 1984).

9. Emanuel Rostworowski, "Podbój Śląska przez Prusy a pierwszy rozbiór Polski," *Przegląd Historyczny* 63 (1972): 389–412.

10. For a reassessment of Russian motivations in the period of the first Polish partition, based on new archival sources, see Michael G. Müller, "Hegemonialpolitik und imperiale Expansion: Die Teilungen Polens," in Eckhard Hübner et al. eds., *Rußland zur Zeit Katharinas II.* (Cologne, 1998), 397–410.

11. The implications of the establishment of Prussian and Habsburg rule in the Polish *zabory* for the emergence of a proto-national conflict in the region are considered by Michael G. Müller, "Adel und Elitenwandel in Ostmitteleuropa. Fragen an die polnische Adelsgeschichte im ausgehenden 18. und 19. Jahrhundert," *Zeitschrift für O (ZfO)* 50 (2001):, 497-513.

12. For a thorough analysis of Russo-Prussian relations and Russia's changing perception of German politics in the eighteenth century, see Martin Schulze Wessel, *Rußlands Blick auf Preußen. Die polnische Frage in der Diplomatie und der politischen Öffentlichkeit des Zarenreichs und des Sowjetstaats, 1697–1947* (Stuttgart, 1995), 27–92.

13. Michael G. Müller, "Rußland, Polen und der Siebenjährige Krieg," *JGO* 28 (1980): 198–219.

14. Wessel, *Rußlands Blick auf Preußen,* 85–97.

15. Erik Amburger, *Fremde und Einheimische im Wirtschafts- und Kulturleben des neuzeitlichen Rußland* (Wiesbaden, 1982); Bartlett, *Human Capital*; Scharf, *Katharina II.*, introduction.

16. Stökl, *Osteuropa und die Deutschen,* 112–15.

17. Joseph Laurence Black, *G.-F. Müller and the Imperial Russian Academy* (Kingston and Montreal, 1986).

18. Michael G. Müller, "Toleration in Poland-Lithuania in the Eighteenth Century," in O. P. Grell, ed., *Religious Tolerance in Enlightened Europe* (Cambridge, 1999), xx–yy.

19. Staszewski, August II Sas, 199–207.

20. Jacek Staszewski, *Polacy w osiemnastowiecznym Dreźnie* (Wrocław, 1986).

21. Andrzej Zahorski, ed., *Warszawa w latach 1526–1795* (Warsaw, 1984).

22. Friedrich, *The Other Prussia*, 189–216; Michael G. Müller, "*Städtische* Gesellschaft und territoriale Identität im Königlichen Preußen um 1600. Zur Frage der Entstehung deutscher Minderheiten in Ostmitteleuropa," *Nordost-Archiv*, N.S., 6, no. 2 (1997): 565–84; Milos Reznik,Pomoři mezi Polskem a Pruskem. Patriotismus a identity v Královských Prusech v době děleni Polska (Prague 2001).

23. See also Peter Oliver Loew, "Geschichtsschreibung und Geschichtskultur in Danzig 1795–1989" (Ph.D. diss., Freie Universität Berlin), 2001.

24. Michael G. Müller, *Zweite Reformation und städtische Autonomie im Königlichen Preußen. Danzig, Elbing und Thorn in der Epoche der Konfessionalisierung, 1557–1660* (Berlin, 1997), 167–90.

# German Writers, Power and Collapse

## The Emergence of *Polenliteratur* in Eighteenth-Century Germany

### ◆ David Pickus ◆

Though they usually attract little notice, little pieces of Poland are scattered throughout European cultural history. For example, at one point in Goethe's novel *Elective Affinities* a round of celebrations is described, and then a proposal is made by one partygoer to the others that they do things "in the Polish style."[1] This meant that they should "come now and eat me out of house and home and continue onward in that fashion."[2] Poland has absolutely nothing to do with the story, but from the perspective of the German reading public's mentality, a reference to "Polish style" as self-destructive excess makes sense. From the late eighteenth through the mid-twentieth centuries, at least, mentioning Poland was a quick and direct way of signifying wild disorder and its consequences. Moreover, Goethe's implicit moral that Polish behavior sows the seeds of its own downfall was hardly unique to him. It was ubiquitous commonplace. For German speakers, references to the "Polish *Reichstag*" (meaning "chaotic tumult") and "Polish economy" (meaning "shambles") literally made proverbial the three-way association between Poland, excessive license and self-induced grief. Even dictionaries accepted this meaning. Dr. Daniel Sanders's *1876 Wörterbuch der deutschen Sprache*, lists under the heading for the adjective "Polish" as a "proverb" a (German) school that became a Polish *Reichstag*, where "everyone did as he pleased." The same definition goes on to tell us that the word is also associated with "uncleanness."[3]

There is something prejudiced about these deprecating images. Moreover, no reminder is needed that such attitudes toward Poland can and were mobilized for purposes of legitimizing violence and aggression.[4] Yet to understand what Germans wrote about Poland to be nothing more than bigotry misses the complexities of the matter. First of all, as we shall see, not every German author took a hostile stance toward Poland. Furthermore, the majority of those who criticized Poland considered themselves to be doing it in the service of some higher ethical end. Perceptions of Poland developed in concrete historical circumstances and were put to a complicated series of ideological uses along the way. We can understand the nature and significance of this cultural phenomenon by looking at how it originated in a distinct body of literature, namely *Polenliteratur*. *Polenliteratur* is simply defined as German writing describing and evaluating Poland and its inhabitants. It is spread out across a number of genres, primarily history, political commentary, novels, poetry, memoirs and travel description.

The honor of identifying *Polenliteratur* as a specific object of study goes to a Habsburg-era Austrian literary critic, Robert Franz Arnold. His 1900 monograph, *Geschichte der deutschen Polenlitteratur,* set a model for all future studies.[5] This book, while clearly dated by scholarly conventions of a bygone era, contains two perceptive hypotheses that continue to be valuable. First, although the subtitle of the volume is "from the beginnings to 1800," the vast majority of its pages is taken up with the era of the partitions, roughly 1760 to 1800. This is due to the straightforward fact that Poland only really attracted the attention of German intellectuals once the consequences of "liberty's folly," or its anti-monarchial aristocratic republicanism, became apparent. As Arnold noted, German interest in Poland in Luther's era was exiguous. This was at a time when German lands were torn apart by internecine religious warfare, and the Polish Commonwealth was both relatively peaceful and at the height of its powers.[6] Only in the late seventeenth century, when Poland underwent a particularly destructive and chaotic series of wars and civil wars called the "Deluge," did depictions of Poland pick up. Nevertheless—and this is the second key point found in Arnold—*Polenliteratur* did not truly acquire a character of its own until the last four decades of the eighteenth century. This is not only because of changes within the Polish lands, but also because of fundamental changes in German intellectual life. During the epoch of 1760–1800 the fate of Poland mattered to German authors as it never had before.

What was it about the late eighteenth century that made it conducive to the creation of *Polenliteratur*? Here, an interesting conjunction should be noted. *Polenliteratur* crystallized as two fundamental historical transformations were taking place. As H. M. Scott aptly observed of the second half of the face of Europe from the Seven Years' War onwards, we should treat the "emergence of the eastern powers as a turning point in the evolution of the modern European states system."[7] Specifically, in East Central Europe changing boundaries not only reflected the predominance of the Russian, Prussian and Austrian regimes, but marked the solidification of a political order that was to last until 1918. In political, economic and military terms, the difference these decades made was profound. Simultaneously, within the German lands, a less tangible, but still profound intellectual development was occurring. This is the era of what is called the "Late Enlightenment."[8] This is more than a continuation of the enlightened ideas that were elaborated and articulated in Germany in the first half of the eighteenth century. Picking up from Lessing onward through the French Revolution, German thinking saw a "coming of age," meaning that intellectual life became more ambitious both in the scope of what it addressed and in the intensity of its demands that the world be reshaped according to the strictures of reason, criticism and imaginative thought. To provide one brief example, in Lessing's 1759 tragedy, *Philotas*, the protagonist commits suicide with the wish of being transported to an Elysium where "all are virtuous friends and brave members of a blessed state."[9] The decades until 1800 saw Germany's first genuinely modern generations of intellectuals trying to create a world where one did not have to wait so long or take such drastic action to achieve this measure of virtue and political happiness.

We can ask if there is any connection between these two transformations. Indeed, *Polenliteratur* shows that there is. However, it is a link that "worked" only in one direction. German authors had little influence on the course of great-power policy in Poland in the course of the eighteenth century. Yet, from the converse direction and judging from the wide range of writers who commented on Poland, what was happening to Poland had an impact on their sensibilities. Even more significantly, their response to Poland's ultimate fall as an independent state reveals a great deal about how they defined themselves, and how they, as subjects of German states, defined themselves vis-à-vis the East. Hence, we must examine the self-understanding of the German writers who propagated it, their anxieties and ambitions. It is quite unlikely that anyone will settle once and for all which evaluations and opinions about Poland were valid and accurate and which were not. Rather, we can look at *Polenliteratur* not so much for what objective facts it reveals about Germany's neighbor to the east, but for what it shows about the German intellectuals who produced it, particularly their own conflict-ridden relationship to the modernity they saw emerging around them.

## An Alliance with Power

The three Polish partitions of 1772, 1793 and 1795 certainly "removed" or abolished Polish sovereignty from a far-flung series of territories.[10] However, contemporaries did not like to think of this as a simple conquest. Instead, they saw it as a defeat of a kind of social and political organization that was once found throughout Europe, and which, by a vicissitude or trick of history, lasted longer in Poland than other places. To summarize briefly: the Polish Republic of Nobles, an aristocratic, magnate-dominated polity, was seen as finally showing that it could not compete with the absolutist states that had emerged around it. The issue for the contemporary thinker was not so much that monarchs like Frederick II or Maria Theresa could completely eliminate the power of landed nobility and feudal political structures (when obviously they could not—and did not necessarily want to). Rather, the key point is that they could mobilize the power of a central bureaucracy and standing army both to contemplate the annexation of Poland and to actually carry it through. As Johann Erich Biester, the editor of the enlightened journal *Die berlinische Monatsschrift* explained, Frederick II was responsible for the first partition, but he was not to blame, and it had to happen, since "the powerful parties were satisfied, and this part of Europe remained quiet. Certainly, this satisfaction came at Poland's expense, which however saw its cruel and fanatical civil war ended."[11]

This discussion of the morality and meaning of the partitions continued through the reign of the last king of Poland, Stanislaw August Poniatowski in 1764 and concluded with his final defeat and Kosciuszko's failed attempt to rescue Poland in the years 1793–95.[12] At that time, the German "intellectual estate" was making more energetic attempts to assert itself than ever before. The population of the German-speaking lands hovered somewhere between 20–24 million. In this, the intellectuals were perhaps some 20,000 individuals, or 0.1% of the population. Yet in its way, this was an active minority. In 1775 about 2,000 German books appeared. By 1790 the number was some 3,560 and the yearly number continued to rise.[13] Moreover, the number of journals and newspaper-like periodicals also grew strongly. The upshot of all this is that Poland afforded the "reading and judging" element of Germany's population ample opportunity to reflect on warfare, leadership and change in the nature of sovereignty.

The results were interesting. Since the age of the Baroque, German writers had been associating what they called "northern Europe" with uncontrolled violence. For instance, a few lines from the verse of Kaspar Stieler (1632–1707) describe a sojourn in Poland where "der scharffe Sebel der Barbaren/ist ofters um mein Haupt gefahren"[14] (roughly: "the barbarians' sharp saber often was aimed at my head"). What Enlightenment-era writers did was take the linkage between Poland and violence and apply it to the changed circumstance of the partitions. To show one instance, in 1773, in the respected journal *Teutsche Merkur* author and editor C. M. Wieland took time from the usual discussion of *belles lettres* and morals and considered Poland's loss. The most significant part of his comment was a wish directed toward the removal of Polish territory, saying, "may the happiness of this otherwise so unhappy land be established by it; may the well being of humanity be advanced by it."[15] German intellectuals had reached the point where they had begun to philosophize about Poland and its fate. The partition was understood by Wieland through this lens: as a potential solution for the problem of disorder which seemed to cause it.

This leads to a fundamental consideration about *Polenliteratur* in the late eighteenth century. The shadow of the partitions hang over it, and whatever particular topic it happened to address, it always had as its background the new principle of state sovereignty that emerged with modernity: the unequal contest between absolutist and feudal polities. In the case of Wieland, it is clear that he seeks to do something that is at least as old as Seneca's literary efforts to influence Nero. Wieland writes as if he is addressing the rulers of the earth, ones who will see the validity of his reasoning and set their course by it. In adopting this tone, he makes Poland into a kind of test case for the validity of the exercise of centralized state power. If it somehow improves mankind and brings about the sort of rational happiness that Enlightenment thinkers desired, then Poland's partition is to be praised. Thus, if Wieland's comment seems to be condoning force, it is because "force" is trying to be shaped into something that is enlisted in the service of intellectual ideals. What interested German writers in Poland was that it appeared to be a country that demonstrated a lesson of some sort.

This lesson took two principal forms. On the one hand, there is an undeniable note of *Schadenfreude*, as German intellectuals gloated or otherwise took some sort of satisfaction at Poland's incapacity to resist what was being done to it. An anonymous poet put this basic sentiment into verse, with a pithy couplet that went: "Polen, deine Missethaten/ haben es dahin gebracht/ dass du itzt zu grossen Schaden/ hast verloren so an Macht."[16] (Poland, your misdeeds have brought you to a point where, to your great misfortune, you have lost so much power.) The poem goes on to blame the aristocratic magnates, who are "swelled with arrogance" for inviting their own destruction. This is a sentiment also echoed by Herder. He wrote that if Poland's magnates were raging that they were being mistreated, then they should just rage on and blame their fathers who got them into such trouble.[17] For the contemporary intellectual, who certainly would have occasion to resent and feel outrage at the exercise of aristocratic power, the spectacle of so many nobles being brought low must have been gratifying.

Yet there was another form the response could take. Instead, of glee, Poland's plight could be approached with pity. A good example of this is a poem called "Polonia" by the social critic and journalist C.D.F. Schubart. The sympathy that Schubart shows toward Poland is predicated upon the notion that Poland's continued existence is untenable. Hence, the poem is an exception that proves the rule. The difference between his view and the majority's is that he is frightened by the recent political changes and thus sees Poland as pitiable rather than laughable. His poem revolves around of the image of a personified female "Polonia," who witnesses "robbers" storming out of the forest to destroy her country and who subsequently wants to die. The conclusion that Schubart draws from this assault is revealed in the poem's final section. It describes a grandfather who, seeing no choice, kills his children and grandchildren, and then commits suicide himself. The suggestion is that this is the only thing that can be done about Poland's misery. "What is a life without freedom?" he asks himself before collapsing on the corpses of his children. The poem's last line is that "Polonia laments."[18] In its own way, this message is also gratifying to the intellectual who wrote it, albeit in a more bitter manner. What it shows is that intellectuals reserve the right to determine when the power of the state is not enlisted of the service of humanity, but rather toward the end of "wild robbery."

Whether lamenting or applauding, this was a specific kind of gratification. To give it a name, it is a "bourgeois" satisfaction. Considering the more negative or gleeful accounts of Poland, the sort of damage to Polish sovereignty or dignity that was celebrated in them was not understood by its exponents to be an improper one. Rather, it was grasped a taming and dismantling of the feudal forces that had undermined progress in Europe, particularly in Europe's East. The come-uppance was that a ruling elite that stood opposed to bourgeois values of rationality and humanity lost its chance to participate in the shaping of the future. It was this that Wieland seemed to be suggesting when he saw the first partition as something that could be a step toward the establishment of human happiness. It was this that Schubart proposed ought to be the case when he saw the defenseless and disappearing Poland set upon.

If we cast our net wider and look at the many other writers who dwelt on either the misery of Poland's inhabitants or the justice of the partitions, we see that what they agreed about most was that what was being attacked in Poland was a retrograde principle, one that would be improper to allow to continue. Friedrich Freiherr von der Trenck wrote a pamphlet in 1773 in which he bluntly stated that if Poland, before the partition, was "truly a happy nation" where everyone "enjoyed their natural and civil rights according to their social estate," then any justification for partition advanced by states like Prussia remain "cheating conclusions of a Machiavellian reasoning."[19] Yet Poland was not this way, and as it continued to outrage the ideals that intellectuals valued, it continued to be seen as something that deserved its own end. It was as this object lesson that the image of Poland had its lasting impression on eighteenth-century intellectual consciousness. Thus, to explain the logic of *Polenliteratur* more fully, we must ask how this object lesson related to the era's wider intellectual goals.

## Anti-Civil Society

Naturally enough, German writings on Poland during the partition era depict a polity in decay. What needs to be emphasized here is how this decay served a bourgeois philosophical agenda. "Bourgeois" is a translation of *Bürger* or *bürgerlich*. Though it does mean "middle class" in the sense of being neither noble nor peasant, it also means "civil" in the sense of "civil society" or *bürgerliche Gesellschaft*. It is an error to accept the view—popular from Rousseau onward—that "bourgeois" must signify some sort of narrowness or selfishness masked over by hypocrisy.[20] This unpleasant element is certainly there, but the ideals of citizenship to which these writers were aspiring were both sincerely held and genuinely bourgeois. A look at the specific charges leveled against Poland shows this.

To explain, in the travel literature and political commentary three common images continually recur. The first is the Polish noblemen who cannot control their own lustful and tyrannizing impulses, but who also cannot unite to pursue rational policy or defend the state as a whole. (One commentator, who had lived in Austria's annexed Polish province of Galicia, wrote that the "law of the jungle in the Holy Roman Empire" was still a "weak second" to what the Polish nobility had done. Their thorough-going destructiveness was "something that can be only be exercised by the wild spirit of a despot, degenerating from republican freedom to licentiousness and wantonness."[21]) Second, there are the representatives of the estates below the nobility, all of whom are in various, but extreme forms oppressed and miserable. (One traveler, on his journey, called the Polish people "the most disgusting beings one can see."[22]) Finally, there is dirt and filth in the most literal and visceral sense. This dirt is the concrete reminder of the disorder reigning in Poland. (A doctor, visiting Warsaw, described seeing naked men and women bury themselves up to the neck in horse manure in the senseless hope that the fumes would cure their venereal disease.[23])

It would take us too far afield to go through each instance where these images appear. What needs exposition is the fact that what was being excoriated in Poland was the opposite of the goals and ideals sought by the "practitioners of civil society,"[24] or the intellectuals seeking to realize the moral promise of bourgeois aims. This is not simply an abstract claim. The dominant political ideal of the age was the converse of what was seen in Poland, namely some centralized authority that restrained and guided itself according to just and philosophical principles. Likewise, the hierarchy sought in society was not supposed to be one like Poland's "society of estates." Instead, it was supposed to be based on a rational delineation of functions, one that encouraged welfare and growth, not stagnation and misery. Finally, it was supposed to be apparent and obvious that this new civil society was well-ordered and well-run. The bourgeois ideal (easily caricatured) about tidy streets and well-scrubbed people is an echo of the eighteenth-century hope that a polity would demonstrate its successful humanity and progressiveness in its every appearance. All this leads to a conclusion: *Polenliteratur* is not simply literature about a country. It is a literature of "bad examples." The point it continually makes is that, in Poland, one sees demonstrated the consequences of not striving toward bourgeois ideals. This message had resonance for the contemporaries who made it.

The area of the Polish-Lithuanian Commonwealth or Republic of Nobles represented the opposite of the bourgeois virtues needed to create a happy and flowering society. Poland captured this complicated formula in a concrete image. If the dream of a realized civil society was difficult to obtain, at least the dangers of having its opposite could be demonstrated.

## Brief Excursus on the East European Context

Although *Polenliteratur* has a scope and valance of its own, some of its impact can be further clarified if we consider it in comparison with the ways German authors treated other Eastern European nations. From the time of Peter the Great onward, Western European public opinion had a strong sense that there was a fundamental struggle in

Eastern and East Central Europe between local, smaller-scale aristocrats and ambitious monarchs who had taken it upon themselves to mobilize their polity's military and bureaucratic power. Simultaneously admiring and apprehensive of this transformation, contemporary German observers had to make sense of the new arrangements these upheavals were creating. *Polenliteratur* was a large part of this project, but alongside it was a continuing stream of literature describing and explaining Eastern Europe's other Slavic and non-Slavic peoples. Indeed, an incidental, but revealing comment Goethe made in *Dichtung und Wahrheit* shows how much Poland was thought of as being part of a larger, more exotic—yet not quite modern—mosaic of peoples. In his autobiography, Goethe was describing his youthful enthusiasm for the market fair at Leipzig when he noted that "what especially attracted my attention, with their unusual clothing, was the inhabitants of the eastern regions, the Poles and the Russians, and above all the Greeks, who, due to their attractive figures and valuable clothing, I went to admire a little too often."[25] This physical presence signals a change in collective mentality as, like the marketplace, nature and fate of each Eastern European nation had to "jostle" for attention in the mind of intellectual observers.

This change in attention had important cultural and political consequences, as German intellectuals looked for basic formulas to relate the conditions and changes they saw. Fundamental themes and tropes that appeared in *Polenliteratur* also recurred, with minor variations, throughout the literature on other Eastern European peoples. An example from Hungary shows how much particular differences were noted and placed under an organizing rubric. In 1781, the prominent Berlin publicist and *Aufklärer* Friedrich Nicolai took a short "side trip" from his thoroughly documented journey through Germany and Switzerland in order to observe the situation in Hungary. Attuned, as ever, to the potential for progress, he spoke of a "land blessed by nature."[26] At the same time, he devoted the thrust of his comments to the ways this potential went unrealized. As he saw it, neither industry nor agriculture was pursued effectively, and an excess of sensuality, as well as to much "papistry, superstition, and bigotry"[27] prevented the Hungarians themselves from making full use of the human and natural resources they had been given. If we return to the vocabulary of *Polenliteratur*, we see also in this response to another Eastern European polity the conviction that an older, aristocratic order needed to be swept away. The literature also expresses the underlying hope that it be replaced with a form of state and social organization that met the intellectual ambitions and demands of the age. *Polenliteratur*, therefore, not only refers to Poland, but also enables us to clarify the ideological aims informing the intellectual responses to other Eastern European peoples.

What was the cumulative consequence of the German intellectual response to Eastern European peoples? The answer to this question requires continued research from a variety of different angles. One tentative conclusion—one that deserves further investigation—does arise. It is that German intellectuals pressed for something to be done about Eastern Europe, but could not reach any consistent and uncontested consensus on what this action was. Take, for instance, the evidence assembled in Klaus Heitmann's *Das Rumaenenbild im deutschen Sprachraum, 1775–1918.*[28] In documenting these German depictions of Romania, Heitmann shows the persistence of negative stereotypes (lack of cleanliness, laziness and unreliability of the local population, etc.). He also quotes several German authors who clearly contradict these negative views. Among them was an observer named Schmidl, who wrote that "the Romanian is a very teachable, employable worker, and who only needs proper leadership."[29] Other authors took up the issue of what needed to be done with Romania in different ways, and reached different evaluative conclusions, but kept returning to the expectation that Eastern Europe was a space where some sort of change should be imposed. This returns the discussion to eighteenth-century *Polenliteratur*. Admittedly, the intellectuals who wrote it could not fully predict the subsequent history of Eastern Europe, nor the role the German people and German states would play in shaping it. Nonetheless, the Polish partitions signaled the kind and quality of changes to be brought to Eastern Europe. By elaborating the basic repertoire of responses to the changes being implemented (and inflicted) on the region's traditional aristocratic polities, *Polenliteratur* deepens our understanding of Germany's interaction not only with Poland, but with Eastern Europe as a whole.

## Conclusion: A Mottled Legacy

The second and third partitions showed that Poland would not be allowed to "reform" itself back to strength. They also demonstrated that any truly sovereign Poland that would eventually emerge would unsettle—perhaps even undermine—the political and military balance in East Central Europe. Poland became what it remained until well into the twentieth century: a potential trouble spot and a sign that Europe's stability was established by force. As the 1790s progressed, and the finality of Poland's collapse became apparent to intellectuals, *Polenliteratur* hardened into ideological schools. There was the *polenfeindlich* majority that saw no virtue in Polish achievements and aspirations, and a *polenfreundlich* minority that equated the Commonwealth's victimization with the wider victimization of all oppressed humanity. Neither school had to start anew, as there was ample material expressing both themes and motifs from the 1770s and 1780s.

To give an example of the political consequences of this ideological divergence, in 1795 and 1797 two countervailing, but logically consistent books concerning the fate of Poland were published. The first, *Untersuchung über die Rechtmäßigkeit der Theilung Polens* (Investigations into the Justice of the Polish Partitions), published in Warsaw (perhaps) in 1795, uses Kantian ethical theory to show the injustice of the partitions. For the author of this book, the governments that partitioned Poland had to be wrong because no leader could elevate himself above morality and "the laws of practical reason."[30] The second book, *Deutschland und Poland: Eine politische Parallele, zur nähern Erforschung des Schicksals von Deutschland seit der Revolution in Frankreich* (Germany and Poland: A Political Parallel Aimed at a Closer Examination of the Fate of Germany Since the Revolution in France), published in "Deutschland" in 1797, explained that Poland necessarily perished, since it had a bad system of government and, furthermore, that something similar should be done to the Holy Roman Empire.[31] Hence, the partitions had to be right because what mattered was not the strength of the moral reasons for "freedom and independence," but the power to prevent foreign incursions.

From these short synopses it is easy to see that since neither accepted the other's basic principles, the two schools of *Polenliteratur* talked past each other. Also mutually exclusive were their images upon which supporters of each side drew. *Polenfreundlich* authors would show emotional scenes of unhappy Poles suffering needlessly. *Polenfeindlich* authors would show the standard scenes of Poles misusing and squandering their freedom, bringing destruction down on their own heads. The large *Polenliteratur* of the nineteenth century was an elaboration on these central tropes.[32] The question is whether this ever-increasing body of literature demonstrated the points about power, freedom and social and political organization that its authors were trying to make.

Indeed, from the standpoint of the intellectuals who first propagated it, the legacy of *Polenliteratur* is ambiguous. On the one hand, *Polenliteratur* did guarantee that German writers could continue to see Poland as a mirror of what civil society was not. If they wished, this could help them define what they wanted it to be. On the other hand, it is hard to see how Poland's failures ever really settled the issue of what German thinkers should strive for and how they should achieve it. There is something depressing about reading a literature that continually sees a lesson in another's suffering. However, that tells us something about German thinkers' troubled relationship with Eastern Europe. As long as these intellectuals were in conflict with themselves, and insecure in relation to power and authority, then their view of Poland—like a distorted mirror—reflected their own anxieties and apprehensions of failure in the creation of a modern and well-ordered civil society.

## Notes

1. G. W. v Goethe, *Die Wahlverwandtschaften* (Berlin, 1951), 177.
2. Ibid., 177.
3. Dr. Daniel Sanders, *Wörterbuch der deutschen Sprache* (Leipzig, 1876), vol. 2, part 1, 571.
4. For the wider context, see Ursula A. J. Becher, Włodzimierz Borodziej, and Robert Maier, eds., *Deutschland und Polen im zwanzigsten Jahrhundert: Analysen, Quellen, didaktische Hinweise* (Hannover, 2001).
5. R. F. Arnold, *Geschichte der deutschen Polenlitteratur von den Anfängen bis 1800* [sic] (Halle, 1900). For other studies of *Polenliteratur,* see David Pickus, *Dying with an Enlightening Fall: Poland in the Eyes of German Intellectuals, 1764–1800* (Lanham, MD, 2001). An im-

portant study of perceptions of Eastern Europe in general is Larry Wolff, *Inventing Eastern Europe: The Map of Civilization on the Mind of the Enlightenment* (Stanford, 1994).

6. Arnold, op. cit., 4–8.

7. H. M. Scott, *The Emergence of the Eastern Powers* (Cambridge, 2001), 1.

8. For an exposition of the Enlightenment's development, see Thomas P. Saine, *The Problem of Being Modern, or, the German Pursuit of Enlightenment from Leibniz to the French Revolution* (Detroit, 1997).

9. G. E. Lessing, "Philotas," in *Die Ehre hat mich mich nie gesucht: Lessing in Berlin, Gedichte, Prosa, Briefe*, Gerhard Wolf, ed. (Frankfurt a.M., 1986), 238.

10. See Michael G. Müller, *Die Teilingen Polens: 1772, 1793, 1795* (Munich, 1984).

11. Johann Erich Biester, *Abriß des Lebens von Katharine der Große* (Berlin, 1797), 134.

12. See Adam Zamoyski, *The Last King of Poland* (London, 1997).

13. The figures come from Horst Möller, *Vernunft und Kritik: Deutsche Aufklärung im 17. und 18. Jahrhundert* (Frankfurt a.M, 1986), 273.

14. Arnold, op. cit., 6.

15. Quoted in Gerhard Kosellek, *Reformen, Revolutionen, Reisen: Deutsche Polenliteratur* (Wiesbaden: Harrasowitz, 2000), 129.

16. Quoted in Arnold, *Polenlitteratur*, 44.

17. Johann Gottfried Herder, "Adrestea," in *Sämmtliche Werke*, vol. 9 (Karlsruhe, 1820), 308.

18. Christian Friedrich Daniel Schubart, "Polonia," in *Deutsche Chronik* (Ulm), May 19, 1774 155.

19. Friedrich Freiherr von der Trenck, *Beantwortung auf die in französischer Sprache erschienenen Schmächschrift betitelt: Anmerkung über die Erklärung der Wiener, Petersburgen und Berliner Höfe, die Zergliederung der Republik Pohlen Betreffend* (Aachen, 1773), 2.

20. There is a great deal of discussion of the meaning of bourgeois ideals in eighteenth-century Germany. A good starting point is Urusla A. J. Becher, *Politische Gesellschaft: Studien zur Genese bürgerlicher Öffentlichkeit in Deutschland* (Göttingen, 1978).

21. Franz Kratter, *Briefe über die itzigen Zustand Galiziens*, vol. 1 (Leipzig, 1786), 198.

22. Johann Friedrich Zöllner, *Briefe über Schlesien, Krakau und die Grafschaft Glatz auf einer Reise im Jahre 1791* (Berlin, 1792), 267.

23. F. L. de la Fontaine, *Chirurgisch-Medizinsche Untersuchungen verschiedenen Inhalts Polen Betreffend* (Breslau and Leipzig, 1792), 140.

24. This coinage is taken from Isabel V. Hull, *Sexuality, State and Civil-Society in Germany, 1700–1815* (Ithaca, 1996).

25. Goethe, *Dichtung und Wahrheit*, II 6 (*Werke*, Weimar Ausgabe, 27, 1889), 48.

26. Quoted in Wolfgang Martens, "Kleine Nebenreise nach Ungarn," in *Kulturbeziehungen in Mittel und Osteuropa im 18. und 19. Jahrhundert: Festschrift für Heinz Ischreyt zum 65 Geburtstag*, Wolfgang Kessler, Henry Reitz, and Gert Robel, eds. (Berlin, 1982), 147.

27. Martens, "Kleine Nebenreise," 151.

28. Klaus Heitmann, *Das Rumaenenbild im deutschen Sprachraum, 1775–1918* (Studia Transylvanica) (Cologne, 1985).

29. Ibid., 136.

30. Anonymous, *Untersuchung über die Rechtmäßigkeit der Theilung Polens* ("Warsaw," 1795), 26.

31. Anonymous, *Deutschland und Poland: Eine politische Parallele, zur nähern Erforschung des Schicksals von Deutschland seit der Revolution in Frankreich* ("Deutschland," 1797), 69.

32. See Helga Whiton, *Der Wandel des Polenbildes in der deutschen Literatur des 19. Jahrhunderts* (Bern and Las Vegas, 1981).

# German Colonization in the Banat and Transylvania in the Eighteenth Century

### ❖ Karl A. Roider and Robert Forrest ❖

German colonization in the eighteenth-century Habsburg Monarchy focused on two areas, the Banat of Temesvar (Timoşoara) and Transylvania. In the case of the Banat, Habsburg policy did not focus exclusively on filling those lands with Germans because they were Germans. There the Habsburgs were eager primarily to provide a population for a recently acquired area depopulated by war and disease. Still, they regarded the Germans as bringing civilization and culture to an area they believed needed some of both. In Transylvania, Habsburg policy-makers, while having a more complex policy of immigration, believed a larger German presence would serve the same purpose. Indeed, there they hoped that mingling and perhaps marriage with the local Magyars might dampen the Hungarian tendency to object to Habsburg rule.

In both cases encouragement of population growth and economic development common to seventeenth- and eighteenth-century Cameralism played roles in Habsburg policy that sent Germans to the East. Cameralism, associated with such Habsburg thinkers as Johann Joachim Becher, Wilhelm von Schroeder, and Philip Wilhelm von Hörnigk, was an economic theory that recognized that real power rested not so much on the strength of the monarchy's army as on the strength of its economy, including the well-being of its subjects. These Cameralists argued that the state must invest in agriculture, manufacturing, commerce, and infrastructure because the wealth derived from those endeavors would enable it to sustain the kind of bureaucracy and military that would assure its safety.

The Banat became a Habsburg possession following the Austro-Turkish War of 1716–1718. In 1699, at the Treaty of Carlowitz (Sremski Karlovci), the Austrians acquired most of old Hungary north of the Danube/Sava River line with the exception of the Banat, a land bordered on three sides by the Danube, Tisza, and Maros (Mureş) rivers. In the subsequent war, the Habsburg armies conquered and secured not only the Banat, but the fortress of Belgrade and a substantial portion of Serbia. The Habsburgs did not declare this land reconquered and thus subject to the Hungarian crown, but rather newly acquired (*neoacquisita*) and liable to direct administration from Vienna. On the advice of his foremost military advisor, Prince Eugene of Savoy, Emperor Charles VI (1711–1740) established a commission to govern the Banat and to recommend policies to improve it.[1]

## The Banat

The Banat offered the Habsburgs the opportunity to conduct a controlled experiment in the implementation of Cameralist ideas. It represented a confined space of approximately 11,150 square miles (28,879 kilometers) which was considerably underpopulated. A census by the *Hofkriegsrat* conducted in late 1718 counted a population of 85,000 in this space, or a rather low 7.62 people per square mile. That census was probably wrong, because later scholarship indicated that the population was more likely 300,000, or 26 people per square mile.[2] The severe undercounting by the *Hofkriegsrat* could have been attributed to all kinds of reasons, but in any case even 26 people per square mile indicates a sparse population. Because of its small population and its status as a land controlled by the crown without interference from estates or a resident nobility, the Banat was a perfect place to see if Cameralist policies worked. The Habsburgs could bring in settlers, provide them with the means to raise crops and livestock, engage in infrastructure improvements—especially in controlling water since the area was marshy and swampy—introduce policies related to disease control, and generally turn it into a model of how a modern state could improve a backward land.

The first task was to find colonists, and in the 1720s the most fertile recruiting ground was the Holy Roman Empire, especially the Rhineland. That area had suffered considerably during the War of the Spanish Succession, was burdened by high taxation, and did not offer much new land to its freehold peasants.[3] In fact, that area had already seen recruiters of various kinds, including British who were looking for settlers in Ireland and North America, French who wished to settle French Guiana, Russians already interested in moving people to the Volga and Black Sea regions, and even Spaniards for the sparsely inhabited Sierra Morena. But there is no evidence that the Habsburgs in this early period were interested in settling only Germans in the Banat. Rather, Germans were the most readily available and had the fewest restrictions on their moving.

The Habsburgs did impose one limit on these early immigrants—they had to be Roman Catholic. In the early eighteenth century, religion, not nationality, was thought to determine a person's loyalty. The assumption was that Catholics would be loyal to the Habsburg Monarchy, Protestants to the king of Prussia, Orthodox to the tsar of Russia, and Jews and Muslims to the sultan of the Ottoman Empire. Political leaders made exceptions, but it was an assumption nonetheless. For that reason, the Habsburgs did not want Protestants in an area so critical to the defense of Hungary.[4] But that also meant that the Habsburgs were willing to accept colonists who were Catholic but not German, and in the 1730s the governor of the Banat found homes for 500 Roman Catholic Albanian families and encouraged "many thousand" Catholic Bulgarians to come as well.[5]

The bulk of the indigenous population was not Catholic but Orthodox, notably Romanians and Serbs. Despite their equation of Catholicism with loyalty, the Habsburgs had no intention of converting the Orthodox, especially since they feared that proselytizing by Catholic orders would alienate the Serbian *Grenzer* so vital to the defense of the monarchy in that area. In 1745 the government of Maria Theresa established the *Kommission* (later *Hofdeputation*) *in Banaticis, Transylvanicis, et Illyricis*, one of whose principal functions was to protect the interests of the Orthodox.[6] Non-Catholic German farmers might not be sufficiently loyal to the state, but they were also not vital to its defense; non-Catholic Serbian border troops were.

More important as settlers than Germans just for being German were people with skills. A main reason the Habsburgs recruited Germans to the Banat was that they possessed superior knowledge in agriculture and mining, and the hope was that they would pass these skills on to native Romanians and Serbs.[7] But the Habsburgs sought other skills as well. The government recruited Italians for their ability to manufacture silk, paper, and olive oil and to grow vegetables and rice. It sought Armenians for their knowledge of leather work, and it even hoped to find some Turks skilled in the weaving of a particular kind of woolens.[8] Again the hope was that these people would pass on their skills to the natives and even to other colonists. However, this hope was not fulfilled because those foreigners who came, including the Germans, tended to group in clusters of their own nationality.

The results of this first period of colonization were not at all promising. As one can imagine, the biggest obstacle was disease. The whole border region between the monarchy and the Ottoman Empire was known as a land infested with disease, notably malaria, smallpox, and plague. Part of the responsibility of the *Grenzer* was maintenance of the *Pestkordon*, which required a period of quarantine for everyone crossing the border from the Ottoman Empire into Hungary. In 1728 the administration of Temesvar, the capital city of the Banat, recorded 51 baptisms and 484 deaths among the Germans, and rumors spread throughout the Holy Roman Empire that the Banat was becoming "the graveyard of Germans."[9]

Disease was not the only difficulty the colonists faced. Things were not cheap in the Banat, and despite the initial gifts of the government to get things started, there seemed to be chronic shortages of items essential to maintain agriculture like draft animals, dairy cattle, and tools. In this early period little progress was made on the control of water, and even if a farmer got all that he needed to begin his family's new life, floods could wash them all away. The presence of a criminal element did not help either. Some of the indigenous people were unhappy to see the arrival of these folks who seemed determined to uplift them economically and culturally, and they stole their livestock and sold it across the Maros River in Hungary.[10]

The Carolinian experiment in the Banat ended with the Austro-Turkish War of 1737–1739 when the area was overrun with military forces and all of the paraphernalia that came with them. That was enough for many of the colonists, who packed up their things and headed for other parts of the monarchy or back to their original lands. By 1740 there was no doubt in any official's mind that this initial experiment in Cameralist population enhancement had ended in disappointment.

The second effort to uplift the Banat came during the reign of Maria Theresa, particularly the 1760s. According to some sources, by 1760 the Banat had a population of 400,000, of whom 24,000 were Germans and 33,000 were Catholics.[11] Once again the Habsburg authorities sent recruiting teams and advertisements to western Germany, where they found a good response owing to some overpopulation and food shortages at that time. But this time the intent of colonization had broadened. Unlike the pre-1740 period, the Theresian government used the Banat almost as a dumping ground for leftover people, such as those convicted of crimes, including prostitutes, who went as "wives" to areas short of females. Those dispatched were generally not perpetrators of serious crimes like robbery and murder but relatively minor offenses such as poaching, begging, or escaping from debt. One *Staatsrat* document of 1771 suggested that these people possessed virtues, describing them as "hard-working people experienced in farming whose crimes resulted not from a vicious heart or from unmitigated wickedness, but from unfortunate prejudice and obstinacy."[12] Still, the administration in Temesvar was not enthusiastic about such colonists because these people did not possess the virtues to take advantage of their new opportunities. In the view of the local bureaucrats, criminals, even those convicted of less than capital crimes, did not make good colonists.[13]

A major source of colonists in the Theresian period were men mustered out of the army following the end of the Seven Years' War (1756–1763). In a colonization decree of 1763 Maria Theresa declared her intention to settle ex-soldiers in Hungary, Transylvania, and the Banat "to win the army personnel for the crown" and to protect the other crown lands from a flood of unemployed soldiers.[14] Just as they were not delighted with criminals settling in the Banat, the administrative officials in Temesvar were not eager to see erstwhile soldiers arrive either. The very fact that they were soldiers, the head of administration wrote, meant that they were "unvirtuous people and vagabonds."[15] His assessment seems to have been accurate, for in 1764 the administration notified the *Hofkammer* in Vienna that the ex-soldiers were not eager to become model citizens but were prone to "drunkenness, indolence, and an evil life."[16] Maria Theresa also settled German-speaking prisoners of war in the Banat, assuming that they would be grateful to any sovereign who gave them an opportunity to find a livelihood. They turned out to be less reliable than the ex-soldiers, most of them fleeing for home as soon as they reached the Banat.

In 1768 Emperor Joseph II, since 1765 co-ruler with his mother Maria Theresa, visited the Banat and expressed great disappointment at what he found. The colonization effort had brought new people, including Germans, to the Banat, but it remained a backward place, not at all a model for civilization that Vienna had hoped it would be, and certainly not a place that would pay back soon on the investment put into it. Joseph criticized especially the officials running the land, complaining that they were of low quality, willing to accept bribes and to ignore crimes. In fact, he was so unhappy with the administration that he suggested that the best way to improve the Banat might be to reverse the whole centralizing process, create estates, and sell the province to them.[17]

Joseph's visit changed the focus of the administration toward the Banat. After 1768 the major effort ceased to be colonization and turned instead to improving the economy and society. This took the form particularly of educational reforms. In 1764 the *Hofkammer* had proposed establishing schools for the indigenous Orthodox population, mainly to install Christian virtues and cure it of the "liabilities of cattle-stealing, murder, and bigamy."[18] At that time the administration in Temesvar rejected the idea of schools, declaring that education would not improve the local people, which would only happen if priests and police "force the people to church and confession."[19]

After Joseph's visit the *Hofkammer* proceeded with its educational reforms, and a number of its officers submitted proposals for consideration. In 1774, six months before the general order regulating schools throughout the entire monarchy, the *Hofkammer* established elementary schools in the Banat. Some members of the *Hofkammer* recommended that the language of instruction be German because they argued that the ultimate goal of the establishment of schools should be to provide recruits for the Habsburg military and civil service. But in the end the *Hofkammer* decided that education should be in the indigenous languages, because its purpose would be to instill the virtues of hard work and obedience to the law and that would only happen in schools where children could learn in their own languages. Higher schools, the *Hofkammer* agreed, would have German as the language of instruction, but no children could learn in German if not well-versed in their own language.[20]

Just as the *Hofkammer* did not envision these schools as vehicles for Germanization, so it did not envision them as vehicles for Catholicization either. The decrees directed that there be religious instruction in the schools, but it would be in Orthodoxy, not Catholicism. The officials conceded that if the teachers tried to force Catholicism on the children, they might not come to school at all, which would defeat the purpose of the educational reforms generally. Still, the instructors in Orthodoxy would not be local priests, not so much because they might be insufficiently loyal to the monarchy, but because they showed "no enthusiasm for education."[21] Therefore, religious instruction would be carried out by secular teachers, who would stress to the children that personal virtue and obedience to the state were characteristics of all religions.

Habsburg colonization in the eighteenth century established a German presence in the Banat, but it was not a particularly aggressive policy and it was certainly not designed to create a German enclave there for the sake of Germanness. It was instead part of a broad experiment to see if the Cameralist policies of population increase, educational opportunity, and economic development could increase the wealth of a province and ultimately contribute to the power of the state. In the eighteenth century the results were not particularly encouraging. In fact, at the end of Joseph's visit in 1768 he wrote, "Never had 900,000 florins been spent worse, more uselessly, or unwisely as in this colonization business."[22]

Still, the Banat in the nineteenth century became prosperous and could be regarded as one of those many places where Habsburg rule produced in the end a cultured, developed, educated area. By the middle of the nineteenth century there were 200,000 Germans in the Banat, which made up about 14% of the population.[23] By then education and religious tolerance had made great strides there and national tensions had not yet made an impact. In many ways Habsburg rule in the Banat was the best time in its history.

# Transylvania

Transylvania, like the Banat, belonged to the Kingdom of Hungary before the Ottomans conquered it in the sixteenth century. Unlike the Banat, it had a centuries-old constitution that solidified, reflected, and legally protected its social, cultural, and religious diversity. Transylvania also basked in prosperity from a well-developed agriculture and commerce that the Banat could only envy. The Turks preserved Transylvania's constitution and nurtured its prosperity so it was relatively well-off when the Austrians conquered it from the Turks during the War of the Holy League (1683–1699).

Transylvania contained 21,297 square miles (55,159 kilometers), slightly less than double the Banat's area. Transylvania's demographic makeup has frustrated scholars for decades. First, the population fluctuated due to movements of Magyars and especially Romanians back and forth across its western and eastern borders to escape problems facing them in their native lands or in Transylvania itself.[24] Second, until 1787, when Joseph II ordered a complete census of the principality's inhabitants, Habsburg officials had prepared only tax or conscription lists of the population by periodically summoning people to their local churches.[25] Third, since conscription censuses counted a smaller portion of the population than tax censuses and a number of people evaded both, they undercounted the population.[26] In fact, all Habsburg Cameralist efforts at enumerating their human resources in Transylvania underestimated them.[27]

While the reader should keep these caveats in mind, Transylvania's eighteenth-century demographic statistics followed Western Europe's upward trend with a steady growth rate of about 1 percent per year.[28] This rate is much lower than that obtained by using the highly inaccurate censuses from the early decades of the eighteenth century. For example, a 1730 conscription census put Transylvania's population at 725,000. A more accurate census taken in 1760–65 found 1,176,454 people living in Transylvania, but another tax census published in 1766 listed 1,453,742 inhabitants, a number larger than that in Joseph II's census.[29] By 1776, a tax census revealed that Transylvania's population had either risen or fallen to 1,359,260.[30] Joseph II's census arrived at a figure of around 1,440,986, or 67.66 people per square mile, a population density considerably greater than that in the Banat.[31] This collective data also included statistics on Transylvania's ethnicity. The three major groups were Romanians, Magyars, and Germans. The volatile Romanian segment constituted a majority ranging from about 65 percent at midcentury to slightly more than 50 percent in 1800.[32] The Magyars and Szeklers together comprised between 33 and 40 percent, with the Saxons between 10 and 12 percent of Transylvania's population.[33]

The Magyars had migrated from the Russian steppes arriving in what became Hungary about 896 A.D., but did not move eastward into Transylvania until 1003.[13] They divided it into counties and introduced a nobility, headed by a *vajda* or prince, to govern the mostly Romanian people living there. During the 1360s, the *vajda* became a semi-independent prince who could summon assemblies of his subjects.

A major reason the Magyars seized Transylvania was to secure their kingdom against seemingly endless marauding bands prowling the Russian steppes. To supplement the local population, the Magyars colonized eastern Transylvania with Szeklers and Germans. The Szeklers had joined the migrating Magyars on the steppes and had almost completely assimilated with them. Hungary's king Géza II (1141–62) invited Germans, known as Saxons, to settle in the southeastern corner of Transylvania.[34] More German settlers followed these pioneers, and in 1224 King András II (1205–35) bestowed self-government on the Saxons. Henceforth, their section of Transylvania became known as the *Fundius regius*, or *Königsboden*. The Saxons farmed but also introduced urbanization and commerce into Transylvania, which largely explains why they preserved their cultural identity against the more numerous Magyar-Szekler group.

The Magyar nobility, the Szeklers, and the Saxons soon became nations in the medieval sense of enjoying political and legal rights. Each nation had separate religious and political organizations that rendered them autonomous from each other and from the central government. A nearly successful peasant revolt in 1437–38 prompted the three nations to establish a formal union to protect their privileges and to prevent any other group, namely the Romanians, from becoming a nation. In short, these three nations, united by a common desire to preserve their autonomy, comprised states within a principality, within a kingdom.

The Reformation came to Transylvania in the midst of the chaos accompanying the Ottoman conquest and reorganization of Hungary following the Battle of Mohács in 1526. Ottoman indifference to their Christian subjects' beliefs and the Protestant inclinations of Transylvania's Prince John-Sigismund Zápolyia (1559–71) facilitated the smooth introduction of Protestantism into Transylvania. During the 1540s the Saxons converted to Lutheranism. Most Hungarians became Calvinists in the 1550s, and in 1564 the Transylvanian Diet accorded these two creeds equality with Roman Catholicism. In that same year, Unitarianism attracted a few Hungarian nobles, and in 1568 it also achieved equality with the other three Christian denominations, now legally designated as accepted religions. Orthodox Christianity, the Romanians' faith and thus the faith of the majority of those living in Transylvania, was tolerated but had no legal standing. Although the diets of 1564 and 1568 spared Catholicism the same fate as Orthodoxy, it had lost its formerly dominant position. Prince Steven Báthory (1571–86) unsuccessfully tried to eradicate Protestantism. His failure insured that religious bigotry would not replace toleration, at least for the accepted faiths, and that Transylvanian autonomy would become inseparable from Protestantism.

This was the Transylvania that the Austrians liberated from the Turks in the 1680s—religiously tolerant for the age, with a heritage of political autonomy managed by three feudal nations, and prosperous. It had also avoided most of the damage and depopulation that the Habsburg-Ottoman wars had visited on Hungary's western provinces. Emperor Leopold I (1658–1705) promised to respect the Hungarian and Transylvanian constitutions, and in his *Diplomum Leopoldinum* in 1691 he confirmed the rights and privileges of Transylvania's three nations and four accepted religions. Although recognizing it as still part of the Hungarian crown, Leopold preserved Transylvania's autonomous diet, administration, and judicial system. He also created a separate chancellory for it in Vienna. [35] A *Gubernium*, consisting of a governor and twelve councillors, replaced the prince as the executive.[36] Each of the three nations and four churches were to be equally represented on the *Gubernium* and in the Transylvanian Aulic Chancellery in Vienna. In practice, however, the Habsburg regime effectively abolished Transylvania's self-government by making all of the major decisions concerning the principality in Vienna conform to the centralizing principles of its absolutism.

Habsburg absolutism entrusted Catholicism with the vital role of spiritually unifying and controlling the monarchy's varied cultures. Given the indispensability of religious diversity for the autonomy of Transylvania's nations, Habsburg political ambitions for Transylvania required Catholic supremacy over the region's other faiths.

Realizing the weakness of the Catholic Church in Transylvania and encouraged by his trusted advisor Leopold Cardinal Kollonics, Leopold I hoped to subject Transylvania to the Counter-Reformation despite Báthory's previous failure.[37] He restored some of the Catholic Church's lost estates, increased its income, built new churches, and reintroduced the Jesuits.[38] Throughout the eighteenth century, the Habsburg regime awarded most of Transylvania's administrative posts to Catholics.[39] It even barred Protestants from obtaining semi-administrative posts. When Martin Hochmeister, a Lutheran printer living in Hermannstadt, sought appointment as Transylvania's imperial printer, Maria Theresa refused to bestow that position on him unless he converted to Catholicism, which he did in 1777.[40] Such methods fortified Transylvania's Catholics, but even with Jesuit help, they could not convert the Protestants.

Regarding the Romanian Orthodox, Cardinal Kollonics proposed a different policy from the one the Austrians pursued in the Banat, by recommending converting the Romanians to Catholicism. The Transylvanian diet had placed the Orthodox under the accepted Calvinist Church. As most of the Calvinists were Magyars and Szeklers, the Habsburgs in one stroke would remove the Romanians from religious rule by non-Romanians, reinforce the Catholic Church, and enfeeble the two Transylvanian nations that caused them the most concern.[41] Kollonics's scheme began in 1699 with the introduction of the Uniate Church in Transylvania. The Council of Florence had sanctioned the Uniate Church in 1439 in order to end the schism between Orthodoxy and Catholicism, but few Orthodox Christians outside Poland had accepted it. As a reward for those Romanian Orthodox priests who became Uniates, Kollonics promised them the same status as Catholic clergy, including the rights as a nation and membership in a legal religion. Kollonics wanted the Uniate clergy to become the vanguard for turning Romanian Orthodox into Uniates. The Jesuits would then convert the Uniates to full Catholics, providing the Habsburgs with a source of leverage against Transylvania's Protestants.

The revolt led by Ferenc Rákóczi in Hungary and Transylvania (1703–1711) dealt a blow to Kollonics's religious offensive from which it never recovered. Austria reaffirmed Transylvania's constitution at the Peace of Szatmár (1711), and for the rest of the century the Habsburg rulers acquiesced in Transylvania's existing social and religious structure in order to avoid further revolts. During the Rákóczi uprising, many Uniates returned to the Orthodox Church, and attempts to revive the Uniate Church after 1711 foundered largely because cautious Habsburg rulers continually ignored the promises Kollonics had made to the Romanians.[42] In fact, census data show that all Habsburg efforts to enhance Catholicism's numbers in Transylvania failed.[43] By 1773, only 8.6 percent of Transylvanians professed Catholicism, while 11.2 percent were Uniates—who, however, identified more with the 52.4 percent Orthodox than with Catholics. Most of the remainder were Protestants.[44]

Given the failure of the Carolinian and Theresian regimes to diminish, if not

.minate, Protestantism from Transylvania, the Habsburg administration turned, as it had in the Banat, to Cameralism and focused on education to improve and unify the Transylvanian subjects. Prior to this point, Cameralism was practiced mainly through efforts to increase population. Transylvania had been less seriously depopulated than central and southern Hungary because it had been spared the worst ravages of the Habsburg-Ottoman wars.[45] Nonetheless, it had shared in the subsequent devastation wrought by the Rákóczi revolt and chronic epidemics, which partly explains the low numbers of its 1730 census. Since both areas needed more people, Vienna proposed to dispatch mostly Catholic Germans. Kollonics had earlier advocated sending Germans because he felt that they would avoid assimilating with Magyars as had the Saxons and would, therefore, become "apostles of civilization, nationality, and religion."[46] Habsburg officials also thought that intermarriage with German colonists would lessen the Magyar proclivity for sedition.[47] German immigration into Hungary and Transylvania began in earnest after the Peace of Szatmár in 1711. As in the case of the Banat, these immigrants were both peasants and artisans, many of the latter migrating from towns elsewhere in Hungary.[48]

Transylvania received around one million immigrants between 1720 and 1787. Between 350,000 and 400,000 may have been Germans; an equal number of Romanians came from the Ottoman provinces of Moldavia and Wallachia, while most of the remainder were Magyars moving from Hungary proper.[49] More research is necessary to account for nearly all of these folks, especially for the Germans. Some Germans were soldiers sent to the Transylvanian *Grenzer* regiments, authorized in 1761/62. Maria Theresa hoped that introducing Catholic soldiers would improve Catholicism's lot in Transylvania and that the addition of more non-Magyars would benefit Habsburg absolutism by undermining the Magyar and Szekler estates. Transylvania's nations unsuccessfully opposed the regiments, but in practice they had no impact on Transylvania's constitution.[50]

Toward the end of the Seven Years' War, Maria Theresa gave the order to form additional *Grenzer* regiments along the Transylvanian border with the Ottoman Empire. At the same time, Saxon political leaders decided to ask the empress to release Prussian and German prisoners of war for settlement in Transylvania. The principality's governor, Samuel von Brukenthal, and commanding general, Baron von Buccow, presented the proposal in Vienna. Its stipulations were that the prospective immigrants be Lutheran and artisans and that they also be too short for service in the Habsburg army.[51] Maria Theresa liked the idea and directed Aegid Freiherr Borié, a member of the Council of State and a strong advocate of absolutism, to draft a plan. Given the possibility that the men would flee for home at the first opportunity, the empress insisted that every effort be made to assure that the prisoners selected for settlement were willing to remain in their new homes.[52] To achieve that goal, the Austrians chose only single men, and they obtained wives for as many of them as possible among

Lutherans living in western Austria.[53] At first, the plan called for sending these Germans to Hungary, the Banat, and Transylvania's *Fundius regius*, but opposition from both the Banat's administrators and Chancellor Wenzel Anton Kaunitz removed the Banat from consideration.[54] Alas, nearly all of the former prisoners of war sent to Hungary fled at the first opportunity, while roughly half of the 1,000–2,000 sent to Transylvania stayed in their new homes.[55] All those who stayed had recently married Austrian women. In his assessment of the program when it ended in 1763, Borié concluded "that the settlement of these Prussian prisoners of war was not useless," but Konrad Schünemann contends that it only contributed to the general dissatisfaction with immigration among the monarchy's subjects.[56]

Slightly over 1 percent of Transylvania's German immigrants were exiled (transmigrated) Austrian Protestants. Between 1734 and 1737 Charles VI authorized the deportation of 624 Protestants from the Salzkammergut and Carinthia to the Saxon *Fundius regius*. His hope was that these people would bring more advanced farming methods to the Saxons, who did in fact adopt some of them. Still, half of these immigrants died shortly after arriving, and most of the others soon left for other parts of the empire.[57] Later on, Maria Theresa gave greater weight to cleansing Austria's western provinces of Protestants than to economic improvement or repopulation in Transylvania. She treated Protestants as criminals and in a series of deportations between 1752 and 1758, sent 2,974 of them to Transylvania from the area around the Enns River, Styria, and Carinthia; between 1773 and 1776 she deported another 188 families from Styria.[58] The empress also intended to remove a large group of Moravian Protestants, but the persuasiveness of Kaunitz and the bitter opposition of her son and co-ruler, Joseph II, persuaded her to send just forty-three to Transylvania in 1780.[59]

Maria Theresa's transmigrations, which involved many more Protestants than those of Charles VI, faced stiff opposition in Transylvania from the *Gubernium,* the Catholic officialdom, and even from the Saxon leadership. The *Gubernium* disliked Vienna telling it its business, but the administrators knew that they could only protest the resettlement, not stop it. The Catholic leadership argued that a large influx of Protestants would weaken its already reduced standing in Transylvania.[60]

The Saxon reasons for opposing the arrival of these fellow German Lutherans were more complicated. They felt culturally much closer to Lutherans from northern Germany, where their ancestors had lived prior to migrating to Transylvania. They recruited pastors for their churches and teachers for their schools from the Lutheran areas of the Holy Roman Empire, and the Saxon elite had sent their sons to universities there.[61] Lutherans from western Austria were not the kind of Lutherans or the kind of Germans the Saxons wanted settled among them. Besides that, these Austrian Lutherans might constitute a formidable political block because Vienna had compelled the *Gubernium* to treat them as full citizens in the Saxon nation.

Eager to dilute the cultural and political influence of these new arrivals, the Saxons scattered them on wasteland where, ostracized by the Saxons and separated from each other, they languished in poverty as day laborers and poorly paid craftsmen. Saxon reports to Vienna complained about the condition and lawlessness of these immigrants, partly to convince Habsburg officials not to send any more.[62] In the end, Transylvania was not in any way hospitable to these immigrants, and more than half of them died within a few years after arriving.[63] The deportations of Protestants to the eastern provinces of the Habsburg Empire stopped with the succession of Joseph II as sole ruler in 1780. He did briefly consider sending some deists to Transylvania, but decided to have them whipped instead.[64]

Habsburg policies failed to achieve their primary goals of homogenizing Transylvania's diverse population and, if not eliminating, then at least neutralizing its constitution. While Vienna did seriously weaken Transylvanian autonomy at the principality level, the legal nations' autonomy, although threatened, survived intact. Imperial vacillations between the punitive approach of the Counter-Reformation and Cameralism's positive encouragements introduced tension into the Habsburg administration. Nowhere was that more visible than in immigration. On the one hand, immigrants could contribute to economic growth; on the other, they threatened the nations' and Protestantism's privileged status. Joseph II tried to end the tension in favor of Cameralism by replacing the Counter-Reformation with religious toleration for all faiths and abolishing the nations' rights through centralizing reforms. However, the three nations joined forces as they had done in 1437 to defend their freedoms and had persuaded the emperor to rescind his reforms before his death in 1790. The Saxons' lack of compassion for fellow Protestants deported into their midst epitomizes the hollowness of this victory. It is noteworthy that the one group of Transylvanians unwilling to welcome those who spoke their language and, in some cases, shared their religion would be the smallest of the recognized nations.

Yet, the Three Estates ultimately fared no better. Between 1784 and 1847 Transylvania's population nearly doubled, from around 1.441 million to 2.5 million. Insofar as immigration played a role in this increase it was largely the Romanians whose numbers rose from 720,000 to 1.2 million, while the Hungarian-Szekler population increased from 576,000 to 830,000, or about 40% of the total compared to between 33 and 40% in 1784. The Saxons grew from 150,000 to 200,000 to about 8% of the total population, which was down from 10–12% in 1784.[65] During these decades, Hungarian and Romanian nationalism burst into full bloom. The national strife between the Hungarian-Szeklers and Romanians deepened as their respective nationalisms intensified until they erupted into open violence during the Revolution of 1848. The Saxons, whose declining percentage of Transylvania's total population made them more determined to preserve their independence, played an increasingly marginal role in this struggle that has never really ended. The ethnic conflict also insured that the Habsburg's eighteenth-century religious and Cameralist goals for Transylvania were never realized.

German migration to the East in the eighteenth-century Habsburg Monarchy had mixed motives and mixed results. Although data remain unreliable, one can suggest that 500,000 Germans moved to the Banat and Transylvania in that period, either from parts of the empire or other lands in the monarchy. In the Banat the purpose was to populate a depopulated area which could become in the long run a source of increased revenue and recruits for the army. In Transylvania the motives were more complex, including a failed plan to make the area more Catholic and to dilute the political power of the three recognized nations. In the nineteenth century, however, German colonization paid off. Both lands became part of the general economic and demographic growth of the monarchy and enjoyed to some degree the educational improvements and social and cultural progress that occurred during that time. The twentieth century was not so favorable to either one, but that is another story.

# Notes

1. The *Hofkammer* in Vienna recommended this course of action, and Prince Eugene agreed. Prince Eugene to *Hofkriegsrat*, 21 June 1717, in *Feldzüge des Prinzen Eugens* (Vienna, 1891), XVII, supplement, 70–72. The commission served as an advisory body to the *Hofkammer* and *Hofkriegsrat*.
2. Sonja Jordan, *Die kaiserliche Wirtschaftspolitik im Banat im 18. Jahrhundert* (Munich, 1967), 17; Josef Kallbrunner, *Das kaiserliche Banat: Einrichtung und Entwicklung des Banats bis 1739* (Munich, 1958), 26–60; and Aurel Tinta, *Colonizarile habsburgice in Banat, 1716–1740* (Timisoara, 1972), 82.
3. Tinta, *Colonizarile habsburgice*, 24–29.
4. Ernst Nowotny, *Die Transmigration ober- und innerösterreichischer Protestanten nach Siebenbürgen im 18. Jahrhundert* (Jena, 1931), 46; Konrad Schünemann, *Österreichs Bevölkerungspolitik unter Maria Theresia* (Berlin, 1935), 73.
5. Kallbrunner, *Das kaiserliche Banat: Einrichtung und Entwicklung des Banats bis 1739*, 37.
6. Gunther Rothenberg, *The Military Border in Croatia, 1740–1881* (Chicago, 1966), 32–33.
7. Fritz Valjevac, *Geschichte der deutschen Kulturbeziehungen zu Südosteuropa* (Munich, 1958), III, 102.
8. Jordan, *Kaiserliche Wirtschaftspolitik*, 24–26.
9. Johann Schwicker, *Geschichte des Temeser Banats* (Grosz-Becskerek, 1861), 317.
10. Ernst Schimscha, *Technik und Methoden der Theresianischer Besiedlung des Banats* (Baden bei Wien, 1939), 100–01. The penalty for stealing livestock was death, but it did not discourage the thieves much.
11. Schünemann, *Österreichs Bevölkerungspolitik unter Maria Theresia*, 73. P. G. M. Dickson believes that Schünemann's figures for 1760 are "unconvincing," but agrees that his colonization figures are probably correct for the 1760s. In that decade 11,000 families settled in the Banat and Batchka, with 2,000 more on cameral estates for a total of 52,000 persons. P. G. M. Dickson, *Finance and Government under Maria Theresia, 1740–1780* (Oxford, 1987), I, 36.
12. Quoted in Schünemann, *Österreichs Bevölkerungspolitik*, 78.

13. Friedrich Lotz, "Die frühtheresianische Kolonisation des Banats (1740–1762)," in *Gedenkschrift für Harold Steinacker* (Munich, 1966), 162. Between 1752 and 1768, 3,130 criminals were transported to the Banat.

14. Alexander Krischan, "Die Kolonisationspatent Maria Theresias von 25 II 1763 als Beitrag zur Besiedlungsgeschichte des altungarischen Raumes," *Deutsches Archiv für Landes- und Volksforschung* 7 (1943): 101.

15. Quoted in Schünemann, *Österreichs Bevölkerungspolitik*, 160–61.

16. Quoted in ibid., 164. The settlement of invalided soldiers in the Banat Military Border proved more successful. Felix Milleker, *Geschichte der Banater Militärgrenze*, 1764–1783 (Pančevo, 1926), 41–42.

17. Sieglinde Neidenbach, "Die Reisen Kaiser Josephs II ins Banat" (Doctoral dissertation, University of Vienna, 1967), 55–63.

18. Quoted from the Bishop of Temesvar, Vinzentius Joannovich Viedek, in Herta Tietz, "Die Einrichtung eines Schulwesens für Romänen und Serben im kaiserlichen Banat (1718–1778)," *Südostdeutsches Archiv* 9 (1966): 195.

19. Quoted in ibid., 188.

20. Ibid., 194–95.

21. A *Hofrat* Kress argued against religious instruction among the Orthodox children because it would make them more knowledgeable of their faith than Catholic children were of theirs. Ibid., 196.

22. Quoted in Konrad Schünemann, "Die Wirtschaftspolitik Josephs in der Zeit seiner Mitregenschaft," *Mitteilungen des Instituts für österreichische Geschichtsforschung* 47 (1934): 30.

23. Schwicker, *Geschichte des Temeser Banats*, 427, 455.

24. Béla K. Király, *Hungary in the Eighteenth Century: The Decline of Enlightened Absolutism* (New York, 1969), 6.

25. Ernst Wagner, *Historisch-Statistisches Ortnamenbuch für Siebenbürgen mit einer Einführung in die historische Statistik des Landes*. Studia Transylvanica Ergänzungsbände des Siebenbürgische Landeskunde (Vienna, 1977), 43–48.

26. For example, the conscription census quite reasonably omitted the *Grenzers,* but the tax censuses included them. The *Grenzer* regiments were fairly large. Estimates for the 1780s range between 133,000 and 244,000. Alfred Gürtler, *Die Volkszählungen Maria Theresias und Josef II., 1753–1790* (Innsbruck, 1909) provides a good explanation of Austrian census methods during the last half of the eighteenth century. The Austrians collected population data in numbers of families rather than individuals. Scholars have adopted a multiplier of five to transform statistics in families into individuals.

27. Dickson, *Finance and Government,* I, 34.

28. The numbers include the border regiments. Ibid., I, 35.

29. Louis Roman, "Démographie et société aux pays Roumanins (XVIe–XIX siècles)," *Nouvelles études d'histoire* 6, part 1 (1980), 293; Elmer Illyés, *National Minorities in Romania* (Boulder, CO, 1982), 17; Natalia Giurgiu, "Populaie Transilvaniei la sfîrsitul secolului al XVIII-lea începutul secolului al XIX-lea," in Stefan Pascu, ed., *Populaie li Societate, studiide demografie istorica* (Cluj, Romania, 1972), I, 102; József Tamásy, "Az 1784–1787, évi elsl Magyarországi népszámlálás család-és háztartásstatisztikai vonatkozásai," *Demografia* 6 (September 1963), 534–35; Angelika Schaser, *Josephinische Reformen und Sozialer Wandel in Siebenbürgen: Die Bedeutung des Konzivilitätsreskriptes für Hermannstadt* ( Stuttgart, 1989), 16.

30. Arhivele Statului Sibiu, Urbarii li conscriplii, Number 1.

31. John F. Cadzow, Andrew Ludanyi and Louis J. Elteto, eds., *Transylvania, The Roots of Ethnic Conflict* (Kent, Ohio, 1983), 19; Wagner, *Historisch-Statistisches Ortnamenbuch*, 163;

Tammásy, "Az 1784–1787," 534–35; Giurgiu, "Populatia Transilvaniei," 102. Giurgiu's and Tammásy's figures are 1,366,680 and 1,372,090 respectively for Transylvania plus 244,534 for the border regiments. Wagner's numbers are 1,245,739 for Transylvania and 133,230 for the border regiments.

32. Illyés, *National Minorities*, 17; Giurgiu, "Populalie Transilvaniei," 102.

33. Illyés, *National Minorities*, 10–11; Robert Forrest, "Martin Hochmeister's Hermannstadt in 1790," in Bernard Cook et al., eds., *Consortium on Revolutionary Europe, 1750–1850. Selected Papers 1995* (Tallahassee, 1995), 27.

34. These German colonists came from northwestern Germany. Most of them hailed from middle Franconia, the Rhineland (Cologne, Trier, Aachen, Lüttich), and Luxembourg. A smaller number emigrated from Westphalia, Hesse, Bavaria, and Thuringia. See Illyés, *National Minorities*, 10–11, 17.

35. Keith Hitchins, *Nation Affirmed: The Romanian National Movement in Transylvania, 1860–1914* (Bucharest, 1999), 4–6.

36. Rolf Kutschera, *Landtag und Gubernium in Siebenbürgen: 1688–1869* (Vienna, 1985), 140–52.

37. Charles Ingrao, *The Habsburg Monarchy, 1618–1815* (Cambridge, 1994), 85.

38. David Prodan, *Supplex Libellus Valachorum or the Political Struggle of the Romanians in Transylvania during the 18th century* (Bucharest, 1971), 115.

39. Friedrich Teutsch, *Geschichte der Siebenbürger Sachsen für das sächsische Volk* (Hermannstadt, 1907–26), II, 202–05. The most notable exception to this rule was the Lutheran Samuel von Brukenthal, a particular favorite of Maria Theresa who served as governor of Transylvania between 1774 and 1787.

40. Adolf von Hochmeister, *Leben und Wirken des Martin Edlen von Hochmeister, königlicher Rath, Senator und Proconsul der k. freien Stadt und des Stuhles Hermannstadt in Siebenbürgen, Besitzer der grossen goldenen Cibil-Ehren-Medaille* (Hermannstadt, 1873), 15, 20–23, 275.

41. Prodan, *Supplex Libellus Valachorum*, 115.

42. Many Uniates returned to Orthodoxy when the rebels controlled Transylvania. The fact that the revolt's leader, Ferenc II Rákóczi, was Catholic helped to save the Uniate Church. Ibid., 129.

43. They harassed Protestants in Transylvania. For example, even under Joseph II (1780–1790), Protestant churches could have neither bells nor a door fronting on a major street. T. C. W. Blanning, *Joseph II* (London, 1974), 74.

44. Schaser, *Josephinische Reformen*, 16.

45. Kiraly, *Hungary in the Eighteenth Century*, 5. Kiraly contends that the kingdom's population had declined 50 percent since the reign of Matthias Corvinus (1458–90).

46. Henry Marczali, *Hungary in the Eighteenth Century* (Cambridge, 1910), 201, 206.

47. John Spielman, *Leopold I of Austria* (New Brunswick, N.J, 1977), 139–40.

48. Marczali, *Hungary in the Eighteenth Century*, 206–09. Subsequently the name "Swabians" was applied to these immigrants. By 1780 they comprised a majority of most of the burgers, even in Buda. Most innkeepers and minor Habsburg officials were also Swabians by 1780.

49. Dickson, *Finance and Government*, I, 34–35.

50. Schaser, *Josephinische Reformen*, 32–34.

51. Schünemann, *Österreichs Bevölkerungspolitik*, 133–34.

52. Ibid., 135.

53. Ibid., 139–40. This enabled the empress to obtain settlers and reduce the Lutheran population of western Austria with one stroke.

54. Ibid., 137–41.

55. Ibid., 140–41. The Austrians arrested some of those who fled Transylvania. They testified that they had received promises of homes and jobs and had received neither.

56. Ibid., 144.

57. Ibid., 98.

58. Erich Buchinger, Die "Länder" in Siebenbürgen: Vorgeschichte, Durchführung und Ergebnis einer Zwangsumsiedlung im 18. Jahrhundert (Munich, 1980), 319–36, 421, 428.

59. Derek Beales, Joseph II. Vol. 1: In the Shadow of Maria Theresa, 1741–1780 (Cambridge, 1987), 466–73; Franz A. J. Szabo, Kaunitz and Enlightened Absolutism, 1753–1780 (Cambridge, 1994), 247–57.

60. Schünemann, Österreichs Bevölkerungspolitik, 101.

61. Forrest, "Martin Hochmeister's Hermannstadt in 1790," 28–29.

62. Joseph Karniel, Die Toleranzpolitik Kaiser Josephs II. (Tel-Aviv, 1986), 59; Buchinger, Die "Länder" in Siebenbürgen, 342, 408–20.

63. Buchinger, Die "Länder" in Siebenbürgen, 421–30.

64. Paul von Mitrofanov, Joseph II. Seine politische und kulturelle Tätigkeit (Vienna and Leipzig, 1910), 725–26.

65. Istvan Deak, "The Revolution of 1848–49 in Transylvania and the Polarization of National Destinies," in Transylvania: The Roots of Ethnic Conflict, ed. John F. Cadzow, Andrew Ludanyi, and Louis J. Elteto (Kent, Ohio, 1983), 122.

# The Long Nineteenth Century

### ❖ Lothar Höbelt ❖

As befits a book organized under the auspices of the Austrian Center, the following essays about Germans in the East during the "long nineteenth century" deal primarily with the Habsburg Monarchy. Yet, as we all know, the Habsburg Monarchy was famous for being a dual monarchy, after 1867 at least. There was one half where Germans and their language occupied a dominant, if no longer privileged position; and the other half, where Germans were just the top dogs among the underprivileged minorities, even if their position in the empire as a whole gave them some residual leverage. Thus, even within the Austro-Hungarian Monarchy, we find the two variants of a political framework that we would encounter in a more extreme fashion if we were to look further north to the position of Germans in Prussia and Russia. In Prussia the state actively supported them (against Poles), while in Russia the state tried—sooner or later—to fight or at least circumscribe the position of the famous Baltic barons.

All of this points to the growing importance of the political dimension for interethnic relations. That is an obvious and yet slightly paradoxical development. After all, the nineteenth century counts as the heyday of liberalism, which ought to have meant less state intervention, rather than more. Yet, as Pieter Judson rightly points out, the interference of state agencies in local matters increased. Modernization and economic integration meant more *Reibungsflächen*, or social friction, as a people began to adopt distinctive identities. Of course, it might be argued that none of our specimen empires was actually run by "true liberals." But looking at liberal practice in most of continental Europe at least, one is still left wondering whether even classical liberals really were all that resistant to the social engineering bug that infected so many of their late-twentieth-century namesakes.

One thing is certain, though. The paradise of St. Benedict of Anderson must surely be Eastern Europe even if it also included a lot of rather hellish spots. The area simply boasted of a surfeit of multilingual people and milieus. Smetana wrote his diary in German, Archduchess Sophie wrote hers in French; Croat poets wrote in both of these languages and in their own, as Drago Roksandić reminds us. The champions of ethnic nationalism had far more in common than they cared to admit. East Europeans were as much indebted to the pompous Germans they resented as the Germans were to the arrogant French who had succeeded in turning a state bankruptcy into an empire earlier in that century. In that fascinating world, clearly, there was a disproportionate number of people who had a choice—once it came to identifying with one nation rather than another, or none at all.

This ethnically rich patchwork tapestry should not let us forget, however, that most nineteenth-century Europeans did not speak (or understand) any language other than their mother tongue. True, most Europeans possibly did not care that much for any high-minded idea of national obligations, either, even if they kept mum about it, as their social betters seemed so crazy about it. Thus we arrive at a possible paradox about the "classes" and the "masses" (to use Gladstone's celebrated Midlothian phrase). The "classes" that maybe had the ability to rise beyond ethnicity did not want to do so, whereas the monolingual "masses" supposedly yearned for (socialist) internationalism or (Catholic) universalism. As the nursery rhyme has it, Man always wants what he has not.

That paradox is compounded by a second, historiographical one, that has to do with the curious love-hate relationship between present-day historians and nineteenth-century nationalists (who incidentally also often dabbled in history). Like atheists, who—at least in Europe—often seem to be the only people around who perversely still care about God (and His inexistence), historians tend to take all too seriously the claims of the people whose agenda they try to deconstruct. Thus Pieter Judson writes, "Being German in Tyrol meant practicing a particularly orthodox form of Catholicism, while in Styria it often implied a skepticism toward the Catholic hierarchy." That sums up superbly the dominant regional orientations on the *Kulturkampf* issues. On the campaign trail, editors would slyly suggest that only firm Catholics (or anti-clericals, as the case might be) could qualify as true Germans. But do we really want to take these statements at face value? Or is it not a typically German philosophical notion that a nation has to have "a meaning" or "a character" at all? Read differently, the same statements could also be interpreted: If Catholics and anticlericals both found it useful to claim that only those who supported their stance could be regarded as true Germans, then to be German must have held a wide appeal, indeed.

We read: "Individuals, families, or even communities may have adopted national identities at certain moments but that did not prevent some of them from adopting different identities at other moments, or from expressing complete indifference to those identities at yet other moments." Quite so. But who, other than the most punch-drunk editor, ever claimed otherwise? Germans do vote for different parties, belong to different churches or social classes, may feel strongly about crazy hobbyhorses, and have disparate views on everything from sex to free trade; but why does this make it difficult to see them as Germans ?

In a multiethnic system there will always be cross-cutting cleavages. It is true—and important to realize—that nation played a bigger part in politics and, presumably, in public life in general in 1900 than in 1848 because of the intrusion of outsiders as modernizing agents, as Judson puts it so well. Xenophobia, the indiscriminate fear of foreigners who were bound to put a strain on scarce resources and spread diseases, probably diminished during the nineteenth century, but was replaced by a politicized rivalry that spread downwards from rulers to "citoyens" whose newly developed aspirations towards "home rule" were bound to come into conflict with one another in any multiethnic environment. Horizontal categories were replaced by vertical ones. Whether you like multicolored maps or not, geography took over. That also means that regional differences played a big part. Indeed, this is one of the aspects where all of us seem to concur: All politics are local.

Again, thoroughbred nationalists used to be vehemently opposed to "amphibians," people who opportunistically sided with one group or the other depending on circumstances. They saw such behavior as a great danger. Today's conventional wisdom likes to regard them as a lost chance for the politics of identity to have branched off into a different direction. But did they actually matter quite that much? "The study of context, of historical contingency and of individual circumstance is key to determining what individuals and communities adopted what national identities." Now, mention context—and I submit. But, of course, context first and foremost means that for Salzburg or the Alföld, even for Eger and the Podripsko, there was not too much of a choice to start with.

As a reactionary it is quite enjoyable to watch all the certainties of "class" and "nation" that progressives of yesteryear, from nationalist freedom fighters to emancipatory class-warriors, used against the old orders fall to pieces under the concentrated attacks of postmodern deconstruction. Yet one still wonders why among all the communities people might want to imagine, or all the cleavages they might like to tumble into, some have been so much more persistent than others. Nation or class are abstractions, like so many other concepts we freely use. So they do not really exist or, if so, only in our imagination. But does that not remind you of the limerick about the consistent empiricist's dilemma?

> There was a faith-healer of Deal
> Who said, "Although pain isn't real,
> If I sit on a pin,
> And it punctures my skin,
> I dislike what I fancy I feel."

Twenty-first-century liberals (or paid-up Europeans of all persuasions) dislike what they fancy is nationalism's puncturing pin. So they comfort themselves with the idea that it is hardly real. While it is certainly true that nations have not been immovable objects since time immemorial, maybe "enlightened discourse" has swung too far in the opposite direction of subjectivity: I am what I want to be. If you take identity seriously, the only members of a nation are the nationalists themselves. People who believe in any authority higher than their nations—church, dynasty, class, not to forget gender, sexual orientation or environmentalism—are no true Germans. I suppose Schönerer might have approved. But does such a definition of nation help us understand the pull nationalism has exercised for most of the last two hundred years ?

There seems to be a certain paranoia about injecting objective criteria into the debate about nationalism. This is strange, as we have no means of knowing what people really thought at the time (and anyone who has worked with pollsters' data wonders whether we are on much firmer ground today). Maybe the reluctance to acknowledge that use of language was indeed a very good predictor of national loyalties has more to do with the Anglo-Saxon world, where "regional" state-building (if on a global scale) has produced political loyalties below the level of the "English-speaking peoples," whereas the Anglo-Saxon community gets submerged in the idea of the "West," which is supposed to be based on values, rather than English. Now, does not that remind us of Germans in 1848 who invited everybody to become one of them, irrespective of nationality? That could mean two things: either that they were still true liberals then and ought to have succeeded—or that they were kidding themselves.

But then the world in which Germans in the East were living was one where it was both easy and convenient to do so. Enjoy. It is a very special world. But do not jump to conclusions.

# Changing Meanings of "German" in Habsburg Central Europe

### ◈ Pieter M. Judson ◈

How might we usefully examine the relations between German and non-German-communities in Eastern Europe during the nineteenth century without imposing a modern nation-centered perspective on those relations? How did German communities or individuals differentiate themselves from their non-German neighbors, if at all? More importantly, how did popular understandings of what it meant to be a German (or German-speaking) change during the nineteenth century? And how did such ideas about national identity become the basis for a cultural and social politics of separation within and among communities in many parts of Eastern Europe? This essay tries to suggest some useful ways of thinking about German-speakers, their changing conceptions of themselves and of their non-German-speaking neighbors in the broad geographic region known as East Central Europe during the long nineteenth century (1789–1914), using examples drawn primarily from the Habsburg Monarchy. In particular the essay contrasts conceptual changes about identity among nationalists to the ongoing realities of daily life in multilingual regions, demonstrating unevenness in the development of a consistent, coherent, and popular German national identity. By the end of the nineteenth century German nationalist media, politicians and organizations all framed daily life in the region in terms of ongoing battles among nations. They attributed local incidents of violence to nationalist animosities and portrayed the local world in terms of nationalist conflict. Yet despite their best efforts the nation remained an object of indifference, ambivalence, and only occasional interest among most inhabitants of East Central Europe.

During the nineteenth century, ideas about national identity first became politicized and popularized among large, socially diverse populations.[1] This process was anything but predictable or linear in nature, nor did it take place in a consistent or similar manner across the region. Despite the claims of nationalists to the contrary, the process did not reflect deeper transhistorical features somehow embedded in the region or in the peoples who have inhabited it. The particular character of local society produced particular local beliefs about national identity, and these often varied widely within broadly defined national communities. Considering oneself to be a German in one part of Eastern Europe, for example, might involve a completely different set of shared or imagined qualities than it did in another part of Eastern Europe.

For social scientists, journalists, and politicians, the challenge of defining who was considered a German national and what political meanings that label conveyed appeared to be solved only by the end of the First World War. Post-1918 European governments increasingly categorized their populations according to particular ethnic attributes, often as a means to determine which groups should enjoy the full rights of citizenship. State policies that linked the full exercise of citizenship rights to membership in a national community helped to popularize national identities among their own populations even more. By the mid-twentieth century, radical policies of ethnic cleansing, discrimination against linguistic or religious minorities, and wholesale expulsions, not to mention genocide, had indelibly imprinted formerly abstract categories on the experiences, relationships, and self-understandings of many Europeans, including the inhabitants of Central and Eastern Europe.

Since our period largely predates the twentieth-century introduction of identity cards, official systems of national ascription or ethnic attribution, it is far more difficult to determine which people considered themselves to be German or German national in the nineteenth century and what exactly they meant by that label.[2] On the other hand, those practices of ethnic or national attribution that underlay twentieth-century government policies certainly developed from ways of thinking about large populations that had originated in the second half of the nineteenth century. Such ways of thinking about populations—in terms of ethnically or linguistically defined nations—in turn originated both at the level of state policy and at the level of popular social movements. They resulted both from state centralization initiatives—often not immediately concerned with determining national belonging—and in many regions from a rise of popular participation in local, regional, and state politics. In this essay I try to suggest how these varied factors taken together produced new understandings of identity, often making those identities into the basis of new forms of politics. After an introductory discussion I propose to analyze debates about the meaning of nation from the Austrian half of the Habsburg Monarchy, drawn from two particular moments: the revolutions of 1848 and the end of the nineteenth century, when politics became both nationalized and popular in character.

Nation itself was a relatively recent form of popular self-identification in the nineteenth-century world. The term "nation" meant many things in 1789, but few of these approached the mass-oriented ethnic, linguistic, religious, or territorial understandings of the term that had become standard by 1914. Some early-nineteenth-century definitions of nations, such as the Magyar or Polish, referred quite specifically to the traditional privileges enjoyed by corporately defined social groups within a polity. In cases such as these "the nation" referred to the gentry and aristocracy of a given state or province. Yet the restless century of industrialization, urbanization, increased communication, consumption, and movement in Europe produced a considerable expansion of the literate public, an explosion of popular media, and the rapid growth of mass politics in the region. These developments both informed and transformed the very meanings of terms like "Magyar," "Polish," and "German," as such terms came to apply to entire populations rather than to specific social groups. Thus the nineteenth-century context of growing mass political involvement helped to produce the ambition both among nationalist activists and some regimes to realize the nation in every individual.[3]

In many parts of Europe imperial regimes had often relied on corporate-based alliances with local elites to impose their rule more effectively among their diverse territories, as, for example, with the Russian government's relationship to Baltic German-speaking communities. During the nineteenth century, however, many regimes turned increasingly to the use of linguistic, religious, or national categories as a way to impose more centralized and consistent forms of administrative rule over local populations. For the centralizing regime, often absolute in its pretensions, the quality of rule, so to speak, had to be consistent and universal, no matter the type of subject to which it was applied. Liberal theory too demanded a legal equality and equivalent treatment among all subjects of a ruler. Both of these developments could well make use of the more universal idea of nation, or even of religion or cultural tradition, as a means of reforging links between government and local society. Clearly none of these newer concepts (nation, religion, culture) was actually universal in scope when applied to real situations. Nor did most regimes take easily to visions of community that differed so radically from earlier understandings of the bases for community or society.

When an imperial government that had largely relied on alliances with local elites began instead to differentiate peoples by means of language use or religion, the change wreaked havoc on previous social alliances, threatening as it did the traditional shape of local social relations. In reaction to such policies, a local elite social group (like those Baltic German-speakers) often redefined its own traditional social status more consciously in terms of linguistic, religious, and cultural traditions rather than according to the privileged functions it had played within the empire. Local social groups could respond both defensively and opportunistically to the ideological and political spaces created when regimes invoked nationalist, cultural, or religious definitions of community. In the Prussian partition of Poland, for example, the government eventually came to use the issue of popular national identity as part of a larger strategy to undermine the power of traditional elites over the local economy. Constructing a greater sense of loyalty to their rulers based on language use or religious practice among the lowest classes, like the transfer of property from its former owners, appeared to enhance the centralizing power of the imperial state. But such a strategy carried with it serious long-term risks linked to the mobilization of a mass base as well. In the Prussian case, policies of Germanization in the late nineteenth century only helped to produce a new, mass-based sense of Polish identity that spread well beyond the traditional members of the Polish nation (the gentry) to peasants, artisans, and workers. This created a much broader and more socially unified basis for opposition to the regime.[4] At the same time, the Prussian regime's focus on policies of Germanization lent ammunition to its German nationalist critics, who contended that only the most extreme policies could effectively achieve the government's goals.

In the new German Empire after 1871, radical activists' own attempts to produce a stronger public appreciation for the importance of Germanness "from below" gained some reluctant support from local, state, and federal government agencies, particularly in multilingual regions. The *Kulturkampf* in its popular dimensions also contributed to the popularization of German nationalist efforts, since Polish nationalism in Prussia rested increasingly on identification with the local practice of Catholicism. Yet in Germany official government efforts to Germanize non-German-speaking peoples remained mitigated by practical concerns of state that outweighed the single-minded engagement of nationalist activists. Nationalist activists consistently demanded more radical policies of Germanization in the East precisely because they rarely gained the degree of financial or ideological support from the government for which they had hoped.[5] In this case we can see that the popular discourses used to debate issues of nationalization and the radical proposals that became policy in the twentieth century did not dominate government policy in the nineteenth century. If the origins of extreme policies of nationalist citizenship can be seen in the nineteenth century, the particular ways in which they became policy in the twentieth century were certainly not inevitable or even foreseeable.

In the case of the Habsburg Monarchy, where political centralization also gradually replaced traditional reliance on local elites, state policy before 1848 was not defined in modern ethnic or national terms. As we shall see, however, linguistic policy linked to administrative centralization did help to produce the rise of mass national identities.

The popularization of German nationalist identities and politics in the Habsburg Monarchy in the nineteenth century proceeded from several complex sources. However, even as we examine processes of nationalization, we also need to consider a different and perhaps more vexing question. What, after all, did the term "German" as a signifier of identity mean to people in communities throughout Central and Eastern Europe? Who could be considered a German, and on what basis? By the end of the nineteenth century was there a common understanding among self-proclaimed Germans about what constituted their unique identity and who might share in it? When we invoke the term "German" or "German nationalist," we are not using terms whose meanings are self-evident to observers or consistently defined throughout the region. Even to those who may have identified themselves as "Germans" in the nineteenth century, whether in the Habsburg Monarchy or in the eastern border regions of Prussia, the meanings of the term were hardly transparent, self-explanatory or uncontroversial. For today's reader, the term conveys a deceptively (easy) empirical sense of familiarity. We presume that Germans are easily recognizable when they appear in the historical record, and we know that they were present in several regions of nineteenth-century Central and Eastern Europe. Yet the empirical confidence we feel in the object of our research tends to dissolve upon closer inspection of the nineteenth-century individuals and communities who constitute the objects of our study. When the historical record yields examples of literate individuals who self-consciously referred to themselves as members of a larger German community or nation, these individuals usually defined their Germanness in ways that neither we nor self-defined Germans from other regions would necessarily find familiar. Germanness as a quality often signified a system of social and cultural values that helped people to mark their particular place in local society. The particularities of local conditions therefore often shaped local understandings of the term "German." The notion that Germans constituted a recognizable and well-defined group of people who shared a common sense of self-identification throughout Central and Eastern Europe derives largely from the efforts of nineteenth-century nationalist activists themselves who sought to create an interregional and unified German nation.

At the outset of the nineteenth century the term "German" would have been understood very differently in particular regions and at different levels of society. At one level the rise of a German literary culture in the eighteenth century spoke to a growing, socially relatively homogenous reading public across Central and Eastern Europe. At another level some activists passionately believed that the inhabitants of the various German states constituted a nation that could potentially form its own unified state to rival France or England. For others, as with Lutherans in northern Hungary or Galicia, being German meant professing a particular religious tradition in a region where most people practiced a different religion. Being German in Tyrol meant practicing a particularly orthodox form of Catholicism, while in Styria it often implied a skepticism toward the Catholic hierarchy.[6] Inhabitants of other regions called themselves Germans because education in and knowledge of German culture constituted a local form of cultural capital that offered social status and mobility to those who adopted it. As a form of identity that was often situationally defined, when it was considered at all, Germanness rarely referred to qualities or interests that transcended a local perspective. This is especially evident from the nature of the task that faced German nationalist activists in both the German Empire and the Habsburg Monarchy: to convince Germans in individual localities to see themselves in terms of their commonalties with a larger interregional nation.

If those who saw themselves as Germans nevertheless used the term in diverse ways to express very different kinds of identities, should we treat them as constituting a single group? If, for example, people who could speak or read German did not think of themselves as Germans, can we usefully refer to them as Germans? We must recall that in the nineteenth century Germans as a group existed only as an analytic tool for our purposes and not as a substantial reality.[7] This caveat also extends to those forms of difference that we presume must have constituted sources of difference in identity for nineteenth-century individuals. To imagine that certain social or cultural differences in the past inevitably produced the national differences we see in the present is to impose a national teleology on the evidence. If nations and national identities are invented, they do not necessarily need to be organized around some transhistorical local form of difference, as the work of several historians of the region remind us.[8] In fact, the search for transhistorical differences (as a key to explaining later ethnic or national conflict) is an ahistoric undertaking that repeats the claims made by nineteenth-century "national awakeners." They, after all, believed that awareness of differences needed only to be aroused among the broader population to produce inevitable forms of national consciousness. In fact, it is the processes outlined earlier, the interactions between state policy and local initiative that gave larger social meaning to local forms of difference like language use.

If Germans in the nineteenth century did not constitute a self-consciously bounded group of people, plenty of activists, social scientists, philosophers, and historians, among others, nevertheless worked hard to realize the goal of creating such a group. As the public sphere of political, economic, social and cultural engagement pushed beyond the walls of rural small towns in the nineteenth century, nationalist activists increasingly worked to forge popular group loyalties to a greater German nation that would be shared by an interregional public. Still, as scholarship on the nineteenth century concept of *Heimat* reminds us, when people called themselves (or others) Germans during the nineteenth century, they often used the term to refer to a set of shared qualities that remained defined by local circumstances and traditions. They did not necessarily think of themselves as part of an interregional culture.[9]

One avenue of approach to investigating the Germans in nineteenth-century Central and Eastern Europe is to analyze the changing popular meanings of the terms "German" and "Germans" as they were used at all levels of public life during the nineteenth century. In the next two sections of this essay I look at specific approaches to this question, one from 1848 and the other from the late nineteenth century in Habsburg Austria. Both of these historical moments witnessed renewed public debate over the meanings of "the Germans" and "Germanness," and a few examples will suffice to show both the early diversity of meaning of the terms, and also the ways the use of the terms and their meanings changed over fifty years.

The conflicts over the meanings of a German nation in 1848 engaged a limited stratum of society. The efforts of this stratum built in part on an appropriation of Habsburg state modernization processes that were rooted in moral, intellectual, and social reform visions of the eighteenth and early nineteenth centuries. As Arnold Suppan points out in his essay, the eighteenth-century reform efforts of Maria Theresa and particularly Joseph II produced policies that treated the German language as the new *lingua franca* (to replace Latin) of the Habsburgs' culturally diverse holdings. The reformers' goals—to increase the coherence of administration, the productivity, loyalty, and moral capacities of their subjects through increased educational and economic opportunities—all produced policies favorable to German language use at every level of society, although not necessarily unfavorable to the use of other local languages as well.[10]

It is not difficult to see how early German nationalists conflated the reformers' focus on the *utility* of the German language with the alleged cultural and later the national *qualities* of those who used this language. German nationalists adopted this sense of cultural leadership in part as a political response to the claims of the Magyar, Polish, and later Czech nationalists who opposed Habsburg centralization and saw their interests best reflected in decentralized structures. The functional importance of the German language to the centralized empire became the foundation for several arguments promoting the political interests of German-speakers as such. But one should be wary of confusing the terms "German-speaker" with "German," since many Magyar and Czech nationalists in the early nineteenth century, for example, spoke German fluently, and did not define their nationalist loyalties in terms of their linguistic competence.[11] Furthermore, since the term "nation" had traditionally referred to a political corporation and not a linguistically defined community, it is not surprising to hear speakers of one language around 1800 declaring their loyalty to a nation represented by a different language. We have only to think of those urban German-speakers in the Prussian partition of Poland who proclaimed their loyalty to Poland against their region's absorption by Prussia.[12] Examples such as this also remind us that throughout the nineteenth century, differences in religious, regional, or class identification often determined social loyalties far more powerfully than differences in language use.

What range of cultural qualities did the term "German" connote in a local social context by 1848? Did it also refer somehow to an interregional community of Germans? The sudden profusion of public political debate unleashed by the revolution sharply conveyed diverse contemporary meanings of concepts like nation, Germans, Germanness, and Germany in the territories of the Habsburg Monarchy. Almost overnight, these concepts became an integral part of the popular rhetoric used to demand political, economic, and social reform in ways that had been impossible before the revolution terminated the *Vormärz* censorship regime. In 1848, most civically engaged people in Austria appear to have agreed that nationhood was inextricably linked to the pressing issues of personal, community, political and social freedom. Most revolutionaries conceded that without the guarantee of such liberal freedoms, national consciousness could not be spread and national greatness certainly could not be attained. Many historians of 1848, however, tended to present liberalism and national rights as alternatives to each other, even if allegedly naïve political actors at the time did not understand the inevitability of this dichotomy. According to this version of events, individuals and parties eventually had to choose between their liberal and their national commitments.[13] The 1848ers, however, did not understand the issues in quite such binary terms. Mid-nineteenth century activists more often than not conceived national development and political freedoms as mutually constitutive of each other. One could not exist without the other; these were not separate or separable issues. Most bourgeois nationalists (Czech, German, Slovene) believed that the development of their nation depended on the moral progress of their people, and such progress—to be accomplished above all through civic education—could not be guaranteed without the benefit of basic civil rights and the experience of political participation.

When the Viennese German nationalist newspaper *Schwarz-Roth-Gold* complained about peasant apathy to the nation in August 1848, it did so in terms that linked national identity inextricably to progressive political and moral values. "Traditional education made people stupid. The majority of Austrian peasants does not even know that there is a Germany and that it is their fatherland! . . . Traditional forms of education did not want to . . . provide our children with the example of the free men of their national past, out of fear that it would teach them [to think] independently."[14] It was the very quality of freedom that characterized everything having to do with nation, and this link of liberal ideas to national identity forged a concept of nation far different from the concepts we encounter around 1900. This may help us to understand why the statutes of several German nationalist organizations in 1848, for example, made membership available to "any Austrian citizen without regard to religion, nationality, or estate."[15] How could membership in a German nationalist organization be open to individuals of "any nationality?" Clearly the activists who formulated these statutes did not wish to limit membership in a German nation to those who were German-speakers or who felt themselves to be German, but rather opened their community to those who shared their cultural values and political commitment.

If political activists understood a German national community as one that was open to all who partook of their idealism, then the second point to understand about 1848 is how very few people actually shared a sense of national consciousness. Not only did very few peasants express a sense of national belonging, as the quotation above demonstrates, but those who did see themselves as part of a nation often defined that nation in highly parochial terms. The prominence of nation in public discussions should not blind us to the deeply local ways in which it was conceived and understood. Rather than speak of the Germans in East Central Europe, when it comes to 1848 we can perhaps speak of those Tyrolers, Upper Austrians, Styrians, Bohemians, or Moravians who also considered themselves to be German. Activists who sought to spread national enlightenment to the peasantry in 1848 usually formulated their appeals in terms of highly localized interests. This constituted a strategic choice, but it also reflected the beliefs and experiences of the nationalists themselves. In very few places (Vienna, Graz) did discussions of nation transcend local understandings to incorporate broader political and social visions. When, for example, the young Karl Stremayr, a law student at the University of Graz, ran for election to the Frankfurt Parliament, a body whose task after all was the construction of a German nation-state, his speech to local peasant voters hardly mentioned Germany. Instead, he focused on the need to end the feudal economic system and the absolutist regime, and on his loyalty to the emperor.[16]

This situational understanding of nation also permeated discussions among activists who held more radical nationalist positions in towns where nationalist conflict between different groups had broken out. The Slovene historian Peter Vodopivec recounts one such example of local tradition shaping nationalist positions in southern Styria, where German-speakers and Slovene-speakers often lived in close proximity. In 1848, Slovene nationalists in Ljubljana/Laibach (in neighboring Krain province) demanded the creation of a new province that would unite all Slovenes in the monarchy. Several Slovene nationalists in Styria, however, opposed the division of their traditional province along national lines. Instead of creating a Slovene province with its own diet, the Styrian Slovenes promoted greater national reconciliation and equality among nations within Styria. A poem dating from 1848 and cited by Vodopivec captures a very different kind of nationalist agenda and includes the following lines (written alternately in Slovene and German):

> How happy are we brothers,
> in beautiful Styria,
> we need not fear any ill,
> our unity makes us strong,
> the knowledge of both languages,
> this promotes commerce,
> to go our separate ways,
> would harm us all.[17]

German-speaking deputies to the Styrian diet charged with creating a new provincial constitution reacted bitterly when Slovene nationalists displayed their Slavic red-white-and-blue colors publicly or founded a Slovene nationalist association in Graz, seeing such actions as public challenges to German and liberal ideals.[18] On the other hand, the German-speaking deputies in Graz treated Slovene *speakers* (as opposed to Slovene nationalists) as trustworthy political allies, agreeing to publish Slovene language translations of the diet's proceedings in local German newspapers in order to make the legislative session more accessible. "Many of the Slovenes who read the Graz papers are very intelligent people," noted one German liberal deputy to the diet, and appending the translations would "give them more trust in us."[19]

These examples suggest that at mid-century, local differences in language use did not define community relations and identities as fully as later nationalists believed they should. In 1848 local relations and familiarity still appear to have counted far more than any abstract interregional sense of nation. At the same time, if local differences in language use did not convey incommensurable differences, and bilingualism often appeared to be the norm, then local examples of intermarriage and social interaction between users of different languages would not have seemed remarkable either. For this reason too, definitions of Germanness remained open and vague, and liberal in their relations to other nations. Again, from the pages of *Schwarz-Roth-Gold*, one writer in July 1848 underlined this openness, claiming that membership in the nation "is based not simply on the soil of birth or language of culture, but rather on . . . nobility of action and the worthiness of conviction." Those who sought out education for themselves and their children and demonstrated their commitment to humanistic values could indeed *become* German. In fact, the 1848ers believed that this same set of moral qualities that defined their nation would enable it successfully to regulate relations among all the other nations within the Austrian Empire. "We want a German Austria . . . a powerful leader for all our brother nationalities, not through [coercive] power . . . but rather through the voluntary respect that we earn when we deal in freedom and humanity."[20]

Yet even as German nationalists conceived their nation in open and liberal terms, they, and their counterparts in other movements, faced serious political issues that appear to us to have almost guaranteed the development of mutual antagonism among movements. The Herculean task of reconstituting political and social order on a new basis, as manifested in the efforts of the Frankfurt and Vienna (later Kremsier) parliaments, the short-lived Slav congress, the town councils and provincial diets, all but guaranteed that practical issues of language use would create a serious political bone of contention. German nationalists had trouble understanding the protests of those who sought to undo the earlier attempts to make German a *lingua franca* for the empire. It is perhaps a testimony to the narrow social basis of nationalist activists, men who had much more in common than they cared to admit, that they maintained a common vision of liberal freedoms in the Kremsier draft and refused to allow their efforts to be derailed by nationalist conflict. It was precisely the issue of language use in government and administration that created a space for the political activism that fundamentally divided nationalists by the late nineteenth century.

In the fifty years following the revolutions of 1848, far more people in the Austrian Empire became actively involved in a public sphere whose limits grew well beyond the boundaries of village or region. Nineteenth-century governments too, continued on the path of centralized state building that had been initiated by their reforming predecessors of the eighteenth century. In the aftermath of the revolution the Habsburg regime had even revived its efforts to impose greater coherence on regional and local administration through expanded use of German in the bureaucracy. This new insistence on German as the language of governance in the 1850s provoked effective opposition in Hungary. Government centralization in Austria, however, went well beyond language use in the civil service to encompass education reform, development of a transportation and communications infrastructure for the entire empire, and targeted investment to promote industrialization.

Constitutional reform in the 1860s loosened censorship, expanded public education and associational life significantly, and increased popular participation in politics. The expansion of communications and transportation infrastructures often recast political questions in interregional as opposed to local terms. Through the efforts of local associations, local media and political parties, more and more Austrians joined public life in some capacity or other. With the Compromise of 1867, the Hungarian half of the Dual Monarchy gradually adopted nationalizing policies typical of nation-states like France, Germany, or Italy. The empire that formed the Austrian half of the Dual Monarchy, however, remained officially anational (later multinational). This state experienced a steady rise in mass political participation, culminating with the implementation of universal manhood suffrage for parliamentary elections in 1907.

In Austrian society, attempts to categorize and mobilize people in ethnic or national terms emerged from popular nationalist political initiatives after 1848 and not directly from the offices of government agencies. Nevertheless, the ongoing modernizing efforts of the state played a critical, if unwitting, role in the nationalization of Austrian society in the late nineteenth century. As nationalist political movements competed within the framework of the new constitutional system to increase their electoral constituencies in an age of growing mass-based politics, they sought to make the idea of national identity relevant to every aspect of life. They succeeded at least in nationalizing political life by demanding the application of constitutional guarantees of linguistic equality to an ever-expanding set of institutions. From educational to judicial institutions, from administrative to commercial practices, no possible corner of public life remained immune to the demands of nationalists. The late-nineteenth-century infusion of nationalist content into public life ranged from the provision of welfare benefits or access to education at all levels to local forms of economic competition and even to patterns of consumption.

To realize this nationalization of public life as fully as possible, however, each group had to define a set of shared qualities that would help newly politicized Austrians to understand to which nation they belonged and why. Additionally, the dynamic of nationalist political competition within Austria after 1867 caused the leaders of each group regularly to insist that its needs were incommensurable with those of competing nations and that a gulf of enormous proportions separated the members of one nation from another. Such claims of differences among populations were made vigorously and often, in part because national belonging continued to mean very little to most nineteenth-century Austrians as they went about their daily routines. And while ordinary Austrians may have reacted with interest or indifference to claims about the importance of national loyalties, nationalist activists continued to develop and refine their claims about national differences, how they manifested themselves in daily life, and how they could be measured scientifically.

By 1900 both ideas about nation and the numbers of people who felt allegiance to nations had changed dramatically throughout East Central Europe. The character of ideas about Germanness changed too, in part because of the growing populariza-tion of politics, in part because of the 1867 Compromise, which had recognized the rights of the Hungarian nation, and in part because of the activism of other nationalist groups in the empire, particularly the Czech nationalists. The role of the German language and culture as a broadly unifying factor in Austrian public life declined considerably as Slav nationalists agitated successfully in the legislatures and the courts for the use of their languages in schools, universities, the courts, and the civil service. German might remain the inner, interregional language of the imperial bureaucracy and of the military, but its advantages as a universal *lingua franca* in the region had diminished.

Many German nationalists clung uneasily to the traditional claim of German language and culture as somehow more culturally advanced and therefore more valu-able than the other languages in public use in the monarchy. With the establishment of Polish and Czech universities at L'viv/Lwów/Lemberg and Prague, with Italian nationalist demands for an Italian-language law faculty and Slovene demands for a university in Ljubljana, the position of German as the undisputed vehicle of culture, progress, and modernity was less self-evident. As a result, German nationalist asser-tions of their nation's *Kulturträger* status in East Central Europe became increasingly strident. As German nationalists became more defensive about the position of their language and culture in the monarchy, they began to adopt new arguments to justify their leading position. They did not abandon arguments about the universality of their nation, and except for the anti-Semites among them, they continued to welcome anyone into its ranks. Yet at the same time, they articulated some new arguments that located specific spaces as German and that stressed the incommensurable differences that separated theirs from other cultures. Speakers of other languages, especially in the cities, seemed less and less likely to choose to become German for the sake of social mobility, now that they had other options available to them in other languages.[21] Consequently, the German nationalist community became more inward-looking and exclusive in its rhetoric. The greater German nationalist focus on national ownership of territory and on the fundamental differences that allegedly separated nations also derived from a growing appreciation of the importance of numbers, rather than of "quality" or cultural status, in influencing local and imperial politics. Elections had to be won if control by one nationalist group or another was to be exercised effectively. Although a curial system that favored wealthier and better-educated citizens dominated local municipal and regional elections, activists nevertheless sought to mobilize every possible voter in every curia for their purposes.[22]

After 1848, many government policies of modernization depended on initiatives in the social sciences that sought to organize and map populations according to their linguistic and religious character, for the purpose of applying social policy more effectively.[23] Categorization of local populations according to language use in the imperial census, for example, became valuable tools for the development of local school and, later, welfare policies after the passage of the 1867 constitution in Austria. Since the constitution had promised equal treatment to the speakers of Austria's different languages, this required setting up schools in native languages wherever possible.[24] Over time, the implementation of this guarantee and its application to other areas of public life (courts, civil service) required increased statistical knowledge about the linguistic make-up of local populations.

In the 1870s, government statisticians developed a census apparatus that would question Austrians, among other things, about their language of everyday use.[25] The imperial government had no wish to promote nationalist agitation or the importance of national identity, however indirectly, through the census. Yet its attempt at linguistic categorization for limited policy purposes produced several unintended side effects, including new opportunities for nationalist politicians. Statistical studies like the decennial census did not automatically produce nations through a kind of Foucauldian effect, but they certainly did produce new opportunities for nation-building, which creative nationalist politicians readily exploited. In early debates over the particular form of the census, nationalists had complained vigorously that it asked respondents for their language of daily use instead of for their mother tongue or their nationality. The nationalists' failure to impose national categories on the census, however, did not daunt activists in the least. They simply used other tools at their disposal—press, political agitation, mass meetings—to link language usage in the census to broader, newly invented mass nationalist identities. The nationalists appropriated census categories like "language of daily use" in order to mobilize people on the basis of common qualities. Already in the 1880s, following the first Austrian census, activists claimed that all those who had listed a particular language on the census form belonged in fact to that nation. This claim, and the counter-claims it provoked, produced powerful effects in Austrian public life. By 1910 many more people believed the language question referred to their nationality—a fixed personal identity—rather than to the *function* of language in their locality. Nationalist activists even turned to the courts to challenge the census results for particular localities where they believed the national enemy had somehow manipulated the outcome.[26]

If nationalists complained that the census did not explicitly ask for the national allegiance of its respondents, historians might complain that it made no allowance for the many people who used *more* than one language in families, businesses, or daily social lives, to report that critical fact. We have no way of knowing whether any of these respondents in fact spoke the language of another nation as well. We historians have also validated nationalist claims about the census, however inadvertently, by reading it ourselves as if it somehow revealed national self-identification among the Austrian population. Histories of the Habsburg Monarchy or East Central Europe invariably include maps depicting the languages that a majority of people reported in a particular region. Almost always these maps identify their subjects as "the Czechs," "the Germans," or "the Slovenes," for example, rather than as "Czech-speakers," "German-speakers," or "Slovene-speakers."[27] This slippage on the printed page—from the individual who reported a single language of daily use in the census to the presumption of national identity—transforms all people into members of nations, whether they felt that way or not. From there it is a small step to territorialize those nations by assigning to them the geographic regions where they appear to have constituted a majority.

Instead of accepting nationalist claims that associated language use on the census with a declaration of national identity, historians might more fruitfully ask what factors induced some respondents to report one language in a given year instead of another language. How might we explain the choices of those individuals, families, and communities who self-consciously practiced a form of bilingualism, marrying their German language skills to Czech, Slovene, Polish, or Hungarian (or marrying their Czech skills to an acquired knowledge of German)? In some regions we know that the same people reported different languages of daily usage in different decennial censuses.[28] What situations caused them to report one language one year and a different language ten years later? Considering these questions in a nineteenth-century context might help us to avoid presuming that such people had already developed a single and consistent sense of national identity. It would also encourage us to follow Rogers Brubaker's productive suggestion that we think of individual national professions of identity—professions of nationness—as an occasion or as an event rather than as an ongoing process or and unchanging, internalized truth.[29] Finally, keeping these questions in mind would help us literally to *see* things differently when we examine the abstract depictions of social scientists that map language use onto territory.

If we consider the information that these abstracted maps, graphs, and charts fail to convey to us (bilingualism, situational reporting of linguistic usage), we can see one reason why it is so difficult to speak of Germans, German communities, or a German nation in nineteenth-century Central and Eastern Europe. Other kinds of choices made by individuals, families, and communities also undercut the clear assertion of national identity proclaimed for them by contemporary nationalist activists. Why, for example, did some parents in multilingual regions choose to rear and school their children in more than one language? Nationalist activists tried to square their version of reality with the social behaviors they encountered by denouncing such people as "amphibians," "national hermaphrodites," and as psychologically deformed opportunists who would sell themselves and their children to the highest national bidder. Or they depicted such people as the unfortunate pawns of oppressive employers and landlords who forced them to adopt a different language from their authentic one in order to save their job or their apartment. [30] By speaking and writing in these terms, nationalists sought to normalize the concept that everyone indeed had one authentic national identity. To us, however, the example of people who did not easily fit into a nationalist schema points to the fundamental difficulty of presuming that language use in the nineteenth century implied a particular national community identity.

Although more people clearly saw themselves as Germans, as part of a larger German nation by 1900, the significance of that choice and the meanings with which they imbued this choice also remained diverse and often contradictory. The generally swift rise of popular literacy and newspapers throughout the empire meant that people far away from each other received their news from sources that presented it in a uniform context. Far more people who adopted a national identity now shared a comparable sense of the meaning of their Germanness and who belonged to their community, than earlier in the century. Nevertheless, regional loyalties remained powerful when it came to those definitions, and activists often scrambled to paper over several conflicts about the character of the German community that had emerged by 1900. Two particularly vexing questions that prevented the formation of an ideologically unified German nationalist movement involved the role of Jews and the Catholic Church within that movement. Several organizations and parties defined their German identity in terms of racial, religious, or economic anti-Semitism. Several, including the largest among them, remained open to Jewish membership and to a non-racial definition of the German community. Many German nationalists in a region like the Tyrol (like Christian Socials in Lower and Upper Austria) continued to define their community identity in terms of loyalty to the Catholic Church, whereas German nationalist organizations and parties elsewhere saw the Church as their nation's enemy. When these latter organizations attempted to unify their efforts, as with the first Congress of German Nationalist Defense Organizations in 1908, for example, they could not achieve the hoped-for unity, precisely due to the powerful disagreements about these issues, particularly the role of Jews.[31] While it is true that far more Austrians saw themselves as belonging to a German nation in 1900 than had been the case in 1848, they did not agree at all on the character or meaning of this nation.

This essay has attempted to demonstrate that terms like "German" or "nation" carried far more diffuse and locally based meanings for diverse nineteenth-century populations than they did to Germans at various points in the twentieth century. The study of context, of historical contingency, and of individual circumstance is key to determining what individuals and communities adopted what national identities over time. So is the idea of nation-ness as event rather than identity. When and in what kinds of situations in the nineteenth century did people tend to see themselves as national? In what kinds of situations were they indifferent or ambivalent about the idea of belonging to a nation? Individuals, families, or even communities may have adopted national identities at certain moments, but that did not prevent some of them from adopting different identities at other moments, or from expressing complete indifference to those identities at yet other moments. Even those who did identify themselves consistently as "Germans" throughout this period would not necessarily have understood themselves as members of a larger interregional German community, one that formed an interconnected, unified cultural and social whole. Their sense of their Germanness may have derived from their particular religious practice, their local social position, or their degree of education. In the context of specific regional and local identities there may indeed have been plenty of self-described Germans to be found, but little sense of a larger connection among such groups of individuals. Imposing the common term "Germans" on these diverse populations risks compromising the accuracy of our representations of people in the past by flattening out their considerable differences to fit them into a broad modern category.[32]

It is also clear, however, that the requirements of modernizing states and the efforts of developing social sciences worked together, however unintentionally, to promote the categorization of populations in terms of language use, religious practice, and eventually according to the abstract concept of nation. While state policies did not alone create nations in the nineteenth century, they often created the available political and social spaces where local or regional activists could articulate particular interests. Even states like Austria, whose policy opposed the recognition of national interests, nevertheless helped to produce the spread of nationalism through promises of linguistic and religious equality. The most egregious example of Austrian state policy that unintentionally encouraged the process of nationalization of populations was undoubtedly the Moravian Compromise of 1905. Undertaken in order to diminish the harmful effects of political nationalism on public life, the compromise created separate Czech and German electoral lists and school systems. The new law required, however, that all Moravians register themselves and their families as either members of the Czech or German nation, thus forcing many who had not previously considered themselves to be part of either nation to join one of them.[33]

From the perspective of the twentieth century, the history of the nineteenth century in Central and Eastern Europe seems to offer a panoramic view of worsening relations among neighboring communities that used different languages or practiced different religions. What we are seeing, however, is neither the awakening of nations nor the end of some kind of idyllic existence characterized by an acceptance of diversity or so-called hybrid identities at the local level. The largely rural communities of East Central Europe in particular knew nothing of hybridity or multiculturalism because they knew nothing of modern nations. What they experienced in their everyday lives was completely normal to them and not exceptional. What was exceptional to them, however, was the gradual intrusion in their world of outsiders, of civil servants, of communications and commercial networks, of new media, of political parties. Even in 1848, when popular politics first exploded the cultural fabric of daily life in the region, the potential for all-consuming nationalist conflicts to tear society apart remained only a potential. Activists in 1848 were not the activists of 1900. The former still defined their world in tangible ways that privileged local interests and interpretations of the world. For this reason, their nationalisms did not necessarily exclude other nationalisms, and given the legal and social conditions of the day, most envisioned a society characterized by personal emancipation. By 1900, however, local conditions had changed radically, thanks to the spread of media, the rise of literacy, and a remarkable political mobilization. So too had the contents of nationalist ideologies. Local interests were now understood by more people to be intimately connected to nationalist interests. A broad and abstract concept of nation (whichever version) had become part of loyalty to the traditions of place, making local conflict on nationalist lines more of a possibility in daily life.

# Notes

1.  For an excellent analysis of recent literature on the nationalization of Eastern European populations, see Larry Wolff, "Revising Eastern Europe: Memory and the Nation in Recent Historiography," *Journal of Modern History* 78 (March 2006), 93–118.

2.  For an excellent account of an early attempt to categorize populations according to ethnicity through the use of identity cards, see Laird Boswell, "From Liberation to Purge Trials in the 'Mythic Provinces': Recasting French Identities in Alsace and Lorraine, 1918–1920," *French Historical Studies* 23, no. 1 (Winter 2000), 129–162. On the question of identity cards producing identities that mark people for death or expulsion, see Timothy Snyder, *The Reconstruction of Nations: Poland, Ukraine, Lithuania, Belarus, 1569–1999* (New Haven, 2002); Gerald Stourzh, *Die Gleichberechtigung der Nationalitäten in der Verfassung und der Verwaltung Österreichs, 1848–1918* (Vienna, 1985); and Tara Zahra, "Reclaiming Children for the Nation: Germanization, National Ascription, and Democracy in the Bohemian Lands, 1900–1945," *Central European History* 37, no. 4 (December 2004). The latter two works examine judicial records in Imperial Austria to illustrate the different

ways that ethnic attribution and national ascription became embedded in nineteenth-
and twentieth-century legal categories.

3. A fine account of the process in West Galicia is Keely Stauter-Halsted, *The Nation in the Village: The Genesis of Peasant National Identity in Austrian Poland, 1848–1914* (Ithaca, 2001). See also Jeremy King, *Budweisers into Czechs and Germans: A Local History of Bohemian Politics, 1848–1948* (Princeton, 2002).

4. For a good account of the relationship between the Prussian government's policy of Germanization and the rise of a strong and self-conscious Polish nationalist movement in West Prussia, see Ralph Schattkowsky, "Nationalismus und Konfliktgestaltung. Westpreussen zwischen Reichsgründung und erstem Weltkrieg," in *Die Nationalisierung von Grenzen: Zur Konstruktion nationaler Identität in sprachlich gemischten Grenzregionen*, ed. Michael Müller and Rolf Petri (Marburg, 2002), 35–79; Schattkwsky, *Identitätenwandel und nationale Mobilisierung in Westpreussen und Galizien* (Marburg, 2002).

5. A superb analysis of the situation in the region around Posen in Prussia is Thomas Serrier, "'Deutsche Kulturarbeit in der Ostmark'. Der Mythos vom deutschen Vorrang und die Grenzproblematik in der Provinz Posen (1871–1914)," in *Die Nationalisierung von Grenzen*, 13–33.

6. The local meanings Tyrolers assigned to Germanness, meanings that differed in the extreme from concepts of Germanness in Bohemia or Styria, for example, are analyzed by Laurence Cole in *"Für Gott, Kaiser, und Vaterland." Nationale Identität der deutschsprachigen Bevölkerung Tirols 1860–1914* (Frankfurt a/M, 2000).

7. Rogers Brubaker, *Ethnicity without Groups* (Cambridge, MA, 2004), 7–12.

8. See especially Gary Cohen, *The Politics of Ethnic Survival: Germans in Prague, 1861–1914* (Princeton, 1981); King, *Budweisers.*

9. Celia Applegate, *A Nation of Provincials: The German Idea of Heimat* (Berkeley, 1990); Alon Confino, *The Nation as Local Metaphor: Württemberg, Imperial Germany, and National Memory, 1871–1918* (Chapel Hill, 1997).

10. Peter Bugge, "Czech Nation-Building, National Self-Perception and Politics 1780–1914" (Ph.D. diss., University of Aarhus, 1994), 16–21; Hugh LeCaine Agnew, "Czechs, Germans, Bohemians? Images of Self and Other in Bohemia to 1848," in Nancy M. Wingfield, ed., *Creating the Other: Ethnic Conflict and Nationalism in Habsburg Central Europe* (New York, 2003), 56–77.

11. On the ignorance of the Hungarian language among some Hungarian nobility, see the first chapter of Istvan Deak's engaging *The Lawful Revolution: Louis Kossuth and the Hungarians, 1848–1849* (New York, 1979). On knowledge and use of the Czech language in early-nineteenth-century Bohemia, see Bugge, "Czech Nation-Building."

12. Michael Müller, "Zur Identitätsgeschichte deutschsprachiger Gruppen in Grosspolen/Provinz Posen und dem Königlichen Preussen/West Preussen vor 1848," in *Die Nationalisierung von Grenzen*, 6.

13. In a thoughtful consideration of the multiple ways in which historians have framed the events of 1848, historian R. J. W. Evans notes that while the causes of the revolution were international in nature, they have been remembered largely in national terms. Given the development of national historical traditions later in the nineteenth and twentieth centuries, the original contemporary understandings of the events of 1848 have often been lost. R. J. W. Evans, "1848 in Mitteleuropa: Ereignis und Erinnerung," in *1848. Ereignis und Erinnerung in den politischen Kulturen Mitteleuropas*, ed. Barbara Haider and Hans Peter Hye (Vienna, 2003), 31–55.

14. *Schwarz-Roth-Gold*, 22 August, 1848.

15. "Statuten des deutschen konstitutionellen Vereins in Teplitz" (Bohemia) in Österreichische Nationalbibliothek: Flugblätter- und Plakate- Sammlung, 1848–1871.

16. Carl von Stremayr, *Erinnerungen aus dem Leben* (Vienna, 1899), 18–19. Stremayr later served in liberal cabinets in the 1870s as Minister for Religion and Education, and for a brief period as Prime Minister in a transitional cabinet.

17. *Celske novine*, 24 August 1849, quoted in Peter Vodopivec, "Mythos und Wirkichkeit des slowenischen Jahres 1848," in *1848. Ereignis und Erinnerung*, 243.

18. Gerhard Pfeisinger, "Die Revolution von 1848 in Graz" (Ph.D. diss., University of Salzburg, 1985), 103–106.

19. *Verhandlungen des Landtages Steiermark*, 14 June, 1848, 12–13.

20. *Schwarz-Roth-Gold*, 11 July, 1848.

21. Cohen, *The Politics of Ethnic Survival*, 138–139.

22. Pieter M. Judson, *Exclusive Revolutionaries: Liberal Politics, Social Experience, and National Identity in the Austrian Empire, 1848–1914* (Ann Arbor, 1996), 193–266.

23. See several of the essays on the categorization, territorialization, and quantification of national populations in Wingfield, *Creating the Other*.

24. Hannelore Burger, *Sprachenrecht und Sprachgerechtigkeit im österreichischen Unterrichtswesen 1867–1918* (Vienna, 1995).

25. The best critical history of the Imperial Austrian census remains Emil Brix, *Die Umgangssprachen in Altösterreich zwischen Agitation und Assimilation: Die Sprachenstatistik in den zisleithanischen Volkszählungen 1880 bis 1910* (Vienna, 1982). For an illuminating study of the debate over whether or not to allow respondents to list more than one language of daily use, see King, *Budweisers*, 58–59.

26. The most famous of these challenges involved the census results for the city and region of Trieste, where a recount was ordered by the government. Brix, *Umgangssprachen in Altösterreich*, 194.

27. Most recently, Robin Okey, *The Habsburg Monarchy c. 1765–1918: From Enlightenment to Collapse* (New York, 2002), xii reproduces such a map, although Okey at least points out that the regions are assigned to various nationalities on the basis of their majority, rather than their sole presence in given regions. Okey's map is labeled "Nationalities of the Habsburg Monarchy in 1848."

28. See the excellent discussion of census-taking by Cohen in *Politics of Ethnic Survival*, especially 86–139.

29. Brubaker, *Nationalism Reframed: Nationhood and the National Question in the New Europe* (New York, 1996), 16–19; Brubaker, *Ethnicity without Groups*, 12–13.

30. On nationalist debates over children, bilingualism, and school choice, see Zahra, "Reclaiming Children for the Nation"; and Zahra, "Your Child Belongs to the Nation: Nationalization, Germanization, and Democracy in the Bohemian Lands, 1900–1945" (Ph.D. diss., University of Michigan, 2005).

31. *Verhandlungsschrift über den 1. Deutschen Schutzvereinstag in Wien am 3., 4., 5. und 6. Jänner 1908*, Vienna, 1908. The German School Association, the German League for the Bohemian Woods, and several organizations in Moravia refused to adopt anti-Semitic membership requirements, whereas the Südmark and the League of Germans in Bohemia were overtly anti-Semitic in their platforms and policies. On the issue of anti-Semitism in the German nationalist movement, see Pieter M. Judson, "'Whether Race or Conviction Should Be the Standard:' National Identity and Liberal Politics in Nineteenth-Century Austria,' *Austrian History Yearbook* 22 (1991). On Catholicism and German nationalism in the Tyrol, see Cole, "*Für Gott, Kaiser, und Vaterland.*" The issue of nationalist relations to the Catholic Church was also highly problematic for the Czech nationalist movement, especially in the early years of the First Czechoslovak Republic. See Cynthia Paces, "Religious Heroes for a Secular State: Commemorating Jan Hus and Saint Wenceslas in 1920s

Czechoslovakia," in *Staging the Past: The Politics of Commemoration in Habsburg Central Europe*, ed. Maria Bucur and Nancy M. Wingfield (West Lafayette, 2001), 209–235.

32. Pieter M. Judson, "When Is a Diaspora Not a Diaspora? Rethinking Nation-Centered Narratives about Germans in Habsburg East-Central Europe," in *The Heimat Abroad: The Boundaries of Germanness*, ed. Krista O'Donnell, Renate Bridenthal, and Nancy Regain (Ann Arbor, 2005), 218–247.

33. King, *Budweisers into Czechs and Germans*, 114.

# Controversies on German Cultural Orientation in the "Croatian National Renewal"

## German Language and Culture in Croatian Everyday Life, 1835–1848

### ◆ Drago Roksandić ◆

Any investigation into German language and culture in Croatian everyday life during the "Croatian national renewal" (1835–1848) presupposes a variety of distinctive scholarly, cultural and ideological assumptions. Whereas it is impossible to discuss such a broad subject comprehensively in an article, I have focused here on what I perceive to be the three most significant aspects of the subject. First, a number of Croatian historians have argued that the very notion of the "Croatian national renewal" was essentially synonymous with the concurrent Illyrian movement. They have, for example, reexamined the social dimensions of the standardization of the Croatian language and the emergence of the modern Croatian culture within the Illyrian movement and (South-) Slavic world, having in mind that Croatian nation-building and the modernization of Croatian society had been a much longer and more complex historical process. Attitudes towards German had been also changing in different periods of that process and, in particular, in different historical contexts. Second, because of changing current scholarly attitudes towards (South-) Slavic contexts of the Croatian nation-building at that particular time, a number of traditional research topics have been redefined without major new empirical knowledge. Attempts to reevaluate (South-) Slavic contexts are also related to reevaluations of German and, in some cases, Italian and other contexts. Third, the recent "revival" of a "neo-romantic" interpretation of Croatian history—insisting primarily on Croatian ethno-confessional continuities in a millennial perspective—has relativized and even marginalized the problematic of the Illyrian movement.

My own approach is to define the "Illyrian movement" in linguistic and cultural terms traditionally recognized by scholars of the period 1835–1848, which can be visualized as part of a long process of Croatian social modernization and controversial cultural reappropriations. That historical experience has been of decisive importance for the self-determination of the "national elite" in a core area around Zagreb that roughly included Varaždin, Križevci, Sisak, and Karlovac. What interests me most is the Croatian national elite's "Illyrian" self-perception, particularly in relation to the role of German in Croatian society and culture at that time and in the contemporary Croatian national imagination. More specifically, did the Croatian "national elite" during this period consider German linguistic communication in the "homeland" to be dysfunctional?

In purely social terms, the elite from the aforementioned core area included individuals and groups from different strata, including lower-middle elements. What was common to them all was Croatian and Slavic literacy and culture, particularly in speech. Understood in such a way, the national elite was basically convinced that the future of the Croatians as a Slavic people depended upon reappropriations of their own linguistic-cultural heritage and its functional uses, as well as future development of the Croatian language as a South Slavic language.

Socially, it was a pretty heterogeneous group, with no clearly defined social agenda. At least initially, the nobility was marginally integrated in this "Illyrian" group, in which middle-class urbanites dominated. Many appear to have been first-generation educated people of peasant origin, particularly from the Military Border. Although the majority were ethnically Croatian, there were others from very different ethnic backgrounds. Even the leading figure of the Illyrian movement, Dr. Ljudevit Gaj (Ludwig Gay), belonged to a family of the typical mixed, but mostly German Central European origin. Roman Catholics were the most numerous, with a noticeable number of Eastern—including Serbian—Orthodox, as well Jews and other confessional minorities.

What mattered much more was their regional background. The large majority of them originated from the aforementioned core region. Since the mid-sixteenth century that part of medieval "Slavonia Superior" was among those few remnants of the territories of the kingdoms of Dalmatia, Croatia and Slavonia known as the *reliquiae reliquiarum* that had escaped Ottoman occupation. Much of it belonged to the Habsburg Military Border against the Ottomans, which was also the region closest to both the Austrian hereditary lands and the rump of Habsburg-controlled Royal Hungary. The rest formed the center of Civil (Provincial) Croatia, comparatively the most developed one in the Croatian "ethnic space." The division between military and civilian roles held important implications for the first half of the nineteenth century. Whereas Military Croatia and Military Slavonia were militarized, agrarian communities under the absolute control of the *Hofkriegsrat* that separated Civil Croatia from Civil Slavonia, as well as from Dalmatia (under continuous Austrian civil rule after 1815), the Zagreb area had the best connections to the Austrian and Hungarian lands, as well as to scattered areas of Croatian "ethnic space," including even Ottoman-held regions like western Bosnia. Additional connections with nearby Slovenian areas and more distant Serbian centers both within and beyond the monarchy (i.e., Novi Sad and Belgrade) ensured that the Zagreb area would take the lead in the processes of social modernization and nation-building in the first half of the nineteenth century.

Such extremely complex socioeconomic and legal circumstances convinced Croatian visionaries of the imperative of rediscovering a "national soul" that manifested itself in a spoken and written "language." Since linguistic practices were also very complicated, orthographic reform and a subsequent linguistic standardization within a larger South Slavic context defined the substance and to a large extent "predetermined" the content of a "national renewal." That made a question of attitudes towards the status and uses of German in Croatia, in particular in the "Illyrian movement," very sensitive and controversial. In order to couch research questions in their appropriate contexts, it is necessary to examine a certain number of them before going to the sources on Illyrianist attitudes towards German.

## Languages of Oral and Written Communication in the Croatian "Ethnic Space" from the Late Middle Ages to 1830s

First of all, what is actually Croatian "ethnic space"? It is a *terminus technicus*, since borders of the Croatian ethnolinguistic community changed considerably over time, as did those of all neighboring communities, including not only Slavic ones like Slovenian and Serbian, but Hungarian, Italian, etc. The biggest changes took place in the fifteenth and sixteenth centuries.

The great majority of the common people spoke various Croatian dialects (Čakavian, Kajkavian, Štokavian) that continuously underwent important changes in linguistic and cultural terms. Both the Ottoman conquests and ethnic- and linguistic-demographic changes narrowed the Čakavian and Kajkavian space to the benefit of Štokavian, which had evolved considerably since the late Middle Ages. Štokavian speakers in Croatia comprised not only Croats, but many early modern Serb immigrants who migrated until the end of the seventeenth century from Ottoman-held Croatian lands to the east and southeast.[1] If there was a literary language integrating such a Croatian "ethnic space," it was primarily Latin, used both by the Roman Catholic Church and for secular purposes, most notably as the official language of the Croatian-Slavonian estates until 1847. The European identity of late medieval and early modern Croatian culture was primarily determined through the use of Latin by the literate stratum of the Croatian estates, which facilitated its acculturation not only with the Mediterranean and Pannonian regions, but with Western Christianity as a whole.

Another language that has to be added to Croatian and Latin is Old Slavonic in its Croatian appropriation, written mostly in Glagolitic and, later on, also in (Western) Cyrillic characters. That language was a "cradle" of the Croatian literary language since the time of Sts. Cyrill and Methodius. Practicing Old Slavonic, written in both alphabets, made possible Croatian linguistic communication among Slavs—irrespective of their particular Western or Eastern confessional differences. Until the fifteenth and sixteenth centuries there was almost half a millennium of continuity in cultivating Croatian Old Slavonic, and nearly as much continuity in using regional written languages in the Croatian culture. During the Renaissance a number of literary mature works were already done in Croatian. Latin characters were gradually introduced to Croatian from the fourteenth century and soon became dominant in writing, particularly following the post-Tridentine Catholic renewal.

Since late medieval Croatia was mostly oriented towards the Adriatic, yet another link to the outside world was provided by Italian, along with autochthonous Dalmatian and Istrian Roman dialects. Italian was not just a "foreign" language for urban Croatians in the Adriatic area of that time, since Italian was already the established *lingua franca* of the Mediterranean. Moreover, the Venetian Republic's acquisition of much of the eastern Adriatic during the fifteenth century assured that its spoken and written dialect would eventually culturally appropriate large parts of Croatia's Adriatic littoral. These were mostly urban populations in the eastern Adriatic, which were used to speaking and even writing Italian. After the Council of Trent, usage of both Latin and Italian initially expanded along with missionary activities. Indeed, Venetian Italian survived the Republic's collapse in 1797, becoming the language of official communication, accepted and even supported by the succeeding Austrian regime.

Of course, the Republic of Dubrovnik/Ragusa was a special case, as befitted its status since the mid-fifteenth century as a virtually independent tributary to the Ottoman sultans. The local Croatian *"slovinski"* dialect, Italian, and Latin coexisted and were used interchangeably in daily communication. As a result *"slovinski"* became linguistically very cultivated, including a series of literary works—unparalleled in its beauty to the present today.

A newcomer in literary terms came from the southeast. Bosnia's Islamic community contributed its own distinctive lingual-cultural practices. Although literary usage of Turkish, as well as Arabic, never attained as high a sociocultural level as Latin, Islamization of a large, sometimes even bigger part of the Bosnian society (which, in the first half of the sixteenth century, included much of Ottoman Croatia), changed substantially the very notion of a Croatian linguistic and cultural "space." Yet another new arrival was German, although in quite another sense than Turkish. In the sixteenth century it was one of the languages spoken in some of the cities of "Slavonia Superior," such as Varaždin and, later on, Zagreb (Gradec). Initially, it was a marginal linguistic phenomenon in proto-urban environments along the Styrian and Carniolan borders that constituted the southeastern frontier of the Holy Roman Empire. But German usage expanded fast in the sixteenth and seventeenth centuries.

Initially it stemmed from the growing importance of the Inner Austrian nobility, as well as of German soldiers in the emerging imperial military borderlands in Croatia and Slavonia. Almost continuous warfare against the Ottomans, which often assumed the form of "small wars" with conditionally negotiated peace settlements, introduced German in Croatia well beyond mere military and political usage.

Given successive Ottoman advances which, by 1592, had reached the vicinity of Zagreb and the nearby Inner Austrian frontier, German assistance assumed paramount importance, despite continuous suspicion of the Habsburgs' "hidden agenda." Another element facilitating expansion of German was the missionary zeal of Catholic religious orders, most notably the Jesuits, which came to Slavonia and Croatia from Bavaria and Austria. The *Brucker Libell* that the Inner Austrian Estates negotiated with Archduke Charles in 1578 led to the gradual territorialization of the Military Border system, with the appointment of supreme commanders for Croatian and Slavonian zones. Although this reduced the expansion of German in Civil Croatia, it expanded it significantly in the regions under direct military rule of Inner Austria's *Hofkriegsrat*. German became the language of communication within the military administration, irrespective of the linguistic background of the speakers all the way from Senj on the Adriatic to Koprivnica on the Drava River.

In spite of the "domestication" of some German linguistic patterns in the dialects of the ordinary people in the Military Border, they employed only very simplistic, limited constructions related to the command language. It was only in the last quarter of the eighteenth century that German began to make real headway among the lower strata following the establishment of a regular system of elementary education. The simultaneous introduction of higher education for military and administrative border officers (*Verwaltungsoffiziere*) also had an important impact on Military Border society. Enlightened upper and middle strata emerged, introducing a new world view and way of life in the small towns of the Military Border from Senj on the Adriatic to Zemun just across the Danube from Belgrade.

The peak of such a development was reached in 1784, when Emperor Joseph II introduced German as an official language in the Habsburg *Gesamtstaat*. For the first time in its history, Civil Croatia and Slavonia were obliged to communicate officially in German. Although the language law was abolished in 1790, it had two major consequences. First, the fiercely proud Croatian-Slavonian nobility was so deeply offended at the challenge to its feudal privileges that it looked and, in a way, pushed to rebuild bridges with its Hungarian counterpart. Second, every innovation in the so-called Age of Enlightenment was in one way or another linked to the German language. It did not matter if it was originally articulated in some other European language, since the language of the transfer was German. In particular Croatian-Slavonian urban culture was permeated with the German language and German culture. Immigration from German territories made their own as well.[2]

One of the causes was migrations of townspeople from German-speaking areas, including those where German was at least partially the language of everyday communication among autochthonous Slavic populations (like Slovene and Czech). Those demographic shifts were part of a proto-modernizational, better to say, civilization and cultural transfer from Central Europe, regularly intermediated by the German language.

In the years following the Peace of Karlowitz/Karlovci (1699), German usage was extended in different forms and practices up to the *Ducatus Syrmiensis*, several hundreds kilometers eastwards from Zagreb. These were mostly new military borderlands where it was used by military and administrative authorities reporting directly to the central government in Vienna. Certainly German was spoken more widely in the *Militärgrenze* than in Civil Croatia and Slavonia, a process that intensified over the next two centuries with new waves of German-speaking colonists. In opposition to that process, urban culture in both "Slavonia Superior" and "Slavonia Inferior," divided by long-established borderlines to the Ottoman Empire up to 1699, became profoundly rooted by the German linguistic communication and cultural patterns typical for Central European citizenry.

Nevertheless, until the Military Border's dissolution and reintegration with Croatia and Slavonia in 1881, German was still spoken by only a very limited number of inhabitants, while illiteracy prevailed in rural areas. Popular speech did, however, include a large number of phonetically and morphologically assimilated words and idioms of German origin.[3] By contrast, the Military Border's urban communities, in spite of their marginal demographic importance, were much more Germanized, regardless of the number of ethnic Germans living in them. Quite often it was the case that ethnic Germans were "Croatianized" by family relations, but still retained German cultural values and patterns that had been more deeply internalized by the community. Needless to say, there were many other cultural transfers of Austro-German origin, which were intermediated only partially by the German language itself.

For a very long period the Habsburg-Ottoman border marked the farthest reach of German usage. Only occasionally did cultural transfers, originating from Central Europe and related to the German linguistic culture, cross that frontier. In particular the Oriental urban culture of Bosnian cities south of the Sava River was very resistant to German influence.[4] The first "breakthroughs" took place in resurgent Serbia under Ottoman rule. Belgrade was on the Sava and Danube rivers and, once under Serbian authorities (for the first time in 1806), the city became the major recipient and intermediary of German linguistic and cultural patterns and values across the northern Balkans.[5]

Meanwhile, German language usage pervaded Croatian "ethnic space" from the northwest to the southeast. Functionally, one can differentiate distinctive usages in different Croatian lands and environments that were not necessarily related to each other. Initially, since the late medieval period, it was mostly used in urban centers along Carniolan and Styrian frontiers from Rijeka to Varaždin.[6] It was spoken by specific

## Population of Croatian lands ca. 1840 (estimated)

| | Croats | Serbs | Other | Total |
|---|---|---|---|---|
| **Banal Croatia** | 689,000 | 141,000 | 17,000 | 847,000 |
| | 81.4% | 16.6% | 2.0% | |
| -Civil Croatia | 519,000 | 3,000 | 4.000 | 526,000 |
| | 98.7% | 0.5% | 0.8% | |
| -Civil Slavonia | 170,000 | 138,000 | 13,000 | 321,000 |
| | 53.0% | 43.0% | 4.0% | |
| **Military Border** | 386,000 | 363,000 | 9,000 | 758,000 |
| | 50.9% | 47.9% | 1.2% | |
| -Croatian Border | 258,000 | 240,000 | | 498,000 |
| | 51.8% | 48.2% | | |
| -Slavonian Border | 127,000 | 123,000 | 9,000 | 259,000 |
| | 49.1% | 47.4% | 3.5% | |
| **Dalmatia** | 300,000 | 74,000 | 16,000 | 390,000 |
| | 77.0% | 19.0% | 4.0% | |

| | Croats | Slovenes | Italians etc. | |
|---|---|---|---|---|
| **Istria** | 130,000 | 30,000 | 55,000 | 215,000 |
| | 60.5% | 14.0% | 25.5% | |

| | Croats | Serbs | Slovenes | Others | Total |
|---|---|---|---|---|---|
| T O T A L S | 1,505,000 | 578,000 | 30,000 | 97,000 | 2,210,000 |
| | 68.0% | 26.1% | 1.5% | 4.4% | |

(Source: Stančić, 1985, 11)

urban groups within particular professions. Its practice showed great resiliency and was reinforced by the arrival of German-speaking colonists, most notably artisans engaged in "German crafts." Trade also contributed. The Catholic renewal, taking place mostly from the beginning of the seventeenth century, was to a large extent linked to the spread of German. Although much of their curriculum was in Latin, relatively numerous Croatian students studied in German academies and universities until the nineteenth century, contributing on their own to German's cultural "domestication." Beginning in the mid-eighteenth century, enlightened absolutist reforms contributed greatly to the modernizing effect of the German language in Croatia.

Not surprisingly the Croatian and Slavonian Military Borderlands exhibited the most direct influence of the German language. Given the less differentiated socioeconomic and cultural structures of the *Militärgrenze*, German linguistic and cultural effects were basically limited to military functions in a broader sense. Nonetheless, from the mid-eighteenth century on there was a constant flow of talented young nobles and commoners from the Military Border to military institutions in Wiener Neustadt and Vienna, which constituted the first, relatively numerous group of individuals of both Croatian and, to a lesser extent, Serbian origin who had been pre-selected for careers as military officers. Although it is not yet sufficiently known in what way they participated in German linguistic and cultural transfers to Croatia, one cannot ignore their relevance to the process.

Another, hierarchically less influential group proved even more important in the transfer process. The central government was determined to build a Military Border system that was self-reliant, particularly in economic terms, in order to minimize the burden that it placed on the treasury. As a result, "pseudo-civil" structures were established and developed whenever necessary. The best example is the stratum of *Verwaltungsoffiziere* who were assigned administrative, economic, fiscal and other responsibilities at the village, company, and even regimental level. For their education a *Grenzverwaltungsinstitut* was established in Graz at the beginning of the nineteenth century that recruited mostly native-born sons from the Military Border. Consequently, there emerged the nucleus of a relatively educated "popular intelligentsia" in a rural society of nearly total illiteracy that was obliged to assume far-reaching responsibilities at the grass-roots level, despite having little chance of career advancement. *Verwaltungsoffiziere* did more for the popular assimilation of Austro-German values and customs than any other group, including priests of German educational background. At the same time, this distinctive military stratum, knowing better than anybody else that the Military Border system was a system without a future, was a major "reservoir" of educated and dissatisfied "lower-middle-class" people for the recruitment of the "national elite" between the revolution of 1848 and the Military Border's dissolution in 1881.

Finally, the languages of three neighboring imperial structures—Italian, German and Turkish—intermingled in Croatia's "ethnic space." Each exhibited a wide variety of linguistic borrowings and cultural transfers which were, in very different ways, important for Croatia's distinctive linguistic and cultural development. The Italian traditions of intercultural communication were by far the longest and richest, but functionally and spatially limited to maritime limitrophic areas. Turkish was already present in the western part of Ottoman Bosnia as a language of administration and high culture, but was only occasionally spoken even among Moslems outside of a limited circle of Islamic-educated people. Still, terminological and idiomatic influences of the Turkish language were widespread in the vernacular, extending even across the Ottoman border. Oriental cultural influences were even deeper among Christian populations as well.

In spite of the obvious fragmentation of Croatian "ethnic space" throughout the early modern epoch, one cannot overestimate its effects on nascent Illyrian movement of the 1830s. With the exception of Bosnia-Herzegovina's Roman Catholic communities, which were indistinguishable from the Croatian ethnic matrix, virtually all Croats lived in distinctive territorial units within the Habsburg borderlands, quite often sharing traditions and aspirations quite different from each other, namely the Civil/Provincial/Banal Croatia and Slavonia under Hungarian tutelage, the Croatian and Slavonian Military Border under direct *Hofkriegsrat* rule, Dalmatia (including Boka Kotorska and Dubrovnik region) and Istria administered from Vienna.[7] The population of Croatia's unquestionable Habsburg loyalty was certainly an agent of integration, not to speak at this moment about other "proto-modern" integrative mechanisms that stemmed from Habsburg policy. The dynasty was perceived as a German one. Although the German language was alien to the dominant Croatian tradition of *iura municipalia,* it was at the same time recognized and assimilated as a language, gradually replacing Latin in communication with Europe and, more significantly, as a vehicle of change and modernization.[8]

## Croatian vs. German and "Conservative Modernization" in the Austrian Empire (1815–1848)

At least in an early modern context, the Venetian, Ottoman and Habsburg empires were all too linguistically diverse to be identified with a single language. The same could even be said for Croatia. Without Venetian printers, the emergence of modern Croatian would have been inconceivable; without Bosnian Franciscan literature, there could have been no universally comprehensible Štokavian standardization of the modern Croatian language; nor would it have been possible to promote literacy among Croatia's lower social strata without *ratio educationis.*

Nevertheless, the languages intermingling with each other in the *Triplex Confinium* of imperial encounters did not enjoy equal footing at any moment in the early modern period. There were different kinds of "winners" and "losers" in every particular situation. In a historical perspective of the three centuries after 1500, the German language made by far the biggest "breakthrough" in the region. The Venetian Republic had already lost its imperial maritime hegemony long before its dissolution in 1797. Although it survived as an empire for more than a century afterward, the slow but steady erosion of Ottoman imperial power in southeastern Europe reinforced the Habsburg Monarchy's contemporary image as "predestined" to establish a new Christian *oikuménē* in the region. Redefined as a *Gesamtstaat* and unburdened by the detritus of the Holy Roman Empire, the Austrian Empire's conservative modernizers implicitly or explicitly preferred to build their state around a single, German language, despite significant resistance to it from its Hungarian, Croatian and other subjects. After 1815, central authorities communicated primarily in German. It was the principal language of higher—particularly university—education. Apart from the classical languages, only Italian enjoyed a certain amount of cachet in some parts of the monarchy as a language of modernity. *Landessprachen* like Croatian were recognized as languages of initial education and bureaucratic communication with the lower strata of the population.[9]

By the end of the eighteenth century, Croatia's entrepreneurial class began to insist upon the importance of the Croatian language, justifying their pretensions by making contemporary comparisons. When a young Croatian from Karlovac, Josip Šipuš, was inspired by Adam Smith to produce *Temely xitne tergovine* (Foundations of the Wheat Trade) in Zagreb in 1796, he devoted the introduction almost exclusively to justifying its publication in Croatian and to extolling the need for Croatian linguistic reform to overcome limited accessibility in a changing world. In order to excuse the pretentious of his approach, he pointed out that both past and present scholars from "our homeland" had no chance to make the "honest" Croatian language "flourish, like languages of the other peoples do." According to him there were only mothers, who by teaching their children to speak in their own language taught them at the same time to "love" both their "nationality" and the "common good." The biggest problem for Šipuš was that Croats were not able to express many of their life experiences in their own language, which had been heretofore innocent of many modern concepts. They were, therefore, obliged to borrow terms and constructs from other tongues. Because this was done locally without any reference to parallel but different formulations taking root in other areas, it was impossible for Croats to understand each other properly.[10]

Actually, structures of the language market in Croatia were polycentric and many-sided during the first half of the nineteenth century. Within early modern Croatia's predominantly illiterate ethnic space, the highly literate—which always included more than Catholic priests—were always readily identifiable. Such erudites were often cultivated speakers of several languages who lacked sufficient opportunities to sustain careers at home. Those interested in linguistic matters were well-represented and contributed in different ways to functional changes of their own "glorious" language, much as they did to linguistic and literary developments elsewhere. Nor were their contributions necessarily just occasional, since the early modern Croatian language inherited a considerable number of grammars, dictionaries, etc.[11]

The major problem was that all too often, the linguistic orientation of these devoted, often talented authors contradicted each other in many ways. As a result, the Viennese court contributed much more to the establishment of standardized Croatian during the eighteenth century than did the Croatian and Slavonian Estates. This had numerous consequences.[12] Regardless of their linguistic skill or institutional (including Catholic) affiliations, talented individuals faced a large variety of problems in the pursuit of linguistic standardization. One had to be aware of social and ethnonational linguistic contexts of such a far-reaching project. Such a future-oriented challenge also had to define itself in relation to relatively rich and obviously controversial linguistic developments that went back to the Renaissance and, even further, to the origins of Croatian Slavic writing. Second, it had to take into account the intermingling of linguistic practices, most notably Latin, Italian, German, and Hungarian. Third, it had to be defined within the broader context of other regional Slavic languages, since the popular Kajkavian dialect was shared with Slovenian, and Štokavian with the Serbs and Bosnians. The problem posed by the alphabet also had to be faced. Despite its romanticism, the Croatian national elite of the 1830s understood that language was about power, both secular and spiritual. Contemporaries were also aware that Croatia was a country at the crossroad of the European West and East. In the words of Count Janko Drašković, "We are in the middle of Europe." In his view both were potentially dangerous for Croatia, the East by its "darkness" (*tamnotom*), the West by its "glitter" (*preizbistrenjem*). Using metaphors, Count Drašković was advocating at that time some kind of a Croatian "third way," based on supreme knowledge (*velika pamet*), better education and the practical skills of public officials in different dominions, including responsibilities of enlightened clerics of all denominations.[13]

In meeting different kinds of challenges, the Croatian national elite preferred at that time to integrate itself within a larger "Illyrian" context. The word "we" (*mi*) referred to Croats as Illyrians, while "homeland" (*domovina*) accorded with the dominant German tradition of equating *Kulturnation* with *Sprachnation* (*Sprache = jezik*).[14] What mattered in the Croatian case was that the challenge of—and solution to—linguistic standardization was perceived as part of a civilizational process. What was less clear was what constituted the "middle way" (*sredoputno popeljanje puka*). Nevertheless, linguistic standardization did its best to follow that "third way." It meant also that modern linguistic structures had to follow patterns already established in those European languages which were closest to the Croatian historical experience. To Drašković these were German and Latin. In order to make his *Disertacija* more accessible, he added a small dictionary to the text of all those Croatian terms that might not have been known to readers. Clarifying those notions, Drašković referred to German and Latin:

> Blagodariti, dankbar lohnen, gratificare.
> Blagopolučje, Glückseligkeit, beata abundantia . . . .[15]

Drašković assumed that literate people spoke German and Latin whenever they had to discuss topics of public relevance and that the challenge was how to make them think and speak Croatian. Josephinist education and culture at the highest levels had to be "domesticated." Drašković's linguistic skills were very modest, in spite of his knowledge of several languages. It was then up to younger, philologically much better educated "Illyrians" to cultivate the language to the level required in contemporary European communication. There were many initiatives, including grammatical contributions by Vjekoslav Babukić (1836) and Antun Mažuranić (1839), as well as a German-Illyrian dictionary by Ivan Mažuranić and Jakov Užarević (1842).[16] Easily the biggest contribution to the Croatian lexicology of the time was the publication of the Mažuranić-Užarević dictionary, which succeeded in bringing together both traditional Croatian lexicographical achievements and coinages for newly emerging needs in spoken communication. The dictionary treated both popular dialects and literary language, as well as issues of modern European culture and civilization.[17]

It was very symptomatic of Croatia's linguistic situation that another, much weaker dictionary, *Ilirsko-němačko-talijanski rěčnik* (Illyrian-German-Italian), published in Vienna by Josip Drobnić in 1846–49, was a much bigger financial success. It is almost certain that the book's translation of Croatian words into the dominant German and Italian—then the preeminent languages of Croatian public communication—facilitated such a market reception.

There is, however, still a question that has never been properly investigated, namely, how numerous those in Croatia and Slavonia who spoke German were in the first decades of the nineteenth century. Although census-taking became quite a professional routine in the second half of the nineteenth century, they were sufficiently haphazard in the preceding decades that their data is unreliable. What is beyond doubt is that these are orders of numeric values. First of all, one has to keep in mind that the German-speaking population lived mostly in urban settlements and that, with the exception of some German-speaking villages in eastern Slavonia and Syrmia, the language was only rarely spoken in the countryside. In 1840, the roughly 30,000 residents of Zagreb (just over 12,000), Karlovac (7,000), and Varaždin (9,000) constituted the majority of the Croatian "national elite," while, Rijeka (10,000), Osijek (12,000), and Split (8,700) did not participate in the Illyrian movement in a way comparable to cities in northwestern Croatia. By 1847, Zagreb had grown to 15,000 inhabitants, which was not the case of other cities.[18] Even in those Croatian cities one has to differentiate very distinctive levels of German-language communication. There was a huge difference between those speaking correct German and those using more or less "broken" provincial dialects or occasionally "borrowing" bits and pieces for everyday communication. It was only in the Military Border that the entire adult male population was expected to understand command German. In any case, it would be impossible to accept a thesis that these were urban majorities without proving it through detailed investigation. As Daniel Baric explains, "Comprise, enseignée, parlée par la majorité de la population urbaine au début du siècle, elle perd en quelques décennies sa place au profit des langues nationales."[19]

It would be more appropriate to say that majorities used to know elementary German, at least at the level of understanding. They were more accustomed to listening to somebody speak German than to speaking it fluently themselves. One cannot forget that the urban majority was illiterate; if anything, they were more apt to "think" in German than to speak it. In that sense it is possible to say that in some environments, German-speaking majorities prevailed. Writing about "Illyrian" entertainment, Vukotinović stated in 1842 that the language used in more decent forms of it was still German.

In 1842, Vukotinović enthusiastically reports on social gatherings again, though he admits at one place that the language "of us Croats or Illyrians is still German."[20]

There is one more aspect that we need to consider. The appropriations of the German language differed from one cultural circle to another, as well as between localities. As Baric explains,

> Every European region preserves a particular attitude towards the German language, depending upon the structure of its population and its situation related to information and culture transmitted by German.[21]

Some of the most educated personalities in the Croatian national elite who had mastered several languages but insisted nonetheless on using Croatian were very sensitive to the vulgar use of intermingling languages. Ivan Kukuljević Sakcinski was the first to address the Croatian estates in the vernacular on 2 May 1843, observing bitterly to his compatriots that Croats were a little bit German, a little bit Italian, a little bit Hungarian and a little bit Slav—altogether right nothing! He insisted in an inflammatory speech that Croats needed to get rid of a "dead" Latin and other "living" languages that were not theirs, while strengthening their native Croatian in their own homeland, making it the ruling language, which, he concluded, was the most important precondition for the Croatian people's survival.[22]

Fundamental questions of Croatian linguistic and cultural self-determination were raised amid comparisons with the neighboring "others," particularly those who were able to respond properly to challenges posed by the *Zeitgeist*. For these *Vorkämpfer* the relationship with language became the most important criterion for analyzing the self-esteem of individuals and society as a whole. All of Croatia's neighbors, whether Germans, Hungarians, or Italians, insisted on their own language's preeminence and had consequently earned not only the respect but the fear of the "Illyrians" as a threat to the future of the monarchy's Slavs. Kukuljević Sakcinski was particularly disgusted that "Croats and Slavonians" were living practically in isolation, without intermingling with the "others" in the monarchy and yet were avoiding using their own language and were even ashamed of it. For Kukuljević Sakcinski, this was a recipe for future "enslavement":

> . . . just look at our neighbors that are under the same Austrian scepter with us. Every one of them, German, Hungarian and Italian, placed his language at the first place. Only we, submissive and humble Slavs that number 17 millions in the Empire, only we, timid Croats and Slavonians, who are not coalesced with any other people [*puk*] in our homeland, we fear of our language like a scarecrow and serve foreigners and foreign will and do only those things that the others consider nice and beautiful and things useful to others.[23]

Of course, the Croatian national elite continued to be genuinely interested in

German and Italian culture, and there was nothing of relevance in their statements and convictions which was not in one way or another derived from readings in these two languages. Those German and Italian personalities who symbolized the values which were found to be of the utmost importance in Croatia were appropriated by Croatian culture. It is a long list, but one name that deserves special mention is the German writer F. Schiller, who was arguably the foreigner most thoroughly "domesticated" by the "Illyrians." He alone accounted for almost a third of all poetry translated from the German![24]

It is difficult to find the name of any Croatian poet of the period who did not translate from German into Croatian, including Lj. Gaj, A. Mihanović, D. Rakovac, D. Demeter, A. Nemčić, S. Vraz, S. Marjanović, I. Kukuljević, M. Bogović, I. Trnski, and P. Preradović.[25] When we consider that there were practically no Croatian poets in the first half of the nineteenth century who did not also write in German, it becomes clear that the Croatian linguistic and cultural emancipation followed primarily Central European patterns rooted in German linguistic and cultural experience. Some of those poets began by writing in German, while the rest kept writing in both languages throughout their lives. That they devoted themselves to Croatian literature did not in any way affect interest in German letters.

It was the same story with the German theater, which was an institution of the utmost importance in Central Europe's national "renewals." At the beginning of the nineteenth century, Zagreb and many other cities in the region were inundated by traveling German theatrical companies. They performed exclusively in German and the repertoire was the same as anywhere else in the monarchy. Pieces written by August von Kotzebue dominated. A Croatian national repertoire emerged slowly, to a large extent by translating, rewriting, and imitating German pieces. Although an amateur, the physician D. Demeter invested enormous energy in establishing Croatian theater. In 1841 he founded a theater book series "Izbor igrokaza ilirskoga kazališta" (Selection of plays from the Illyrian theater), which featured mostly Croatian translations of German works.[26]

Gradually, German theatrical companies realized that Croatian audiences wanted to enjoy performances not only in German, but also in Croatian. A certain number of artists decided to establish themselves in Zagreb and other Croatian cities while performing in the national language. This tendency was much more common in music. At the beginning of the nineteenth century, there were traveling musicians who played for Croatian magnates. A national "revival" required a musical culture, and there were quite numerous public concerts done by those guests. It did not take too long before some of them began to compose popular pieces based on national motifs. Needless to say, some of them became very popular in Zagreb:

> Residents of Zagreb could attend performances of flute players Anton Ebenhöch and Wilhelm Kiltray from Pest in 1836, of a violin player from Petrograd and a

student of Paganini Eleonora Naumann in 1838, of a singer Marija Fisch from
Odesa in 1839. On July 27, 1846, Franz Liszt held a concert.[27]

Those Croatian students of music who studied abroad were educated in the German
tradition. The most talented among them, Vatroslav Lisinski, after studying in Prague
and coming back, wrote two Croatian operas, *Ljubav i zloba* (1843–45) and *Porin*
(1848–51), both of which are still performed today.[28]

## Conclusion

One could enumerate all of the other domains of "renewalist" innovations. It is possible to identify German elements in all of them. Although the major objective of
the Croatian "national renewal" was emancipation from German cultural domination, the achievement of such an objective depended more on the "domestication"
of German values and patterns in Croatian and (South) Slavic terms. Starting with
orthographic reform, Ljudevit Gaj, the leading personality of the Croatian "national
renewal," aimed at a "construction" of a South Slav literary language, based on Slavic
frameworks (again, following a Herderian model), but structurally imitated examples
of long-established European languages, above all German. Even more significantly,
theoretical justifications were almost regularly transferred from German culture,
including those related to the necessity of emancipating the Slavic languages from
German. Frequent reference was made to Arndt, who wrote that "a nation is lost as
soon as its preference for foreign language becomes dominant."[29]

Thus the horizon of the initial period of Croatian nation-building was limited.
With the beginning of the Croatian "national renewal," the upper strata of Croatian
society largely opposed the central government's attempts to promote the use of German, since it was incompatible with the nobility's *iura municipalia*. At the time, the
nobility's potential for reform was very weak, for which reason Croatia's conservative
but pragmatic entrepreneurial stratum instinctively followed another strategy that
became prevalent in the Croatian "national renewal." The Croatian culture had to
be nationalized—"domesticated"—but not in all-exclusive opposition to German.
Quite the opposite: whatever was linked to essential societal changes, reforms, progress, etc., and intermediated by German was soon recognized, internalized in the
Croatian collective experience, and gradually linguistically transferred into Croatian.
It was a long process that was only initiated in the period 1835–48. But, as Šafařík
explained in his *Abkunft der Slaven,* Croatian, like Czech, was supposed to develop
a "fraternal relationship" with both Latin and German. Ivan Derkos accepted this
in Croatia in 1832:

> Its brotherly connection (kinship) with modern German and Latin cannot be
> denied. In his *Abkunft der Slaven* Šafařík says: "An entire being and content as
> well as the structure of the Slavic language is primarily Greek-Latin-German.
> With regard to this, the Slavic language belongs to an affiliation of languages

which is formed when initially akin languages, influenced by various internal and external factors, develop independently, taking a lasting shape over time while, afterwards, they borrow words with foreign imprint to one another through trade, war, and other ways of communication."[30]

Although different in so many ways, European languages depended on each other in terms of civilization and modern mentalities, since they historically experience comparable challenges. The Croatian national elite was deeply convinced of this, even if it did not often publicly state it in such terms. Emotional mobilization in the first half of the nineteenth century necessitated another public message.

# Notes

1. Brozović, Dalibor. Ivić, Pavle. Jezik, srpskohrvatski/hrvatskosrpski, hrvatski ili srpski. Jugoslavenski leksikografski zavod "Miroslav Krleža." Zagreb, 1988.
2. Count Janko Drašković wrote about it in his "Disertacija" (1832), insisting that it was only with the eighteenth-century Habsburg reforms that the German language was "imposed" (z silum upeljaše) everywhere in Hungary and Croatia ("hodna učine nimačkog jezika i nimačke običaje u sve kuće preštimanje"), provoking Hungarian and Croatian resistance, but also opposing Hungarians and Croats to each other. (Drašković, Janko. "Disertacija . . . ," in Miroslav Šicel, ed., Programski spisi hrvatskog narodnog preporoda [Zagreb, 1997], p. 59.) In short, among Croats and Hungarians the German language was considered to be a "novelty." At the same time, it was perceived to be a language of the "privileged"!
3. It is a pity that there has never been a more systematic investigation of those "borrowings."
4. Circumscribed as they were by mechanisms of "repressive toleration," even Christian communities in Bosnian cities largely acclimated to Oriental cultural forms. After 1699 closer proximity to the Pannonian and Adriatic "worlds" doubtless influenced Bosnian everyday life, with some controversial patterns being rejected, while others were accepted. Although it would be wrong to minimize such limited transfers, it was only after the Austro-Hungarian occupation of Bosnia-Herzegovina in 1878 that the latter was integrated into "Central Europe" in terms of linguistic communication.
5. It is difficult to overestimate this role, even as Belgrade preserved much of its Oriental character throughout the nineteenth century. The most important intermediaries were invariably Serbs and occasionally Croats coming from the Habsburg Monarchy, who were popularly referred to as Švabe (Swabians).
6. The German linguistic impact was very weak along the eastern coast of the northern Adriatic from Rijeka to Senj, even in parts which used to be under military jurisdiction, at least partially, since the beginning of the sixteenth century on. Italian dominated in public and official usage, although Croatian was always in use, either written in Latin or Glagolitic characters.
7. Nikša Stančić, "Hrvatski narodni preporod 1790–1848," in Hrvatski narodni preporod 1790–1848. Hrvatska u vrijeme Ilirskog pokreta. Muzej za umjetnost i obrt (Zagreb, 1985), 11.
8. Hungarian never achieved the same level of acceptance among Croats and other Slavs, since it was perceived to be a language of Asian origin.
9. See Encyclopaedia Jugoslaviae 6, Zagreb, 1965, 333.
10. See the introduction to the reprint of Ivan Erceg, ed., Temelj žitne trgovine, published by Matica hrvatska (Karlovac, 1993). It make sense to refer at this point to Pierre Bourdieu's

"economy of symbolic exchanges," insisting upon the fact that linguistic exchanges represent at the same time symbolic power, realized as power relations between speakers and groups to which they belong. Pierre Bourdieu, *Što znači govoriti: Ekonomija jezičnih razmjena* (Zagreb, 1992), 13–14.

11. See Zlatko Vince, *Putovima hrvatskoga književnog jezika: Lingvističko-kulturnopovijesni prikaz filoloških škola i njihovih izbora* (Zagreb, 2nd ed., 1990).

12. Whereas Vince's synthesis remains the standard, there is a need for a new monograph on the subject.

13. "We are in the center of Europe, East and West threatens us, the first by the darkness, the second by the enlightenment, the first by the subordination from which we liberated ourselves a century ago rejecting the mental slavery once and forever, the second by the brightness, which still cannot be gazed by the feeble eyes of our people. Therefore, one needs to guide the people through a middle way as well as to have educated and trained officers. In order to prevent evil it requires better schooling and complete education of priests of all confessions." ("Mi usried Europi ležimo, nama se prieti istok i zapad, on tamnotom, ov preizbistrenjem, on stopom iz kojega prije jednoga vieka se oslobodili jesmo ne tijući više u sužanjstvo umno zapasti; ov sjanjem, kojega gledat još odviš nejake oči puka našega jesu. Tu daklje sredoputno popeljanje puka, tomu pako vrlo velika pamet i uvježbanje u časnikih potrebna jest. Ovo pako zagteva za priečenje svega zla bolje školovanje i svršenije naučenje popovah sviuh bogoštovjah.") Janko Drašković, *Disertacija . . .* (Karlovac, 1832), quoted in Miroslav Šicel, *Programski spisi hrvatskog narodnog preporoda* (Zagreb, 1997), 72.

14. "Perception of the homeland among the younger generation owes its profundity and scope to Humboldt's viewpoint that the real homeland is the language" ("Pojam o domovini u mlade generacije duguje dubinu i širinu humboldtovskom gledištu da je prava domovina jezik.") Namely, "Die wahre Heimat ist eigentlich die Sprache." Josip Bratulić, *Hrvatski narodni preporod 1790–1848. Hrvatska u vrijeme Ilirskog pokreta* (Zagreb, 1985), 32.

15. Janko Drašković, *Disertacija . . .* (Karlovac, 1832), quoted in Šicel, *Programski spisi hrvatskog,* 72.

16. Stančić, "Hrvatski narodni preporod," 23.

17. "It is a dictionary that reflects language 'not just as a popular communication in everyday use, but as a language of literacy and a decoder and transmitter of European education and civility' as stated in the subscription invitation." ("Rječnik je to u kojem se jezik odražava 'ne samo kao pučki govor u potrebi svagdanjoj, već i kao književni jezik i tumačnik i provodič izobraženja i uglađenja europejskoga', kako stoji u Pozivu k pretplati.") Bratulić, *"Hrvatski narodni preporod 1790–1848,"* 35.

18. All these figures have to be relativized by comparing them with those of the Habsburg Monarchy's major cities at mid-century, including Vienna (400,000), Prague (115,000), Pest (110,000), and Trieste (slightly over 80,000). Stančić, "Hrvatski narodni preporod," 9).

19. Daniel Baric, "La langue allemande en Croatie dans la première moitié du XIX$^c$ siècle: une prédiminance contestée," Mémoire de DEA présenté par Daniel Baric, Université de Paris—Vincennes—Saint-Denis, Paris 1996–97, 1.

20. "Godine 1842. Vukotinović ponovo s mnogo zanosa izvještava o zabavama, no na jednom mjestu priznaje da je jezik 'kod nas Horvatah ili Ilirah uvěk još němački.'" Nada Premerl, Hrvatski narodni preporod 1790–1848. *Hrvatska u vrijeme Ilirskog pokreta* (Zagreb, 1985), 136.

21. "Chaque région d'Europe central entretient un rapport particulier avec l'allemand, reflétant la composition de sa population et sa situation face aux informations et à la culture transmises par l'allemand." Baric, "La langue allemande en Croatie," 1.

22. "We are partly Romans, partly Germans, partly Italians, partly Hungarians and partly Slavs, and in total (to be honest) we are nothing at all! Dead Roman language and living Hungarian, German and Italian, these are our tutors, those alive fright us, the dead one clutches our throat, suffocates us, conveys and surrenders us, feeble as we are, to the hands of the living; at the present we only have so much force to withstand the dead, before long we will not be able to conquer the alive if we do not stand at our feet, that is, if we do not reinforce our language in our homeland and proclaim it dominant." ("Mi smo malo Latini, malo Nijemci, malo Talijani, malo Mađari i malo Slavjani, a ukupno (iskreno govoreći) nismo baš ništa! Mrtvi jezik rimski, a živi mađarski, njemački i talijanski, to su naši tutori, živi nam se groze, mrtvi nas drži za grlo, duši nas i nemoćne nas vodi i predaje živim u ruke; sada imamo još toliko sile da se suprotstavimo mrtvomu, zamala nećemo moći nadvladati žive ako se čvrsto ne stavimo na svoje noge, tj. ako svoj jezik ne utvrdimo u domovini i ne postavimo ga vladajućim.") Ivan Kukuljević, "Prvi od davnina zastupnički govor na hrvatskom jeziku koji je održao Ivan Kukuljević 2. svibnja 1843. u Hrvatskom saboru," in Miroslav Šicel, *Programski spisi hrvatskog narodnog preporoda* (Zagreb, 1997), 157–58.

23. ". . . pogledajmo samo na susjede, koji su s nami pod istim žezlom austrijskim, svaki od njih: Njemac, Mađar i Talijan postavio je svoj jezik na prvo mjesto, samo mi ponizni i krotki Slavjani kojih u carstvu imade 17 milijunah, samo mi plašljivi Hrvati i Slavonci, koji u svojoj domovini nismo s nikojim drugim pukom smiješani, bojimo se našega jezika kao kakovog strašila i služimo tuđemu i tuđoj volji i činimo samo ono, što se drugim lijepo i krasno biti vidi, i što je drugim hasnovito." Ivan Kukuljević, "Prvi od davnina zastupnički govor na hrvatskom jeziku koji je održao Ivan Kukuljević 2. svibnja 1843. u Hrvatskom saboru." *Ibid.*, 157–59.

24. Encyclopaedia Jugoslaviae 6, Zagreb, 1965, 343–344.

25. Encyclopaedia Jugoslaviae 6, Zagreb, 1965, 344.

26. Encyclopaedia Jugoslaviae 6, Zagreb, 1965, 344.

27. "Zagrepčani su 1836. slušali flautista Antona Ebenhöcha i Wilhelma Kiltraya iz Pešte, 1838. petrogradsku violinisticu, Paganinijevu učenicu Eleonoru Naumann, 1839. pjevačicu Mariju Fisch iz Odese, a 27. srpnja 1846. koncert je održao i Franz Liszt." Zdravko Blažeković, *Hrvatski narodni preporod 1790–1848. Hrvatska u vrijeme Ilirskog pokreta* (Zagreb, 1985), 117.

28. Ibid., 118.

29. Josip Mayer, "Glas rodoljubca," in Ivan Krtalić, *Polemike u hrvatskoj književnosti.* in Kolo I—Knjiga I. Pet slova rogatih (Zagreb, 1982), 1, 131; *Danica ilirska,* 1 (Zagreb, 1836).

30. "A ne može mu se zaniekati bratski vez (srodstvo) sa modernim germanskim (njemačkim) i latinskim. Šafařík veli u svom Abkunft der Slaven. "Čitavo biće, sadržaj i gradja slavenskoga jezika ipak je u prvom redu grčko-latinsko-njemačka. Slavenski se jezik nalazi s obzirom na to u onom srodstvu jezika, koje nastaje u tom slučaju, kad izprva srodni jezici, pošto su se tekom vremena pod uplivom različitih unutrašnjih i spoljašnjih tvornih elemenata samostalno razvili i stalno uobličili, kasnije s pomoću trgovine, rata i drugačijega obćenja jedan drugomu posudjuju rieči, kojima se strani biljeg poznaje." Ivan Derkos, "Duh domovine nad sinovima svojim, koji spavaju," in Šicel, *Programski spisi hrvatskog,* 100.

# "Germans" in the Habsburg Empire

## Language, Imperial Ideology, National Identity, and Assimilation

### ◆ Arnold Suppan ◆

The peoples of the Habsburg Empire—beginning with the "Germans"—experienced between 1770 and 1914 similar processes as many other western European peoples: a population explosion, enlightenment, an industrial boom, bureaucratization, urbanization, *embourgeoisement*, and the formation of mass society; mass education and the growth of communications; the transition from absolutism to constitutionalism; and the transition from religious prescription to competing secular and clerical norms—altogether a huge social modernization within three or four generations. After the "Germans," mainly German Austrians, had succeeded in pushing into the background the Spanish, Italian, and French cultural influences that had dominated the imperial court and the life of the aristocracy well into the eighteenth century, they attained social, cultural, and political dominance as a direct consequence of their superior achievements. More important was the fact that "Germanism" represented a specific language and culture, whereas "Slavism" in the eyes of the West was only a somewhat hazy, generic term applied jointly to several diverse groups. But the Habsburg Monarchy could not develop into a nation-state like France, Great Britain, Italy or Germany, for it was an empire with eleven major nationalities (Germans, Magyars, Czechs, Poles, Ruthenians/Ukrainians, Romanians, Croats, Serbs, Slovaks, Slovenes, and Italians) and seven major confessions (Roman Catholics, Greek Orthodox, Greek Catholics/Uniates, Calvinists, Lutherans, Jews, and Bosnian Muslims). Hence the question in modern historiography first raised by Oscar Jászi's *The Dissolution of the Habsburg Monarchy:* "How did social and ethnic factors come to interact there?"[1]

# The Leading Role of the German-Speaking Population

Because of the prevalence of their language and the way the state apparatus was constituted, at the end of the eighteenth century the "Germans" were without doubt the leading group among the different nationalities in the Habsburg Empire. Their dominant position was partly supported by tradition that dated back to a time when mainly German-speaking lands that were later lost—Lusatia (1635), Alsace (1648), the major part of Silesia (1742), "Vorderösterreich" or the "Vorlande" from the Breisgau to the Burgau (1805)—belonged to the Habsburg Monarchy. The acquisition of the Inn district (1779) and Salzburg (1805/15) in no way compensated for these losses. At any rate, with the partitions of Poland (1772/95) and the Congress of Vienna (1814/15) the German part of the Habsburg domains was considerably weakened, while the non-German areas were further increased (Lombardy, Venetia, the Venetian part of Istria, Dalmatia, Ragusa, Galicia, and the Bukovina). Although these territorial adjustments accompanied the process of a political disengagement in Germany, the Austrian Empire was able to renew its connection with the German states through its position as the presiding power over the Germanic Confederation (*Deutscher Bund*). Both the Austrian Hereditary Lands (*Deutsche Erblande*) and the Bohemian lands (*Böhmische Länder*) were added to this new, rather weak political construction in central Europe.[2]

The geographical distribution of the German Austrians in the Habsburg Monarchy was a source of a number of difficulties and contradictions. Numerically speaking, the strongest block of Germans inhabited the old patrimonial dominions of Lower and Upper Austria, Styria, Carinthia (Salzburg), Tyrol, and Vorarlberg. Together with the German-speaking regions in southern Bohemia, southern Moravia and the four westernmost Hungarian counties of Pressburg (Pozsony), Wieselburg (Moson), Ödenburg (Sopron), and Eisenburg (Vasvár), the Germans in these lands constituted a strong and, except for some linguistic enclaves and urban minorities, clear-cut majority that assured its national existence. Meanwhile, the capital city of Vienna provided them with a center of gravity, despite the occasional expression of antipathies towards it. Of course, a more or less pronounced regional patriotism (*Landesbewusstsein*) existed among these German Austrians, especially in Tyrol, Carinthia and Styria. Therefore, the political views remained different: predominantly conservative in Tyrol, more nationalistic in Carinthia and Styria, which were affected by the nationality question. Nevertheless, the friction between the Germans and the Slovenes did not reach the same intensity as it did in the Bohemian lands. But the anxiety of the German minority groups in Carniola (especially in the Gottschee), in the Littoral (especially in the cities of Trieste, Görz and Pola), in Galicia and in the Bukovina fostered centralistic tendencies everywhere.[3]

The Germans who lived in the Bohemian lands—Bohemia, Moravia, and Austrian Silesia—constituted strong minorities in Bohemia and Moravia and were the strongest of the three ethnic groups in Austrian Silesia. As the German Bohemians (*Deutsch-Böhmen*), German Moravians (*Deutsch-Mährer*), and German Silesians (*Deutsch-Schlesier*) represented the most modern and most wealthy German group in the whole monarchy, its group consciousness, and later its national identity, was extremely high. Therefore, until the mid-nineteenth century, the German milieu dominated also scholarship, technology, the arts and literature in the Bohemian lands. The "Czech world" was rather a "semiosphere," something "precultural" or "extracultural." The Czech language could serve an educated "cultured" person as a means of communication with a member of the "lower" classes of native speakers who did not know enough of the more prestigious German language. As the Germans held important positions in commerce, crafts and industry and played an important role in intellectual life, they refused to go along with efforts of some Bohemian and Moravian aristocrats and of some Czech intellectuals around the historian František Palacký to unify and attain a special position for their provinces with the idea of the Bohemian *Staatsrecht*. Provincial patriotism existed until the mid-nineteenth century, but its political importance declined continuously.[4]

The reform period under Maria Theresa and Joseph II anchored relatively fair and efficient bureaucratic traditions, German cultural traditions of its educated classes, the conjunction of manufacturing and agrarian zones, and the toleration of the Lutheran, Calvinist, Orthodox, and Jewish religious minorities. In 1762, the Austro-Bohemian lands counted seventy-two larger towns—but only Vienna and Prague as substantial cities. Hungary had only forty or so Royal Free Towns, with Pressburg (Pozsony, Bratislava) as the largest. In the bigger towns with a competition between the aristocracy, the richer burghers and some religious orders, the German language became more and more the means of communication between the monarchy's interlocking elites. Already by the mid-eighteenth century, the bulk of the Bohemian, Moravian and Silesian upper middle classes and almost the entire aristocracy, including the minority of Czech descent, had made German their first language. The same happened in the towns of Carniola and Lower Styria, as well as in some regions of upper and western Hungary, supported by Lutheran *lycea*.[5] One should not forget that since the 1760s the influence of the Saxon and Prussian Enlightenment increased, especially in nearby Bohemia. A secular-minded bourgeois intelligentsia was emerging in Vienna and Prague, in Pressburg and Buda. Joseph von Sonnenfels, son of a Jewish rabbi from Moravia, tended to take the bourgeois values of the German Enlightenment as the standard for a civil society; and the Transylvanian Saxon Ignaz Born promoted the foundation of the Learned Society in Prague. Habsburg enlightened absolutism even broadened the vision of many young Hungarian nobles, training them in the Theresianum or the Royal Hungarian Bodyguard in Vienna, and employing them on missions into the western centers of social and intellectual ferment.[6]

Under the influence of the Dutch Gerard van Swieten and Joseph von Sonnenfels, Queen Maria Theresa demanded that schools should produce good, loyal and civically useful "subjects." Therefore she instructed the former Silesian Abbot of Sagan (Žagań) Ignaz Felbiger to prescribe general regulations for German higher, middle, and elementary schools mandating obligatory schooling of all male inhabitants and the separation of schools from the church. Felbiger worked out blueprints for the establishment of a primary school (*Trivialschule*) in every village, with grammar schools (*Hauptschulen*) in the larger centers and a sufficient number of training colleges (*Normalschulen*). The *Allgemeine Schulordnung* for the Austrian and Bohemian lands in 1774 also made German an obligatory subject in all elementary schools in Czech and "Illyrian" (e.g., South Slavonic) districts (including the imperial Military Border) as well as the language of instruction in the *gymnasia;* nevertheless, Czech was allowed in four of the sixteen Bohemian *gymnasia.* On the other hand, when Felbiger's guidelines were applied to Hungary in 1777, the *Ratio educationis* provided that elementary education should be given in the pupil's mother tongue—and most interestingly, the orders gave Hungarian no preference over the six other languages (German, Slovak, Croat, Ruthene, "Illyrian" and "Wallachian") which they described as current in Hungary. But they still declared it especially important that every elementary schoolchild should be taught German, and—while the basic language of instruction in the *gymnasia* maintained Latin—the greatest weight was to be attached to the teaching of German in these higher establishments too. Finally, the *Ratio* expressed the hope that this would gradually lead to German developing "as the Court hand long wished" into the "national language" of Hungary.[7]

The German language was also introduced at the universities of Prague, Pest and Lemberg (Lwów, L'viv), as well as in the Mining Academy (*Bergakademie*) at Schemnitz, founded in 1762/1770. After the dissolution of the Jesuit order in 1773, the university of Tyrnau (Nagyszombat, Trnava) was taken under state supervision and was moved first to Buda in 1777 and then to Pest in 1784. Until 1773, Prague University was located in the *Clementinum* with the faculties of philosophy and theology in Jesuit hands, and in the *Carolinum* with the faculties of law and medicine, where the professors were laymen. Then all faculties became state establishments, and in 1784, a new syllabus was introduced into all faculties, with German replacing Latin as the language of instruction.[8]

Of course, the goal of spreading the German language all over the Habsburg Monarchy was an "overstretch," when we calculate that in the year of Maria Theresa's death (1780), the roughly 24 million inhabitants were divided between 5.8 million Germans, 3.35 million Magyars, 2.55 million Czechs, 2 million Flemish and Walloons, 1.8 million Ruthenes, 1.6 million Romanians, 1.6 million Italians, 1.2 million Slovaks, 1.1 million Poles, 950,000 Croats, 900,000 Slovenes, 650,000 Serbs, 400,000 Jews, 150,000 Gypsies, and a small number of Armenians, Ladins, Bulgars, etc. Nevertheless, treating the Austro-Bohemian and Hungarian lands as one united state (*Gesamtstaat*), Emperor Joseph II made German the official language of the bureaucracy in 1784. Few realized it at the time, but a fateful link had been forged between Germanization and centralization. In the Bohemian lands, the reaction of some estates and burghers to this decree led to the emergence of a defensive component in Bohemian-Czech patriotism, which laid stress on historical, constitutional, and cultural traditions. Therefore, they began to emphasize elements of their enlightened "territorial patriotism" (*Landespatriotismus*) and especially the emblematic of Czech language.[9] The reaction in Hungary was violent: county officials declared that they were incapable of learning German within three years; the Hungarian nobility began systematically to patronize Hungarian literature; the counties protested against a national census in the form of a German conscription, which the nobility suspected as a precursor to the lifting of its tax exemption. Virtually every county remonstrated, with resistance increasing when the emperor ordered a new administrative division of Hungary in ten districts. While the completion of the census was an apparent success for Joseph II, it was not possible to put the language decree into practice. On the contrary, it gave impetus to the unfolding movement for the modernization and embellishment of the Hungarian language. In February 1789, Joseph II imposed a uniform tax on all landed property in the country: even nobles would have to pay 12.25% of their income from the land into the treasury. But in the same year, when Joseph II needed recruits and supplies for a new war against the Ottomans, the Hungarian nobles, their peasants, and the intelligentsia revolted. In January 1790, the disillusioned and dangerously ill emperor revoked most of his reforms.[10]

Nevertheless, when Emperor Leopold II made some compromises with the nobility in Hungary, Bohemia and Austria, "the Habsburg dynasty had fulfilled with distinction at least three missions in central and eastern Europe: It had reconverted southern Germany to Roman Catholicism, it had withstood the Ottoman Turks, and it had disseminated western civilization deep into the Balkans. Failure to renew any of these missions after 1800 threatened survival at the very time when success at westernizing subject peoples was turning some of them into bitter opponents." And many "Josephists"—including professors, bureaucrats, statisticians, lawyers, economic theorists and politicians—maintained and started to work in new functions and committees.[11]

## The French and German Challenges

Once the French Revolution started to equate "people" with "nation" and "state" and to teach that sovereignty rested with the community of citizens, the Habsburg Empire was confronted with the fundamental question of whether to raise a new state nationalism or to promote new ethnic nationalisms. Johann Gottfried Herder's *Ideen zur Geschichte der Philosophie der Menschheit* (1784) prompted many Slavonic scholars, poets, artists, and politicians to construct the people (*Volk*) as the most important collectivity and to build a new national self-consciousness anchored in history, language, folklore, and religions of their peoples. Although nations were not natural phenomena, rather products and projections of national self-confidence that had been partly developed from traditions since the Middle Ages and partly invented from enlightened intellectuals, Herder's ideas cast the mold for the creation of national identities for all peoples in east central and southeastern Europe. Therefore, since the failure of Joseph II it was more and more questionable whether the German-oriented central dynastic, administrative, economic, and cultural institutions of the Habsburg Empire would be able to assimilate the weaker, linguistic-ethnic non-German groups into a socially formed and structured "nation-state" with the language of the ruling social elite—like in France or in the United Kingdom.[12]

As the French raised citizen armies unprecedented in size and dedication that generated a new national energy and political will, the beheaded Queen Marie Antoinette's nephew Archduke Charles wrote a treatise entitled "On War against the New Franks" while his elder brother, Emperor Francis II, launched repressive policies against writers, professors, officers, civil servants, businessmen, and against the clubs, secret societies, and even some of the religious organizations to which they belonged. When a former professor of natural history at the University of Lemberg and former spy in Leopold's secret police, Ignác Martinovics, organized two secret societies in Pest and Buda at the end of July 1794, fifty-three "Jacobins" were arrested and accused of high treason. Seven ringleaders were executed a year later, while many others were sentenced to imprisonment in the notorious dungeons of Kufstein, Spielberg and Munkács (Mukačeve). The "Franciscan repression" thereby provided the basis for the stereotype of a reactionary Austria that alienated many progressive Germans, both inside and outside the monarchy.[13]

On 10 August 1804, three months after Napoleon's self-proclamation as "Hereditary Emperor of the French" in May 1804, Francis declared himself to be "Hereditary Emperor of Austria," meaning the Austrian lands, the Bohemian lands, Hungary, and Galicia, using the Bohemian crown crafted two centuries earlier for Emperor Rudolf II. Once Napoleon created the Confederation of the Rhine and issued an ultimatum to Francis, the herald of the "Holy Roman Empire of the German Nation" read a proclamation on 6 August 1806 in Vienna announcing that Francis II, "by God's grace elected Roman Emperor, for all times guardian of the *Reich*, Hereditary Emperor of Austria, King in the Germanies," had laid down his imperial crown and released the members of the *Reich* from their constitutional obligations. Napoleon's reorganization of central Europe permanently transformed German and Austrian politics. Many German intellectuals like the Prussians Friedrich Gentz and Adam Müller, and the Hannoverans August Wilhelm and Friedrich Schlegel moved to Vienna and formulated the new state ideology of the "patriarchalic Politeia Austria." Archduke Charles tried to mobilize the Germans in 1809, exclaiming that "We are fighting for the autonomy of the Austrian monarchy, in order to recreate Germany's independence and national honor." Yet only the Tyrolean innkeeper Andreas Hofer responded with an uprising against the French and the Bavarians. And when the young German national movement under the spiritual guidance of Johann Gottlob Fichte, Ernst Moritz Arndt, and

Friedrich Jahn imprinted the ideal of a German nation-state on its banners, Austria could not follow this decidedly powerful trend, because a national counter-movement of Magyars, Poles, and Italians had already begun to develop.[14]

At this point, the paths of Austria and Germany diverged. While State Chancellor Clemens Lothar Prince Metternich never accepted Herder's idea of the "nation," even less its wider political implications, Baron Carl vom und zum Stein, the chief minister in Prussia, considered himself a member of a "German people" (*Volk*). Wilhelm von Humboldt, the Prussian Minister and Envoy at the Congress of Vienna, was convinced that greater unity among Germans would certainly come: "It will never be possible to stop Germany from wanting to be One state and One nation." And his wife wrote at the same time: "Austria is so diversely and heterogeneously mixed in its strengths, in the nationalities of which it consists, that I would like to wager everything that it will cease to be a great German power before the end of this century. Evidently the national Germanity is still growing and Austria cannot keep up."[15]

Even as the "Holy Alliance" between Russia, Austria and Prussia demonstrated the fraternal solidarity of the peoples and rulers as the basis of both domestic and foreign policy, Prince Metternich had the reference to the solidarity of peoples erased from the text. Tsar Alexander I's ambivalent acknowledgment of the participation of the people on the one hand and the authority of the princes as representatives of the will of the people on the other hand made it easier for Metternich to transform the idea of the Holy Alliance, rooted in enlightened and liberal thinking, into a confirmation of the former absolute system of government. The "Concert of Powers"—Britain, Russia, Austria, Prussia and, after 1818, France once more—agreed upon the founding of a German Confederation. Of course, the areas of the Prussian East—East and West Prussia and Posen (Poznań)—belonged to it as little as Austrian Galicia, the kingdom of Hungary, the kingdom of Dalmatia-Croatia-Slavonia and the kingdom of Lombardo-Venetia. Nevertheless, not only were the Habsburgs' Austrian Hereditary Lands including the Slovene Carniola, the mainly Italian-speaking Littoral and Trentino absorbed but also the Bohemian lands with a majority of Czechs. Although the German Confederation had accommodated increasingly fewer of the current liberal and national aspirations since the reactionary turning point of 1819/20, in the age of an upwardly mobile bourgeoisie, industrialization and the national idea, the supranational Habsburg Empire could hardly solve its own problems or point out the way for Germany's future development.[16]

## State Nationalism and Ethnic Nationalisms in the Metternich System

In the new age of European nationalism, the Austrian Empire either had to build on its own (German-Austrian) base to create a strongly centralized "westernized" state that could reduce regional particularism and minority linguistic groups, or accept the empire's ethnic and cultural diversity and reconcile the differences between the diverse national cultures with the idea of a supranational monarchy. It was a fundamental weakness of the Habsburg Empire that only five of its twelve major peoples—the Magyars, Czechs, Croats, Slovaks, and Slovenes—lived exclusively within its borders, while a majority of the other seven—the Germans, Italians, Poles, Ruthenes/Ukrainians, Romanians, Serbs, and Jews—lived outside the monarchy. In 1837, the Habsburg Empire included not only 6.4 million Germans and 4.6 million Italians, but 14.8 million Slavs, 5.3 million Magyars, 1.6 million Romanians and 600,000 Jews. Since the early nineteenth century, the opposition of the "old and historic" nations—the Italian, Hungarian, Polish, Bohemian, and Croat nobility, as well as the Italian bourgeoisie—limited the political efforts of the governing "Austrian" elites to the imperial court. On the other hand, the absolutist reforms in education had already created a new Slavonic *Bildungsbürgertum* by the first half of the nineteenth century that fostered important linguistic and cultural activities even among "non-historic" ethnic groups that commenced a "maturation" process that ultimately coalesced into culturally and politically vigorous nations desiring to keep and strengthen their national individuality.[17]

Like the nation itself, the traditional social order was anything but stable. Thanks to the monarchy's parlous finances and slow pace of industrzialiation, its economy, towns and middle classes lagged behind those of western Europe, while perpetuating the long-lasting political and legal domination of the nobles, and unresolved peasant question. Otherwise, even the conservative forces of the Habsburg Empire were receptive to modern ideas, to English products and machines, to French—though, of course, not Jacobin—culture. By 1800, Vienna's 232,000 inhabitants still made it the largest city in central Europe, much larger than Buda-Pest and Prague, but also larger than Berlin (150,000) or Hamburg (100,000). The capital of the Austrian Empire—since 1816 concentrated in the "Privileged Austrian National Bank" after the four brothers Rothschild helped to stabilize the currency—was dominated by the Court, the aristocracy, the new German-dominated entrepreneurial elites (bankers, wholesalers, industrialists) as well as the German-dominated *Mittelstand* (Eduard von Bauernfeld): on the one hand the *Besitzbürgertum* of the manufacturers, merchants and economists, on the other hand the *Bildungsbürgertum* of the higher officials, professors, priests and artists. Out of a group of 242 Viennese entrepreneurs, 45 came from the "Old Reich" (König, Dreher, Thonet, Lohner), 21 from Switzerland (Geymüller), 14 from Italian lands, and 6 each from France and Britain. Given the social barriers erected by the aristocracy, bankers, entrepreneurs and high officials formed a "second society" that entered the estates of Lower Austria.[18]

Although the Metternich regime promoted the foundation of technical schools and colleges, as well as Vienna's Austrian Academy of Sciences (with forty Austrian Germans, Slavs, Italians, and Magyars as members), Viktor Baron Andrian-Werburg's influential *Österreich und dessen Zukunft* (1841) envisioned a process of dissolution amid the elites and lower classes of the various nationalities. Austria "signifies no solid *Volk,* no land, no nation." Andrian-Werburg believed that there was only one way out, and that was through the creation of a public spirit (*Gemeinsinn*). In Tyrol-Vorarlberg, Lower and Upper Austria and in the Bohemian lands, more than 95 percent of the children attended schools, against only 76 percent in Styria, 55 percent in Lombardy, one-third in Carinthia, Carniola and Venetia, and 14 percent in Galicia and Bukovina. Liberal aristocrats and burghers founded opinion-forming organizations like the *Juridisch-Politischer Leseverein.* Crop failures of 1846–47 and outbreaks of social unrest in cities and villages across the empire increased feelings of hopelessness and spiritual distress, with even Metternich predicting the onset of "fatal diseases." No less pessimistic was one of the champions of Magyar liberalism, Nicholas Baron Wesselényi. Although he was never able to overcome the constitutional biases of his class, he remained sensitive to the intricacies of the nationality question, predicting as early as 1842 that "Austria's existence can be maintained best by peace [but that] war, even a victorious war, may well annihilate her."[19]

## German Austrians between Frankfurt and Vienna 1848/49

In March 1848, almost no one in Europe expected Austria to assert itself against the combined onslaught of liberalism and nationalism. On Monday, 13 March, students, workers—and rowdies—marched in Vienna, the garrison intervened, the demonstrators demanded the dismissal of Metternich, and Emperor Ferdinand agreed. Outside the walls, in the city's crowded and depressed suburbs, workers and artisans settled old scores against unpopular landlords and factory owners, tax collectors and government officials. An imperial proclamation confirmed the abolition of censorship, the establishment of the National Guard and the convocation of representatives of all provincial Estates—with increased representation of the burghers.[20]

German liberals and radicals alike were convinced that the existing political order in central Europe was intolerable. Both groups believed that Metternich's Confederation was an inadequate foundation for German public life. But on the national question, the political opposition was divided. At the end of March, a so-called *Vorparlament* in Frankfurt am Main called for national elections on the basis of unified and unrestricted suffrage, and in the first half of May parliamentary elections were carried out in all 39 member-states of the German Confederation. On 18 May the 585 newly elected members were already convened in the Frankfurt *Paulskirche*, which would remain the site of their deliberations for most of the next eleven months. While the Constitutional Committee began its discussions of the basic rights such as national citizenship, civil equality, freedom of speech, and religious freedom, the plenum had to deal with the problems of German nationhood. Neither in Tyrol and Styria, nor in Bohemia nor in Moravia could clear national boundaries be drawn. The challenge from the German National Assembly in Frankfurt affected not only the German Austrians, but also the Czechs and Poles in the Bohemian lands, the

Slovenes in Interior Austria, and the Italians in the Littoral and Trentino. Many of their delegates followed the example of the Czech historian František Palacký, who rejected his invitation to the *Vorparlament*—"I am not a German, at least I do not feel myself to be such, I am a Bohemian of Slav race and have dedicated myself with my possessions and abilities to the service of my people for all time."[21] All told, seventy Austrian electoral districts, mostly in Bohemia, but also in Moravia, Lower Styria, Carniola, and Trentino, were not represented at Frankfurt, either because no elections were held there or because the elected delegate did not show up.[22]

Meanwhile, the German Bohemian towns between Karlsbad (Karlovy Vary) and Reichenberg (Liberec) elected the "hard core" of the Bohemian leftists, while the voters in Eger (Cheb), Rumburg (Rumburk), and Troppau (Opava) decided for "Black-Yellows" (*Schwarzgelbe*). Conservative delegates dominated in Alpine regions like Upper Austria and Styria, where six Graz University professors were elected. Laibach (Ljubljana) elected Anton Alexander Count Auersperg and the poet Anastasius Grün, Trieste sent Karl Ludwig Freiherr von Bruck, and Görz (Gorizia, Gorica), Adelsberg (Postojna), Gottschee (Kočevje), Rudolfswerth (Novo Mesto) and Stein (Kamnik) all elected German delegates.[23] The great majority of the German-Austrian members of the Frankfurt parliament did not anticipate that joining the nation would require that they abandon their old allegiances or give up their special position in the Habsburg Empire. But in the end, the German-Austrian delegates at Frankfurt had to decide between the Habsburg "Black-Yellow" (*Schwarz-Gelb*) or the German "Black-Red-Gold" (*Schwarz-Rot-Gold*). When in late October 1848 the plenum adopted articles of a draft constitution, which called for a nation composed exclusively of German states (although German princes might still rule non-German territories) the Schwarzenberg government in Vienna made clear that the Habsburg Monarchy would make no accommodations to German national aspirations, terming "the maintenance of Austria's political unity a German and European necessity." Whereas most of the 115 Austrian delegates had come to Frankfurt as *Großdeutsche*, they now returned home as *Großösterreicher*, where many now served as members of the newly elected Austrian *Reichstag*.[24]

Elections to a new Austrian *Reichstag* had already been announced in May and carried out in the second half of June. Of the 383 elected only 160 were "Germans" from the Austrian Empire, the others being Czechs, Poles, Ukrainians, Slovenes, Croats, Serbs, Italians, and Romanians. Among the German delegates representatives of the *Gesamtmonarchie* predominated, typically landowners, administrators, lawyers and peasants. When Archduke John opened the first Austrian parliament on 22 July 1848 in Vienna, the delegates quarreled immediately over a common language for negotiations. The majority were educated middle-class professionals who spoke German, but almost a quarter (94) were peasants, of whom some 30 were illiterates, including a dozen who did not understand German and were possibly visiting Vienna for the first time. In general, neither the Galician nor the Dalmatian delegates were familiar with German. After some debate, the *Reichstag* adjourned without making a decision.[25]

When it reconvened in November in the Moravian town of Kremsier (Kroměříž) to discuss a new constitution for the peoples of Austria, Prime Minister Felix Prince Schwarzenberg told the assembled delegates that he favored a settlement that would "unite all the lands and peoples of the monarchy into one great state." Discussions in the gorgeous Kremsier palace of the Olmütz (Olomouc) archbishop were dominated by the question of whether the monarchy should be a centralized state or federation. The Bohemian delegate from Saaz (Žatec), Ludwig Löhner, proposed five nation-states, while the Slovene Matija Kavčič proposed fourteen national units, and the Czech leader Palacký demanded that the monarchy be reconstituted on a very modern principle of nationality, that would divide it along ethnic-linguistic lines consisting of eight units divided between (1) Germans from the Austrian and Bohemian lands, (2) Czechs and Slovaks merged from the Czech parts of the Bohemian lands and Slovak Upper Hungary, (3) Poles from Galicia, combined with the Ukrainian parts of Bukovina and the Carpathian Rus', (4) Illyrians from Carniola and the Slovene parts of Styria, Carinthia, and the Littoral, (5) Italians from Lombardy, Venice, Trentino, and the Italian parts of the Littoral, (6) South Slavs from Dalmatia, Croatia-Slavonia, and Vojvodina, (7) Magyars from central Hungary, and (8) Romanians from eastern Hungary (including Transylvania) and Bukovina). In the end, both the Hungarians and the German Tyroleans, Styrians and Carinthians refused to consider partition-ing their historic crown lands, while the Poles and Ukrainians struggled over eastern Galicia. A large majority emerged in favor of retaining the existing "historic units" and accepted only the proposal of Kajetan Mayer, a German lawyer from Brünn (Brno), that the larger crownlands should be subdivided into *Kreise*, delimited on an ethnic basis.[26]

The national political strategy of the Czechs, Slovaks, Ukrainians, Slovenes, and Croats was based on the conviction, known as Austroslavism, that the Austrian Empire was a suitable system for small nations situated between Germany and Russia—provided that the Habsburg Monarchy was radically restructured along federal lines. Alas, the 1848/49 revolutions demonstrated the mutual incompatibility of the various central European nationalist movements: While the German Bohemians and Moravians sent delegates to Frankfurt, the Czechs boycotted and organized a Slavic congress in Prague; the Slovenes demanded a "United Slovenia," while the German Styrians and Carinthians emphasized the unity of Interior Austria, and the Italians proclaimed autonomy for Trieste, Gorizia, Istria, and Dalmatia; last but not least, the Croatian *Sabor* strove for exactly the same rights and privileges that the Hungarian parliament had wrested from King Ferdinand. And while their representatives traded demands, the people of the Habsburg Empire were massacring one another for the first time in their common history in the name of nationality, especially in southern Hungary and Transylvania. Hence it was understandable that Interior Minister

Philipp Count Stadion announced at the beginning of March 1849 the dissolution of the Kremsier parliament and the promulgation of a territorially comprehensive and strongly centralist constitutional *octroi,* albeit one that postulated equal rights for all nationalities.[27]

## Neo-Absolutist Reaction and Liberal Reform

Prime Minister Schwarzenberg and his minister of trade Karl Ludwig Freiherr von Bruck believed that the Habsburg Empire, strengthened by a German-speaking central administration, would be able to regain its European position. They abolished the internal customs barrier with Hungary and planned to create a central European economic entity, hoping this plan would attract not only the Germans in the Austrian Empire but also those living beyond its borders, creating an empire with seventy million inhabitants. But France and Russia resisted, while Prussia promoted the "German Customs Union" (*Deutscher Zollverein*). By 1842 the *Zollverein*'s architect, Friedrich List, had already recognized the profitable exchange of industrial and agricultural products between western and east central Europe and for that reason demanded a central European economic unit under German hegemony extending as far as the Black Sea. Chancellor Metternich had recognized early on the danger of such a development for Austria's position in Germany, but by 1850 not only had the north German states spoken out against Austrian membership of the Customs Union, but also a majority of Austrian industrialists from Lower Austria, Bohemia, Moravia, Styria and Carinthia. Thus Bruck's appeal to the "moral weight of an alliance of seventy million people" was equally useless.[28] The Austrian politics in the age of neo-absolutism stood in contrast to the prevailing *Zeitgeist.* The internal policy of all-powerful Interior Minister Alexander Bach was characterized by unrestrained absolutism and empire-wide centralization, which never called into session the legislature and abolished the self-governing institutions of the provinces and municipalities that had been introduced in 1848. But

> the centralizing, Germanising new Austria was, at the same time, a civic state, which retained the basic achievements of the bourgeois revolution: the freeing of the serfs, the legal equality of citizens, and proportional taxation. The government placed middle-class specialists into offices previously occupied by elected officials and attempted to separate consistently administrative and judicial functions.[29]

In 1855, Bohemian, Austrian and Hungarian princes and counts, as well as Jewish financiers and German industrialists, founded the famous *Credit-Anstalt für Handel und Gewerbe.* Moreover, since the 1840s a railway network was built radiating outward from Vienna and connecting Brünn in 1841, Prague in 1845, Cracow in 1848 (*Nordbahn*), Pest in 1850 (*Ostbahn*), Graz in 1854, Trieste in 1857 (*Südbahn*), Innsbruck in 1858 (*Westbahn*), Lemberg in 1861, and Zagreb in 1862. Some decades after István Count Széchenyi had pleaded for railway development, a Hungarian network radiating outward from Budapest was created too. But just as fiscal pressure generated by the Crimean War obliged the government to sell the state railways to a French bank, the additional burden of the Italian war in 1859 ruined the imperial fisc. Nevertheless, from the 1860s onward masses of people were transported by railroad, and while the national capital and political energy radiated outward from Vienna and Buda-Pest, products flowed inward from a "tributary" countryside.[30]

With a population of more than 75 percent Roman and Greek Catholics, the Habsburg lands constituted the largest Catholic realm in Europe. During the era of neo-absolutism, disputes over church policy centered around the Concordat of November 1855, which had placed all marriages under the jurisdiction of canon law and had given the church supervision over elementary schools. The Austrian May laws of 1868 restricted canon law to marriage between Catholics, while withdrawing marriage disputes from ecclesiastical courts. Although nearly all elementary schools were placed now under state direction, the state paid priests to dispense religious instruction in the schools. Parish priests continued to be appointed by local secular authorities, while bishops were appointed by the emperor and confirmed by the Holy See. On 30 July 1870 Austria-Hungary declared the Concordat to have lapsed on the grounds that the Declaration of Papal Infallibility had altered the character of the contracting party. In May 1874, the Concordat was formally replaced by legislation giving the Roman Catholic Church privileged but not monopolistic status.[31]

By 1859 the state's fiscal collapse and defeat at Solferino had emboldened the German bourgeoisie and *Bildungsbürgertum* to take the lead in demanding political participation. Two years later the February Patent created a new constitution with the establishment of a two-chamber parliament and new diets in the crownlands that favored the German *Bürgertum* in the second and the third curia. Prime Minister Anton Schmerling wanted to build a centralized constitutional monarchy under German-Austrian leadership; but the Hungarians continued to reject the idea of a centralized state. Liberal notions of public virtue and visions of economic development began to dominate the German-Austrian, Czech, Magyar, and Italian public. The growth of urban population intensified the diversity of the monarchy's ethnic structure, especially in Vienna, but also in Buda-Pest, Prague and Trieste.[32]

In 1866 Emperor Francis Joseph I still ruled over 34 million subjects, nearly twice the 19 millions governed by his Prussian rival, King William I. Yet it was known that "the Prussians usually mobilized and utilized their military and fiscal resources more efficiently, ruthlessly and intelligently than the Austrians."[33] Sharpened by Prussian Prime Minister Otto Prince Bismarck, the distrust and antagonism between the Habsburg and Hohenzollern dynasties reached the final round of their long "struggle for supremacy in Germany." On 3 July 1866, at the Bohemian fortress Königgrätz (Hradec Králové) a combination of better logistics, more modern weapons and superior generalship decided a battle of about 440,000 men in favor of Prussia. But the problem of national identity, which had become so pressing for German-Austrian intellectuals since the beginning of the nineteenth century, did not go away. "You claim that you have founded a *Reich*," the poet Franz Grillparzer berated Bismarck, "but all you have done is to destroy a *Volk*." Writing in 1896 Max Weber judged that "from Bismarck's point of view, dynastic Austria [was] an institution which sacrificed the membership of ten million Germans to the [Habsburg] Empire, in order to politically isolate thirty million non-Germans."[34]

## The Preponderance of the Germans in Cisleithania

The central European turning points of 1866 and 1871 are not always clearly distinguished from each other in our historical memory. Therefore it is difficult to say whether it was Königgrätz or Sedan that played the more decisive role in the fall of the Imperial Austrian and Greater German federal system of rule and the rise of Prussian and Little German predominance. As early as 1871 the Viennese government envisaged a dominant central European bloc in cooperation with Prussia-Germany and hoped that Bismarck would promote its interests in the Balkans. Although in 1878 the majority of Czechs, Poles, Slovaks and South Slavs greeted the occupation of Bosnia and Herzegovina as a means of strengthening the Slav population in the Dual Monarchy, the commitment to the German *Reich* in foreign policy expressed in the "Dual Alliance" (*Zweibund*) displeased above all the Czechs, even though most of their foreign trade was shipped to Hamburg via the Elbe.[35]

When Emperor-King Francis Joseph I tried to reach a compromise with the representatives of the liberal Hungarian nobility, Ferenc Deák and Gyula Count Andrássy, the German-Austrian liberal bourgeoisie began to understand that the conditions prevailing in the other half of the empire were of importance for them too. The new Habsburg foreign minister and former Saxon prime minister Friedrich Ferdinand Count Beust was convinced that the Habsburg Empire's great power position, which the emperor regarded as the *raison d'être* of its existence, could be only guaranteed by dualism, with its acknowledgment of German and Magyar hegemony against Panslavism. So the Compromise (*Ausgleich*) of 1867 became the basic law of a new country, the "Austro-Hungarian Monarchy." But it was not only a compromise between the newly crowned King and the Hungarian nation but also a power-sharing arrangement between the liberal Hungarian nobility and the German-Austrian liberal bourgeoisie, for the latter recognized that the dualism guaranteed them a modern constitution, as well as a centralized, German-dominated Austrian half of the monarchy in the face of a "real possibility of provincial or national federalism."[36]

The adoption of the December constitution in 1867 roughly coincided with the Austrian administration's transition from Bach's absolutism to a new era of mild liberalism. In contrast to the famous Austrian article XIX/1867, which endowed equal rights for all nationalities (*Volksstämme*), the Hungarian Nationality Law XLIV/1868 employed the French nation-state model in recognizing only one "nation," the

Hungarian, but withheld larger collective rights or political institutions from the "nationalities." While in Cisleithania (*Die im Reichsrate vertretenen Königreiche und Länder*) no state language was fixed and each crownland maintained its *Landessprachen* and *landesübliche Sprachen*, Hungarian became the state language in Transleithania to be used in the parliament, the courts, and higher education. In principle, other languages were admissible in churches, county and municipal governments, as well as in primary and secondary schools. The Budapest government's only important concession to national interests was the Hungarian-Croatian Compromise of 1868, "an agreement unlike the Austro-Hungarian Compromise concluded not between political equals but unequals." In its interpretation by the Vienna government, the semi-autonomy granted to the (Polish) Galician administration in 1868 was less restrictive than the provisions of the Hungarian-Croatian Compromise. However, the different constitutional laws made an empire-wide reform of the nationality problems almost impossible.[37]

Nevertheless, the new double state retained the most important role in the "modernization" of the national societies. In 1868/69, the liberal Austrian government of "Carlos" Prince Auersperg passed laws on universal military service, compulsory school attendance, and the status of the Roman Catholic Church. The army became a melting pot of nationalities, toward which officers and men felt a *Schwarz-Gelb* loyalty transcending national origin. An eighty-word German vocabulary constituted the language of command (*Kommandosprache*), although many officers spoke the different vernaculars of their soldiers. Nevertheless, as late as 1910 the national differentiation of the active officer corps of the imperial and royal (*k.u.k.*) army showed 78.7% Germans (including the majority of the Jews), and only 9.3% Magyars, 4.8% Czechs, 2.5% Poles, 2.4% Croats and Serbs, 0.9% Romanians, 0.7% Italians, 0.5% Slovenes, and 0.2% Ukrainians. The percentage of reservists with the *Matura* fell among the Germans (60.2%), Croats, Serbs, and Slovenes (2.1%), Romanians (0.6%) and Italians (0.5%), while it increased among Magyars (23.7%), Czechs and Slovaks (9.8%), and Poles and Ukrainians (3.1%). On the other hand, the German percentage of all the soldiers in 1910 amounted to only 25.2%, compared to Magyars (23.1%), Czechs (12.9%), Serbo-Croats (9.0%), Poles (7.9%), Ukrainians (7.6%), Romanians (7.0%), Slovaks (3.6%), Slovenes (2.4%), and Italians (1.3%).[38]

Ostensibly the bureaucracy's mission was to extend uniformity throughout the empire, westernizing the non-German peoples and regimenting everyone to obey edicts of the crown. The complex of constitutional laws of December 1867, valid in the Austrian half of the monarchy, ensured a wide range of civil and human rights and liberties, including the right to unhampered national and linguistic development. Emblems of uniformity blanketed the empire: every district captainship, courthouse, post office, and railroad station bore a yellow shield with a double-headed eagle. Friedrich Kleinwaechter, two times rector of the university of Czernowitz (Cernăuţi, Černivci) in Bukovina and one of the best analysts of the imperial administration, described the ideal of an Austrian official as "a man who had a perfect command of the German language but having no kind of national consciousness, not even a German if he happened to be a German; a man who was devoted to the dynasty as a blind instrument without a semblance of criticism."[39]

When Austria modernized its secondary and higher education after 1848 (with universities, technical colleges, classical *gymnasia*, *Realschulen*, and *Realgymnasia*), as well as the Benedictine, Piarist and Jesuit *gymnasia*, enrollments grew remarkably and expansion paralleled developments in much of western Europe. German speakers owed their continuing overrepresentation among students in higher education to their longstanding social, economic, and political advantages over the other ethnic groups. Nonetheless, enrollments among German-speaking peasant and craft families in the Alpine provinces were limited by slower economic transformation, the survival of traditional values, and greater distances to educational institutions than for residents of Lower Austria, or the Bohemian crown lands. On the other hand, the German-speaking students (including Jews) could study at the universities of Vienna, Graz, Innsbruck, Prague, and Czernowitz, while the Czech language was used at the Czech part of the Charles University (since 1882), Polish at the universities of Cracow and Lemberg, and Romanian at the faculty of theology in Czernowitz. After 1900, there were also seven Austrian technical colleges in Vienna, Prague (Czech and German), Brünn (Czech and German), Graz and Lemberg (Polish). Whereas instruction in Pest, Klausenburg (Kolozsvár, Cluj), Debrecen and Pressburg was in Magyar, while Zagreb employed Croatian, neither Italians, Slovenes, Serbs, Slovaks nor Ukrainians had the possibility of studying in their language. The Italians demanded a university in Trieste, as did the Slovenes in Ljubljana, and the Ukrainians in L'viv, but the German-Austrian and Polish-Austrian authorities rejected such demands, although the Italians and Ukrainians got some chairs at Innsbruck and Lemberg after prolonged debate. Therefore, the Italian, Serbian, Romanian and Ukrainian youth studied more and more abroad, strengthening the irredentist movements.[40] Having achieved nearly complete religious equality in the 1860s, members of Austria's German-speaking Jewish and Lutheran religious minorities looked to secondary and higher education as a means of social advancement. To a great extent both groups had survived by finding various economic niches, whether in petty commerce, services, and some minor crafts for Jews, or in craft production, entrepreneurial functions, and farming in isolated districts for the small Lutheran population. Now the Jewish youth flocked to secondary schools (like the Vienna and Prague *Akademisches Gymnasium*) and higher education in such numbers that they were significantly overrepresented relative to their share of the total population throughout the pre-World War I era; by 1914, they accounted for 41 percent of medical and 26 percent of law students of the University of Vienna. The Protestants' historic experience also motivated them to use education to achieve greater economic and social security. Already in 1850, the government recognized the Protestant theological institute in Vienna as an independent faculty in a demonstration of tolerance for religious minorities. By the end of the decade Lutherans had a share of university and technical college enrollments between two and three times larger than their proportion of the total population, and they continued to be overrepresented in higher education throughout the late nineteenth century.[41]

David Good calculated the levels and growth rates of per capita income in twenty-two regions of the Habsburg Empire between 1870 and 1910 and presented some surprising results. Not surprisingly Lower Austria (including Vienna) enjoyed the highest income level in 1870 ($1,382), followed by Bohemia, Silesia, Salzburg, Moravia, the Littoral (with Trieste), Upper Austria, Tyrol/Vorarlberg, and Carinthia. Therefore, income in most of the Austro-Bohemian lands exceeded that of the top Hungarian region, Danube-Tisza (with Pest), in tenth place with $640 income per capita. Until 1910 Lower Austria (now with $2,290 income per capita), Bohemia, Silesia, and Salzburg held their places, but the Danube-Tisza region ($1,506) rose to fifth place, followed by the Littoral and Moravia. No doubt, the German Austrians held the best economic positions and, next to the Italians, were the highest per capita taxpayers. Just as British, Dutch, French, Swiss, western German, and Italian capitalist pioneers got the industrialization process off to a good start in the monarchy, so German-Austrian entrepreneurs, engineers, and technicians did their share to put this process in motion in non-German areas. Although the Habsburg Empire grew more rapidly in the late nineteenth century than most European economies, including even Germany, its Alpine lands showed lower growth rates than central Hungary. But the southern and eastern borderlands remained the poorest, particularly those inhabited by Croats, Serbs, Ukrainians, and Romanians.[42] That much of the capital invested in Hungary came from German-Austrian and other non-Hungarian investors can be seen from the structure of Hungary's national debt. On the eve of World War I nearly 8.4 billion Austro-Hungarian crowns, or about 55 percent of this debt, was in "foreign" hands, including 4.7 billion crowns from Cisleithania. In fact, Austria itself was a debtor country that borrowed money not only to lend it at a higher interest rate in Hungary, but also to make use of its better credit rating abroad to help meet its junior partner's need for capital.[43]

## Between Challenge and Power-Sharing

The Compromise of 1867 had given the German-Austrians preponderance in Cisleithania and secured them socioeconomic preponderance, intellectual leadership, and the majority of diplomatic, administrative and army positions. Yet between 1867 and 1910 the German-speaking middle and upper strata in both Hungary and Austria's Slavic territories lost its dominance due to a combination of emigration and the natural transformation from a society of ranks and orders to a modern class structure. In Prague, Pilsen (Plzeň) and Budweis (České Budějovice), Budapest and Fünfkirchen (Pécs), Güns (Kőszeg) and Wieselburg (Moson), Tyrnau (Trnava) and Kremnitz (Kremnica), Kronstadt (Braşov) and Bistritz (Bistriţa), Esseg (Osijek), Semlin (Zemun) and Pantschowa (Pančevo), Laibach (Ljubljana) and Cilli (Celje), the German-speaking urban elites (*Besitz- und Bildungsbürgertum*) were challenged by the new mass politics of the Czech, Magyar, Slovak, Romanian, Serbian, Croatian or Slovene national movements. The perceived threat from such formerly subordinated groups prompted them to convert their purely status-group identities into a new ethnic solidarity, creating networks of voluntary associations (*Turnvereine, Schulvereine*, etc.). Even after the ethnic differentiation and separation, most Germans cultivated a self-image as a property-holding and cultural elite with a strong belief in German superiority over the Czechs, Slovaks, Romanians, Ukrainians, and South Slavs. Fortunately, ethnic differences did not cut off all interactions in private affairs. Migration and social mobility made it impossible for any modern urban minority to remain socially and economically homogeneous.[44] In the 1880s, the Slavophilic policies of Eduard Count Taaffe's conservative government transformed the Czech campaign against dualism into advocacy of the Austrian state. Realizing that there was no immediate prospect for achieving their maximalist State Rights Program, Czech policy focused on more readily attainable demands for placing of the German and Czech languages on equal official footing. Like the Prague Polytechnic in 1869, Prague's Charles University was divided in 1882 into two separate Czech and German branches, while several dozen Czech *gymnasia* and modern technical and trade schools were founded. In 1880, the Czech language became co-equal with German as the language of "external" communication (*äußere Amtssprache*) in Bohemia and Moravia between bureaucrats and citizens. Once the Czechs had won control of the Bohemian diet in 1883, German-Bohemians expressed a new fear of Czechization by demanding a separate German-speaking borderland territory. Indeed, when the Czechs gained the upper hand in Prague in the 1860s, the loss of a central base placed the Bohemian-Germans at a real disadvantage. Many of them left for Vienna, where a good many obtained positions in government, education, or professional services. The move only reinforced the Bohemian-Germans' affinity for centralization. By contrast, the "Young Czech" movement demanded that Bohemia should be all Czech. In 1897, the Czechs thought they had achieved a breakthrough when Prime Minister Kasimir Count Badeni put their language on an equal plane with German in "internal" communications with and among public officials in Bohemia and Moravia and between Bohemian and Moravian officials and Vienna; as a result, all civil servants were required to know Czech as well as German within three years. In effect, this would have meant hiring almost exclusively Czechs, who were the only Bohemians likely to be fluent in both the provincial languages.[45]

After these concessions had been retracted in the face of German disruption of the Austrian parliament and violent demonstrations in the Bohemian and Austrian lands, Czech-German relations were subject to constant conflicts that defied all attempts at compromise. The fundamental positions of both national groups now became non-negotiable as each side engaged in a kind of a bureaucratic and psychological guerrilla warfare for minimal gains along the extended, and often hardly recognizable, linguistic boundaries. Just as Czech officials could not be prevented from using their native tongue, German-Bohemians could not be prevented from ignoring orders from Prague in their home districts. In 1913 negotiations on a Bohemian compromise failed once more, even as national compromises were achieved in Moravia (1905), Bukovina (1910), Galicia (1914), and the Bohemian city of Budweis (1914).[46]

Surprisingly the Austrian parliament was able to agree on universal suffrage law in 1906 that established five curias with 516 single-deputy electoral districts, while respecting the interests of tax payers, the national majority and the population at large. The ensuing May 1907 elections brought 232 German, 108 Czech, 79 Polish, 32 Ukrainian, 24 Slovene, 19 Italian, 11 Croat, 5 Romanian, 4 Zionist, and 2 Serb members into parliament. The *Reichsrat's* Lower House was dominated by five blocks, each numbering between 70 and 100 representatives: the German Clericals and Christian Socials, the German Liberals and Nationalist groups, the Czech parties, the Polish Club, and the Social Democrats. The German deputies were further differentiated between the middle classes and the workers. While the Christian Social Karl Lueger explicitly argued that the most powerful contribution Vienna made to German culture was its capacity to nurture voluntary assimilation (especially of hundreds of thousands of Czechs and Jews), German urban voters in most provincial towns voted for one of the anti-clerical liberal and nationalist groups. While the German *Nationalverband* won the parliamentary elections in 1911, the Christian Socials lost Vienna after the death of Lueger, as did the Social Democrats and their Austro-Marxist *Kulturkampf* in the Austrian provinces.[47]

By contrast, a "Central European Economic Association" (*Mitteleuropäischer Wirtschaftsverein*) had already been founded in Berlin in 1904, with the purpose of paving the way for the economic integration of Germany, Austria-Hungary and, perhaps, Switzerland, Belgium and the Netherlands. By 1912 the German-Bohemian newspaper *Deutsche Arbeit* noted that "The watchword 'Central Europe for German-dom' must become the lode star of Germany's overall policy." No matter how much these plans were influenced by Germany's aspirations for great power status or even by the "bid for world power," the fact remains that they were not devoid of economic rationale. Since the last decades of the nineteenth century a rapidly industrializing Germany had experienced a dramatically increased demand for food and raw materials that sucked in exports from the monarchy's Polish, Hungarian, Romanian and South Slav territories. Meanwhile, capital flowed in the other direction from Germany and the Austrian-Bohemian lands to east central and southeast Europe. Therefore, at the beginning of World War I, German and German-Austrian economic circles discussed economic plans for a stronger cooperation of Germany and Austria-Hungary within *Mitteleuropa*.[48]

# Assimilation and Integration of the Germans in Hungary

After several migrations during the Middle Ages and the eighteenth century, Germans lived in ten different parts of the Kingdom of Hungary:

- the western counties of Pozsony, Moson, Sopron and Vas;
- Pest-Pilis-Solt-Kiskun, Esztergom, Komárom and Fejér counties, as well as the twin cities of Buda and Pest;
- Veszprém county with the Bakony woods;
- the southwestern counties of Tolna, Somogy and Baranya, the so-called Swabian Turkey;
- the southern counties of Bács-Bodrog, the so-called Batschka/ Bácska/Bačka; Torontál, Temes and Krassó-Szörény, the so-called Banat/Bánát; and Arad;
- the Croatian counties of Virovitica and Srijem/Srem;
- the Transylvanian counties of Szeben, Alsó-Fehér, Kis-Küküllő, Nagy-Küküllő, Brassó, Maros-Torda, Kolozs and Besztercze-Naszód;
- the northeastern counties of Máramaros, Szatmár, Ugocsa and Bereg;
- the eastern Slovak counties of Szepes and Sáros, the so-called Zips;
- the central Slovak counties of Turócz, Nyitra and Bars.[49]

The Germans' ancestors had migrated from different regions in Germany and Austria. Medieval Hungarian kings had invited "Bavarians" (*Heanzen, Bohnenzüchter*) to settle along the kingdom's western rim and in the Slovak *Hauerland*, as well as "Saxons" to settle in the Zips (*Zipser Sachsen*) and Transylvania (*Siebenbürger Sachsen*). Since the late seventeenth century, Habsburg monarchs Leopold I, Charles VI, Maria Theresa, and Joseph II, as well as some Hungarian aristocrats, had brought "Swabians" first to the counties of Transdanubia (*Donaubaiern*) and Szatmár (*Sathmarer Schwaben*), then to "Swabian Turkey" (mostly from Hesse and Fulda), and last but not least to the Batschka (*Batschkaer Schwaben*) and Banat (*Banater Schwaben*). There were significant differences in dialect, social class and confession between the "Bavarians," "Saxons" and "Swabians," with the great majority of the "Bavarians" and "Swabians" being Catholic, while almost all "Saxons" were Lutherans. Therefore, it was not possible to develop a common consciousness of Germanity and to build up a common national group. Nevertheless, the more educated and socially sophisticated Hungarian-Germans typically maintained contact with the Germans in the Austrian lands or even in Germany.[50] Although no exact data are available of the ethnic and linguistic distribution at the end of the eighteenth century, ethnic relations can nevertheless be traced from a register ordered by Queen Maria Theresa in 1772–73 that recorded the confession and language spoken by the population. In 44 counties and districts of Hungary proper (without Transylvania, the Partium, Croatia, the Military Frontier and the Eastern Banat) there were 8,920 settlements (among them 3,507 Magyar, 2,563 Slovak, 802 Romanian, 699 Ruthene, 637 German, 275 Croatian, 144 Slovene, 99 Serb, 24 Polish, 1 Bulgarian and 1 Czech) as well as 62 ethnically mixed communities (20 Magyar-German, 14 German-Serbian, 6 Slovak-German, 6 German-Ruthene, 11 Magyar-German-Serb, 3 Magyar-German-Slovak, 1 Magyar-German-Croat and 1 Slovak-German-Serb.[51]

In the Reform Era, Elek Fényes investigated the distribution of the population by mother tongue and nationality recorded in county and diocesan registers. From a total of 12,880,406 inhabitants Fényes calculated a total of 4,812,759 Magyars (37.36%), 2,202,542 Romanians (17.10%), 1,687,256 Slovaks (13.10%) and 1,273,677 Germans (9.89%). This data coincided more or less with the Austrian census in 1850, but the figure for the Germans increased to 1,356,652 (10.28%), with 756,420 Germans living in Hungary proper (9.62%), 335,080 in the Serbian Vojvodina (23.49%), 219,374 in Transylvania (10.58%), 37,875 in the Military Frontier, and 7,903 in Croatia-Slavonia. Because we have no official data on ethnic distribution for the next thirty years, the census of 1850 (as rectified by the head of the Office for Statistics in Vienna, Karl von Czoernig) remained the most important for the first decades of modernization.[52]

After 1830, the political leadership of the Hungarian nation passed from the old aristocracy—especially the families Andrássy, Apponyi, Batthyány, Bethlen, Csáky, Draskovich, Erdődy, Esterházy, Festetics, Hadik, Károlyi, Pálffy, Széchényi, Szécsen, Teleki, Wesselényi, and Zichy[53]—to landowners with medium-sized property holdings, the *bene possessionati*. This upper segment of the untitled nobility consisted of between twenty to thirty thousand families, or a quarter of the total nobility. They typically lived as country gentlemen in relative economic security and exercised great influence on the outlook of the incipient bourgeoisie. Members of the increasingly influential lesser nobility, or gentry, which constituted approximately half of the noble estate, also participated in the diet and county government. Significantly, writers, publicists, and politicians like Lajos Kossuth, Ferenc Deák, Francis Pulszky, and Joseph Eötvös belonged to the gentry, which had to work in order to make a living. As minor officials in the county administration, lawyers, doctors, educators, or priests, they mingled with the non-noble stratum of professional people referred to as *honoratiores*. It was mainly the middle and lesser nobility who set out to achieve bourgeois status and its cultural attributes. Fear of the "northern colossus" and of presumed Russian support of the Pan-Slav and Pan-Orthodox inclinations of the numerically superior Hungary's non-Magyar nationalities were among the chief motivating factors, because Wesselényi, Eötvös, and Kossuth alike stressed the need for solidarity between the kingdom's German and Magyar "elements."[54]

While most Royal Free Towns had a German-speaking majority at the beginning of the nineteenth century, the "Magyarization" of the German *Bürgertum* had begun in earnest by the 1830s in Raab (Győr), Stuhlweißenburg (Székesfehérvár), Fünfkirchen (Pécs), Ofen (Buda) and Pest. In 1844, Magyar became the kingdom's official language. At the end of the decade Buda counted 30,000 German and 7,500 Magyar inhabitants, Pest 30,000 each. But in Pressburg, Ödenburg, Temeschburg (Temesvár, Timişoara), as well as in the Saxon towns of Transylvania and Zips the German majority held fast. In the "lawful revolution" of 1848, the Hungarians got an independent ministry that was responsible to parliament and elected on a suffrage based chiefly on educational and property qualifications. All feudal privileges and obligations were eliminated, while the newly emancipated peasantry acquired approximately two-thirds of the land. Religious freedom was expanded, although the Orthodox and Jewish faiths were still not on a fully equal footing with the Catholic, Calvinist, Lutheran, and Unitarian confessions. But by the late summer of 1848 Hungary was consumed by two wars for an independent Magyar nation-state. One was a fight for national independence from the Habsburgs and the Austrian government, the other a civil war fought between the Magyars and the majority of the kingdom's non-Magyar peoples. It was only at the end of July 1849 that Kossuth's revolutionary government was ready to make serious concessions on the nationality question by granting complete self-government for the Serbs, Croats, and Romanians, together with more restricted autonomy for the Slovaks and Germans that included linguistic, religious, and educational freedom.[55]

Nevertheless, during the Hungarian revolution and the war of independence of 1848–49 most of the "Swabians" fought on the side of Lajos Kossuth, while most of the Transylvanian Saxons supported the Austrian forces. *Banater Schwaben* defended Ungarisch-Weißkirchen (Bela Crkva) against Serb frontier guards, "Swabians" defended the fortress Komorn (Komárom, Komárno), and "Swabians" as well as "Saxons" from Zips fought in Honvéd battalions. Of thirteen Honvéd generals executed at Arad in 1849, five were Germans: one each from Pressburg, Zombor (Sombor), County Turócz, Vienna and Germany. Only the Honvéd commander-in-chief, Zips Saxon Artúr Görgey, survived—because of a personal appeal to Francis Joseph from Tsar Nicholas I—to live in political exile in Viktring at Klagenfurt. The Austrian commander-in-chief, General Julius Haynau, expressed the court's disappointment in the Hungarian Germans "that those who are by language and custom German also supported the delusion of a Hungarian republic."[56]

The years 1848/49 showed not only the futility of controlling liberal aspirations by the police methods of the Habsburgs and the Romanovs, but also the mutual incompatibility of competing national movements. When the new Habsburg centralism divided Hungary into five districts and separated Transylvania, Croatia-Slavonia and the new *Serbische Woiwodschaft und das Temescher Banat*—with an ethnic mixture of Romanians, Serbs, Germans and Magyars—German became the official language of the whole country. The Imperial Minister of the Interior, Alexander Bach, ran the land with his "Bach hussars" (mainly German, Czech and Slovene administrators), sixteen regiments of Austrian gendarmes and a network of police informers. But the new absolutist regime also abolished the customs barrier separating Hungary from Austria and introduced the Austrian Civil Code, together with detailed regulations on tariff, taxation, weights and measurements, postal services, and the emancipation of the serfs (1853). But after the humiliating defeats of the Austrian armies at Solferino and Königgrätz, both the emperor and German-Austrian bourgeoisie accepted the idea of a real compromise with Hungary in each each half of the double monarchy would be transformed into a state under one nation's leadership. Thus Hungary's Nationality Law XLIV of 1868 postulated the idea that "all Hungarian citizens constitute a nation in the political sense, the one and indivisible Hungarian nation" and, with it, the fiction of a Magyar nation-state on the western European model. It denied the political existence and, thus, the "nationalities'" claims to collective rights and political institutions, offering instead the assertion that "every citizen of the fatherland . . . enjoys equal rights, regardless of the national group to which he belongs" as meager compensation.[57]

Beginning in 1880, decennial Hungarian censuses collected statistics for every person's mother tongue. According to these figures, the German-speaking population totaled 1,953,911 (12.5%) in 1880, and 2,037,435 (9.8%) in 1910. While the percentage of the "Germans" fell in all regions, the absolute figures increased in southern Hungary and Transylvania. Germans maintained an absolute majority only in the county of Moson and the town of Ödenburg, a relative majority in the county of Nagy-Küküllő and in the towns of Pressburg, Temeschburg, Werschetz, and Semlin. But they were still a strong minority (over 25%) in the counties of Sopron, Vas, Tolna, Baranya, Bács-Bodrog, Torontál, Temes, Szeben and Brassó, as well as in the towns of Esseg (Eszék, Osijek) and Pantschowa (Pancsova, Pančevo). By confession, two-thirds of all Hungarian "Germans" were Catholic, one-fifth Lutheran, and 10% Jewish. But particularly at the beginning of the twentieth century, the term "mother tongue" did not necessarily refer to the language picked up in infancy, usually from one's mother; it was rather "the language the person in question considers his own, the language he masters best and uses most willingly," the language acquired at the *Kindergarten*, at school, in social life. Thus the category of mother tongue was suitable to mark eventual changes in language usage during the lifetime of an individual. Of course, this official Hungarian definition worked in favor of increasing the Hungarian language.[58]

Comparing the census figures concerning mother tongues between 1880 and 1910, German reached its peak in 1900 with 2,135,181 inhabitants (11.1%). During the six decades between 1850 and 1910, the number of people speaking Hungarian as their mother tongue more than doubled (107.10%), while the number of German-speakers grew only by 48.76%. Whereas the kingdom's 252,665 Jews had been classified as a separate nationality in 1850, by 1880 more than 90% were counted as Magyars or Germans. On the other hand, emigration was particularly high among the Slovaks, Ukrainians and Germans, totalling 16.73% of all emigrants between 1899 and 1913). As of 1910, 11.0% of the total population spoke both Hungarian and German, 5.3% Hungarian and Slovak, 4.2% Hungarian and Romanian—altogether 23.5% Hungarian and some minority language.[59]

The "Magyarization" of the Germans increased especially in the cities and towns over 5,000. Although the Germans recorded in 1910 were the most literate and exhibited the most developed and differentiated social structure of all nationalities, 72.45% of the population of the 156 Hungarian towns declared themselves as Magyars, only 9.86% as Germans. Even in districts where a non-Magyar people was in absolute majority, 24 out of 77 towns had a Magyar majority. Hence Jászi's thesis that urbanization was an organic part of the process of assimilation or "Magyarization." In the case of the Germans and Jews, assimilation was mainly a voluntary process, while other non-Magyars were probably motivated both by external pressures and a desire to get ahead. At any rate, the forcible "Magyarization" of the educational system was aimed at preventing the non-Magyar nationalities from developing an educated elite of their own. One apparent consequence of "Magyarization" in the cities and towns of Hungary proper was that 59.57% of the voters in the parliamentary elections in 1910 were Magyars, versus only 11.74% Germans. Similarly, only a few Transylvanian "Saxons" took seats in the Hungarian parliament.[60]

Because the new industries needed more and more specialists and skilled workers, between 1869 and 1900 the number of Germans in Hungary increased. Yet this figure decreased in Budapest from 123,308 (34.2%) in 1880 to 78,882 (9.0%) in 1910. Nevertheless, only a quarter of them were born in Budapest, half of them coming from the countryside and a quarter from Austria, Germany or Switzerland. The "Germans" dominated especially the building industry, the metalworking industry and gastronomy. In the countryside, the richer "Swabian" peasants became the master (*Herren*) of their villages, where children were typically educated in both German and Hungarian. Nor did they protest when the kingdom's government and the Catholic Church changed the language of instruction in hundreds of elementary schools from German to Hungarian. The *Lex Apponyi* of 1907 obliged non-Hungarian elementary schools—whose teachers received salary raises—to ensure that their pupils knew Hungarian by the end of the fourth year. In the same year, knowledge of Hungarian became a precondition for employment at the state railways. Only the Lutheran Transylvanian Saxons successfully defended their private school system and *gymnasia*.[61]

No doubt, the Magyar upper and middle class exploited its advantage in the new Hungarian nation-state. The governments of Gyula Count Andrássy and Kálmán Tisza welcomed foreign capital and specialists, giving them a free hand to modernize the backward Hungarian economy. The rapid "Magyarization" of the emerging German and Jewish bourgeoisie was another consequence of this process. On the other hand, in the 1890s dissatisfaction was voiced primarily by the increasingly impoverished eastern Hungarian nobility, who could not adjust to the new economy; they also found a ready-made scapegoat in the "foreign" German and Jewish entrepreneurs. After the Millenary Celebration of 1896—which tried to present the chimera of a "unified Hungarian nation state"—Magyar chauvinism increased against the nationalities through the Magyarization of public schools, the names of localities, and the state railroads. Between 1880 and 1910, about half a million Germans, some 300,000 Slovaks, and tens of thousands of Ukrainians, Romanians, Serbs, and Croats became Hungarian in speech and culture.[62]

## German Irredenta in the Habsburg Empire?

As long as the term "German nationality" remained a cultural and ethnic concept, it did not imply a political theory about the relationship of nationality and state and it posed no problem of divided loyalties. The Austrian "Greater Germans" at the Pauls-kirche saw no essential difference between their ideal and Austrian patriotism. Politi-cally, the Germans of the Habsburg Empire were "Austrians," and Austrian citizenship did not amount to denial of German nationality. In 1848, the German Austrians did not rebel so much against the Austrian emperor as in opposition to absolutism. But after 1866, German-Austrian history was thenceforth strongly influenced, as Otto Bauer observed, by "the conflict between our Austrian and our German character." And after 1871, the "Greater German" idea in Austria became a servant or "seconder" of a Prussian Germany and a danger to the Habsburg Monarchy. So a group of intel-lectuals—including five men who were destined for widely divergent careers—Georg Ritter von Schönerer, Viktor Adler, Engelbert Pernerstorfer, Robert Pattai, and the historian Heinrich Friedjung—formulated the famous "Linz program," in 1882, a manifesto of reforms intended to transform Austria (without Galicia, Bukovina, and Dalmatia) into a democratic nation-state with a German majority. They disapproved of German domination over foreigners, but in the provinces of mixed nationality, like the Bohemian lands and Interior Austria, they became ruthless integral nationalists.[63]

Since the proclamation of the German Empire in 1871, a new German national-ism began to emerge among the German Austrians. Organizations like the German *Turnverein* found growing swarms of followers in Austria-Hungary. For thousands of German-Austrian students Bismarck's Protestant, anti-Slavic Germany and not the Catholic, multi-national empire of the Habsburgs became their spiritual home. The "German School League" (*Deutscher Schulverein*), founded in 1880, and the *Schulverein Südmark*, founded in 1889, began to spread Pan-German ideas among the scattered German groups in the Bohemian and South Slav lands. Georg von Schönerer, the son of an ennobled Viennese engineer and, since the early 1870s, a German Liberal member of parliament, offered a blend of Germanic paganism and racial anti-Semitism. In 1885, Schönerer added the Aryan Clause to the Linz Program and soon initiated the "Away from Rome" (*Los-von-Rom*) movement against the state church. In Styria and Carinthia this movement attracted Germans who disliked their Slovene priests, while in Bohemia it expressed hostility of Germans and Czechs to Habsburg hegemony.[64]

At the end of the nineteenth century, radical German nationalists and Pan-Germans (*Alldeutsche*) began to preach a new German identification based on membership in a racially defined German *Volk* with claims to German national political rights or outright unification with Germany. Although the members of Austria's *Deutschnationale Vereinigung* sang the Prussophilic *Wacht am Rhein* and joined the cult of Bismarck, they believed that a policy of moderate demands and willingness to compromise offered the best defense for the German cause. This course continued, more or less, with the *Deutsche Volkspartei* (1895) and the *Deutscher Nationalverband* (1911). The *furor teutonicus* in 1897 against Badeni's decrees showed very clearly that most of the German Austrians wanted to maintain the Austrian state with the historical, political, economic, social, and cultural dominance that constituted the German *Besitzstand*.[65] At the beginning of the twentieth century the Pan-German association (*Alldeutscher Verband*) formulated the demand "Away from Hungary" (*Los-von-Ungarn*), but this irredentist propaganda did not succeed. Although some German-Hungarian intellectuals like Lutz Korodi from Kronstadt, Edmund Steinacker from Debrecen, and Adam Müller-Guttenbrunn from the Banat had to emigrate to Vienna or Germany, the *Ungarländisch-Deutsche Volkspartei* was established in 1906 in the southeastern Banat town of Werschetz. The following year, this German-national party joined Romanian politicians in protesting against Apponyi's Magyarizing school law. But the party failed in the *Reichstag* election in 1910, and only Rudolf Brandsch from Hermannstadt and Ferdinand Riester from Ruma won seats in the Hungarian parliament.[66]

Oscar Jászi was convinced "that there never was a serious German irredentistic movement in Austria, that it signified rather a sentimental attachment to Germany or at best a sulky protestation against the growing influence of the Slavs which menaced German hegemony." He estimated the force of the dynasty, army, and Catholic Church was so strong under the German Austrians that a real German separatist movement could not develop. Neither *Los-von-Rom,* with its outspoken anti-Habsburg tendencies, nor the Pan-German idea ever constituted a truly revolutionary movement, particularly since the leading political circles of Berlin never sympathized with them. Until 1914 official German policy followed the conception of Bismarck, who with his keen sense of *Realpolitik* understood very well that the union of the German Austrians would lead not only to a renewed armed conflict between the Habsburgs and Hohenzollerns, but could kindle a world war as Austria's Slavs would refuse to accept such an outcome. On the other hand, the German Austrians could better serve the whole German nation from outside the German Empire than inside; in the words of Bismarck, "The German Austrian is justified to aspire for political leadership and should safeguard the interests of Germandom in the Orient, serving as the tie of contact between Germans and Slavs by hindering their collision."[67]

When Karl Max Prince Lichnowsky replaced the German ambassador in Vienna, in 1898, he alluded to the prevalence "in the Ostmark" [sic] of the idea of Austro-German unification even in the more moderate German circles. But in June 1898, Bernhard von Bülow, the German foreign secretary, gave a categoric instruction:

> Our political interest, to which all platonic sympathies should be subordinated . . . lies in the maintenance of Austria-Hungary in its present independence as a Great Power. This interest demands that we be on our guard to discourage disintegrating tendencies in Austria whether they come from the Czech, Polish, or German side. The German Austrians should not remain in doubt that as long as their struggle for the German cause is animated by an effort to safeguard Germandom as a cement for the inner cohesion and further maintenance of the Austrian state in its present form, we follow their aspirations with the most complete sympathy. But at the same time they should know that as soon as this struggle has as its final aim the separation of the German provinces from Austria and with this a return to the status quo of before 1866, the German nationalists cannot count on the promotion of their plans from our side.[68]

## The Austrian and Hungarian Census of 1910

According to the Austrian census of 1910, which classified citizens by colloquial language, the Austrian half of the Habsburg Monarchy contained 9,950,266 Germans (35.6%), 6,435,983 Czechs (23.0%), 4,967,984 Poles (17.8%), 3,518,854 Ruthenians/Ukrainians (12.6%), 1,252,940 Slovenes (4.5%), 783,334 Croats and Serbs (2.8%), 768,422 Italians and Ladins (2.7%), as well as 275,115 Romanians (1.0%) and 10,974 Magyars; 608,062 of the 28,571,934 inhabitants were "foreigners," the majority "Hungarians" (Magyars, Slovaks, Croats, Germans, etc.), over and above that "Russians" (Poles, Ukrainians, Jews, etc.), Romanians, Serbs, Bulgarians, Greeks, Turks, Italians (mostly in Trieste), *Reichsdeutsche*, Swiss, etc. The census also profiled Cisleithania's population by religion: 79% Roman Catholic, 12% Greek Catholic (Uniate), 4.6% Jewish, 2.3% Greek Orthodox, 1.6% Lutheran, and 0.5% Calvinist.[69] The parallel Hungarian census, which classified all inhabitants by mother tongue, counted 10,050,575 Magyars (48.1%), 2,949,032 Romanians (14.1%), 2,037,435 Germans (9.7%), 1,967,970 Slovaks (9.4%), 1,833,162 Croats (8.8%), 1,106,471 Serbs (5.3%), 472,587 Ruthenians/Ukrainians (2.3%), 121,097 Gypsies/Roma (0.6%), 93,174 Slovenes (0.5%), 88,209 Bunjevci and Šokci (0.4%), 63,812 Czechs (0.3%), 40,537 Poles (0.2%), 33,387 Italians (0.2%), 23,267 Bulgarians (0.1%), and some others—altogether 20,886,487 inhabitants. The confessional breakdown was 52.1% Roman Catholic, 14.3% Greek Orthodox, 12.6% Calvinist, 9.6% Greek Catholic, 6.4% Lutheran, 4.5% Jewish, and 0.4% other. In Bosnia-Herzegovina, around 96% of the 1,898,044 inhabitants spoke Serbo-Croatian; 43.5% were Orthodox, 32.25% Muslim, and 22.9% Catholic.[70] In sum, the 51,356,465 inhabitants of Austria-Hungary in 1910, living on a territory of 676,365 km², comprised eleven major "nationalities" (*Volksstämme*) and seven major confessions. The majority were not only concentrated in homogeneous regions but also in many mixed areas and "linguistic islands." Therefore, we can be certain that about 20% of all inhabitants spoke two or even more languages more or less equally, including not only civil servants, officers, lawyers, professors, teachers, priests, journalists, administrators, merchants, traders, innkeepers, craftsmen and landowners, but also a larger part of the population in Vienna, Budapest, Prague, Pilsen (Plzeň), Budweis (České Budějovice), Brünn (Brno), Olmütz (Olomouc), Troppau (Opava), Cracow, Lemberg (Lwów, L'viv), Czernowitz (Cernăuţi, Černivci), Preßburg (Pozsony, Bratislava), Ödenburg (Sopron), Kaschau (Kassa, Košice), Klausenburg (Kolozsvár, Cluj), Kronstadt (Brassó, Braşov), Temeschburg (Temesvár, Timişoara), Maria-Theresiopel (Szabadka, Subotica), Neusatz (Újvidék, Novi Sad), Fünfkirchen (Pécs), Esseg (Eszék, Osijek), Agram (Zágráb, Zagreb), Fiume (Rijeka), Triest (Trieste, Trst), Laibach (Ljubljana), and Sarajevo, as well as in many smaller towns and markets in Bohemia, Moravia, Austrian Silesia, Galicia, the Bukovina, Transylvania, Upper Hungary, southern Hungary, Croatia-Slavonia, Lower Styria and the Littoral.[71]

The two most widely distributed nationalities were the Germans and Jews (most of whom spoke Yiddish, but German in the western crownlands). Even outside the territory of the present Austria, many areas contained respectable proportions of German-speakers in 1910, particularly in Bohemia (2,467,724—36.76%), Moravia (719,435—27.62%), Austrian Silesia (325,523—43.90%), Bukovina (168,851—21.24%), Lower Styria (73,148—15.0%), Carniola (27.915—5,36%) and Trieste (11,856—6.21%). In Hungary, the Germans lived scattered in many regions, such as western Hungary (332,148—27.6%), "Swabian Turkey" (186,673—30.1%), the Batschka (190,697—23.5%), Banat (387,545—24.5%), Transylvania (234,085—8.7%), Budapest (78,882—9.0%), Zips (38,434—22.2%) and Croatia-Slavonia (134,078—5.1%). Altogether, in those parts of the Austrian crownlands outside today's Republic of Austria there were roughly 4,125,000 "German-speaking" inhabitants, in Hungary (excluding the later Burgenland) almost 1.8 million.[72]

# Summary

Beginning with the Carolingian and Ottonian colonization, "Germans"—mainly Bavarians—settled in present-day Austria, becoming Austrians, Styrians, Carinthians, Salzburgers, and Tyrolians. In the High Middle Ages Bohemian and Hungarian kings settled "Germans" in the Bohemian lands (*Deutsch-Böhmen, Deutsch-Mährer, Deutsch-Schlesier*), in Upper Hungary (esp. *Hauerländer, Zipser Sachsen*), and in Transylvania (*Siebenbürger Sachsen*). Since the tenth century German bishops and aristocrats settled

Germans in Lower Styria (*Untersteirer*) and Carniola (esp. *Gottscheer*). Following Hungary's reconquest from the Turks (1683–1718), the Habsburgs settled "Germans" on the Hungarian plain (*Donauschwaben*), as well as in Galicia (*Galizien-Deutsche*), and the Bukovina (*Buchenländer*). Up to the mid-nineteenth century, many of these groups enjoyed positions of privilege and leadership among their Slavic, Magyar and Romanian neighbors, especially as the burghers of medieval cities and towns with German city law, in Hungary's Royal Free Towns. Most German-speakers defined their group identity in terms of the privileged status derived from their social order, occupation (*Zünfte*), place of residence, or religion. "Speaking a distinct language was commonly understood to be a function of the corporate groups to which they belonged and/or the communities in which they lived."[75]

Once the reforms of Maria Theresa and Joseph II had strengthened state administration and common education, the German language assumed the leading role in the whole Habsburg Monarchy. Ten of thousands of "Josephists" abetted the modern centralization process through their work as bureaucrats, administrators, professors, teachers, lawyers and economists. By the mid-nineteenth century, the bulk of the educated middle classes in Carniola, the Bohemian crownlands, Upper Hungary, Transylvania, southern Hungary, Croatia-Slavonia and the Bukovina had made German their first language. In the decade of neo-absolutism, German was even made the official language in the whole Austrian Empire. From the mid-nineteenth century onwards, the new railway system spread Viennese newspapers like *Die Presse*/*Neue Freie Presse* across the monarchy, where they joined numerous regional German-language newspapers in almost all crownland, including the *Agramer Tagblatt* (Zagreb), *Bohemia* (Prague), *Krakauer Zeitung, Laibacher Zeitung, Pester Lloyd* (Budapest), *Pressburger Zeitung, Kronstädter Zeitung, Siebenbürgisch-Deutsches Tageblatt* (Hermannstadt), and *Czernowitzer Zeitung*. After the Austro-Hungarian Compromise of 1867 German prevailed as Cisleithania's first—though not official—language, whether in the *Reichsrat,* central administration, and high courts, or in the economy, or even among the educated classes (with *Matura*) and the outlets of high culture (such as the many *Deutsche Theater* between Karlsbad, Czernowitz and Temeschburg).[76]

After the Silesian wars and the forced cession of the greater part of Silesia, the German Austrians harbored strong reservations about the Prussian Germans. The old antagonism between Austria and Prussia was coupled with the rivalry between Vienna and Berlin, even though the longstanding confrontation between Catholics and Protestants was no longer applicable. As the Greater German sentiment increased after 1809 and began to dominate the liberal and democratic movements among students and intellectuals, German Austrians were divided by strong tensions between pro-Austrian and pro-German elements. Under the threat of Napoleon efforts were made to create an Austrian state-nation (*Staatsnation*), which were repeated after 1849. But these efforts were not in conformity with the general trend in Europe, which led neither towards a multiethnic state-nation nor regional patriotism (*Landespatriotismus*) but, on the contrary, in the opposite direction towards nation states (*Nationalstaaten*) with a state-nation speaking the same language.[77]

In the first half of the nineteenth century, problems of divided loyalty between the Austrian Empire and Germany were minimal. Although the Habsburg monarch resigned as the Holy Roman Emperor in 1806, he held the presidency of the German Confederation until 1866. In 1848, German-Austrian representatives at the Frankfurt parliament could argue for German unification on a *grossdeutsch* basis. Although there was no great conflict between the interests of the German Austrians and those of the citizens of the other German states, at the end they had to decide between the Austrian and German empires. No doubt, the unification of Germany in 1871 came as a shock to many German Austrians, since now the Protestant Prussian Hohenzollern, rather than the Catholic Austrian Habsburgs, presided over a new second *Reich* as German emperors. Although the old Habsburg dynasty was of Alemannic descent, since the dawn of the early modern era, many Habsburgs had preferred to consider themselves Burgundians, Netherlanders, Spaniards or Lorrainers. But some members of the dynasty, such as Maria Theresa, Joseph II, and the Archdukes Charles and John, were imbued with a strong feeling of loyalty to the German cause. And Emperor-King Francis Joseph regarded himself as a German prince—even after the loss of Austria's position in Germany.[78]

The "enlightened" absolutist monarchy had deprived the feudal estates of many political privileges, but it appointed a large number of aristocrats, including members of both old and high-ranking "feudal" families and newly knighted nobles, to top positions in the army, diplomatic corps and administration. But when all manorial dues were abolished in 1848 and in the 1860s the nobleman's relationship to the soil changed from that of a feudal lord of the manor (*Herrschaft*) to that of a mere proprietor of extensive landholdings. Although a sizeable number of aristocratic families came from German states (Schwarzenberg, Thurn and Taxis, Schönborn, Metternich, Stadion, Henckel-Donnersmarck, Wessenberg, and Rechberg) and another part from the Austrian Habsburg lands (Liechtenstein, Dietrichstein, Harrach, Khevenhüller, Trauttmannsdorff, Seilern-Aspang, Lamberg, Starhemberg, Thun-Hohenstein, Auerspergs, Herbersteins, and Windisch-Grätz), there was no ethnic German aristocracy like Hungary's Magyar nobility. Independent of their ethnic origin, many aristocratic families in the Bohemian lands regarded themselves as "Bohemian" or "Moravian lords," including old "Czech" families like the Lobkowitz (Lobkovic), Waldstein (Valdštejn), Czernin (Černín), Kinský, Sternberg (Šternberk), Nostitz (Nostic), Martinitz (Martinic), Kaunitz (Kounic), and Kolowrat (Kolovrat). Most of these aristocrats preferred a federal form of government for the crownlands and were imbued with a feeling of provincial patriotism.[79]

The newly knighted nobility, which comprised descendants of the bourgeoisie and peasantry who had been knighted for distinguished military or administrative service or for comparable success in the financial, industrial and commercial world, established a "second social class" (*zweite Gesellschaft*) that played an important role in the monarchy's political and cultural life. The German-speaking "bureaucracy"—especially the officials of the central government in Vienna—first served "enlightened" absolutism, the pre-1848 restoration system, neo-absolutism, and, finally, the constitutional monarchy before and after 1867. The conviction that they represented the state, whether in a literal or even narrower sense, made up a large part of the civil servants' professional ethics. Consequently, the German or German-speaking had an advantage over the other nationalities. After the middle of the nineteenth century the large majority of the officials in the interior ministry and judiciary came from the middle class. Even the powerful Interior Minister Alexander Bach came from peasant stock. But his bureaucratic regime was not restricted to German employees, including Magyars who took pleasure in grumbling about the Czech "Bach hussars."[80]

There is hardly doubt that there was considerable tension between Catholicism and the German element in the so-called "Catholic empire Austria." But one cannot speak of as far-reaching an identification between the two as that which existed between Catholicism and the Poles, Slovenes and Croats. There were no prominent national champions of the German cause among the high clergy such as Bishop Anton Martin Slomšek was for the Slovenes, Bishop Josip Juraj Strossmayer for the Croats, or Bishop Cölestin Endrici for the Italians in Trentino. Liberal and German nationalist circles were offended when members of originally German families of the high aristocracy like the cardinals and prince-archbishops of Prague Friedrich Prince Schwarzenberg and Franz Count Schönborn sided with the Czechs. Old resentments that stretched as far back as the Counter-Reformation were revived whenever the conservative German Catholic People's Party of the Alpine districts voted with the Slavs. Indeed, this was to become one of the reasons for Georg von Schönerer's "Away from Rome" (*Los-von-Rom*) movement. This anticlericalism could be directed not only against the Catholic Church but also against the monarchy or at least against the dynasty. Whenever the more prominent spokesmen of the German-Austrian clergy turned their attention to the nationality problem they generally sought to promote mutual reconciliation and understanding. Wenzel Frind, the suffragan bishop of Leitmeritz, and Ignaz Seipel, the Austrian federal chancellor in the 1920s, exerted themselves to reconcile the different nationalities, as did devoted Catholic laymen like Max Hussarek and Heinrich Lammasch, the last prime ministers of imperial Austria.[81]

The German Lutherans were distinctly more German-nationalist in attitude than the Catholics. In 1910, 268,621 German Lutherans lived in Cisleithania as minorities in scattered settlements in the Sudeten and Alpine lands, especially in Austrian Silesia, in northwestern Bohemia, Vienna, Graz, and in Upper Carinthia. After 1831, Leipzig's *Gustav-Adolf-Stiftung* and, after 1862, Vienna's *Gustav-Adolf-Verein* gave huge financial support to many Austrian, Bohemian and Galician communities. In Hungary, the 410,663 German Lutherans recorded in the 1910 census were numerically stronger, especially those in the western Hungarian counties (Pozsony, Moson,

Sopron, and Vas), Zips, Transylvania, and the Bácska. The largest and best organized German Lutheran group was the Transylvanian Saxons (*Die evangelische Landeskirche A.B. in Siebenbürgen*), with approximately 226,000 members in 1900. If a larger figure of German Lutherans in Hungary displayed a greater power of resistance to "Magyarization" than their Catholic counterparts, this is likely because the Magyar Lutherans were relatively few in number. It was certainly not because the Lutheran clergy was more loyal to the German cause than the Catholic, because there were also numerous Lutheran "Magyarones."[82] In general, there was a strong pro-German feeling among the German-speaking Jews in the western half of the empire, while in the eastern part they were unmistakably pro-Magyar and spoke mainly Hungarian. In the first instance language was largely responsible for this feeling; but in both cases the attitude of the Jews was also motivated by the Josephist legacy of tolerance and emancipation and the revolutionary movement of 1848. Since the 1880s, German-speaking and, on the whole, German-oriented Jewry became involved in a two-front struggle. The German nationalists accused them of putting on German airs without having a right to do so, of crowding the universities with foreigners, and of actually constituting an unreliable international element; while the non-German nationalities, who usually resented them, found in the pro-German attitude of a large percentage of the Jews another reason to reject them. The supposition that, with relatively few exceptions, the Jews—and not just the German-speaking Jewry—would have, to the very end of the monarchy, preferred its continued existence to its dissolution seems to be justified.[83]

It was a part of the national revolutions of 1848 that the elections to the first German parliament in Frankfurt challenged the Magyar, Czech, Polish, Italian, and Slovene intelligentsia—and that Magyar, Italian, Czech, Slovak, Polish, Romanian, Serb, Croat and Slovene political leaders would respond by challenging the superiority of the German Austrians. The increasing industrialization and railway construction since the 1850s in the Bohemian, Hungarian and Slovene lands started a new economic competition between the non-German majorities and the German minorities that steadily eroded the social and economic boundaries that had separated them from the majority populations and helped preserve them as distinct groups. These changing circumstances gave the German minorities an impetus to redefine themselves, to articulate new and narrower ethnic or national identities, and to organize for defense of their group interests if they were to retain any semblance of their old special status and community life. These smaller German-based provincial organizations were primarily concerned with regional national controversies or with the question of their relationship with the central administrations in Vienna or Budapest.[84]

Until the 1880s, the German Austrians had no need to establish organizations to defend their own nationality or to challenge others. Moreover, as long as national identity was a matter of culture and language alone, the German-Austrians did not feel endangered. Self-determination, a fine principle for most of the monarchy's nationalities, was rather a destructive force for the Germans, who were not compelled to consider its implications until 1871. Therefore, in Austria a regional consciousness (*Landesbewusstsein*) as German-Bohemians, German-Moravians, German-Silesians, German-Styrians, German-Carinthians or German-Tyrolians prevailed until the last decade of the nineteenth century. Not before the Badeni crisis in 1897 did a common national consciousness as German-Austrians (*Deutsch-Österreicher*) develop. To be "German" or "Czech" or "Slovene" in Austria after the Badeni crisis "gave one a special 'ethnic' political license that allowed one not only to draw upon the constitutional and administrative prerogatives of the 1860s, but to blend those privileged identities into the new material and class interests of the 1890s." But the two great mass parties, the Christian Socials and the Social Democrats, both of which were chiefly German in membership, had official programs designed to appeal to class rather than to national interests. The question of German or German-Austrian national feeling was to a degree inhibited by the question of the appropriate relationship of the German-Austrian to the German Empire: "Should he look to Vienna or to Berlin as his national capital?"[85] The official nationality statistics show that we cannot speak about any extensive "Germanization" during the period from 1880 to 1910, from which we have exact and generally reliable figures. During this period the percentage of Germans in the Austrian half of the empire declined from 36.8 to 35.6 percent (in Lower Austria from 96.9 to 95.9, in Bohemia from 37.2 to 36.8, in Moravia from 29.4 to 27.6, and in Silesia from 48.9 to 43.9 percent). Thus, on the basis of statistical evidence, it can be said that with the exception of various regions like the German-Slovene border area (where the percentage of the Germans grew from 70.2 to 78.6 percent in Carinthia, and from 67.0 to 70.5 percent in Styria), it was precisely during the period when the nationality struggle was most intense that "Germanization" no longer played an important role. Between 1860 and 1914, the Germans lost several important positions, of which Prague was the foremost, and their quota of citizens in most towns of central Bohemia dropped. By contrast, hundreds of thousands of Czech migrants to Vienna and their descendants were "Germanized."[86]

In Hungary the percentage of Germans declined between 1880 and 1910 from 12.5 to 9.8 percent; in the same period, the German element of Budapest disintegrated. The kingdom's "Germans" increased to more than two million, but without a common national consciousness as Hungarian-Germans (*Ungarndeutsche*) until World War I. The Lutheran Transylvanian Saxons possessed the strongest regional consciousness, followed by the confessionally mixed western Hungarian-Germans, the more Catholic Danube Swabians and the Lutheran Saxons in Zips. But it must be said that the majority of the Catholic bishops supported the official policy of "Magyarization." While the "German" village peasantry and artisans sustained their pre-modern political mentality, most of the more highly educated "Germans" assimilated in the Hungarian cities, especially in Budapest. The "Magyarization" of the Germans also worked because almost 40 percent of Hungarian-Germans spoke the

Hungarian language. The "Saxons" and "Swabians" only tried to organize national-political movements after the Hungarian governments launched a forced assimilation policy in the last decades of the nineteenth century.[87]

In the immediate prewar years, the German-Austrians—together with the assimilated German-speaking Jewish and Slavic families—still held the strongest political, economic, social und cultural position in the Dual Monarchy. Yet, in most respects, their national movement had not developed as far as those of other nationalities like the Magyars, Czechs, or Poles. Nevertheless, the German-Austrians spoke the major language, which was that of the Austrian parliament, the Austrian ministries, the joint ministries with Hungary, the Austrian supreme courts, the *k.u.k.* army and navy, the Austrian Catholic hierarchy, and the higher educational institutions. It was similarly the language of business and industry, as well as of the predominant culture of Vienna. German-Austrians also held the top positions in the bureaucracy, professions, and finance. Most German-Austrians accepted this privileged situation as natural; "it seemed to show that among the Habsburg nationalities they worked harder, were smarter, and had more highly developed civilization. It must also be remembered that German-Austrian superiority was not class-based." The aristocracy, the bourgeoisie, the *Besitz-* and *Bildungsbürgertum*, the lower middle class, peasantry, artisans, and industrial working class all tended to be better off than their counterparts among the other nationalities.[88]

By the time the war came in 1914, there was no common German-Austrian consensus about the future. The majority were undoubtedly most concerned about maintaining their position intact, and they supported the dynasty, the empire, and the army. Only a small minority wanted to break up the monarchy, with the German regions, including the Bohemian lands and Trieste, joining the German *Reich.* It should be noted that although other national groups like the Czechs, Poles and South Slavs drafted blueprints for territorially discrete autonomous or independent administrations, the German-Austrian mass parties did not formulate similarly detailed plans. The Christian Socials wanted to keep things as they were; the Social Democrats stood for a federal solution, but were deeply aware of the problems in drawing new boundaries. German-national parties concentrated on defending the status quo against the attempts of other nationalities to improve their positions. Of course, in 1914 the German-Austrians did not expect to lose the war; even the most pessimistic could not have foreseen the extent of the catastrophe that occurred four years later. The German *Reich* as a strong ally backed the Habsburg decision to attack Serbia, and the two empires fought against Russia, Italy, Romania, and the Western Powers until the end. Although there were some disagreements about the conduct of military operations and the postwar settlements, nothing could prepare the German-Austrians for the formation of a German-Austrian republic.[89]

"Germans"[72] in Bohemian, Moravian, Silesian, Galician, Hungarian, Upper Hungarian, Transylvanian, Southern Hungarian, Croatian-Slavonian, Littoral, Carniolan and Lower Styrian cities and towns, 1880–1910–1920/21

| | Austrian or Hungarian census of 1880 | | Austrian or Hungarian census of 1910 | | Czechoslovak or Polish or Hungarian or Romanian or Yugoslav census of 1920/21 | |
|---|---|---|---|---|---|---|
| | total population | Germans | total population | Germans | total population | Germans |
| **Bohemia** | | | | | | |
| Prag (Praha) | 162,323 | 32,657 | 223,741 | 18,753 | 676,657 | 30,429 |
| Pilsen (Plzeň) | 38,883 | 6,827 | 80,445 | 10,036 | 88,416 | 6,757 |
| Budweis (České udějovice) | 23,845 | 11,829 | 44,538 | 16,903 | 44,022 | 7,006 |
| Aussig (Ústí nad Labem) | 16,524 | 15,019 | 39,301 | 35,607 | 39,830 | 30,544 |
| Reichenberg (Liberec) | 28,090 | 24,742 | 36,350 | 32,893 | 34,985 | 27,929 |
| Gablonz (Jablonec) | 9,032 | 8,782 | 29,521 | 26,343 | 26,929 | 21,982 |
| Eger (Cheb) | 17,148 | 15,477 | 26,682 | 23,029 | 27,524 | 23,125 |
| Teplitz (Teplice) | 14,841 | 13,429 | 26,777 | 23,729 | 28,892 | 22,489 |
| Warnsdorf (Varnsdorf) | 15,162 | 14,595 | 23,220 | 21,887 | 20,328 | 18,237 |
| Karlsbad (Karlovy Vary) | 10,579 | 10,266 | 17,466 | 16,783 | 19,480 | 17,173 |
| Leitmeritz (Litoměřice) | 10,854 | 9,263 | 15,421 | 13,165 | 16,988 | 11,015 |
| Brüx (Most) | 10,136 | 8,943 | 25,692 | 21,372 | 27,239 | 17,014 |
| Komotau (Chomutov) | 10,111 | 9,499 | 19,129 | 18,414 | 21,123 | 18,245 |
| Asch (Aš) | 13,209 | 11,796 | 21,880 | 19,826 | 19,525 | 17,812 |
| Saaz (Žatec) | 10,425 | 9,616 | 17,130 | 16,295 | 16,211 | 13,979 |
| Trautenau (Trutnov) | 11,253 | 9,460 | 16,106 | 14,379 | 14,584 | 11,412 |
| Böhmisch-Leipa (Česká Lípa) | 10,170 | 9,892 | 12,065 | 11,326 | 11,737 | 10,083 |
| Rumburg (Rumburk) | 10,142 | 9,818 | 10,544 | 10,250 | 9,093 | 8,458 |
| Graslitz (Kraslice) | 7,850 | 7,784 | 13,857 | 13,579 | 12,526 | 12,249 |
| Bodenbach (Podmokly) | 5,862 | 4,620 | 13,412 | 11,556 | 15,103 | 12,117 |
| Tetschen (Děčín) | 5,612 | 4,825 | 10,640 | 9,885 | 11,244 | 9,289 |
| Dux (Duchcov) | 7,363 | 4,872 | 12,399 | 8,048, | 12,619 | 6,324 |
| Weipert (Vejprty) | 6,433 | 6,223 | 11,898 | 11,360 | 10,422 | 9,996 |
| Oberleutensdorf (Litvínov) | 5,727 | 5,582 | 10,658 | 9,294 | 9,429 | 7,287 |
| Turnau (Turnov) | 2,863 | 2,472 | 15,086 | 11,983 | 15,485 | 10,578 |
| **Moravia** | | | | | | |
| Brünn (Brno) | 82,660 | 48,591 | 125,737 | 81,617 | 221,758 | 55,816 |
| Olmütz (Olomouc) | 20,176 | 12,879 | 22,245 | 13,253 | 57,206 | 15,818 |
| Mährisch-Ostrau (Ostrava) | 13,448 | 3,682 | 36,754 | 17,299 | 41,765 | 9,879 |
| Iglau (Jihlava) | 22,378 | 18,745 | 25,914 | 20,523 | 28,179 | 13,420 |
| Znaim (Znojmo) | 12,254 | 10,636 | 18,825 | 16,090 | 21,197 | 7,988 |
| Sternberg (Šternberk) | 14,243 | 14,108 | 14,601 | 14,357 | 12,925 | 11,520 |

| | Austrian or Hungarian census of 1880 | | Austrian or Hungarian census of 1910 | | Czechoslovak or Polish or Hungarian or Romanian or Yugoslav census of 1920/21 | |
|---|---|---|---|---|---|---|
| | total population | Germans | total population | Germans | total population | Germans |
| Neutitschein (Nový Jičín) | 10,274 | 9,017 | 13,859 | 11,575 | 13,226 | 8,635 |
| Mährisch-Schönberg (Šumperk) | 8,562 | 8,416 | 13,329 | 12,765 | 13,117 | 10,571 |
| Lundenburg (Břeclav) | 5,681 | 3,442 | 8,517 | 4,696 | 12,500 | 2,028 |
| Witkowitz (Vitkovice) | 2,591 | 992 | 23,151 | 15,990 | 27,358 | 6,940 |
| **Silesia** | | | | | | |
| Troppau (Opava) | 20,562 | 16,149 | 30,762 | 27,240 | 33,457 | 22,008 |
| Jägerndorf (Krnov) | 11,792 | 10,127 | 16,681 | 15,390 | 21,129 | 18,635 |
| Bielitz (Bielsko) | 13,060 | 10,778 | 18,568 | 15,144 | 19,785 | 12,247 |
| Teschen (Český Těšín, Cieszyn) | 13,004 | 6,091 | 22,489 | 13,244 | 8,068 | 3,406 |
| Galicia and Bukovina: | | | | | | |
| Krakau (Kraków) | 66,095 | 4,590 | 151,886 | 4,817 | 183,706 | 435 |
| Lemberg (Lwów, L'viv) | 109,746 | 8,911 | 206,113 | 5,922 | 219,388 | 1,650 |
| Czernowitz (Cernăuți, Černivci) | 45,600 | 22,720 | 87,128 | 41,360 | 90,000 (approx.) | 18,000 (approx.) |
| **Hungary (proper)** | | | | | | |
| Budapest | 360,551 | 119,902 | 880,371 | 78,882 | 928,996 | 60,425 |
| Fünfkirchen (Pécs) | 28,702 | 5,121 | 49,822 | 6,356 | 47,556 | 5,034 |
| Ödenburg (Sopron) | 23,222 | 16,425 | 33,932 | 17,318 | 35,248 | 16,911 |
| Raab (Győr) | 20,981 | 1,420 | 44,300 | 1,167 | 50,036 | 1,389 |
| Steinamanger (Szombathely) | 10,280 | 1,167 | 30,947 | 1,354 | 34,699 | 1,707 |
| Baja | 19,241 | 2,073 | 21,032 | 1,735 | 19,371 | 1,590 |
| Saróksar | 7,541 | 5,477 | 13,345 | 5,460 | 16,253 | 7,101 |
| Güns (Kőszeg) | 7,301 | 5,290 | 8,423 | 3,066 | 8,492 | 3,314 |
| Tolnau (Tolna) | 7,723 | 4,364 | 8,851 | 1,952 | 8,239 | 3,084 |
| Wieselburg (Moson) | 4,903 | 3,583 | 6,258 | 2,567 | 6,336 | 2,557 |
| **Upper Hungary (Slova)** | | | | | | |
| Pressburg (Pozsony, Bratislava) | 48,006 | 30,440 | 78,223 | 32,790 | 93,189 | 25,837 |
| Kaschau (Kassa, Košice) | 26,097 | 4,218 | 44,211 | 3,189 | 52,898 | 2,145 |
| Neutra (Nyitra, Nitra) | 8,660 | 1,969 | 16,419 | 1,636 | 19,118 | 723 |
| Tyrnau (Nagyszombat, Trnava) | 10,824 | 2,758 | 15,163 | 2,280 | 17,745 | 894 |
| Preschau (Eperjes, Prešov) | 10,139 | 1,889 | 16,323 | 1,404 | 17,577 | 817 |
| Zipser Neudorf (Igló, Spišská Nova Ves) | 7,521 | 2,249 | 10,525 | 1,786 | 11,608 | 1,689 |

| | Austrian or Hungarian census of 1880 | | Austrian or Hungarian census of 1910 | | Czechoslovak or Polish or Hungarian or Romanian or Yugoslav census of 1920/21 | |
|---|---|---|---|---|---|---|
| | total population | Germans | total population | Germans | total population | Germans |
| Kremnitz (Körmöczbánya, Kremnica) | 8,550 | 6,178 | 4,515 | 1,514 | 4,805 | 886 |
| **Transylvania** | | | | | | |
| Klausenburg (Kolozsvár, Cluj) | 29,923 | 1,423 | 60,808 | 1,676 | 83,542 | 2,073 |
| Kronstadt (Brassó, Braşov) | 29,584 | 9,599 | 41,056 | 10,841 | 40,335 | 11,293 |
| Hermannstadt (Nagyszeben, Sibiu | 19,446 | 14,001 | 33,489 | 16,832 | 45,670 | 20,960 |
| Bistritz (Besztercze, Bistriţa) | 8,063 | 4,954 | 13,236 | 5,835 | 12,364 | 5,163 |
| Schäßburg (Segesvár, Sighişoara) | 8,788 | 4,963 | 11,587 | 5,486 | 11,561 | 5,620 |
| Mediasch (Medgyes, Mediaş) | 6,489 | 3,470 | 8,626 | 3,866 | 10,124 | 4,691 |
| **Southern Hungary (Banat, Batschka)** | | | | | | |
| Temeschburg (Temes-vár, Timişoara) | 33,649 | 18,539 | 72,555 | 31,644 | 82,689 | 29,188 |
| Arad | 35,556 | 5,448 | 63,166 | 4,365 | 62,490 | 3,012 |
| Lugosch (Lugos, Lugoj) | 11,287 | 4,533 | 19,818 | 6,151 | 20,036 | 5,983 |
| Werschetz (Versecz, Vršac) | 22,329 | 12,354 | 27,370 | 13,556 | 27,011 | 13,244 |
| Groß-Betschkerek (Nagybecskerek, Zrenjanin) | 19,529 | 6,356 | 25,470 | 6,682 | 27,522 | 7,888 |
| Groß-Kikinda (Nagykikinda, Velika Kikinda) | 19,845 | 4,531 | 26,356 | 5,838 | 25,774 | 5,774 |
| Pantschowa (Pancsova, Pančevo) | 17,127 | 6,356 | 20,201 | 7,388 | 19,407 | 7,255 |
| Ungar.-Weißkirchen (Fehértemplom, Bela Crkva) | 9,845 | 6,644 | 11,524 | 6,062 | 9,650 | 5,194 |
| Maria Theresiopel (Szabadka, Subotica) | 61,367 | 1,479 | 94,610 | 1,913 | 101,857 | 2,424 |
| Neusatz (Újvidék, Novi Sad) | 21,325 | 5,159 | 33,590 | 5,918 | 39,122 | 6,486 |
| Zombor (Sombor) | 24,693 | 2,672 | 30,593 | 2,181 | 31,342 | 2,996 |
| Apatin | 11.973 | 10,668 | 13.136 | 11.661 | 13,435 | 12,252 |
| **Croatia-Slavonia** | | | | | | |
| Agram (Zágráb, Zagreb) | 28,388 | 2,678 | 79,038 | 4,458, | 108,674 | 3,545, |
| Esseg (Eszék, Osijek) | 18,201 | 8,970 | 31,388 | 11,269 | 34,485 | 10,077 |

| | Austrian or Hungarian census of 1880 | | Austrian or Hungarian census of 1910 | | Czechoslovak or Polish or Hungarian or Romanian or Yugoslav census of 1920/21 | |
|---|---|---|---|---|---|---|
| | total population | Germans | total population | Germans | total population | Germans |
| Semlin (Zimony, Zemun) | 11,836 | 5,254 | 17,131 | 6,559 | 18,528 | 6,631 |
| Ruma | 8,541 | 4,741 | 12,148 | 6,943 | 12,463 | 6,993 |
| Vukovar (Vukovár) | 8,741 | 3,128 | 10,359 | 3,502 | 10,242 | 2,671 |
| Winkowitz (Vinkovce, Vinkovci | 5,277 | 1,832 | 9,220 | 3,160 | 10,162 | 2,667 |
| **Littoral:** | | | | | | |
| Fiume (Rijeka)[73] | 20,981 | 895 | 49,806 | 2,196 | 45,680 | 1,828 |
| Pola (Pula) | 31,683 | 3,829 | 70,948 | 9,500 | 49,323 | n.f. |
| Triest (Trieste, Trst) | 144,844 | 5,141 | 229,510 | 11,856 | 238,655 | ca.3,000 |
| Görz (Gorizia, Gorica) | 20,920 | 2,149 | 30,995 | 3,238 | 28,134 | n.f. |
| **Carniola:** | | | | | | |
| Laibach (Ljubljana) | 26,284 | 5,658 | 46,630 | 6,742 | 53,294 | 1,826 |
| Gottschee (Kočevje) | 1,332 | 1,187 | 2,531 | 1,859 | 3,359 | 1.266 |
| **Lower Styria:** | | | | | | |
| Marburg (Maribor) | 17,628 | 13,517 | 27,994 | 22,653 | 30,662 | 6,595 |
| Cilli (Celje) | 5,393 | 3,301 | 6,919 | 4,625 | 7,602 | 859 |
| Pettau (Ptuj) | 4,257 | 2,729 | 4,630 | 3,672 | 4,449 | 968 |

Sources: K.K. Statistische Central-Commission (Ed.), Special-Orts-Repertorien der im Reichsrate vertretenen Königreiche und Länder, bearb. auf Grund der Ergebnisse der Volkszählungen 1880, 1890 und 1900 (Wien, 1883–1905); Die Ergebnisse der Volkszählung vom 31. Dezember 1910 in den im Reichsrate vertretenen Königreichen und Ländern 1/1: Die summarischen Ergebnisse der Volkszählung (Österreichische Statistik, Neue Folge 1/1, Wien, 1912); A magyar szent korona országainak 1910. évi népszámlálása VI: Végeredmények összefoglalása (Magyar Statisztikai Közlemények, Új sorozat 64, Budapest, 1924) [Census 1910 in the Lands of the Hungarian Holy Crown VI: Summary of the final results (Reports on Hungarian Statistics, New serial 64, Budapest, 1924)]; Statistický lexikon obcí v Čechach [Statistical lexicon of the communities in Bohemia] (V Praze, 1923); Statistický lexikon obcí na Moravě a ve Slezsku [Statistical lexicon of the communities in Moravia and Silesia] (V Praze, 1924); Statistický lexikon obcí v Republike Československej, III: Slovensko [Statistical lexicon of the communities in the Czechoslovak Republic, III: Slovakia] (V Prahe, 1927); Definitivni rezultati popisa stanovništva od 31. jan. 1921. godine [The final results of the census from 31 January 1921] (Sarajevo, 1932); Wilhelm Winkler, Statistisches Handbuch des gesamten Deutschtums (Berlin, 1927), pp. 186–189.

# Notes

1. Oscar Jászi, *The Dissolution of the Habsburg Monarchy* (Chicago, 1929, ²1961); Josef Redlich, *Das österreichische Staats- und Reichsproblem* (3 vols. Leipzig, 1920–1926); Robert A. Kann, "The Dynasty and the Imperial Idea," *Austrian History Yearbook* 2/1 (1967), pp. 11–31, here 19; Helmut Rumpler, "Eine Chance für Mitteleuropa. Bürgerliche Emanzipation und Staatsverfall in der Habsburgermonarchie, in *Österreichische Geschichte 1804–1914* (Wien, 1997); Wim Blockmans, *A History of Power in Europe: Peoples, Markets, States* (Antwerp, 1997), pp. 315–361; Robin Okey, *The Habsburg Monarchy c. 1765–1918: From Enlightenment to Eclipse* (Houndmills and London, 2001), pp. vi–vii.

2. Erich Zöllner, "The Germans as an Integrating and Disintegrating Force," in *The Nationality Problem in the Habsburg Monarchy in the Nineteenth Century: A Critical Appraisal,* part 1: "Centripetal Forces, Nationalism as a Disintegrating Force, The Ruling Nationalities," in *Austrian History Yearbook* III/1 (1967), pp. 201–233, here 201–203; Robert A. Kann, *Das Nationalitätenproblem der Habsburgermonarchie: Geschichte und Ideengehalt der nationalen Bestrebungen vom Vormärz bis zur Auflösung des Reiches im Jahre 1918,* 2 vols., Veröffentlichungen der Arbeitsgemeinschaft Ost 4 (Graz and Köln, 1964), vol. 1, pp. 57–108, 362–363.

3. Zöllner, "The Germans," p. 204; cf. Josef Riedmann, *Geschichte Tirols* (Wien, 1982); Wilhelm Neumann, *Bausteine zur Geschichte Kärntens,* Das Kärntner Landesarchiv 12 (Klagenfurt, 1985); *Die Steiermark. Brücke und Bollwerk. Katalog zur Landesausstellung 1986,* Veröffentlichungen des Steiermärkischen Landesarchivs 16 (Graz, 1986).

4. Jiří Kořalka, *Tschechen im Habsburgerreich und in Europa 1815–1914. Sozialgeschichtliche Zusammenhänge der neuzeitlichen Nationsbildung und der Nationalitätenfrage in den böhmischen Ländern,* Schriftenreihe des Österreichischen Ost- und Südosteuropa-Instituts 18 (Wien and München 1991), pp. 23–75; Grete Klingenstein, "Was bedeuten 'Österreich' und 'österreichisch' im 18. Jahrhundert? Eine begriffsgeschichtliche Studie," in *Was heißt Österreich? Inhalt und Umfang des Österreichbegriffs vom 10. Jahrhundert bis heute,* ed. Richard G. Plaschka, Gerald Stourzh, and Jan Paul Niederkorn (Wien, 1995), pp. 149–220, here p. 177; Vladimír Macura, "Problems and Paradoxes of the National Revival," in *Bohemia in History,* ed. Mikuláš Teich (Cambridge, 1998), pp. 182–197.

5. In Pressburg, Schemnitz/Selmecz és Bélabánya/Banská Štiavnica, Zipser Neudorf/ Igló/Spišská Nova Ves, Käsmark/Késmárk/Kežmarok, Leutschau/Lőcse/Levoča, Preschau/Eperjes/Prešov, Bistritz/Beszterce/Bistriţa, Schässburg/Segesvár/ Sighişoara, Kronstadt/Brassó/Braşov, Hermannstadt/Nagyszeben/Sibiu, Oberschützen/Felsőlövő, and Ödenburg/Sopron.

6. Robert A. Kann, *Geschichte des Habsburgerreiches 1526–1918* (Wien, 1977), pp. 162–184; Okey, *Habsburg Monarchy,* pp. 12–33; Jiří Kroupa, "The Alchemy of Happiness: The Enlightenment in the Moravian Context," in *Bohemia in History,* pp. 164–181; Eva Kowalská, "Slovakia in a Period of Structural Changes 1711–1848," in *A Concise History of Slovakia,* ed. Elena Mannová (Bratislava, 2000), pp. 178–184.

7. László Kontler, *A History of Hungary: Millennium in Central Europe* (Houndmills and New York, 2002), pp. 211–212; cf. Helmut Engelbrecht, *Geschichte des österreichischen Bildungswesens,* 5 vols. (Wien, 1982–88).

8. Kontler, *Hungary,* p. 211; Jan Havránek, "The University Professors and Students in Nineteenth-century Bohemia," in *Bohemia in History,* pp. 215–228.

9. Kořalka, *Tschechen,* pp. 51–52, 64.

10. Carlisle A. Macartney, *The Habsburg Empire, 1790–1918* (London, 1968), pp. 75–82;

Kontler, *Hungary,* pp. 215–218; cf. Horst Haselsteiner, *Joseph II. und die Komitate Ungarns: Herrscherrecht und ständischer Konstitutionalismus* (Wien, 1983).

11. William M. Johnston, *The Austrian Mind: An Intellectual and Social History, 1848–1938* (Berkeley, 1972), p. 1.

12. Peter Alter, *Nationalism,* 2nd ed. (London, 1994), pp. 39–43.

13. James J. Sheehan, *German History 1770–1860* (Oxford, 1989), pp. 227, 230, 279–280; Macartney, *Habsburg Empire,* pp. 157–158; Kontler, *Hungary,* 221–222.

14. Rumpler, "Mitteleuropa," pp. 57–68; Sheehan, *German History,* pp. 235, 249.

15. Sheehan, *German History,* p. 404; Helmut Rumpler, "Austria and Europe from a Historical Perspective," in *Austria—So Much to Offer,* ed. Herbert Krejci (Wien, 1995), pp. 7–25; William D. Godsey, *Nobles and Nation in Central Europe: Free Imperial Knights in the Age of Revolution, 1750–1850* (Cambridge, 2004), p. 226; cf. Dieter Langewiesche, *Nation, Nationalismus, Nationalstaat in Deutschland und Europa* (München, 2000).

16. Rumpler, "Mitteleuropa," pp. 133–140.

17. Heinrich Lutz, *Zwischen Habsburg und Preußen. Deutschland 1815–1866* (Berlin, 1986), pp. 20–21; Robert A. Kann and Zdeněk V. David, *The Peoples of the Eastern Habsburg Lands, 1526–1918* (Seattle, 1984), pp. 185–291.

18. Ernst Bruckmüller, *Sozialgeschichte Österreichs* (Wien and München, ²2001), 233–236; Erich Zöllner, *Geschichte Österreichs. Von den Anfängen bis zur Gegenwart* (Wien and München, 8th ed., 1990), pp. 368–371.

19. Rumpler, "Mitteleuropa," 248–259; Sheehan, *German History,* 629–631, 657; George Barany, "Hungary: The Uncompromising Compromise," *Austrian History Yearbook* 3/1 (1967), pp. 234–259, here 236.

20. Cf. Wolfgang Häusler, *Von der Massenarmut zur Arbeiterbewegung. Demokratie und soziale Frage in der Wiener Revolution von 1848* (Wien and München, 1979); *1848—Ereignis und Erinnerung in den politischen Kulturen Mitteleuropas,* ed. Barbara Haider and Hans Peter Hye (Wien, 2003).

21. Jiří Kořalka, *František Palacký (1798–1876). Životopis* [Curriculum vitae] (Praha, 1998), pp. 265–273.

22. Lutz, *Habsburg und Preußen,* pp. 264–265.

23. Lothar Höbelt, "Die politische Geographie der Deutschen in Österreich: Ein Vergleich der Frankfurter und Kremsierer Abgeordneten," in *Der Reichstag von Kremsier,* pp. 115–120; Arnold Suppan, *Zwischen Adria und Karawanken,* Deutsche Geschichte im Osten Europas 7 (Berlin, ²2002), p. 291; Vasilij Melik, "Frankfurtske volitve 1848 na Slovenskem" [The Frankfurt elections in the Slovenian lands], *Zgodovinski časopis* 2/3 (1948/49), pp. 69–134.

24. Sheehan, *German History,* pp. 683–691; Rumpler, "Mitteleuropa," pp. 305–313.

25. Berthold Sutter, "Die politische und rechtliche Stellung der Deutschen in Österreich 1848 bis 1918," in *Die Habsburgermonarchie 1848–1918,* 3/1, pp. 154–339, here 169–175; Barbara Jelavich, *Modern Austria: Empire and Republic, 1815–1986* (Cambridge, 1987), pp. 44–45; Sheehan, *German History,* pp. 696–701.

26. Rumpler, "Mitteleuropa," pp. 313–315; Helmut Slapnicka, "Der Plan nationaleinheitlicher Kreise (§ 3 des Kremsierer Verfassungsentwurfs) und die Versuche seiner Verwirklichung," in *Kroměřížský sněm 1848–1849 a tradice parlamentarismu ve střední Evropě. Der Reichstag von Kremsier 1848–1849 und die Tradition des Parlamentarismus in Mitteleuropa,* ed. Josef Harna, Milan Hlavačka, Jana Starek [et al.] (Kroměříž and Kremsier, 1998), pp. 55–63.

27. István Deák, *The Lawful Revolution: Louis Kossuth and the Hungarians, 1848–1849* (New York, 1979), pp. 209–234; Suppan, *Zwischen Adria und Karawanken,* pp. 203–211.

28. Klaus Koch, "Österreich und der Deutsche Zollverein (1848–1871)," in *Die Habsburgermonarchie 1848–1918,* vol. 6/1: *Die Habsburgermonarchie im System der internationalen*

*Beziehungen* (Wien, 1989), pp. 537–560; cf. Harm Hinrich Brandt, *Der österreichische Neoabsolutismus: Staatsfinanzen und Politik 1848 bis 1860,* 2 vols. (Göttingen, 1978).

29. Éva Somogyi, "The Age of Neoabsolutism, 1849–1867," in Peter F. Sugar, Péter Hanák, and Tibor Frank (eds.), *A History of Hungary* (Bloomington, 1990), pp. 235–251.

30. Iván T. Berend and György Ránki, *East Central Europe in the 19th and 20th Centuries* (Budapest, 1977), p. 180.

31. Johnston, *Austrian Mind,* pp. 56–62; cf. Peter Leisching, "Die römisch-katholische Kirche in Cisleithanien," in *Die Habsburgermonarchie 1848–1918,* vol. 4: *Die Konfessionen,* ed. Adam Wandruszka and Peter Urbanitsch (Wien, 1985), pp. 1–247.

32. Rumpler, "Mitteleuropa," pp. 380–385; Lutz, *Habsburg und Preußen,* pp. 366–368.

33. Dominic Lieven, *Empire: The Russian Empire and Its Rivals* (London, 2000), p. 166.

34. Sheehan, *German History,* p. 911; Max Weber, *Gesammelte Schriften* (Tübingen, ³1971), p. 449; Lutz, *Habsburg und Preußen,* pp. 452–477.

35. Lutz, *Habsburg und Preußen,* pp. 477–479; cf. *Österreich und die deutsche Frage im 19. und 20. Jahrhundert: Probleme der politisch-staatlichen und soziokulturellen Differenzierung im deutschen Mitteleuropa,* ed. Heinrich Lutz and Helmut Rumpler (Wien, 1982).

36. Somogyi, "Neoabsolutism," pp. 247–251; cf. Mirjana Gross, "The Character of Croatian Autonomy in the First Decade after the Hungarian-Croatian Compromise of 1868," in *The Mirror of History: Essays in Honor of Fritz Fellner,* ed. S Wank, H. Maschl, B. Mazohl-Wallnig, and R. Wagnleitner (Santa Barbara and Oxford, 1988), pp. 275–294.

37. Cf. Gerald Stourzh, *Die Gleichberechtigung der Nationalitäten in der Verfassung und Verwaltung Österreichs 1848–1918* (Wien, 1985); László Péter, "Die Verfassungsentwicklung in Ungarn," in *Die Habsburgermonarchie 1848–1918,* vol. 7: *Verfassung und Parlamentarismus,* ed. Helmut Rumpler and Peter Urbanitsch (Wien, 2000), pp. 239–540.

38. István Deák, *Der k.(u.)k. Offizier 1848–1918* (Wien, ²1995), pp. 215–224.

39. Jászi, *Dissolution,* p. 164.

40. Gary B. Cohen, *Education and Middle-Class Society in Imperial Austria* (West Lafayette, 1996), pp. 75–83; cf. *Dějiny university Karlovy* [History of the Charles University], vol. 3, 1802–1918, ed. Jan Havránek (Praha, 1997).

41. Cohen, *Education,* pp. 258–259, 274–275; Steven Beller, *Vienna and the Jews, 1867–1938. A Cultural History* (Cambridge, 1989), pp. 34–37.

42. David Good, *The Economic Lag of Central and Eastern Europe: Evidence from the Late Nineteenth-Century Habsburg Empire,* (Working Papers in Austrian Studies 93-7 (Minneapolis 1993), pp. 1–36.

43. Barany, "Hungary," pp. 253–254; cf. Frigyes Fellner, *Ausztria és Magyarország nemzeti vagyona* [The National Wealth of Austria and Hungary] (Budapest, 1913), pp. 60–68.

44. Gary Cohen, *The Politics of Ethnic Survival: Germans in Prague, 1861–1914* (Princeton, 1981), pp. 274–282; Peter Vodopivec, "Über die sozialen und wirtschaftlichen Ansichten des deutschen Bürgertums in Krain vom Ende der sechziger bis zum Beginn der achtziger Jahre des 19. Jahrhunderts," in *Geschichte der Deutschen im Bereich des heutigen Slowenien 1848–1941: Zgodovina Nemcev na območju današnje Slovenije 1848–1941,* ed. Helmut Rumpler and Arnold Suppan (Wien and München, 1988), pp. 85–119; cf. Peter Judson, *Inventing Germanness: Class, Ethnicity, and Colonial Fantasy at the Margins of the Habsburg Monarchy,* Working Papers in Austrian Studies 93-2 (Minneapolis 1993); Jeremy King, *Budweisers into Czechs and Germans: A Local History of Bohemian Politics, 1848–1948* (Princeton, 2002).

45. Otto Urban, "Czech Society 1848–1918," in Mikuláš Teich (ed.), *Bohemia in History* (Cambridge, 1998), pp. 198–214; cf. Otto Urban, *Die tschechische Gesellschaft 1848 bis 1918,* 2 vols. (Wien, 1994); Hugo Hantsch, "Die Beziehungen der Sudetendeutschen zu den Hochschulen Österreichs," *Der Donauraum* 4 (1959), pp. 145–153.

46. Jan Křen, *Konfliktní společenství: Češi a Němci 1780–1918* [Conflict community. Czechs and Germans 1780–1918] (Praha, 1990), pp. 270–279; *Člověk na Moravě 19. století.* Resümee: *Der Mensch im Mähren des 19. Jahrhunderts,* ed. L. Fasora, J. Hanuš, J. Malíř (Brno, 2004), pp. 473–494; Kořalka, *Tschechen,* 159–173; cf. Heinrich Rauchberg, *Der nationale Besitzstand in Böhmen,* 3 vols. (Leipzig, 1905).

47. Lothar Höbelt, "Parties and Parliament: Austrian Pre-War Domestic Politics," in *The Last Years of Austria-Hungary: Essays in Political and Military History 1908–1918,* ed. Mark Cornwall (Exeter, 1990), pp. 41–43; Rumpler, "Mitteleuropa," pp. 553–560.

48. *Deutsche Arbeit,* 12 (Prag 1912/13), p. 525; cf. Friedrich Naumann, *Mitteleuropa* (Berlin, 1915); Henry Cord Meyer, *Mitteleuropa in German Thought and Action 1815–1945* (Den Haag, 1955).

49. Peter Urbanitsch, "Erläuterungen zur Sprachen- bzw. Nationalitätenkarte der österreichisch-ungarischen Monarchie," in *Die Habsburgermonarchie 1848–1918,* vol. 3: *Die Völker des Reiches,* ed. Adam Wandruszka and Peter Urbanitsch (Wien, 1980).

50. Friedrich Gottas, "Die Deutschen in Ungarn," in *Die Habsburgermonarchie 1848–1918,* vol. 3: *Die Völker des Reiches,* part 1 (Wien, 1980), pp. 340–410, here 340–342; Karl Manherz, *Die Ungarndeutschen* (Budapest, 1998), pp. 3–7.

51. *Lexicon universorum locorum Regni Hungariae populosorum anno 1773 officiose confectum* [Topographical lexicon of the communities of Hungary compiled officially in 1773] (Budapest, 1920); László Katus, "Multinational Hungary in the Lights of Statistics," in Ferenc Glatz (ed.), *Ethnicity and Society in Hungary,* Etudes Historiques Hongroises 2 (Budapest, 1990, p. 116; Kontler, *Hungary,* p. 220.

52. Elek Fényes, *Magyarország statisztikája* [The Statistics of Hungary] (Pest, 1842); "Übersichtstafeln zur Statistik der österreichischen Monarchie 1850," in *Mittheilungen aus dem Gebiete der Statistik* 1/1 (Wien, 1852).

-54. Barany, "Hungary," pp. 236–237; cf. Joseph Eötvös, *Die Reform in Ungarn* (Leipzig, 1846).

55. Barany, "Hungary," pp. 240–242; cf. Deák, *The Lawful Revolution;* Emil Niederhauser, *1848. Sturm im Habsburgerreich* (Wien, 1990).

56. Manherz, *Die Ungarndeutschen,* pp. 26–28.

57. Kontler, *Hungary,* pp. 263–283.

58. Gottas, "Die Deutschen," pp. 344–362; *Volkszählung in den Ländern der Ungarischen Heil. Krone im Jahre 1910. 6. Teil: Zusammenfassung der Endergebnisse,* ed. Kön. Ungarischen Statistischen Zentralamt, Ungarische Statistische Mitteilungen, Neue Serie 64 (Budapest, 1924), pp. 59–60.

59. Katus, "Multinational Hungary," pp. 112–129; Gottas, "Die Deutschen," pp. 348, 353–356.

60. Barany, "Hungary," pp. 254–255; cf. Gyula Szekfű, *Három nemzedék* [Three Generations] (Budapest, ²1922).

61. Ferenc Glatz, "Das Deutschtum in Ungarn im Zeitalter der industriellen Entwicklung," in *300 Jahre Zusammenleben—Aus der Geschichte der Ungarndeutschen,* ed. Wendelin Hambuch (Budapest, 1988), pp. 74–86; Manherz, *Die Ungarndeutschen,* pp. 29–34; Kontler, *Hungary,* p. 298.

62. Ferenc Glatz (ed.), *A magyarok krónikaja* [The Chronicle of the Hungarians] (Budapest, 1995), pp. 436–37; cf. Péter Hanák, *Ungarn in der Donaumonarchie. Probleme der bürgerlichen Umgestaltung eines Vielvölkerstaates* (Wien, 1984).

63. Kann, *Nationalitätenproblem,* vol. 1, pp. 98–102; Andrew G. Whiteside, "The Germans as an Integrative Force in Imperial Austria: The Dilemma of Dominance," *Austrian History Yearbook* 3/1 (1967), pp. 157–200; Jelavich, *Modern Austria,* p. 82.

64. Johnston, *Austrian Mind,* p. 62; Eduard G. Staudinger, "Die Südmark. Aspekte der Pro-

grammatik und Struktur eines deutschen Schutzvereins in der Steiermark bis 1914," in *Geschichte der Deutschen*, pp. 130–154.

65. Sutter, *Die Deutschen in Österreich*, pp. 222–232. On 31 October 1897, in the *Neue Freie Presse* Theodor Mommsen published his notorious letter "An die Deutschen in Österreich" and recommended: "Seid hart! Vernunft nimmt der Schädel der Tschechen nicht an, aber für Schläge ist er auch zugänglich."

66. Günter Schödl, *Alldeutscher Verband und deutsche Minderheitenpolitik in Ungarn 1890–1914,* Erlanger Historische Studien 3 (Frankfurt/Main 1978), pp. 98–100, 124–128, 135–139, 142–147; cf. Paul Molisch, *Geschichte der deutschnationalen Bewegung in Österreich von ihren Anfängen bis zum Zerfall der Monarchie* (Jena, 1926); Berthold Sutter, *Die Badenischen Sprachenverordnungen,* 2 vols. (Graz and Köln, 1960–1965); Lothar Höbelt, *Kornblume und Kaiseradler: Die deutsch-freiheitlichen Parteien Altösterreichs 1882–1918* (Wien, 1993).

67. Richard Charmatz, *Österreichs innere Geschichte*, vol. 2 (Leipzig and Berlin, 1918), p. 95; Jászi, *Dissolution*, pp. 384–85.

68. Jászi, *Dissolution*, pp. 158, 385.

69. Wandruszka and Urbanitsch, *Habsburgermonarchie*, 3/1, tables 1, 5, 29.

70. Katus, "Multinational Hungary," pp. 111–130.

71. Paul Robert Magocsi, *Historical Atlas of East Central Europe* (Seattle, 1993), pp. 104–109.

72. Peter Urbanitsch, "Die Deutschen," in *Die Habsburgermonarchie 1848–1918,* 3/1, pp. 33–153; Gottas, "Die Deutschen," pp. 340–410.

73. The Austrian census of 1880 and 1910 counted inhabitants with German colloquial language, the Hungarian census of 1880 and 1910 inhabitants with German mother tongue; the census in Czechoslovakia, Poland, Hungary, Romania and Yugoslavia in 1920/21 counted inhabitants with German mother tongue and/or nationality.

74. Fiume (Rijeka) was until 1918 a corpus separatum of the Hungarian kingdom, 1920–1924 a free state, and from 1924 onwards divided between Italy und Yugoslavia.

75. Gary B. Cohen, "Ambiguous Identities: German Minorities in East-Central Europe, 1848–1945," in *18th International Congress of Historical Sciences 1995,* ed. International Committee of Historical Sciences (Montréal, 1995), pp. 126–27.

76. Cf. Adam Wandruszka, *Geschichte einer Zeitung: Das Schicksal der "Presse" und der "Neuen Freien Presse" von 1848 bis zur Zweiten Republik* (Wien, 1958); Hannelore Burger, "Mehrsprachigkeit und Unterrichtswesen in der Bukowina 1869–1918," in *Die Bukowina. Vergangenheit und Gegenwart,* ed. Slawinski and Joseph P. Strelka (Bern, 1995), pp. 93–127.

77. Alter, Nationalism, pp. 1–15; Zöllner, "The Germans," pp. 202–203; cf. Joseph Alexander von Helfert, *Über Nationalgeschichte und den gegenwärtigen Stand ihrer Pflege in Österreich* (Prag, 1853).

78. Zöllner, "The Germans," pp. 210–211; cf. Jean-Paul Bled, *François-Joseph* (Paris, 1987).

79. Zöllner, "The Germans," pp. 216–219; Roman Sandgruber, *Österreichische Agrarstatistik 1750–1918,* Materialien zur Wirtschafts- und Sozialgeschichte 2 (Wien, 1978), pp. 234–238; cf. Hannes Stekl and Marija Wakounig, *Windisch-Graetz. Ein Fürstenhaus im 19. und 20. Jahrhundert* (Wien, 1992), pp. 9–19; Ralph Melville, *Adel und Revolution in Böhmen: Strukturwandel von Herrschaft und Gesellschaft in Österreich um die Mitte des 19. Jahrhunderts* (Mainz, 1998); Pavel Cibulka, "Eine Herrschaft in Mähren," in *Grenze und Staat. Passwesen, Staatsbürgerschaft, Heimatrecht und Fremdengesetzgebung in der österreichischen Monarchie 1750–1867,* ed. Waltraud Heindl and Edith Saurer (Wien, 2000), pp. 719–787.

80. Zöllner, "The Germans," pp. 219–220; Urbanitsch, "Die Deutschen," pp. 149–153.

81. Zöllner, "The Germans," p. 213; Friedrich Engel-Janosi, "The Church and the Nationalities in the Habsburg Monarchy," *Austrian History Yearbook* 3/3 (1967), pp. 67–82; Adam Wandruszka, "Katholisches Kaisertum und multikonfessionelles Reich," in *Die Habsburgermonarchie 1848–1918*, 4, pp. xi–xvi.

82. Friedrich Gottas, "Die Geschichte des Protestantismus in der Habsburgermonarchie," in *Die Habsburgermonarchie 1848–1918*, 4: *Die Konfessionen*, pp. 489–595.

83. Zöllner, "The Germans," pp. 215–216; cf. Robert S. Wistrich, *The Jews of Vienna in the Age of Franz Joseph* (Oxford, 1989).

84. Cohen, "Ambiguous Identities," p. 126.

85. John W. Boyer, *Culture and Political Crisis in Vienna: Christian Socialism in Power, 1897–1918* (Chicago, 1995), p. xii; Jelavich, *Modern Austria*, pp. 145–146.

86. Zöllner, "The Germans," pp. 207–208.

87. Ungarische Volkszählung 1910, p. 80; Moritz Csáky, "Die römisch-katholische Kirche in Ungarn," in *Die Habsburgermonarchie 1848–1918*, 4: *Die Konfessionen*, pp. 248–331, here 281–289; cf. Günter Schödl (ed.), *Land an der Donau*, Deutsche Geschichte im Osten Europas 6 (Berlin ²2002), pp. 349–454; Magocsi, *Historical Atlas*, p. 105 (map 32a).

88. Jelavich, *Modern Austria*, pp. 144–145; cf. Friedrich von Wieser, *Über Vergangenheit und Zukunft der österreichischen Verfassung* (Wien, 1905); Michael Hainisch, *Einige neue Zahlen zur Statistik der Deutschösterreicher* (Leipzig and Wien, 1909).

89. Jelavich, *Modern Austria*, pp. 146–147.

# The Age of Total War

## ❖ Ronald Smelser ❖

In the context of this volume, it is interesting how the time frame has been narrowing. The initial part of the book examines the Germans in the framework of a thousand years, as the relationship of the Germans with their eastern neighbors developed gradually in many contexts over many generations and with many permutations. Then the time frame narrowed to the "long century," a period from the mid- to late eighteenth century to the early twentieth, when changes which would be fateful for the era of total war were set in motion, often imperceptibly, but with a tendency to accelerate over time.

In this section of the volume the time frame narrows to a brief thirty years, during which a number of factors, which emerged during the "long century," came together to create a critical mass of destructive power, which would strain to the breaking point and beyond Germany's relations with its neighbors. These factors include the following:

1.  an exclusivist, intolerant ethnic and racial nationalism, among Germans and non-Germans alike, which eventually would detonate structures—such as the Habsburg and Romanov empires—which had provided mutual homes—at many levels—for Germans and their neighbors. It also destroyed or eclipsed many historical common loyalties—church, town, region, monarchy—which had bound disparate peoples together. This radical nationalism, initially espoused by intellectuals, eventually percolated down in society thanks to the advent of

2.  mass politics, which produced political leaders who were adept at playing on the baser fears, prejudices and emotions that had hitherto lurked beneath the surface of society. The gradual expansion of the suf-frage base in many parts of Europe during the late nineteenth century, including in Germany itself, as well in the Habsburg Empire and, after the revolution of 1905, even in Russia, provided radical nationalist politicians with a large and growing mass of voters who, through their

vote, brought those very prejudices to politics at all levels from locality
to capital. The outcome of the First World War only exacerbated this
tendency and eventually brought to power in countries, both venerable
and newly constructed, regimes which instrumentalized the political
passions in new ways, not the least of which were

3. social/political movements which, breaking the bounds of traditional
   politics, took the form of surrogate religions and brought a quasi-re-
   ligious fervor to the task of creating heaven on earth for their own
   people—and hell for the others. Clearly, the most dramatic example of
   this was Nazi Germany, although we find in smaller formats analogous
   phenomena in many neighboring countries. That the Nazis could aspire
   to their apocalyptic goals was, in turn, made possible by both the

4. bureaucratic power of the modern state, civilian and military, which
   could make the marginalization , or conquest, or annihilation of whole
   peoples a matter of public policy, and

5. the technology of death, which enabled the Nazi regime, using twentieth
   century innovations in areas like transportation, communication, chemi-
   cals, incarceration, and war making to turn on neighbors of centuries,
   bringing destruction to millions—on the battlefield, on the home front,
   and in concentration camps.

One important issue emerges with regard to the periodization of the age of
total war. The traditional pattern is to view World War I, then the interwar period
of the successor states, and then World War II as discrete periods. The organization
of this section of the volume generally follows that pattern, focusing on Poland and
Czechoslovakia in the second period. But this breakdown obscures the serious issue
of continuity versus discontinuity, which appears in the essays that follow. More
specifically, do the two world wars represent, taken together, the Thirty Years' War of
the twentieth century? Or are they separate and very different conflicts, as the great
historian Gerhard Weinberg would argue?

Advocates of the first viewpoint maintain that the first stage of the Thirty Years'
War left many issues hanging fire, which made another, related conflict likely, if not
inevitable. These issues, all of which involve to one extent or another Germany and
the East include, the question of whether the Germans or the Russians would dominate the Europe of the future, particularly in the East; the viability of the Successor
States with respect to their economic, political and ethnic makeup; international
order versus international anarchy—would the Germans and their neighbors find
an umbrella in the League of Nations and its minority treaties or would national
sovereignty continue to be trump; the larger viability of the Versailles settlement and
those powers charged with its maintenance. These unresolved issues link the two
conflicts, leading from one to another.

Moreover, they also argue that the ideology which would prescribe Nazi behavior during World War II in the East had already been developed by the time of World War I, and that it would be men who were socialized to brutality and death in World War I who would carry out the genocide of the next war. Moreover, as Sven Lindquist points out in his book, *Exterminate the Brutes*, most of the Nazi practices in the East had already been anticipated by Europeans in Africa in the nineteenth century, including slave labor, genocide, death marches, cultural obliteration, etc. In this light, the wars in Europe, which witnessed an increasing level of barbarization, were, in a sense, the continuation of colonial practices in other parts of the world transferred back to Europe.

On the other hand, one can view the war in the East from 1914 to 1918 as of a different quality and magnitude than its counterpart from 1939 to 1945. In comparison to Nazi goals in World War II, German goals in the First World War seem almost benign. One can view the plans of the High Command within the context of a traditional colonial power. The people out there, said the German officer in 1917, are culturally benighted, economically impoverished and socially primitive. But several generations in contact with our superior *Kultur* will enable them to lift themselves. By contrast, the contents of *Generalplan Ost* in 1941 called for brutal racial subjugation and annihilation on a massive scale; a death toll through attrition of 30,000,000 people was assumed. In short, in World War I the Germans viewed the peoples to the East as living in filth; by World War II they were the filth. In neither case were they viewed as equals. In either event, the result was the same in the end—the mass murder of former neighbors at the hands of the Germans during the war, followed by the disappearance of large communities of German-speaking people through forced expulsion afterwards.

As we regard the first two contributions in this section, there has been astonishingly little work done on Germany with respect to its attitudes, aims and practices in the East during the First World War, since a spate of writings, several of them spawned by Fritz Fischer, appeared in Germany in the 1960s and early 1970s. These included Martin Broszat, *Zweihundert Jahre deutsche Polenpolitik*, Peter Borowsky, *Deutsche Ukrainepolitik*, Immanuel Geiss, *Der polnische Grenzstreifen*, Hans-Erich Volkmann, *Die deutsche Baltikumpolitik*, Winfried Baumgart, *Deutsche Ostpolitik*, Werner Conze, *Polnische Nation und deutsche Politik im ersten Weltkrieg*. Since then very little has appeared, save for a few studies of the strategy and tactics of the German and related armies, such as Norman Stone's *The Eastern front, 1914–1917* and Gunther Rothenberg's *The Army of Francis Joseph*, both in the 1970s.

Vejas Liulevicius addresses the issue of continuity/discontinuity in his essay on German military administration in areas seized from Russia early in World War I called *Oberost*. In these territories the Germans found what they regarded as a kind of *tabula rasa* (*Unkultur*), on which the German army, primarily desirous of exploiting the area for its own needs, also hoped to put its stamp in the form of beneficent and elevating policies for the various nationalities inhabiting this territory. Already possessed of a long term sense of superiority over the peoples to the east, the German officers in charge of this vast territory found their stereotypes only confirmed by the disordered state of the land after military action had laid it waste. So, the military set about through "German work" reorganizing the vast *Oberost* territory and planning the future of the inhabitants: a kind of "nations-building" under German hegemony. The mission failed, partly owing to the resistance of the "natives," partly to German defeat in 1918. The Germans, frustrated by resistance to their plans and resentful of failure, felt they had learned their lesson. The relatively benign vision of "lands and peoples," to be reorganized and uplifted, gave way to a far more lethal one of "races and spaces," to be conquered, exploited, enslaved and annihilated, which became the Nazi vision of the next war.

Dennis Showalter goes back further in time in his essay to examine the "institutional culture of ethnic stereotypes." Stereotypes, which developed in the German military in the nineteenth century, were sharpened in the course of the First World War and culminated in the destruction of the Second World War. Anti-Slavism emerged in Germany in the second half of the nineteenth century, partly reflecting negative attitudes toward increasingly visible peripatetic Polish agricultural labor; partly owing to strong anti-Russian biases emerging from liberal and socialist ideologies; and partly due to racial concepts that reached the level of public policy in Prussia in the 1880s and 1890s. These negative stereotypes were extended to Polish recruits in the German army, exacerbated by the fact that for most of these recruits German was a second language, often leading to misunderstanding, confusion and substandard performance. Similar mechanisms led to stereotyping of Jews as well in the German army—the "pathetic Jew" joined the "stupid" Pole, thus setting up the two main target groups of the future Nazi regime. World War I sharpened these stereotypes; the Pole became dangerous, the Jew treacherous. These newer, more lethal stereotypes festered during the interwar period and reappeared in deadly fashion during the next war. Both authors, then, seem to lean in the direction of continuity in their approaches.

The next contributions deal with the theme of ethnic Germans in the Successor States, which produces equally daunting interpretive problems. How does the nature of German self-understanding and identity change when Germans, who had, by and large, been the overlords in Poland and Bohemia, become minorities in newly constructed nations run by those who had previously been subordinated to them—from *Herrenvolk* to *Volksdeutsche*? To what extent did these Germans come to accept the new polities during the 1920s and under what terms? What was the effect on them of the rise to power in Germany of Hitler and the Nazis? By what process did the ethnic Germans turn away from the polities in which they had so recently been embedded and embrace a more encompassing form of Germanic identity? How did the Poles and Czechs who were themselves trying to forge a national identity and nation building view them?

Part of the problem in the past in dealing with these issues lay in the fact that historians on both sides of the ethnic divide were not able to break out of the "we vs. them" mentality. Former generations of Czech and Polish as well as German scholars could not shed the straitjackets of a narrowly conceived ethnic/national perspective to understand the tragedy for both sides in the events preceding and during World War II (just as the protagonists in the interwar period were unable to get beyond the practice of ethnic/national exclusivity). For example, in the area of Czech-German relations (which even today are not as cordial as those between Germany and her other eight neighbors), even a younger generation of scholars is having difficulty escaping the older patterns. A 1996 essay by a German, Christoph Boyer, and a Czech, Jaroslav Kucera, evoked a strong response from a senior German scholar, who observed that the article "was ideologically in line with the old Czechoslovak state ideology." The two scholars took up the challenge in the pages of the journal *Bohemia* and the old Manichean struggle continued. Outside historians suggested other more useful approaches and frames of reference than the traditional ones. For example, comparative studies, that would transcend "we versus them," or the formation of identity among Czechs and Germans; peace studies, to examine time periods in which the worst did not happen and explain why; environmental and regional history, which examines the common experiences of several ethnic groups; interdisciplinary studies, such as gender; to mention only the most obvious.[1]

Some historians have taken up this challenge, and are among the authors of essays in this volume. Elizabeth Drummond in her essay examines the shifting nature of German nationalist expression in Posen/Poznań from the late nineteenth century to the interwar period as portrayed in the activities of nationalistic pressure groups such as the German Eastern Marches Society and the Pan-German League. Although biological-racial nationalism seems to have been the currency of the league in the years prior to the First World War, the Marches Society tended to reject racism and represent a cultural nationalism, which at least offered the Poles, busy asserting their own national identity, the opportunity to be "raised up" to a civilized level. This policy largely backfired however, as the Germans discovered that educating the Poles did not make good Germans out of them, but rather middle class Poles loyal to their own nationality. The outcome of the First World War reversed the roles of the two peoples however, and the Germans, those who did not emigrate to Germany proper, found themselves trapped in a reconstituted Poland, where the Polish government used many of the same techniques against them as they had used against the Poles in the prewar period. The result was a radicalization of the German minority, a wholesale embracing of the biological-racial model and, eventually, support for the Nazis, once Hitler had come to power. This set the stage for the disasters of the Second World War.

The destruction of dynastic states and the emergence of "national-ethnic" ones after World War I often led to the mass migration of minority populations out of the host country, as for example in Posen/Poznań after 1918, a pattern which continued during and after World War II and as recently as the 1990s in the former Yugoslavia. In some cases, though, as James Bjork points out in his essay, that migration did not happen, owing to relative liberality on the part of the dominant group, or to the method of land transfer, or to the relative 'rootedness' of the minority population. Bjork, in his essay, goes on to offer religious affiliation as an additional factor. Religious affiliation, often a marker for ethnicity, could exacerbate differences between majoritarian and minority populations—and usually did. Occasionally, however, shared confession could facilitate cultural transmission and hence better relations between unequal partners, thus obviating the perceived need for a rude sorting out of populations. He tests his hypothesis on the basis of the mixed Polish-German populations of Upper Silesia, a contested area, which, by most indications, should have witnessed a "sorting out" of the two nationalities. Both Poles and Germans in this area were overwhelmingly Catholic. But, although many priests were reshuffled according to nationality, most remained devoted to traditional utraquist pastoral work, so that the nationalizing dreams of both Poles and Germans were frustrated. There obtained a kind of permeability of the language barrier in the churches that prevented full-scale nationalization. This represented a pointed, but all too often neglected, example of a potential third course between "absolute assimilation on the one hand and identification as a defiant and irreducible minority on the other." This seems to have been one case where the strict formula "we versus them" broke down to an extent, aided by the practices of a universal institution.

If a common confession prevented complete nationalization, so could common language, as Richard Blanke points out in his essay. Here he deals with a Polish-speaking German minority in interwar Poland (the Masurians and Upper Silesians). He points out that for many of these people a national consciousness developed counter to native language, an interesting exception to the general rule. Even under fairly strong Polish political pressure, these people clung to their German identity; eventually in the 1920s many of them adopted the German language as an expedient and most fled the country in 1945, although the Poles still laid claim to them as "Poles." This essay, like the one before, demonstrates how contingent, fluid and, often, negotiable, rather than set in stone, nationality often can be.

Eagle Glassheim's essay on the Sudeten German nobility demonstrates that hypernationalism could be just as pronounced in post-World War I Czechoslovakia as in Poland. Even though the German nobility in Bohemia prior to the war had been a supranational elite, resisting radical nationalism on both sides, this stance did not save them from a Czech nationalism, which identified them with the German enemy and attempted to confiscate their estates as part of a land reform program. In this climate, even the large landowners, many of them Czechs, broke down into rivaling Czech and Sudeten German camps, something they never did prior to the war, and pursued their interests within this context. The German landowners in their organization (the *Landbund*) soon began talking in terms of the German national *Besitzstand* in Bohemia, language reserved to the nationalists prior to the war, and eventually found themselves caught up with most of the rest of the Sudeten Germans in the Nazi wave of the 1930s.

The final set of essays in his part of the volume examines Nazi Germany and the war in the East, particularly the Nazi-Soviet conflict of 1941–1945. In contrast to the relative paucity of studies on Germany's goals and practices in the East during World War I, here we are confronted with an embarrassment of riches. Just as a young generation of American (and British) scholars is investing the field of ethnic relations with new interpretive concepts, so a young generation of German (and American) scholars is transforming our understanding of what the Nazis were about in the East in World War II.[2]

Equipped with language skills in several Eastern European languages and experienced in researching in often obscure Polish or Russian or Ukrainian archives, these scholars have sorted through the mountains of documents which have become available since the collapse of the Soviet Union and shaped useful and insightful studies. What are the issues involved here? Again, as mentioned earlier, they are the issues of continuity and discontinuity; of decision-making, to what extent central, to what extent on the ground; of motivation, social background, and ideological training on the part of perpetrators at several levels; of tensions between economic motives and genocidal intent; and of the role of the German military as opposed to that of the SS, SD and other police agencies in mass murder.

Much of the work on Nazi policies and practices in the East has been subsumed under the rubric of Holocaust studies—and rightfully so. One major motive behind Hitler's invasion of the Soviet Union in 1941 was, after all, the destruction of what the Nazis called the "Jewish-Bolshevik" regime. Nor should one forget, that although Jews were the central target of Hitler's regime and were to be annihilated to the last person, an additional important motive lay in traditional anti-Slavism, which imperiled that large group of people who had been neighbors of the Germans in the East since time immemorial. If the Nazis were eventually to kill 6,000,000 Jews in the death camps, they also would take the lives of 28,000,000 people in the Soviet Union alone, not counting those in other more neighboring countries. The second largest number of deaths after the Jews was over 3,000,000 Soviet POWs.

With the Nazi regime and World War II the vision of empire in the East took on gargantuan, destructive and ahistorical proportions. As Peter Black demonstrates in his essay, the Nazis abused history by depicting their empire building as a resumption of medieval patterns. Once again, they maintained, there would be a great *Drang nach Osten* to expand the economic, political, cultural and, above all, racial *Lebensraum* of the German people to the East. This time, however, there would not be a sharing of culture, a pattern we have seen as recently as World War I, not to mention a wave of Christianization. Rather, the Jews were to be annihilated; the Poles and other Slavic peoples "decapitated" of their intellectual elites and reduced to modern day helots, with enormous human losses by attrition assumed as a matter of course. This destruction and enslavement would be accompanied by a transfer of German settlers, who, in league with ethnic Germans already living throughout Eastern Europe (but themselves subject to transfer), would provide the foundation for an ever-expanding German "racial state." As Black points out in the Polish context, to undertake the enormous administrative task of reordering the East, the Nazis availed themselves of "auxiliaries," many of them drawn from the ethnic German population, but many others from the "native" population, including Soviet POWs, Ukrainians, Lithuanians, etc., who served as auxiliary police or camp guards.

Geoffrey Megargee indicates in his essay that it was not just Hitler, the SS and the party that envisioned and carried out the war of racial destruction in the east. Rather, the German army itself was deeply involved. There has been a persistent myth going back to the immediate postwar period and strengthened during the Cold War, that the *Wehrmacht* basically fought a decent, clean war, while the Nazi SS and SD did all the dirty work. Recent scholarship has confirmed what we briefly realized at the end of World War II—and then forgot—namely that the German generals agreed with the basic propositions of the regime. These included the need to use war to acquire *Lebensraum*, the need to destroy the "Jewish-Bolshevik" regime whatever the cost, the need to reduce the Slavic peoples to servitude and the willingness to do whatever it took to achieve these goals. Accordingly, the German army was deeply implicated in mass murder in the east through its occupation policies, through its cooperation with the Nazi police and, above all, through its toleration of the death by starvation, exposure and disease of millions of prisoners under its control.

"Hitler moves east" has been a common theme of historical research; but Hitler also moved southeast, which is the topic of Béla Bodo's essay. Hitler could deal with the Soviet Union in one great, devastating strike. The situation in southeastern Europe both before 1939 and during the war was infinitely more complex. There were a number of countries there to deal with, each had a different history and nationality mix; each was at a different geographic proximity with Germany; some were pro-revisionist with respect to the World War I settlement, some were not. Relations between these countries and Nazi Germany resemble a kaleidoscope, as a fluid situation in the prewar period put one or the other country on a pro- or anti-German basis, often with a quick change in sides. Hitler dealt cleverly with these countries, beginning already in 1933 to sign bilateral trade agreements with them, partly to cut them of from the West. These agreements were always advantageous to the Germans. Hitler also preferred to deal with national or ethnic states, not because he appreciated the nationalities of Southeast Europe—the opposite is the case—but because he hated diversity and found unitary states easier to control. Before and during the war he also exploited nationality conflict by using border changes or the threat of them as carrot and stick. The most dramatic examples of this were the former Yugoslavia and Czechoslovakia.

Bodo goes beyond just detailing German policies toward southeastern Europe country by country, he puts the entire era in a larger context by asking some fundamental questions about how or to what degree Nazi Germany's foreign policy is or is not on a continuum of nineteenth- and twentieth-century European imperialism in general. Did Hitler's support for ethnic boundaries in Southeast Europe have an ideological base or was it simply an example of his opportunism? What was the relationship between Nazi racism and Hitler's attempt to economically exploit the area? Did his temporary redrawing of the ethnic map unwittingly complete Wilson's conception of the nationality state? Finally, he also notes the relevance of partisan warfare, particularly as it was practiced in Greece and Yugoslavia during the war, to more recent examples of guerilla warfare.

The barbaric Nazi policies against the peoples of eastern and southeastern Europe were not just a matter of *Reich* German agencies and its military imposing their ideological will on the ethnic enemy. There was another important element in the wartime mix: the ethnic Germans (culturally and linguistically German but citizens of the various eastern and southeastern European countries). These *Volksdeutsche* had, in many cases, lived for centuries in much of Europe to the east of Germany, indeed, deep into Russia itself. Many of these people found themselves deeply distressed by the settlement of the First World War, when the dramatic political and geopolitical changes often left them in a position where they were powerless minorities ruled by people who, in many cases, they themselves had dominated. The Nazi regime made an active effort to court these people during the 1930s and in a number of countries pro-Nazi political parties and groups emerged among the ethnic Germans, enabling them in some cases to function as Trojan horses against the countries of which they were nominally citizens.

With war and occupation, the ethnic Germans often collaborated with the Nazis, gaining temporary advantages by virtue of belonging to the "master race." Most dramatically, the Waffen-SS was able to recruit hundreds of thousands of young ethnic Germans for its military units, which, in turn, were often used in anti-partisan campaigns. By the end of the war, the *Volksdeutsche* were etched in the minds of the newly liberated peoples as followers of Hitler and accomplices in his war of racial annihilation and enslavement. As a result, more than 13 million ethnic Germans were expelled from their ancestral homelands, a dramatic development which ended in many areas the centuries long, often hostile, sometimes cooperative, always symbiotic relationship between Germans and the peoples of the East. John C. Swanson in his essay gives us a country-by-country overview of ethnic German populations before and during the Second World War culminating in their dramatic fate after 1945.

## Notes

1. See Ronald Smelser, "Alte Argumente im neuen Licht," and the response "Von alten und neuen Fragestellungen," *Bohemia* 38/2 (1997), 358–371.
2. Representative here would be the work of Dieter Pohl, Christian Gerlach, Johannes Huerter and Christian Hartmann.

# German Military Occupation and Culture on the Eastern Front in World War I

### ◈ Vejas Gabriel Liulevicius ◈

*Kultur* was a central slogan and one of the organizing principles of German occupation policies in Eastern Europe during the First World War. While fighting raged on the Eastern Front, an expansive German military administration was set up behind the lines, in the occupied territories wrested from the Russian Empire from 1915 on (in present day Lithuania, Latvia, and Belarus, later also Estonia). This state, called Ober Ost, represented a military utopia in which the army could organize the administration along its own principles, exercising a monopoly of control. Through strict military organization, Ober Ost established a close surveillance of the varied peoples and lands under its control, using techniques that anticipated the authoritarian total states of the following decades of the twentieth century, and exploited the territory economically for the benefit of the army and the German homefront. Accompanying these measures was a striking emphasis, in a time of total war, on cultural policies in these Eastern European lands. Such policies aimed to set the terms for the post-war future, binding the areas to the sphere of German culture. The German administration's propaganda announced that it was undertaking the work of *Kultur* here and celebrated this as "German Work," linking its policies to a wider German cultural mission in the East. Such propaganda was directed not only at the natives, but also at the German home front, and most of all at the German soldiers in the territories, who contended with the day-to-day realities of occupation and the experience of the Eastern Front. The encounter with Eastern Europe, framed in terms of culture, transformed German views of the lands and peoples of the East during World War I and in its aftermath. During the Second World War, the Nazis would return to this region with a radicalized version of the visions of control and transformation broached in Ober Ost.[1]

The start of the war in 1914 and 1915 in the East was a set of surprising, contradictory experiences for Germany: invasion and repulsion, defeat and victory. German officials were horrified at the unexpectedly quick mobilization of Russian armies that bore down on Prussia, threatening to destroy the gamble of the Schlieffen Plan in the west. Refugees streamed away from the exposed border areas. However, at the titanic battles of Tannenberg and the Masurian Lakes, generals von Hindenburg and Ludendorff defeated the invading forces, and would be hailed as the saviors of East Prussia.[2] A renewed Russian incursion into East Prussia took place again in October of 1914 and would finally be repulsed only in the winter of 1915.

The trauma of the Russian invasion was lovingly cultivated and reinforced by German propaganda. Claims of widespread systematic atrocities against the civilian population were made: the charges included arson, deportation, summary executions, and other forms of abuse. In fact, according to historians today, in spite of the legends of Cossack depredations, the reality of the Russian occupation "was significantly less dramatic."[3] But the images used in propaganda were deliberate and lurid, aiming to use the experience. This invasion, the only significant occupation of German territory, was taken as evidence for the government's claim that Germans were fighting a war of defense against a "world of enemies." Such arguments helped in the integration of the Social Democratic movement into the war effort, as one of its revolutionary passions was a determination to fight the autocratic Tsarist regime.

Appeals for aid to refugees and later for help in reconstruction in East Prussia were in the spirit of the *Burgfrieden* announced at the start of the war. The "Ideas of 1914" (of which the *Burgfrieden* notion was one) were espoused by countless journalists, professors, historians, and writers (among them Thomas Mann). They included a statement of the values for which Germany was supposed to be fighting. In the West, it was claimed, German *Kultur* (said to be deep-rooted, idealistic, authentic, and profound) faced off against French and English *Zivilisation* (seen as commercial, technologically-oriented, and superficial). By contrast, the Russian invasion was presented as an elemental onslaught of sheer barbarism. German propaganda images showed destroyed towns, homes, and domestic interiors, claiming that such actions were the essence of Slavic nature. Over the following years, one other function of dwelling on the alleged atrocities of the Russian forces was to offset the spreading conviction in the West and in neutral countries that the German invasion of Belgium and Northern France had been marked by violence against civilians, as well as the destruction of landmarks like the library of Louvain.[4] The Allied stereotypes of "Huns" and "Barbarians" would be met by an insistence that in the East, against the Tsarist allies of the Western powers, the Germans represented the force of culture.

In 1915, the Eastern Front saw remarkable movement, which often stood in stark contrast to the immobility and blood-soaked stagnation of the Western Front. In the summer months, German armies advanced far into the western borderlands of the Russian Empire in what was called the "Great Advance." Poland was placed under a civil administration, but the lands to the northeast (today Lithuania, southern Latvia, parts of Belarus, and northern portions of Poland) were placed under a purely military rule. There was no extensive planning for the military occupation, so much would be left to improvisation on the spot. First impressions were to be very important. Though ordinary Germans from the eastern provinces had some knowledge of the neighboring lands, the immediacy of being surrounded by so many foreign impressions left an impact on many soldiers. The sociologist Norbert Elias, then a student, later testified to his unfamiliarity with the East, though it had been just over the border.[5] The soldiers also saw territories that had just been scoured by the front passing through, often after being subjected to the scorched earth policies of the retreating Russian forces. Some towns and cities were crowded with refugees, often wracked with disease and hunger, while other areas were left depopulated in the evacuation. The first impressions here of the East showed lands where terrible acts seemed almost normal.

In the occupied territories, the Germans set about the urgent task of establishing order and a working administration. At the same time, beyond these immediate imperatives, the control of the region also offered some tantalizing future prospects to Hindenburg and especially his Quartermaster General, Ludendorff. The area was named *Das Land Ober Ost* after Hindenburg's title as *Oberbefehlshaber Ost*, the Supreme Commander in the East. As envisioned by its staff, this was to be a novel form of state: rule of the army, by the army, and for the army, using its possibilities to the utmost. The lands and peoples of the East were to be taken in hand by the army. The natural resources and productive capacities of the land would be exploited, while the diverse peoples of the region would be cultivated as well. The army's role would be that of cultural mentor and teacher. The very diversity of the ethnic mix here (including Lithuanians, Jews, Latvians, Poles, Belarusians, Estonians, Russians, Tatars and many others) made outside rule natural, the administration's propaganda argued. The result of these ambitions would be an extensive set of policies intended to harness the region physically and culturally.

Here in the East, the "Ideas of 1914" were given a different twist, as the German forces were said here to confront not an inimical *Zivilisation*, but rather sheer absence of culture, *"Unkultur."* Such a judgement, however, did not spring into being fully formed only in World War I. Rather, these statements built on earlier stereotypes of Eastern Europe, such as the supposed existence of a cultural gradient (*Kulturgefälle*) or an alleged essential chaotic nature of Eastern European peoples, summed up in the words *"polnische Wirtschaft."*[6]

To these older stereotypes and oppositions were added the immediate, first-hand impressions of the German soldiers and officials themselves in Ober Ost. These impressions were obviously not monolithic nor exactly the same for all of the two to three million men who served on the Eastern Front and the occupied territories, but certain common themes emerge. Eastern Europe, its lands and peoples, encountered for the first time immediately after the ravages of modern war, often seemed disordered and primitive, dirty and diseased, and in many ways dangerous. The scenes of combat and the devastation wrought on homesteads left one officer dispirited, who wrote in a letter of seeing "empty gables torn up as if by madness, destroyed human habitations, open cadavers and gray heaps of corpses, fires, foreign, foreign faces pressed to the ground, lying as if branches broken by a storm." As a result of such impressions, he declared, "How the world has changed and become empty!"[7] The openness of the landscape left a strong memory for soldiers. A realistic novel by another officer described the impact of "the size of the land, which had swallowed them, as a big fish swallows many smaller ones, and which held them here against their will. Only a few thought more clearly. But they, too, felt at this hour only a vague, crippling helplessness, coming from the land and lying on them like fetters, binding them."[8] The poor quality of the roads, which turned into bottomless seas of mud during the rains, was one of the central images mentioned in accounts of the East. The potential for epidemics and disease was also remarked on often. In a photo album of souvenir pictures published by the 58th infantry division, a picture depicts a military bath jokingly labeled a "Louse-oleum."[9] Poems written by soldiers for army newspapers summed up the impressions of the Eastern Front:

### "On the Advance March"
Like a dark gray coat/ The heavy night lowers itself.
Without respite, restless, ever further/ Eastwards we carry the battle.
The smell of burning and rubble and corpses./Pestilence is every pull of breath.
And the jackdaws, hoarsely croaking,/ Reel by in heavy flight.
And with wild greed a vulture/ Breaks out of the dark realm of clouds.
Horror and terror lie/ Over the blood-soaked field.
Let it lie, let it be!/ Battle is battle and war is war!
Cheerful and without respite, restless,/ Eastwards we carry victory.[10]

The cycle of images thus showed an East that seemed threatening in its nature and the wartime dangers it held.

At the same time, these impressions were tempered by a conviction, encouraged in the propaganda of Ober Ost, that the region was in fact even now undergoing transformation. The German army was said to be improving the underdeveloped region, bringing order and cultivation to Eastern Europe. An amateur poet, Sergeant Hamm, summed it up thus:

### "A Look Backwards"
Even still I hear the pounding of heavy steps/ In the rubble of the cities—hear people pleading.
Villages moaning, condemned to death in flames./ All about my eyes still see the misery,

Which the disgrace of the Russian army inflicted/On their own
land, on works of nature!
That, which seemed forever lost, was created anew by- /The German battalions of *Kultur*!

Many thousands of hands I see serving duty,/ The German spirit
blows through the poor land;
And new life rises up out of the ruins,/ Which noble mind snatched
from decline.
The golden bridge of the future is erected,/ Waiting for the spring,
field and meadow breathe.
We have carried eastwards stone upon stone/ We German pioneers
of *Kultur*!

Here an unshakable grip writes history,/ The sun turns itself back
smiling.
The henchmen's misdeed, it came to nothing,/ Upon the desolate
ruins there blooms a new joy.
And even if we leave this land one day,/ Many an imperishable
monument shows the tracks
Which we cleared for ourselves through the dirt of the alleys- / We
German battalions of *Kultur*![11]

In making this argument, officials of Ober Ost resorted to the concept of
"German Work" (*Deutsche Arbeit*). The term was taken from the Romantic father of
Volkskunde of the nineteenth century, Wilhelm Heinrich Riehl, who had argued that
each people possessed its own kind of work. The Germans were said to be endowed
with a genius for a kind of work that organized and administered. Under German
direction, Ober Ost was to be remade as a "Neuland," showcasing the creative powers of the German army, the school of the nation. The trophy which was awarded to
Hindenburg and Ludendorff to memorialize their founding of Ober Ost presented
this conceit in a visual image: atop it stood the goddess of victory with laurels and a
sheaf of wheat, metaphors for conquest and harvest. The stand for the trophy showed
a German soldier training the growth of a tree.

This concept of German Work gave a blank check for ambitious programs to
reorganize the territory and to set the terms for the future of the peoples living there.
The Ober Ost administration on the one hand pursued a program of *Verkehrspolitik*,
or "movement policy," which sought to control and direct the movement of resources,
goods, and people in its realm through modern means. An array of techniques was
used for this purpose: the issuing of Ober Ost passes, censuses, the drawing of new
administrative borders, police surveillance, orders severely restricting movement. The

constructive side of this ambition was to be the building of a network of transport projects in the region, binding it to Germany economically and administratively: new roads, train lines, waterways, telegraph and telephone networks. The other realm of policy, which sought to achieve similar imperatives on a spiritual plane, was the cultural program pursued by Ober Ost.

The Ober Ost administration devoted a striking degree of attention to issues of culture in a time of total war mobilization. This dedication reflected a sense of future prospects that would be yielded by such investment. The army would cultivate the native peoples and draw them closer to German cultural influence. By making the Germans mentors of the cultural development of Eastern European peoples in the zone between Russia and Germany, the terms of their future would be set. Ludendorff announced that on its own, "the motley population cannot create any *Kultur*."[12]

The army could pursue a cultural program in many dimensions, which would cultivate the peoples. The administration published newspapers in the local languages and translators labored to create terms for modern administrative measures missing in the respective tongues. A censorship office banned books and periodicals deemed dangerous. The school system was regulated, schools inspected, and their subjects dictated, especially emphasizing the teaching of German. Army reviewers surveyed native arts and especially native theater, evaluating it for its promise. Military scholars evaluated the unfamiliar art treasures and architectural landmarks of the region, revealing the history of the place to the locals who actually lived there. Even archaeological excavations were organized. The native cultures were put on display at living museums called Work Rooms (*Arbeitsstuben*) in Wilna, where visitors could observe craftsmen at work at their traditional trades.

Parallel to these efforts ran another set of initiatives directed at the German soldiers who did the day-to-day work of the occupation regime. They were to be confirmed in a sense of purpose here in Eastern Europe, a larger German cultural mission in the East. The newspapers of the army, soldiers' guidebooks to cities of the region, front theater and front movies, and special Soldiers' Homes to provide a sense of home away from home for the occupiers in alien surroundings contributed to this aim.

Predictably, given the importance placed on culture, the friction that emerged between the occupiers and the occupied native peoples would thus also have a cultural dimension and would on occasion be a culture clash over the meaning of central values. The German concept of order, *Ordnung*, for instance, contrasted with the concepts of order held by the largest ethnic group in the territory, the Lithuanians. Ober Ost's own "constitution," the *Verwaltungsordnung* of 1916, spelled out its mission: "The task of the Administration is the establishment and maintenance of ordered political and economic circumstances in the occupied territory," followed by the sentence, "The interests of the army and the German Empire always come before those of the occupied territory."[13] *Ordnung* was a function of state authority here, turned to the task of cultivating the anarchic occupied area. Lithuanian activists, by contrast, emphasized a different conception of order, *tvarka*, whose meanings were opposed to those of the German *Ordnung*. As was natural for a peasant people, the concept of *tvarka* grew out of the concept of the farming homestead. It denoted an order that was supposed to be natural, unforced, and homegrown, not imposed from above. The first political manifestos of the nationalist movement would offer *tvarka* as an alternative to any foreign domination. A cultural conflict also flared up almost immediately over the native schools. In the first months of the German occupation, different ethnic groups in the territory had founded a thousand new schools in the countryside. Fearing the political potential of these schools in an ethnically mixed territory, Ober Ost often fell back on simply closing schools. Irregular attempts at Germanization or ethnic manipulation turned the schools, precisely because of their cultural importance, into a constant battleground throughout the years of the regime. It was also evidence of a disconnect, as the cultural policies and initiatives of the administration either did not reach the native populations or were regarded with great suspicion as harbingers of greater regulation yet to come. By 1917, a shift in mood took place among the native populations. As the economic exploitation of the region and anxieties about what the regime's policies (among them the cultural) portended for the future intensified, locals now frequently felt that neither a return to Russian rule nor German occupation were livable alternatives.

The importance of ideas of culture to the German administration of the occupied East had significant consequences after the Ober Ost regime came crashing down in November 1918 due to defeat in the West. This reversal came after what had seemed to many to be victory in the East, sealed in the Treaty of Brest-Litovsk, and seemed thus all the harder to assimilate. German mercenary units, the *Freikorps*, stayed on to fight in the *Baltikum* area against the Red Army as well as the young republics of Estonia, Latvia, and Lithuania in 1919. The *Baltikumer* claimed to be defending the culture of the world. In Germany, a variant of the "Stab-in-the-Back Legend" grew up around the experience of occupation in the East: supposedly, generous policies had been met with ill will and ignorance, or had run up against some intractable, unreformable essence of the East and its peoples. Some former Ober Ost officials considered the cultural efforts to have been a mistake, unappreciated and spurned. Over the next decades the Nazis would form a radicalized version of the mission in the East, which drew on some of the perceived "lessons" of the First World War. If the lands and peoples could not be cultivated, they must instead be viewed as spaces and races to be administered, reordered, and cleansed or removed. The Jewish populations of Eastern Europe were to be destroyed immediately, in the Nazi program of genocide, the "Final Solution." As for the other native peoples of the region, Hitler insisted that they were not to be cultivated. The German soldiers would not be "school-masters," he declared. Completing the Nazis' perverse instrumentalization of ideas of a cultural mission, Himmler would announce that the peoples of Eastern Europe would be "slaves for our *Kultur*."[14] Ober Ost's failed rule and its propagation of the cultural mission the German army had to perform in the occupied East had crucial consequences, calling forth from its failure visions more extreme and violent.

# Notes

1.  Vejas Gabriel Liulevicius, *War Land on the Eastern Front: Culture, National Identity and German Occupation in World War I* (Cambridge, 2000).
2.  Dennis E. Showalter, *Tannenberg, Clash of Empires* (Hamden CT, 1991).
3.  Showalter, *Tannenberg*, p. 159.
4.  John Horne and Alan Kramer, *German Atrocities 1914: A History of Denial* (New Haven, 2001).
5.  Norbert Elias, *Reflections on a Life*, trans. Edmund Jephcott (Cambridge, MA, 1994), pp. 19–20.
6.  Michael Burleigh and Wolfgang Wippermann, *The Racial State: Germany 1933–1945* (Cambridge, 1991), p. 26.
7.  Otto Grautoff, ed., *Bernhard von der Marwitz. Eine Jugend in Dichtung und Briefen* (Dresden, 1923), pp. 121–23.
8.  Victor Jungfer, *Das Gesicht der Etappe* (Berlin, 1919), pp. 16–19.
9.  Dr. Portius, ed., *Gedenkblätter der 58. Infanterie-Division. 2. Teil* (Strassburg i. Els, n.d.).
10. Bundesarchiv/Militärarchiv Freiburg i. Br. (BAMA) PHD 8/73, Gefr. Benny Kippes, "Im Vormarsch," *Wacht im Osten. Feldzeitung der Armee-Abteilung Scheffer*, no. 440 (13 February 1917).
11. BAMA PHD 8/73, Sergt. Max Hamm, "Ein Rückblick," *Wacht im Osten*, no. 819 (28 February 1918).
12. Erich Ludendorff, *Meine Kriegserinnerungen, 1914–1918* (Berlin, 1919), p. 138.
13. BAMA (Bundesarchiv-Militärarchiv Freiburg i.Br.) PHD 8/20, "Ziffer 259. Verwaltungsordnung für das Etappengebiet im Befehlsbereich des Oberbefehlshabers Ost (Ob. Ost)," in *Befehls- und Verordnungsblatt des Oberbefehlshabers Ost*, Nr. 34 (26 June, 1916), 269–89.
14. Quoted in Michael Burleigh, *Germany Turns Eastwards: A Study of "Ostforschung" in the Third Reich* (Cambridge, 1988), p. 8.

# Comrades, Enemies, Victims

## The Prussian/German Army and the Ostvölker

### ◆ Dennis Showalter ◆

Recent writing on Nazi Germany stresses public and institutional acceptance of the Reich's racist ideology and involvement in even the worst of its genocidal crimes. The motivating power of Nazi principles in military contexts has been demonstrated comprehensively by Omer Bartov.[1] So much, indeed, has been done to establish Wehrmacht complicity in National Socialism's genocidal policies in Eastern Europe that the roles of the SS and the *Einsatzgruppen* run a certain risk of marginalization. But while demolishing the "clean shield" myths of the immediate postwar years, the weight of contemporary analysis stresses the armed forces' Nazification by a mixture of generalized sympathy for National Socialist ideology and the mass mobilization that brought into uniform ever larger numbers of potential, if not necessarily eager, executioners.[2]

This pattern applies above all to Eastern Europe, where centuries of cultural influence and political rule generated prejudices sharpened by the First World War and honed to a genocidal edge under National Socialism.[3] It is not necessary to deny that approach to suggest another dimension. Germany's military, the army in particular, had developed over the preceding two centuries an institutional culture of ethnic stereotypes, reflecting internal experiences and judgments that during and after the Great War served to structure and process defeat and its consequences. The purpose of this chapter is to outline the nature of that culture, and the passage of those it objectified from comrades, through enemies, to victims.

## I.

The link between war and ethnicity in the Western world can be traced at least to the Greek city states, and their system of locally raised, homogeneous hoplite contingents. Beginning with the Alexandrian era, identity also came to be associated with behavior rather than birth. A cohort of Roman auxiliary troops, for example, might specialize as slingers or light cavalry, with its official ethnic identity as "Batavian" or "Iberian" gradually becoming nominal as its ranks refilled from wherever it might be stationed.

During the Middle Ages and the early modern period, contingents were distinguished more by particular skills than by cultural or linguistic identity.[4] In the eighteenth century, French and British regiments often had regional designations alongsid their numerical ones, but the designation was seldom anything but nominal.[5]

Sweden's introduction of locally based conscription provided an alternative, as regiments identified with the province from which they drew the bulk of their manpower, and socialized "outsiders" into the territorial system.[6] Prussia's cantonal system also served to develop provincial identities in the army's infantry and cavalry regiments, though the higher proportion of "foreigners" and long-service men in Prussia's peacetime ranks tended to make that identity regimental as opposed to local.[7] Of more significance was the emergence in the course of the eighteenth century of a certain "pecking order," by which men from some parts of the kingdom were considered better soldiers than those from others. That hierarchy reflected to a degree the relative length of time a particular region had been part of the Prussian kingdom. Regiments recruited in Silesia, annexed by Prussia in 1740, were initially regarded as less effective than formations from the "old provinces." Even more crucial was the personal judgment of Frederick the Great—a judgment that as often as not depended on performance at maneuvers as opposed to combat and, once rendered, was seldom revised. For purposes of this paper the important point is that the regiments raised, and the soldiers recruited, from the Polish territories incorporated after 1773 were incorporated into the existing matrix. There is no significant indication that Poles were regarded as inherently less effective or reliable than the rest of the army. Polish units were assigned to "counterinsurgency" operations in Poland and former Poland during the 1790s on a basis of availability; no significant distinctions in either employment can be established from the records.[8]

The Prussian army's matrix began to change with the introduction of the Conscription Law of 1815. It institutionalized the principle of universal manhood suffrage, and in consequence transformed the active army into a training cadre for annual classes of conscripts. That development in turn required a revolution in training methods. Since the days of Frederick William I, the army's norm had been the accession of relatively small numbers of recruits at any one time. In consequence, training processes had been almost individual. Recruits were put under the wing of an old soldier, who showed them the daily routines. Drill itself involved small squads: a half-dozen or so, under the direct supervision of a noncommissioned officer. The entire process involved a high degree of osmosis and imitation; and most recruits were already accustomed to this kind of instruction—the early modern norm for learning anything.[9]

The new conscription policy meant half to two-thirds of every regiment were recruits. Since recruits were inducted only once a year, training became a mass, collective process. Instead of focusing on individuals, officers and NCOs were impelled to treat their new intakes as entities, to be dealt with as groups and given collective identifications. That development was fostered by the principle of territorial recruiting: keeping conscripts in their home regions and provinces. Common sense and experience alike indicated that, taken in the aggregate, men from Berlin and men from Pomerania were likely to respond differently to similar stimuli.[10]

Collective identification was encouraged as well by the rapid decline—arguably the strangulation—of the "Landwehr spirit," that generalized enthusiasm for peacetime military service the military reformers had expected would infuse the men of the new Prussia.[11] Instead the government deliberately discouraged such populist attitudes in favor of a "well ordered police state."[12] Increasingly, moreover, military budgets failed to keep pace with birth rates—which meant relatively fewer eligible men were actually conscripted into the active army, and those who were seldom regarded it a a stroke of good fortune. The annual recruit contingents were correspondingly best described as "tractable." Products of a deferential, patriarchal society and an authoritarian state, they were unlikely to stage individual or collective acts of resistance. Neither could they be expected systematically to cooperate proactively with the army system. They would do what they were told—period. Exceptions, negative or positive, seem to have been few and far between.

In the early stages of this new pattern of collective identification, the system's negative focus was instead directed westward, towards the Rhineland and Westphalia. These territories had been given to Prussia over significant protest—in particular from the army, which disliked the strategic focus on France that accompanied the territorial realignment, and questioned the loyalty and reliability of units raised initially from men who had often fought on the other side. The western regiments' performance in the Waterloo campaign was sufficiently mixed to sustain an image of limited effectiveness into the postwar years. That image was reinforced by an officer's-mess conviction, particularly strong in individuals who were transferred from "old Prussian" formations, that Rhenish draftees were unable or unwilling to meet Prussian standards of drill and discipline. Urbanism, liberalism, Catholicism—all were blamed for the phenomenon. Some uniformed sociologists even ascribed the difference to drinking wine instead of honest Prussian beer.[13]

The general level of Old Prussian alienation from the newly acquired western provinces was so high that in some ways they resembled an occupied territory during the quarter century preceding the revolutions of 1848. And while the active units from the region remained loyal during that year of upheaval, the performance of the

Landwehr was sufficiently dubious to inspire a significant overhaul of the military system in the provinces.[14] That, however, was part of a general refurbishing of the Prussian Army, beginning in the 1860s and with the familiar Roon reforms being only the final stage. The key aspect of the revitalization for purposes of the present essay is that it involved fully integrating the Rhineland and Westphalian elements into the army proper. That policy was validated by the performance of the western formations in 1866, correspondingly followed when the *muss-Preussen* of the territories annexed in that year were "coordinated" into the army. raising its strength from nine corps to twelve, plus the Saxon contingent, and vindicated beyond reasonable dispute in 1870–71.[15] In the latter conflict, the differences in performance among the various Prussian contingents involved no more than bragging rights.

## II.

Until mid-century, then, the army's principal internal negative stereotype had been not ethnic but regional. Slavs and Jews had remained, if not quite invisible, under the army's institutional radar. Even the insurrections in Posen in 1848 had been suppressed easily enough that the dominant image of Polish revolutionaries was that expressed in the last third of Gustav Freytag's *Soll und Haben:* as barbarians from whom German settlers were rescued by the cavalry in the fashion of an American western movie.[16]

That began to change in the last quarter of the nineteenth century—but in two different paradigms. The growth and spread of anti-Slav prejudice in the Second Reich is well documented. Conservative admiration for Russia's stability was being eroded by a liberalism critical of Russian absolutism, and by a socialism strongly influenced by Marx's contempt for Russian "character." Freelance intellectuals like Paul de Lagarde and university academics like Theodor Schiemann increasingly described Russians as degenerate primitives, whose women lacked the emotional resources to be successful call girls and whose men could not manage to use modern plumbing correctly.[17]

While the officer corps was scarcely recruited overwhelmingly from Junker aristocrats, East Elbian influences were nevertheless disproportionately predominant, and East Elbian attitudes were widely copied. An anti-Polish nationalism fostered by Bismarck and reinforced by the ethnic patrioteers of the HKT Society was reinforced by the growing importance of seasonal gang labor in a rural eastern Germany whose population was declining. The Poles and Russians who brought in the harvests were nameless and faceless, coming with the dust, going with the wind.[18]

It would have been surprising had such attitudes not have extended to Slavs in German uniforms. Almost all of these were Poles, most of them living in Posen and Silesia. Some Polish conscripts were resident in the territory of I Corps, recruited in East and West Prussia. Others were sons of Polish migrants to the western industrial centers, doing their time in Saxon, Rhenish and Westphalian regiments. Particularly in the latter cases, linguistic and cultural differences tended to make them easy scapegoats. More than abstract stereotyping, however, was involved. As the century progressed, increasing numbers of Poles passed through the empire's elementary school system and acquired at least fundamental literacy in German. It remained, however, a second language for most of them—a pattern enhanced, paradoxically, by the increasing emphasis of Polish nationalists on fostering the everyday use of Polish as a response to linguistic Germanization.[19]

A common result in the army was a disproportionate number of Polish recruits who literally did not get the word—or even worse for them, responded in a way that led the drill instructor to believe he was being mocked. The problem was exacerbated because, as more and more recruits entered service functionally literate, increasing amounts of instruction were delivered in classroom models, as opposed to the often literally hands-on, hayfoot-strawfoot techniques of an earlier era. Moreover, recruits who underperformed for any reason were likely to bring down disproportionate amounts of collective punishment on their comrades, as sergeants and corporals struggled to bring their recruits up to unit standards. Time spent shoveling manure as a punishment for poor performance was frequently accompanied by an after-taps "visit from the Holy Ghost," a beating administered by the barracks room as an incentive to improve performance.[20]

Suicide rates in the Posen and Silesian corps regularly stood high in the army's list.[21] Obviously, not every Polish conscript was subjected to such treatment. Those whose German was adequate, those who were strong and quick enough to compensate for lack of comprehension, were folded into the mass of conscripts and became anonymous. Skill in polishing extra boots in barracks, willingness to carry extra rifles on a route march, could do much to overcome the disadvantage of extra consonants in a surname. At the same time the "Polack," whose dull wits, two left feet, and unkempt uniform made him the despair of his superiors and his squad mates alike, became a stock figure of German army humor generally characterized by crudeness rather than sophistication.[22]

The army's Jews were a different story. Their first significant presence came during the Wars of Liberation, when significant numbers of acculturated, urban young men volunteered for service despite a persistent hostility depicting them as "outsiders" in the emerging Prussian and German national communities.[23] For sixty years afterward the Prussian Jewish community continued to furnish sons to the draft, but in a context where Jews were frequently more anxious to serve than the army was to have them. A term in uniform was understood to have social values: developing the Jew physically and expanding his cultural horizons. At the same time a growing army stereotype depicted Jews collectively less as shirkers than as unable to meet the physical demands of duty in a rifle company and the emotional demands of barracks life.[24]

Scholars of the Second Empire use slander trials and church sermons to argue that public attention was focused so constantly and negatively on the "Jewish Question" that seemingly minor anti-Semitic manifestations could have significantly wider repercussions.[25] Stereotype and reality were linked in this case by the institution of the one-year volunteer. These were men with higher levels of education, able to pay their own expenses for a year of service. The system is usually analyzed in terms of its role as a source of reserve officers. In principle, volunteers were eligible to apply for a commission. It is well known that not only Jews, but Gentiles with the wrong political orientations or social origins were excluded from that process. But being a one-year volunteer had advantages apart from prospects of a commission. It was a mark of middle-class status. It saved a year or two of time embarking on a profession or learning a business. Not least, it offered prospects of better treatment while in service—at least of treatment different from that accorded the ordinary soldier

Such considerations continue to move society's privileged classes even in the twenty-first century. Large numbers of Jewish boys—as many as 30,000 between 1885 and 1914—joined their Gentile counterparts in applying for and receiving the status of *Einjaehriger*. Once in the regiments, however, the volunteers were frequently in for a rude surprise, whatever their ethnic or religious identification. The army had never quite known what to make of the "one-years." Despite their nickname of "of-ficers' chicklets" they were not really officer candidates. At the same time they had enough of a special status, enough exceptions were made for them in regulations and practice, that they were a running challenge to the noncoms. In some regiments, the volunteers were allowed to live at home. Their time was free as long as they attended the specific classes prescribed for them.[26]

Such advantages did not make them exactly popular with fellow soldiers serving longer terms in uniform. A volunteer who was willing to take his turn on the unpleas-ant details, who took some time to build himself up and improve his endurance in the local *Turnverein* before reporting, and who, not least, knew when to laugh at a dirty joke and when to buy a round of drinks for his squad, could have a memo-rably enjoyable year.[27] Those who did not adapt, the physically weak, the "mama's boys" (*Muttersoenchen*), or simply those unfortunate enough to become "designated scapegoats" could be driven to collapse or suicide.[28] The point for present purposes is that the German army's "visible Jew" was likely to be one of those unfortunates. Like their Polish counterparts those Jewish one-years able to blend into the general collective attracted limited notice. Those who stood out bore burdens sometimes enhanced because, since they could never become officers, there was no chance of their returning to collect payback from former *Schinder*.

Thus by 1914 the Kaiser's army had in place direct, coherent, sustainable, and credible stereotypes of two of the Third Reich's principal victim groups. They were also safer targets than Social Democratic conscripts, who increasingly could count on the support of their party in pursuing cases of abuse and harassment.[29] But, of more significance for this essay, neither stereotype was dangerous. As a soldier the Pole was stupid. The Jew was pathetic. The relative benignity of these images is highlighted by the army's much more negative images of its third visible ethnic community: soldiers from Alsace-Lorraine. Even before the Zabern Affair, these were stereotyped as disaffected at best, potentially disloyal at worst. The army coped in part by assigning significant numbers of Alsatian recruits to the Prussian Guard, stationed in Berlin—apparently in the mixed and contradictory hopes that the splendor of the Reich's capital would impress the Wacke bumpkins, and that good old Potsdam discipline would drive the nonsense out of their heads. The issue was further ameliorated because, as a crucial frontier sector, Alsace-Lorraine had a garrison several times larger than the population could support—two, later three corps instead of one. Alsatian conscripts could be correspondingly diluted—until the mobilization of 1914 brought reservists into the ranks.[30]

## III.

The surprising thing about the Great War is the durability of the three stereotypes. From the beginning of hostilities the German army successfully fostered disaffection and disloyalty among its Alsatian soldiers by expecting it. The argument of Dominick Reichert, that most reluctant of the Reich's Alsatian defenders, that Alsatians were less willing than other Germans to kill wounded and prisoners in cold blood is best taken with at least a grain of salt.[31] But beginning with the Battle of Verdun, Alsatians on the Western Front were subjected to special treatment based on suspicion of disloyalty: excluded from patrol assignments, teamed with presumably more reliable men from other regions. By 1917, divisions transferring from the Russian front were combing out their Alsatian elements. Desertions increased, to be met with announcements of increasingly stern punishments, despite the War Ministry's concern. By 1918, the disaffection in Alsaian ranks was beyond the army's capacity to remedy directly.[32]

Germany's Jewish soldiers were front-line targets less of the army's stereotyping than of the growing spread in Germany of anti-Semitic propaganda unchecked by an otherwise rigorous censorship. The "civil truce" Kaiser William proclaimed in 1914 was complemented by enthusiastic, and highly visible, Jewish participation in the war effort. Jews were eventually made eligible for reserve officer commissions, and more than a few of the long-derided one-year volunteers proved themselves brave and canny platoon sergeants (*Vizefeldwebel der Reserve*) under fire. The challenge came from a home front showing increasing signs of stress as a war originally marketed as ending in weeks demanded unexpected numbers of victims and levels of sacrifice. An improvised mobilization of a fragmented society encouraged mutual acquisitions of shirking. The anti-semites focused a diffuse hostility on the Jews. In October 1916 the Prussian War Ministry issued an order to perform a census of Jews serving in the military, subject to conscription, released from service, or found unfit. The order was in part a response to the national mobilization ordered by the new Chief of Staff, Paul von Hindenburg. It was also a self-protective response to a drumfire of accusations that the army was careless or complicit in allowing Jews to escape the rigors of the trenches.[33]

The census results were never made public, and the *Judenzählung* was not by itself sufficient to transform the army's institutional image of the Jew. It did reinforce the long-established stereotype of the Jew as a useless soldier, expressing it now in terms of seeking safe jobs in rear areas while his Gentile comrades bled for the Fatherland. The accompanying sense of alienation and exclusion felt by many Jewish soldiers nevertheless encouraged a growing consciousness of significant cultural gaps between Jew and Gentile even in the rifle companies.[34]

The Reich's Polish soldiers, in contrast, underwent a fundamental redefinition of image: from stupid to dangerous. The process did not begin with disaffection at the front. Regiments from Posen and Silesia performed no less well than those from other provinces throughout most of the war. The army did not undertake a *Polenzaehlung*, nor did it systematically transfer Polish soldiers for reasons of suspected unreliability. The key to the change was rather the role Russian Poland, conquered in the summer of 1915, came to play in the postwar visions of the German government and high command. Politicians projected an autonomous Polish kingdom, client of the Central Powers. Generals hungry for manpower sought to use that promised land as a lever to raise volunteers from the former Russian provinces.

On November 5, 1916, Germany proclaimed an independent Poland—and thereby created an objective conflict of loyalty in its own Polish soldiers. Nationalism in German Poland was less an affair of elites than a grass-roots process, based on businessmen, teachers, lawyers, and independent smallholders—the kinds of local notables who during the war became reserve officers or senior NCOs. They paid attention to such developments as Austria-Hungary's creating an autonomous Polish Legion. They paid attention as well to home-front developments. Compared to the western and central provinces, Posen and Silesia seem to have suffered from even worse shortages, even less sympathetic management, and even more hamfisted application of mutually contradictory government regulations. Both provinces were splitting along ethnic lines well before the Allies proclaimed their support for an independent Poland, and well before the December 1918 uprising that de facto transferred Posen to the new Polish state.[35]

The regional German authorities and the local German population fought back. The image of the postwar volunteer formations, the *Freikorps*, has been shaped on one hand by their role in Germany proper, as a spearhead of the antidemocratic, anti-Republican Right; and on the other by the post-Armistice *Baltikumer*, the *Landsknechts* who dreamed of carving out an Eastern redoubt for a saving remnant of true Germans. There was a middle ground along the ethnic frontier between Poles and Germans, occupied by locally raised German forces who saw themselves fighting for their homes and their liberties no less than their Polish counterparts. The difference was that the German home guards and militias were increasingly supported, and for practical purposes supplanted, by *Freikorps* from outside the region. These latter formations, better armed and with higher percentages of men who enjoyed fighting, were more effective than the locals in the mid-intensity fighting characteristic of the border. The Poles nevertheless gave them all they could handle, even at the Annaberg, the May 1921 stand-up fight in Silesia that became for the *Freikorps* what Woodstock was for America's counter-culture: if every German *had* been there who *claimed* to have been, the Poles would have disappeared in the mass![36]

What the *Freikorps* brought to the ideology of ethnicity in the German east was a developing sense of the East European—whatever his specific identity—as "other," as alien. This objectification reflected to a degree the *Freikorps*'s increasingly solipsistic sense of themselves as "others," cast out from a Germany ruled by socialists, traitors, and fat little men with briefcases. It reinforced as well a sharpening of ethnic lines reflected, for example, in the propaganda tabloid *Pieron*, aimed at German Silesians, which consistently depicted Poles as dirty apes, adept only at murdering Germans.[37] Objectification, however, had another context : the experiences of the Russian front.

From Tannenberg in 1914 to Riga in 1917, the Russian soldier acquired an image of being hard to kill, but easy to defeat. The 1915 battle of Gorlice-Tarnow was a prototypical Eastern Front battle. Pitting comprehensive planning and high-tech, heavy artillery and chlorine gas against numbers and inertia, a handful of German divisions tore open the front on a thirty-kilometer sector, captured a third of a million prisoners and exhausted Russia's available resources in everything from anesthetics to ammunition. From the perspective of the Germans on the ground, the Russian army survived only because it ran faster than the Germans could chase it.

Rear security was seldom a problem. Large numbers of potential partisans had been evacuated by the Russians themselves as part of a general policy of scorched earth.[38] The German army paid for most of what it took. Its soldiers usually behaved themselves; the level of atrocities in the intital stages of the war in the West was significantly worse.[39] Germans were, however, collectively shocked by their first experiences, visual and olfactory, of the newly occupied territories. As the front stabilized, the German army initiated what amounted to a civilizing campaign behind its lines. This reflected both an arguably distinctive German work ethic, and a belief, common in most armies, that planned activity keeps soldiers out of trouble.[40] Since the eighteenth century, moreover, European armies had paid increasing attention to at least surface cleanliness, latrine discipline, and other forms of what might be called preventive sanitation. One officer put the matter bluntly. It was, he said, a question of "Soap. Only when the population has learned to wash themselves can we think of political measures."[41] Wherever the Germans went, they scoured. They cleaned streets, disinfected bathhouses, established public toilets. First schoolchildren, then whole communities, were deloused and bathed, in mass processes more effective than polite.[42]

German behavior is easy to describe dismissively, as a bourgeois/Freudian obsession, or symbolically, as prefiguring other kinds of "cleansing."[43] But the Russian

defeats and retreats of early 1915 resulted in a near-breakdown of public welfare and
utility systems that were none too elaborate to begin with. The consequences were
enhanced by the previously mentioned deliberate evacuation of civilians from the
fighting zones. As a consequence masses of dispossessed people drifted more or less
aimlessly behind both front lines. Refugees with no access to toilet facilities polluted
water. Refugees with no opportunity to wash became lousy. With lice came disease.
Typhoid and cholera were endemic in the Eastern theater of war by 1915. During
the year they were joined by a massive typhus epidemic.

Lice bit Germans too. The German army in the East suffered almost four times
as many sick as wounded.[44] Nor were German doctors, most of them from established
communities in the Fatherland, prepared emotionally or professionally for the conditions they found in Russia. The normal coping measures for typhoid, typhus, and their
relatives were—and remain—the kinds of no-nonsense public health measures that
fit the German army's institutional framework. Refugees were collected and deloused,
their possessions disinfected or burned, their persons confined in abandoned buildings or open-air camps. Sanitary and hygiene regulations were at times enforced with
persuasion, at others with fines and jail terms, and not infrequently by applications of
boots, fists, and rifle butts, seasoned with barrack-room insults.[45] At the same time,
while typhus and related dirt-and-hunger diseases never disappeared from German
zones of occupation, they did not explode into pandemics.[46]

The connections of the above material to World War II policies describing
Jewish ghettos as quarantine areas, and World War II propaganda equating lice with
death, scarcely requires elaboration. Worth emphasizing, however, is the widespread
conviction among the Germans engaged in the anti-typhus campaign and similar
efforts that they were doing good—albeit good *de haut en bas*—for people unable to
care appropriately for themselves. The question of Germany's ultimate responsibility
for the situation by invading Russia in the first place emerged only among particular
centers of advanced social consciousness like the army newspapers published in the
larger cities.[47]

On one level this was a process of distancing the occupiers from a strangeness
they found disorienting at all levels. On another it was a way of imposing order on a
cultural mixture as frightening as it was exotic. Some German Jewish soldiers—and
some non-Jews—came to admire the "authenticity" of a Jewish life lived by Jews
who neither questioned nor apologized for their identity. Arnold Zweig emerged a
Zionist. Victor Klemperer on the other hand found his identity as a German visiting
a Talmud school in Vilna. The "repellent fanaticism "of that environment convinced
him ". . . I did not belong to these people even if one proved my blood relation to
them a hundred times over . . . I thanked my creator that I was a German."[48]

Army stereotyping of Slavs was less conflicted. They were overwhelmingly cast
as primitives, as simple-minded as they were good-hearted. One of the best yarns

emerged from the POW camps. A prisoner who has been working for two years on a Russian farm returns to camp white-faced from fear. The husband is coming home—and thanks to a little intimate fraternization, the family has grown in his absence. When POW and muzhik meet, however, the Russian is effusive: "how can I thank you for all you have done? The fields are planted, the cows are giving milk—and the baby is a prize boy!"[49]

The anecdote suggests a deeper form of "colonial" discourse that informed much of the German army's eastern experience in the Great War. In the shtetl of Eishyshok near Vilna, made famous by Yaffa Eliach's Tower of Life in the Washington DC Holocaust Museum, the Germans are described as caring for victims of hunger and disease, painting houses, constructing sidewalks, planting trees—even introducing new crops like tomatoes and strawberries. The occupiers receive credit for inaugurating a cultural renaissance by supporting and participating in local art and theater groups. Eliach—who, it hardly needs to be said, is anything but Teutonophilic—especially praises the German army for the "civil order and well-being" it sustained.[50]

Colonialism had an imperialist counterpoint. German generals and politicians played with the East in a manner inviting comparison with Charlie Chaplin's "Great Dictator" and his balloon. A Central European customs union, new thrones in the Baltic states and Poland, German colonization of lands vacated by wartime migrations—these and similar grandiose projects increasingly became the stuff of memoranda and conferences at the highest levels.[51]

## IV.

Each in its own way, colonialism and imperialism validated and reinforced the army's ethnic stereotyping of *Ostvölker*. Yet there was another side to the story. For men who prior to 1914 had seldom been beyond the sound of their church bells or factory whistles, Russia was big. Russia was strange. Russia was foreboding. In German forests the trees seemed to stand to attention. Russian forests were vast, uncultivated, seemingly impervious to human influence.[52] Even in towns, Germans felt a sense of open horizons, a certain agoraphobia.[53] An argument might indeed be made that the cultural activities Germans introduced to places like Eishyshok were successors to the fires made by primitive man to provide a focus against the night.

This sense of physical alienation was reinforced by the large-scale, near-bestial ferocity that accompanied the collapse of the tsar's empire. Suddenly Russia and its peoples were dangerous—dangerous in an alien way, best expressed in the increasingly widespread myth of *Flintenweiber*. According to legend these women of the *Ostvölker* not only carried guns. They used their sexuality to trap unwary Germans in a variety of bizarre scenarios that say more about the psychology of their authors than any realities of irregular warfare in post-tsarist Russia. The mythology has been described as "woman as castrator."[54] A more developed approach might suggest "woman as transgressor"—or rather, woman as symbolizing transgressive behavior in a land where increasingly the very stones and trees seemed hostile. The *Flintenweib*, like the woman sniper in the Vietnam War film *Full Metal Jacket*, incorporates the sense of facing the alien, the unnatural, that in the end overwhelmed German efforts to "civilize" the East with band concerts and delousing stations supported on bayonets.

The Great War and the postwar *Freikorps* experience thus combined to provide a new, far less benign image of the Slav. Now he was malevolently dangerous. The Jew underwent a similar metamorphosis during the revolutions of 1918–1920. The spectrum of supporting stereotypes, from lank-haired revolutionary conspirator to Bolshevik commissar with the obligatory Mauser pistol belted over his coat, is all too familiar. So is the reinforcing of those stereotypes not only through radical-right propaganda and rhetoric, but by the ethnically based politics of Poland's German minority.[55] Think-tanks, the *Institut für Ostforschung* in particular, which addressed in more or less abstract contexts the possibilities inherent in managed population transfers, as opposed to the Great War's more random processes. The repeated deportation of Jews under the Third Reich was only part of—indeed merely a preliminary to—the comprehensive resettlement of the east: a mixture of ethnic cleansing and ethnic domination.[56]

More significant for this paper, however, is the disappearance of prewar ethnic stereotypes from the Reichswehr. That hundred-thousand-strong volunteer force, created in matrices established by the Versailles treaty, was for practical purposes entirely German. It did not exclude Poles and Jews as a matter of policy. That was unnecessary: prospective recruits screened themselves. A young adult of Jewish or Polish ethnicity who successfully joined the Reichswehr as an enlisted man, or who earned a commission as some of both groups did, was pre-acculturated to the point of invisibility. The Reichswehr, though not an elite in the sense of its own myths or the standards of later airborne and special operations forces, chose its enlisted men with a good deal of care. There was no room in its ranks or its master story for either stupid soldiers or ineffective ones.[57]

The disappearance of those long-standing cultural niches left the Reichswehr without an institutional counter to the racist ideologies increasingly current in the wider society. Efforts to use regulations exclude their political manifestations had at best marginal success even before 1933.[58] As the Reichswehr became the Wehrmacht and restructured itself as a mass conscript force after 1935, even those barriers collapsed. Generalized concepts of the "East" as an object of German manifest destiny, long present in the culture, were integrated with National Socialist conceptions of the east as "living space. " Soldiers were informed that they were the vanguard of Germany's destiny, with the missions of conquering the new territory, settling it as "soldier-farmers (*Wehrbauern*), and ruling over the primitives who inhabited it.[59]

To an average draftee the first task might seem dangerous and the second far-fetched. The third proved congenial from the early days of September 1939. Negative, derogatory attitudes towards Polish and Jewish cultures informed the army's official reports, its private correspondence, and its public behavior. Troops used Nazi jargon to describe the people: "subhuman" or "inhuman." This was still a far cry from genocide. It was, however, an even longer distance from drill-ground insults and *Kasino* jokes. The army did not fall gleefully and immediately on the conquered Poles and Jews. Even during the initial fighting, however, as an institution it showed consistent willingness to initiate reprisals, to implement terror, to translate vague authorizations into fists, boots, and firing squads. It stood beside the SS rather than apart from it as an instrument of repression.[60]

Sebastian Haffner once raised the question whether pre-Nazi anti-Semitism had a certain homeopathic effect, inoculating its adherents against the extreme, genocidal Nazi version. The point is highly debatable.[61] National Socialism was at best an incomplete ideological system, whose essential nihilism depended heavily on the capacity to insert itself into other traditions and experiences. But Nazism filled voids and vacuums as well. It offered, to cite familiar examples, a sense of community in an age of anomie and *accidie*. It promised change at a time of gridlock. It appealed to heroic virtues in an era privileging the mundane.[62] This essay, more modestly, has shown how a key institution in the Nazi system, the army, developed over a century and a half a structure of negative prejudices and stereotypes towards Slavs and Jews in its ranks. The essay also suggests the possibility that these negatives, established in a specific context, diminished or denied the general dangers both groups posed to "Germany" as a constructed concept.

Events during and after World War I altered the general paradigm, establishing Jews and Slavs as dangerous, able and willing to threaten Germany by violence. Simultaneously the army lost touch with its countervailing stereotypes: the Slav too stupid and the Jew too hopeless to pose any real risks. Contempt is not a particularly nice emotion. But is it unreasonable to speculate that contempt did to a degree act in the German army as a counterpoint to, and possibly insulation against, other, more deadly stereotypes?

## Notes

1.  Omer Bartov, *Hitler's Army: Soldiers, Nazis, and War in the Third Reich* (New York, 1991).
2.  Cf., among many possible examples, *Die Wehrmacht: Mythos und Realitaet*, ed. R.-D. Mueller and H.-E. Volkmann (Munich, 1999); and Michael Burleigh, *The Third Reich: A New History* (New York, 2000).
3.  Cf. recently, *inter alia*, Vejas Gabriel Liulevicius, *War Land on the Eastern Front: Culture, National Identity, and German Occupation in World War I* (Cambridge, 2000); and Paul Julian Weindling, *Epidemics and Genocide in Eastern Europe, 1890–1945* (Oxford, 2000)
4.  See Dennis E. Showalter, "Caste, Skill, and Training: The Evolution of Cohesion in European Armies from the Middle Ages to the Sixteenth Century," *The Journal of Military History*, 57 (1993), 407–430.

5.  Andre Corvisier, *L'Armee francaise de la fin du xviie siecle au ministere de Choiseul. Le Sol-dat*, 2 vols. (Paris, 1964), I, 410 ff.

6.  Alf Aberg, "The Swedish Army from Luetzen to Narva," in *Sweden's Age of Greatness, 1632–1708*, ed. M. Roberts (New York, 1973), pp. 265–287.

7.  Willerd Fann, "Peacetime Attrition in the Army of Frederick William I, 1713–1749," *Central European History*, 11 (1978), 323–334. A good proportion of those "foreigners" were actually Prussian subjects who joined outside the cantonal system.

8.  Cf. Christopher Duffy, *The Army of Frederick the Great* (Newton Abbott, 1974); and Curt Jany, *Geschichte der preussischen Armee von 1500 bis 1914*, vol. 3, *1763–1907*, 2nd ed. (Osnabrueck, 1967), pp. 314 ff.

9.  See the forthcoming article by Robert Rush and Dennis Showalter, "Der gute Kamerad: The Prussian Soldier in the Age of Frederick the Great."

10. For the new military order cf. Dierk Walter, "Preussische Heeresreformen, 1807–1870: Militaerische Innovation und der Mythos der 'Roonschen Reform'," Dissertation, Bern, 2001, esp. pp. 168–282; and Dennis E. Showalter's forthcoming *The Wars of German Unification*, chap. 1 passim.

11. Heinz Stuebig, "Heer und Nation: Zur Entwicklung der paedagogisch-politischen Ideen Hermann von Boyen," *Militaergeschichtliche Mitteilungen*, 59 (1999), 1–22.

12. Alf Luedtke, *Police and State in Prussia, 1815–1850*, tr. P. Burgess (Cambridge, 1989).

13. For background cf. Manfred Koltes, *Das Rheinland zwischen Frankreich und Preussen: Studien zur Kontinuitaet und Wandel am Beginn der Preussischen Herrschaft (1814–1822)* (Koeln, 1992); Jeffry Diefendorf, *Businessmen and Politics in the Rhineland 1789–1834* (Princeton, 1980); and Jonathan Sperber's magisterial *Rhineland Radicals: The Democratic Movement and the Revolution of 1848–49* (Princeton, 1991). All are more or less sharply critical of Berlin's policies towards the new territories.

14. Robert Sackett, "Die preussische Landwehr am linken Niederrhein um die Mitte des 19. Jahrhunderts," *Annalen des Historischen Vereins fuer den Niederrhein*, 190 (1991), 167–188.

15. Klaus-Dieter Kaiser, "Die Eingliederung der ehemals selbststaendigen norddeutschen Truppenkoerper in die preussische Armee in den Jahren nach 1866," Dissertation, Berlin, 1972.

16. See the historiographically oriented essay by Krzysztof Makowski, "Das grossherzogthum Posen im Revolutionsjahr 1848," in *1848/49*, ed. R. Jaworski and R. Luft (Munich, 1996), pp. 140–172; and for the military aspects, Hermann Kunz, *Die kriegerische Ereignisse im Grossherzogthum Posen in April und Mai 1848* (Berlin, 1899).

17. The images are from Viktor Hehn, *De Moribus Ruthenorum. Zur Charakteristik der russischen Volksseele*, ed. Theodor Schiemann, reprint ed. (Osnabrueck, 1966).

18. William W. Hagen, *Germans, Poles, and Jews: The Nationality Conflict in the Prussian East, 1772–1914* (Chicago, 1980).

19. Richard W. Tims, *Germanizing the Poles: The H-K-T Society of the Eastern Marches, 1894–1914* (New York, 1941).

20. Hartmut Wieder's comprehensive analysis, "Soldatenmisshandlungen im Wilhelmischen kaiserreich," *Archiv fuer Sozialgeschichte*, 22 (1982), 159–199.

21. In 1895, for example, V Corps was second at 8.87 per thousand, VI Corps stood sixth of sixteen at 8.17. "Zur Selbstmordsterblichkeit in der Preussischen Armee," *Militaerwochenblatt* 9, 1896.

22. *Untertan in Uniform. Militaer und Militarismys im Kaiserreich 1871–1914. Quellen und Dokumente*, ed. B. Ulrich, J. Vogel, and B. Ziemann (Frankfurt, 2001), does not address the "Polish question" specifically but is a useful compendium of primary sources on the

army's internal structure at this period despite the editors' unconcealed distaste for their subject.

23. Karen Hagemann, "*Mannlicher Muth und Teutsche Ehre.*" *Nation, Militaer und Geschlecht zur Zeit der Antinapoleonischen Kriege Preussens* (Paderborn, 2002), pp. 255 ff. In the context of this essay it is worth noting that the Jews of Posen tended to acculturate to German rather than Polish patterns. Cf. *The Naturalized Jews of the Grand Duchy of Posen, 1834–1835*, compiled by David Luft, foreword by Malcom Stern (Atlanta, 1987).

24. The best overview of the century's first half is Horst Fischer, *Judentum, Staat und Heer in Preussen im fruehen 19. Jahrhundert* (Tuebingen, 1968).

25. See Barnet Peretz Hartston, "Judaism on Trial: Antisemitism in the German Courtroom (1870–1895)," Dissertation, University of California, San Diego, 1999; and Zvi Bachrach, *Anti-Jewish Prejudices in German Catholic Sermons* (Lewiston, NY, 1993).

26. Cf. L. Mertens, "Das Privileg des Einjaehrig-Freiwilligen Militaerdienst im Kaiserreich und seine Gesellschaftliche Bedeutung," *Militaergeschichtliche Mitteilungen* 39 (1986), 59–66, and Hartmut John, *Das Reserveoffizierkorps im deutschen Kaiserreich 1890–1914* (Frankfurt, 1981).

27. As did the future Protestant clergyman Adolf Clarenbach, *Heitere Erinnerungen aus dem Leben eines westfaelischen Landesgeistlichen* (Borgeln, 1981), pp. 31–32.

28. This is by mo means a German phenomenon. Drill instructors in all mass armies not infrequently deliberately single out such a recruit as a warning to the rest that their lot can always get worse.

29. See Alex Hall, *Scandal, Sensation, and Social Democracy: The SPD Press and Wilhelmine Germany, 1890–1914* (Cambridge, 1977), pp. 116 ff.

30. Cf. generally David Schoenbaum, *Zabern 1913. Consensus Politics in Imperial Germany* (London, 1982); and J. G. Morrison, "The Intransigents: Alsace-Lorrainers against the Annexation," Dissertation, University of Iowa, 1970.

31. Dominik Reichert, *Beste Gelegenheit zum Sterben. Meine Erlebnisse im Kriege 1914–1918* (Munich, 1989), pp. 20 passim.

32. Arnold Kramer, "*Wackes* at War": Alsace-Lorraine and the Failure of German National Mobilization, 1914–1918," in *State, Society, and Mobilization in Europe during the First World War*, ed. J. Horne (Cambridge, 1997), pp. 105–121.

33. Cf. Christhard Hoffmann, "Between Integration and Rejection: The Jewish Community in Germany, 1914–1918," ibid., 89–104; and Werner Angress, "Das deutsche Militaer und die Juden im Ersten Weltkrieg," *Militaergeschichtliche Mitteilungen*, 19 (1976), 77–146.

34. See for example the brief memoir of David Katz, "Frontjahre im Ersten Weltkrieg," *Bulletin des Leo Baeck Instituts*, 80 (1988), 13–17.

35. Cf. especially Werner Conze, *Polnische Nation und deutsche Politik im Ersten Weltkrieg* (Cologne, 1958); and T. Hunt Tooley, *National Identity and Weimar Germany: Upper Silesia and the Eastern Border, 1918–1923* (Lincoln, 1997).

36. R. G. L. Waite, *Vanguard of Nazism: The Free Corps Movement in Postwar Germany, 1918–1932* (Cambridge, Mass., 1952), remains standard in English. Hagen Schulze, *Freikorps und Republik, 1918–1920* (Boppard, 1969), is also excellent; for the Baltic experience see Dominique Venner, *Histoire d' un fascisme allemand: Les corps-francs du Baltikum et la Revolution* (Paris, 1996).

37. Tooley, 336. *Pieron* was the Upper Silesian counterpart to the American South's "good old boy": a commonsensical working man.

38. Cf. Daniel Graf, "The Reign of the Generals: Military Government in Western Russia, 1914–1915," Dissertation, University of Nebraska, 1972; and Peter Gatrell, *A Whole Empire Walking: Refugees in Russia during World War I* (Bloomington, 1999), pp. 16–23.

39. John Horne and Alan Kramer, *German Atrocities 1914: A History* (New Haven, 2002).
40. Joan Campbell, *Joy in Work, German Work: A National Debate* (Princeton, 1989).
41. Steven Aschheim, *Brothers and Strangers: The East European Jew in German and German Jewish Consciousness, 1800–1923* (Madison, 1982), p. 148.
42. Weindling, 90 ff.
43. See for example Theo Schwarzmutter, *Zwischen Kaiser und "Fuehrer": Generalfeldmarschall August von Mackensen*, 2nd ed. rev. (Paderborn, 1996), pp. 111–113; and Weindling, essentially passim.
44. Liulevicius, 22.
45. Use of physical force in these contexts was part of an escalating pattern of individual violence by Germans, especially officers, against "eastern peoples." Lieulevicius, 107, sees this ideologically, as part of a larger program of control built on force. As a counterpoint it should be noted that until very recently in the Western world generally, drill instructors, straw bosses, schoolteachers, and not least athletic coaches took affirmative views of corporal punishment as a motivator and an instructional device.
46. R. Otto, "Fleckfieber (Typhus exanthematicus)," in *Handbuch der aerztlichen Erfahrungen im Ersten Weltkrieg*, ed. W. Hoffmann (Leipzig, 1922), pp. 403–460; Alfred Cornebise, *Typhus and Doughboys: The American Polish Typhus Relief Expedition, 1919–1921* (Newark, NJ, 1982), shows no significant differences between racist German and democratic American approaches to the disease.
47. Even there solidarity of any kind with the locals was generally limited. Dennis E. Showalter, "The Homesick Revolutionaries: Soldiers' Councils and Newspaper Propaganda in German-Occupied Eastern Europe, 1918–1919," *Canadian Journal of History*, 9 (1976), 69–88.
48. Arnold Zweig, *Das ostjuedische Antlitz* (Berlin, 1920); Victor Klemperer, *Curriculum Vitae. Erinnerungen, 1881–1918,* vol. 2 (Berlin, 1996), pp. 684, 687. The best general treatment of this subject is Aschheim, *Brothers and Strangers*, pp. 143 ff.
49. This particular version is modified slightly from the one in Alon Rachamimov, "Marginalized Subjects: Austro-Hungarian POWs in Russia, 1914–1918," Dissertation, Columbia, 2000, p. 119.
50. Yaffa Eliach, *There Was Once a World. A 900-Year Chronicle of the Shtetl of Eishyshok* (Boston, 1998),p. 57.
51. Cf. Holger H. Herwig, "Tunes of Glory at the Twilight Stage: The Bad Homburg Crown Council and the Evolution of German Statecraft, 1917/1918," *German Studies Review*, 6 (1983), 53–63; and Winfried Baumgart, *Deutsche Ostpolitik 1918* (Vienna and Munich, 1966).
52. Liulevicius, 27–28.
53. Klemperer, 462.
54. Klaus Theweleit, *Male Fantasies*, tr. S. Conway et. al. (Minneapolis, 1987), pp. 70 ff.
55. Richard Blanke, *Orphans of Versailles: The Germans in Western Poland, 1918–1939* (Lexington, 1993).
56. Michael Burleigh, *Germany Turns Eastwards: A Study of "Ostforschung" in the Third Reich* (Cambridge, 1988).
57. William Mulligan discusses the beginnings of the process of making the Reichwehr into a military community in "Restoring Trust Within the *Reichswehr*: The Case of the *Vertrauensleute*," *War & Society*, 20 (2002), 71–90.Adolf Reinicke, *Das Reichsheer, 1921–1934* (Osnabrueck, 1986), is good for the Reichswehr's inner dynamics.
58. As shown in detail by Peter Bucher, *Der Reichswehrprozess. Der Hochverrat der Ulmer Reichswehroffiziere, 1929–1930* (Boppard, 1967).

59. Cf. Jost Hermand, *Old Dreams of a New Reich*: *Volkish Utopias and National Socialism*, tr. P. Levesque and S. Soldovieri (Bloomington, 1992); and Rolf-Dieter Mueller, *Hitlers Ostkrieg und die deutsche Siedlungspolitik: Die Zusammenarbeit von Wehrmacht, Wirtschaft und SS* (Frankfurt, 1991).

60. Alexander B. Rossino, "September 1939: The German Army in Poland," Dissertation, Syracuse, 1999.

61. Sebastian Haffner, *The Meaning of Hitler*, tr. E. Osers (Cambridge, Mass., 1979), pp. 91–92. Cf. Shelley Baranowski, "Conservative Elite Anti-Semitism from the Weimar Republic to the Third Reich," *German Studies Review*, 19 (1996), 525–537. Hans-Heinrich Wilhelm, "Die 'Nationalkonservativen Eliten' und das Schreckgespenst vom 'juedischen Bolschewismus'," *Zeitschrift fuer Geschichtswissenschaft*, 43 (1995), 333–349, offers a more direct challenge to Haffner's hypothesis, and by extension to this paper.

62. Cf. Peter Fritsche, *Germans into Nazis* (Cambridge, Mass., 1998).

# From "verloren gehen" to "verloren bleiben"

## Changing German Discourses on Nation and Nationalism in Poznania

### ❖ Elizabeth A. Drummond ❖

On the eve of World War I, Poles and Germans in the Prussian province of Poznania[1] had become firmly polarized into two opposing nationalist camps. Increasingly rigid notions of Germanness and Polishness as well as stereotypes about the "national other" gradually crowded out any meaningful room for peaceful national coexistence. For their part, German nationalists, adopting the architect of German unity, the former Prussian and German chancellor, Otto von Bismarck, as their spiritual father, often invoked a Bismarck quotation as one of their slogans: "No foot of German land shall be lost nor shall any aspect of German law be sacrificed, that is our policy."[2] The quotation continued to be used after World War I and the loss of most of the province to the new state of Poland, but in a slightly altered form: "No foot of German land shall remain lost."[3] The change from "shall be lost [*verloren gehen*]" to "shall remain lost [*verloren bleiben*]" might seem to be merely a slight reworking of Bismarck's quotation in acknowledgment of the changed postwar territorial situation. The change, however, mirrored a change in attitude towards the "Polish question," one that reflected a more aggressive German nationalism and greater ease of recourse to chauvinistic and racialist discourses.

Of the myriad patriotic societies which emerged in Imperial Germany in the last two decades of the nineteenth century, the Pan-German League (Alldeutscher Verband)[4] and, in particular, the German Eastern Marches Society (Deutscher Ostmarkenverein)[5] engaged their energies in debating the so-called (Polish question.) Both societies claimed to serve as guardians of national symbols and the interests of

*Deutschtum. Deutschtum*, the German *Volk*, at least before the war, was defined by a common language, culture, and history; that is, ethnicity was a cultural rather than a biological-racial category. While the Pan-German League, particularly after Heinrich Class ascended to the chairmanship of the League in 1908, increasingly embraced a discourse of scientific racism and anti-Semitism, the Eastern Marches Society generally refrained from employing such language, preferring *Volk* to *Rasse*.[6]

German nationalists justified German rule in the eastern provinces by asserting the superiority of German *Kultur*, a superiority that warranted political dominance as well. The publications of the Eastern Marches Society and the Pan-German League repeatedly highlighted the differences between Germany's *Kultur* and Poland's *Unkultur*.[7] Images of German culture (*Kultur*), intelligence (*Intelligenz*), diligence (*Fleiß*), honesty (*Ehrlichkeit, Redlichkeit*), honor (*Ehre*), and constancy (*Stetigkeit*) contrasted starkly with images of Polish wantonness (*Übermut*), mismanagement (*Mißwirtschaft*), unruliness (*Ungebärdigkeit*), impudence (*Frechheit*), ill-breeding (*Unerzogenheit*), and impertinence (*Unverschämtheit*).[8] For German nationalists, the cultural inferiority of the Poles and their inability to maintain a functioning political system, therefore, justified the partition of Poland in the late eighteenth century and German dominion over Poznania and West Prussia. For Germans living in the eastern provinces, the *Ostmärker*, this German dominance was to be eternal, regardless of whether Poznanian Poles eventually proved themselves culturally worthy of statehood.

Indeed, German nationalists pointed to the emergence of a Polish middle class in the late nineteenth and early twentieth centuries as evidence that German culture, German schools, and German administration had raised Polish society in the eastern provinces out of its natural, primitive state. But this emergent middle class did not, as hoped, become German, but rather developed into a bilingual pillar of Polish nationalism, now equipped with the weapons with which better to further Polish-national claims. For *Ostmärker*, the emergence of a recognizably Polish middle class symbolized the growing threat of the Polish movement. At the same time, however, it also reinforced the superiority of German *Kultur*. This tension in the ideology of prewar German nationalism—criticism of the growth of the Polish middle classes, considered the most dangerous arm of Polish nationalism, but ardent support for Germanization policies, to which they attributed the emergence of a Polish middle class—was apparent already before World War I. As the Pan-German Paul Samassa himself noted at the annual meeting of the managing committee in 1906, "Experience has taught us that the so-called 'cultural policy' in the Prussian East has merely led us to providing the enemies of our people with the weapons with which to fight. From the national standpoint we have no interest in a higher level of education among the Poles, which almost without exception raises their national consciousness and makes them more competitive in the economic struggle."[9] While this opinion was loudly acclaimed by the other members of the committee, it did not preclude calls for the continuation of Germanization policies. Samassa himself made a plea for stronger

Germanization measures only six year later.[10] Despite recognizing the ideological paradox, German nationalists proved unable to divorce themselves from the notion of Germanization and its corollary, the notion of Germanness as a cultural construct, until after World War I.

Both the Eastern Marches Society and the Pan-German League declared in their statutes that anyone who "felt himself" German would be welcomed in the nationalist camp.[11] As Heinrich von Tiedemann, the chair of the Eastern Marches Society, declared at a meeting of the Society's general committee in 1905: "The German Eastern Marches Society is nothing other than a national German society that knows no political or confessional bias or partisanship, that campaigns [*zur Felde ziehen*] against nothing other than un-German [*undeutsches*] behavior and welcomes and supports any endeavor that aims at the maintenance and cultivation of Germandom [*Deutschtum*]."[12] For the *Ostmärker*, then, the only preconditions for membership in the German nation were German behavior and German self-consciousness.[13] Membership in the German national community, therefore, entailed the acceptance of certain values that *Kultur* and *Bildung* entailed order, control, honesty, industriousness, education, culture, rationality, the rule of law, masculinity, etc., in short, the cultural values associated with the German bourgeoisie.[14] The German bourgeoisie, in turn, in particular, the *Bildungsbürgertum*, were leading members of the Eastern Marches Society and the Pan-German League. These leaders extended their own cultural consciousness to embody the "ideal German." On the basis of the authority that *Kultur* and *Bildung* conferred, moreover, these men claimed to speak for the nation.

Simple declarations that the Pan-German League and the Eastern Marches Society accepted all those men who thought and acted German, however, did not resolve the tensions around the question of who or what constituted a German. That, in the Prussian East, at least before the defeat in World War I and the loss of the eastern provinces, the notion of Germanness was flexible, is best exemplified by the Eastern Marches Society's attitude toward Poznania's Jews. Although many German nationalists viewed Jews as cultural, religious, and even national "Others," the society and its leadership were careful not to exclude Jews from membership in the society or in the German nation. In marked contrast to the Pan-German League, which became openly anti-Semitic with the rise of Heinrich Class first to executive secretary of the league in 1901 and then to chairman in 1908, the Eastern Marches Society consistently discouraged racialist language, employing instead a notion of "culture" that made room for German Jews.[15] The attitude was not necessarily benign, and many *Ostmärker* themselves sympathized with or espoused anti-Semitic beliefs. Leading members of the Eastern Marches Society, however, recognized the significance of Jews for the German cause in Poznania. As Fritz Vosberg, the general secretary of the Poznanian provincial committee of the society, stated, "the Jews are staunchly German and also represent this standpoint publicly."[16] The national chair

of the society, Heinrich von Tiedemann, moreover, repeatedly made impassioned appeals to the membership to reject anti-Semitism and to welcome "German-national
Jews" into the national community.[17] The Eastern Marches Society's condemnation
of anti-Semitism was motivated primarily by political and demographic concerns.
With Jewish support at the polls, Germans would be able to stave off Polish advances.
Without Jewish support either because of Jewish emigration or because Jews would not
vote for anti-Semitic candidates German candidates were left vulnerable to defeat by
a united Polish voting bloc.[18] Nonetheless, the society's appeals to Jews acknowledged
the flexibility of the concept of Germanness and highlighted the cultural aspects of
Germanness over any religious or biological "racial" aspects.

The fact that Tiedemann had to issue repeated condemnations of anti-Semitism
in the ranks of the Eastern Marches Society points to the fact that many members
were, indeed, moving toward the logical conclusion of nineteenth-century *völkisch*
nationalism. To wit, it did not go without saying that all those who identified themselves as German were, in fact, German. To define who or what constituted a German meant excluding all those people who were not and, by implication, could not
be German. As such, ethno-cultural nationalism became increasingly exclusive and
rigid. Flexible, pragmatic, and inclusive notions of national identity simply did not
offer the same power, either in providing for a cohesive notion of a national community or in mobilizing Germans in the service of the nation, and in opposition to
"the Other." While culture continued to be the dominant discursive mode for the
Eastern Marches Society and German nationalists in the Prussian East throughout
the wartime years and beyond, it increasingly became an essentialist and racialized
notion, bringing *Ostmärker* closer in their ideological outlook to their co-nationals in
the Pan-German League and the other radical nationalist organizations which sprang
up in the wake of German defeat in World War I.

Even before the actual outbreak of hostilities in Europe in 1914, the *Ostmärker*,
like German nationalists throughout the Reich, considered themselves in a state of
war. The German-Polish national conflict was, for German nationalists in the eastern
provinces, nothing short of a "hard national fight [*schwerer völkischer Kampf*]."[19] Fearful
of the "growing power of *Polentum*,"[20] which was seen as constituting nothing short
of a "Slavic invasion,"[21] German nationalists stressed time and time again that the
situation was, indeed, one of "life or death [*Lebensfrage*]."[22] When war came in 1914,
however, it did not come, as some *Ostmärker* had feared and forewarned, on the heels
of Polish nationalist agitation. While spontaneous mass celebrations accompanied
the declaration of war in other German cities, the streets of Poznania's cities stayed
relatively quiet.[23] Living in a borderland made both Germans and Poles uncertain
about the prospect of war. Any war in the East would, to be sure, occur in part on
their own land, thus unsettling soldiers and civilians alike. Poznania's Poles, moreover,
faced an inauspicious choice: to fight with Germany and Austria-Hungary against
Russia or to hitch their fate to the wagon of Russian-led pan-Slavism. In the end,

the vast majority of Poznanian Poles joined the German and Austrian cause, albeit reluctantly, preferring a known enemy to an unknown and—given developments in the Congress Kingdom—potentially far worse enemy. As a result, young Poznanian Poles boarded the trains alongside their fellow German soldiers in August 1914. The nationalist fervor that usually accompanied such departures was attended, instead, in the Polish case, by prayers. Only the Germans sang "Deutschland, Deutschland, über Alles."[24]

The Poles had good reason to approach the coming war with a measure of reluctance. While Germans experienced a sense of national community that transcended the divisions of political parties, confession, and class, the Poles clearly recognized that this national community excluded them. They could hardly think that Emperor William II's declaration on the evening of Friday, 31 July 1914 that "I no longer recognize parties or confessions. Today we are all German brothers, and only German brothers" applied to Poles as well.[25] The war was fought in the name of the German nation and German national pride, not in the name of the Hohenzollern dynasty and its subjects.

In honor of the *Burgfrieden*, German nationalist organizations in the Prussian eastern provinces called a halt to their anti-Polish activities in the East. The Polish patriotic societies, in particular, the gymnastic societies, had little choice but to suspend operations, as their memberships increasingly boarded the trains for the front.[26] Nonetheless, activities continued, particularly at the level of the national and regional coordinating committees, if a bit quieter. Polish nationalists cooperated with fellow Poles in Galicia, in the Congress Kingdom, and in the West in hopes of winning recognition for an independent Polish state after the end of the war. The wartime proclamation of a Polish state by the German and Austrian governments was confined only to former Russian territories and, as a result, did not change the situation for Poznanian Poles, but it did embolden them. For German nationalists, the birth of a Polish state transformed their prewar declaration of war on the Poles from a rhetorical strategy, aimed at awakening a German population perceived to be in a national slumber, into a sense of actual war, a true state of emergency. Meetings of the Eastern Marches Society's executive committee were referred to as *Kriegssitzungen*, a practice that extended even after the armistice and the signing of the Versailles Treaty.[27] Disdain and prejudice morphed into pure hatred.[28] Poles were no longer described merely as primitive or impudent, but as a "conquering people [*Eroberungsvolk*]."[29] Germans, the Eastern Marches Society argued in the midst of the war, must now take their national conflict to a higher state of war, a sign that the fundamental nature of the conflict had evolved.[30] This shift was part and parcel of a more general change in German attitudes to the East, one effected by occupation of formerly Russian lands.

As we now know from the work of Fritz Fischer and his students, German war aims in the east were extensive. As Vejas Liulevicius's excellent study of German occupation policies in Lithuania during World War I reveals, German war aims for the East entailed not only territorial acquisitions but also the complete reconstruction of society in the East according to a program of "German work." This program of "German work" built on and went beyond the policies of Germanization already well established in the Prussian eastern provinces. As Liulevicius argues, "the eastern front-experience and practices of the military administration formed in German soldiers a specific view of the East and the sort of things that might be done there. Increasingly, the area was seen not as a complicated weaving of 'lands and peoples' [*Land und Leute*], but as 'spaces and races' [*Raum und Volk*] to be ordered by German mastery and organization. For many, a new German identity and mission directed against the East grew out of the eastern front-experience."[31]

The postwar territorial settlement, stipulated both by Treaty of Versailles signed on 28 June 1919 in Paris and by later agreements on borders, transferred most of Poznania and West Prussia to the new Republic of Poland. Poland reborn was different both in its territorial expanse and its national and confessional constellation than its ancestor, the Commonwealth of Poland-Lithuania. While the borders were drawn beyond the frontier of ethnic Poland and, hence, interwar Poland had to deal with considerable national minorities, the new state was nonetheless dominated by the new form of Polish nationalism that had emerged in the nineteenth century, one that stressed national homogeneity and the privileges of the co-national at the expense of the non-national rather than the more fluid definition of Polish citizenship that had prevailed in the Commonwealth.[32] In the immediate postwar years, Józef Piłsudski, Roman Dmowski, and other Polish leaders set about to build a new Polish state and to secure its borders. In doing so, they enacted policies of Polonization, remarkably similar to the German Empire's policies of Germanization, in their own western and eastern borderlands.

In a situation where the "dominant-subordinate" relationships were, as Richard Blanke argues, reversed, with Germany's eastern provinces becoming Poland's western provinces, Poles used their new-found dominance to enact anti-German and Polonizing policies, which they considered essential for the survival of the young Polish republic.[33] These policies were, in large part, copies of the anti-Polish and Germanization policies enacted by the Prussian and German governments before World War I. Poland's language policy, for example, declared Polish the sole official language of the state. Even in the western, formally German, provinces of Poland, German was not accorded any legal standing. Just as Germans had attempted to use the schools as a vehicle for Germanization, so, too, did the Poles for Polonization. Instruction in Polish was required as of the fourth year, with opportunities for learning German reduced as children advanced into higher levels. History, politics, and geography were all taught from the Polish perspective. The Polish government also sought to undermine the strength of the German minority in the economic life of the western provinces through the expropriation German property. The Versailles

Treaty empowered the Polish government to seize property that had formally been owned by the German government, but required financial compensation for the seizure of private property of German citizens. Nonetheless, the Polish government quickly moved to expropriate the property of German citizens, without sufficient compensation, which prompted some of the first complaints brought by the German minority to the League of Nations.[34] The goals of these measures were to weaken the economic foundations of the German minority in Poland and to undermine the sense of a German-national community, with the ostensible goal of integrating the German minority into the Polish state. Whether Germans could ever, however, become good Poles remained a question unanswered. In theory, Polonization policies could achieve the integration of the German minority, although many of the proponents of Polonization, like their earlier German counterparts, believed that Germans would remain a "fifth column" within the country.

The loss of the Prussian eastern provinces created strong feelings of fear and disappointment coupled with a strong hatred for all things Slavic among the *Ostmärker*. Many Germans simply fled the region. Some 600,000 Germans had left Poznania and West Prussia, now known as Pomorze, by the end of 1921. The remaining German population in Poland constituted only 3.9 percent of the population of the state. The bulk of this German minority lived in the formerly German regions of Poznania, Pomorze/West Prussia and Silesia, but there were also smaller German communities in other parts of the Polish state. In the province of Poznania, Germans amounted to 16.7 percent of the population.[35] Whether the German exodus was voluntary or coerced lies beyond the scope of this article.[36] The exodus was significant, however, both because there was now a large group of aggrieved Germans in the Weimar Republic who spoke loudly about reclaiming their previous homeland and because the numerically weakened German minority in Poland increasingly felt itself an endangered national outpost. Both of these forces served to radicalize the discourse surrounding the Polish question. As a result, a noticeable shift occurred in the discourse of German nationalists active in the Polish question, both those who remained behind in the new Republic of Poland and those who departed for the West.

The German minority in Poland quickly moved to organize themselves politically. Just as the Poles used the weapons of their former Prusso-German masters, so, too, did the German minority employ the weapons of Polish "organic work."[37] Efforts at creating a unified German-national community had originated in the revolutionary chaos following the armistice. In response to the announcement of the creation of a Polish "National Council" in November 1918, German nationalists moved to establish their own national councils (*Volksräte*) to defend German interests and to prevent the loss of German territories to the new state of Poland. These councils were fighting another two-front war, against the forces of Polish nationalism, on the one hand, and the new government in Berlin, which showed little support for German nationalists in the eastern provinces, on the other. These various councils united in a *Deutsche*

*Vereinigung* (German Association) in December 1918, which was led by a prominent member of the Eastern Marches Society, Georg Cleinow.[38] The loss of Poznania and Pomorze/West Prussia to Poland led to the disbanding of these organizations and the emigration of much of the leadership, who were unwilling to live under Polish rule.

Following the dissolution of the national councils, two main lines of political orientation emerged among Germans remaining in the former eastern provinces. The first, the *Zentralarbeitsgemeinschaft der politischen Parteien* (Central Coordinating Committee of the Political Parties), was essentially an outgrowth of the Weimar government and found little support among Germans in Poznania and Pomorze/West Prussia, who generally fell far to the right of the parties in the Weimar coalition. Poznanian Germans, therefore, united the various German national councils into a new organization, the *Deutscher Volksrat* (German National Council), under the leadership of Eugen Naumann. The West Prussian German national councils united into the *Landesvereinigung des deutschen Volkstums in Polen* (Provincial Association of Germans in Poland), which was first led by Cleinow and, following his departure for the West, by Kurt Graebe. These two groups merged in August 1919, taking the *Landesvereinigung* name and establishing their headquarters in Bromberg/Bydgoszcz, long a stronghold of Germanness in Poznania; Naumann became chair, and Graebe served as his deputy. In December 1920, the *Zentralarbeitsgemeinschaft*, bowing to the political tendencies of the region, agreed to merge with—or, rather, be subsumed by—the *Landesvereinigung*; the new organization later took the name *Deutschtumsbund zur Wahrung der Minderheitenrechte* (German League for the Protection of Minority Rights). Similar to the Polish "organic work" movement, the German League spawned a variety of organizations to deal with specific issues of interest to the German minority, including school, teacher and student, welfare, agricultural, artisan, trade, and women's organizations.[39] The Polish government cracked down on the German League in 1923, but it reemerged shortly thereafter as the *Deutsche Vereinigung in Sejm und Senat* (German Union in Sejm and Senat), which represented German interests in the Polish parliament. The auxiliary organizations also reappeared within a couple of years of being repressed.[40]

Given the breadth of the German League's activities, prewar organizations such as the Eastern Marches Society lost much of their prominence. Many of the leading members of the Eastern Marches Society, moreover, had formed the first wave of the exodus and became loud proponents of revisionism in Weimar Germany. The Eastern Marches Society, however, remained in existence, albeit in affiliation, after 1922, with the *Deutscher Ostbund* (German Eastern Union), which was, in turn, affiliated with the *Deutscher Schutzbund für das Grenz- und Auslanddeutschtum* (German Protective Union for Germans in the Borderlands and Abroad), established in 1919 to protect the interests of German minorities abroad and of former members of those minorities now living in Germany itself.[41] While the German League and its successor, the German Union, represented the German minority vis-à-vis the Polish government, the *Ostbund*, the Eastern Marches Society, and other similar societies such as the *Verein für das Deutschtum im Auslande* (Society for Germandom Abroad) continued to play a significant role in constructing images of "the Pole" and "the German" in opposition and in lobbying the government for harsher policies vis-à-vis Poland, namely, for the revision of borders.

Both in Weimar Germany and in Poznania, German nationalist organizations adopted an increasingly militant and racialized discourse. The reformulation of the Bismarck quotation by the Eastern Marches Society cited at the beginning of this article from "No foot of German land shall be lost" to "No foot of German land shall remain lost" was indicative of the transformation. Not content merely to defend German interests, German nationalists after World War I advanced a more aggressive program, seeking to undo the postwar territorial settlement and to effect the reintegration of the lost eastern territories into Germany. Moreover, whereas the German *Volk* before the war had been defined by a common language, culture, and history, that is, along ethnic or cultural rather than racial lines, the postwar period saw a gradual shift in this discourse, away from notions of culture and by extension, the possibility that Poles could become more "civilized" towards essentialist notions of race and biologically-determined inferiority. In doing so, German nationalists active in the "Polish question" moved closer to the ideological radicalism of the Pan-German League, which had adopted the vocabulary of race and racial theory even before World War I. Attempts, such as those of the Eastern Marches Society, to discourage Germans from adopting discursive and political strategies that would alienate real or potential "cultural" Germans in particular, Poznanian Jews, but also Germanized Poles disappeared from pages of nationalist publications. As a result, the tension in the ideology of prewar German nationalism between a discourse of culture and a notion of Germanness based on the adoption of certain "German" values and emerging discourses of race and biology largely evaporated after World War I, as culture itself became essential and unchanging, tied to blood and biology rather than to consciousness or behavior.[42]

In light of such a shift, it is not surprising that the German minority in Poznania as well as German nationalist organizations concerned with the Polish question adopted a more militant stance during the interwar period. Again, the history of the Eastern Marches Society provides a useful example. While some members of the society urged loyalty to the new Polish state and supported attempts to work within the state for the protection of the German minority, the society as a whole and the vast majority of both the leadership and the membership rejected such a conciliatory approach. Instead, Germans were encouraged to adopt a policy of active obstructionism vis-à-vis the Polish state and to work in the interests of the true German fatherland by acting as a fifth column in Poland. That the society continued to herald Bismarck and to fly the Imperial German flag at its meetings gave clear indication that Weimar Germany itself, in the eyes of the Society's members, was not the true Germany.[43]

Given the opposition of most *Ostmärker* to the Weimar regime, the Eastern Marches Society found natural, if at times uncomfortable, allies in the myriad radical, extremist, right wing organizations that emerged in the interwar period. Already in December 1918 the society had thrown its support behind the *Freikorps* in combating an uprising of Polish nationalists in Poznań/Posen.[44] Throughout the 1920s individual *Ostmärker* solidified the organizations ties to other organizations of the radical right. The alliance was formalized in 1930, when Major a.D. Siegfried Wagner, son of the former vice-chair of the society, Franz Wagner, and head (*Bundeskanzler*) of the *Stahlhelm*, encouraged the society to adopt an explicitly revisionist and right-extremist position. The members were ready to do so and elected Wagner chair of the Eastern Marches Society on 15 November 1930. From 1930 on, then, the Eastern Marches Society was largely subordinated to the politics of the *Stahlhelm* and, later, the Nazi Party, until the society was dissolved in 1935 during the Nazi *Gleichschaltung*.[45]

On the whole, the German minority in western Poland quickly moved to support the National Socialists following their rise to power. Throughout the interwar period the German minority in Poland remained alienated from the Polish state and saw the revision of the Versailles Treaty as the only feasible solution to their plight. National Socialist organizations had already been founded in Poznania before Hitler came to power in 1933. The *Deutscher Nationalsozialistischer Verein für Polen* (German National Socialist Society for Poland), later renamed the *Jungdeutsche Partei in Polen* (Young German Party in Poland), was founded in 1921, and the NSDAP established its own presence in western Poland in the early 1930s. While these two organizations enjoyed only limited support before the Nazi seizure of power, after 1933 support for National Socialism among the German minority in Poland spread quickly. These tendencies among Germans in Poland were institutionalized, both in the myriad nationalist organizations and in the political leadership of the German minority itself, namely, the German Union in Sejm and Senat.[46]

The German government encouraged the creation of a unified German political bloc in Poland. Early efforts, such as the *Deutscher Jungblock in Polen* (German Youth Block in Poland) and the "Jägerhof Circle," foundered because they were not seen as radical enough by the Young Germans. More successful was the *Deutsche Vereinigung für Westpolen* (German Union for Western Poland), founded in July 1934 and ostensibly a union of the German Union in Sejm and Senate and the Young Germans; the organization was led first by Erik von Witzleben and then by Hans Kohnert. The German Union, which sought to represent the German minority in Poland as a whole, adopted a program declaring itself to be true to the National Socialist ideological program but slightly less "revolutionary," a nod to the traditional, conservative political leadership of the German minority.[47] Many Young Germans, however, remained hostile to the more moderate German Union for Western Poland. As Richard Blanke argues, this hostility was more a rivalry between competing factions within National

Socialism than between two competing ideological movements.[48] While the Young Germans were more aggressive in their agitation, they failed to attract the same kind of popular support as did the German Union. In the end, the more conservative variant of National Socialism proved more appealing to Germans in Poznania and Pomorze/West Prussia, in large part because it was more familiar to them, the result of the evolution of German nationalism in the *Ostmarken*.[49]

German nationalist organizations such as the German Eastern Marches Society and the Pan-German League had initially been founded as (supposedly) defensive organizations designed to prevent the victory of Polish nationalism and to protect and preserve the superiority of German culture, and German rule, in the Prussian East. Despite their repeated claims to be "for Germandom and not against Polentum," they had, from their very inception, adopted ideological positions hostile to Poles. German nationalists in Poznania sought not only to prevent further Polish gains, but also to roll back previous gains, a policy that proved a dismal failure, both in the short-term (for example, the policy of settling Germans in the province) and in the long-term (that is, the eventual loss of the territory to the new Polish state after World War I). Key weapons in the rolling back of Polish-national gains were German educational, language, and economic policies, the pillars of Germanization. These policies, however, in "civilizing" Poles created two tensions, one practical and one ideological. On the one hand, German policies, especially educational policy, often helped to strengthen the Polish middle classes and, thus, the Polish nationalist movement, thus proving the policies to be counterproductive. On the other hand, the ideological justification for Germanization that Germanness was an open and flexible notion and that Poles could be made into good Germans proved consistently problematic for German nationalists whose natural urges were to exclude all Poles from potential membership in the German national community. After World War I, both of these tensions disappeared. Germanization, as a policy, was necessarily abandoned. Germanization, as an ideology, was also abandoned in favor of an exclusive and racialist sometimes explicit, sometimes implicit approach to the national question. Both the changed geopolitical situation and the changed ideological foundation led to a more aggressive, revisionist, and chauvinistic German nationalism in Poznania. No longer content to protect and preserve German culture, German nationalists in the lost eastern provinces devoted themselves to winning back those lands. *"Fest und beständig"* was one of the old slogans of the Eastern Marches Society; after World War I, just as with the Bismarck quotation, the Society now added "'The eastern marches shall be German again [*Die Ostmark soll wieder deutsch sein*]!"[50] Twenty years after the end of World War I Adolf Hitler led his troops into Poland to reclaim "German" territory and to conquer more *Lebensraum* for the German national community in the East, opening up a new and horrific chapter in German-Polish relations.

# Notes

1. Unfortunately, no English equivalents exist for most Polish towns and regions. As a result, I use both versions of a given place name throughout the text, giving preference to the name used by the majority of the population at the time, hence Poznań/Posen and Bromberg/Bydgoszcz. For the sake of simplicity and to distinguish the province from the city, I use the term 'Poznania' to refer to the region known by Germans as the *Provinz Posen* (*prowincja poznańska* or the province of Poznań/Posen) and by Poles as the *Wielkie Księstwo Poznańskie* (*Großherzogtum Posen* or Grand Duchy of Poznań/Posen) or as *Wielkopolska* (*Großpolen* or Greater Poland). However, when discussing German or Polish discourse, I use the place name used by those activists. The solution is cumbersome but warranted given the politicization of place names both then and now.

2. Geheimes Staatsarchiv Preußischer Kulturbesitz (henceforth GStA PK), I. HA, Rep. 195, Deutscher Ostmarkenverein, Nr. 140, Flugblatt entitled "Die praktische Arbeit des Deutschen Ostmarken-Vereins"; and Nr. 72, Vol. I, Posener Ortsgruppe letterhead (M).

3. See, for example, GStA PK, I. Ha, Rep. 195, Deutscher Ostmarkenverein, Nr. 38, Bl. 62 (M).

4. The Pan-German League was founded in 1890 with the stated goal of "the stimulation of German-national character [*Gesinnung*] around the world, the preservation of German place and custom in Europe and overseas and the integration of everything German [*Deutschtum*]." See Bundesarchiv Berlin (henceforth BA Berlin), R8048, Alldeutscher Verband, Nr. 4, Bl. 11–13, Satzungen des Alldeutschen Verbandes. For a history of the Pan-German League, see Roger Chickering, *We Men Who Feel Most German: A Cultural Study of the Pan-German League, 1886–1914* (Boston, 1984).

5. The German Eastern Marches Society was founded in 1894 in Poznań/Posen. Its goal was "the strengthening and fortification [*Befestigung*] of German-national feeling and the economic strengthening of the German nation [*Volk*]." See the *Satzungen des Vereins zur Förderung des Deutschtums in den Ostmarken* (Posen, 1894) and GStA PK, I. HA, Rep. 195, Deutscher Ostmarkenverein, Nr. 72, Vols. I & II; Nr. 90; and Nr. 140 (M). For a history of the Eastern Marches Society, see Adam Galos, Felix-Heinrich Gentzen and Witold Jakóbczyk, *Die Hakatisten: Der Deutsche Ostmarkenverein (1894–1934). Ein Beitrag zur Geschichte der Ostpolitik des deutschen Imperialismus* (East Berlin, 1966); and Sabine Grabowski, *Deutscher und polnischer Nationalismus. Der deutsche Ostmarken-Verein und die polnische Straż 1894–1914* (Marburg, 1998).

6. For a discussion of the radicalization of Pan-German ideology, see Chickering, *We Men Who Feel Most German*, pp. 230–245.

7. See, for example, GStA PK, I. HA, Rep. 195, Deutscher Ostmarkenverein, Nr. 9a (M).

8. Such images are scattered throughout the pages of *Die Ostmark*, the organ of the Eastern Marches Society, and the *Alldeutsche Blätter*, the organ of the Pan-German League, which often concerned itself with the Polish question as well as the internal documents of both organizations. See, for example, *Die Ostmark* 1904, 78–79; *Mitteilungen des Alldeutschen Verbandes,* 1892: 53; *Alldeutsche Blätter* 1894: 75 and 1901: 451; GStA PK, I. HA, Rep. 195, Deutscher Ostmarkenverein, Nr. 9a, Nr. 140 and Nr. 174, Bl. 19 (M); BA Berlin, R8048, Alldeutscher Verband, Nr. 504, "Kundgebungen, Beschlüsse und Forderungen des Alldeutschen Verbandes 1890–1902," lecture by Paul Samassa on "Die slawische Gefahr in den Ostmarken" at the Verbandstag in Eisenach on 25 Mary 1902, S. 113. Cf. Dietrich Schaefer, "Geschichtliche Einleitung," in *Die Ostmark*, ed. Deutscher Ostmarkenverein (Lissa, 1913), pp. 1–62; GStA PK, I. HA, Rep. 195, Deutscher Ostmarkenverein, Anh. 71, "Festschrift zum 10-jährigen Stiftungsfest" (M); BA Berlin, R8048, Alldeutscher Verband,

Nr. 506, "Die Bilanz des neuen Kurses," lecture by Heinrich Class at the Verbandstag in Plauen on 12 September 1903, p. 41 and Nr. 522, "Der Kampf um das Deutschtum: Die preußischen Ostmarken," by Christian Petzet (Munich, 1898).

9. BA Berlin, R8048, Alldeutscher Verband, Nr. 57, Sitzung des Geschäftsführenden Ausschusses, Berlin, 17/19. November 1906, Bl. 18.

10. BA Berlin, R8048, Alldeutscher Verband, Nr. 84, Sitzung des Geschäftsführenden Ausschusses, Hannover, 13/14 April 1912, Bl. 13–16, letter from Samassa to the Hauptleitung of the Pan-German League, dated 1 April 1912.

11. See *Satzungen des Vereins zur Förderung des Deutschtums in den Ostmarken* (Posen, 1894); GStA PK, I. HA, Rep. 195, Deutscher Ostmarkenverein, Nr. 34, Bd. 1, Bl. 1–2, Satzungen der Berliner Ortsgruppe der Deutschen Ostmarkenvereins (M); and BA Berlin, R8048, Alldeutscher Verband, Nr. 4, Bl. 11–13, Satzungen des Alldeutschen Verbandes.

12. GStA PK, I. HA, Rep. 195, Deutscher Ostmarkenverein, Nr. 2, Vol. I, Bl. 111ff, Tiedemann's speech at the Gesamtausschuß meeting on 29 October 1905 (M).

13. Such membership requirements—or lack thereof—were also typical of German associations in the Habsburg Empire. See Gary B. Cohen, *The Politics of Ethnic Survival: Germans in Prague, 1861–1914,* 2nd ed. (West Lafayette, 2006); and Pieter M. Judson, *Exclusive Revolutionaries: Liberal Politics, Social Experience, and National Identity in the Austrian Empire, 1848–1914* (Ann Arbor, 1996).

14. The work on the cultural consciousness of the German *Bürgertum* is extensive. See, for examples, the essays in David Blackbourn and Richard J. Evans, eds., *The German Bourgeoisie: Essays on the Social History of the German Middle Class from the Late Eighteenth to the Early Twentieth Century* (London/New York, 1993). Cf. Pierre Bourdieu, *Distinction: A Social Critique of the Judgement of Taste* (Cambridge, MA, 1984).

15. For a discussion of the radicalization of Pan-German ideology, in particular, its turn towards racial anti-Semitism, see Chickering, *We Men Who Feel Most German*, pp. 230–245.

16. GStA PK, I. HA, Rep. 195, Deutscher Ostmarkenverein, Anh. No. 36, Bl. 13–19, Vosberg's report about Gostyn (18 February 1913) (M).

17. See GStA PK, I. HA, Rep. 195, Deutscher Ostmarkenverein, Nr. 90, Bl. 36–37, Tiedemann to Konrad Plehn (22 December 1894); Nr., 90, Bl. 82, Tiedemann to Max von Binzer (8 January 1895); and Nr. 132, Vol. 1, Bl. 92, report by Tiedemann) 14 July 1914) (M). Cf. *Im deutschen Reich* 1902: 97–100 & 1903: 708–715.

18. See *Im deutschen Reich* 1902: 171, 457 and 1908: 72–75; and GStA PK, I. HA, Rep. 195, Deutscher Ostmarkenverein, Anh. Nos. 88 and 63, Bl. 290–295 (M). I have examined this dynamic in more detail in Elizabeth A. Drummond, "On the Borders of the Nation: Jews and the German-Polish National Conflict in Poznania, 1886–1914," *Nationalities Papers* 29/3 (2001): 459–475.

19. GStA PK, I. HA, Rep. 195, Deutscher Ostmarkenverein, Nr. 72, Vol. I, Bl. 21 (M).

20. GStA PK, I. HA, Rep. 195, Deutscher Ostmarkenverein, Nr. 72, Vol. I, Bl. 2 (M).

21. GStA PK, I. HA, Rep. 195, Deutscher Ostmarkenverein, Nr. 140 (M).

22. GStA PK, I. HA, Rep. 195, Deutscher Ostmarkenverein, Nr. 140 (M). Cf. BA Berlin, R8048, Alldeutscher Verband, Nr. 522, "Der Kampf um das Deutschtum: Die preußischen Ostmarken" by Christian Petzet (Munich, 1898), p. 1.

23. See, for example, Peter Fritzsche, *Germans Into Nazis* (Cambridge, MA, 1998), pp. 13–28.

24. See GStA PK, I. HA, Rep. 195, Deutscher Ostmarkenverein, Nr. 161, Bl. 92–98, "Der August 1914 in einem polnischen Dorf Posens: Eine Skizze" by Gertrud Flatau of Bialoschwein.

25. "Zweite Balkonrede des Kaisers, 1. August 1914," in Ulrich Cartarius, ed., *Deutschland im Ersten Weltkrieg* (Munich, 1982), p. 15. Cf. Fritzsche, *Germans Into Nazis*.

26. See the membership lists of the "Guard" Society and, in particular, the gymnastic organizations; Archiwum Panstwowe w Poznaniu (APP), Towarzystwo "Straż," Nrs. 28–31 and APP, 879, Związek Sokołów Polskich w Pa stwie Niemieckim, Nrs. 17–19 & 82–170. The sheer number of names drawn through with a black line indicates how much of the membership of these organizations was lost not only to the battlefront but to the war.

27. GStA PK, I. HA, Rep. 195, Deutscher Ostmarkenverein, Nr. 2, Vol. II, Bl. 157–201, minutes of the Kriegssitzungen des Geschäftsausschusses des Hauptvorstandes from the second half of 1919 (M).

28. See, for example, GStA PK, I. HA, Rep. 195, Deutscher Ostmarkenverein, Nr. 4, Bl. 2–5, meeting of the general committee in Posen, 1918; and Nr. 9a (M).

29. GStA PK, I. HA, Rep. 195, Deutscher Ostmarkenverein, Nr. 4, Bl. 11, Tiedemann at the general committee meeting in Posen, 1918 (M).

30. GStA PK, I. HA, Rep. 195, Deutscher Ostmarkenverein, Nr. 13, Bl. 30–43, Denkschrift des Posener Provinzial-Vorstandes des Deutschen Ostmarken-Vereins zur Frage der Neuorientierung der preußischen Polenpolitik, 1916 (M).

31. Vejas Liulevicius, *War Land on the Eastern Front: Culture, National Identity and German Occupation in World War I* (Cambridge, 2000), p. 8. See also Fritz Fischer, *Griff nach der Weltmacht: Die Kriegszielpolitik des kaiserlichen Deutschland 1914–1918* (Düsseldorf, 1961).

32. See Brian Porter, *When Nationalism Began to Hate: Imagining Modern Politics in Nineteenth-Century Poland* (Oxford, 2000).

33. Richard Blanke, *Orphans of Versailles: The Germans in Western Poland 1918–1939* (Lexington, 1993). An excellent analysis of German-Polish national relations before, during, and after World War I, one of the very few studies to span the wartime years, is Mathias Niendorf's *Minderheiten an der Grenze: Deutsche und Polen in den Kreisen Flatow (Złotów) and Zempelburg (Sępólno Krajeńskie) 1900–1939* (Wiesbaden, 1997). A good study of the German minority in Poznania is Dariusz Matelski's *Mniejszość niemiecka w Wielkopolsce w latach 1919–1939* (Poznań, 1997). Much of the earlier Polish scholarship on the German minority in interwar Poland has justified these Polonization measures, a debate which Blanke succinctly describes in *Orphans of Versailles*, pp. 1–8. Cf. Marian Drozdowski, "The National Minorities in Poland, 1918–1939," *Acta Poloniae Historica* 22 (1970): 226–251; Przemysław Hauser, *Mniejszość niemiecka w województwie pomorskim w latach 1920–39* (Wrocław, 1981); Jerzy Krasuski, *Stosunki polsko-niemieckie*, 2 vols. (Poznań, 1962–1964); Stanisław Potocki, *Położenie mniejszości niemieckiej w Polsce 1918–1939* (Gdańsk, 1969); and Jerzy Tomaszewski, "Konsekwencje wielonarodowościowej struktury ludności Polski 1918–1939 dla procesów integracyjnych społeczeństwa," in *Drogi integracji społeczeństwa w Polsce XIX–XX w.*, ed. H. Zieliński (Wrocław, 1976), pp. 109–138.

34. Ibid.

35. Blanke, *Orphans of Versailles*, p. 32.

36. Blanke ably summarizes the historical debate on the question in chapter 2 of his *Orphans of Versailles*, pp. 32–53.

37. "Organic work" was the name given to the various Polish-national organizations that emerged in the nineteenth century. Eschewing armed uprising, the "organic work" movement focused on education and economic "self-modernization." It sought to overcome the traditional social and economic weaknesses of Polish society and to integrate the Polish population into a unified nation, which would challenge the partitioning powers and pave the way for future Polish independence. See William W. Hagen, "National Solidar-

ity and Organic Work in Prussian Poland, 1815–1914," *Journal of Modern History* 44/1 (1972): 38–64; Witold Jakóbczyk, *Studia nad dziejami Wielkopolski w XIX w. (Dzieje pracy organicznej)*, 3 vols. (Poznań, 1951–1967); William W. Hagen, *Germans, Poles, and Jews: The Nationality Conflict in the Prussian East, 1772–1914* (Chicago, 1980); Stanislaus A. Blejwas, "The Origins and Practice of 'Organic Work' in Poland, 1795–1863," *Polish Review* 15/4 (1970): 22–55; and Stanislaus A. Blejwas, *Realism in Polish Politics: Warsaw Positivism and National Survival in Nineteenth-Century Poland* (New Haven, 1984).

38. See Blanke, *Orphans of Versailles*, pp. 54ff.; and Matelski, *Mniejszość niemiecka w Wielkopolsce w latach 1919–1939*, pp. 72–77.

39. See Blanke, *Orphans of Versailles*, pp. 54ff.; and Matelski, *Mniejszość niemiecka w Wielkopolsce w latach 1919–1939*, pp. 77–88.

40. Blanke, *Orphans of Versailles*, pp. 73ff.; and Matelski, *Mniejszość niemiecka w Wielkopolsce w latach 1919–1939*, pp. 88–95. The same two political tendencies emerged in the German minority in interwar Czechoslovakia—the cooperative *Arbeitsgemeinschaft* (Association for Work) and the oppositional *Kampfgemeinschaft* (Association for Struggle)—although the former proved much more successful in winning the support of significant segments of the German population in Czechoslovakia than did its counterpart in Poland. For a history of the German minority in interwar Czechoslovakia, see Rudolf Jaworski, *Vorposten oder Minderheit? Der sudetendeutsche Volkstumkampf in den Beziehungen zwischen der Weimarer Republik und der CSR* (Stuttgart: Deutsche Verlags-Anstalt, 1977), especially pp. 15–70.

41. Blanke, *Orphans of Versailles*, pp. 150ff. Cf. Galos, Gentzen, and Jakóbczyk, *Die Hakatisten*, pp. 265–418.

42. See, for example, GStA PK, I. HA, Rep. 195, Deutscher Ostmarkenverein, Nr. 4, Bl. 36–40, Ginschel at the general committee meeting in Posen, 1918; and Nr. 3, Vol. I, Bl. 4–5, report from the general committee meeting on 26 October 1918 (M).

43. See Galos et al., *Die Hakatisten*, op. cit., pp. 334ff. and 372ff.

44. Ibid., pp. 342f.

45. Ibid., pp. 395ff. The society was in formal contact with the Nazi Party at least as early as 1932, and individual members had already initiated contact even before that time; see GStA PK, I. HA, Rep. 195, Deutscher Ostmarkenverein, Nr. 278 (M).

46. Blanke, *Orphans of Versailles*, pp. 163–206; and Matelski, *Mniejszość niemiecka w Wielkopolsce w latach 1919–1939*, pp. 95–133, 308–339.

47. Blanke, *Orphans of Versailles*, pp. 163–206, esp. p. 174; and Matelski, *Mniejszość niemiecka w Wielkopolsce w latach 1919–1939*, pp. 95–133, 308–339.

48. Blanke, *Orphans of Versailles*, pp. 163–206, esp. p. 174.

49. Blanke, *Orphans of Versailles*, pp. 163–206; and Matelski, *Mniejszość niemiecka w Wielkopolsce w latach 1919–1939*, pp. 95–133, 308–309.

50. GStA PK, I. HA, Rep. 195, Deustcher Ostmarkenverein, Nr. 9a (M).

# The National State and the Territorial Parish in Interwar Poland

### ❖ James Bjork ❖

The years immediately following the First World War witnessed a major escalation in the grim narrative of ethnic cleansing that unfolded in East-Central Europe between the Balkan Wars of 1912–1913 and the Wars of the Yugoslav Succession in the 1990s. From the Baltic to the Aegean, hundreds of thousands of people whose national affiliations clashed with the titular nationality of their state of residence either fled or were forcibly sent packing in a brutal attempt to translate the "nationality principle" into reality. The scale of these refugee movements, however, varied dramatically across the region. Some groups—Germans in Poznania and West Prussia; Turks, Bulgarians, and Greeks on the wrong side of borders in the Balkans and Anatolia—emigrated *en masse*. In other regions, including almost all of the Habsburg successor states, only a small portion of the newly created national minorities left their homes.

What accounted for this striking variation in the fate of the minorities that emerged after the First World War? A wide range of factors played a role, of course: the way in which a given block of territory changed hands; the stringency of the successor states' policies toward national minorities; the relative "rootedness" of the minorities themselves.[1] But I would suggest that one of the most important variables in determining which minorities stayed put and which migrated was religion—specifically, whether religious affiliation separated a particular group from the majority population or, alternately, provided a point of cultural transmission between them. The first half of this thesis, that religious divisions tended to accentuate and exacerbate the perception of ethnic/national difference, will likely make intuitive sense to most scholars. Religious difference, after all, was often one of the chief markers that *defined* national difference, especially in Eastern Europe, and it has often been noted that cultural distinctions that were ostensibly based on linguistic, "racial," or "ethnic" criteria were, on the ground, actually extrapolated from membership in different religious communities. In the Greek-Turkish population transfers, for example, the norm was for all Muslims to be defined as "Turks," whether or not they spoke any form of Turkish, while the category of "Greeks" could expand to encompass any Orthodox population, from Serbs to Arabs.[2] Similarly, in Poznania and Polish Pomerania, many scholars, both in the nineteenth century and more recently, have resorted to using confessional statistics as a proxy for analyzing nationality on the assumption that Catholics were overwhelmingly Polish and Protestants overwhelmingly German.[3] In these as well as other these cases, nationality was so closely linked with membership in religious communities that Protestant, Catholic, Orthodox, and Muslim clerics often emerged the most vociferous nationalist agitators and/or the most zealously targeted symbols of national distinction.

But if many students of nationalism are familiar with such examples in which overlapping, mutually reinforcing religious and national identifications led to heightened national conflict, the alternative possibility—of cross-cutting religious and national categories resulting in a blurring and amelioration of national distinctions and a reduction in pressure on national minorities to emigrate—might not seem as immediately plausible. In part, I think, this skepticism stems from an assumption that ethnic and linguistic groups have generally *not* "shared" the same religious community in a meaningful or robust way, even if they formally adhered to the same religious confession. In the Balkan Wars of 1912–1913, to take one particularly striking example, Serbs, Bulgarians, and Greeks may have held a common allegiance to the Orthodox faith, but different organizational hierarchies clearly delineated national varieties of Orthodoxy, facilitating campaigns of ethnic cleansing rather than impeding them.[4] Catholics in the United States, though spared such violent confrontations, were also often formally divided along national lines, as new "national" parishes—Polish, German, Italian, Czech—were established specifically to minister to particular groups of immigrants. It is important to remember, however that this kind of formal demarcation of religious communities in national terms, routine among American Catholics and among the Orthodox population of the Balkans, was *not* sanctioned by the Catholic church on the European continent. European parishes were defined strictly by geographic contiguity, meaning that linguistically mixed populations frequently ended up in the same parish and were provided with pastoral care by the same local clergy. This simple but often overlooked fact—that there were, officially, no "German" or "Polish" or "Czech" or "French" parishes in the polyglot borderlands of Catholic Europe—had significant consequences. It meant that the everyday activities of local parish life, rather than doing the work of national activists in demarcating who was who in national terms, instead tended to muddy the issue, as individuals were allowed to move across linguistic/national lines while remaining in the same religious space and interacting with the same religious personnel.

In order to understand how this model of the bilingual religious community worked in practice and how it could provide a counterweight to pressures on national minorities to emigrate, it is helpful to look more closely at one of the most spectacular examples of this phenomenon: the German-Polish borderland of Upper Silesia. Here was a region that, according to many criteria, should have produced a decisive "sorting out" of populations along national lines following the postwar re-drawing of boundaries. Other German territories ceded to Poland, after all, had witnessed a massive emigration of members of the new German minority. In addition, as the most densely populated and economically important of all the contested interwar borderlands, Upper Silesia had been the setting for a particularly grueling and hard-fought plebiscite campaign, which went in Germany's favor by a vote of 59 percent to 41 percent. And yet, after the region was divided between the two states in 1922, the level of migration of Germanophile residents from the Polish portion of Silesia was far less than in the other parts of the Prussian East that had been awarded to Poland after the Paris peace settlement. In the provinces of Poznania and West Prussia, roughly 70 percent of the German minority population emigrated;[5] in Polish Upper Silesia, by contrast only a minority (about 25 percent) of the Germanophile residents moved to Germany.[6]

An important clue in explaining this discrepancy lies in the differing confessional profiles of these borderlands. In Poznania and West Prussia, where the vast majority of Germans were Protestant, daily religious life worked to separate the minority population from the Catholic majority, while in Polish Upper Silesia, where the majority of the German population was Catholic, German and Polish Catholics shared local religious communities and daily religious practices.[7] And "shared" is, indeed, the proper term in this case. Since the late nineteenth centuries, the urban parishes that served the overwhelming majority of Upper Silesians had been thoroughly bilingual or (to use the contemporary term) "utraquist." In these "double parishes," bilingual priests routinely delivered homilies, heard confessions, staged popular missions, and led parish association meetings in both German and Polish.

In the aftermath of the plebiscite of March 1921, as the contours of the new German-Polish border running through Upper Silesia became clear, the future of this "utraquist" model seemed in some doubt. In keeping with a longstanding practice of adjusting diocesan boundaries to conform to state boundaries, the Vatican set in motion the process of establishing a new diocese for Polish Silesia, gradually separating it from the jurisdiction of the bishop of Breslau, Adolf Cardinal Bertram. From October 1921 through November 1922, the areas to be ceded to Poland were placed under the administration of an episcopal delegate, Father Jan Kapica, who remained under the formal authority of Cardinal Bertram. In November 1922, Pope Pius XI appointed Father August Hlond of the Salesian order to take over the ecclesiastical governance of Polish Silesia as an apostolic delegate, answerable directly to Rome. Three years later, a separate diocese of Katowice was established, including both the

Polish portion of "Prussian" Silesia as well as the areas of "Austrian" Silesia devolving to Poland in the peace settlement.[8] As this division of the region into a "Polish" and a "German" diocese proceeded, the question naturally loomed of whether this would involve a more thoroughgoing nationalization of individual parishes on either side of the new frontier. There was considerable evidence that it might. Of the 550-odd parish priests working in the region at the time, over 100 migrated from Polish Silesia to German Silesia or vice-versa because they were on the "wrong" side of the new frontier—in other words, because their national loyalties clashed with the state in which they now found themselves.[9] Before this wave of migration, the Upper Silesian portion of the Breslau diocese and the Katowice diocese-in-the-making had clergies with nearly identical national profiles. Now German Silesia was assured an overwhelmingly German-oriented clergy, Polish Silesia a decidedly Polonophile one. It seemed a significant step in the direction of a full-scale cultural nationalization of the new borderlands.

It was a significant step, but, nonetheless, very far from the ultimate destination. For this partial "sorting out" of scores of Upper Silesian priests did not produce anything like the cultural payoff that nationalizing German or Polish state officials envisioned. Not only did a number of avowedly Polonophile priests stay in their parishes in German Silesia, as well as a greater number of vocally Germanophile priests in the parishes of Polish Silesia, but the largest single ideological grouping among the region's clergy—the nationally indifferent—remained essentially unaffected by the informal priest-exchange of 1921–1922. These priests, along with a surprising proportion of the incoming "refugee" clergy, remained wedded to the traditions of "utraquist" pastoral work and showed little interest in either pressuring minority-language parishioners to emigrate or encouraging their systematic cultural assimilation. A combination of principle, inertia, and sheer stubbornness resulted in a striking degree of continuity in linguistic practice in Upper Silesia's parishes, particularly in the industrial parishes clustered along either side of the new border. This linguistically latitudinarian religious milieu, as I will be illustrating in detail below, contributed to the relatively low rate of cross-border migration by lay Catholic Upper Silesians during the interwar period, as well as the limited success of efforts at systematic assimilation.

When one looks more closely at the profile of the priests that remained in their pastoral posts after the 1922 frontier shift, one sees that the post-plebiscite shift toward national homogenization was less impressive that it seemed at first blush. This was particularly true in Polish Silesia, where the Polonophile Father Lewek estimated that only about 50 of the 200-odd priests involved in pastoral work at the time of the plebiscite were reliably Polish-oriented.[10] Even after adjusting for an influx of 50 or so conationals from the west and the exodus of about 50 German-oriented priests over the next few years, one is left with a formidable contingent of up to 100 "nationally suspect" priests—i.e., with Germanophile sympathies or indifferent—among the clergy of the Apostolic Delegacy of Katowice. The proportion of non-Germanophile clergy remaining in German Silesia was no doubt significantly lower, but it seems likely (based on earlier estimates of 200 or more nationally neutral priests in the plebiscite region as a whole)[11] that at least 100 of the roughly 350 priests on that side of the frontier also had uncertain national inclinations.

The non-Polish-national clergy who remained in parishes in Polish Silesia included more than 50 who considered themselves German,[12] though these ran the gamut from the abrasively German-national to the diplomatically Germanophile. One the priests who might have been expected to be among the first to join the exodus out of Polish Silesia was Father Josef Zientek, the longtime pastor (since 1904) of the predominantly working-class, Polish-speaking parish of Roździń/Rödzien. Already in the middle of the plebiscite campaign, his own church council had voted 48 to 7 to have him replaced by someone more "impartial."[13] And yet Zientek weathered the change of sovereignty in Rödzien with surprising equanimity and continued to serve as senior pastor of the parish, as well as secretary of the deanery of Katowice, for the next decade. Like many other pro-German clergymen, Zientek felt less comfortable with the Polish language than with German (he later explained to Bishop Adamski that his mother had never prayed with him in Polish).[14] But unlike some of his émigré colleagues—who, despite their "utraquist" label, actually had quite limited Polish proficiency[15]—Zientek seemed to have little difficulty in switching to Polish in corresponding with his new superiors in Katowice. He did, however, remain unabashedly German-oriented in his own sympathies and was regularly denounced by the more Polish-patriotic of his parishioners as a "Hakatist of the purest kind" who is "ashamed of everything Polish."[16] Zientek responded to such criticism caustically, complaining to the curia that "peasants and women," often "coming from the lowest level of society," now felt like they owned the church.[17]

Father Zientek's tense relationship with the dominant nationality of his new home state was rather extreme, but not at all unique. Many priests who remained in Polish Silesia maintained such pronounced Germanophile sympathies that they came under the scrutiny of both government officials and local patriots. Father Alojzy Dyllus, a curate in Załęże, held meetings of German minority organizations in the local parsonage and made fun of Polish figures in the German-language press. Father Paweł Gediga in Leszczyny reportedly maintained a clandestine broadcasting station in his parsonage (with the implication of sinister cooperation with German propaganda). Father Karol Hübner campaigned to preserve the name Deutsch-Weichsel for his parish, which now went by the Polish Wisła Mała.[18] Over the course of the interwar period, confrontations between Germanophile priests and Polish patriotic groups sometimes grew so heated that the former either stepped down or were transferred by the diocesan hierarchy. A considerable number of these priests eventually abandoned Polish Silesia altogether, belatedly joining the earlier exodus of Germanophile priests heading west.[19] But many other priests who were cited as "anti-Polish" troublemakers remained firmly ensconced in their parishes. Indeed, in an illustration of how loose the relationship between national sentiment and migration could be, at least two of the priests who later came under fire for their Germanophile sentiments (Karol Arndt and Franciszek Florek) had actually migrated *into* Polish Silesia in 1921–1922—and were also duly listed among "Polish" refugees from German terror![20]

Most of the Germanophile clergy who did remain in parishes in Polish Silesia kept somewhat lower profiles than the priests mentioned above and were generally on better terms with their diocesan superiors and Polish-speaking parishioners, if not always with government officials. The church hierarchy's model of the "good" German minority priest was undoubtedly Father Josef Kubis, the pastor of Załęże and head of the deanery of Katowice. In the spring of 1922, Kubis had met with Ludwig Skowronek, his one-time mentor, and several other moderate Germanophile clergymen to discuss how to deal with the onset of Polish rule. They agreed that the only viable policy was conscientious loyalty to their new ecclesiastical superiors and scrupulous national impartiality in pastoral work.[21] This attitude earned Kubis the trust of his Polish colleagues and new superiors; when the diocese of Katowice was officially organized in 1925, he was one of six clergymen appointed as canons of the cathedral chapter.[22] In his own parish of Załęże, Kubis fiercely protected local traditions lest any precipitous innovations trigger a sense of class or national grievance. Even before the war, he had protested attempts to make local schoolchildren attend classes on day of the parish festival (St. Joseph's name day), noting that "the faithful are very attached to their holidays."[23] And when municipal authorities complained about his demands that they pay gravediggers for the burial of the poor, Kubis insisted that such payments were necessary to ensure the continuation of Załęże's longstanding custom of burying poor parishioners with the same level of ceremonial as rich parishioners.[24] This meticulously localist perspective seemed to shield Kubis from most national controversies while giving him more credibility at those moments when he did take on certain demands of Polish-national parishioners. When, for example, he firmly rejected repeated requests by veterans of the Polish insurgencies to have an armed honor guard at a funeral service, Kubis characteristically defended his decision by referencing communal opinion. The insurgent representatives, he argued, were "young men, as yet unmarried, with no weight in the community" and often prone to drinking and fighting; giving them a position of honor would only provoke unrest.[25]

Most German-oriented priests seem to have followed a cautious course roughly similar to that of Father Kubis and rarely provoked the displeasure of Polonophile parishioners or their superiors.[26] Indeed, some priests known to be "German" in their personal cultural orientation raised the ire of the *German* press by failing to lobby for German language instruction or promote German minority institutions. Father Ernest Bresler, the pastor of Mysłowice, provides an interesting illustration of this phenomenon. He had earlier been the target of complaints by pro-Polish parishioners, who claimed that he was "not stopping the abuses of his [pro-German] curates and himself mistreats the Poles."[27] A couple years later, however, a German parishioner was writing to the *Oberschlesische Kurier* to report that Bresler had become a "vehement Polish agitator" in order to preserve "his good [i.e., financially lucrative] position." This "agitation" consisted of allowing a service commemorating the anniversary of one of the Polish uprisings and telling parishioners after the Polish-language mass that "Polish parents should send their children to Polish schools."[28] Such changes in national tone—often subtle to an outside observer but obviously noticeable to contemporary residents—were a part of many Germanophile priests' adjustment to changed circumstances.

The line separating these discreetly German-leaning clerics from the genuinely "neutral" clergy was a very fine one. Thomas Szczeponik, a parliamentary leader of the Silesian German minority, went so far as to argue that if one were to ask an Upper Silesian priest if he is a German or a Pole, a Polonophile priest would simply respond that he is a Pole, while the evasive response "'I am a priest' . . . usually means attachment to German nationality."[29] Leaving aside the tendentious implication that Poles are inherently more "nationalist" than Germans, Szczeponik's story was based on an undeniable fact: the rhetorical strategy of claiming national "neutrality" was one pursued disproportionately by priests who might otherwise be classified as "German." One can see the close connection between self-characterization as nationally indifferent and assurances of one's ability to conduct conscientious Polish-language pastoral work in Father Paweł Michatz's correspondence with diocesan delegate Jan Kapica. During the widespread jockeying for pastoral posts following the division of Upper Silesia, Michatz's top priority was finding a post near his elderly mother (in Mysłowice), and he carefully positioned himself as a "neutral" to keep as many options open as possible:

> Regarding my national disposition, I follow the example of St. Paul, my patron, and want to devote myself to everything that has been entrusted to me. I do not meddle in politics, because I practice obedience to the authorities of the church, though it would be easier for me after my entry into Upper Silesia [presumably he meant the Polish part of Upper Silesia] to portray myself as a die-hard Pole, above all because the Polish general consul in Berlin has more than once sent me a complimentary letter or some kind of expensive gift in recognition of my work among Poles.

"For idealistic and aesthetic reasons," Michatz reiterated, he tried to avoid politics and instead "devote myself to pastoral work, which soothes the disharmony and injury opened by fratricidal war."[30] After a few abortive bids for various pastoral posts in the industrial region, in which moderately Germanophile clergymen seemed more favorably disposed toward his candidacy than Polonophile ones,[31] Father Michatz succeeded in becoming pastor of a new parish in an industrial suburb of Katowice.

His claim of national neutrality, however, was vigorously contested by Polish state officials. Seizing on the fact that he spoke German in private life and that he seemed especially solicitous toward German-language parish associations, the local Department of Public Safety labeled him a "fervent German" and concluded that his removal from the parish would be highly desirable.[32]

Another priest who took pains to represent himself as nationally impartial was Father Josef Knossalla. In writing in support of his candidacy for the pastoral post in Radzionków (Radzionkau), one longtime Center politician had stressed that Knossalla would be "agreeable to both [national] sides."[33] At least some Polonophile residents of Radzionków, however, were not convinced. A representative of the local community council protested that, when Father Knossalla served in the parish as a curate, he had shunned subscribers to Polish-national newspapers during the post-Christmas pastoral visitations (*kolęda*); defended membership in the German veterans association (*Kriegerverein*); and discouraged people from wearing their "national costumes" (*strój nardowy*). Knossalla managed to weather these charges and was installed in Radzionków as pastor, but he subsequently came under intensive government scrutiny. After rumors circulated that the pastor of Radzionków was making anti-Polish statements, the curia in Katowice came to his defense, assuring the office of the Silesian governor (*wojewoda*) that Knossalla "had Polish convictions, though he has not manifested them politically."[34] As with Father Michałż, Father Knossalla's national "neutrality" was accepted much more readily by his ecclesiastical superiors than by nationalizing state officials or grass-roots national activists.

Indeed, particularly after Marshall Józef Piłsudski's 1926 coup and the appointment of the *Sanacja*-affiliated Michał Grażyński as provincial governor of Silesia, government officials' suspicions of national heterodoxy tended to extent to almost the entire native clergy of Upper Silesia, not just its avowed German minority. Father Kapica, after all, had reassured Cardinal Bertram that "the greatest part of the clergy [of Polish Silesia] feels inwardly German."[35] And diocesan officials, in their efforts to neutralize complaints by the German minority, had stressed that "all the priests of Polish Upper Silesia have the German abitur and German university studies behind them."[36] How could one expect the diocese to take a hard line on Polonizing the new borderlands when the local "Polish" clergy had so many personal bonds with the "German" clergy, when even the apostolic delegate August Hlond—by 1926 the Archbishop of Gniezno and Primate of Poland—fondly remembered being the *Pfarrkind* ("parish child") of a leading Germanophile pastor (Skowronek) while growing up in the industrial region?[37]

Tensions between the Polish state and the Silesian clergy were also evident in their differing approaches to the basic question of just how many "Germans" there were among the Catholic population of the diocese of Katowice. An official diocesan estimate in 1926 placed the number of German Catholics in former Prussian Poland at approximately 140,000,[38] while a parish-by-parish survey conducted in 1928 recorded some 180,000 "Catholics of German speech."[39] Both figures were noticeably higher than the official census tally of 1931, which claimed there were fewer than 50,000 German Catholics in the region.[40] None of these figures, of course, can be taken as an authoritative measure of how many Catholics were "really" German. Other indices of national sentiment, after all, such as provincial election results in 1930, suggested that some 300,000 Catholics had Germanophile sympathies.[41] What was more interesting about the diocesan nationality statistics was not the precise figure they provided, but instead their ambivalence, almost agnosticism, about the whole question of who was "German" or "Polish." Many local priests noted that the "German Catholics" included in their estimates were composed "mostly" or "almost entirely" of "Germanized Poles" or "Germanized locals." Diocesan officials underlined these observations by noting at the end of the statistical survey that these parishioners "could take part in a Polish service with at least as much benefit [as a German service]."[42] Rather than imagining their flocks as discrete German and Polish congregations that used the same church building but otherwise occupied separate worlds, clerics assumed that many parishioners could—and sometimes did—switch between Polish and German worship services or parish associations if one or the another seemed more convenient or inviting, just as the clergy themselves were expected to preach or teach in either language as context dictated.

This permeability of linguistic boundaries at the level of parish life had complex implications. On the one hand, it meant that nationalizing pressures in society as a whole—including state-driven assimilation efforts—were often translated into religious practice as well, with local clergy doing little to counter-act them. The balance between German and Polish sections of (clerically taught) confession-and-communion classes, for example, had shifted steadily in favor of the German language up through the First World War, reflecting the habituation of school-age children to classroom instruction in German.[43] The incorporation of part of Upper Silesia into Poland simply redirected this pattern of deference, as parish-based religious education quickly started to reflect the reality of mass Polish-language education.[44] We have already seen one example of the change in emphasis in Father Bresler's transformation into an "agitator" for Polish-language religious instruction, and it seems that the shift in the balance of confession-and-communion classes was, indeed, both widespread and rapid. In the parish of St. Peter and Paul in Katowice, for example, 342 of the children who had offered their first confession in 1913 did so in German, while 138 confessed in Polish.[45] By 1926, only 200 children at St. Peter and Paul were enrolled in the German sections of confession-and-communion instruction, while 400 were enrolled in the Polish sections.[46]

This dynamism in the linguistic balance of educational activity contrasted with a general inertia in the provision of German and Polish worship services and associational opportunities. As the diocesan authorities in Katowice frequently reiterated in responding to charges of anti-German discrimination, the proportion of German- and

Polish-language worship services changed only modestly during the interwar period, and provisions for German-language associational activity actually *increased* in many parishes.[47] Even the statistics published by German minority organizations (and intended to be alarmist) suggest a rather underwhelming shift in the linguistic balance of worship activity. In the districts of Katowice and Świętochłowice, home of most of Polish Silesia's German-speaking minority, the number of Sunday morning Polish masses was reported to have risen from 58 to 75 between 1918 and 1926, while the number of Sunday morning German masses was said to have declined from 33 to 28.[48] This represented, to be sure, a noticeable prioritizing of new Polish-language services as new parishes were founded and pastoral care expanded, as well as a certain curtailment of those German-language services—in particular, the so-called "school masses" for students and teachers—that were deemed to have been introduced under pressure from the German government prior to 1918. In most large parishes, however, the prewar schedule of one German-language mass and two or three Polish-language masses every Sunday remained very much the norm, in spite of considerable German emigration and Polish immigration.

The parish of Rödzien provides an example of how even rather minor tinkering in the schedule of worship services was hotly contested and scrutinized for national advantage and disadvantage. In 1923, Polish activists in Roździń lobbied Apostolic Delegate Hlond to have the 8 AM German-language Sunday mass switched with the 11 AM Polish-language mass since, it was argued, Polish-speaking workers returning from late shifts in the mines, as well as their wives, would find it easier to attend the earlier service. If the schedule of Polish-language services did not accommodate them, the head of the local Union for the Defense of the Western Marches (*Związek Obrony Kresów Zachodnich* – ZOKZ) warned, these workers might attend the German-language mass and thereby "easily succumb to Germanization."[49] Zientek took issue with this logic in his response to the apostolic delegate's office, suggesting that it was actually easier for miners to attend the *later* service, but the apostolic administration—apparently at the initiative of Father Teofil Bromboszcz, the most militantly pro-Polish figure in the hierarchy—deferred to the (apparent) preferences of the Polish-speaking workers. Father Zientek was characteristically acerbic in his commentary. "Polishness," he wrote to Hlond, "will neither gain nor lose anything by this change."[50]

Various indices of linguistic practice at the parish level do, indeed, give the impression of striking continuity, despite a prevailing rhetoric (whether hortatory or alarmist) of a decisive nationalization of the region. In the spring of 1924, a pair of popular missions, one German-language and one Polish-language, was staged in the parish of St. Jadwiga's (Hedwig's) in Królewska Huta. A total of 12,104 men and women offered confessions in German, while 9,225 men and women confessed in Polish.[51] This linguistic balance roughly corresponded to the national breakdown reported in diocesan statistics four years later (50 percent German, 50 percent Polish),[52] but differed sharply from the Polish census figures of 1931, which claimed the German proportion of Królewska Huta's total population (including Protestants and Jews) had fallen to only 13 percent.[53] The clergy, placing more faith in their own internal statistics, maintained the traditional worship schedule of two German and two Polish masses, confident that this balance roughly reflected the preferences of parishioners and that any major alteration would be needlessly provocative. It was not that the clergy was particularly convinced of the essential "Germanness" of those who attended German-language masses; as we have seen, church documents routinely referred to the bulk of the German minority as "Germanized Poles" who, for the most part, knew Polish well. But if these parishioners were habituated to a German-language mass, a German-language mass they would have.

It was all the more significant—and, for Polish officials, all the more distressing—that the pastor defending the status quo in St. Jadwiga's was not a Germanophile holdover from the Wilhelmine era but a newly installed, impeccably "Polish" priest, Father Jan Gajda. Father Gajda sparred with state officials about various national controversies in the parish at least as frequently as his more German-oriented colleagues: e.g., over concerns that German parishioners were receiving more recognition for their financial contributions, that church employees were disproportionately Germanophile, or that Polish choral singing was receiving insufficient support.[54] Father Gajda was generally dismissive of such complaints. The church employees in question, he emphasized, were not "Germans" but simply "Upper Silesians" who "only speak broken German." As for the parish's "Polish" organist, who had allegedly been pushed aside, Father Gajda argued that the gentleman in question had in fact consistently neglected the Polish choir and had been replaced by another "Upper Silesian" who was "not only a Polish citizen but felt himself to be sincerely Polish." After thus underlining the slippery and contentious nature of national labels in this context, Father Gajda invoked what was, for the local clergy, a much more "real" and pertinent division, that between representatives of the church and those of the state. Gajda's letter to the police directorate of Królewska Huta took exception to the fact that state officials were "pok[ing] their noses into church affairs." He continued: "I lived for 20 years under the watch of the Prussian police, and I do not fear being under the watch of the Polish police. But I protest energetically against this 'protection.' If you gentlemen among the police would simply fulfill your religious obligations, that would be enough for me."[55]

Such episodes illustrated the considerable gulf that persisted between the priorities of the local Catholic clergy and both the nationalizing agenda of the interwar Polish state and the claims of the more militant leaders of the German minority community. In the eyes of state officials or of German minority politicians, the huge discrepancy between the low and high estimates of the German Catholic population in Silesia (50,000 vs. more than 300,000) was clearly a matter of "falsification," generated (according to the respective interpretation) by the pressure of overbearing

Polish bureaucrats or the enticements of German employers. To Upper Silesia's clergy, however, the ubiquity of ambiguous "Pole-Germans" in the region was not a bewildering statistical artifact but rather a self-evident sociological reality, corresponding to the large group of more or less bilingual residents who navigated various paths through the linguistic smorgasbord of parish life. Determining these parishioners' "national identities"—beyond the immediate issue of which parish association they wished to join or in which catechism class they wished to enroll their children—was simply not a matter of great interest to this regional elite.

The ambiguity of the church's role in simultaneously preserving and eroding German minority culture should not seem particularly strange to those familiar with the histories of "national" parishes in the urban neighborhoods of the United States, which could also be said to have both helped to segregate and to assimilate "ethnic" Catholics. But while there was generally a clear trajectory to these process in an American context—an initial cultivation of immigrant languages steadily giving way to a growing use of English and other aspects of "Americanization"—the geopolitical uncertainties of the German-Polish borderlands through much of the 20th century made the positing of any inexorable long-term "transition," whether German-to-Polish or Polish-to-German, far more dubious. In this uncertain context, bilingual Upper Silesians might explain away either their Germanophile or Polonophile traits as temporary, superficial accommodations to "foreign" rule while proclaiming the other national culture as authentically "theirs." Or, alternately, they might begin look at *all* expressions of national identity with ironic detachment. Regardless of how individuals subjectively understood the national ambiguities of their behavior, however, the persistence of those ambiguities through the interwar period effectively provided a viable "third way" between absolute assimilation on the one hand and identification as a defiant and irreducible national minority on the other. The cultural repertoire that made possible this navigation between "Germanness" and "Polishness" was, of course, the product of all the various complexities of Upper Silesian history. But as I have argued here, it was especially critical that an institution with the weight and authority of the Roman Catholic Church provided both the ideological framework and the social space to maintain ties to ostensibly irreconcilable cultures. By defining linguistic hybridity as normal rather than pathological, Upper Silesia's "utraquist" parishes could serve as counter-model to the nationalizing state, suggesting to the region's amorphous German minority that it might not be necessary to "sort themselves out" according to definitive national criteria.

## Notes

1. See, for example, the brief but thoughtful analysis in Roger Brubaker's *Nationalism Reframed* (Cambridge, 1996), pp. 148–78.
2. Michael Marrus, *The Unwanted: European Refugees in the Twentieth Century* (Oxford, 1985), p. 104.

3. For an example of contemporaries conflating religion and nationality in the Prussian East, see Max Weber, *The National State and Economic Policy*, translated and reprinted in part in *Nineteenth Century Europe: Liberalism and Its Critics,* Jan Goldstein and John W. Boyer, eds., (Chicago, 1988), pp. 438–460. For a recent example, see William Hagen's *Germans, Poles, and Jews: The Nationality Conflict in the Prussian East 1770–1914* (Chicago, 1980).

4. *The Other Balkan Wars* (Washington, DC: Carnegie Endowment for International Peace, republished 1993).

5. Based on calculations by Richard Blanke (*Orphans of Versailles* [Lexington, 1993], pp. 33–34, 244–245).

6. My estimate of the total number of Germanophile residents (400,000) is based on doubling the number of votes cast for Germany in the plebiscite (to take residents under voting age into account) and subtracting the roughly 50,000 "outvoters" who had voted in the plebsicite (overwhelmingly for Germany according to most reports) but who no longer lived in the region. (plebiscite statistics from Sarah Wambaugh, *Plebiscites since the World War* (Washington, 1933), vol. 1, pp. 250, 244–245). It is generally estimated that 100,000 people emigrated from Polish Silesia after the drawing of the new frontier (e.g., Wambaugh, p. 269, fn. 1; *Województwo Śląskie (1922–1939)*, Franciszek Serafin, ed. (Katowice, 1996), p. 179).

7. It is worth stressing that, in Upper Silesia, references to "daily" religious practice are meant rather literally, since the region was one of the most religiously observant on the continent. The boast of one local priest, that Upper Silesians were "the most religious nation [*sic*] in the world" (Memorandum on the Religious Aspect of the Upper Silesian Problem, n.d. [1921], signed by Prelate Tylla, Clerical Councillor Buchwald, and Vicar Strzyz), was, perhaps, a bit hyperbolic. But based on the usual statistical measures of popular piety, Upper Silesia has, indeed, consistently ranked higher than most other regions of either Germany or Poland. This phenomenon has remained noticeable up to the present day. Church attendance and participation in communion have consistently been well above the Polish national average in the dioceses of Katowice, Gliwice, and Opole and sometimes close to twice the level of observance in the neighboring (formerly Russian) Dąbrowa industrial basin. See statistical tables in *Kościół i Religijność Polaków, 1945–1999*, Witold Zdaniewicz and Tadeusz Zembruski, eds. (Warszawa, 2000), pp. 479–547. For most Upper Silesians, then, whether German or Polish, parish-based religious activity represented an extensive part of their overall social lives and, therefore, a crucial component of their sense of "belonging" in a local community.

8. A concise but exhaustively documented narrative of the formation of the diocese of Katowice can be found in Henryk Olszar's *Duchowieństwo katolickie diecezji Śląskiej (Katowickiej) w drugiej Rzeczypospolitej* (Katowice, 2000), pp. 42–56.

9. One more precise estimate is that 51 parish priests emigrated from German Silesia and 56 from Polish Silesia in the immediate post-partition period: Olszar, pp. 74–80. The estimate of the total number of clergy engaged in pastoral work is taken from "Oberschlesische kirchliche Verhältnisse," *Germania*, 29 October 1921, p. 2. To reconcile Olszar's figures with the statistics for priests engaged in strictly pastoral activities, I have subtracted the number of clergy serving in a teaching capacity (3 of the migrating Polish priests, 9 of the migrating German priests).

10. Lech Krzyżanowski, *Kościół katolicki wobec mniejszości niemieckiej na Górnym Śląsku w latach 1922–1930* (Katowice, 2000), p. 40.

11. An estimate of 200 pro-German and 200 neutral priests was given in "Die katholische Geistlichen in Oberschlesien," *Gazeta Ludowa*, 1 January 1920, quoted in *Gesamtüberblick über die Polnische Presse*, p. 11. A situation report of the Polish insurrectionists classifed

50 percent of the clergy (or 250–300 priests) as neutral and only 20 percent (or 100–125 priests) as truly pro-German, cited in Olszar, pp. 202–3.

12. Olszar gives a suspiciously precise figure of 58 German priests working in the diocese of Katowice in 1926, p. 203.

13. Msgr. Ratti (papal nuncio in Warsaw) to Bertram, 10 October 1920, I.A.25.o.29 (Bertram Nachlass), AAW.

14. Olszar, p. 209.

15. It is extraordinarily difficult to categorize priests according to their linguistic proficiency, especially there is no independent way to access their speaking abilities. Complaints about the quality of local priests' Polish were ubiquitous, but some of these were at the level of criticizing orthography or felicity of style. There were, however, some priests whose official "bilingual" status (indicated by a double cross next to their names in the diocesan handbook) was extremely dubious, even by their own admission. Pastor Alois Reif of St. Barbara's in Königshütte, for example, begged off heading the local Polish-language workers' association because he "had far too little mastery of the Polish language" to lead the group. Pfr. Reif to Bertram,15 August 1915, Acta der Fb. G. K. betreffend die Parochie Königshütte, 1876–1930, (Akta lokalne), AAK.

16. The term "hakatist" was a reference to the members of the German Eastern Marches Society, also known, according to the initials of its founders, as the H-K-T Society or, in the Polish abbreviation, "hakata." "Hakatist" was the preferred pejorative term for arch-German nationalists. "Parafianie" to Arcypasterzu, 10 August 1927, Acta der Fürstbischöflichen Geheimen Kanzlei betreffend die Kuratie Rozdzien, 1875–1930 (Akta lokalne, Rozdzien), AAK.

17. Zientek to Kurji Biskupiej, 22 March 1926, Acta der Fürstbischöflichen Geheimen Kanzlei betreffend die Kuratie Rozdzien, 1875–1930 (Akta lokalne, Rozdzien), AAK.

18. Examples from Olszar, pp. 203–5. Olszar mentions fifteen priests who were considered "anti-Polish" by the Polish government.

19. Olszar lists 30 priests who transferred to the diocese of Breslau from the diocese of Katowice between 1922 and 1939, p. 92. These include priests engaged in purely educational posts, as well as priests who were trained in the diocese of Katowice (i.e., were not yet ordained in 1922). For a detailed account of some of the controversies that led to these resignations/transfers, see Jarosław Macała, *Duszpasterstwo a narodowość wiernych: Kościół katolicki w diecezji katowickiej wobec mniejszości niemieckiej, 1922–1939* (Wrocław/Katowice, 1999), pp. 61–65.

20. From cross-referencing of lists of "Polish" emigrants (pp. 73–74) and list of "anti-Polish" German priests (pp. 203–4). Olszar does not comment on this striking juxtaposition. Father Lewek, however, had admitted in his own reminiscences that the 1921–22 emigration from German Silesia included a few cases in which "priests were forced to flee not because of their Polishness but for some other reason" (p. 37).

21. Jerzy Myszor, *Historia Diecezji Katowickiej* (Katowice, 1999), p. 30.

22. Ibid., p. 84.

23. Kubis to Kopp, 4 March 1913, Acta der Fürstbisch. Geheimen Kanzlei zu Breslau betreffend die Seelsorgstelle in Zalenze, 1899–1930 (Akta lokalne, ogólne), AAK.

24. Kubis to Kurji, 17 November 1927, Acta lokalne Zalenze, AAK.

25. Kubis to Kurji Biskupiej, 14 June 1928, Acta lokalne Zalenze, AAK.

26. Olszar specifically cites ten priests who were deemed "loyal" Germans, but he considers this to have been the "most numerous group" among the Germanophile clergy (pp. 206–8).

27. Ratti to Bertram, 10 October 1920, I.A.25.o.29 (Bertram Nachlass), AAW.

28. "Das gehört nicht auf die Kanzel," *Oberschlesische Kurier*, 22 August 1922, reprinted in Szczeponik, p. 180.
29. Myszor, p. 110.
30. Michatz to Kapica, 13 May 1922, Delegatura, vol. 4, AAK.
31. Father Skowronek in Bogucice had noted his preference for Michatz as his successor, but Apostolic Delegate Hlond argued that some unspecified "imprudence" by Michatz had turned a large number of the local parishioners against him, Hlond to Skowronek, 11 January 1923, Personal-Akten (Ludwig Skowronek), AAK. Father Lewek was also ill-disposed toward Michatz's candidacy in Wirek, for reasons that are not entirely clear. Lewek to Kapica, 9 May 1922, Delegatura, vol. 6, AAK.
32. Myszor, pp. 111–12.
33. Prezes koła radzieckiego (Radzionków) to Kapica, 14 June 1922, Delegatura, vol. 2, AAK.
34. *Słownik biograficzny katolickiego duchowieństwa Śląskiego xix i xx wieku*, Mieczysław Pater, ed. (Katowice, 1996), pp. 174–75.
35. Kapica to Bertram, 24 April 1922, I.A.25.o.32 (Bertram Nachlass), AAW.
36. *Die Wahrheit über das Martyrium der deutschen Katholiken in Polen*, in Szczeponik, p. 87.
37. Hlond to Skowronek, 11 January 1923, Personal-Acten, Ludwig Skowronek, AAK.
38. Myszor, p. 104. I have deducted the German-speaking population of former-Austrian Silesia from the overall diocesan estimate.
39. Calculated from parish-specific statistics given in *Die statistischen Erhebungen über die deutschen Katholiken in den Bistümern Polens*, Kazimierz Śmigiel, ed. (Marburg, 1992), pp. 16–56.
40. The 1931 Polish census recorded 68,755 Germans in the province of Silesia, of whom 68 percent were Roman Catholic (Blanke, *Orphans of Versailles*, pp. 82, 244–245).
41. The German electoral list won 183,000 votes in this provincial election, over 160,000 of these in the former Prussian parts of the province. After extrapolating from voting-age population to total population and deducting German Protestants and Jews, this result suggests approximately 300,000 Germanophile Catholics. Election figures from Blanke, p. 98.
42. *Die statistischen Erhebungen über die deutschen Katholiken in den Bistümern Polens*, Kazimierz Śmigiel, ed. (Marburg, 1992), quote from p. 56.
43. On this process, see my "Everything Depends on the Priest? Religious Education and Linguistic Change in Upper Silesia," in *Die Grenzen der Nationen: Identitätenwandel in Oberschlesien in der Neuzeit*, Kai Struve and Philipp Ther, eds. (Marburg: Herder-Institut, 2002), pp. 71–102.
44. I am not doing justice here to the very long and heated controversy during the interwar period about the scale of enrollment in German minority schools. Suffice it to say that these schools could, at best, only provide a shadow of the universal and mandatory German-language instruction of the *Volksschulen*, though they remained a much more formidable force than Polish-language schools in German Silesia. See Blanke, "Polish-speaking Germans under Polish Rule: Polish Silesia, 1922–1939," *Canadian Review of Studies in Nationalism*, 21/102 (1994), 25–32.
45. Acta Visitationis Archipresbyteratus Myslowitz, vol. 10 (1910–1915), AAK.
46. Reported in *Die Wahrheit über das Martyrium*, printed in Szczeponik, p. 97. Given the round numbers offered here, these statistics must be taken as rough estimates rather than precise figures.
47. *Rocznik Diecezji Katowickiej* (Katowice, 1936), pp. 52–53, 61.

48. Calculated from the parish mass schedules printed in Szczeponik, pp. 172–78. I have not been able to verify these schedules independently, so it is possible they exaggerate the number of changes made to the detriment of German-language worship.
49. Kalinowski, Prezes, Zarząd Z.O.K.Z., to Hlond, 6 September 1923, Acta der Fürstbischöflichen Geheimen Kanzlei betreffend die Kuratie Rozdzien, 1875–1930 (Akta lokalne, Rozdzien), AAK.
50. Zientek to Admin. Apostolska, 15 October 1923, Acta der Fürstbischöflichen Geheimen Kanzlei betreffend die Kuratie Rozdzien, 1875–1930 (Akta lokalne, Rozdzien), AAK.
51. Visitation report from 1924, Acta der Fb. G. K. betreffend Grundsachen der Curatie St. Hedwigs in Königshütte, 1889–1934 (Akta lokalne), AAK. Children, interestingly, are grouped in a separate category and not divided by language.
52. *Die statistischen Erhebungen*, pp. 30–31.
53. Census figure for Królewska Huta (Chorzów) from Olszar, p. 196.
54. "Kilka polskich parafjan" to *Głos Poranny*, 2 July 1926.
55. Gajda to Dyrekcji Policji Król. Huta, 30 August 1926, Acta parafialne, Königshütte (St. Hedwig), AAK.

# Interwar Poland and the Problem of Polish-speaking Germans

### ❖ Richard Blanke ❖

The large Polish state that emerged after the First World War was at least one-third non-Polish, and included (to begin with, at least) more than two million Germans. They had not been consulted, of course, about this assignment, and would probably have been unhappy with it, even under the best of conditions. What made their situation especially difficult, particularly in the formerly Prussian areas, was the fact that it meant a sudden and radical transposition of two peoples who were fully aroused nationally, mutually antagonistic (and with some good reasons for being so), and pretty sharply defined in opposition to each other. For the most part, at least; for the German-Polish borderlands were also inhabited by as many as one million people whose national orientation was *less* clearly defined; and whose final national disposition remained in doubt, and therefore in dispute.

I refer to these people, for lack of a better term, as "Polish-speaking Germans," not a label that everyone will want to accept, but one that seems to have been largely verified by subsequent developments. Included in this group are virtually all of the 440,000 or so Masurians (i.e., the Polish-speaking Protestants in East Prussia—although most of the 45,000 Polish-speaking, but Catholic, Warmians would also qualify) and a substantial minority of the c. 1.4 million Polish-speaking Silesian. (Not included, however, for reasons discussed below, are the c. 175,000 Cashubes in West Prussia.)[1] But the Masurians and many of the Silesians (i.e., the Polish-speaking Upper Silesians, in what follows) still seemed to be "in play" in 1918. At least, this was the view of most Polish nationalists, for whom national identity was normally determined by native language; and if this was not yet the case, it was just a matter of time until it became so under the new political arrangements. But when this did not happen—when the German identities of most of these people proved pretty tenacious, even under Polish rule—government-minority relations in these two regions, and majority-minority relations on the popular level as well, acquired a special, and especially acrimonious character. For this reason the problem of Polish-speaking Germans seems to warrant its own special place in any consideration of the German minority in interwar Poland, and represents an interesting twist to the larger problem of "Germans and the East."

Aside from their place in German-Polish relations, these Polish-speaking Germans have also attracted the attention of scholars far removed that field, because of the light they shed on general questions of nationalism and national identity. The Masurians, in particular (as I have argued more extensively in a recent monograph),[2] present the clearest and best-documented example anywhere in Central or Eastern Europe of national consciousness developing counter to native language. Indeed, one searches the ethnographic map of Central and Eastern Europe in vain (with the possible exception of Upper Silesia) for even one additional case with which they might be compared. Although the Masurians spoke Polish and lived for centuries adjacent to Poland, they remained almost unanimous in their apparently unforced identification with, first, the Prussian state, and then the German nation. And they did so at a time when the rest of eastern Europe was moving strongly toward national communities defined by language and ethnicity. That this singular exception should have occurred in the home province of Johann-Gottfried Herder, the greatest prophet of linguistic nationalism, is just an additional piquancy.

To be sure, the trend in nationalist theory, especially during the past half-century, has clearly been away from the traditional assumption, which traces back *to* Herder and the Romantics, that language and ethnicity connote, and provide the objective foundation for, both nationality and (eventually) national consciousness. Most modern scholarship on nationalism stresses the subjective, or "political," sources of national identity; and so the idea of "Polish-speaking Germans" does not create an immediate problem. It is also clear that some pretty prominent nations, including Switzerland, Ireland, Canada, and the United States, have emerged either from just part of a language community or on the basis of more than one such community. As Max Weber noted with specific reference to the Polish-speaking but pro-German Upper Silesians and Masurians, neither the fact of common language nor even "sentiments of ethnic solidarity" suffice by themselves to "make a nation" in the modern, political sense. A common language, culture, and territory may provide the basis for a shared ethnic consciousness; but for that consciousness to become "national" it has to become explicitly political.[3] Some contemporary students of nationalism also cite the Masurians and Upper Silesians to make much the same point, e.g., Eric Hobsbawm, who notes that while the idea of Polish-speaking Germans was "*a priori* inexplicable" to adherents of the ethnic-objective view of national identity, the existence of significant numbers of "linguistic Poles" who, "for whatever reason, preferred to consider themselves politically German, . . . who preferred living in Germany to living in reborn Poland," cannot be denied; and was made "incontrovertible" by the several post-World War I plebiscites, which demonstrated that quite a few people "spoke one language but opted to join the state of those who spoke another."[4]

It is simply an empirical fact, however, that throughout most of Eastern Europe language *has* usually denoted ethnicity, and ethnicity national identity, and never more so than today. And nowhere has this connection been more generally accepted than in Poland,[5] where until quite recently it was the near-universal view, among scholars as well as the general public, that the very idea of a Polish-speaking German was an oxymoron, and the phenomenon itself obviously just a superficial and unnatural reflection of unequal power relationships.[6] For this reason interwar Poland considered that it had every moral as well as legal right to force back into line those Masurians and Silesians over whom it acquired political control.

These two principal groups of Polish-speaking Germans did not have that much in common otherwise, except that each was the majority population in a part of Prussia that had not been part of the pre-1772 Polish Commonwealth. The Masurians were Protestant and lived mostly as small farmers in something of a rural backwater, whereas the Silesians were Catholic and at home in Germany's second most important industrial region.[7] They also differed in that the Polish effort to win over the Masurians had been essentially an exercise in futility, whereas the Polish campaign in Upper Silesia seemed to have caught fire shortly before the First World War. In Masuria, a significant Polish-national mobilization effort had been underway for some decades prior to 1914, but it enjoyed virtually no success, primarily because the Masurians remained essentially immune to any kind of Polish-national appeal. As of 1914, the Polish-national presence in Masuria consisted of little more than a single newspaper with a paid circulation of about 400, one small bank, and a political organization that usually attracted only 1–2 percent of the vote in parliamentary campaigns. In Upper Silesia, by contrast, where Polish nationalists did not even run candidates of their own until the 1890s, they were attracting 40 percent of the vote by 1907 and had captured five of the region's twelve Reichstag seats.

Some may also wonder, within this general context, about the Cashubes, a third small ethnic group that inhabited the hilly region west of Danzig and sometimes (e.g., in Günter Grass's *Blechtrommel*) appear between the lines of the German-Polish conflict. In some respects, the Cashubes may have been less-than-complete Poles; some linguists consider that their dialect has a much stronger case than Masurian or Upper Silesian to be considered a distinct language apart from Polish. They are also thought to be descended, not from medieval Poles (as is the case with Masurians and Upper Silesians), but from one of the other, now-extinct West Slavic peoples of the Middle Ages.[8] In some social and economic respects, the Cashubes resembled the Masurians: they were mostly small farmers, with little urban life and a landed nobility and professional class that was mainly German. But the differences were also fundamental: the Cashubes had belonged to Poland until 1772 and remained

Catholic. As such, they remained under the influence of a Polish-run church that used standard Polish and reinforced a sense of solidarity with Poland. Even the Prussian state, when it introduced Polish-language instruction into Cashubian schools after 1842, used standard Polish.[9]

There were occasional signs that at least some Cashubes, including Florian Ceynowa in the 1850s and a group of "Young Cashubes" led by Alexander Majkowski after 1900, wanted recognition of Cashubian cultural distinctiveness. Ceynowa argued most strongly for the preservation of the Cashubian language and fashioned a Cashubian grammar. He also challenged the predominantly noble and clerical Polish political establishment on populist grounds. But he did not attract much of a following and never moved into the area of political separatism—Poles remained for him the Cashubes' "older brothers."[10] After 1871, Bismarck's *Kulturkampf* only reinforced the ties between Cashubes and the Polish national movement. Subsequently, the Cashubes were treated simply as Poles under Prussian Polish policies, participated fully in the Polish "organic work" movement, and voted consistently for Polish candidates. From the time the Reichstag was established in 1867, the "Cashubian" Reichstag district (Neutstadt-Karthaus-Putzig) sent only Polish-national representatives to Berlin.[11] In short, while the Cashubes may occasionally have thought of themselves as distinct from Poles proper, this did not take the form of alignment with German nationalism, as it did in Masuria (especially) and Upper Silesia. At no time, either before or after the transfer of Cashubia (a.k.a. the "Polish Corridor") to Poland in 1920, can the Cashubes be said to have approached the condition of "Polish-speaking Germans."

The war years witnessed a marked increase in Polish interest in both Masuria and Upper Silesia. Despite the discouraging results of the prewar mobilization effort in the former region, Masuria (and East Prussia generally) appeared on many of the wartime wish lists prepared by advocates of a resurrected Poland. Polish Protestants, as represented by the Augsburg Lutheran Church in Russian Poland, were especially interested in acquiring Masuria, for it was home to the largest single population of Polish-speaking Protestants. As Germany's defeat beckoned, Polish National Democratic leaders, led by Roman Dmowski, asserted a claim to both Masuria and Upper Silesia, as well as to that part of the German Empire that had belonged to the old Polish Commonwealth. Dmowski justified this claim on grounds that most people in these places spoke Polish; if they did not also "feel" Polish, they would surely come to do so after just a brief period of Polish rule.[12]

Dmowski intended, of course, for Poland to receive Masuria and Upper Silesia outright, local sentiment counting for no more here than in the Sudetenland or South Tyrol. But while all three of the major powers at the Paris Peace Conference were prepared at first to award Upper Silesia to Poland, only France supported the Polish position on Masuria. First Britain, and then the United States, insisted that some effort be made to learn what the Masurians themselves thought of the idea of becoming part of the new Poland. In keeping with the recommendations of the Conference's

Commission on Polish Affairs, the draft Treaty of Versailles assigned only part of one Masurian *Kreis* (Neidenburg), the town of Soldau/Działdowo and its surroundings, to Poland, on grounds that it lay astride the direct rail route between Warsaw and Danzig. Otherwise, an internationally supervised plebiscite would be conducted to help the Conference decide what to do with the bulk of Masuria. But the real blow to Poland's aspirations came when Britain and the United States, after agreeing to a draft treating that awarded Upper Silesia to Poland outright, had second thoughts: their most significant concession to the numerous German objections to the draft treaty was a plebiscite for Upper Silesia as well.[13]

While Poland could look forward with at least some optimism to the vote in Upper Silesia, few Poles imagined that they had any chance in Masuria. The population of the Upper Silesian plebiscite district was approximately 2/3 Polish-speaking and (as noted) had shown considerable receptivity to Polish nationalism. Masuria, on the other hand, was included in an "East Prussian Plebiscite District" in which Polish-speakers (i.e., "Poles," "Masurians," and "bilinguals" combined, as counted by the 1910 Prussian census) numbered only 47.4 percent of the total population; the remainder claimed German as their native language.[14] Even in Masuria alone, where Polish-speakers still maintained a 54 percent majority as of 1910 (and persuasive arguments have been advanced that the actual figure was closer to 75 percent), no one familiar with the history of Masurian political attitudes can have had any illusions regarding the likely outcome of a plebiscite choice between Germany and Poland, regardless of Germany's currently unsettled condition. Those Polish nationalists who had actually spent some time in Masuria, however much they believed in the underlying justice of Poland's cause, were especially pessimistic about its plebiscite prospects. Masurians had yet to give any indication, even in the wake of Germany's defeat, that they saw themselves as part of *Polonia irredenta* or were looking for deliverance from a "Prussian yoke." The only Polish journal in this region of c. 450,000 people was a thrice-weekly, four-page sheet with a circulation of less than 500.[15] And the silence from Masuria was all the more notable in contrast to the surge of Polish-nationalist activity elsewhere in Prussian Poland; most notably in Poznania and West Prussia, but also in Upper Silesia. Polish representatives in Paris attributed this silence to "the cruel persecution of Masurians just because they desire to belong to the common motherland Poland."[16] To the extent that they really believed this, however, they were only setting their country up for a major disappointment.

In retrospect, the best course of action for Poland, and the only way to avoid major embarrassment, would have been to respond to the proposed plebiscite in Masuria with a "thanks, but no thanks." But having proclaimed to the world (as it were) that the Masurians were really Poles, there was no graceful way to just drop the claim now that it was to be put to a vote. Besides, if one had really internalized the ethno-linguistic view of nationality, as many Poles had done, one could always hope against hope that proper Polish feelings must eventually emerge among the

Masurians. In fact, however, Poland lost both plebiscites, although the defeat in East Prussia (July 11, 1920) was by far the more humiliating: with 90 percent of eligible voters participating, they cast 99.3 percent of their votes for Germany. Surely, no other contested ethnic group has ever, under un-coerced conditions, issued so one-sided a statement of its national preference. Nor can one attribute this entirely to the Masurians' Protestantism, for Polish-speaking, but Catholic, Warmians also gave more than 85 percent of their vote to Germany. In Upper Silesia the following year (March 20, 1921), the outcome was much closer, and most ethnic Poles did vote for Poland. Nonetheless, it was the 40 percent of them who sided with Germany who determined the outcome, and gave Germany its 60 percent majority.

Subsequently, the Peace Conference (led now, following the refusal of the United States to ratify the Versailles Treaty, by Britain, France, Italy, and Japan) decided to divide Upper Silesia between Germany and Poland. Despite its defeat, Poland seemed to get the better of the deal, i.e., 48 percent of the people, the two largest cities, and the bulk of the industrial plant. But while Poland's share of Upper Silesia was less than 30 percent German by language, 44 percent of its votes had just gone to Germany in the recent plebiscite. In other words, Polish Silesia had a sizeable "German" minority of some 330,000 people (at least to begin with), except that many of them were of the "Polish-speaking" variety. In the case of Masuria, the lopsided plebiscite vote provided no grounds for dividing the spoils—only a few small communities, which had voted for Poland and were adjacent to Poland, became Polish in 1920—but the Soldau District, transferred without a plebiscite, contained an additional 18,000 "Germans" (c. 75 percent), most of them Polish-speaking.[17]

The problem for Polish nationalists, most of whom saw ethno-linguistic nationality as the only authentic kind, is that they could not help but view such "Polish-speaking Germans" as just so many Poles who had been duped by a German power structure into thinking that they were something else, and an especially annoying legacy of the despised Prussian regime. Now that the local power structure had become Polish, it was expected that the underlying Polishness of these people would reemerge; and that Poland had both the right and the duty to expedite this conversion. This was all the more the case because Silesia province, although Poland's smallest, was perhaps its most vital economically, accounting for about two-thirds of Polish coal and steel production. The problem was that most of these Polish-speaking Germans remained surprisingly steadfast in their identification with Germany. This persistence, and the resulting official frustration, is surely the main reason why government-minority relations were especially bitter in Polish Silesia and in the Soldau District.[18] In other words, it was not just that Polish officials in these two regions were unusually aggressive or chauvinistic; if one was steeped in ethno-linguistic nationalism as the only proper kind, and convinced that nationality was something inherited rather than chosen, then it really was hard to accept the idea of Polish-speaking Germans. Nor was this problem limited to Polish officials, as can be seen in the bewildered question posed by the League of Nations' Brazilian point man for minority issues, Pedro de Azcarate: "How were we supposed to know that part of the majority would try to pass itself off as belonging to the minority?"[19]

In fact, the problem of Polish-speaking Germans seems rather to have grown under Polish rule. In both Silesia and the Soldau District, the departure for the Reich of most ethnic Germans during the 1920s left a "German" minority population that was *mostly* Polish-speaking. Even in absolute terms, its numbers may actually have increased under Polish rule. Thus German parties in Polish Silesia regularly drew several times as many votes as the number of ethnic Germans would seem to justify, e.g., in the 1930 elections to the provincial parliament, German parties received 183,000 votes (34 percent) vs. the 69,000 German speakers of all ages (6 percent of the province's total population) recognized by the official census of 1931; more votes even than the 180,000 members (again, of all ages) claimed by the minority's own leaders.[20] One can imagine the reaction of Polish officials when more than 50,000 Polish-speaking parents tried to enroll their children in the German-language minority schools that Poland was obliged (under the 1922 Geneva Convention) to operate.[21]

Especially after 1926, when the former insurgent leader Michał Grażyński became governor of Silesia province, Poland became ever more determined to "re-Polonize" its Polish-speaking Germans, regardless of the restrictions imposed by the Geneva Convention, or by the League of Nations (which undertook to enforce that convention), or by the World Court (which also ruled in favor of the minority on more than one occasion). The result was that this small province soon became the scene of one of interwar Europe's harshest anti-minority regimes, but one directed less at the small and rapidly declining population of ethnic Germans than at the larger and more vexing problem of Polish-speaking Germans. Discriminatory state policies were supported (if not dictated) by chauvinistic mass organizations, including the Union of Silesian Insurgents (ZPS) and the Union for the Defense of the Western Borderlands (ZOKZ). The percentage of children admitted to minority schools dropped from 15 percent to 5 percent. Elections were simply set aside if too many votes were cast for German parties. Most devastating of all was the regime's systematic effort to reduce minority employment in the province's factories and mines: one by one, it took control (or, less often, ownership, which was a more expensive proposition) of German firms and proceeded to reduced the number of minority employees; and minority status adhered to those, regardless of native language, who patronized minority schools. By 1938, when Polish Silesia had an overall unemployment rate of 16 percent, minority unemployment ranged between 45 percent and 60 percent, and apparently serious plans for the wholesale removal of the minority to Germany, or even to third countries, were being discussed in Berlin.[22]

In the formerly East Prussian Soldau District, three-quarters of the region's

24,000 people were Masurian (i.e., Polish-speaking Protestants), and they seemed to share the same national-political orientation as those Masurians allowed to vote in 1920 (thus the German candidate received 75 percent of the vote in the first Polish parliamentary election). Poland's effort to use the Soldau District as the base for its Masurian plebiscite campaign also turned out badly: a single mass meeting was scheduled, but most of the audience took up the chant, "We are German" and then filed out of the hall singing "Deutschland über alles"![23] Worse yet, when Red Army units penetrated as far as Soldau during the Polish-Soviet War of 1920–1921, they were greeted as liberators, with flowers and (German) flags, by much of the local population. Nonetheless, Polish officials persisted in the belief that changed political conditions, especially the establishment of an apparently powerful Polish state, would yet turn the tide and allow the underlying Polish consciousness of the Masurians, in Germany as well as in the Soldau District, to awaken.[24] A number of state institutions aimed at Masurians across the border, including a "Masurian People's Home," a Masurian Museum, and a Protestant teachers seminary, were established in Soldau and Polish-Protestant civil servants were recruited to work there.[25] As in Silesia, Poland insisted that Polish-speaking Masurians, regardless of their political sympathies, attend Polish-language schools. When a group of parents petitioned to have their children receive at least their religious instruction in German, officials denied the request on grounds that the children were "Masurians, and so Poles." The parents then appealed to the League of Nations (as they were entitled to do under Poland's Minorities Protection Treaty), arguing that the state had no right "to determine our nationality. . . . We declare explicitly that, though of Masurian descent, we all belong to the German nationality."[26]

Before long, in the face of official chicanery, worsening economic conditions, an influx of poorer Polish workers, and the prospect of conscription into the Polish army, Masurians began to leave the Soldau District for Germany. And they did so at about the same rate as "German-speaking Germans" in the rest of western Poland, i.e., about two-thirds of each group left western Poland during the first decade of Polish rule.[27] The Soldau teachers' seminar, supposed to train "a cadre of Polish intelligentsia for Prussian Masuria," never managed to recruit even ten students at a time, despite generous scholarships, and was liquidated in 1932. Use of the German language and adherence to German organizations by Soldau Masurians seemed only to increase. The Polish Lutheran Church also failed in its campaign to woo Masurians away from the (formerly Prussian-state) United-Evangelical Church; and while the latter body continued to offer services in Polish as well as German, attendance at the Polish-speaking services continued to decline in favor of the German-language offerings. Thus the Polish campaign to win over the Masurians already consigned to its rule ended in apparent failure.[28] Indeed, Poland's interwar experience with the Soldau Masurians seemed only to prefigure its experience with the remainder of the Masurians after World War II.

Meanwhile, on the German side of the frontier, Germany seemed to have ample grounds to just declare victory in the battle for the hearts and minds of the Polish-speaking Germans in Masuria and Upper Silesia, as officials regularly did when speaking publicly. Behind the scenes, however, they continued to fret; even about the Masurians, among whom there no longer existed any indigenous Polish-national movement to speak of. But just the fact that so many Masurians and Silesians continued to use Polish in their day-to-day private affairs remained a source of concern; and this was just as true of Prussia's Social-Democrat-led state government as of more conventional German nationalists.[29] For all the confident official talk about the Polish-speaking Germans' firm attachment to Germany, and powerful evidence that this was indeed the case, it turned out that a lot of German as well as Polish nationalists continued to suspect that language and ethnicity might be the more reliable bases of nationality, after all.

But such residual concerns were soon rendered moot, at least in the Masurians' case, by their accelerated and apparently purposeful abandonment of their native language in favor of German, which they did, moreover, at a more rapid pace under the liberal-democratic Weimar Republic than under the previous semi-authoritarian regime. It was as though the Masurians had resolved that if their language was to be cited as grounds for being taken from the only country they had ever known and given to Poland, then they would simply change their language; and transform themselves from Polish-speaking Germans into something more like Germans of Masurian descent. Most of them were now fluent in German—according to the 1925 census, 83 percent of native Masurian speakers claimed fluency also in German—and increasingly favored its use in public settings. In other words, while the 1920 plebiscite marked the culmination of the Masurians' political identification with Germany, the following period witnessed their most rapid cultural-linguistic assimilation. Indeed, they rather overshot the mark after 1930, when they provided Hitler with his largest majorities anywhere in the country. In the July 1932 Reichstag election, which saw the Nazi vote climb sharply to 37 percent in Germany as a whole, in the three Masurian Reichstag districts it reached, respectively, 58, 66, and (in Lyck-Johannisburg) 71 percent! By contrast, a mere 147 Masurian votes (0.06 percent of the total) went to Polish candidates in this same election.[30]

All of which raises the question: how oblivious—or how trusting in the ethnolinguistic view of nationality—must Polish leaders have been to think that people, whatever their native language, who had delivered a 99 percent vote against Poland in 1920, and then largely abandoned their use of Polish, and then supported the NSDAP in such numbers, could still be won over? Because that is the only conclusion one can draw from Poland's insistence in 1945 that up to one million "ethnically Polish autochthons," as Polish-speaking Germans were now called, be exempted from the vast ethnic cleansing project envisioned for the rest of its newly acquired lands; and invited, required even, to remain behind while the "real" Germans were sent packing.

In any case, the result was a second explicit opportunity (the other being the plebiscites of 1920–1921) for Masurians and Upper Silesians to reconsider their orientation to Germany; and under conditions where all those political, material, or opportunistic factors that may have inclined previous generations toward Germany and away from Poland pointed now in the opposite direction. Indeed, option for Poland was usually the only way to avoid having to leave one's homeland.

Only a minority participated in this experiment, however; at least in the Masurian case. 75 percent of Masurians fled in advance of the Red Army without even waiting to see what Polish rule would be like. In fact, although these Polish-speaking Germans were not obliged to leave, their rate of departure was just about the same as for "German-speaking Germans." But the behavior of the 25 percent of Masurians who remained behind (or who returned) provides an interesting and instructive conclusion to this survey, in the sense that it basically reinforces the major lesson of the interwar period; namely, that the German national identity of most Masurians and many Silesians proved to be pretty tenacious. While both groups were officially recognized as Poles, offered Polish citizenship, and celebrated even as a source of historical-demographic justification Poland's acquisition of otherwise German lands, it soon became clear that most of them, while wanting to remain where they were, did not want to become Poles. Many Masurians, in particular, refused even to accept Polish citizenship, despite its benefits, and their thoughts soon turned instead to emigration to what was left of Germany. After 1956, when it became easier to leave Poland, most of them did so. According to recent reports, only a few thousand Masurians, i.e., less than 1 percent of the 1890 figure and no more than 5 percent of those who were there in 1946, remain in Poland today. Equivalent figures for Silesia are harder to come by, since Polish-speaking Germans were always just a part of Silesia's Polish-speaking population and not differentiated as such in official statistics. But most of the hundreds of thousands of *Spätaussiedler* who have relocated to Germany during the past four decades have come from Upper Silesia. Since many of these people no longer spoke much German, even as a second language, it was now the Germans' turn to deal with the counter-intuitive phenomenon of "Polish-speaking Germans"; and many Germans seemed to agree with most Poles that most of these "late resettlers" were motivated more by economic self-interest than by a genuine and deep-seated sense of German national identity. But as this survey has sought to demonstrate, the identification of these Polish-speaking Germans with Germany has a long history, has been put to the test on more than one occasion, and has exacted a considerable price (e.g., forfeiture of homeland, preceded by years of discrimination and mistreatment); for which reason, it is time that the depth and authenticity of this commitment were recognized.

Well into the 1980s, official Poland denied that it even had a German minority of any significant size, primarily because only Germans-by-native-language counted as such. So it doubtless came as quite a surprise when a "German Bloc" attracted 40 percent of the vote in Opole wojewodship (and 2.5 percent of the vote nationwide) in the first post-Communist parliamentary elections in 1990. Subsequently, these numbers declined as ever more Polish-speaking Germans left for Germany itself. In other words, while Poland finally acquired Masuria and Upper Silesia, it no longer has many Masurians and the number of indigenous Upper Silesians is much diminished. In Germany, where most of these people have relocated, they have not made much of an effort to preserve their ethnic identities (consisting essentially of a German superstructure and a Polish base); and so they have largely disappeared as identifiable ethnic groups. In the case of the Masurians, in particular, their history has essentially come to an end.

In conclusion, the story of the Polish-speaking Germans is interesting not just for its own sake, but also within the larger context of eastern European nationalism, not because language does *not* necessarily regulate national identity, but because throughout *this* vast region it *has* generally done so. The historical experience of the Masurians and Silesians demonstrates pretty clearly that national identity of the political or "subjective" (sometimes referred to as the "Western European") type, based on allegiance to a long-established polity and its dominant national group rather than native language, manifested itself also in the otherwise hostile climate of eastern Europe. Their twentieth-century history demonstrates also that national identity *of this type*, far from being just the coerced, unnatural, and presumably correctable result of unequal power relationships, can be just as tenacious and authentic as national identity of the more "normal" kind, based on ethno-linguistic community. For even after they came under Polish rule, whether in 1920–1922 or in 1945, many Silesians and virtually all the Masurians persisted in their German national-political orientation to the point of ethnic self-negation and abandonment of their homeland.

## Notes

1.   Population figures, based upon the 1910 Prussian census: "Masuria" (i.e., the eight Masurian core *Landkreise*): 441,000, of which c. 62% Polish-speaking = 273,000 + Masurians in 3 neighboring counties (3300) = 276,300 + 150,000-175,000 Masurians in western Germany = a Masurian (i.e., Polish-speaking, East Prussian Protestant) population of c. 440,000; Polish-speaking Warmians: c. 43,000; Cashubes: c. 175,000; Upper Silesians: 2,207,981, less three overwhelmingly German counties (Neisse, Falkenberg, and Neustadt) with a population of c. 137,000), leaving an Upper Silesian Plebiscite District (1921) of 1,356,000 Polish speakers (67%) and 657,000 German speakers. Judging, however, *from* the 1921 plebiscite, the district's population is better described as 40% Polish, 33% German; and 27% "Polish-speaking German."
2.   *Polish-speaking Germans? Language and National Identity among the Masurians (since 1871)* (Cologne, 2001).
3.   Quoted by Walker Connor, in *Ethnonationalism* (Princeton, 1994), p. 45.
4.   Eric Hobsbawm, *Nations and Nationalism since 1780* (Cambridge, 1992.), pp. 59, 134.
5.   Peter Brock, "Polish Nationalism," in *Nationalism in Eastern Europe*, ed. Peter Sugar et al. (Seattle, 1969), pp. 310–372.
6.   Actually, most German nationalists also equated language with nationality—in some

older works on nationalism, the ethno-linguistic form is referred to *as* the "German" type—as opposed to the political-subjective form favored in Western Europe and North America. But German leaders soon discovered that the political-subjective version served their interests better, at least in the German-Polish borderlands.

7. Actually, a good quarter of all the Masurians also worked in heavy industry, but they did so far from home in the Ruhr District; cf. Hans-Ulrich Wehler, "Zur neueren Geschichte der Masuren," *Zeitschrift für Ostforschung* 11 (1962), 147–172.

8. Peter Böhning, *Die nationalpolnische Bewegung in Westpreußen 1815–1871* (Marburg, 1973), p. 17; Friedrich Lorenz, *Die Geschichte der Kaschuben* (Berlin, 1926), passim.

9. Böhning, p. 189.

10. Böhning, p. 192.

11. Dietrich von Oppen, "Deutsche, Polen, und Kaschuben in Westpreußen, 1871–1914," *Jahrbuch für die Geschichte Mittel- und Ostdeutschlands* 4 (1955), 212; Günther Dettmer, *Die ost- und westpreußische Behörden im Kulturkampf* (Heidelberg, 1958), p. 23; Richard Blanke, *Prussian Poland in the German Empire* (New York, 1981), pp. 33f.

12. Kay Lundgreen-Nielsen, *The Polish Problem at the Paris Peace Conference* (Odense, 1979), pp. 48ff. Sarah Wambaugh, *Plebiscites since the War* (Washington, 1933), I, 103; Wojciech Wrzesiński, *Warmia i Mazury w polskiej myśli politycznej 1864–1945* (Warsaw, 1984) p. 527.

13. Lundgreen-Nielsen, pp. 197ff.

14. Wambaugh, I, 99ff., II, 48ff.; Wojciech Wrzesiński, *Plebiscyty na Warmii i Mazurach oraz na Powiślu w 1920 roku* (Olsztyn, 1974), p. 84.

15. Kazimierz Jaroszyk, *Wspomnienia z Prus Wschodnich* (Olsztyn, 1969), p. 87.

16. Wrzesiński, *Plebiscyty,* p. 58.

17. Poland's defeat in a third plebiscite in the West Prussian Marienwerder District, through which the Warsaw-Danzig rail line also passed, removed the original rationale for Soldau's transfer to Poland, but its disposition was not reconsidered.

18. Cf. Richard Blanke, *Orphans of Versailles: Germans in Western Poland, 1918–1939* (Lexington, 1993), pp. 37ff., 96ff.

19. Pedro de Azcarate, *The League of Nations and National Minorities* (Washington, 1945), p. 147.

20. Henryk Rechowicz, *Sejm Śląski, 1922–1939* (Katowice, 1971), appendix; Otto Ulitz, *Oberschlesien: Aus seiner Geschichte* (Bonn, 1971), pp. 81ff.

21. Edward Wynot, "The Case of German Schools in Polish Upper Silesia, 1922–1930," *Polish Review* 19 (1974); 50; Tomasz Fałęcki, *Niemieckie szkolnictwo mniejszościowe na Górnym Śląsku (1922–1939)* (Katowice, 1970).

22. Blanke, *Orphans*, p. 213.

23. *Plebiscyty na Warmii, Mazurach i Powiślu w 1920 roku,* ed. Piotr Stawecki et al. (Olsztyn, 1986), pp. 157f.

24. Thus Kazimierz Smogorzewski (*Dziennik Gdański*, Dec. 13, 1921): "With each generation [Polish] national consciousness [in Masuria] will awaken in ever wider circles," for this was the "basic, unavoidable effect . . . of the idea of nationality"; and a second plebiscite thirty years hence would turn out "quite differently from the parody of July 11, 1920."

25. Wojciech Wrzesiński, "Kwestia mazurska na Działdowszczyźnie w latach 1920–1930," *Komunikaty Mazursko-Warmińskie* 4 (1959), 268ff.

26. *Deutsche Rundschau* (Bromberg/Bydgoszcz), March 28, 1926. The Polish-nationalist press could scarcely contain its irritation, e.g., *Gazeta Olsztyńska* (March 31, 1926): the petitioners were "poisoned, sick people," examples of the "disgraceful, shameless, and clever manner" by which Prussian Germanization policies had managed to "destroy the Polish

sentiments of the Masurians," leading to "stupidity, alcoholism, superstition, and religious sectarianism" on both sides of the frontier.

27. Horst Jablonowski, "Wieviel Polen hat es vor dem 2. Weltkrieg in Ostpreußen gegeben? " *Acta Prussica. Beiheft zum Jahrbuch der Albertus-Universität Königsberg* (Würzburg, 1968), p. 313.

28. Wojciech Wrzesiński ("Kwestia," p. 291) and Andrzej Sakson (in *Mazurzy - Społeczność Pogranicza* [Poznań, 1990], pp. 62f.) use the same phrase, "Poland suffered a painful defeat," to summarize developments in interwar Soldau.

29. Cf. Blanke, *Polish-speaking Germans?* pp. 233ff.

30. Dieter Hertz-Eichenrode, "Die Wende zum Nationalsozialismus im südlichen Ostpreußen 1930–1932," *Olsztyńskie Studia Niemcoznawcze* (1986), 70.

# The Birth of a Sudeten German Nobility, 1918–1938

### ◆ Eagle Glassheim ◆

At the turn of the century, the Bohemian nobility held a towering position in Habsburg society and government. Great magnates such as the Schwarzenbergs, Thuns, and Lobkowiczs alternated between the glittering halls of the Hofburg in Vienna and their sprawling country estates in Bohemia. In all, barely 300 noble families owned over a third of the land area of the Habsburgs' Bohemian Crownlands, a material base that supported brilliant careers in the Foreign Office, government, and parliament. An imperial, supra-national elite, the Bohemian nobility resisted nationalism and its more virulent Czech and German advocates.

Ultimately, these imperial stalwarts could not save the Monarchy from the divisive forces of war and nationalism. When the Habsburg Monarchy collapsed in 1918, the Bohemian nobility became both a symbolic and real target of Czech revolutionaries, who sought to build a post-imperial identity for their new state. Czechoslovakia's middle-class leaders portrayed nobles as a national and social enemy, a living symbol of the German-dominated Monarchy that, as one legislator put it, had to be "expunged" from the history of the Czech nation.[1] In 1919 the National Assembly passed a massive land reform aiming to transfer noble estates into the hands of Czech small farmers.

With their political power largely destroyed after 1918, nobles turned their energies to an all-out defense of their property against land reform, to save "what could be saved" in the words of Bedřich (Prince) Schwarzenberg (1862–1936).[2] As the National Assembly debated the nature of the reform in early 1919, prominent nobles met in the Schwarzenberg Palace in Prague to discuss the creation of a landowners' defense organization. Two groups emerged from these talks, each with a distinct agenda: the Union of Czechoslovak Large Landowners (*Svaz československých velkostatkářů*) and the Association of German Large Landowners (*Verband der deutschen Grossgrundbesitzer*). The *Svaz*, the larger of the two groups, favored a policy of cooperation with the Czechoslovak state in the hopes that loyalty would bring lenience. The *Verband* took a more confrontational position, adopting a complex defense strategy combining Sudeten German nationalism and German internationalism. In this paper, I'll show how these identifications emerged and how they ultimately led many Verband nobles to support National Socialism in the 1930s.

A Czech-German divide among landowners was already apparent in early 1919. While negotiations over the formation of the *Svaz* were beginning in March of 1919, Bohemian Germans still hoped that the Paris peace treaties would grant them autonomy or independence. When Bedřich Schwarzenberg urged Adolf (Count) Waldstein to recruit German landowners for the emerging *Svaz*, Waldstein complained that the group's insistence on using the Czech language would drive away potential supporters. "Especially in North Bohemia," he wrote, "so long as the borders there are not certain, there is still the hope [among German landowners] that they will not end up attached to the Czechoslovak Republic."[3] Even if the borderlands were to be included in Czechoslovakia, Waldstein objected to the *Svaz*'s Czech emphasis. Instead of minority status in a Czech organization, he hoped for a bi-national "utraquist" union that would represent all landowners equally, with equality of both the Czech and German languages in administration. This view in fact mirrored the emerging position of the German minority in Czechoslovakia: the claim that Czechoslovakia should be organized as a nationalities state (with no dominant nationality) like Switzerland, and not a national state like France.[4]

In spite of Waldstein's reservations, *Svaz* founders insisted that it be a statewide interest group, include Czechoslovak in its title, and use Czech as its official language. At first, some members opposed inviting Germans and Hungarians to join the group, as it could give non-Czechs a majority in the organization. "In a republic," Bedřich Schwarzenberg told a meeting of the *Svaz*'s directorate in June, "only an association with a Czech leadership can prosper. One with a German tint is incapable of survival."[5] Other members, including Bedřich (Prince) Lobkowicz and Ervín Nádherný, pressed for a more inclusive policy, accepting all those "who will stand faithfully by the Republic." In the end, the *Svaz* issued a broad invitation to all landowners, regardless of nationality and political affiliation, to join. Even so, the *Svaz*'s basic Czech character and acceptance of the Czechoslovak state were non-negotiable.

Not satisfied with the *Svaz*'s linguistic concessions, German landowners formed the *Verband* in September of 1919.[6] The goals of the *Verband*—moderation of land reform, full compensation for confiscated land, et al.—were at first similar to those of the *Svaz*, and the two groups cooperated through a joint Central Committee.[7] But by the early 1920s, they differed substantially over strategy, with the *Svaz* stressing its corporate nature and loyalty to the Czechoslovak state and the *Verband* emphasizing its German character and the discriminatory nature of land reform against Czechoslovakia's German minority.

These differences in strategy emerged in 1921, with the Verband's Wilhelm Medinger arguing for the internationalization of the land reform issue through propaganda in England and elsewhere.[8] With a massive forest confiscation plan in the works in 1922, the *Verband* called an emergency meeting in July to discuss possible responses. The organization's president Eugen Ledebur introduced the meeting by declaring that "the war of extermination (*Vernichtungskampf*) against large landowners has become acute" and that defense efforts must be intensified. Medinger outlined a two-pronged counterattack the *Verband* would use. First, the *Verband* would attempt to tie the cause of large landowners to that of Sudeten-Germandom as a whole. "The German nation has already recognized" he argued, "that the threat to German large landowners is at the same time a threat to Germans' national, *völkisch* existence." Second, the *Verband* would use its identification with Sudeten Germans to propagandize internationally. Through two German organizations that supported the League of Nations, *Völkerbund* and *Völkerbundliga*, the *Verband* would "bring our just struggle before the international forum. . . . We shall not neglect any foreign political means at our disposal."[9]

The Czech *Svaz* steadfastly resisted efforts of the *Verband* to draw it into Medinger's national strategy. In response to the *Verband*'s 1922 change of direction, both Jan Lobkowicz and Zdeněk Kolowrat insisted that the *Svaz* must "rule out politics and the national approach and generate only topical and specialized propaganda."[10] The Svaz subsequently avoided overt collaboration with the Verband, which Lobkowicz feared would antagonize the Czechoslovak government and give the *Svaz*'s enemies "a dangerous weapon, such that they could show that all large landowners in Czechoslovakia are Germans."[11]

Nonetheless, the *Verband* took its minority rights case to international forums without the *Svaz*'s help. Working through Medinger's *Völkerbundliga*, the *Verband* began preparing a series of petitions to the League of Nations. Medinger delivered the first official complaint on behalf of German landowners to the League in September 1922. Land reform was in direct violation of Czechoslovakia's minority treaty, the petition argued, because it treated members of a minority differently from those of the majority.[12] In its implementation, the land laws were not "directed at large estate owners as such, but far more against only those large land owners who are not members of the majority nation."[13] More specifically, the laws aimed at the "expulsion of Germans" from certain regions through the "redistribution of confiscated German land to Czech colonists and especially through the nationalization of German border forests." The petition urged the League to intervene to stop the State Land Office from continuing this conscious policy of "denationalization."[14]

The *Völkerbundliga*'s 1922 complaint tied the land reform to a general discrimination of the Czechoslovak government against Germans in a range of fields, including education, finance, and the bureaucracy. "A gloomy feeling of powerless despair has seized our co-nationals (*Volksgenossen*)," the petition lamented, "now that they are also to be forcefully driven off of their ancestral land."[15] The petition offered scores of quotations from Czech sources—including the National Assembly, newspapers, and public officials—betraying the national impetus of the reform. Using a vocabulary common to German nationalists, Medinger wrote of a threat to German "national assets" (*Nationalvermögen*) and "national property" (*nationaler Besitzstand*).[16] The petition appended a resolution from the German town of Graslitz repeating the point that land was vital to German national survival: "The attack on the German homeland (*Heimat*) will push the whole German population to unanimous resistance, because our German *Volk* is inseparably bound to its land and its forests."[17] This kind of rhetoric became typical, both in future communications to the League of Nations and in *Verband* propaganda at home and abroad.[18] With its new national strategy Medinger and the *Verband* managed to tie the fate of German nobles to that of the German minority as a whole in Czechoslovakia.

The *Völkerbundliga* thus became an important international lobbying organization for both noble landowners and the German minority more broadly. It counted as members prominent German nobles such as Ledebur, Max Egon Fürstenberg, Karl Buquoy, Alain Rohan, and Adolf Schwarzenberg.[19] Other than Medinger, the most active Bohemian noble was Alfons (Prince) Clary-Aldringen (1887–1978), who eventually served as president of the group after 1937. Clary was a noted internationalist, with a host of contacts and friends in England. As early as 1921, German political parties, and in particular Ledebur, looked to Clary as a propagator of the Czechoslovak German cause in London and kept him supplied with statistics relating to German minority complaints.[20] Clary used this information to good effect, winning support from a number of British aristocrats for the Sudeten Germans, including Lord Henry Bentinck, who offered to spread the word "among the Labour, Liberal and other centers of public opinion in England, as well as among the League of Nations." Another contact, Sir Felix Doubleday arranged for Clary to meet with representatives of the British Foreign Office.[21] Clary also managed, through the help of Adalbert Sternberg, to win the ear of the new owner of the *New York Herald*, Frank Munsey.

After 1921 Medinger, Clary, and Ledebur regularly gave speeches at home and abroad raising complaints over land reform and treatment of the German minority in Czechoslovakia. Skillfully marshalling the Wilsonian rhetoric of self-determination, Medinger's speeches portrayed the Sudeten Germans as a beleaguered minority that, denied its fatherland, only sought autonomy and linguistic rights on the Swiss model. Land reform was the most prominent of many national injustices: "The socialization practices which have penetrated into Czechoslovakia from Russia, give a lever to the Czechs for open and disguised national oppression. . . . The Czechs, abusing their political preponderance, have encroached upon German national property." Germans, Medinger declared in 1922, had faith in the League of Nations, refusing "to consider it a humbug intended only to nourish fallacious hopes among the national minorities." He urged the League to act to fulfill its mandate to protect minorities, before "radical and desperate elements on both sides are strengthened."[22]

Ledebur sounded a similar note, arguing that the land reform violated international law, as defined in the minority treaties, by discriminating against Czechoslovakia's Germans. "Nation and land are inseparable concepts," he wrote in a 1925 article entitled "Land Reform and International Law." He added that confiscation of a minority's landed property (*Besitzstand*) was equivalent to an attack on its very existence. The land reform violated Czechoslovakia's minority treaty in two ways: by targeting German landowners for confiscation and by favoring Czech farmers for redistribution. As an egregious example of the former, Ledebur cited the 1923 forest reform, which had affected 33 minority owners and only two Czechs. The Land Office's colonization policy was, Ledebur wrote, evidence of an anti-German bias in the parcelization process. Taken together, the two policies were shrinking substantially the amount of land in German hands. "The hopeless political situation of the national minorities offers no possibility of a parliamentary defense," he complained. "Only international law, in its latest form, the minority treaty, offers the possibility of an effective remedy."[23]

In spite of the efforts of Medinger and Ledebur to internationalize the Sudeten German question in the 1920s, they achieved little more than occasional admonitions from abroad over land reform. Even so, the *Völkerbundliga* built a strong following in Czechoslovakia and secured powerful connections in Geneva and Britain. In 1935, Konrad Henlein and the Sudeten German Party (SdP) recognized in Medinger's organization a useful tool for developing its own foreign policy, independent of that of Czechoslovakia's Foreign Minister Edvard Beneš. Increasingly dominating Sudeten German politics, the SdP quickly took control of the *Völkerbundliga* and used it and its noble members' connections in England to promote the Sudeten German cause. In effect, the SdP adopted and expanded the German internationalism espoused by Clary and Ledebur in the 1920s. In return, well-connected nobles became some of the SdP's most valued propagandists abroad.

The rest of this story is well known. As Ronald Smelser has so ably documented, the SdP became a willing tool of Hitler's campaign to dismember Czechoslovakia in 1938. Like most SdP supporters, Bohemia's German nobles welcomed the annexation of the Sudetenland to the German Reich. For these nobles, the biggest draw of National Socialism was its potential for bringing together the scattered Germans of Central Europe into a greater German economic and cultural community. Nobles such as Clary-Aldringen lamented the inward-looking cultural and economic autarky of nation-states such as Czechoslovakia, and they yearned for a return to the cosmopolitan German-dominated culture and common market of the Habsburg Empire. As the League of Nations seemed ever less capable of protecting minorities or diminishing the cult of borders in Europe, many German nobles turned to National Socialism as a vessel for their German internationalist aspirations.

In order to "save what could be saved" Czechoslovakia's nobles adapted themselves to the post-imperial national political order. Both the Czech oriented Svaz and the German Verband employed a national rhetoric in their lobbying efforts against land reform. But both groups grafted this heightened national identification onto longstanding noble traditions in Bohemia. Svaz leaders commonly invoked Bohemian historic rights tradition, leavening their Czech national vocabulary with a cosmopolitan territorial and state patriotism. The Verband pursued a German international strategy, in the hopes of re-forming a greater German cultural and political community under the aegis of the League of Nations. Sudeten German fascists hijacked this vision in the 1930s, and Sudeten German nobles could not escape the nationalist/German internationalist rhetoric that had become central to their post-imperial self-understanding. Many became Nazi sympathizers, and none escaped the destruction and retribution consequential to Hitler's creation of a new German Empire.

# Notes

1. František Modráček in the National Assembly on 16 April 1919 (session 46). Text at Elektronická knihovna—Český parlament: dokumenty českého parlamentu [Electronic Library—Czech parliament: documents of the Czech parliament] <http://www.psp.cz/cgi-bin/win/eknih/1918ns/ps/stenprot/046schuz/>.
2. Bedřich Schwarzenberg to Adolf Waldstein 29 March 1919. SOA Praha, RA Valdštejn, VI-59, k 170.
3. Adolf Waldstein to Bedřich Schwarzenberg 5 April 1919. SOA Praha, RA Valdštejn, VI-59, k 170.
4. For a succinct statement of this argument, see Wilhelm Medinger's article "The Situation of the Germans in the Czecho-Slovak State," *Reconstruction*, 1 June 1922. My copy of the article is from an unpaginated reprint. Ironically, Edvard Beneš would promise to create a Swiss-style nationalities state in a memorandum to the Paris Peace Conference in May 1919. It was to prove an empty promise. See Elizabeth Wiskemann, *Czechs and Germans* (Oxford, 1938), 92–93.
5. Protokoly o schůzích představenstva SČV (Minutes of meetings of the directorate of the SČV), 3 June 1919. SOA Třeboň, RA Schwarzenberg Sekundogeniture, ic 1571, k 332.
6. Verband der deutschen Grossgrundbesitzer (VdG) to SČV, 6 September 1919. SÚA, SČV, ic 390, k 46.
7. On the Verband's early goals, see "Denkschrift des Verbandes der deutschen Grossgrundbesitzer Böhmens," 12 December 1919, SOA Praha, RA Valdštejn, signature V-1/VI#2/document 4.
8. Protokol schůze Ústředního výboru Svazů [Minutes of the meeting of the Central Committee of the Svazs], 30 June 1921. SÚA, SČV, ic 88, k 4.
9. "Bericht über die am 11. Juli 1922 stattgefundene Sitzung der Grossgrundbesitzerverbände zur Abwehr gegen die Kündigung." SÚA, SČV, ic 117 k 7.
10. Zdeněk Kolowrat at Porada mezisvazové komise 16 October 1922. SÚA SČV ic 88, k 4.
11. Protokol schůze Ústředního výboru Svazů, 23 March 1927. SÚA, SČV, ic 88, k 4. See also Protokol of 16 October 1922 for the Svaz leadership's opposition to using nationality arguments in international courts.
12. This refers to Article 8:1 of the Treaty of St. Germain en Laye, 10 September 1919. See

"Beschwerde der deutschen Grossgrundbesitzer der Tschechoslowakischen Republik, die die Ankündigung der Konfiskation ihres Eigentumes für den 1. Jänner 1923 erhalten haben, gerichtet an den Völkerbund" (Prague: die Deutsche Völkerbundliga in der Tschechoslowakischen Republik, September 1922), 6.

13. Ibid., 9–10.

14. Ibid., 27.

15. Ibid., 4.

16. Ibid., 20–21.

17. "Kundgebung der Stadtgemeinde Graslitz vom 18. Juli 1922," in ibid., 61.

18. See, among many examples, Wilhelm Medinger, "Landwirtschaft: Die Waldverstaatlichungs-Pläne," *Prager Tagblatt*, 3 March 1922. Copy in SÚA MZV-VA #1379 k 2701. It is clear in other German newspapers, such as *Bohemia*, that much of their information on the forest confiscations came from Medinger and/or the Verband. New petitions and memoranda to the League of Nations followed in 1924, 1925, and 1926.

19. Membership and donation lists in SOA Litoměřice (Děčín) RA Clary-Aldringen, k 447. Franz Clam-Gallas also made substantial donations. He was listed as a "founding" donor in 1922. See SOA Litoměřice (Děčín) RA Clam-Gallas, "Vereine," k 156 ic 468.

20. See Deutschpolitische Arbeitstelle to Alfons Clary-Aldringen, 28 July 1921 and Eugen Ledebur to Alfons Clary-Aldringen, 11 August 1921. SOA Litoměřice (Děčín) RA Clary-Aldringen, k 446.

21. Lord Henry Bentinck to Alfons Clary-Aldringen, 12 September 1921 and copy of letter from Felix Doubleday to Sir William Timell, 4 August 1921. SOA Litoměřice (Děčín) RA Clary-Aldringen, k 448.

22. Wilhelm Medinger, "The Situation of the Germans in the Czecho-Slovak State," speech delivered at the Conference of the Committee for the Protection of National Minorities of the League of Nations Unions, reprinted in *Reconstruction: International Economic Monthly* (Vienna), 1 June 1922.

23. Eugen Ledebur-Wicheln, "Bodenreform und Völkerrecht," *Wochenschrift für Kultur, Politik, und Volkswirtschaft* 7, nos. 20–21 (14 and 21 February 1925): 483. Copy of article in SOA Litoměřice (Děčín) RA Ledebur, ic 190 k 14.

# Askaris in the "Wild East"

## The Deployment of Auxiliaries and the Implementation of Nazi Racial Policy in Lublin District

### ❖ Peter Black ❖

To conquer the "living space" from the eastern borders of the Reich to the Ural Mountains that the National Socialist leadership perceived the very biological survival of the German race to require was a core goal of Hitler's National Socialist ideology. Based on what Gerhard Weinberg has identified as prewar general National Socialist consensus,[1] the German leaders intended, within this newly won territory, to eliminate entirely or intellectually decapitate peoples perceived to be of "alien" and "inferior" race—and hence a danger to the German Reich—leaving behind a "residue" to provide manual labor for German settlers. In German-occupied Poland, Nazi race and settlement policy involved murdering the Jewish population, enslaving the Polish population, and settling Germans on militarized agricultural bases, from which a "master race" would rule the region for a thousand years, converting it to German "living space." From the first days of the occupation of Poland in 1939 until the evacuation of Polish territory in 1944–1945, the Germans relied upon auxiliaries to enforce their decrees and to implement their vision of racial restructuring in the East, including the removal of unwanted "racial material" and dangerous political and "biological" enemies.[2]

The notion of German settlers—"colonists"—on the eastern borders of the Reich as defenders of German empires and as bearers of an allegedly superior German culture goes back to the establishment of the Hanseatic League and the proselytizing crusades of the Teutonic Knights. Historical interaction between Germans and the peoples of Eastern Europe rarely coincides with aims and goals perceived through

---

Opinions and conclusions expressed herein are those of the author and do not necessarily represent the official opinion of the United States Holocaust Memorial Museum.

later popular images. Nineteenth-century nationalists presented proselytization, late medieval warfare, and voluntary German migration, without political or cultural ambitions, at the behest of east European kings and lords as a "slow, but unstoppable natural process" in which a "superior" people brings order and culture to the "uncivilized hoards" of the East.[3]

In the late nineteenth century, the image of German settlement in the East was driven in part by a conservative, nationalist interpretation of what Woodruff D. Smith has labeled "migrationist colonialism." Migrationist colonialism was originally a liberal response to the maintenance of German culture among the waves of emigrants fleeing political oppression or lack of economic opportunity in Germany. After Bismarck unified Germany under conservative auspices and the depression of 1873 finalized the divorce of the traditional German middle classes from free trade liberalism, pro-colony activists in Germany perceived the acquisition of colonies not only as a symbol of national strength, but also as a haven against the social effects of industrial capitalism, where the pre-industrial middle-class virtues could be preserved. Competing with this vision of white farming colonies were pro-industry demands to establish colonies as trading areas and adjuncts to the German economy. These Wilhelmine trends—"settlement ideology" and "economic colonialism" would devolve for some into the intellectual wellspring of Nazi imperialism, trends that Woodruff Smith has defined as *Lebensraum* expansionism and *Weltpolitik* expansionism.[4] Absorbed in Germany's late century scramble for overseas colonies and efforts to Germanize the population of Prussian Poland in part through land sales to German settlers, German nationalists increasingly perceived colonial settlements as opportunities to recreate the fatherland, preferably in the East, through trade with Germany, preservation of German culture, and, for those so inclined, maintenance of racial purity within a ethnic milieu perceived, as Wolfgang Wippermann has written, in terms of interaction between a "civilized Germany and the more or less cultureless East."[5] German settlements in Eastern Europe, regardless of the degree of assimilation to local culture (a factor that racists deemed irrelevant) were, in this mindset, bases from which the German nation could launch pro-active, preventative strikes against Slavic, and after 1917, Bolshevik hordes threatening Central Europe.

After the unexpected collapse of the German Reich in 1918 and the imposition of the hated Versailles Treaty, imperial visions of a cultural/racial mission to civilize the "wild East" and maintaining a defensive bulwark against a "wildly agitated, restless Slav and semi-Slav flood," now pushed westward by Bolshevism, were integrated on the radical right of the Weimar political spectrum with efforts to revise and adequately defend Germany's eastern borders. This racially redefined "march of the Teutonic Knights of old"[6] necessitated the removal of those peoples who resisted or who, by virtue of their race might be likely to resist German rule. Hitler and other National Socialist ideologues, including Heinrich Himmler, redefined the complex and varied motivations of previous German migration to the East as the unconscious fulfillment of a biologically determined racial impulse.[7] Now racially conscious, as they claimed themselves to be, the National Socialists intended to follow the path of their forebears and fulfill this biological destiny. When he became *Reichsführer-SS* in 1929, Himmler infused the SS, which had previously functioned as a Nazi Party security force, with a mission of race and settlement.[8]

In the context of conquest and settlement, the use of indigenous auxiliaries in Poland and, later, in the occupied Soviet Union, recalled practices of Germany's short colonialist period, particularly in German East Africa.[9] Locally recruited mercenaries, called *askaris*, were first deployed in German East Africa during the 1888–1889 Abushiri rebellion of the Kiswahili speaking indigenous population against German rule. During World War I, five thousand *askari* soldiers fought loyally under German command, tying down an Anglo-French army of 130,000 in East Africa in a campaign that Woodruff Smith has called "the most significant contribution that the colonial empire ever made to Germany."[10]

Though his visions of a future German garden of Eden lay further to the east, in Ukraine, the Crimea, and the Caucasus, and though his foreign policy in the 1930s permitted the existence of a Polish satellite state, Hitler decided to conquer Poland in 1939, after the Polish government refused to accept its prescribed role in a German-dominated Europe.[11] Indeed, German goals in Poland were vague, but explicitly violent.[12] Nevertheless, Hitler told his top military advisers on October 17, 1939 that Germany must wage a "ruthless" national struggle to "prevent a Polish intelligentsia from forming a ruling class" and offer the remainder of the population "only the scantiest means of livelihood" sufficient to permit its survival as a "source of labor."[13] Postponement of the ideologically ordained racial crusade against the Soviet Union until Germany dealt with the Western Powers rendered prostrate Poland an ideal experimental field for the establishment of National Socialist rule: the annihilation of unwanted and enemy "races" and the establishment of German outposts, populated by "retrieved" German "blood," supported by manual labor from leaderless masses of "inferior" indigenous populations, and guarded in part by indigenous police auxiliaries whose blood was "acceptable" if not desirable and whose willingness to serve their German masters was unquestioned.

After Poland's defeat, Germany directly annexed Danzig, West Prussia, Poznań, and Upper Silesia, and designated the remainder of German-occupied Polish territory as the Government General (*Generalgouvernement*). Immediate settlement and security goals involved the deportation of hundreds of thousands of Poles and Jews from the annexed territories to the Government General in order to make room for the settlement of ethnic Germans from Soviet-occupied or Soviet-coveted territory. The German invaders also aimed to kill or deport to concentration camps the members of Poland's political and cultural elite and to mobilize and exploit the vast potential for manual labor in the Government General by instituting compulsory labor requirements for both Poles and Jews.[14]

In his infamous memorandum "Some Thoughts on the Treatment of Those of Foreign Race in the East," submitted to Hitler on May 25, 1940, Himmler envisioned a race of German settlers, police, administrators, and racial anthropologists to "sift through" a "race mish-mash" to identify German blood and transport those "racially valuable" persons to Germany for assimilation. Those without racial value or presenting a danger to German rule, such as the Jews, would be removed altogether, leaving behind an "inferior population" that would exist at the disposal of the Germans as a "leaderless nation of laborers for special construction tasks." "Mired in its own cultureless existence," these laboring masses would be "summoned under the strict, consistent, and just guidance of the German nation to work on the latter's everlasting cultural achievements and construction projects."[15]

After the fall of France in the summer of 1940, Nazi Germany refocused attention on destroying the Soviet Union, giving new impetus to experimental planning for long-term German rule in Poland. Himmler's appointments as Chief of German Police on June 17, 1936 and as Reich Commissar for the Strengthening of German Nationhood (*Reichskommissar für die Festigung deutschen Volkstums*—RKFDV) on October 7, 1939 established his SS and police as the primary executive apparatus for this "racial restructuring of Eastern Europe," of which the elimination of the Jewish population formed "an integral part."[16]

The SS apparatus in Poland involved several central authorities as well as a regional command structure that permitted planning, and pushed the agenda for the racial restructuring of occupied Poland. The Reich Central Office for Security (*Reichssicherheitshauptamt*—RSHA) was established in September 1939 under the leadership of *SS-Gruppenführer* Reinhard Heydrich through the amalgamation of the Security Service (*Sicherheitsdienst*—SD) and the Security Police (*Sicherheitspolizei*). An agency of the Nazi Party, the SD had been the political intelligence agency of the Reich from 1934. The Security Police had been established in June 1936 and consisted of the German political police detective forces, unified in 1935 into the Secret State Police (*Geheime Staatspolizei-Gestapo)*, and the Criminal Police detective forces (*Kriminalpolizei*—Kripo), which were unified in 1937. The RSHA was responsible for the "racial" and preventative security of the nation: using perceived collective "racial" criteria, its mission was to "uncover," neutralize or eliminate both actual and potential opponents of Nazi rule in Germany and German-occupied Europe.[17] The Main Office Order Police (*Hauptamt Ordnungspolizei*—HA Orpo), established in 1936 as the central agency for all uniformed police forces in Germany, supplied the manpower, under guidance of the RSHA and the direct command of regional SS and police leaders, to destroy enemies, round up "good" candidates for Germanization and recruit and train auxiliary police.[18] The SS Race and Settlement Main Office (*SS-Rasse- und Siedlungshauptamt*—RuSHA), originally founded in 1931 under R. Walther Darré and led during the war by *SS-Gruppenführer* Otto Hofmann, was responsible for the so-called physical-racial evaluations of persons deemed to be of "retrievable" German blood.[19] Himmler's RKFDV staff, raised to main office status in 1941 under *SS-Gruppenführer* Ulrich Greifelt, was responsible for coordinating the efforts of RSHA and RuSHA to plan and populate proposed German settlements and for managing the details of the settlement operations.[20] Finally, the SS Main Offices Administration and Economy (*Verwaltung- und Wirtschaft*) and Budget and Facilities (*Haushalt- und Bauten*), established in 1939 under *SS-Gruppenführer* Oswald Pohl and reorganized in 1942 with the concentration camp system into the SS Economic-Administration Main Office, *SS-Wirtschafts-Verwaltungshauptamt—WVHA*), developed construction concepts and plans and budgeted for the future settlements.[21]

Each of these central institutions had offices or representatives throughout occupied Europe, whose activities were coordinated and, in times of emergency, commanded by regional Higher SS and Police Leaders (*Höhere SS- und Polizeiführer—HSSPF*) and, at the lowest regional level, by SS and Police Leaders (*SS- und Polizeiführer—SSPF*).[22] Attached to the staff of the HSSPF for the Government General, *SS-Obergruppenführer* Friedrich-Wilhelm Krüger, were commanders of Security Police (*Befehlshaber der Sicherheitspolizei—BdS*) and Order Police (*Befehlshaber der Ordnungspolizei—BdO*), and officials designated to represent the RKFDV, the VWHA (later WVHA), and the RuSHA. At the level of the SSPF were assigned commanders (*Kommandeure*) of Security Police and Order Police (KdS, KdO).

Himmler's planning initiatives for German settlements in the Government General were entrusted to his SSPF for District Lublin, *SS-Brigadeführer* Odilo Globocnik.[23] Globocnik's staff in Lublin attained specific strategic significance in Nazi planning due to his ideological fanaticism, due to provisional plans in 1939 to concentrate central European Jews on a "reservation" in his District, and due to Lublin's geographical position along the Nazi-Soviet demarcation line. As such, District Lublin was an ideal laboratory for the development of Nazi racial policy.[24]

Himmler's appointment as RKFDV lent the SS and police the jurisdictional potential, but not the undisputed power to steer race and settlement policy in the Government General. Hitler's racist war against Poles and Jews, who together made up more than 90 percent of the population of the Government General,[25] demanded manpower. For example, between 1939 and 1942, approximately two million Jews resided in the Government General.[26] In District Lublin, there resided between 250,000 to 320,000 Jews, with 47,000 Jews in Lublin and 16,000 in Chełm.[27] Reich German manpower in the District was limited. The civilian occupation bureaucracy had slots for between 1,600 and 1,900 employees (including chauffeurs, porters, and clerical support personnel), while resources for the SS and police included between 500 and 600 Security Police and SD officials (more than two thirds of whom were stationed in Lublin), 441 permanently stationed German gendarmes, two detachments of Municipal Order Police (*Schutzpolizei*) in Lublin and Chełm, and 1,315 Polish police officials.[28] Since the fulcrum of executive power was concentrated in the cities of the Government General, successful implementation of policy required a reliable and ruthlessly trained cadre of auxiliaries prepared to go into the countryside in force.

Both the Jews and members of the Polish elite were top priority "enemies" requiring executive attention, both to secure the Government General and to initiate settlement plans. While the Security Police and SD, with their mobile units, known as *Einsatzgruppen*, had the advantage of past intelligence operations to target Polish leaders, SS authorities clashed with their civilian counterparts over the mechanics of "managing" the Jewish population and over the manpower required for implementation of German ordinances. Even as the Germans were conquering Poland in September 1939, the SS sought exclusive control over the Jewish communities. Security Police chief Reinhard Heydrich ordered his *Einsatzgruppen* commanders to establish Jewish Councils, made up of leading Jewish citizens, which would be responsible for carrying out German orders and through which roving Security Police and SD units would coordinate their efforts to concentrate the Jewish population.[29] After the establishment of the civilian authority of the Government General on October 26, 1939, Governor General Hans Frank issued a decree requiring the establishment of Jewish Councils responsible to the civilian authorities.[30]

In their effort to usurp the implementation of anti-Jewish policies in the Government General, the SS and police authorities were the first to recruit indigenous auxiliaries. In District Lublin the SSPF recruited an ethnic German *Selbstschutz* (literally: self-defense) from the fragmented ethnic German populations living in the countryside, particularly in the vicinity of Chełm.[31] Like its counterparts in other districts of the Government General, the *Selbstschutz* in Lublin advanced two key components of long-term German planning: the recruits were conscripted in the process of identifying German families and hence determining the existence of retrievable German "blood"; and they served as a vehicle for the SS and police to monopolize the indigenous manpower available to enforce German decrees. From the *Selbstschutz* recruits in Lublin, Globocnik and his staff created an auxiliary police battalion, stationed in Lublin, but capable of deployment anywhere in the district where executive muscle was required.[32]

Globocnik did not invent the idea to recruit auxiliary police among local ethnic Germans. On the day of his appointment as RKFDV, Himmler had authorized the German Order Police headquarters to establish locally based *Selbstschutz* units in the annexed western territories of Poland. For the Government General, he appointed an SS and *Selbstschutz* commander, subordinate to Krüger as HSSPF. Between November 1939 and April 1940, SS and police authorities recruited some 12,600 ethnic German men into *Selbstschutz* units under command, respectively, of the SSPF for each of the four districts of the Government General.[33] These *Selbstschutz* units generally remained under the strict supervision and discipline of the district commanders of the Order Police (KdO). Only in District Lublin did Globocnik as SSPF retain direct control over the unit, utilizing it more or less as a private police force.

By December 1939, SS and police authorities in Lublin had established a *Selbstschutz* battalion of between 800 and 1000 men divided into five companies.[34] With this battalion as armed support, Globocnik sought to usurp for the SS and police control over policy towards the Jews of Lublin District. In theory, the deployment of Jewish labor was the responsibility of German Labor Office officials and coordinated locally by the civilian authorities at the *Kreis* level, the *Kreis-* and *Stadthauptmänner*[35]; in practice, officials often seized Jews out of their homes, off the street and even from the worksites of their rivals. Taking advantage of these conditions, Globocnik established in early December a string of workshops in a field on Lublin's Lipowa Street. The *Selbstschutz* administered and the guarded this so-called Lipowa Lager, and the Jewish Council financed it.[36] On December 8, 1939, SSPF officials encouraged *Wehrmacht* representatives to seek laborers for military construction projects not from the civilian labor offices, but directly from the SSPF. Globocnik's men announced that in the future the tasks of the *Selbstschutz* in Lublin would involve the "registration . . . and supervision of hundreds of thousands of Jews" who would be "concentrated in forced labor camps" to facilitate the provision of labor for road construction and river regulation sites. In order to handle requests for labor and to coordinate his Jewish labor policy at one station, Globocnik established a "Jewish desk" (*Judenreferat*) on his staff under *SS-Obersturmführer* Dr. Karl Hofbauer.[37] Though he operated on his own timetable, Globocnik's initiative was consistent with Himmler's general plans for the exploitation of Jewish labor in Poland. On January 30, 1940, Security Police Chief Reinhard Heydrich told a gathering of SS, SD and police officials of his intention to deploy, under SS and police supervision, thousands of male Jews at hard labor. A week later, Himmler discussed with Colonel General Walther von Brauchitsch, the commander in chief of the army, plans to compel all male Jews to work on border fortifications in eastern Poland.[38]

On occasion, the SSPF could cooperate with the civilian authorities. For instance, its officials deployed the *Selbstschutz* in support of German Labor Office officials rounding up Polish peasants for deportation to the increasingly labor-starved Germany. The ethnic Germans cordoned off rural villages, seized the men capable of work and guarded them in two transit camps on Lublin's Krochmalna Street.[39]

Globocnik's real goal, however, was control over Jewish life and labor. In a meeting with district civilian officials on April 22, 1940, he announced that *Selbstschutz* units would henceforth conscript Jewish labor. He proposed to house Jewish workers in camps financed by the Jewish Council in Lublin and named *SS-Standartenführer* Willi Stemmler to command the *Selbstschutz* guard detachments so deployed. Eventually, the *Selbstschutz* would guard and supervise the labor of 2,700 Jews in six camps working on river regulation projects along the Bug River under contract for the

Water Economy Inspectorate (*Wasserwirtschaftsinspektion*) for *Kreis* Biała-Podlaska alone. Altogether, Stemmler's units guarded at least twenty camps throughout Lublin District and were deployed to conscript laborers for them.[40]

Globocnik's pet project for Jewish labor was the ill-conceived border fortifications project that Heydrich had mentioned in January 1940. By early spring, SS and police authorities in Lublin had chosen the village of Bełżec (*Kreis* Zamość), located eight miles from the Nazi-Soviet demarcation line, as the central location for a series of camps to house Jewish laborers deployed in the excavation of anti-tank ditches along that part of the demarcation line not marked by the Bug River.[41] Approximately 1,140 Gypsies, deported from Hamburg and Bremen, were the first prisoners to arrive at Bełżec, on May 22–24, 1940[42]; a transport of Jews from Lublin followed within a week. In early August, three subsidiary camps were established to accommodate the influx of Jews conscripted for labor from Radom, Cracow, and Warsaw districts. The Jewish Council in Lublin reported in September the presence of more than 11,000 Jewish laborers in the border camps. *Selbstschutz* units guarded the border fortifications camps and worksites from May 1940 until the civilian authorities secured their dissolution in October. The closing report of the Jewish Council in Lublin, which bore fiscal responsibility for feeding and housing the prisoners, estimated that 300 persons died during the course of the project.[43] Though the practical military value of the fortifications was nil and their defensive purpose was rendered superfluous by Hitler's December 18 operational order to attack the USSR, the project supported SS and police efforts to control the deployment of Jewish labor in the Government General and set a precedent for the dependence on auxiliaries to manage population policy.

Globocnik also deployed the *Selbstschutz* on his own initiative in minor population movements. In early May 1940, he ordered the destruction of the so-called small ghetto, a mixed Polish-Jewish neighborhood in west Lublin, reportedly because he was "not pleased to have a Jewish settlement in the vicinity of his staff headquarters."[44] Teams of security police officials and selected *Selbstschutz* recruits, operating within a moving cordon of *Selbstschutz* units (anticipating the ghetto deportation operations of 1942), broke into the homes of Jews, forced them out onto the street and transported them by truck or on foot to the Majdan-Tatarski suburb of Lublin. SS and *Selbstschutz* men shot at least eight Jews during the operation, including an elderly, blind woman. They also engaged in characteristic plunder: a widow with seven children later pleaded with the SS and *Selbstschutz* headquarters to return three milking cows that had been confiscated and which had been her only means of income.[45]

The Selbstschutz also participated independently in punitive reprisal operations. In April 1940, at Globocnik's insistence, *Selbstschutz* men murdered more than 150 civilians and torched 27 farms in Józefów (*Kreis* Radzyń) in retaliation for the murder of five ethnic German residents of the village. Despite the protests of his superiors in Cracow (HSSPF Krüger and Governor General Hans Frank) over this incident, Globocnik sent the *Selbstschutz* out on another mission in June to massacre some 27 Polish and Jewish civilians at Radawiec, a village located a few miles west of Lublin.[46]

These massacres, ongoing corruption, and the unwillingness of the police at any level to take up stations in the countryside increased the demand of local civilian occupation administrators for small enforcement units of their own, an option that Frank and Krüger had been discussing since March 1940. On May 6, 1940, Frank established a *Sonderdienst* (Special Service), which was to deploy small units of armed ethnic Germans at the disposal of the *Kreishauptmänner* to perform various police functions. To coordinate the individual units, Frank established within the office of the Governor General an Inspectorate of the *Sonderdienst*, run by an administrator named Hermann Hammerle.[47] In order to counter SS concerns about the development of a policing force independent of SS and police, Frank and Krüger agreed on a compromise: though deployment of the *Sonderdienst* units fell to the Inspectorate and to the individual *Kreishauptmänner*, Globocnik and his cronies would maintain a *Sonderdienst* Replacement Battalion based in Lublin, which would supervise recruitment, training, placement, equipment, supply, discipline and reward.[48]

By mid-July, complaints from the civilian authorities forced Krüger to dissolve the *Selbstschutz* and to accelerate the deployment of the *Sonderdienst* under the authority of the individual *Kreis-* and *Stadthauptmänner*.[49] Officially dissolved throughout the Government General on August 31, 1940, the *Selbstschutz* in Lublin that briefly became the lynchpin of the persecution of Jews and Poles in Lublin District was composed of young ethnic German residents of that District. The typical recruit was male, between 18 and 35 years of age, overwhelmingly Lutheran, and engaged in agriculture.[50] His youth, lack of education, pride in being German and uneasy relationship with his Polish neighbors rendered him susceptible to the blandishments and threats of Globocnik's recruiters. He was less likely to identify with Nazi aims and policies than his counterparts in western Poland, who, as German citizens prior to 1918, tended to feel outrage at having to become Polish citizens, or his counterparts in the USSR, for whom relentless Stalinist oppression in the 1930s made the Nazi invader in 1941 appear as liberator.[51] Nevertheless, many recruits committed themselves unequivocally to the Third Reich. Others were attracted by career opportunities, extra rations, or adventure. Still others feared to disobey an official summons and were bullied into service by recruiters or by zealous parents. Other indirect pressures may have included: concern about unemployment or starvation, unbearable family relationships, concern about status within the ethnic German community, and, perhaps, simple boredom.[52] Whatever the combination of motives for enlisting, once enrolled, the recruits proved, with rare exceptions, to be pliable tools of the SSPF leadership in Lublin. Though the *Selbstschutz* experiment in Lublin in 1940 failed, its significance is threefold: its history (1) reflected the bitter struggle between SS-police and civilian authorities over scarce manpower resources and police power at the local level in the Government General; (2) underscored the first attempt of the

SS and police to gain exclusive control over the implementation of Hitler's "ruthless national struggle" in the Government General; and (3) demonstrated that under ruthless and ideologically committed leadership, raw recruits, equipped at the most with a cultural attachment to Germany, could be fashioned into an efficient machine for Nazi population policy, including mass murder.[53]

After six months, the compromise on the *Sonderdienst* collapsed; in February 1941, Krüger granted Globocnik his request to be relieved of any responsibilities for the organization.[54] Though he had to accept former *Selbstschutz* personnel specialist and *SS-Hauptsturmführer* Karl Streibel, who continued to report to Globocnik in Lublin, as a "consultant," and had to depend on SS and police personnel as non-commissioned officers for six more months, Hammerle reported a reduction of tension between the *Sonderdienst* Inspectorate and the SS and Police.[55] The real source of this tension and the significance of the *Sonderdienst* experiment lay in the efforts of the civilian authorities in Poland to establish enforcement units independent of the SS and police apparatus. Since the *Kreishauptmänner* lacked the authority to dispatch police units in small groups to implement German occupation policy in the countryside, the *Sonderdienst* men represented the only reliable force available to local civil officials. No doubt, too, the latter came to depend on the *Sonderdienst* men because they were ethnic Germans, or at least persons of potentially suitable "blood" who could speak enough of the language to make the administrators feel comfortable in a stressful and increasingly dangerous environment. The *Kreishauptmann* in Siedlce (District Warsaw) noted in summer 1940 the urgency with which he awaited the arrival of his *Sonderdienst* men, who "both with their eager German hands and with their Polish language ability form an indispensable support for the Reich German police officials."[56] Frank confided to Hammerle on December 14, 1940 that the significance of the *Sonderdienst* as an executive was so great that the civilian authorities "must consciously minimize its importance . . . to distract the attention of other circles."[57]

The civil authorities had intended the *Sonderdienst* to consist of ethnic Germans who would eventually make their careers in the German administration and contribute to the Germanization of occupied Poland. During its first year, the Inspectorate of the *Sonderdienst* trained 4,000 men. Though the genealogical pedigree of many did not conform to the strictest Nazi standards, civil administrators aimed to create a consciousness of being German sufficient to inspire active commitment to Hitler's war against Jews and Bolsheviks, Poles and Russians. *Sonderdienst* recruits endured lectures on German history, Nazi ideology, and "geography in alignment with German principles." Articles in the Inspectorate's periodical seem reflective of themes that the German trainers hoped to reinforce. Among these themes was "race consciousness." *Sonderdienst* men were instructed, often condescendingly, that the blood of all the Germanic "races" flowed in their veins. They were praised for having been able to sustain their Germanness against the "influence of alien blood" and promised that they would be lifted to the "educational-cultural level of their German racial compatriots [*Volksgenossen*] from the Old Reich."[58]

Urged to identify completely with the fate of Adolf Hitler and the German Reich, the *Sonderdienst* man was instructed to become "battle conscious" (*kampfbewußt*), understanding that he was "not to vegetate without resolution," but to fight "for the light against the darkness," that is, to fight "for National Socialism against Bolshevism and world Jewry." The arch-enemy in this struggle was identical to that which their Reich German counterparts fought: Jews and the "Jewish spirit [*Geist*] that had crept into Europe from the Orient" and had throughout history "maliciously and destructively sought to annihilate the races, nations, politics and the economy."[59]

The *Sonderdienst* units, numbering between thirty and thirty-five men for each *Kreis*, enforced local ordinances and maintained a "German" presence in the Polish countryside. Armed with whatever ideological training they absorbed, the *Sonderdienst* men were deployed not only on "routine" enforcement, such as collecting taxes, requisitioning agricultural goods, interdicting illicit trade, monitoring pricing, and enforcing forced labor obligations for Jews and Poles, but also in operations to concentrate the Polish Jews prior to March 1942 and to deport and shoot Polish Jews within the framework of Operation *Reinhard* in 1942–1943.[60] As such, their deployment underscored the necessity of auxiliary support for the implementation of core race and settlement policy in occupied Poland.

Though they miscalculated the ability of the civilian authorities to fashion a police executive, Himmler and Krüger understood by 1941 that the *Sonderdienst* threatened SS and police interests in the Government General. They sought to destroy it in the summer of 1942, but in the absence of an equivalent service to the *Kreishauptmänner*, they failed to pry the local detachments loose from the civilian authorities.[61] Nevertheless, one should not make too much of this jurisdictional struggle. Both civil administrators and police authorities shared the "National Socialist consensus" in occupied Poland: (1) to exterminate the Jews and the Polish intelligentsia; (2) to exploit the labor potential of the Polish masses; and (3) to turn the Government General into a region of German settlement. As a part of this vision, the *Sonderdienst* served not only as a police executive, but also as a stepping stone to full acceptance into the German "racial community." When it came to core race, settlement and security issues, SS and police and civil authorities cooperated more than they fought, with disastrous results for their victims.

Whether Globocnik was privy to Heydrich's January 1941 submission to Hitler regarding a "solution" to the European "Jewish question,"[62] when he withdrew permanently from the *Sonderdienst* argument in February, remains unknown; certain is that, during the course of 1941, Globocnik received dynamic new tasks that required the recruitment of a new auxiliary police force. In late October 1940, Himmler and Globocnik discussed "race consciousness" training programs for residents of German settlements in Poland to prepare them for relocation in the Reich.

The *Reichsführer* also authorized a massive search for German blood throughout occupied Poland and the detail of SS men from the RuSHA for the establishment of so-called SS and Police Bases (*SS- und Polizeistützpunkte*), the establishment of which Himmler ordered in November 1940. The *Reichsführer* conceived of the SS and Police bases as armed industrialized agricultural complexes located throughout the conquered territories of eastern Poland and, eventually, the Soviet Union. In addition to increasing agricultural production for the German "race," these bases would serve the "maintenance of order and the stabilization of political power" in the East, representing the "extended arm of the German leadership."[63] In February 1941, on the suggestion of Lublin *Stadthauptmann* Fritz Sauermann, Globocnik established a "Research Institute for East Facilities" (*Forschungsinstitut für Ostunterkünfte*) as a brain trust for base planning.[64]

On July 17, 1941, Hitler entrusted Himmler with exclusive authority for security matters in the occupied Soviet Union. That same day, the *Reichsführer-SS* appointed Globocnik his "Commissioner for the Establishment of the SS and Police Bases in the New Eastern Area" (*Beauftragter des Reichsführers-SS und Chef der deutschen Polizei für die Errichtung der SS-und Polizeistützpunkte im neuen Ostraum*).[65] On July 20, Himmler visited Lublin and ordered Globocnik to establish a major concentration camp to house forced laborers who would construct facilities for German settlement in the East. Himmler also designated Lublin and Kreis Zamość as initial areas for German colonization.[66] Two weeks later, on August 6, 1941, *SS-Obersturmbannführer* Josef Nemec from the staff of the SSPF Lublin and *SS-Obersturmbannführer* Gustav Maubach of the police base commissioner's staff, met in Lublin with *SS-Obersturm-führer* Gustav Hanelt, the chief of the *SS-Mannschaftshaus* in Lublin.[67] They discussed the division of labor in the initiation of German settlement plans in Poland and the USSR. Among Hanelt's responsibilities was to be planning for the establishment of the SS and Police bases and for the "clearing out of the Jews" while working closely with an "ethnic-political desk" (*Volkspolitisches Referat*) of the Nazi Party in organizing the Germanization of the designated areas.[68]

On the previous day, August 5, 1941, Order Police Chief *SS-Obergruppenführer* Kurt Daluege instructed the HSSPFs in the East and Globocnik in Lublin to establish SS and police bases in the occupied USSR before the onset of winter and to speed up the formation of indigenous auxiliary police forces.[69] One response to the SSPF's search for manpower was a training camp on the grounds of a sugar factory outside the town of Trawniki, twenty miles east southeast of Lublin. Globocnik's deputy, *SS-Hauptsturmführer* Hermann Höfle, had established the Trawniki facility in early July as a holding center for Jews, Ukrainians and Soviet prisoners of war selected from *Wehrmacht* prisoner of war camps as potential collaborators or as dangerous persons.[70] From the summer of 1941 until March 31, 1942, the Trawniki Training Camp was subordinate to Globocnik in his capacity as SS and Police base commissioner; the auxiliaries trained there were formally named "the Guard Forces [*Wachmannschaften*] of the Commissioner for *Reichsführer SS* and Chief of German Police for the Establishment of SS and Police Bases in the New Eastern Area"; the recruits themselves were nicknamed *askaris* after the indigenous units deployed in German East Africa.[71]

On the basis of general instructions from Himmler and Heydrich to select from among captured Soviet soldiers "persons who appeared particularly reliable and [were] . . . therefore suitable for deployment in the reconstruction of the occupied [Soviet] territories,"[72] Globocnik's staff initially recruited former Soviet prisoners of war for training as police auxiliaries in Trawniki. As the SSPF staff lacked even the managerial manpower, let alone the engineering and construction expertise, to deal with settlements proposed for the occupied Soviet Union, Himmler removed Globocnik from this position at the end of March 1942 and transferred responsibility for the planned bases in the USSR to the WVHA. From the summer of 1942, Trawniki and the auxiliaries trained there were subordinated to Globocnik in his capacity as SS and Police Leader in Lublin District.[73] If indeed these *askaris* were conceived as indigenous troops for the colonists of the Nazi "racial state," they certainly became embroiled quickly in operations deemed vital to the security of the future German Reich, particularly the plan to murder the Jews of the Government General, known as "Operation *Reinhard*."

When Himmler tasked Globocnik with what came to be called Operation Reinhard remains unclear. Surviving documentation leaves few clues as to the exact parameters of the operation in 1941. Nevertheless, in his concluding report on its purpose, aims and activities, Globocnik described four aspects of the program: (1) extermination of the Polish Jews; (2) exploitation of the remaining Jewish labor potential; (3) evaluation of property and valuables (including cash and jewelry) taken from the murdered Jews; and (4) retrieval of the hidden assets (such as stocks and bonds) and stationary property (real estate, factory plant) that belonged to the Jews.[74] In the autumn of 1941, Globocnik established what later became known as the Operation Reinhard Staff in the SSPF Lublin office. He appointed *SS-Hauptsturmführer* Hermann Höfle as his "Expert for Jewish Matters in the 'Special Action Reinhardt.'" Höfle, supported by Hanelt's staff at the *SS-Mannschaftshaus* and members of the SS and police base commissioner's staff, planned major deportation operations to specific sites in Eastern Poland.[75] A second department, later known as the Inspectorate of the SS Special Detachments (*Inspektion der SS-Sonderkommandos*), was led by Christian Wirth and tasked with the construction and maintenance of stationary killing facilities at three sites in eastern Poland: Belzec, Sobibor and Treblinka II. Wirth arrived in Lublin in the autumn of 1941 with personnel detailed from the Führer Chancellery (*Führerkanzlei*), who until August 1941 had systematically killed institutionalized persons with physical and mental disabilities under the code name "*Tiergartenstrasse 4* (T-4)" at stationary killing centers throughout the Reich. As early as November 1941, small squads of guards trained at Trawniki arrived at Belzec, Sobibor, and Treblinka. There they guarded Jewish, Polish, and Soviet prisoner of war labor under the supervision of SSPF technical personnel, who had been transferred in part from the T-4 operation to construct stationary killing centers. With the arrival of more personnel from T-4, integrated with selected non-commissioned SS officers from Globocnik's staff in Lublin, the three notorious killing centers were up and running in March 1942 (Belzec), May 1942 (Sobibor) and July 1942 (Treblinka II).[76]

To deport the Polish Jews and murder them in the killing centers, the Operation *Reinhard* staff required a loyal, reliable, ruthlessly trained and led cadre of men; the Trawniki auxiliaries fulfilled this need. On October 27, 1941, Globocnik recalled former *Selbstschutz* personnel officer Karl Streibel to Lublin to command the Trawniki Training Camp. Already in late August, German police recruiters had begun to screen Soviet soldiers in German prisoner of war camps; the first recruits had received their status as auxiliary police guards at Trawniki in early September. By mid-September, nearly 1,000 recruits were training in the camp, including ethnic Germans, German language-speakers, soldiers of non-Russian nationality whom the Germans presumed to have reason to hate the Bolshevik regime, and, eventually, persons who looked healthy, despite the dreadful conditions in the camps. Many of the ethnic Germans came from Ukraine, the Volga Republic, or the scattered communities of eastern Russia, including Siberia.[77]

As the SSPF administrators realized the magnitude of the task in front of them, they selected Ukrainians, Estonians, Latvians, Lithuanians, Belarussians, Russians, Romanians from the North Bukovina and Bessarabia, Tartars and the occasional Chuvash, Eurotin and Komi.[78] One Trawniki man, who served as the orderly for the commandant of the Treblinka labor camp, was later known to have been half-Jewish.[79]

By March 1942, the Trawniki Training camp had roughly 1,250 recruits, virtually all selected from among the Soviet prisoners of war captured during the 1941 campaign. In June and July 1942, Streibel selected another 1,200 Soviet soldiers from among those captured in the south Ukraine and in the Crimea in May 1942 along with a smattering of Baltic nationals captured in 1941 and incarcerated in Germany.[80] The murderous treatment of Soviet prisoners of war in German custody during the winter of 1941–1942 and German military reverses after the summer of 1942 dried up the supply of Soviet soldiers to recruit as collaborators. From August 1942 until the end of 1943, Streibel's men therefore conscripted civilians from groups thought to be politically and racially "reliable": e. g., the young men of the west Ukraine (Galicia and Podolia) in February and April 1943, persons working for other German authorities,[81] Goralian mountaineers from the Tatra region between Poland and Slovakia in January 1943, ethnic Ukrainians from Lublin District in June–July 1943, and a sprinkling of ethnic Poles in November 1942.[82] When Globocnik left Lublin in September 1943, he reported that approximately 3,700 men were serving in the Trawniki system.[83]

The Trawniki-trained guards provided support for all aspects of Operation

*Reinhard.* Commanded by small units of German SS and police, they were deployed at company strength (90 to 120 men) to staff the SS Special Detachments at the killing centers Belzec, Sobibor, and Treblinka. There they guarded the killing centers and supervised the surviving "work Jews" who "assisted" new victims into the gas chambers, disposed of the corpses, and sorted and packed the loot for shipment to Lublin or to Berlin.[84] Units from company to battalion size were dispatched to deportation sites throughout the Government General and the Białystok District to assist German Municipal Police and Security Police in clearing major and minor ghettos. The Trawniki men were instrumental in emptying the Lublin and L'viv ghettos in March–April 1942, and participated in at least one mass shooting of Jewish men, women, and children on the outskirts of Lublin in April.[85] Trawniki-trained guards were deployed on at least two (and probably three) occasions in the Warsaw Ghetto (June–September 1942, January 1943, and April–May 1943),[86] during the deportations from Częstochowa and other Radom District ghettos in September–October 1942, and during the uprising in the Białystok ghetto in August 1943.[87] Though generally commanded by the SSPF, supervised on the spot by the personnel of the KdS, and supported by local German municipal police or gendarmerie detachments, ghetto clearing operations were coordinated by Höfle and his small staff, supported by the violence, brutality, and increasing expertise of the Trawniki-trained guards, who cordoned off the ghettos and assisted Order Police and Jewish policemen in moving the Jews out of their apartments to train stations.[88] Trawniki-trained guards also carried out operations in smaller ghettos throughout District Lublin.[89]

The Trawniki men also guarded Operation *Reinhard* labor camps throughout Lublin District, including the Lipowa Lager and the Airstrip Camp in Lublin city and the labor camps at Trawniki, Poniatowa, Budzyń, and Kraśnik.[90] As Globocnik later wrote to Himmler's adjutant, the purpose of the this labor camp system was four-fold: (1) to relieve the burden of increased war production from the industrial plant of the Reich; (2) to release German workers for other purposes and to reduce the acute labor shortage in the Reich; (3) to relocate key and sensitive industries and plant damaged by or vulnerable to Allied bombing; and (4) to increase production through tighter supervision as well as to eliminate profit skimming in the war industry.[91] For a time in the winter of 1941–1942 and 1942–1943, Trawniki-trained units guarded the Prisoner of War Camp Lublin on the edge of the city, which officially became the Lublin Concentration Camp on February 15, 1943 (and which the Polish and Jewish prisoners called Majdanek).[92] Small detachments also guarded the estates in District Lublin slated to be future SS and Police bases, many of which engaged Jewish forced laborers.[93] Finally, Trawniki men guarded the collection sites for booty taken off the murdered Jews, including the *Bekleidungslager* in Lublin and a barrack established at Trawniki in the summer of 1942 to store the clothing of the Jews murdered during Operation *Reinhard.*[94]

Under Globocnik's leadership, the Trawniki-trained guards responded to needs in other regions. From November 1941, Trawniki men guarded the Treblinka Labor Camp under the leadership of the SSPF in Warsaw District.[95] From January 1942 to November 1943, a Trawniki-trained detachment guarded the notorious forced labor camp for Jews under the jurisdiction of the SSPF for Galicia District on Janowska Street in L'viv, and participated in the dreadful liquidations of Jewish workers there.[96] Both before and after the forced labor camp for Jews in Płaszów was incorporated into the WVHA concentration camp system, a Trawniki-trained detachment guarded the camp, first for the SSPF in Cracow and, later, as part of the SS Death's Head Battalion, for the WVHA. Trawniki-trained guards served the staff of the SSPF in Radom. One detachment was even sent to Germany to guard laborers at the Heinkel Works in Rostock; while another was sent in March 1943 to supplement the SS Death's Head Battalion at the Auschwitz Concentration Camp complex.[97]

The Operation *Reinhard* staff was responsible for the deaths of between 1.5 and 1.7 million Jews, and undetermined numbers of Gypsies, Poles and Soviet prisoners of war.[98] That the Trawniki men played a central role in Operation *Reinhard* is apparent from the awards and promotions received by the German officials who commanded them. Globocnik praised Streibel for commanding the Trawniki Training Camp "with the greatest discretion and understanding for the special leadership needs of this unit" and noted that the Trawniki men had "proved themselves in the best way . . . especially in the framework of the Jewish resettlement."[99] After a visit to Sobibor and Treblinka in February 1943, Himmler approved the promotion of several German SS and police officials involved in Operation *Reinhard*, including Wirth, Höfle, and killing center commandants Stangl, Hering, and Reichleitner.[100] Nor were the Trawniki men themselves neglected. In 1942, Wasil Chlopecki became eligible for family support benefits in part based on his "missions" in "the resettlement of the Jews." Fedor Jaworow received a service award for having "been especially deserving," in that for two years, "he belonged to the Special Detachments in Belzec, Sobibor, and Treblinka and conducted himself there to the greatest satisfaction." Trawniki man Alexej Milutin "belonged for a long time to the Special Detachment Treblinka and conducted himself well there."[101]

As necessary as the Trawniki-trained guards were to this "negative" aspect of German race and settlement policy, they were also deployed in the few efforts, limited by the worsening fortunes of war and by the brutality with which those efforts were carried out, to place German settlers in the areas designed by Himmler in July 1941 for German settlement, specifically in *Kreis* Zamość. Globocnik had been studying the issue since the autumn of 1940 and had recruited teams of young SS professionals—engineers, architects, agronomists, population experts, climatologists, etc.—to join the SS-*Mannschaftshaus* efforts to plan the future bases, prompting the commander of Security Police and SD (KdS) in Lublin to state after the war that it was "unique in the entire history of the occupation all of that that Globocnik did."[102]

During his visit to Lublin in July 1941, Himmler approved a Globocnik proposal that the city of Lublin and *Kreis* Zamość, where Globocnik claimed to have discovered 6,000 "polonized" Germans, form a link in a chain of proposed ethnic German settlements from the Baltic States to the ethnic German communities of Transylvania. Globocnik intended that this ring of settlements would "encircle" and "gradually strangle, economically and biologically, the remainder of the Polish nation [*verbleibende Polentum*] in the western border zone." After Himmler declared *Kreis* Zamość to be the "first region for German settlement in the Government General" on November 12, 1942, Globocnik initiated operation with the forcible removal of around 108,000 Poles and Ukrainians from 300 villages in *Kreise* Zamość, Hrubieszów, Biłgoraj, and Tomaszów-Lubelski; around 9,000 ethnic Germans from Bessarabia were the first ethnic Germans to replace the evacuees.[103] Supported by Trawniki-trained auxiliaries, SS and police authorities carried out the deportations between late November 1942 and March 1943 with such poor planning, chaotic haste, and unconscionable brutality that the operation created "war in the [Lublin] District."[104] District Governor Zörner, whom Globocnik had kept in the dark, argued with Governor General Frank's endorsement that both security and agricultural production would collapse if the SS did not halt the deportations.[105] Though Himmler instructed Frank that one should not "be over anxious about these intentions,"[106] Globocnik's population policy in Zamość undoubtedly contributed to his ouster in September 1943. In July 1943, with *Kreise* Zamość and Biłgoraj in total disarray, the Governor of District Lublin, Himmler's brother-in-law *SS-Gruppenführer* Richard Wendler, who had replaced Zörner in May, denounced the Zamość operation as a "spectacular failure . . . so that one can only speak now of a pigsty as a result of the movement of populations back and forth."[107] Under these circumstances and with Operation *Reinhard* virtually concluded, Himmler thought it prudent to transfer Globocnik from Lublin.

As in the case of the WVHA concentration camp commanders, who between 1942 and 1944 were required to act both "negatively"—eliminating dangerous enemies of the Reich—and "positively"—supplying the Reich with capable forced laborers—the German SS and police apparatus in the field was much more effective at murder and destruction than at production, construction and settlement. Jan Erik Schulte's analysis of proposed postwar SS settlements indicates that the planners envisioned significant space for prisoners and forced labor, indicating that both terror and racial selectivity were to be an integral part of SS rule in the East. Bases were to have space for ongoing racial evaluations and testing as well as RuSHA offices for approving future marriages. SS planning foresaw the existence of an SS and police base at each *Kreis* seat in the Reich Commissariat Ukraine, proposing some 20,000 German SS and police personnel for Ukraine alone. Even if Nazi exhortations to produce large families had truly been effective in the ranks of the SS and police,[108] the German nation could not, in a generation, produce enough potential SS and policemen to guarantee the protection of even some of the cities, let alone the rural areas. Given visions of border forts similar to idealizations of those in the U.S. "wild West" of the nineteenth century and the intention to periodically Germanize selected members of the "inferior" races (and to routinely kill others, perhaps at facilities such as Auschwitz and Majdanek) to augment the outposts of "white settlements" guarded in part by *askaris* in the German colonial tradition, SS planning, as Schulte has written, "was far removed from reality."[109]

The new order planned by the National Socialists in occupied Poland and points further east depended upon ruthless elimination of real and perceived enemies of Germany, conceived of in racial terms, and the settlement of the future core of an ever-expanding German-Germanic "racial group." From the beginning, the SS and police had the advantage among German agencies in the strength of their ideological concept and the devotion of personnel, financial and administrative resources to "resolving" these questions. Hence, Himmler's agencies took the lead in postwar "planning," both in Poland and the Soviet Union. As the experience in Lublin District of the Government General was to show, the German authorities lacked the manpower to effect the desired population changes without indigenous help. Given the practical and ideological importance of police work for maintaining security both in the present and in the long-term future and the leading role of the SS in both defining and preventatively eliminating collective enemies and determining the characteristics of racial acceptability, the SS and police needed and obtained the services of the indigenous populations. With the exception of the *Sonderdienst*, the SS alone was able to deploy the auxiliary units, at least in the Government General, to begin the implementation of the long-term goal of ethnic restructuring in the East through mass murder and resettlement. In District Lublin, Globocnik sought first to use the ethnic German *Selbstschutz* and the somewhat more diverse *Sonderdienst* as tools to establish SS supremacy in both security concerns and population control. With the attack on the Soviet Union, however, the National Socialist regime embarked on the murderous adventure that its leaders had conceived; Globocnik's apparatus assumed responsibility for the first permanent SS and police bases which would secure—by eliminating enemies, settling Germans, and selecting and breeding new Germans from the best indigenous "racial material"—that long-term expansion of German "racial stock" that Hitler deemed necessary for the nation's survival. Although the geography and the race-based ideology harked to the *Lebensraum* element in Nazi imperialism identified by Woodruff Smith, the facilities and the auxiliaries were more reminiscent of the *Weltpolitik* trend of brutal colonial exploitation.[110] With his Trawniki *askaris*, who, like their African namesakes, served the Germans until the evacuation of Poland in 1944–1945, Globocnik appeared for a time to have that reliable police auxiliary force to help Himmler realize his murderous vision for the occupied East. Due to military reverses and the sheer absence of reality checks in the planning process, the SS and police bases remained largely on paper; but the SS and police in the Government General succeeded dreadfully in eliminating Polish Jewry and annihilating approximately twenty percent of the 1939 Polish population. The result of German race and settlement policy in occupied Poland was not, however, the establishment of one thousand years of German rule, but the elimination of a thousand-year German cultural presence in Poland.

# Notes

1. Gerhard L. Weinberg, *The Foreign Policy of Hitler's Germany: Starting World War II, 1937–1939* (Chicago, 1980), p. 664.

2. German dependence on auxiliaries in other regions they occupied during World War II had been amply demonstrated. For Lithuania, see Michael MacQueen, "Nazi Policy Towards the Jews in the *Reichskommissariat Ostland*, June-December 1941: From White Terror to Holocaust in Lithuania," in *Bitter Legacy: Confronting the Holocaust in the USSR*, ed. Zvi Gitelman (Bloomington, 1997), pp. 91–103; and Knut Stang, "Kollaboration und Völkermord: Das Rollkommando Hamann und die Vernichtung der litauischen Juden," in *Die Gestapo im zweiten Weltkrieg: "Heimatfront" und besetztes Europa*, edited by Gerhard Paul and Klaus-Michael Mallmann (Darmstadt, 2000), pp. 464–480. For Estonia and Belarus, see Ruth Bettina Birn, "Collaboration with Nazi Germany in Eastern Europe: The Case of the Estonian Security Police," *Contemporary European History*, vol. 10, no. 2 (2001), pp. 181–198; and Martin Dean, *Collaboration in the Holocaust: Crimes of the Local Police in Belorussia and Ukraine* (London, 2000). More generally, see Richard Breitman, "Himmler's Police Auxiliaries in the Occupied Soviet Territories," *Simon Wiesenthal Center Annual*, vol. 7 (1990), pp. 23–39. The role of auxiliaries in Latvia, Serbia and Greece requires more research. For Latvia, see the unsatisfying volume by Andrew Ezergailis, *The Holocaust in Latvia, 1941–1944: The Missing Center* (Riga, 1996). The German occupation regimes in Serbia and Greece are handled by Walter Manoschek, *"Serbien ist 'judenfrei'": Militärische Besatzungspolitik und Judenvernichtung in Serbien 1941/42* (Munich, 1993); and Mark Mazower, *Inside Hitler's Greece: The Experience of Occupation, 1941–1944* (New Haven, 1993).

3. Wolfgang Wippermann, *Der"Deutsche Drang nach Osten": Ideologie und Wirklichkeit eines poltischen Schlagwortes* (Darmstadt, 1981), p. 41. Wippermann dates the earliest such writings from the decade before the 1848 revolutions. For the best introduction to these issues, see still Günther Stökl, *Osteuropa und die Deutschen: Geschichter und Gegenwart einer spannungsreichen Nachbarschaft* (Munich, 1970), pp. 33–46, 59–60. For the political spin put on these late medieval settlements by nineteenth century German nationalists, see Wippermann, *Der "Deutsche Drang,"* pp. 9, 29, 38–46.

4. Woodruff D. Smith, *The German Colonial Empire* (Chapel Hill, 1978), pp. 17–19; Woodruff D. Smith, *The Ideological Origins of Nazi Imperialism* (Oxford, 1986), pp. 21–40, 52–111. For the establishment of German colonies in Africa and the Pacific, see Smith, *Colonial Empire*, pp. 51–115; and the introduction in Sara Friedrichsmeyer et al., eds., *The Imperialist Imagination: German Colonialism and its Legacy* (Ann Arbor, 1999), pp. 10–18.

5. Wippermann, *"Deutsche Drang,"* p. 9. See also pp. 85–116, for late-nineteenth-century German perspectives.

6. Adolf Hitler, *Mein Kampf,* trans. Ralph Manheim (Boston, 1943), p. 140.

7. Himmler expressed an early fascination with the East in a November 1921 entry in his diary, written on the evening after he heard a speech from *Freikorps* commander Ernst Rüdiger von der Goltz in the Munich Löwenbräukeller. Richard Breitman, *The Architect of Genocide: Himmler and the Final Solution* (New York, 1991), pp. 15–16.

8. For Himmler's impact on the early SS, see Robert Lewis Koehl, *The Black Corps: The Structure and Power Struggles of the Nazi SS* (Madison, 1983), pp. 47–51.

9. See Woodruff D. Smith, *The German Colonial Empire* (Chapel Hill, 1978), pp. 222–224; Juhani Koponen, *Development for Exploitation: German Colonial Policies in Mainland Tanzania, 1884–1914* (Helsinki, 1994), pp. 133–134, 568–569.

10. Smith, *Colonial Empire*, pp. 222–224. The German command staff made up about 10 percent of the entire *askari* force. For example, in 1904–1905, 218 German personnel commanded and administrated 2,140 *askaris*. See Koponen, *Exploitation*, pp. 133–134, 569.

11. For Hitler's consistent musings on the German settlement in this *Lebensraum*, see Hitler, *Mein Kampf*, pp. 641–664; *Hitler's Secret Book*, translated by Salvator Attanasio (New York, 1961), pp. 74, 78, 139, 145; *Hitler's Secret Conversations*, introduction by H. R. Trevor-Roper (New York, 1953), pp. 4–5, 13–14, 56–57. With regard to Poland as a satellite of Nazi Germany, there is some debate as to whether Hitler ever really intended to work with Warsaw. See Klaus Hildebrand, *The Foreign Policy of the Third Reich* (Berkeley, 1973), pp. 33, 82; Weinberg, *Foreign Policy*, pp. 497–499, 503–504; Charles Bloch, *Das Dritte Reich und die Welt* (Paderborn, 1993), pp. 250–251. In conversations on the evenings of July 27, 1941 and October 17, 1941, Hitler explicitly referred to the non-German "natives" in regions destined for German settlement as "Indians" and "Redskins."

12. In the late 1920s, Hitler had decried nineteenth-century Wilhelmine policy, arguing that Germany should not make Germans out of Poles, but rather should "seal off" these "alien racial elements" or remove them in order to prevent further "corruption" of German blood." See Hitler, *Secret Book*, pp. 47–48; Alexander B. Rossino, *Hitler Strikes Poland: Blitzkrieg, Ideology, and Atrocity* (Lawrence, 2003), pp. 3–4.

13. "Besprechung des Führers mit Chef OKW über die künftige Gestaltung der polnischen Verhältnisse zu Deutschland (Vom 17.10.1939, abds.)," October 20, 1939, 864-PS, International Military Tribunal, *Trial of the Major War Criminals*, vol. 26 (Nuremberg, 1947), pp. 378–379 (hereafter cited as IMT, 26).

14. Martin Broszat, *Nationalsozialistische Polenpolitik, 1939–1945* (Frankfurt am Main, 1965), pp. 41–51, 84–98; Götz Aly, *"Endlösung": Völkerverschiebung und der Mord an den europäischen Juden* (Frankfurt/Main, 1995), 59–135; Czesław Madajczyk, *Die Okkupationspolitik Nazideutschlands in Polen, 1939–1945* (Berlin, 1987), pp. 356–364. Between 1939 and the spring of 1941, German authorities deported between 325,000 and 365,000 non-Jewish Poles and approximately 100,000 Polish Jews from the annexed territories into the Government General. For German settlement planning for the annexed territories, see Michael A. Hartenstein, "Neue Dorflandschaften: National-sozialistische Siedlungsplanung in den "eingegliederten Ostgebieten' 1939 bis 1944," Ph.D. dissertation, Reinisch Friedrich-Wilhelms-Universität Bonn (Berlin, 1998). For decrees requiring forced labor, see "Verordnung über die Einführung der Arbeitspflicht für die polnische Bevölkerung des Generalgouvernements," October 26, 1939, *Verordnungsblatt des Generalgouverneurs für die besetzten polnische Gebiete* (after January 1941, *Verordnungsblatt für das Generalgouvernement*—hereafter VOBl. GG), no. 1, October 26, 1939, pp. 5–6; "Verordnung über die Einführung des Arbeitszwangs für die jüdische Bevölkerung des Generalgouvernements," ibid., October 26, 1939, p. 6.

15. See the original document, published in Helmut Krausnick, "Denkschrift Himmlers über die Behandlung der Fremdvölkischen im Osten (Mai 1940)," *Vierteljahrshefte für Zeitgeschichte* 5, no. 1, (January 1957), 194–198. See also Koehl, *RKFDV*, 75.

16. Peter R. Black, "Rehearsal for 'Reinhard'? Odilo Globocnik and the Lublin *Selbstschutz*," *Central European History*, 25, no. 2 (1992), 204–226, here p. 204. See also Christopher R. Browning, "Nazi Resettlement Policy and the Search for a Solution to the Jewish

Question, 1939–1941," *German Studies Review* 9, no. 3 (1986), 501; Robert Lewis Koehl, *RKFDV: German Resettlement and Population Policy, 1939–1945: A History of the Reich Commission for the Strengthening of Germandom* (Cambridge, MA, 1957), pp. 49–70; Hans Mommsen, "Umvolkungspläne des Nationalsozialismus und das Holocaust," in Helge Grabitz, Klaus Bästlein, and Johannes Tuchel, eds., *Die Normalität des Verbrechens: Bilanz und Perspektiven der Forschung zu den nationalsozialistischen Gewaltverbrechen* (Berlin, 1994), pp. 68–84. For pre-war SS forays into settlement planning with the Czech Land Office in Prague in 1939 and the proposed resettlement of the Germans of the South Tyrol, see Koehl, *RKFDV*, pp. 45–46. Generally on the leadership of the SS in settlement planning and authorization, see Jan Erik Schulte, *Zwangsarbeit und Vernichtung: Das Wirtschaftsimperium der SS. Oswald Pohl und das SS-Wirtschafts-Verwaltungshauptamt, 1933–1945* (Paderborn, 2001), p. 242; Rolf-Dieter Müller, *Hitlers Ostkrieg und die deutsche Siedlungspolitik: Die Zusammenarbeit von Wehrmacht, Wirtschaft und SS* (Frankfurt am Main, 1991), p. 86.

17. For the formation and role of the RSHA, see Michael Wildt, *Generation des Unbedingten: Das Führungskorps des Reichssicherheitshauptamtes* (Hamburg, 2002), especially pp. 209–276, 419–499, 654–679. See also Jens Banach, *Heydrichs Elite: Das Führerkorps der Sicherheitspolizei und des SD, 1936–1945* (Paderborn, 1998), and the two works by George C. Browder: *Foundations of the Nazi Police State: The Formation of Sipo and SD* (Lexington, 1990) and *Hitler's Enforcers: The Gestapo and the SS Security Service in the Nazi Revolution* (Oxford, 1996). On the Gestapo, see the two volumes of essays edited by Gerhard Paul and Klaus-Michael Mallmann: *Die Gestapo: Mythos und Realität* (Darmstadt, 1995), and *Gestapo im Zweiten Weltkrieg*. For the Criminal Police, see Patrick Wagner, *Volksgemeinschaft ohne Verbrecher: Konzeptionen und Praxis der Kriminalpolizei in der Zeit der Weimarer Republik und des Nationalsozialismus* (Hamburg, 1996). The RSHA also housed the immigration and naturalization agency of the Third Reich, since its political clearances (after a racial examination found suitable blood) ultimately permitted the issuance of Reich citizenship. See Koehl, *RKFDV*, pp. 54–55, 104–107; Valdis O. Lumens, *Himmler's Auxiliaries: The Volksdeutsche Mittelstelle and the German National Minorities of Europe, 1933–1945* (Chapel Hill, 1993), pp. 189–192.

18. See Hans-Joachim Neufeldt, Jürgen Huck, and Georg Tessin, *Zur Geschichte der Ordnungspolizei, 1936–1945* (Koblenz, 1957); Friedrich Wilhelm, *Die Polizei im NS-Staat. Die Geschichte ihrer Organisation im Überblick* (Paderborn, 1997); Florian Dierl, "Das Hauptamt Ordnungspolizei 1936 bis 1945: Führungsspitze und die Befehlshaber in den Wehrkreisen," in Alfons Kenkmann and Christoph Spieker, eds., *Im Auftrag: Polizei, Verwaltung und Verantwortung* (Essen, 2001), pp. 159–175.

19 For a history of the RuSHA, see Isabel Heinemann, *"Rasse, Siedlung, deutsches Blut": Die Rasse- und Siedlungshauptamt der SS und die rassenpolitische Neuordnung Europas* (Göttingen, 2003).

20. For the RKFDV, see Koehl, *RKFDV*.

21. On the WVHA, see Schulte, *Zwangsarbeit*, particularly pp. 239–331.

22. On the HSSPFs and the regional structure of the SS, see Ruth Bettina Birn, *Die Höheren SS- und Polizeiführer: Himmlers Vertreter im Reich und in den besetzten Gebieten* (Düsseldorf, 1986).

23. Schulte, *Zwangsarbeit*, p. 246. There is no scholarly biography of Globocnik as yet. See Peter R. Black, "Odilo Globocnik—Himmlers Vorposten im Osten," in *Die Braune Elite 2: 21 weitere biographische Skizzen*, Ronald M. Smelser, Enrico Syring, and Rainer Zitelmann, eds. (Darmstadt, 1993), pp. 103–115. For Globocnik's activity in Lublin, see Zygmunt Mańkowski, *Między Wisłą a Bugiem, 1939–1944* (Lublin, 1978); Bogdan Mu-

sial, *Deutsche Zivilverwaltung und Judenverfolgung im Generalgouvernement: Ein Fallstudie zum Distrikt Lublin 1939–1944* (Wiesbaden, 1999), pp. 200–208.

24. See in particular the works of Dieter Pohl, *Von der "Judenpolitik" zum Judenmord: Der Distrikt Lublin des Generalgouvernements, 1939–1944* (Frankfurt am Main, 1993); and Bogdan Musial, *Zivilverwaltung*. On the so-called reservation for Jews in District Lublin, see Browning, "Resettlement Policy," pp. 3–12; Christopher Browning, *Nazi Policy, Jewish Workers, German Killers* (Cambridge, 2000), pp. 7–19; Peter Longerich, *Politik der Vernichtung: Ein Gesamtdarstellung der nationalsozialistischen Judenverfolgung* (Munich, 1998), pp. 249–272; Seev Goshen, "Eichmann und die Nisko-Aktion im Oktober 1939: Ein Fallstudie zur NS-Judenpolitik in der letzten Etappe vor der Entlösung," *Vierteljahrshefte für Zeitgeschichte* 29, no. 1 (January 1981), 74–96.

25. Jews and Poles constituted 92 percent of the population of the Government General in 1940, before the addition of Galicia brought in significant numbers of Ukrainians. See "Die Unterabteilung Bevölkerungswesen und Fürsorge: Trägerin der volkspolitischen Arbeit im Generalgouvernement" (hereafter: "Unterabteilung . . .,"), n.d. [internal evidence indicates late 1941], proceedings against Josef Bühler (hereafter: Bühler Trial), NTN 282, p. 52, Archive of the Główna Komisja Badania Przeciwko Narodowi Polskiemu, Warsaw (hereafter: AKG); office of the Governor General, "Bericht über die Aufbau im Generalgouvernement bis 1. Juli 1940," July 1940, ibid., NTN 277, pp. 17–18 (hereafter referred to as: "Bericht").

26. Prior to the German invasion, approximately 2 million Jews resided on what would become the territory of the Government General, including Galicia, which was occupied by the Soviet Union between 1939 and 1941. Approximately 300,000 Jews fled or were killed during the military campaign, leaving between 1.1 and 1.2 million Jews in the Government General at the end of 1939. To this must be added approximately 100,000 Jews deported from the annexed territories and from the Reich as well as 540,000 Jews residing in Galicia in the summer of 1941. See Frank Goleczewski, "Polen, " in Wolfgang Benz, ed., *Dimensionen des Völkermords: Die Zahl der jüdischen Opfer des Nationalsozialismus* (Munich, 1991), pp. 418–419, 426; Dieter Pohl, *Nationalsozialistischen Judenverfolgung in Ostgalizien, 1941–1944: Organisation und Durchführung eines staatlichen Massenverbrechens* (Munich, 1997), pp. 43–45. In January 1942, at the Wannsee Conference, Heydrich cited a figure of 2,284,000 Jews residing in the Government General. Excerpt from minutes of the Wannsee Conference, January 20, 1942, Document NG-2586, reproduced as Document No. 143 in T. Berenstein et al., eds., *Eksterminacja Żydów na ziemiach polskich w okresie okupacji hitlerowskiej: Zbiór dokumentów* (Warsaw, 1957), pp. 268–272.

27. Musial, *Zivilverwaltung*, pp. 102–103. See also Pohl, *Judenmord*, p. 63.

28. Dieter Pohl, *Judenmord*, pp. 38–39. In 1942, Lublin District actually employed around 1,000 Reich German and ethnic German civilian employees, excluding employees of central agencies such as the *Ostbahn*, the Reich Postal Service, and the German Army. Musial, *Zivilverwaltung*, p. 87.

29. Secret Decree of Heydrich to Einsatzgruppen commanders, September 21, 1939, RG-242, T-501/230/18-23, National Archives and Records Administration, College Park (hereafter: NARA). On the activities of the Einsatzgruppen in Poland, see Rossino, *Hitler Strikes Poland*, pp. 29–57, 88–120.

30. "Verordnung über die Einsetzung von Jüdenräten," VOBl.GG, November 28, 1939, no. 9, December 6, 1939, pp. 72–73, LC.

31. In 1940, 24,038 ethnic Germans resided in District Lublin (1.018 percent of the population). See "Bericht...," July 1940, Bühler Trial, NTN 277, pp. 17–18, AGK.

32. Black, "Rehearsal," pp. 204–226.

33. "Working Conference on April 23, 1940," Service Diary of Governor General Hans Frank

(hereafter: Frank Diary), vol. 9, pp. 40–41, RG-238, 2233-PS, NARA. Extensive excerpts from the Service Diary are available in Werner Präg and Wolfgang Jacobmeyer, eds., *Das Diensttagebuch des deutschen Generalgouverneurs in Polen, 1939–1945* (Stuttgart, 1975). On Himmler's orders regarding the establishment of the *Selbstschutz* in Poland, see circular of the RFSS and Chief of German Police [signed Daluege], "Vorläufige Richtlinien für die Organisation des Selbstschutzes in Polen," October 7, 1939, file Polizei-Batallion 104, 314, sygn. 8, pp. 1–4, Wojewódzkie Archiwum Państwowe, Lublin (hereafter cited as: WAPL); order of Himmler, "Stellenbesetzung der SS- und Polizei im Generalgouvernement," November 1, 1939, K. Hintze SS officer file, A3343/SSO, Reel 100A, frame 648, NARA. For the formation of the *Selbstschutz* in general, see Christian Jansen and Arno Weckbecker, *Der"Volksdeutsche Selbstschutz" in Polen, 1939/1940* (Munich, 1992), passim; Hans Umbreit, *Deutsche Militärverwaltungen 1938/39: Die militärische Besetzung der Tschechoslowakei und Polens* (Stuttgart, 1977), pp. 176–181; Broszat, *Polenpolitik*, pp. 62–64.

34. Krüger to Gunst, November 14, 1939, W. Gunst SS officer file, A3343/SSO, Reel 043A, frame 321, NARA; judgment in proceedings against Friedrich Paulus, May 26, 1977, p. 6, file 4 Ks 1/74, State Prosecutor's Office in Frankfurt am Main (hereafter: Paulus Proceedings, StA Frankfurt). An SS officer, Paulus is not to be confused with his unrelated namesake, Field Marshal Friedrich Paulus, who commanded the German 6th Army at Stalingrad.

35. Each District (*Distrikt*) of the Government General was subdivided into smaller districts, called *Kreise*. The local administrative unit was called the *Kreishauptmannschaft* and the chief administrator was known as the *Kreishauptmann*. For the larger cities (e.g., Lublin and Chełm), the administrative unit was known as the *Stadthauptmannschaft* and the administrator as the *Stadthauptmann*. Since both *Kreis* and *Distrikt* translate as "district" but cannot be used interchangeably and since the term "captaincy" has a misleading military connotation in English, I will, to avoid confusion, refer to these positions and administrations by their German terms.

36. "Wydatki obozu pracy," December 7, 1939, file Judenrat, sygn. 43, p. 1, WAPL; "Alhaltungskosten des Arbeitslagers" [*sic*], December 19, 1939, ibid., p. 9; Eduard Dziadosz and Józef Marszałek, "Więzienia i obozy w dystrykcie lubelskim w latach 1939–1944," *Zeszyty Majdanka* 3 (1969), 81; Schulte, *Zwangsarbeit*, p. 248. On responsibility of the Labor Offices, see Musial, *Zivilverwaltung*, p. 116.

37. [Orts-] Kommandantur [I/524] to Department I [Deployment Security], "Auszug aus der Niederschrift von der Besprechung mit Polizei-Kommandeuren beim H.[eeres] K.[ommando]s XXXII am 8.12.1939," December 10, 1939, file Ortskommandantur I/524, sygn. 31, pp. 378–379, WAPL; Globocnik to Chief, District Lublin, February 13, 1940, file Gouverneur, Distrikt Lublin, sygn. 891, p. 10, WAPL.

38. Breitman, *Architect*, p. 96.

39. On Germany's labor needs, see Ulrich Herbert, *Fremdarbeiter: Politik und Praxis des "Ausländer-Einsatzes" in der Kriegswirtschaft des Dritten Reiches* (Berlin, 1985), pp. 67–80. On the *Selbstschutz* role, see Globocnik to Zörner, March 6, 1940, file Gouverneur, Distrikt Lublin, sygn. 755, pp. 4–5, WAPL; Natter to Jache, April 1, 1940, ibid., pp. 6–7; memorandum of Jache, April 8, 1940, ibid., sygn. 759, p. 138; and Dziadosz and Marszałek, "Więzienia," pp. 99, 101.

40. "Protokoll über die am 22.4.40 beim SS- und Polizeiführer stattgefundene Besprechung betreffend den Einsatz jüdischer Zwangsarbeiter," signed Hofbauer, no date, file Gouverneur, District Lublin, sygn. 891, p. 90–94, WAPL; service evaluation for Willi Stemmler, August 10, 1940, W. Stemmler SS officer file, A3343/SSO, Reel 156B, frames 242–243, NARA. When the director of the Biała-Podlaska labor office learned of the impending

dissolution of the *Selbstschutz*, he queried his superiors in Lublin as to "how to guarantee in the future that the Jews would be guarded and selected for forced labor." See Labor Office, Biała-Podlaska to Labor Department, Lublin, July 18, 1940, file Gouverneur, District Lublin, sygn. 746, pp. 41–43, WAPL.

41. Recommendations for War Meritorious Service Cross with Swords, signed Globocnik, November 30, 1940, Zbiór wniosków na odznaczenia/file SSPF Lublin, VII/1, pp. 9–17, AGK; Globocnik to Higher SS and Police Leader East, August 13, 1940, H. Dolp SS officer file, RG-242, A3343/SSO, Reel 160, frame 21. NARA; report of Kreishauptmann Zamość in "Lageberichte der Kreis- und Stadthauptleute für den Monat Mai 1940," June 17, 1940, Bühler Trial, NTN 269, p. 148, AGK; Black, "Rehearsal," p. 215. The labor camp site was near the site of the later killing center at Bełzec.

42. Cable from BdO Cracow [signed Major Ragger] to Government General, Office of Population and Welfare, May 18, 1940, file Gouverneur, District Lublin, sygn. 203, p. 4, WAPL; memorandum of Damrau, no date [July 18 or July 19, 1940], file Gouverneur, District Lublin, sygn. 63, p. 26, WAPL.

43. For further details on camps and conditions, see Black, "Rehearsal," pp. 215–218; Christopher R. Browning, "Nazi Germany's Initial Attempt to Exploit Jewish Labor in the General Government: The Early Jewish Work Camps, 1940–1941," in Grabitz/Bästlein/Tuchel, *Normalität*, pp. 171–186. Dieter Pohl has identified 76 forced labor camps for Jews located in Lublin District, in which between 50,000 and 70,000 Jews were incarcerated in summer/autumn 1940. See Dieter Pohl, "Die grossen Zwangsarbeitslager der SS- und Polizeiführer für Juden im Generalgouvernement 1942–1945," in Ulrich Herbert, Karin Orth, and Christoph Dieckmann, eds., *Die Nationalsozialistischen Konzentrationslager: Entwicklung und Strutkur* (Frankfurt am Main, 2002), pp. 416–417.

44. Interrogation of Friedrich Sch., March 1, 1966, Paulus Proceedings, vol. 4, pp. 643–644, StA Frankfurt; Musial, *Zivilverwaltung*, p. 129.

45. Chana Zylbersztayn to SS Selbstschutz Command, May 30, 1940, file Judenrat, sygn. 20, p. 80, WAPL.

46. For details on the Józefów and Radawiec killings, see Black, "Rehearsal," pp. 219–222; Mańkowski, *Między*, p. 113.

47. Frank Diary, entry for March 16, 1940, vol. 3, pp. 207–214, NARA; "Verordnung über die Einrichtung eines Sonderdienstes," signed Frank, May 6, 1940, VOBl. GG, May 10, 1940, no. 38, 1940 (Part I), p. 186, LC; report of the Inspectorate of the Sonderdienst [signed Hammerle], September 24, 1941, Bühler Trial, NTN 283, pp. 14–26, AGK. For more detail on the Sonderdienst, see Peter R. Black, "Indigenous Collaboration in the Government General: The Case of the *Sonderdienst*," in Pieter Judson and Marsha Rozenblit, eds., *Constructing Nationalities in East Central Europe* (New York, 2004).

48. The literature on the *Sonderdienst* remains minimal. In addition to Black, "Sonderdienst," see Martin Broszat, "Der 'Sonderdienst' im Generalgouvernement," in *Gutachten des Instituts für Zeitgeschichte*, vol. 1 (Munich, 1958), pp. 408–410. For an example of Globocnik's continued influence, see his signature on the recommendation for commendation for Emil Komarek, who served in the auxiliary police in Radom City, in the Warsaw Selbstschutz and later in the *Sonderdienst* for Kreis Radom (and hence never served in Lublin District). SSPF Lublin, List of Recommendations for the Award of the War Meritorious Service Cross, 2nd Class with Swords, no date [November or December 1940], Zbiór wniosków na odznaczenia/File SSPF Lublin, 1940–1944, VII/1, pp. 25–26, AGK.

49. "Polizeisitzung, 30. Mai, 1940,"*Diensttagebuch*, p. 217; Frank Diary, entry for June 27, 1940, ibid., p. 246; Frank Diary, entry for July 10, 1940, ibid., p. 248; "Besprechungspunkte für den Reichsführer-SS mit Dr. Frank," no date [probably July 1940], file Fa-74/Krüger, Institute für Zeitgeschichte, Munich. On the official date of dissolution, see

Service Evaluation, August 31, 1940, G. Stolle SS officer file, RG-242, Reel 163B, frames 673–674, NARA; order of Himmler, August 9, 1941, RG-242, T-175/150/2679287, NARA.

50. Many came from families that had been deported to Siberia by the tsarist government during the First World War; nearly 10 percent of the recruits were actually born in Siberia. See calculations based on a sample of 281 German immigration files of Lublin *Selbstschutz* recruits available in the *Einwandererzentrale* personnel files, RG 242, NARA. Black, "Rehearsal," pp. 209–210.

51. For the ethnic Germans in the Soviet Union, see Fleischauer, *Sowjetunion;* Meir Buchsweiler, *Volksdeutche in der Ukraine am Vorabend und Beginn des Zweiten Weltkrieges—Ein Fall doppelterLoyalität?* (Gehrlingen, 1984). For the ethnic Germans of western Poland, see Jansen and Weckbecker, *Selbstschutz,* passim.; and Umbreit, *Militärverwaltungen,* pp. 200–204.

52. Black, "Rehearsal," pp. 210, 225.

53. Ibid., p. 208.

54. Frank Diary, entries of December 13 and December 14, 1940, vol. 6, pp. 1127, 1128; interrogation of Hermann Hammerle, March 29, 1963, Paulus Proceedings, vol. 2, p. 225, StA Frankfurt; interrogation of J.O., February 26, 1964, ibid., p. 339.

55. Report of the Inspection of the Sonderdienst [signed Hammerle], September 24, 1941, Bühler Trial, NTN 283, pp. 14–26, AGK; Frank Diary, entries for March 29, 1941 and April 8, 1941, vol. 10, pp. 172, 255. On continued *Sonderdienst* dependence on SS and police personnel, see Office of the Government General, "Bericht . . . ," July 1940, Bühler Trial, NTN 277, p. 87, AGK; interrogation of Karl Streibel, October 16, 1962, Paulus Proceedings, vol. 2, pp. 171–172, StA Frankfurt.

56. *Kreishauptmann* Siedłce to Office, Governor General, July 9, 1940, Bühler Trial, NTN 273, 157, AGK.

57. Frank Diary, December 14, 1940, vol. 6, p. 1128.

58. "The *Sonderdienst*: The University of Ethnic German Consciousness in the Government General," in *Mitteilungsblatt für den Sonderdienst, Hilfspolizei im Generalgouvernement* (hereafter: *Mitteilungsblatt*), no. 6, 1943, p. 4, National Library in Warsaw (hereafter NLW); "The *Sonderdienst* as the Primary School of Ethnic German Men," *Mitteilungsblatt,* no. 7, 1943, p. 4, NLW.

59. "Education in the *Sonderdienst,*" *Sonderdienst GG,* 1942 (May 1942), pp. 5–6, NLW; "Adolf Hitler: Life, Work, and Struggle," *Sonderdienst GG,* 1942, no. 2 (June), p. 16, NLW; "Physical Education: On Military Education in the *Sonderdienst,*" *Sonderdienst GG,* 1942, no. 4, (August), p. 61, NLW; "Germany's Right to Lebensraum," ibid., no. 3 (July), p. 36; "The Battle for Europe," pt. 1, *Sonderdienst GG,* 1942, no. 4 (August), pp. 56–57, NLW. For more discussion of anti-Semitic themes in the *Sonderdienst* newsletter, see Black, "Sonderdienst."

60. For involvement of the *Sonderdienst* personnel in carrying out the Warsaw ghetto deportations in summer 1942, the shooting operations in Galicia in spring 1943, and in deportations from Lublin district, see circular of SSPF Warsaw [signed von Sammern-Frankenegg] to *Kreishauptmänner* in Warsaw District, March 13, 1943, document no. 275, in Tatiana Berenstein et al., *Faschismus—Getto—Massenmord: Dokumentation über Ausrottung und Widerstand der Juden in Polen während des zweiten Weltkrieges* (Berlin, 1961), p. 352; report of SSPF Galizien [signed Katzmann] to HSSPF Ost [Krüger], "Lösung der Judenfrage in Galizien," June 30, 1943, L-18, IMT, XXXVII, pp. 401, 404; Musial, *Zivilverwaltung,* pp. 250–251, 253, 259–260, 291, 309, 335; and Black, "Sonderdienst."

61. In October 1941, Reich minister for the occupied eastern territories Alfred Rosenberg expressed interest in the *Sonderdienst* as an institution with potential for the occupied

Soviet territories. See memorandum of October 14, 1941, appendix to Frank Diary, entry for October 13, 1941, XIII, p. 932. Apparently there was an unconfirmed flicker of interest from the civilian Reich Commissar in Ukraine, Erich Koch, to have a civilian-administrative executive unit at his disposal. Memorandum of RSHA IV D to chief, Amt IV, RSHA, and Chief of Security Police and SD, January 15, 1942, R 43 II/1341b, Bundesarchiv, Berlin. In the summer of 1944, the *Wehrmacht* absorbed the *Sonderdienst*. The events can be followed in Black, "Sonderdienst."

62. The actual content of Heydrich's submission is unknown. For two differing opinions as to the specifics of this solution, see Breitman, *Architect*, pp. 151–162; and Longerich, *Vernichtung*, pp. 285–292.

63. Unsigned and undated report on the Construction of SS and Police Bases [internal evidence indicates authorship in the spring of 1941], O. Globocnik SS officer file, RG-242, A3343/SSO, Reel 016A, frames 989–996, NARA; "Aktenvermerk über die Besprechung mit dem Reichsführer SS am 26.10.40 in Krakau," signed Globocnik, November 5, 1940, RG SSPF Lublin, file CSW 891/6, pp. 16–17, AGK.

64. Michael Esch, "Die Forschungsstelle für 'Ostunterkünfte' in Lublin," *1999*, vol. 11, no. 2 (1996), pp. 62–96, here p. 62.

65. "Erlaß des Führers über die polizeiliche Sicherung in den neu besetzten Ostgebieten" [signed Hitler, Keitel, and Lammers], July 17, 1941, RG-242, T-454/100/680, NARA; Himmler to Globocnik, July 17, 1941, O. Globocnik SS officer file, RG-242, A3343/SSO, Reel 016A, frame 961, NARA. In this capacity, Globocnik was subordinate not to Krüger, who was his superior as HSSPF, but to the Order Police chief Daluege in Berlin, a status that effectively nullified the efforts of either authority to control him.

66. Having given these orders orally on July 20, 1941, Himmler signed written notations of their content on the next day. Two memoranda signed by Himmler, July 21, 1941, O. Globocnik SS officer file, RG-242, A3343/SSO, Reel 016A, frames 1058–1059, 1163–1164, NARA; Peter Witte et al., eds., *Der Dienstkalender Heinrich Himmlers, 1941/42* (Hamburg, 1999), entries for July 20–21, 1941, p. 186 and ftn. 17; Broszat, *Polenpolitik*, p. 165; Schulte, *Zwangsarbeit*, pp. 262–263; and Elizabeth B. White, "Majdanek: Cornerstone of Himmler's SS Empire in the East," *Simon Wiesenthal Center Annual* 7 (1990), 3–21, here pp. 4–5.

67. In October 1940, Himmler agreed to provide a sum of RM 5000 to establish an *SS-Mannschaftshaus*, which would be tasked with "conducting research into all basic issues in the District [Lublin] and the mission [to identify German blood] and furthermore for the intellectual stimulation of our SS men." The term literally translates as "men's house," but in this context meant a collection of academically trained SS intellectuals who concerned themselves with future planning and research geared to that effect. Three months later, in February 1941, Globocnik and two members of his staff met with the *Stadthauptmann* of Lublin City, Fritz Sauermann, who suggested the establishment of a "Research Institute for the East" with the help of the most "active, intellectual groups" stationed in Lublin. That Hanelt and his staff took over the Research Institute is clear from an undated memorandum of Hanelt's describing its proposed research sections. See "Aktenvermerk über die Besprechung mit dem Reichsführer SS am 26.10.40 in Krakau," signed Globocnik, November 5, 1940, CA MSW 891/6, pp. 16–17, AGK; Memorandum regarding a discussion between Globocnik and Sauermann on February 3, 1941, no date, ibid., pp. 14–15; "Forschungsstelle Lublin," signed Hanelt, n.d., ibid. pp. 4–6. See also Esch, "Forschungsstelle."

68. Memorandum signed by Hanelt for Globocnik, August 9, 1941, CA MSW 891/6, p. 11, AGK, copy in RG 15.027, SSPF Lublin, Reel 2, Archive of the United States Holocaust Memorial Museum (hereafter USHMM) and published without the date in Esch,

"Forschungsstelle," pp. 68–69. Hanelt's duties were spelled out in the following way: "Planung und wissenschaftlicher Einsatz mit ständigem Vertreter Brigadeführers [i.e., Globocnik] (SS-Obersturmführer Hanelt) hat den Gesamtplan der SS- und Polizeistützpunkte, die Judenbereinigung, den wissenschaftlichen Einsatz im Rahmen des SS-Mannschaftshauses theoretisch zu erarbeiten."

69. Chief of the Order Police [signed Daluege] to HSSPFs in the Occupied USSR and Globocnik, August 5, 1941, and September 3, 1941, fond 1323, opis 1, delo 50, *Gosudarstvennyy Voennyy Arkhiv Rossiyskoy Federatsii* (State Military Archives of the Russian Federation; hereafter: 1323/1/50, RGVA), copy in RG-11.001M.15, Reel 80, USHMM.

70. Letter from Section Population Matters and Welfare [initialed by Türk] to Department Internal Administration, District Lublin with attached "Bericht über die Besichtigung des Auffanglagers in Trawnicki [*sic*]," July 9, 1941, Record Group Persecution in the Government General, Ordner 30, pp. 209, 210a, Bundesarchiv-Zentral Stelle der Landesjustizverwaltungen zur Aufklärung nationalsozialistischen Verbrechen, Ludwigsburg (hereafter: BA-ZdL).

71. See p. 279 above. For the official name, see Service Obligation, October 23, 1941, Eduard Chrupowitsch Trawniki Personnel File (hereafter: E. Chrupowitsch TPF), Trial of Edvard Khlopetskij, Case 6105, Archival No. 11043, p. 130, *Derzhavnyy Arkhiv Sluzhby Bezpeky Ukrainy* (State Archive of the Ukrainian Security Service), L'viv (hereafter: Khlopetskij Trial, 6105/11043, p. 130, ASBU L'viv); interrogation of Friedrich F., March 4, 1969, Proceedings against Karl Streibel, file 147 Js 43/69, vol. 81, p. 15476, State Prosecutor's Office in Hamburg (hereafter: Streibel Trial, StA Hamburg); Judgment in Proceedings against Karl Streibel et al., June 3, 1976, pp. org 121–122, file 208 AR 643/71, BA-ZdL. In contemporaneous official documentation, the Trawniki men were most often referred to as *Wachmänner* or *Trawniki-Männer*. For a contemporaneous use of the term *askaris*, see memorandum to file, "Beurteilungs-Notiz über Lagerleiter SS-Hauptsturmführer Streibel" [internal evidence indicates dictated by von Herff, the chief of the SS Personnel Main Office, on the occasion of his visit to the Government General in May 1943], June 8, 1943, K. Streibel SS officer's file, RG-242, A3343/SSO, Reel 166B, frame 205, NARA.

72. "Richtlinien für die Aussonderung von Zivilpersonen und verdächtigen Kriegsgefangenen des Ostfeldzuges in den Kriegsgefangenenlagern im besetzten Gebiet, im Operationsgebiet, im Generalgouvernement und in den Lagern im Reichsgebiet," attachment 1 to Deployment Order no. 8 of the Chief of Security Police and SD, July 17, 1941, Nuremberg Document NO-3414, RG-238, NARA; RFSS and Chief of German Police [signed Himmler] to HSSPFs and SSPF Globocnik, July 25, 1941, RW 41/4, pp. 816–817, Bundesarchiv-Militärarchiv, Freiburg (hereafter, BA-MA); circular of RFSS and Chief of German Police [signed Daluege], re: Defense Formations in the New Occupied Territories, July 31, 1941, ibid., pp. 824–825.

73. Himmler to Globocnik, March 27, 1942, O. Globocnik SS officer file, RG-242, A3343/SSO, Reel 016A, frame 1135, NARA. See also order of Himmler, May 15, 1942, ibid. See Schulte, *Zwangsarbeit*, pp. 262–331, esp. pp. 262–278 on Pohl's involvement in SS and police base planning in the Government General and the occupied Soviet Union. After March 1942, the Trawniki-trained units were named the "Guard Forces of the SSPF in District Lublin." See Service Obligation, June 23, 1942, W. Amanawitschius TPF, June 23, 1942, fond 1173, opis 4, delo 55, p. 3, *Lietuvos Valstybines Archyvas* (Lithuanian State Archives), Vilnius (hereafter: 1173/4/55, p. 3, LVA Vilnius); Service Obligation, June 23, 1942, J. Kondratenko TPF, Proceedings against Ivan Kondratenko, 6056/57800, ASBU Kiev.

74. Report from Globocnik to Himmler, January 5, 1944, 4024-PS, IMT XXXIV, pp. 72–

75. Most historians now agree that the operation was named after Reinhard Heydrich to commemorate his assassination in Prague in June 1942. Historians Dieter Pohl and Bogdan Musial have argued that the operation was Globocnik's initiative. Musial, *Zivilverwaltung*, pp. 201–208; Bogdan Musial, "The Origins of 'Operation Reinhard': The Decision-Making Process for the Mass Murder of the Jews in the Generalgouvernement," *Yad Vashem Studies* 28 (2000), 113–153, here pp. 115–123; Dieter Pohl, "The Murder of Jews in the General Government," in Ulrich Herbert, ed., *National Socialist Extermination Policies: Contemporary German Perspectives and Controversies* (New York, 2000), p. 87. See also Pohl, *Judenpolitik*, pp. 129, 130, ftn. 94; Peter Witte and Stephan Tyas, "A New Document on the Deportation and Murder of Jews during Einsatz Reinhardt 1942," *Holocaust and Genocide Studies* 15, no. 3 (Winter 2001), 474–475. For a more traditional interpretation, see Peter R. Black, "Central Intent or Regional Inspiration?: Recent German Approaches to the Holocaust," *Central European History* 33, no. 4 (2000), 533–549, especially pp. 546–549.

75. On Höfle, see "Stellungbesetzung d. Stabes d. SS- und Polizeiführers i. Distrikt Lublin i. Personalunion m. Arbeitsstab d. Allg. SS i. Distrikt Lublin," no date, H. Höfle SS officer file, RG-242, A3343/SSO, Reel 102A, NARA. On the role of the SS-Mannschaftshaus in planning the deportations, see undated memorandum of Hanelt [internal evidence indicates early spring 1942], RG SSPF Lublin CSW 891/6, pp. 18–23, AGK, reprinted in Esch, "Forschungstelle," pp. 69ff.

76. On the use of personnel from the Führer Chancellery, which oversaw the so-called euthanasia program, see Henry Friedlander, *The Origins of the Nazi Genocide: From Euthanasia to the Final Solution* (Chapel Hill, 1995), pp. 296–298. For the killing centers, see Yitzhak Arad, *Belzec, Sobibor, Treblinka: The Operation Reinhard Death Camps* (Bloomington, 1987); Eugen Kogon et al., eds., *Nazi Mass Murder: A Documentary History of the Use of Poison Gas* (New Haven, 1993), pp. 102–138; Adelbert Rückerl, ed., *NS-Vernichtungslager im Spiegel deutscher Prozesse* (Munich, 1977), pp. 132–242. Christian Gerlach and Bogdan Musial have documented that the construction team arrived in Belzec in November 1941. See Christian Gerlach, "The Wannsee Conference: The Fate of the German Jews, and Hitler's Decision in Principle to Exterminate All European Jews," *Journal of Modern European History* 70 (December 1998), 759–812; Musial, "Origins," pp. 142–143. Musial and Pohl suggest, based on the postwar testimony of the commander of the German gendarmerie in Lublin District, Ferdinand Hahnzog, that construction on Sobibor began at approximately the same time. See interrogation of Ferdinand Hahnzog, January 31, 1963, file 208 AR 914/63, pp. 22–28, BA-ZdL, cited in Pohl, *Judenmord*, pp. 105–106. In this context, it seems significant that Trawniki-trained guards arrived at the Treblinka Labor Camp (Treblinka I) during the first week of November 1941. See Personnel Sheet and other correspondence in A. Rige TPF, November–December 1941, RG-20869: "Guards," vol. 8, pp. 185–189, *Tsentralnyy Arkhiv Federalnoy Sluzhby Bezopastnosti* (Central Archives of the Federal Security Services; hereafter: TsA FSB, Moscow). Why construction at Belzec received priority remains a mystery, though it may have reflected Globocnik and Höfle's priorities to murder the Jews of Lublin and L'viv.

77. On Streibel's appointment, see Globocnik to HSSPF East, March 6, 1942, K. Streibel SS officer file, RG-242, A3343/SSO, Reel 166B, frame 220–221, NARA; on early ethnic German recruits, see Naturalization Application, February 28, 1944, T. Heinrich Einwandererzentrale (hereafter: EWZ) file, RG-242, NARA; letter from Streibel to the Commander of Security Police in Thorn (Toruń), West Prussia, January 19, 1943, K. Schubrich TPF, RG-20869: "Guards," vol. 11, p. 141, TsA FSB Moscow; Personnel Sheet no. 865, J. Reimer TPF, *Derzhavnyy Arkhiv Zaporiz'koi Oblasti* (State Archives of the Zaporizhzhya Oblast, Ukraine; hereafter DAZO); Personnel Sheet no. 26, F. Swidersky TPF,

1367/1/239, p. 1, RGVA; Personnel Sheet no. 81, E. Binder TPF, RG-20869: "Guards," vol. 2, pp. 282–284, TsA FSB Moscow; and Personnel Sheet no. 55 for Heinrich Schütz, November 1, 1941, RG K-779, 16/"312 e"/411, p. 411, TsA FSB, Moscow.

78. Commander of Security Police and SD in Lublin/Field Office Krasnik to Commander of Security Police and SD Lublin, August 23, 1943, RG K-779, 16/312 "e"/409, p. 228, TsA FSB Moscow; Personnel Sheet no. 1628, June 23, 1942, L. Kairys TPF, 1173/4/51, p. 1, LVA, Vilnius; Personnel Sheet no. 443, no date, K. Demida TPF, RG-20869: "Guards," vol. 24, p. 116, TsA FSB Moscow; Personnel Sheet no. 1996, July 22, 1942, A. Rumjanzew TPF, ibid., vol. 23, p. 186; Personnel Sheet no. 206, February 27, 1942, V. Danko TPF, ibid., p. 190; Service Identity Card for Nurgali Kabirow, No. 1337, ibid., vol. 22, p. 318; Personnel Sheet no. 2182, July 13, 1942, J. Kusmin TPF, ibid., p. 374; SSPF Lublin/ Training Camp Trawniki to Commander of Security Police and SD for District Lublin, May 6, 1943, RG K-779, 16/"312 e"/411, pp. 78–79, TsA FSB Moscow.

79. Excerpt from interrogation of Emil Gutharz, November 30, 1949, Proceedings against Kurt Franz, file 208 AR-Z 23/59, vol. 21, pp. 5649–5650, BA-ZdL.

80. For the first group of recruits, see SSPF Lublin to HSSPF East, re: Recommendation for Promotion of Karl Streibel, March 6, 1942, K. Streibel SS officer file, RG-242, SSOA, A3343/SSO, Reel 166B, frames 220–221, NARA. For the summer 1942 recruits, see, for example, S. Jeromen TPF, RG-20869, "Guards," vol. 4, pp. 156–161, TsA FSB Moscow; L. Kairys TPF, 1173/4/51, pp. 1–4, LVA Vilnius.

81. For examples of civilians recruited from west Ukraine, see Personnel Sheet No. 3227, February 18, 1943, I. Merenda TPF, RG-20869: "Guards," vol. 6, p. 203, TsA FSB Moscow. For examples of Ostbahn, Organization Todt, and German Labor Service employees, see interrogation of Richard N., October 4, 1968, proceedings against Hermann Weinrich, 197 Js 38/65, file 206 AR-Z 15/65, vol. 17, p. 3562, BA-ZdL; service book for Bonifacy Pawlowski, No. 069964, file SSPF Lublin/891, sygn. 18, p. 75, AGK; Trawniki Personnel Sheet no. 3641, B. Pawlowski TPF, February 19, 1943, ibid., p. 73; interrogation of Michael M., February 25, 1969, Streibel proceedings, vol. 81, p. 15545, StA Hamburg.

82. For an example, respectively, of a Polish recruit and a Ukrainian recruit from Lublin District, see Personnel Sheet no. 2795, November 16, 1942, T. Denkewicz TPF, RG-20869, vol. 5, p. 2, TsA FSB Moscow; Personnel Sheet no. 4405, no date, I. Ridzij TPF, 3676/4/329, p. 247, *Tsentralnyi derzhavnyi arkhiv vyshchykh orhaniv vladu ta upravlinnia Ukrainy* (Central State Archive of the Higher Organs of Power and Government of Ukraine), Kiev. For an example of a Goralian recruit, see Personnel Sheet no. 3068, M. Bachulski TPF, RG-20869: "Guards," vol. 19, p. 98, TsA FSB Moscow. The Goralian recruitment turned out to be a bust. Most of the Goralians were dismissed within a month as "unsuited for duty." See Personnel Sheet no. 3066, J. Rutyna TPF, ibid., vol. 14, p. 147.

83. Globocnik to von Herff [Chief of the SS Personnel Main Office], October 27, 1943, J. Schwarzenbacher SS officer file, RG-242, A3343/SSO, Reel 123B, frames 408–409, NARA. Actually more than 4,710 Trawniki men had been recruited by this time, but the force had been thinned out by deaths, disciplinary actions, mutinies, and desertions. Approximately 5,081 men went through the Trawniki system between September 1941 and July 1944. The identification number 5081 appears on "Kompanieliste der 1. Kompanie" (Streibel Battalion), April 6, 1945, file 114-242-6, p. 7, *Státní ústřední archiv v Praze* (Central State Archive in Prague), Czech Republic.

84. SSPF Lublin/Trawniki Training Camp to SS Special Detachment in Sobibor, March 26, 1943, RG K-779, 16/312 "e"/411, pp. 271–272, TsA FSB, Moscow; SSPF Lublin/ Trawniki Training Camp to SS Special Detachment in Sobibor, April 11, 1943, 16/312 "e"/410, p. 277, TsA FSB, Moscow; Commander of SS Special Detachment Sobibor to

SSPF Lublin/Operation Reinhart/Inspector of the SS Special Detachments, July 1, 1943, 16/312 "e"/409, p. 42, TsA FSB, Moscow; SS Special Detachment Belzec to Training Camp Trawniki, May 19, 1943, ibid., p. 150; SS Special Detachment Belzec [signed Hering] to SS-Hauptsturmführer Streibel, March 2, 1943, ibid., p. 376. For Treblinka, see SSPF Lublin/Inspector of SS Special Detachments to Commander of Gendarmerie, Commander of Security Police and SD, and Commander of the Trawniki Training Camp in District Lublin, March 17, 1943, ibid., p. 27. See also Arad, *Belzec*, pp. 68–124, 199–214.

85. For Lublin, see interrogations of Mikhail Egorovich Korzhikov, April 9 and April 21, 1947, RG 20869, "Guards," vol. 23, pp. 306–311, 312–316, TsA FSB Moscow; interrogation of Mikhail Egorovich Korzhikov, September 9, 1964, Matvienko Trial, 4/100366, vol. 10, pp. 118–128, *Arkhiv Upravieniya Federalnoy Sluzby Bezopastnosti po Krasnodarskomu Krayu* (Archives of the Management of the Federal Security Services in Krasnodar Region); interrogations of Nikolaj Semjenovich Leont'ev, June 30, 1964, August 17, 1964, ibid., vol. 1, pp. 37–43 and vol. 10, pp. 49–58; testimony of Abram Thießen, September 6, 1971, Lothar Hoffmann Trial, Main Proceedings, vol. 3, pp. 710–711, Abt. 468, No. 362, Hessisches Hauptstaatsarchiv, Wiesbaden (hereafter: HHA); testimony of Hermann Reese, September 7, 1971, ibid., p. 723. For L'viv, see Judgment in Proceedings against Lothar Hoffmann et al., file 8 Ks 1/70, vol. 4, Abt. 468, Nr. 362, HHA Wiesbaden.

86. Interrogation of Georg Michalsen, January 24, 1961, Streibel Trial, vol. 4, p. 487, StA Hamburg; interrogation of Georg Michalsen, June 29/30, 1961, ibid., vol. 6, pp. 1092–1093; interrogation of Karl Prefi, September 26, 1960, proceedings again Ludwig Hahn (Hahn Proceedings), 141 Js 192/60, vol. 5, pp. 920–921, StA Hamburg; Helge Grabitz and Wolfgang Scheffler, *Letzte Spuren: Getto Warschau, SS-Arbeitslager Trawniki, Aktion Erntefest. Fotos und Dokumente über Opfer des Entlösungswahn im Spiegel der historischen Ereignisse* (Berlin, 1993), pp. 151, 164; memorandum of SSPF Lublin/Trawniki Training Camp, "Aufstellung über die an das Kdo. Warschau abgestellten Wachmänner (S. B.)," April 17, 1943, RG K-779, 16/"312 e"/411, pp. 127–130, TsA FSB Moscow; Report of the SS and Police Leader in Warsaw, SS-Brigadeführer Jürgen Stroop, "The Warsaw Ghetto Is No More," May 16, 1943, RG-238, 1061-PS, IMT XXVI, p. 632 and the appended daily reports on pp. 642–694; casualty report, April 29, 1943, B. Odartschenko TPF, RG 20869, vol. 10, p. 76, TsA FSB Moscow; interrogation of Vladimir Ivanovich Terletskij, June 17, 1948, Terletskij Trial, 5134/2345, pp. 22–25, ASBU Ivano-Frankivsk. Though the evidence is insufficient to make a determination, an entry of January 20, 1943 in the War Diary of the Armaments Detachment in Warsaw referring to a "large action carried out by the Lublin SS, which has appeared in the strength of two companies" would indicate the participation of Trawniki men in the abortive effort to clear the Warsaw ghetto in January 1943. Citation in Grabitz and Scheffler, *Spuren*, p. 182.

87. For Częstochowa, see Personnel Sheet no. 26, F. Swidersky TPF, 1367/1/ 239, p. 1, RGVA, Moscow; Personnel Sheet no. 865, J. Reimer TPF, p. 3, DAZO; interrogation of Semen Efremovich Kharkovskij, September 10, 1971, pp. 1–3, Proceedings against Franz Swidersky, file 8 Ks 4/70 Landgericht Düsseldorf. For Białystok, see [SS Training Camp Trawniki]/Lublin Detachment] [signed Basener] to Białystok Labor Camp, August 14, 1943 with cover letter from Detachment Lublin [signed Basener] to SS Training Camp Trawniki, August 20, 1943, RG-779, 16/312 "e"/411, pp. 85–87, TsA FSB Moscow; SSPF Lublin/SS Training Camp Trawniki/Detachment Poniatowa [signed Schwarzenbacher] to *SS-Hauptsturmführer* Michalsen in Białystok, August 14, 1943, ibid., pp. 94–95.

88. For the general practice, see interrogation of Georg Michalsen, January 24, 1961, Streibel Proceedings, vol. 4, pp. 486–490, StA Hamburg. See also Arad, *Belzec*, pp. 54–62.

89. For the deportations from Międzyrzec-Podlaski, see Christopher Browning, *Ordinary Men:*

*Police Battalion 101 and the Final Solution in Poland* (New York, 1998), pp. 134–135. For procedure in a small-scale deportation, see notation of telephone call to Training Training Camp Trawniki from SS-Hauptsturmführer Michalsen, May 3, 1943, RG K-779, 16/312 "e"/409, p. 106, TsA FSB Moscow.

90. For Trawniki and Poniatowa, see SS-WVHA/SS Training Camp Trawniki/Detachment Poniatowa to SS Training Camp Trawniki, October 10,1943, RG K-779, 16/312 "e"/411, pp. 102–105, TsA FSB Moscow; SSPF Lublin/Trawniki Training Camp to SS Labor Camp Poniatowa, May 25, 1943, RG K-779, 16/312 "e"/410, pp. 291–292, TsA FSB Moscow. For Budzyn, see SSPF Lublin/Trawniki Training Camp to SS Labor Camp/Heinkel Works Budzyn, June 24, 1943, ibid., pp. 302–303; SSPF Lublin/SS Labor Camp Budzyn to SSPF Lublin/Training Camp Trawniki, July 1, 1943, RG K-779, 16/312 "e"/409, pp. 96–99, TsA FSB Moscow. For Krasnik, see SS-WVHA/SS Training Camp Trawniki (signed Franz) to SSPF Lublin/SS Labor Camp Krasnik, October 19, 1943, RG K-779, 16/312 "e"/411, p. 158, TsA FSB, Moscow.

91. Undated report of June 1943, attached to letter from Globocnik to R. Brandt [Personal Staff, Reichsführer SS], June 21, 1943, RG-238, NO-485, NARA. For the establishment of these camps and generally on the regionally based systems of forced labor camps for Jews in the Government General, see Dieter Pohl, "Zwangsarbeitslager," pp. 415–438, especially pp. 419–421.

92. SSPF Lublin/Trawniki Training Camp to Detachment Prisoner of War Camp Lublin, February 15, 1943, RG K-779, 16/312 "e"/410, p. 286, TsA FSB Moscow.

93. For example, at the SS and Police Base on the Jabłon Estate in Kreis Radzyń. See SSPF Lublin/Training Camp Trawniki to SS and Police Base in Jabłon, January 6, 1943, RG K-779, 16/"312 e"/410, p. 85, TsA FSB Moscow; and SSPF Lublin/Training Camp Trawniki to SS and Police Base Skierbieszów, July 27, 1943, ibid., p. 135.

94. For the anticipation of these tasks and Höfle's responsibility for them, see SSPF Lublin memorandum to file, February 16, 1942, RG SSPF Lublin CSW file 891/6, p. 46, AGK. For procedures for storing and shipping the loot, see SS Special Detachment Belzec to Training Camp Trawniki, May 19, 1943, RG K-779, 16/312 "e"/409, p. 150, TsA FSB; SSPF Lublin [signed Globocnik], "Anordnung zur Führung einer Kartei bei den Lagern Trawniki, Chopinstr. 27, Cholm, Bekleidungswerk d. Wa-SS und Abt. IVa b. SS-u. Pol. Führer," September 16, 1942. After collection, Reinhard booty was to be transferred to the WVHA. Circular of R. Brandt to HSSPFs in the Eastern Territories, August 12, 1942, RG-238, NO-3192, NARA. For details on how the loot was to be distributed, see August Frank [WVHA] to Operation Reinhard Headquarters and Concentration Camp Auschwitz, September 26, 1942, NO-724, NARA; Arad, *Belzec*, pp. 154–155; Schulte, *Zwangsarbeit*, pp. 415–418. In 1943, a barrack was set aside at the Poniatowa Forced Labor Camp for the storage of clothing of the murdered Warsaw Jews. See SSPF Lublin/Labor Camp Poniatowa/Administration, signed Hantke, to W.C. Többens, March 25, 1943, G. Michalsen SS Officer file, RG-242, NARA.

95. SSPF Lublin/Training Camp Trawniki to SS Labor Camp Treblinka, March 22, 1943, RG K-779, 16/"312 e"/411, pp. 299–300, TsA FSB Moscow; Personnel Sheet No. 120, A. Poppe TFP, RG-20869: "Guards," vol. 23, p. 142, TsA FSB Moscow.

96. Commander of Trawniki Training Camp/Detachment Lublin to SSPF Lemberg, May 17, 1943, RG K-779, 16/312 "e"/410, pp. 270–272, TsA FSB Moscow; Commander of Trawniki Training Camp/Detachment Lublin to SSPF Lemberg, May 19, 1943, ibid., p. 274; SSPF Lemberg to Commander of Trawniki Training Camp, July 13, 1943, RG K-779/312 "e"/409, p. 133, TsA FSB Moscow. See also Thomas Sandkühler, "Das Zwangsarbeitslager Lemberg-Janowska, 1941–1944," in Herbert, *Konzentrationslager*, pp. 606–635, here p. 621.

97. For Forced Labor Camp and, later, Concentration Camp Krakau-Płaszów, see SSPF Lublin/Training Camp Trawniki to SSPF, District Krakau, March 17, 1943, RG K-779, 16/312"e"/411, pp. 291–294, TsA FSB Moscow; SSPF Krakau/Commander of the Forced Labor Camp for Jews at Krakau-Płaszów to Commander of the Training Training Camp, May 12, 1943, RG K-779 16/312 "e"/410, p. 71, TsA FSB Moscow. For the SSPF Radom, see Roster of the Guard Company of the SSPF Radom, March 30, 1944, RG K-779, 16/312 "e"/410, p. 257, TsA FSB Moscow. For Rostock and Auschwitz, see SSPF Lublin/Training Camp Trawniki to Ernst Heinkel Airplane Works, Inc./Plant Security Management in Rostock, January 13, 1943, RG K-779, 16/312"e"/411, p. 261, TsA FSB Moscow; SSPF Lublin/Trawniki Training Camp to Concentration Camp Auschwitz, March 29, 1943, RG K-779, 16/312 "e"/410, pp. 179–182, TsA FSB Moscow.

98. This estimate derives from a review of Kogon, *Mass Murder*, p. 137; Arad, *Belzec*, p. 379; Rückerl, *NS-Vernichtungslager*, pp. 150–158, 197–200; and a radio intercept of statistics sent by Höfle to the RSHA and the BdS Cracow in January 1943, discussed in Witte and Tyas, "New Document," pp. 468–473.

99. SSPF Lublin [signed Globocnik] to HSSPF East, May 15, 1943, K. Streibel SS officer file, RG 242, A3343/SSO, Reel 166B, frames 206–207, NARA.

100. See "Beförderungsliste: Mitglieder des SS-Sonderkommandos 'Einsatz Reinhard' auf Befehl des Reichsführers-SS," n.d. C. Wirth SS officer file, RG 242, A3343/SSO, Reel 251B, frames 328–329, NARA; memorandum from Himmler's field headquarters to the SS Personnel Main Office, August 19, 1943, ibid., frame 313; and other relevant correspondence in C. Wirth SS officer file, ibid., frames 292–347. For Himmler's visit, see Arad, *Belzec*, pp. 165–167.

101. See SSPF Lublin/Trawniki Training Camp [initialed by Streibel] to Department Population and Welfare, Kreishauptmannschaft Złoczów (Galicia), August 12, 1942, W. Chlopeckyj TPF, Proceedings against Vasiliy Khlopetskij, 6105/11043, p. 118, ASBU L'viv; SSPF Lublin/SS-Training Camp Trawniki [signed Streibel], "Vorschlagsliste Nr. 4 für Tapferkeitsauszeichnungen für Angehörige der Ostvölker 2. Kl. I. Bronze m. Schw.," June 7, 1944, file Wnioski Odznaczenia, sygn. VII/1, pp. 96–99, AGK; SSPF Lublin/SS-Training Camp Trawniki [signed Streibel], "Vorschlagsliste Nr. 5 für Verdienstauszeichnungen für Angehörige der Ostvölker 2. Kl. in Bronze o. Schw.," June 7, 1944, ibid., pp. 100–101.

102. Interrogation of former KdS Lublin chief Johannes Hermann Müller, November 5, 1947, RG-238, M-1019/49/868, NARA; unsigned, undated report on "Construction of SS and Police Bases," O. Globocnik SS officer file, RG-242, A3343/SSO, Reel 016A, frames 989–996, NARA.

103. Müller [RuSHA Lublin] to Hofmann [RuSHA Berlin], October 15, 1941, O. Globocnik SS officer file, RG-242, A3343/SSO, Reel 016A, frames 1141–1143, NARA. For a general overview of "Germanization" projects in Lublin District, see Bruno Wasser, "Die 'Germanisierung' im Distrikt Lublin als Generalprobe und erste Realisierungsphase des 'Generalplans Ost,'" in *Der "Generalplan Ost": Hauptlinien der nationalsozialistischen Planungs- und Vernichtungspolitik*, ed. Mechtild Rössler, Sabine Schleiermacher, and Cordula Tollmien (Berlin, 1993), pp. 271–293; Czesław Madajczyk, ed., *Zamojszczyzna—Sonderlaboratorium SS: Zbiór dokumentów polskich i niemieckich z okresu okupacji hitlerowskiej* (Warsaw, 1979).

104. Interrogation of J. Müller, November 5, 1947, RG-238, M-1019/49/868, NARA. For data on the operations, see Wasser, "'Germanisierung,'" pp. 272–275, 286–290.

105. Excerpt from memorandum signed by Zörner, February 24, 1943, Document no. 133, in *Die faschistische Okkupationspolitik in Polen, 1939–1945* (Berlin, 1989), pp. 250–253; Frank to Hitler, May 25, 1943, Document no. 148, ibid., pp. 267–270.

106. Himmler to Frank, July 3, 1943, RG-238, NO-2444, NARA.
107. Wendler to Himmler, July 27, 1943, O. Globocnik SS officer file, RG-242, A3343/SSO, Reel 016A, frames 1000–1002, NARA.
108. Michael Wildt suggests that they were not, at least among the higher ranks of the RSHA. See Wildt, *Generation*, p. 194.
109. Schulte, *Zwangsarbeit*, pp. 302–304, 307. On a conversation on the evening of October 17, 1941, Hitler referred to the indigenous populations of the Soviet Union as "Redskins." See *Secret Conversations*, p. 57.
110. Woodruff Smith, *Nazi Imperialism*, pp. 234–258.

# A Blind Eye and Dirty Hands

## The Sources of Wehrmacht Criminality in the Campaign against the Soviet Union

### ◆ Geoffrey P. Megargee ◆

During and after the Second World War, German military and civilian leaders successfully propagated a number of myths concerning the role of the German armed forces in that conflict. The most insidious of those myths held that the Wehrmacht fought a "clean" war, in accordance with international norms, while the SS and other Nazi organizations committed the terrible crimes that form such a large part of the Third Reich's legacy. In truth, the Wehrmacht was the willing tool of the National Socialist regime; in the eastern campaigns especially, it aided and abetted the SS in the commission of some crimes, and committed others of its own accord, as part of a genocidal war upon which it embarked enthusiastically. Millions died, and further tens of millions suffered, as a result. Forty years of careful research have documented the Wehrmacht's actions, often in the minutest detail.[1] We know much of what happened and, perhaps more important, we are in a position to discern the complex, synergistic interaction of broader forces that made the crimes possible. An analysis of those forces shows that the events of 1941 to 1945 represent a culmination, rather than a turning point, in German thought and policy. By the time the campaign against the Soviet Union began, a pattern of ruthlessness and prejudice had developed, a pattern that, if it did not determine the German military's actions, certainly shaped them.[2]

The main point of this paper is to examine those broader forces: the beliefs, attitudes and assumptions that formed the dominant intellectual and moral environment within the top levels of the Wehrmacht and made the war in the east a *Vernichtungskrieg,* a war of extermination. These included ideas on race, nationality and culture; on domestic and international politics; on leadership and responsibility; on war in general as well as the particulars of strategy and military operations; and on the Soviet Union as a military adversary. In reality these ideas all acted together, but for the sake of clarity I will address them individually. I will then provide an overview of the plans and orders through which the Wehrmacht leadership put its attitudes into concrete form.

Since at least the nineteenth century, ideas concerning race, culture and nationhood had taken an increasingly aggressive, narrow, and xenophobic turn in Germany. Quite simply, many Germans had come to believe in their complete superiority, and they looked upon other peoples, especially the Slavs and Jews of Poland and Russia, with increasing distrust and hostility.[3] Those feelings intensified as a result of the Great War which, in this connection as in so many others, acted as a cultural crucible. For the first time, a large number of Germans experienced the east directly during their military service, and what they saw often deepened their prejudices. Many Germans held the people there to be latently criminal, dirty, and diseased. Even many German Jews reacted to their eastern brethren with distaste. The German army entered the eastern lands with a sense of purpose, a civilizing mission, but that mission gave way in part to feelings of frustration, hopelessness and disgust as attempts to "reform" the inhabitants—attempts that were often clumsy, offensive, and even brutal—failed.[4]

Following the war, many Germans' attitudes hardened still further. Race-based immigration controls went into effect at the eastern borders, where masses of refugees were trying to enter. Germanic refugees gained admittance, while easterners faced greater scrutiny. Eastern Jews, if they got in at all, had to cope with registration and sometimes internment in concentration camps, where the terrible conditions led to high rates of sickness—thus tending to confirm, in some German minds, that the Jews were disease carriers to begin with.[5] Meanwhile the *Freikorps* fought running battles with Poles on the frontier, while within the state itself, right-wing activists—including some army officers—targeted prominent Jews for assassination. More broadly, Jews found themselves excluded from a range of organizations, including veterans' groups and the army. According to the Weimar constitution they could join the officer corps, but anti-Semitism had deep roots there; General Hans von Seeckt, who did more to shape the *Reichswehr* than any other individual, was himself strongly anti-Semitic. As a result of his and others' efforts, no practicing Jew was able to serve as an officer, and very few served as enlisted men.[6]

Adolf Hitler thus found fertile ground when he came to power and began to encourage the military to apply racial criteria in selecting and promoting personnel. Between June 1933 and February 1934, Minister of Defense Werner von Blomberg gradually brought army personnel policies in line with the so-called Aryan Paragraph of the civil service regulations. At the end of that process, all officers and men who could not establish their Aryan background had to leave the service; at least seventy did so, and on grounds of race, not religious practice. To some extent the Reichswehr's competition with the *Sturmabteilung* (SA) encouraged these measures; the numbers of service personnel involved were insignificant, after all, and the military's leaders might have left well enough alone without that additional incentive, at least temporarily. At the same time, only one officer, Colonel Erich von Manstein, is known to have protested, and his concerns did not reflect any fundamental disagreement with the regime's policy, only a sense that the expulsion was unfair to honorable members of the Reichswehr. Meanwhile, Blomberg also began to introduce anti-Semitic education throughout the army, in a further effort to strengthen ties with a government that he believed represented "a broad national desire and the realization of that toward which many of the best have been striving for years."[7]

On the political level, racism dovetailed neatly with hatred and fear of Marxism to form a key element in the military's dominant ideology. This development had its roots in the imperial period, but here again, the Great War and its aftermath served as catalysts. While the war was going on, suspicion of Jews and Leftists became increasingly prevalent, and the Right—of which most senior army officers counted themselves a part—began attaching those labels to any perceived foe. The suspect groups became the scapegoats when, to the profound shock of nearly every German, the Reich lost the war. In place of a realistic assessment of that defeat, the military propagated the myth of the "stab in the back." The army had not been beaten in the field, the generals insisted; instead, Jews and Leftists first weakened civilian and military resolve with Bolshevik propaganda and then signed a traitorous peace. A new racial-political epithet, "Jewish-Bolshevik," came into being to describe the villains. The loss of the war, the Revolution of 1918, the Weimar Republic, the rise of the Soviet Union, and a host of other plagues now appeared to some to have a common, dangerous source.[8]

The urge to fight "Jewish Bolshevism" helped form the basis for a natural alliance between the military and the Nazi Party; the supposed link between Jews and the Left gave the military added incentive to carry out its own anti-Semitic measures and to support those that the regime implemented in civilian society. Moreover, as the conflict with the Soviet Union approached, the concept of "Jewish Bolshevism" colored the army's view of that nation and its inhabitants. According to Hitler, Germans had once ruled the Russian Empire, but with the Bolshevik Revolution, the Jews had taken over—the Slavs being incapable of ruling themselves. On one level or another most officers accepted that premise, and given that Bolshevism was, by its nature, an avowedly expansionist ideology, the combination persuaded most German officers that the Soviet Union represented a threat to civilization. In their Weltanschauung, anti-Semitic, anti-Marxist and anti-Slav elements came together in a new way to support eastward expansion, which was a long-held goal of the Right in any case.[9]

The fact that such expansion would call for an aggressive war was one that the military accepted as a matter of course, for a variety of reasons. First, many Germans accepted the Social Darwinist premise that conflict was inevitable, between nations as between animal species, and that only the strong deserved to survive. Hitler wrote in his second (unpublished) book that politics must always be "the struggle of a nation for its existence"; in such a struggle, the distinctions between peace and war, on the one hand, and between politics and strategy, on the other, became purely academic.[10] So too did concerns over the rights of other peoples: since Germans were clearly superior, they deserved to take what they needed, by force if necessary, no matter what the consequences for their opponents.

In the period after the Great War, the brutality inherent in such an approach became a leitmotif in itself, and it informed a broad social movement of which the Nazis took advantage. In a concrete sense, the war had brought heretofore-unimagined violence and destruction into people's lives. The effects were profound. For the Right, especially, war became a paradigm for life, and in general people became more used to brutality, regardless of the target. Political discussion in the Weimar era took on aggressive, militaristic overtones, and actual political violence reached new heights. The paradoxically named "conservative revolutionary" thinkers promoted war as a positive good, a force that would eliminate society's weaklings and create a "New Man," who would embody self-discipline, ruthlessness, courage and nationalism. These were the values of the *"Front-"* or *"Kampfgemeinschaft,"* the community of warriors—largely mythical—that shared the trenches during the Great War. They promised a new, more egalitarian society, cultural rejuvenation, and an end to the corruption and privilege of the old regime. The Nazis used these themes, which they reinforced with violence, to establish a strong political base that the military admired and coveted. When the next war came, moreover, the politics of brutality would also carry over seamlessly into military and occupation policy.[11]

Such cultural undercurrents, in combination with conservative racial and political beliefs, found more concrete expression in the military's vision of the coming war. First and foremost, for Germany's senior officers, war was virtually the only, and certainly the final, arbiter of international affairs.[12] More specifically, they believed that war was inevitable if Germany hoped to ensure its future, first as a state and then as a European and, ultimately, a world power. In fact, in their eyes (like those of conservatives in general) the Great War had never really ended. Germany still faced powerful enemies, both within and without, whose destruction was essential. In May 1925 a Defense Ministry document stated, "That Germany will in the future have to fight a war for its continued existence as a people and state is certain."[13] For that reason Hitler's generals shared his goal of rearming Germany, materially and psychologically, and then putting that military strength to use. The new chancellor made that intention clear to his senior military leaders only three days after he assumed power; at a dinner on February 3, 1933 he told the assembled officers that he planned, among other things, to rebuild a standing army, to regain a position of power for Germany, and to use that power, in all likelihood, to expand to the east.[14] That was exactly what his audience wanted to hear.

The new chancellor's intentions fit perfectly with plans that the military started developing long before Hitler came on the scene. Their intellectual starting point was the concept of "total war," a vague but broadly accepted set of assumptions about the nature of the conflict to come.[15] Those assumptions had existed for some time before 1914, even if the term itself had not, and the Great War strengthened them by calling on society's resources to an unprecedented degree. According to the military, however, Germany had never achieved its potential in that conflict, and the failure to mobilize society completely had paved the way for the "stab in the back." There could be no such failure the next time. The regime would have to reshape society in every aspect: political, ideological, economic and military. No source of weakness or disunity—such as pluralism, pacifism, or racial mixing—was tolerable. Propaganda would hammer home the absolute nature of the struggle and highlight every perceived grievance and supposed threat. Economic preparations would have to meet the needs both of the military and of the home front so as to provide the physical and psychological stamina the nation would need for a long fight.[16] In broad terms, the military sought a *Volksgemeinschaft*, a racial community in which homogeneity of blood and thought would provide the strength and support for an aggressive, expansionist, and protracted war—or, put another way, a *Wehrgemeinschaft*, a completely militarized society. The role of forming such a society was one that the generals were willing to leave to the civilian government, having attempted unsuccessfully to perform it themselves during the Great War. The Nazis, for their part, were ready to provide just such assistance: hence their initial appeal to officers who otherwise viewed some aspects of Nazism with suspicion. "The young, the entire *Volk*, must be adjusted to the idea that struggle alone can save us," said Hitler in his February 3, 1933 address.[17] "Total war" meant total commitment.

The "total war" idea was also significant for strategy, for military operations, and for occupation policy. Since it encompassed not just the activities of the fighting forces but the material and moral foundations of the nation's war effort as well, in offensive terms it targeted every source of enemy strength for destruction or exploitation. There would be no distinction between soldiers and civilians in any future war, since the latter supported the former. In a battle for the survival of the race and the nation, any measure that would break the enemy's will, deprive him of the means to fight, or add to Germany's fighting power at his expense was, ipso facto, not only allowable but necessary. Some theorists even argued that such methods would be more humane in the long run, since ultimately they would shorten the fighting. Here the connections between the "total war" idea and some long-evolving trends in German military theory and practice become evident. At least since the Franco-Prussian War, Germans had been developing an approach to warfare that emphasized the maximum application of violence. On the battlefield this meant the "battle of annihilation," in which the goal was not just to induce the enemy's surrender but also to destroy them as a fighting force. Behind the lines it meant extraordinarily harsh repressive measures to crush any resistance on the part of the civilian population. The military might still observe the rules of warfare, but as a matter of convenience, not of principle. Even before 1914, German legal and military theorists were denying the legitimacy of international laws of war. They believed that "military necessity" would always overrule any limitations on violence.[18] During the Great War the army's actions in Belgium and France demonstrated that this was not just idle talk: although on a much lesser scale than in the Second World War, in 1914 the Germans executed prisoners of war and civilian hostages, pillaged and burned towns, and even used groups of civilians as human shields, all in contravention of international agreements.[19]

The Germans' approach to warfare was not unique for the time, but it would combine with racism and political ideology to make the coming war extraordinarily brutal, especially in the east. Hitler made his intentions clear in his first meeting with his senior officers: the best use of Germany's reestablished political power would be "the conquest of new living space in the east and its ruthless Germanization."[20] This was an ideological constant, not a political expedient. Before another gathering of officers on February 10, 1939, he re-emphasized that Germany's present living space was too small; the only solution would be to take more. And he left no doubt as to the nature of the coming conflict: "a purely ideological war, i.e. consciously a national and racial war." On November 23 of that year he again told his commanders, "A racial struggle has erupted about who is to dominate in Europe and the world."[21] Certainly the audience could have had no doubt as to the seriousness of Hitler's intentions by that time, since the Wehrmacht and the SS had been acting with unprecedented viciousness in occupied Poland for nearly three months.[22] What little opposition there was had no effect whatsoever on policy.

Shortly before the eastern campaign, on March 30, 1941, Hitler explained his goals yet again, to two hundred and fifty of the key commanders and staff officers who would soon lead the Wehrmacht into the Soviet Union. This time he was more explicit than ever before. The war against the USSR would be a war of extermination, he said. Communism was inherently asocial and represented an enormous danger for the future; its leaders were criminals and would have to be dealt with appropriately. The usual rules would not apply; the concept of comradeship between soldiers would have to be discarded. The Bolshevik commissars and intelligentsia would be eliminated, and no new intellectual class would be allowed to arise. Harshness today would mean lenience in the future; alternatively, the danger existed that Germany could beat the enemy today but have to fight him again in thirty years. Most of the officers accepted the speech at face value, apparently. These were ordinary officers, not SS fanatics, but few protested, and none to any effect.[23]

This is a good point, before examining the foundations of military strategy and operations in the east, at which to look at the Germans' ideas on leadership and responsibility, in broad terms. The subject is complex, but it helps to explain why those officers who did not share the most radical parts of Hitler's Weltanschauung were nonetheless willing to carry out his orders. It also helps us to understand how those officers who supported the regime and participated in its crimes attempted to justify their actions to themselves and to posterity.

Earlier in its history, the Prusso-German officer corps had demonstrated a capacity for intellectual and moral independence, even at the political level. From 1812, when General Hans von Yorck's defection turned Prussia back against Napoleon, to 1918, when the Supreme Army Command forced the Kaiser to sue for peace, German officers had demonstrated that, when they considered the issue to be important enough, they would stand up to even the highest authority. Within a narrower military sphere, moreover, the General Staff, which dominated the post-Great War officer corps, had long recognized the need for a kind of disciplined, institutionalized independence, according to which staff officers bore joint responsibility for the orders their commanders issued and could appeal orders with which they disagreed. Additionally, German officers could and often did exercise authority out of proportion to their rank, depending on the circumstances.[24] That being said, they also valued obedience and loyalty, as do officers in most armies; they did not, on the whole, lightly question their orders or assume authority to which they were not entitled.

Plainly, the officer corps demonstrated little independence in its relationship with Hitler. After the war, the officers made much of the personal oath of loyalty that they swore to the *Führer*; it did not differ substantially from that which officers had sworn to the king and emperor in times past, and on its face it called for unconditional obedience. It also meshed perfectly with one of the central tenets of Nazism: the *Führerprinzip*, or Leader Principle, according to which all authority and responsibility flowed from the top downward, and the subordinate's only duty was to carry out his orders to the letter, without question. If we believe their memoirs, the generals chafed under this system but were powerless to do anything about it, because of the oath they had sworn and their duty as military men. They also tried to portray themselves as apolitical servants of the regime who had restricted their activities to strictly military matters.

The fact that German officers had acted independently on the political level in the past weakens those arguments, however; a more complete explanation for the officer corps' obedience to Hitler must include other elements. Certainly the interests and attitudes that the generals shared with their *Führer* were central to their performance, but shared leadership philosophies were also a factor. There was more at work within the officer corps than a simple collision between General Staff traditions and the *Führerprinzip*. First of all, the General Staff officially abandoned the principle of joint responsibility, and eliminated an officer's right to appeal orders, as early as 1939. Those measures did not equate to a call for blind obedience, but they did represent the General Staff's acceptance of the idea that the commander had ultimate authority and responsibility.[25] Also, a more nuanced examination of the *Führerprinzip* reveals that the commander's decisions had to reflect the will of his subordinates, and the form of their obedience, as well as any initiative on their part, had to reflect the will of the group as a whole. "The *Führer* is the Party and the Party is the *Führer*," Hitler said in one of his speeches, and this principle applied at every level.[26] In other words, as Michael Thad Allen has explained it, "individual leadership grew out of collective identity."[27] Allen was referring to the SS bureaucracy, but the military worked in nearly the same way. The *Führerprinzip* did not eliminate initiative, but rather emphasized a common purpose and shared responsibility. Hitler wrote that the leader bears "the highest unlimited authority" but also "the ultimate and heaviest responsibility"; the state must "implant joy of responsibility . . . in the hearts of youth."[28] More explicitly, at the March 30, 1941 briefing he told his senior commanders that in eliminating Communist functionaries in the Soviet Union, the troops must not get out of hand, but rather that "the commander must give orders which express the common feelings of his men."[29] There are parallels here to the General Staff's personnel selection and training systems, which had for decades ensured nearly homogeneous political views and also attempted to instill a common *Gedankengang*, a way of thinking, that combined accepted principles with initiative and flexibility.[30] There are also connections to the army's efforts, following the Great War, to break down the barriers that had separated officers and men in that conflict, as well as to later steps that made officers responsible for political indoctrination.

The Germans' understanding of leadership and responsibility gave soldiers and civilians alike a convenient degree of moral as well as practical flexibility. Those who agreed with their orders could carry them out with initiative and imagination. An oath, in and of itself, meant little; after all, the Wehrmacht's senior officers had often ignored their oath to the Weimar government, with which they had felt no bond. The oath to Hitler was different precisely because most officers believed in the individual, and hence the system, to which they were swearing allegiance. The oath could also provide a cover, as well: those who had qualms could tell themselves—and others—that they were just following orders, and that "political affairs" were none of their concern anyway. Members of the army used such reasoning quite unselfconsciously. In a July 1938 letter to Chief of the General Staff Ludwig Beck, Manstein dismissed his former boss's concerns about an attack on Czechoslovakia: if that is the *Führer's* order, Manstein wrote, then he, not the army, will have to accept the responsibility.[31] Such reasoning also came in handy after the war, when the Allies put senior military figures on trial.

One other factor deserves mention in connection with the officers' personal motivations. While most senior generals did not normally face incarceration or execution if they failed to carry out their orders, there *were* costs associated with disobedience, as the officers were well aware. General Johannes Blaskowitz, for example, was the only senior officer to complain to Berlin about atrocities in Poland in autumn 1939. Not only was he relieved of his post, but he was the only *Generaloberst* not promoted to Field Marshal in August 1940; this was an object lesson to anyone who wanted to keep climbing the career ladder. Additionally, beginning in 1940, officers in the top two ranks received secret, tax-free payments from Hitler's personal funds, payments that more than doubled their salaries, and they were told quite explicitly that the money would stop if they did not toe the line. Selected individuals also received large gifts of money or property on significant occasions.[32] While one cannot point to these bribes as a causal factor in any particular decision or set of actions, we also know of no general who refused them, and few ever lost the privilege, either. We are left with the strong impression that, for those few senior officers who might have felt uncomfortable with Nazi aims or methods, the money and the promise of advancement helped them to overcome their doubts.

Having explored the military's attitudes toward various broad issues, we can now move on to the core professional functions at the senior levels: strategy and operations. To begin with, the terms require some brief explanation. Strategy is the realm of thought and action that is concerned with war in its broadest context, with the way in which a nation or group uses military force, or the threat of force, to achieve its political goals. Strategic planning defines the timing, targets, and purposes of war; it involves calculation of the risks involved, of society's economic and moral ability to support military action, and of the military's ability to execute the strategy successfully. Operational planning then picks up where that last element of strategic planning leaves off. At the operational level, military leaders plan campaigns—sequential series of major movements and battles—to achieve strategic goals. They must take into account the nature of those goals; their own force structure and military doctrines; the enemy's strengths, weaknesses, and plans; and the geographic and climatic features of the area where they will be operating. Military intelligence, logistical planning, and personnel management play important roles in operational planning.[33]

Several points about German strategy and operations stand out.[34] First and foremost, the generals had no real say in the strategic realm, even before the war began. Hitler made the decisions, usually without consulting his senior commanders. Furthermore, German military men tended not to understand strategy in its full scope; in their minds, strategy consisted of operations on a grand scale. Proper assessment of national ends and means seems to have been beyond them. In place of such an assessment, they combined demands for unlimited resources with a blind faith in the power of their operational virtuosity to overcome any strategic difficulties. Win enough battles, in other words, and the war will take care of itself. One should note, too, that after some initial resistance in the late 1930s they made no great effort to have a say in strategic decisions, instead limiting themselves to narrower operational questions, and also that they often (and contrary to their postwar assertions) approved of their *Führer's* strategic plans, including the decision to attack the Soviet Union.

To the extent that the German military did any kind of strategic planning for the war against the USSR, their planning process mirrored their intellectual failings. It started with their preconceptions about the enemy, in which two seemingly contradictory views prevailed. First, as previously described, many Germans believed that the Soviet Union represented an existential threat to Germany. Second, however, Russia also appeared to many Germans to be a colossus with feet of clay: politically unstable, filled with discontented minorities, ineffectually ruled, and militarily weak. Knowledge of Stalin's recent purge of his senior military leaders, observation of the Red Army's performance in Finland and Poland, and belief in the inherent inferiority of the "subhuman" Jews and Slavs reinforced this impression and persuaded the generals that the Soviet regime would collapse after one good blow. They neither understood the political power of the totalitarian Stalinist state—a curious blind spot in officers who served the Nazis—nor the resilience and abilities of the Soviet people, nor the USSR's vast economic potential. They did not even make plans to tap into the disaffection they expected to find in various western nationalities, except in the most superficial and temporary ways. Instead the military based its expectations for success entirely upon the assumption that the Wehrmacht would defeat the Red Army easily, after which the regime would simply dissolve. Apparently no one at the top of the command structure ever asked the simple question: what if the Soviets refuse to give up?[35]

On the operational level, the German generals considered themselves the masters of their trade, and they have somehow retained that reputation in many people's eyes to this day. They were indeed talented at modern mobile warfare in a limited sense, and before their enemies learned the same lessons, that talent (along with the army's tactical abilities) gave them a decisive edge. Their early victories brought on hubris, however, even as they masked fatal flaws in the Wehrmacht's operational system. For the Germans, the operational concept—that is, the scheme of maneuver, the plan according to which particular forces would move and give battle—was everything. Logistics, personnel management, and intelligence were purely secondary; they existed only to support the scheme of maneuver. The German operational planning method was first to figure out where they wanted the armies to go, and then to demand the necessary support from the supply and personnel officers, while the intelligence staffs figured out what enemy units the planned operation would encounter. Such an approach functions well when resources of men, equipment and supplies are sufficient, and when the enemy is so inferior that his plans do not matter. In other environments it is more problematic.

The maneuver plan for Operation Barbarossa (the codename for the invasion of the USSR) called for deep penetrations and encirclements by mobile armored spearheads in order to isolate and destroy the Soviet armies in the western part of the country, after which resistance would be negligible, presumably; the Germans believed that the whole thing would be over long before winter. The plan entailed enormous risks, which the generals recognized only incompletely. Most significantly, the offensive would have to go forward on a logistical shoestring. Supplies of men, fuel, ammunition, equipment and transport were sparse, and the distances over which the armies would have to travel were enormous. Supply priority would have to go to ammunition and fuel, while the army lived off the land, at the expense of the local populace. Even then, the Wehrmacht would have to pause for some weeks halfway into the campaign to rest, refit, and re-supply. Moreover, behind the army's fast motorized vanguards, millions of men would march on foot at the same pace as Rome's legions (or less, since Rome had had better roads than Russia), and their supplies and heavy equipment would travel no faster than horses could pull them. The spearheads would have to move fast enough to surround the enemy and prevent them from escaping, but not so fast that the armies behind would lose touch. If the Red Army managed to prolong the fight, the Germans would find themselves running out of resources in short order. Despite the dangers, however, and although hard information about the Red Army and its capabilities was lacking, the planning went forward in an atmosphere that was almost carefree. In fact, as the senior military leaders recognized the increasing constraints that logistical difficulties would place on the length of the campaign, they reacted not by questioning the feasibility of the operation but by shortening their estimates of the time they would need to complete it![36] Such was the hubris that had come to dominate German planning.

This, then, was the constellation of beliefs, attitudes and assumptions that shaped the war in the east on the German side: faith in their own superiority; loathing of Jews and Slavs; fear and hatred of Marxism and its conflation with Jewishness; belief in existential struggle and in Germany's right to use any means to win; attachment to ideals of brutality and ruthlessness; a desire for another war; the assumption that such a war would be "total"; particular hostility toward the Soviet Union; moral flexibility in principles of leadership and responsibility; straightforward greed and ambition; the assumption that the Soviet Union would make an easy target; and a risky plan of attack with inherent dangers for Soviet civilians. Each of these was an element in an explosive compound, whose detonation would destroy the lives of millions. No single element, or even a combination of several, could have brought about the same result. Their synergistic interaction becomes plain when we examine some of the details of the Germans' plans for their war with the Soviet Union.[37]

After the war, former members of the Wehrmacht sometimes tried to explain away their crimes—when they acknowledged them at all—by saying that the campaign was, by its nature, a brutal one, hard-fought by both sides, and that the horrible things that happened were really just an inevitable outcome of such a war. This argument falls flat for several reasons, one of which is that the Germans planned for an especially vicious, even exterminationist campaign long before the invasion opened. We already know of the guidance that Hitler gave to his senior officers on March 30, and of the lack of any significant protest it elicited. But the planning process did not begin or end with that speech. As Jürgen Förster has pointed out, planning for the military campaign and for the control, administration and exploitation of the occupied territories went forward together, starting in the summer of

1940.[38] In actuality, the military and administrative aspects of the invasion were inextricably linked.

To begin with, the Germans' strategic and operational plans put a fatal burden on the Soviet people. The consequences of the army's supply situation were obvious. At the same time, the Reich Food Ministry was worried about shortages in Germany itself. Arguments of "military necessity" now combined with concerns about German civilian morale; obviously the troops had to eat, and no one wanted to see a repetition of the hunger and unrest that had weakened the home front in the Great War. Over the longer term, moreover, Hitler was also looking ahead to an extended conflict with Great Britain and, in all likelihood, the United States; for that, Germany would need the vast resources of Eastern Europe and European Russia. The solution, upon which the military and the regime agreed in early May 1941, was what historians have come to call the "hunger plan": Germany would take the "surplus" food from the more agriculturally productive southern areas of the USSR to feed the Wehrmacht's troops and the Reich. "Surplus," in this context, referred to food that normally went to feed the people in the cities and the USSR's less productive northern zone. By agreeing to this plan, the German military and civilian authorities quietly accepted that up to thirty million Soviet citizens would starve to death.[39] Here was a level of cynicism and brutality that eclipsed anything of which the Germans had been guilty to date.

The "hunger plan" was, moreover, only one of several such measures that the German military authorities planned for their campaign in the Soviet Union. On March 13, 1941 the Armed Forces High Command (*Oberkommando der Wehrmacht* or OKW) had issued a supplement to the Barbarossa directive that defined key administrative responsibilities. Conquered territory would come under "Reich Commissars" as quickly as possible, it stated; each new state would have a Wehrmacht commander and military occupation forces to maintain security. Within the relatively narrow and shifting zone of military control behind the front, meanwhile, the army would concentrate on exploiting the region's resources, while SS agencies would carry out certain "special tasks" independently and on their own responsibility. Negotiations began that same day between General Eduard Wagner, the army's senior logistician and the man responsible for rear area security, on the one hand, and *SS-Gruppenführer* Reinhard Heydrich, chief of the Security Police and the Security Services (SD), on the other. The negotiations resulted in an order from the Army High Command (*Oberkommando des Heeres* or OKH) of April 28, according to which special task forces (*Einsatzgruppen*) would operate with and behind the armies. The *Einsatzgruppen* would receive their operational instructions from the SS command but would coordinate their activities closely with the army, which would also provide supplies, transport, and housing. This was a fine arrangement, as far as the army was concerned, since it would help relieve overextended army units of responsibility for rear area security. And certainly the OKH had neither doubts nor qualms about the measures that the SS units would undertake: they would be there to preemptively eliminate those "enemies of the state and the Reich" that might create problems behind the front, much as similar formations had in Poland. Field Marshal Walther von Brauchitsch, the army's commander-in-chief, had already told his senior commanders on March 27 that the troops "have to realize that this struggle is being waged by one race against another, and proceed with the necessary harshness."[40]

Wagner also addressed the army's own security measures in an OKH order dated April 3, 1941, the "Special instructions on supplies, part c." According to Wagner, the troops were to suppress any resistance with the utmost brutality: "Self-assured and ruthless behavior towards anti-German elements will prove an effective preventive means." The order also regulated the treatment of POWs, which was to be proper, but with the proviso that the troops had to be on the alert for insidious behavior: "Total liquidation of any active or passive resistance!"[41] Another, even more fundamental order followed on May 13, this one from Hitler himself via the OKW, based on a draft from the OKH: the Decree on the Exercise of Military Jurisdiction in the 'Barbarossa' Zone and on Special Measures for the Troops. The decree began by saying that the shortage of personnel and the "special nature" of the enemy meant that the troops would have to defend themselves "mercilessly" against any threat from the civilian population. It then went on to stipulate that civilians accused of crimes would not be tried by military courts; that "guerrillas are to be finished off ruthlessly in battle or while attempting to escape"; and that all other attacks by civilians were to be "crushed by the troops on the spot using the utmost means, until the attacker is annihilated." Those civilians whom the troops merely suspected of an offense were to be brought before an officer, who would decide whether or not they were to be shot. Where individual offenders could not be identified, "collective measures" could be taken against a locality from which an attack came, with the approval of a battalion commander or higher. Furthermore, there was no obligation to prosecute a member of the Wehrmacht for crimes committed against civilians, even if such crimes constituted offenses against military law. If such actions *were* prosecuted, the authorities were to take into account the fact that Bolshevism had contributed to the collapse of 1918, the subsequent sufferings of the German people, and the National Socialist movement's bloody losses.[42] Although Brauchitsch issued an order on May 24 that modified the decree somewhat, it clearly aimed at maintaining discipline and did not otherwise interfere with Hitler's intent.[43] In effect, the highest German authorities all but gave their soldiers *carte blanche*. And just to make sure that the soldiers got the point, on May 19 the OKW also issued a document entitled Guidelines for the Behavior of the Troops in Russia. The battle against Bolshevism, it stated, "demands ruthless and energetic action against Bolshevik agitators, saboteurs, and Jews, and the total elimination of all active or passive resistance." It then went on to warn the troops, among other things, to watch out for enemy agents and to exercise the greatest care when dealing with POWs, especially those of Asian origin, whom it called "devious, unpredictable, underhanded and unfeeling."[44]

One other order constituted perhaps the most explicit statement of the Germans' intentions in their fight against the "Jewish-Bolshevik" enemy: the Guidelines for the Treatment of Political Commissars, which the OKW issued on June 6, 1941, again based upon an OKH draft. The political commissars in the Red Army occupied positions parallel to the military commanders; they were responsible for overseeing the commanders' actions and for indoctrinating the troops. The Germans saw them as the core of the Communist military system and the "originators of barbaric Asiatic fighting methods"; their elimination would make the liberation of the east easier and also help with the control of POWs by preventing the spread of Bolshevik propaganda among the prisoners. For those reasons the so-called Commissar Order called on the front-line troops to immediately shoot any commissars they captured. This was a clear violation of international laws to which Germany was a signatory, but it aroused no protest on the part of the army's leaders, who again only expressed concern about the possible effect on discipline. Halder's comment when he first saw the drafts of the order was that the troops "must do their share in the ideological struggle of the eastern campaign." The order went in writing to the two most senior levels in the chain of command below the OKH, with instructions to pass it on verbally from there.[45]

The orders concerning the treatment of Soviet civilians and soldiers demonstrate that, long before the campaign opened, the military's senior leaders could have had no illusions as to the nature of the war they were about to launch. On the contrary, there is every indication that they not only agreed with the regime's goals but also favored using the most extreme measures in support of them. The Soviet people were about to experience levels of death and destruction that bore only a minimal relationship to the exigencies of war.[46]

The war in the east, like so many other aspects of the Third Reich's history, comes close to defying understanding. The attempt to enter the minds of the men who prosecuted that war can be only partially successful. The best we can produce is a mixture of logic, evidence, and imagination, a collection of generalizations about people whose innermost thoughts we can seldom know. All the same, the fact of the war remains, the deaths remain, the suffering remains, all to be explained somehow. They did not arise from a vacuum. Some people would paint all the Germans of that era as either evil or naive, but those labels explain nothing satisfactorily; they are too simple. And so we look for patterns and connections in people's ideas and experiences, as we experience them, in turn, through the evidence. What we find is a synergistic interaction of dangerous attitudes, assumptions and beliefs, a combination of ruthlessness and prejudice, operating in a critical mass of officers and men to produce the most extreme of outcomes. The "clean Wehrmacht" is indeed a myth, for reasons that we can perceive, even if only in their outlines.

324 ◆ GEOFFREY P. MEGAREE

# Notes

1. For an overview of the literature on this subject, see Rolf-Dieter Müller and Gerd R. Ueberschär, *Hitler's War in the East: A Critical Assessment*, 2d ed. (New York, 2002), esp. parts C, D, & E. Wolfram Wette also examines the genesis of the myth of the "clean Wehrmacht"; see *Die Wehrmacht: Feindbilder, Vernichtungskrieg, Legenden* (Frankfurt a.M, 2002). I am indebted to Peter Black, Wendy Lower, Alex Rossino, and Dennis Showalter for their help in crafting this paper. Thanks also to the New York Military Affairs Symposium and the fellows of the Center for Advanced Holocaust Studies for providing forums in which I could hone my ideas. The opinions in this paper are my own and do not necessarily reflect those of the United States Holocaust Memorial Council or Museum.

2. In this context, "ruthlessness" refers specifically to a willingness to inflict any amount of suffering on any group that stands in the way of final victory, regardless of generally accepted laws or moral standards. "Willingness" is a key term: the Germans did not always exhibit the harshest possible behavior, but they demonstrated that they were willing to. "Prejudice" is, as Webster's defines it, "unreasonable feelings, opinions, or attitudes, especially of a hostile nature, regarding a racial, religious, or national group." Note that the definition says *especially*, not exclusively, of a hostile nature; prejudice often has two faces. In the Germans' case, they certainly exhibited hostile attitudes toward their enemies, but they also held onto unreasonably *favorable* attitudes toward themselves.

3. George Mosse, *Fallen Soldiers: Reshaping the Memory of the World Wars* (Oxford, 1990), 173–74; Ian Kershaw, *Hitler, 1889–1936: Hubris* (New York, London, 1998), 76; Wette, *Die Wehrmacht*, 24.

4. Steven Aschheim, *Brothers and Strangers: The East European Jew in German and German Jewish Consciousness, 1800–1923* (Madison, 1982), 143–48, 173–81; Julian Weindling, *Epidemics and Genocide in Eastern Europe, 1890–1945* (Oxford, New York, 2000), 96–102; Vejas Gabriel Liulevicius, *War Land on the Eastern Front: Culture, National Identity, and German Occupation in World War I* (Cambridge, 2000), esp. chaps. 6, 7. German soldiers in World War II would display many of the same reactions, but with Nazi ideology to egg them on. See Alf Lüdtke, "The Appeal of Exterminating 'Others': German Workers and the Limits of Resistance," in *Resistance Against the Third Reich 1933–1990*, ed. Michael Geyer and John W. Boyer (Chicago, 1994); also Alexander B. Rossino, "Destructive Impulses: German Soldiers and the Conquest of Poland," *Holocaust and Genocide Studies* 11/3 (Winter 1997), 353–54.

5. Weindling, *Epidemics*, 111–18.

6. Wette, *Wehrmacht*, 72–73; Mosse, *Fallen Soldiers*, 176. See also Johannes Hürter, "'Es herrschen Sitten und Gebräuche, genauso wie im 30-jährigen Krieg': Das erste Jahr des deutsch-sowjetischen Krieges in Dokumenten des Generals Gotthard Heinrici," *Vierteljahrshefte für Zeitgeschichte* 48 (2000), 335–36 on officers' attitudes toward Slavs as well as for a more general examination of dominant beliefs.

7. Klaus-Jürgen Müller, *Das Heer und Hitler: Armee und nationalsozialistisches Regime 1933–1940* (Stuttgart, 1969), 78–84; Jürgen Förster, "Complicity or Entanglement? Wehrmacht, War, and Holocaust," in *The Holocaust and History: The Known, the Unknown, the Disputed, and the Reexamined*, ed. Michael Berenbaum and Abraham J. Peck (Bloomington, 1998), 268–270; Wette, *Wehrmacht*, 74–94. The quote is from an address that Blomberg delivered to the group and military district commanders on February 3, 1933; in Thilo Vogelsang, "Neue Dokumente zur Geschichte der Reichswehr, 1930–1933," *Vierteljahrshefte für Zeitgeschichte* 2 (1954), 432.

8. On the stab-in-the-back myth, see Gottfried Niedhart, "Kriegsende und Friedensordnung als Problem der deutschen und internationalen Politik, 1917–1927," in *Der Erste Weltkrieg:*

*Wirkung, Wahrnehmung, Analyse,* ed. Wolfgang Michalka (Munich, 1994), 180–84; Holger Herwig, *The First World War: Germany and Austria-Hungary, 1914–1918* (London, New York, 1993; Oxford, 1995), 425–26; Roger Chickering, "Sore Loser: Ludendorff's Total War," in *An der Schwelle zum totalen Krieg. Die militärische Debatte über den Krieg der Zukunft, 1919–1939,* ed. Stig Förster (Paderborn: Schöningh, forthcoming). On "Jewish-Bolshevism," see Mosse, *Fallen Soldiers,* 179; Wette, *Wehrmacht,* 51.

9.   Wette, *Wehrmacht,* 22–27. See also Fritz Fischer, *Germany's Aims in the First World War* (New York, 1967).

10.  Manfred Messerschmidt, "Foreign Policy and Preparation for War," in *Germany and the Second World War,* ed. Militärgeschichtliches Forschungsamt (Research Institute for Military History), vol. 1, *The Build-up of German Aggression* (Oxford, 1990), 544–45; J. Förster, "Complicity," 269.

11.  Omer Bartov, *Mirrors of Destruction* (Oxford, New York, 2000), 13–21, and *Hitler's Army: Soldiers, Nazis, and War in the Third Reich* (Oxford, 1991, 1992); Mosse, *Fallen Soldiers,* 159–67, 180–85; Richard Bessel, *Germany after the First World War* (Oxford, 1993, 1995), 260–63; Chickering, "Sore Loser"; see also Peter Fritsche, *Germans into Nazis* (Cambridge, Mass., 1998); and Robert Gellately, *Backing Hitler: Consent and Coercion in Nazi Germany* (Oxford, 2001). A cautionary note is necessary: Bessel points out the weaknesses in the proposal that there was a "front generation" of social misfits who flocked to right-wing groups. The vast majority of the eleven million men who returned from service in the war blended back into civilian life smoothly, and their political beliefs spanned the entire spectrum. See *Germany after the First World War,* 257–59.

12.  On that belief and its historical roots, see Wette, *Wehrmacht,* 141–50.

13.  Paul Heider, "Der totale Krieg—Seine Vorbereitung durch Reichswehr und Wehrmacht," in *Der Weg deutscher Eliten in den Zweiten Weltkrieg,* ed. Ludwig Nestler (Berlin, 1990), 43–44. See also Geoffrey P. Megargee, *Inside Hitler's High Command* (Lawrence, 2000), 12.

14.  Handwritten record of Generalleutnant Liebmann, in Vogelsang, "Neue Dokumente," 434–36. See also Wilhelm Deist, *The Wehrmacht and German Rearmament* (London, 1981), 26; J. Förster, "Complicity," 267.

15.  Debate continues over the concept of "total war." From my standpoint, this was not a coherent theory from which everyone drew the same concrete conclusions, and although it called for essentially limitless efforts, practical considerations prevented its implementation in any absolute sense. See Stig Förster, *An der Schwelle zum totalen Krieg.*

16.  See Heider, "Der totale Krieg"; Wolfram Wette, "Ideology, Propaganda, and Internal Politics as Preconditions of the War Policy of the Third Reich," in *Germany and the Second World War,* 1:105; Wilhelm Deist, "The Road to Ideological War: Germany, 1918–1945," in *The Making of Strategy: Rulers, States and War,* ed. Williamson Murray, MacGregor Knox, and Alvin Bernstein (Cambridge, New York, 1998), 364; Wilhelm Deist, "'Blitzkrieg' or Total War? War Preparations in Nazi Germany," in *An der Schwelle zum totalen Krieg;* Richard Overy, "Hitler's War and the German Economy: A Reinterpretation," in *Total War and Historical Change: Europe 1914–1955,* ed. Arthur Marwick, Clive Emsley, and Wendy Simpson (Buckingham, Philadelphia, 2001); Eleanor Hancock, *The National Socialist Leadership and Total War, 1941–5* (New York, 1991).

17.  Manfred Messerschmidt, "The Wehrmacht and the Volksgemeinschaft," trans. Anthony Wells, *Journal of Contemporary History* 18/4 (Oct. 1983), 720–22; J. Förster, "Complicity," 268.

18.  Heider, "Der totale Krieg"; Wette, *Wehrmacht,* 13; Manfred Messerschmidt, "Völkerrecht und 'Kriegsnotwendigkeit' in der deutschen militärischen Tradition," in *Was damals Recht war-: NS-Militär- und Strafjustiz im Vernichtungskrieg,* ed. Manfred Messerschmidt

and Wolfram Wette (Essen, 1996); Stig Förster, "Der Vernichtungsgedanke in der militärischen Tradition des Deutschen Kaiserreichs. Überlegungen zum Problem historischer Kontinuität," in *Krieg, Frieden und Demokratie. Festschrift für Martin Vogt zum 65. Geburtstag,* ed. Christoph Dipper, Andreas Gestrich, and Lutz Raphael (Frankfurt a.M., 2001); J. Förster, "Complicity," 274.

19. See John N. Horne and Alan Kramer, *German Atrocities, 1914: A History of Denial* (New Haven, 2001).

20. Vogelsang, "Neue Dokumente," 434.

21. Both quotes are from Jürgen Förster, "Hitler's Decision in Favour of War Against the Soviet Union," in *Germany and the Second World War,* ed. Militärgeschichtliches Forschungsamt (Research Institute for Military History), vol. 4: *The Attack on the Soviet Union,* 34–35 (Oxford, 1998).

22. On the Wehrmacht in Poland, see Rossino, "Destructive Impulses," and also *Hitler Strikes Poland: Blitzkrieg, Ideology and Atrocity* (Lawrence, 2003).

23. This description of Hitler's points is a synopsis of the notes taken by General Franz Halder, chief of the Army General Staff; see Franz Halder, *Kriegstagebuch: Tägliche Aufzeichnungen des Chefs des Generalstabes des Heeres 1939–1942,* ed. Arbeitskreis für Wehrforschung, Stuttgart, 3 vols. (Stuttgart, 1962), entry for 30 March 1941. On the speech and the audience's reaction, see Wette, *Wehrmacht,* 95–97.

24. See Bradley J. Meyer, "Operational Art and the German Command System in World War I" (Ph.D. diss., Ohio State University, 1988), chaps. 5, 6; David T. Zabecki, *Steel Wind: Colonel Georg Bruchmüller and the Birth of Modern Artillery* (Westport, Conn., 1994).

25. Megargee, *Inside Hitler's High Command,* 64.

26. The quote comes from a speech Hitler gave at Nuremberg, probably in September 1935; a film of the speech is on view at the United States Holocaust Memorial Museum.

27. Michael Thad Allen, *The Business of Genocide: The SS, Slave Labor, and the Concentration Camps* (Chapel Hill, 2002), 12–13. See also Gellately, *Backing Hitler,* 257.

28. Adolf Hitler, *Mein Kampf,* trans. Ralph Manheim (Boston, 1943, 1971), 344–45, 418.

29. Halder *KTB,* entry of March 30, 1941.

30. See David N. Spires, *Image and Reality: The Making of the German Officer, 1921–1933* (Westport, 1984), esp. 36, 47.

31. Kommandeur der 18. Division, 21.7.1938, in Bundesarchiv-Militärarchiv N28/3. Nor was such reasoning unique to the army. Heinrich Himmler reassured members of an SS killing squad in August 1941 that the ultimate responsibility for their actions lay with the Führer. See Richard Breitman, *The Architect of Genocide: Himmler and the Final Solution* (New York, 1991), 195–96.

32. Norman J. Goda, "Black Marks: Hitler's Bribery of His Senior Officers during World War II," *Journal of Modern History* 72/2 (June 2000), 413–52; Winfried Vogel, *Dienen und Verdienen: Hitlers Geschenke an seine Eliten* (Frankfurt, 1999).

33. See Allan R. Millett, Williamson Murray, and Kenneth H. Watman, "The Effectiveness of Military Organizations," in *Military Effectiveness,* ed. Allan R. Millett and Williamson Murray (Boston, 1989), 1:1–30; also Meyer, "Operational Art," 2.

34. See Megargee, *Inside Hitler's High Command,* for an overview of the Germans' strategic and operational beliefs and practices.

35. On the Germans' preconceptions, see Andreas Hillgruber, "Das Russland-Bild der führenden deutschen Militärs vor Beginn des Angriffs auf die Sowjetunion," in *Russland-Deutschland-Amerika. Russia-Germany-America. Festschrift für Fritz T. Epstein zum 80. Geburtstag,* ed. Alexander Fischer, Günter Moltmann, and Klaus Schwabe (Wiesbaden, 1978); also Wette, *Wehrmacht,* 22–32. On the effect on the planning process, see Megargee, *Inside Hitler's High Command,* chap. 6.

36. See Megargee, *Inside Hitler's High Command*, esp. chap. 7. For a more in-depth examination of the planning process, see *Germany and the Second World War*, vol. 4.

37. For an overview of many of the Wehrmacht's crimes themselves, including documentary and photographic evidence, see Hamburger Institute für Sozialforschung, ed., *Verbrechen der Wehrmacht: Dimensionen des Vernichtungskrieges 1941–1945. Ausstellungskatalog* (Hamburg, 2002); also Theo J. Schulte, *The German Army and Nazi Policies in Occupied Russia* (Oxford, 1989).

38. Jürgen Förster, "Operation Barbarossa as a War of Conquest and Annihilation," in *Germany and the Second World War*, 4:481.

39. Christian Gerlach, *Krieg, Ernährung, Völkermord: Forschungen zur deutschen Vernichtungspolitik im Zweiten Weltkrieg* (Hamburg, 1998), 15–17, and *Kalkulierte Morde: Die deutsche Wirtschafts- und Vernichtungspolitik in Weißrußland 1941 bis 1944* (Hamburg, 1999), 46–50; Rolf-Dieter Müller, "From Economic Alliance to a War of Colonial Exploitation. 2(a). Economic Aspects of the Operational Plan," in *Germany and the Second World War*, 4:136–42, and "The Failure of the Economic Blitzkrieg Strategy. 4. The Food-supply Issue: Starvation Strategy or Pragmatism," in ibid., 4:1141–79; J. Förster, "War of Conquest," 481.

40. See J. Förster, "Operation Barbarossa as a War of Conquest," 481–93; the quote is on 485. See also the order "Regelung des Einsatzes der Sicherheitspolizei und des SD im Verbände des Heeres," reproduced in *Verbrechen der Wehrmacht*, 58–60; Helmut Krausnick and Hans-Heinrich Wilhelm, *Die Truppe des Weltanschauungskrieges. Die Einsatzgruppen der Sicherheitspolizei und des SD 1938–1942* (Stuttgart, 1981), 107–72; Christian Hartmann, *Halder. Generalstabschef Hitlers 1938–1942* (Paderborn, 1991), 241–54.

41. J. Förster, "War of Conquest," 485–86.

42. The decree is in *Verbrechen der Wehrmacht*, 46–48; see also ibid., 501–02.

43. Order on "Behandlung feindlicher Zivilpersonen und Straftaten Wehrmachtangehöriger gegen feindlichen Zivilpersonen," in *Verbrechen der Wehrmacht*, 50. See also J. Förster, "War of Conquest," 503–04.

44. The guidelines are in *Verbrechen der Wehrmacht*, 54.

45. The order is in *Verbrechen der Wehrmacht*, 52–53. See also J. Förster, "War of Conquest," 507–11 (the Halder quote is on 508), and "Complicity," 274.

46. Unfortunately, for reasons of space this paper does not address many areas of eastern and southeastern Europe where the Germans also perpetrated atrocities. Readers should note that there were both similarities and significant differences in German motivations and actions in the various countries they occupied. Some of the best new studies are Mark Mazower, *Inside Hitler's Greece: The Experience of Occupation, 1941–44* (New Haven, 1993; Yale, 2001); Bernd J. Fischer, *Albania at War, 1939–1945* (West Lafayette, Ind., 1999); Jozo Tomasevich, *War and Revolution in Yugoslavia, 1941–1945: Occupation and Collaboration* (Stanford, 2001).

# Nazi Foreign Policy towards Southeastern Europe, 1933–1945

## Béla Bodo

Historians of Nazi Germany regularly complain of their difficulty in keeping up with new literature in their field. The number of books published on Nazi foreign policy alone indeed runs into the hundreds, nonetheless, the majority focus on a limited number of themes: continuity and discontinuity in German foreign policy from Bismarck to Hitler; the scope of Hitler's power and ambitions and the nature of decision-making processes in the Third Reich. Two metaphors of the Nazi state dominate such discourse; some historians imagine Germany as a pyramid with Hitler at the apex, decisions flowing from the top down; others see it as a molecule under a microscope, cells dividing, multiplying, and destroying one another randomly. In this short essay, I will ignore organizational history; instead, I will focus on questions that I believe more relevant to general readers: did Hitler's foreign policy fall into the tradition of European diplomacy and late ninetieth and early twentieth-century Western imperialism? Second, did Hitler's foreign policy toward Southeastern Europe represent, as most historian believe, a departure from the Wilsonian idea of national states or did Hitler, by helping to destroy the multi-ethnic states of Yugoslavia and redrawing the borders of Romania and Greece and, at the same time, by preventing the revival of old Hungary, in fact help to complete Wilson's work? Did Hitler's support for ethnic boundaries in Southeastern Europe have to do with his proverbial opportunism or did it stem from ideological convictions? Were there conflicts between ideologically based foreign policy and traditional diplomacy with its focus on economic exploitation and indirect control, and between the means that the Nazis used to achieve their goals and the traditional techniques of Western diplomacy? Did Nazi racism promote or hinder the effective economic exploitation of the region? In short, were Nazi policies toward Southeastern Europe truly an aberration or simply a continuation of traditional European diplomacy?

My goal is to put Nazi foreign policy in an international frame and at the same time increase readers' interests in the history of Southeastern Europe. While the essay is historical in nature, I hope that it also encourages readers to think about general issues such as the nature of alliances between small and larger states and the techniques that great powers often use to pacify world public opinion, keep traditional allies on their sides and obtain new allies. The history of German foreign policy towards Southeastern Europe provides a perfect example not only of victimization but also of the tendency of small states to exploit great power conflicts and act as accomplices to their crimes. The partisan wars in Yugoslavia and Greece between 1941 and 1945 are highly relevant: they shed light on the evolution of guerilla warfare from Chinese revolution to Algiers, Kenya and Vietnam and the present conflict the Middle East.

## The Evolution of Nazi Policy towards Southeastern Europe before 1939

For both political and economic reasons, until the early 1930s, the Weimar Republic showed only limited interest in the Southeastern Europe. The success of German economic policy in the 1920s was predicated upon increased overseas trade and the maintenance of strong economic ties with England and France. The Weimar Republic also looked to the West for political ideas; its democratic politicians had only contempt for the corrupt authoritarian regimes in the region. This Western orientation lasted until the coming of the Great Depression in 1929, which sealed the fate of the international trading system, discredited the idea of free trade and, at same time, changed German attitudes towards Southeastern Europe. The success of the new economic doctrine, i.e. protectionism and autarchy, hinged upon the development of trading blocs dominated by large states. Full sovereignty in this model was given only to the large states; small and medium-sized powers, on the other hand, were expected to follow the lead and adjust their policies to economic and political realities set by great power rivalries and the imbalance of power between rich and poor states. Because of a drastic decline in overseas export and growing trade deficit after 1929, the German government and majority of big businesses felt that trading blocks would serve their interest better than free competition. Their choice was made easier by the crisis of democracy and the concentration of power in the hands of the President and his close advisers brought the Weimer Republic closer to the authoritarian regimes of Eastern and Southeastern Europe.

Outside of sporadic contact with radical authoritarian and fascist groups in Southeastern Europe since the early 1920s, the Nazis knew little about, and had only a limited interest in, the countries of the region. Hitler barely mentioned Southeastern Europe in his *Mein Kampf*, written in the mid-1920s. However, his *Table Talks*, recorded in the early 1940s, show his lack of solid knowledge about the region and its peoples. Hitler seems to have believed in the Germanic origins of the Croats;

typically, he blamed the poverty of Hungarian peasants on their ethnicity and "eastern laziness" and perceived the unwillingness of Romanian soldiers to die for Nazi Germany as a further sign of their Latin background, and hence lower racial value. The outlandishness nature of his beliefs notwithstanding, Hitler's attitude towards the region and its peoples reflected important trends in German political culture. Since the time of Metternich, German statesmen often voiced their disdain for the various ethnic groups in Southeastern Europe. These statesmen's opinions closely matched that of the German public. In spite of the political and cultural domination of the region by Germany, the presence of thousands of foreign students and tourists from the region in both the Second Reich and the Weimar Republic, the German public remained blissfully ignorant about the history and culture of their poor Southeastern European neighbors. In their attitude towards their poor neighbors they resembled the American and British public, which held Central and Latin Americans, and in the case of the British, the Irish, in low regards. What separated the Nazi politicians from traditional German politicians and the German public on the one hand, and politicians and the public in the United States and Great Britain, on the other hand, was the degree to which notions of race impacted their diplomacy. On a practical level, their ideology made it difficult for Nazi leaders to put themselves in the shoes of their negotiating partners and take their interests seriously. Lack of empathy and regard for foreign representatives and nations favored the use of heavy handed methods, including bulling and the threat and the actual employment of force. The Nazis were not only more likely than liberal or conservative politicians to insult and mistreat their guests from south Europe, but they were also prone to underestimate their opponents, ignore political and military realities and be drawn into reckless foreign adventures.

In 1933, however, few statesmen in Southeastern Europe were aware of the extent racism informed Nazi foreign policy. Events between 1933 and 1936 showed that the Nazis were in fact able to tone down their rhetoric and if necessary treat Southeastern Europeans as equals. Indeed, in this period, despite their intense prejudices, the Nazis, mainly for economic reasons, showed more interest in Southeastern Europe than their Weimar predecessors. Hjalmar Schacht, the president of the Reichsbank and the architect of German economic policy between 1933 and 1937, devised an indigenous mechanism to solve the shortage of foreign currency and make German industrial products attractive to agriculturally based countries of Southeastern Europe. Instead of paying hard currency for foodstuffs and minerals, Germany provided her trade partners with industrial goods. Barter agreements seemed to offer advantages to both parties: Germany gained access to cheap agricultural goods and obtained a new market for its industrial products; the countries of Southeastern Europe, on the other hand, could dump their low quality agricultural products on the German market above the world price. By forcing the weaker partners to coordinate their foreign-trade policy with the German system of import controls, the barter deals gave German firms a clear advantage over their Western competitors in Southeastern Europe. By linking exports to imports, barter deals created unusually strong economic ties between Germany and her weaker neighbors, ties that poor countries could ill afford to break and which could be easily be converted into political capital.

The signing of barter agreements, first with Hungary in 1933 and every country in Southeastern Europe over the next three years, helped Nazi Germany to overcome the Great Depression and regain her dominant position in the region. The Nazis' interest in the region seemed first to be economic in nature; like politicians and businessmen in Imperial Germany, they recognized the advantages that the region offered: Southeastern Europe was close and thanks to the development of the modern transportation system its natural riches were easily accessible; the elite spoke German as their second language; they often studied in Germany, and were familiar with German customs, laws and lifestyle. The Nazis naturally recognized the connection between politics and economics; however, they were also careful to not offend these trade partners through over-exploitation. The goal of Nazi foreign policy between 1933 and 1936 was also relatively moderate: they sought to reduce French influence and weaken the power of the Little Entente. Their political goals were wholeheartedly supported by the two revisionist states in the region, Hungary and Bulgaria. Both Hungary and Bulgaria were traditionally pro-German; they fought and lost the war on the side of Germany and hoped to reverse their fortunes with German help. Like Nazi Germany, both Bulgaria and Hungary were diplomatically isolated, and surrounded by hostile neighbors. The Hungarian Prime Minister, the fascist sympathizer Gyula Gömbös, shared Hitler's obsession with the Jews and his hatred for the French, Czechs and Russians. Even in this early stage, however, German interests did not fully coincide with those of her potential allies. The Bulgarian population was pro-Russian, which did not go down well with the anti-Communist Nazis who had design on Eastern Europe. Hungary, on the other hand, had a relatively large German minority, which, deprived by the Budapest regime of collective rights and ignored by the various Weimar governments, looked to the Nazis for protection. Unable to see the connection between its demand for minority right for Hungarians in the neighboring states and its treatment of the German minority at home, the regime in Budapest failed to listen to and was certainly not prepared to fulfill the demands of German-speaking Hungarians. To add insult to injury, the German minorities in the neighboring states opposed Hungarian revisionism and had the audacity to publicize their views. Finally, the Hungarian demand to reincorporate the Burgenland into the land of Saint Stephen and the German desire to keep the province, taken from Hungary in 1919, under its control, continued to create unease on both sides throughout the 1930s.

The status quo states in the region, which had been awarded entire provinces by the victorious powers in Paris after the First World War, were even more suspicious of German intentions. Serbia and Montenegro fought against Germany during the

Great War, while Romania switched sides several times, ultimately ending up in the camp of the victors. The political elite in both countries feared that the Nazis were out to destroy the Versailles system and revise the borders in the favor of their Hungarian and Bulgarian allies. The open admiration that some of the home-grown fascist groups, such as the Serb Zbor, Croatian Ustasha and the Romanian Iron Guard, had for the Nazi system only increased their suspicion. In order to demonstrate their good faith, the Nazis reduced financial support for the Croatian Ustasha in 1934, and maintained only sporadic contact with the Romanian Iron Guard. Still, German-Yugoslav relations remained cool until 1936, despite the signing of an important trade deal in 1934. Similarly, the German origins of the Romanian ruling house notwithstanding, the Nazis made little headway in Romania until 1936. Neither in Romania nor in Yugoslavia were improved trade relations able to dispel suspicion and ill feeling towards Germany. Relations were even worse with Greece and Turkey, with whom Germany had few economic ties and which remained politically outside of the German orbit.

The nature and intensity of Nazi involvement in the region changed dramatically after the start of German rearmament in 1936. Because of its geographical proximity and wealth in strategically important minerals, the value of Southeastern Europe increased rapidly in Nazi eyes. The Nazis recognized that without access to Romanian oil, Hungarian and Yugoslav bauxite and antimony and Turkish chrome, they could not create a modern army and, more importantly, would no be able to wage a modern war. Moreover, the region was nearby; it was relatively easy to defend and the flow of mineral resources and agricultural goods could not be cut off by a naval blockade. The new barter agreements signed after 1936 not only intensified contacts but also changed the very nature of trade relations between Nazi Germany and Southeastern Europe. The import of mineral resources increasingly overshadowed the import of agricultural goods, which, however, also increased in this period. Dependence was further structured by the type of industrial goods that Germany exported into Southeastern Europe: between 1936 and 1939, the countries in the region, especially Romania, Bulgaria and Greece, began to import large quantities of German military equipment. Thus a fateful nexus between natural resources, especially oil, and military equipment was forged. Increased arms imports had serious political consequences: the security of the small states became dependent on German favor; the German military acquired a strategic familiarity with the strength and weakness of the small states' arm forces; German equipment and training made these armies more attractive in the eyes of local military elites and facilitated their integration into the invading German armies during the war.

The incorporation of Austria into Germany in March 1938 and the destruction of Czechoslovakia in the spring of 1939 had serious economic and political consequences. Austria and Czechoslovakia were important to the region as importers of agricultural goods, creditors and providers of industrial equipment and consumer goods. The incorporation of the Austrian and the Czech economies into the German economy drastically increased German economic influence in Southeastern Europe. After 1939, on the average, German shares in the foreign trade of the individual states of Southeastern Europe was about 50 percent. After the German takeover of Austrian and Czech banks, the Third Reich also increased its role as the suppliers of capital. Only in three states were the Germans unable to achieve a position of economic dominance before the war. Albania, as a quasi-Italian colony, was not permitted to develop strong ties with the Third Reich. Greece and Turkey increased their trade with Nazi Germany after 1936; both imported large quantities of war material, and the fascist Metaxas government in Greece harbored strong sympathies for Hitler's regime. However, they continued to maintain strong economic, political and cultural ties with the Western states, which, coupled with strong popular sympathies for Britain and France, kept both countries out of the German political sphere.

After 1936, in contrast to earlier years, close economic ties implied increased political contact and greater dependence on Berlin. Nazi Germany used both economic power and diplomatic tools to overcome lingering distrust for its intentions among Romanian and Yugoslav politicians. Nazi leaders told their Romanian and Yugoslav counterparts that they had more to gain from a friendly relationship with Germany than a hostile one and that the government in Berlin did not necessarily support Hungarian and Bulgarian revisionism. The Hungarians were obviously angered by what they saw as Nazi betrayal and, at the same time, worried about the Nazi intention to annex Austria. Hungary, like Italy, would have favored the continued existence of Austria as a quasi-buffer state between Germany and Southeastern Europe. After the Abyssinian adventure in 1935 and Italian-German rapprochement, however, Hungary had no other option but to swallow the pill and accept the imminent annexation of its sister state. The Rhineland Crisis of 1936, the *Anschluss* in March 1938 and the Sudeten crisis in the fall convinced Germany to reannex the lands that it had lost in 1919. Nazi Germany, however, proved to be a very difficult friend: while it was ready to hand Slovakia to Hungary, the price it demanded was very high. The Nazis wanted the Hungarian government to take military action against Czechoslovakia and, in effect, to accept the odious task of starting a new war. The Nazi leaders failed to empathize with their Hungarian counterparts and did not guarantee that Yugoslavia, with whom Nazi Germany had developed excellent ties after 1936, would not attack Hungary in the case of a Hungarian-Czechoslovak war. Frustrated by Hungarian refusal to play the role of a wall breaker and cut her ties with the Western states, Hitler, under strong pressure from his Italian ally, allowed the return of only southern Slovakia to Hungary in November 1938. He was further angered by unilateral Hungarian occupation of what was left of Ruthenia and the creation of a Hungarian-Polish corridor in March 1939. Hungarian refusal to allow passage of German troops to the Polish front after September 1939 seemed to have permanently cooled relations between Berlin and Budapest. The Hungarians were convinced that Nazi Germany would lose the war; while they remained Nazi Germany's ally, they were also careful not to alienate England and the United States.

Recent political events also forced Yugoslavia and Romania to rethink their ties with both the Western states and Germany. Italy's invasion of Abyssinia in 1935 dealt a heavy blow to the prestige of the Western states and the League of Nations. Even more important was the German occupation of the Rhineland in March 1936, which demonstrated that France and Britain were not willing to go to war in order to defend the postwar international order. The lessons of these two events were not lost on Yugoslavia and Romania, which became increasingly doubtful about the value of their existing treaties with France and the fellow member states of the Little Entente. Romanian and Yugoslavian statesmen believed that normalizing relations with Germany would deprive their revisionist neighbors of their Great Power supporter. Since they had more to offer Nazi Germany, in terms of strategically vital mineral resources, than their competitors, Romania and Yugoslavia could realistically hope that stronger ties with Nazi Germany, if counterbalanced by continued good relations and possible alliance with the Western powers, would strengthen their position in the region. Rational calculation was reinforced by ideological affinities: the regimes of both Romania and Yugoslavia, while never democratic or even liberal by Western standards, moved towards the authoritarian Right after 1936. Still, suspicion of German intentions remained and was reinforced by the incorporation of Austria into Germany in March 1938, the destruction of Czechoslovakia and German support for Polish and Hungarian revisionism. Admiration for German military prowess and maintaining and strengthening existing economic ties was counterbalanced by an even more intense desire to keep out of the Great Power conflicts and maintain their countries' territorial integrity. In order to achieve these goals, both Yugoslavia and Romania, in violation of their treaty obligations, abandoned Czechoslovakia and Poland to their fates in 1938 and 1939 and moved towards armed neutrality. At the same time, they tried desperately to reengage the Western states in the region by concluding new economic agreements and, in the case of Romania and Greece, military alliances with France and England in the spring of 1939. These alliances were not meant to be taken seriously by either parties but served only to deter Nazi aggression. The Nazi attack on Poland, and later on France, forced these to readjust their policies to changed realities.

## Southeastern Europe during the First Stage of the War, 1939–1943

Between 1936 and 1939 Nazi Germany became a dominant power in Southeastern Europe. It achieved this dominant position because the Western powers and fascist Italy were both unwilling and unable to satisfy the economic and security needs of the countries in the region. While Nazi statesmen used every available tool in their arsenal to bring the countries in the region into the German orbit, their most important weapon was the barter agreements that regulated trade between Nazi Germany and the region. After 1939, while economic interests remained important, it was Nazi political and military power that set the tone and determined the outcome of negotiations. The Nazis considered the ethnic groups in the region of generally low racial value. In contrast to the fate assigned to the East Central and Eastern Europe, the Nazis, at least in the short run, did not plan to cleanse the region of its original inhabitants and resettle their homes and farms with ethnic Germans. National states were to survive to ensure the smooth economic exploitation of the region and the recruitment, if the need arose, of auxiliary troops. Nazi Germany refused to conclude a formal alliance with any of its friends in Southeastern Europe even before the war. After the outbreak of the hostility, it tightened its political control; its goal was to turn the countries of the region into satellite and puppet states.

While economic pressure remained important, it was the promise of border revisions that proved to be the Nazis' most powerful diplomatic carrot during the war. The Nazis had a complex attitude towards border revisions and the survival of national states in the region. Hitler held the multi-ethnic Austro-Hungarian Empire in low regard: he had no intention of reviving either Austria-Hungary or the Kingdom of Saint Stephen, in which the Magyars barely made up half of the population. The Nazis preferred national states to multi-ethnic empires not only because they distrusted diversity in any form, but also because they recognized that culturally and linguistically homogenous states were easier to control. At least in theory, the Nazis also admitted that every ethnic group has the right to its own "living space," unless of course this "living space" lay in the German path. Thus, in their attitude towards national states, the Nazis, their hatred of the Versailles system notwithstanding, followed in the footsteps on Wilson, who likewise had little respect for historical rights and boundaries. In two respects, however, the Nazis differed from Wilson in their attitudes towards state formation. First, as strong believers of ethnically homogenous states, the Nazis had no need of nor respect for ethnic minorities and minority rights and were prepared to use or tolerate every means, including transfer of population, ethnic cleansing and genocide, to harmonize ethnic and state boundaries. Second, the Nazis did not consider state boundaries permanent but were ready to award additional "living space" to any ethnic group at its neighbors' expense that had demonstrated its worth in battle or distinguished itself in the service of Nazi Germany. In other words, Nazi attitude towards border revision was guided by the same Social Darwinist ideology that prevented Hitler from getting involved in turf fights between state and party bureaucracies in the Third Reich.

The flexible Nazi approach to border revisions did not stem from unbridled opportunism and lack of principles; it was, rather, the product of Hitler's racism and his unbroken faith in the laws of the jungle. Hitler was a gambler by nature and was prepared to reward foreign states that did not hesitate to take bold actions to advance their interests. Thus, he dangled Burgenland, the whole of Slovakia and Ruthenia before the eyes of Hungarian statesmen in the summer of 1938 in return for Hungarian military commitment to a possible war against Czechoslovakia. When the Hungarian leaders failed to take on the challenge, Hitler immediately retracted his offer and allowed Hungary to reannex only southern Slovakia in early November 1938. Even this limited concession came, however, with a heavy price: Hungary had to leave the League of Nations in February 1939 and, after the grudging German acceptance of the Hungarian annexation of part of Ruthenia in March 1939, it was forced to join the Anti-Comintern Pact. As a result of Nazi pressure, the Hungarian government also introduced harsher anti-Semitic laws and provided more room for fascist parties to organize themselves.

The competition between the revisionist and status quo states for Hitler's favors began in earnest after the conclusion of the Polish Campaign in September 1939. To ensure German support for the upcoming war against its south-eastern neighbor, Hungary increased food deliveries to Nazi Germany in the spring of 1940. Seeking to avert the fate of Czechoslovakia and Poland, Romania, on the other hand, radically increased oil delivery to the Third Reich in early 1940. In return, they wanted Nazi Germany to increase arms sales and restrain both the Soviet Union, which had been a Nazi ally since the signing of the Nazi-Soviet Pact in August 1939, and small revisionist states, such as Hungary and Bulgaria. On July 1, 1940 Romania renounced the Anglo-French guarantee of its frontiers and left the League of Nations less than two weeks later. The king also reshuffled the government to include three members of the Iron Guard, as well as its disputed leader Horia Sima, and introduced anti-Semitic legislation. The Romanians rightly guessed that Hitler had little sympathy for the Hungarians and that he wanted peace in the Balkans to ensure the steady flow of foodstuffs and strategically vital mineral resources into Nazi Germany. Moreover, political stability in the region would deprive both the British and the Soviets of a pretext to get militarily involved in the region, which could threaten the security of the Romanian oil fields.

While the Romanian accurately gauged Hitler's intentions and his lack of support for the Hungarian reannexation of Transylvania, they overestimated his leverage on Stalin. The Russians, on the basis of the Nazi-Soviet Pact, transmitted an ultimatum to Romania on June 26 and a few days later took military control of Bessarabia, Herța and northern Bukovina. Romania immediately requested German occupation but Hitler, recognizing that the whole region could easily explode into a war, suddenly changed his mind and demanded that Romania first reach an agreement with Hungary and Bulgaria. After brief negotiations, Romania accepted the handover of South Dobrudja to Bulgaria but failed to reach a compromise with Hungary on Transylvania. Fearful of the collapse of the Romanian state, which could leave Romanian oil in Russian hands, the Germans were forced to find a peaceful solution to the crisis. With the help of their Italian ally, they finally imposed a compromised settlement on the feuding parties: according to the Second Vienna Award, northern Transylvania, with its Hungarian majority, was to return to Hungary, while southern Transylvania was to remain in Romanian hands. Germany's resort to the ethnic principle as a basis of settlement satisfied, of course, neither the Hungarians nor the Romanians. They felt that Hitler failed to appreciate their love and historical attachment to the entire province. Hitler merely wanted peace in the region and believed that a quick and relatively equitable settlement of outstanding border issues would serve his goal better than the maintenance of the status quo.

The Transylvania issue was kept alive during the war in order to ensure Hungarian and Romanian compliance with Hitler's wishes. Typically, Hitler used the Second Vienna Award to tie both regimes closer to Berlin. In the fall of 1940, Hungary turned from a reluctant ally into a satellite state. It gave up its independent foreign policy, participated in the invasion of Yugoslavia in the spring of 1941 and welcomed the Nazi invasion of the Soviet Union in July. The Romanians were also quick to draw the necessary conclusions from the loss of their territories. In early September, with German support, Marshall Ion Antonescu deposed King Carol, who was unjustly blamed for these disasters, and established a military dictatorship, in which the fascist Iron Guard shared political power with Antonescu's radical conservatives. Impressed by Romanian resolve, Hitler finally complied with their request and sent a military mission to Romania in October. The official purpose of the mission was to train Romanian forces and defend Romania against a possible Soviet or British attack. Its real goal, however, was to protect the oil fields and make the necessary preparations for the invasion of the Soviet Union. Romania was also forced to enter the Tripartite Pact at the end of November 1940, to increase German shares in Romanian oil companies and to increase oil production for the German market. After September 1940, Romania became Hitler's favorite ally in Southeastern Europe and Marshall Antonescu his favorite foreign statesman. He sought and greatly valued Antonescu's advice and met him more often than any other allied leader, Mussolini included. Certainly, politically rational considerations guided Hitler's leanings in this regard: Marshall Antonescu and the Right Radical Conservatives were more popular than the Romanian fascists. Nonetheless, personal sympathy most likely played an important role in Nazi support for the destruction of the Iron Guard in January 1941. While a victim of Nazi state-building in 1940, because of its oil reserves and military contribution to the war against the Soviet Union Romania was poised to profit from a Nazi victory, and Antonescu could realistically expect that Hitler would in the end settle the Transylvania issue in Romania's favor.

Italian response to these events was mixed; while the success of Hungarian and Bulgarian revisionism against Romania in August 1940 encouraged Mussolini, Germany's mission to Romania in early October, without prior consultation with Italy, angered him. Italian power had been on the wane in Southeastern Europe since 1935, when fascist Italy gradually had to give up the title of a dominant power in the

Danubian Basin and the Balkans and accept the role of a junior partner. The invasion of Greece in late October was meant both to impress the Nazis and to regain respect for the fascist regime at home. As predicted by German military experts, the Greek campaign turned out to be a complete disaster. By February 1941, the Greeks had not only ousted the Italians but also conquered one third of Albania. Having been deeply humiliated and her status effectively reduced from that of an ally to a satellite state, Italy was now compelled to ask for German help. Thus Nazi Germany was led into a war that had not been on its agenda and, indeed, one that Hitler had wanted desperately to avoid. Now he felt that Germany had to act not only to save its Italian ally but also to protect the Romanian oil fields from an imminent attack by the British, who had come to Greece's aid. The Germans got militarily involved in the Balkans to expel the British from the continent and also to secure their southern flank on the eve of the Barbarossa Campaign. Although the Greek government was prepared to make painful concessions, including the renunciation of the military alliance with Britain and satisfying at least some of Italy's territorial demands, Hitler could not tolerate the existence of a quasi-neutral state in the Balkans. For the same reason, Hitler decided to combine the Greek campaign with an attack on Yugoslavia. The pretext for this attack had been provided by a successful military coup against a pro-German regime in March 1941. The coup and an anti-German demonstration in Belgrade rekindled Nazi prejudices against both the Serbs, whom the Austrian Hitler blamed for the First World War, and the Yugoslav states, which he considered as a monstrous product of the French-sponsored international order.

The Balkan Campaign achieved its immediate goals: it led to the expulsion of the British from the continent, the destruction of Yugoslavia and the creation of puppet regimes in Croatia, Serbia and Greece. The campaign was effectively over by late April; it was, therefore, not a factor in delaying the attack on the Soviet Union and the subsequent German defeat. The Yugoslav War, nevertheless, marked an important stage in the history of the Second World War: the mistreatment of Serbs, Jews and Gypsies in the spring of 1941 foreshadowed both the murder of millions of Soviet POWs and Communists in the second half of 1941 and the beginning of the Jewish genocide. The war further strengthened Nazi control over its satellite states in Southeastern Europe. Hungary not only allowed German troops to launch their attack on Yugoslavia, with which it had concluded a non-aggression pact only a few months earlier, from its territory but also took military action against its southern neighbor. In return for its services it was allowed to reannex the western part of the Bácska region. Bulgaria acted likewise and was rewarded with the Greek province of Trace and Yugoslav Macedonia. Romania did not profit from the destruction of its former allies. However, it registered with satisfaction that the Nazis did not hand over the eastern part of the Bácska region, which Romania claimed on ethnic grounds, to Hungary but kept it under German military occupation. Hungary and Romania finally threw their lot unequivocally with the Nazis: they came to believe that the

Nazi war machine was unstoppable and recognized that territorial gains were the rewards for active German alliance. On the basis of these perceptions, the Romanian and Hungarian governments offered to participate in the Barbarossa Campaign early in the summer of 1941.

## From Political Hegemony to Total Defeat

Since the late 1930s, Nazi planners had put forward drafts that advocated the creation of an economically and politically unified Europe under German control. Nazi planners described Southeastern Europe as the future "co-prosperity sphere" that would provide Germany with agricultural goods and mineral resources, as well as function as a reservoir of cheap labor. They recognized the need to modernize the region's infrastructure, such as building new roads and establishing more banks, but promoted industrialization only to the extent that it suited the region's agricultural profile. Had they been realized, Nazi plans would have both perpetuated the region's relative backwardness and kept it permanently dependent on Germany. Nazi plans were not only inherently unfair but also unrealistic: they grossly overestimated the economic potential of the region, especially its mineral reserves. Southeastern Europe was not in the position to satisfy the demands of Germany's needs for agricultural goods and mineral resources. Because of its poverty, the region was even less capable of absorbing the industrial surplus of the major continental states.

The Balkan Campaign and the subsequent chaos that ensued put these modernization plans on a back burner. The Nazis continued to talk about the creation of a "European confederation" under German leadership after 1941; however, their short-term goal was to ensure Nazi victory in the war by maximizing the exploitation of foreign nations. Germany continued to export consumer goods and industrial equipment in exchange for strategically vital mineral resources and foodstuffs. It was, however, reluctant to increase the export of military equipment, as well as badly needed iron and coal. Germany's trading partners in Southeastern Europe were angered by the rapid decline in the quality of German industrial goods during the war. They were even more frustrated by the Nazi tendency to run up large debts at their expense.

The degree of Nazi exploitation depended on a number of factors: geographical distance from the Third Reich, the nature of political ties with Nazi Germany (political neutrality or satellite status, for example), the type of mineral resources it exported to Nazi Germany and the negotiating skills of business and political leaders in the region. As a general rule, geographical proximity to Germany meant heavier control over local economic and political systems and greater exploitation. Neighboring states, such as Slovakia and Hungary, were forced to integrate their economies closely into the German war economy. Slovak and Hungarian factories produced mainly for the German market and the better part of their agricultural exports also ended up there. Their mineral resources fueled the Nazi war machine, and they were required to send tens of thousands of laborers into the Third Reich. Hitler's Germany purchased their exports on credit, and since the Nazis had no intention of settling their accounts, the Nazi import of industrial and agricultural goods from these countries in effect amounted to sheer robbery. On the other hand, Turkey, a geographically more distant and politically neutral state, was able to drive a hard bargain with the Germans, receiving up-to-date military and industrial equipment, in addition to iron and steel, in exchange for mineral resources and agricultural products. Turkey kept German debt within acceptable limits, because no German troops were stationed on its soil, and it possessed a mineral that Germany could not do without: chrome iron. German clearing debt in Bulgaria also remained low because this Balkan satellite state had little to offer to the German war economy; much of the debt, in fact, came from the stationing of German troops in the country.

Romania occupied a somewhat intermediary position between Hungary and Slovakia, on the one hand, and Turkey, on the other. Like Hungary, Romania was a satellite state; it was, moreover, Germany's most important military ally in Southeastern Europe against the Soviet Union. On the other hand, it was geographically more distant from Germany and possessed a strategically vital natural resource, crude oil, which it could exchange for modern military equipment, industrial machinery and coal. Highly conscious of the importance of oil to the operation of the German war machine, Romanian negotiators always drove a hard bargain, threatening several times during the course of the war to reduce grain exports to the Third Reich and demanding that the Germans settle their accounts in weapons and gold. Because of these factors, German clearing debt remained under control until 1943, but it skyrocketed afterwards. While the Nazis extorted more goods and services from Hungary than any other nation in the region, it was the puppet states of Croatia and Serbia that, in relation to their size and wealth, had to pay the heavier price for the war. They had to cover the cost of German occupation, send tens of thousands of foreign workers into the Reich, and were forced to put their natural resources at the disposal of the German and Italian governments. The gross exploitation of satellites and puppets was bound to fail and in the end proved both economically and politically counterproductive. The piling up of German debt soon translated into run-away inflation, which, in turn, led to rapid decline in real wages and to higher prices and shortages of consumer goods. The increased misery of the population increased tensions between the allied governments and the Third Reich and, especially in Serbia and Croatia and after 1944 in Slovakia, boosted the armed resistance. The growing insurgency, in turn, made occupation more costly, both in human and material terms, and further hindered the economic exploitation of the former Yugoslav states. In addition, the rapid decline in the export of militarily important mineral resources, such as copper and oil had a negative effect of the Nazi war effort and forced the German government to import these resources from other, mainly northern European, states. German economic policies, then, increased the alienation of the countries in the region from Nazi Germany and contributed to the Nazi defeat in the war.

Economic exploitation was only one of the many causes for the growing insurgency in the former Yugoslavia and Greece. In Yugoslavia, the Wehrmacht finished its mission within a few weeks; however, it was never able to pacify the country. The Germans neglected postwar planning and failed to consider the impact of their military campaign. The use of terror tactics, including the blowing up of trains and public buildings, attacks on army barracks and assassinations of military and political leaders could have been foreseen; such tactics, after all, had a long tradition in the Balkans and continued to be used by various political groups in the interwar period. Second, the redrawing of the map in favor of Italy, Croatia and Bulgaria disaffected the Serbs and Greeks and alienated them from the German occupiers. Third, Nazi support for the murderous Ustasha regime and German toleration of Italian atrocities could not but further alienate the Serb population. Moreover, Nazi backing of the Ustasha regime precluded a lasting truce between Germany and the Serbian nationalist partisans, making it difficult for the German military leaders to play the nationalists off the dangerous and uncompromising Communist insurgents. Fourth, the multiplicity of bureaucracies with overlapping areas of oversight, a phenomenon typical of Nazi rule, only increased chaos and lawlessness in both the former Yugoslavia and Greece. Lack of cooperation between army commanders and the SS and the local police forces in combating the insurgency was particularly harmful to the German war effort, while SS brutality, supported and constantly encouraged by Hitler and other top Nazi leaders, only drove the local population even deeper into the arms of the partisans. There were military commanders, especially after 1943, who warned against supporting the Ustasha regime and about the adverse effects that use of torture, the burning down of entire villages, imposing higher levies, the summary execution of civilians and sending women and children to concentration camps had on the fight against the partisans. While registered by Hitler and his colleagues, however, such advice had little effect on overall Nazi policy. Hitler and top policy makers believed that the Serbs, and to a lesser extent the Greeks, knew and respected only naked power and violence. The same distrust prevented Nazi leaders from handing over more power to the collaborationist regimes and arming their police with heavier weapons. The Nazis ignored their repeated requests to end the indiscriminate killing of civilians and to lower the financial burden of the military occupation. Unable to prove to their people that they would gain more from cooperating with the German army than from resisting them, the collaborationist governments quickly lost the trust that they had originally enjoyed, at least among some civilians, thus removing the last buffer that stood between the occupying forces and the insurgents.

The Germans did achieve some important victories over the partisans. During the second half of 1941 they dealt a crushing defeat to the insurgency, a blow from which Serbia was unable to recover until 1944. The partisans were not eliminated, however, but moved the center of resistance to other parts of the former Yugoslavia, including Montenegro, Bosnia and eastern Croatia. The Germans were able to win individual battles and capture and kill tens of thousands of insurgents and their real or alleged supporters, without, however, extinguishing the movement. They failed to eliminate the insurgency for a number of reasons. First, the German troops in the former Yugoslavia were of generally low quality. Second, they were in the country to deter a possible landing of Allied forces, which was seen as a real possibility, and to protect factories, mines, roads, railway lines and other venues of communication. The Germans simply did not have the manpower to fulfill these tasks and, at the same time, deal effectively with the partisan threat. Third, as mentioned above, their heavy-handed tactics and the economic exploitation of the land drove the local population into the arms of the insurgents. Fourth, the partisans could always recover from their setbacks, while the Germans increasingly lost heart and had difficulty replenishing their forces after 1943. German reports of progress against the insurgency were based on meaningless body counts, which were meant to impress the Nazi military and political leaders. Such statistics, however, were misleading, because many of the victims were innocent civilians caught between the two opposing forces, and masked real failures. The insurgency would only gain steam as the war turned against the Germans and the population could see the end of the conflict. By late 1943 most people supported the partisans and waited eagerly for the arrival of Allied troops.

The Nazis were more likely to achieve their economic and political goals in countries that were not under German military occupation. Traditional Russo-phobia, hatred of Communism and, most importantly, the desire to gain or regain territories, mainly at one another's expense, kept Hungary, Slovakia and Romania solidly in the Nazi camp until the end of the Battle of Stalingrad in early February 1943. The heavy human and material losses that the Romanians and Hungarians suffered in this battle, combined with the news of Allied successes in Italy and the Far East, made the two satellite states and the puppet regime of Slovakia more cautious during the last two years of the war. The Nazis wrenched up their anti-Soviet and anti-Communist rhetoric during the last stage of the conflict. Nonetheless, their slogans about common destiny and shared European civilization that had to be defended against the invading barbarians failed to convince anyone about the sincerity of their intentions. By mid-1943, the elites in Southeastern Europe were looking for an honorable way out of the conflict. They wanted to be on the side of the victors or at least be seen as the victims of Nazi aggression, rather than accessories to Nazi crimes. The Serbs, Slovaks, Romanians and Greeks sought the restoration of their prewar borders, and, if possible, the conquest of additional lands at their neighbors' expense. The Hungarians and the Bulgarians, on the other hand, expected to keep at least part of the territories that they had gained during the war. Finally, the elites in the region looked forward to an Anglo-Saxon, rather than a Soviet, victory, because they recognized that Soviet control would lead to the dismantling of the political and economic elite, social engineering and the loss of national independence. The Nazis were prepared to take extreme measures to prevent their allies' desertion. They tended to be successful in countries closest to the Third Reich, such as Hungary and Slovakia. The Nazis knew these countries the best and had succeeded, by 1943, to completely penetrate their bureaucracy and army. Since the Nazis had less interest in Bulgaria and their power had been essentially limited to a few strategic points in Serbia and Greece by early mid-1944, the loss of these countries in the course of 1944 was a foregone conclusion. Because of its oil reserves and strategic location, Romania was vital to the German war effort. However, thanks to the conspirators' shrewdness and the ineffectiveness of the Gestapo, part of the old elite and the army succeeded in deposing Antonescu's regime in August 1944. Romania fought the rest of the war on the side of its traditional enemy, the Soviet Union, and in return for its sacrifice, was rewarded with northern Transylvania and the Bánát. The defeat of the Slovak uprising and the installation of an Arrow Cross regime in Hungary in the late fall of 1944 could not hide the fact that Nazi Germany had been abandoned by all of its allies. If the success of a great power's foreign policy is measured by its ability to build and maintain alliances, then the foreign policy of Nazi Germany proved to be a failure.

## Conclusion

This short survey of Nazi foreign policy towards Southeastern Europe suggests that in foreign policy it is often impossible to separate economic interests from strategic and ideological considerations. In modern foreign policy economic considerations are colored by personal prejudices and cultural proclivities. In regards to Nazi foreign policy towards Southeastern Europe, economic interests seem to have overshadowed other concerns before 1939. Still, political goals, such as the weakening of the Little Entente and the elimination of French and British influence, were not far below the surface. After 1936, economic contacts with Southeastern Europe were closely tied to strategic interests and rearmament. Whereas economic dominance paved the way for political domination before 1939, during the war it was political and military events that determined the forms that business contacts took. The fact that the economic exploitation of Southeastern Europe served a larger and essentially ideological goal, i.e. the conquest of *Lebensraum* in the East, makes the relationship between economics and politics look even more complicated (even though the Nazi obsession with "living space" also contained both rational or economically based and irrational or ideological elements). The Nazis did not stop at restoring German economic dominance in the region: they had long-term plans that foresaw the creation of a European Union with Nazi Germany at its center. In this new continental economy, Southeastern Europe was assigned the role of a supplier of raw materials and agricultural goods and a provider of cheap labor. Had these plans been realized, Southeastern Europe would have been reduced to the status of a semi-colony without any chance of every moving from the semi-periphery to the center of the economic system. This vision was both economically and ideologically motivated: the role the Nazis allotted to these countries reflected the low regard they had for the various peoples in the region. The gross exploitation of the region during the war was not dictated by military considerations alone. War was, after all, the Nazis' natural element, and murder and slave labor were, according to Nazi ideology, the rightful lot of people of lesser worth. The gross exploitation of the region was not an aberration; it provided only a foretaste of what was awaiting the peoples of the region after Nazi victory. Similarly, the techniques that the Nazis used to combat the growing insurgency cannot be blamed exclusively on military logic and on partisans' cruelty. While terrorism had a long history in the Balkans, after 1941 it was primarily a reaction to the Nazi mistreatment of the population and the violation of their ethnic and national identities. Thus, the partisan war in Yugoslavia and Greece bore a close resemblance to the anti-colonial insurgencies of the twentieth century in Asia, Latin America and the Middle East.

In Nazi foreign policy, ideological and economic considerations went hand-in-hand, mutually reinforcing, rather than excluding, one another. This short essay has also shown, however, that a similar overlapping of motives informed the Nazi decision to redraw the map of Southeastern Europe. The Nazis did not act as traditional conservatives when it came to changing borders and creating new states. They had no desire to turn the clock back and restore the multi-ethnic empires or feudal states in the region. The Nazis accepted the idea of national states for two reasons: first, they distrusted diversity in any form; second, they recognized that states in which the elites shared the language and culture of their subjects tended to be more stable. As modern nationalists, Nazis supported the establishment of state boundaries that followed more closely ethnic lines, despite their barely hidden distaste for some of the beneficiaries, such as the Hungarians. Strategic and economic considerations again complemented and reinforced, rather than displaced, ideological concerns: the fear of Soviet occupation of Romanian oil fields or British landing in the Balkans may have acted as a stimulus to settle the Transylvanian issue between Hungary and Romania, but the form of the final decision reflected an essentially modern nationalist outlook. The Nazis were, of course, no liberals, and in their ideal state they had no place for minorities and, therefore, no need for minority rights. Unlike Western liberals, the Nazis were prepared to use every available means to harmonize state and ethnic boundaries, including the transfer of population, ethnic cleansing and genocide. Strong believers in the idea of the survival of the fittest, the Nazis, moreover, did not see, as most modern politicians do, state boundaries as permanent and anchored in international law and treaties. The metaphor that they followed was the ancient *limes* that separated the tribes in Roman times and the early Middle Ages and that changed according to the economic needs and military prowess of individual tribes.

They were ready to readjust the borders if their allies had proved themselves victorious in the struggle for the survival of the fittest and if they distinguished themselves in the service of Nazi goals. In other words, the Social Darwinist ideology that informed Hitler's approach to turf fights in the Third Reich also colored his attitude towards the question of state boundaries. As his *Final Testament*, dictated just before he committed suicide in the bunker of the Chancellery suggests, Hitler remained an ideologue until the bitter end. To him, defeat in the war only proved that the German people were unworthy of him and that, since the law of the jungle had favored the Russians, the German people were ripe for extinction. Consistent in his political beliefs, this father of the Second World War and Jewish genocide most likely died with a clear conscience.

# References

Ádám, M. *A kisantant (1920–1938)*. Budapest, 1981.

Berend, T. I., and Gy. Ránki. *Economic Development in East-Central Europe in the 19$^{th}$ & 20$^{th}$ Centuries*. New York, 1974.

———, eds. *Hungarian Economy in the Twentieth Century*. New York, 1985.

Browning, C. *The Path to Genocide*. New York, 1992.

Bracher, K. D. *The German Dictatorship*. New York, 1970.

Carr, W. *Arms, Autarchy, Aggression*. London, 1979.

Czettler, A. *A mi kis élethalál kérdéseink: A magyar külpolitika a hadba lépéstől a német megszállásig*. Budapest, 2000.

Fülöp M., and P. Sipos. *Magyarország külpolitikája a XX. században*. Aula, 1998.

Haynes, R. *Romanian Policy towards Germany, 1936–40*. New York, 2000.

Heinen, A. *Die Legion "Erzengel Michael" in Rumänien: Soziale Bewegung und politische Organisation*. Munich, 1986.

Hilberg, R. *Destruction of the European Jews*. New York, 1985.

Hildebrand, K. *The Foreign Policy of the Third Reich*. London, 1973.

Hillgruber, A. *Hitler, König Carol und Marshall Antonescu: Die deutsch-rumänischen Beziehungen, 1938–1944*. Wiesbaden, 1965.

Hitchins, K. *Rumania, 1866–1947*. Oxford, 1994.

Jellinek, Y. *The Parish Republik: Hlinka' Slovak People's Party, 1939–1945*. Boulder, 1976.

Juhász, Gy. *Magyarország külpolitikája 1919–1945*. Budapest, 1969.

Lackó, M. *Nyilasok, nemzetiszocialisták 1935–1944*. Budapest, 1966.

Maier, K., et al. *Germany and the Second World War*, vols. 1–5/2. Oxford, 1991–2003.

Miller, M. L. *Bulgaria during the Second World War*. Stanford, 1975.

Nagy-Talavera, N. M. *The Green Shirts and the Others*. Stanford, 1970.

Nebelin, M. *Deutsche Ungarnpolitik 1939–1941*. Opladen, 1989.

Nemeskürty I. *Requiem egy hadseregért*. Budapest, 1972.

Ormos, M. *Magyarország a két világháború korában 1914–1945*. Debrecen, 1998.

Paris, E. *Genocide in Satellite Croatia, 1941–1945*. Chicago, 1960.

Payne, S. *A History of Fascism 1914–1945*. Madison, WI, 1995.

Pritz, P. *Magyarország külpolitikája Gömbös Gyula miniszterelnöksége idején 1932–1936*. Budapest, 1982.

Ránki, Gy. "Hitlers Verhandlungen mit osteuropäischen Staatsmännern, 1939–1944." In *Deutsche Frage und europäisches Gleichgewicht*, ed. K. Hildebrand and R. Pommerin, pp. 195–228. Vienna, 1985.

Ránki, Gy, et al. *Magyarország története*, vol. 8/2. Budapest, 1978.

——. *A Harmadik Birodalom Árnyékában*. Budapest, 1988.

Sakmyster, T. *Admirális Fehér Lovon: Horthy Miklós, 1918–1944*. Boulder, 1994.

Schlarp, K.-H. *Wirtschaft und Besatzung in Serbien 1941–1944*. Stuttgart, 1986.

Schmider, K. *Partisanenkrieg in Jugoslawien 1941–1944*. Hamburg, 2002.

Streit, C. *Keine Kameraden: Die Wehrmacht und sowjetische Kriegsgefangenen, 1941–1945*. Stuttgart, 1978.

Sugar, P., ed. *Native Fascism in the Successor States, 1918–1945*. Santa Barbara, 1971.

Szakály, S. *Hadsereg, politika, társadalom*. Budapest, 1991.

Tomasevisch, I. *War and Revolution in Yugoslavia, 1941–1945: The Chetniks*. Stanford, 1975.

Trevor-Roper, H. R. *Hitler's Secret Conversations 1941–1944*. New York, 1953.

Weinberg, G. *The Foreign Policy of Hitler's Germany: Diplomatic Revolution in Europe, 1933–1936*. Chicago, 1970.

——. *The Foreign Policy of Hitler's Germany: Starting World War II, 1937–1939*. Chicago, 1980.

——. *A World at Arms: A Global History of World War II*. Cambridge, 1994.

# The Second World War and Its Aftermath

## Ethnic German Communities in the East

### ◆ John C. Swanson ◆

Does the expression "German" refer to citizens of Germany or members of the larger German cultural sphere? The editors of this volume acknowledge that this is a fundamental question, especially since in 1910 nearly a quarter of Europe's German speakers lived outside the German Reich. After World War I and the redistribution of territory, there were even more "Germans" outside of what was called Germany.[1] Today we would label these "Germans," as the League of Nations did in the first half of the twentieth century, as minorities. Reich Germans saw them as *Volksdeutsche*, in contrast to *Reichsdeutsche*.

Discussions of "Germans in the East" usually emphasize the ethnic identity of these individuals as "Germans," often in reference to some kind of connection to the mother country. But the category of "German," or in this case "German minority," refers to a plastic expression that can be molded to mean various things, from numerous perspectives. One should always keep in mind that when discussing a minority the perspective of the mother country differs from the point of view of the leadership of the minority. And in addition to the perspective, or level of understanding, of the mother country and that of the leadership, there is also the viewpoint of the nation-state in which the minority lives, as well as that of the mass of the minority, which often does not correspond equally with that of its leadership.[2]

Discussing a minority, such as the Germans in the East, requires some finesse, since the concepts of "German" and "Germany" can carry various meanings. Such a study also necessitates a foundation in the chronology. The following article will provide a general overview of the leadership of the German minorities in Eastern Europe and its understanding of the "imagined community" of Germans. The emphasis will be on the transition from a more nuanced sense of what "German" meant, at least in local contexts, to a more ethnic understanding of German as part of a larger Germandom, especially as affiliated with Nazi Germany. The article is based mainly on secondary material, and its focus is on the "Germans" in former Habsburg lands not adjacent to Germany or post-1918 Austria: that is, in Hungary, Romania, and Yugoslavia. The German speakers in Poland and Czechoslovakia have received attention in other articles in this volume.[3]

Among the German minorities in Hungary, Romania, and Yugoslavia, as well as those in Poland and Czechoslovakia, there was a clear move in the 1930s into the camp of the National Socialists. In all countries Nazi-type organizations were created, which not only received funding and other forms of assistance from the Reich,[4] but also followed its lead in many ways. Yet this drift toward the right was often the outcome of a clash between an old and new guard among the German speakers in these countries. In telling this story it needs to be emphasized that these German minorities were minorities, in the plural. There were various groups and organizations, representing various interests.

## Germans in Hungary

According to the Treaty of Trianon in 1920, the Kingdom of Hungary was officially reduced to one-third its original size. The multi-national Kingdom, in which the ruling Magyars had represented slightly less than 50 percent of the population in the early twentieth century was replaced with a fairly homogeneous, Magyar nation-state, where only 10.4 percent of the inhabitants did not speak Magyar as their native tongue. In post-World War I Hungary, the German speakers were the largest minority, consisting of 521,211 individuals—6.9 percent of the population—according to the 1920 census.

These German speakers were (and are) collectively referred to as Swabians, even though a small percentage of their forefathers came from that part of southwest Germany,[5] and the majority of these Swabians were peasants—smallholder peasants. Upwardly mobile German speakers often assimilated during the nineteenth and early twentieth centuries, when Magyardom welcomed almost anyone who embraced the Magyar language and culture, and many Hungarians of Swabian origin became super-Magyar patriots.[6] Unfortunately, this meant for the German-speaking minority the loss of highly educated and political active members.

The leadership of the German speakers within Hungary's pre-1920 borders therefore had been Transylvanian Saxons or Swabians from the Banat—two areas that were given to neighboring, successor states at the end of the war. The individual who would emerge after 1918 as the new leader of the Hungarian Germans was Jakob Bleyer (1874–1933), a professor of German literature in the years before the war.[7]

Bleyer, a Swabian from a rural village in the Bacska, came to symbolize the majority of the peasant Swabians, much more than some of the more assimilated Germans who would also fill leadership roles during the interwar years, especially Gustav Gratz (1875–1947).[8]

For a short tenure between 1919 and 1920, Jakob Bleyer served as the minister of nationalities, but after the failure to convince all German speakers in Western Hungary (Burgenland) to support unification with Hungary, the ministry and Bleyer's position were terminated. Afterwards Bleyer's goals were to support and enhance the cultural rights of the Hungarian Germans, especially the ability to use their language in school and church. Both of these rights had theoretically been guaranteed before the war in the nationalities law of 1868 as well as in subsequent legislation. The minority treaties supported by the League of Nations, to which Hungary was a signatory, also upheld such rights. But the policy of Magyarization—of forced assimilation, which had begun in the nineteenth century, was intensified after Trianon.[9]

In order to reach the German-speaking peasants, Bleyer began publishing in 1921 a German-language newspaper, *Das Sonntagsblatt*, which he directed to the German-speaking peasants of Hungary, as well as to those in the lost territories. In 1923 the German minority created a cultural organization, *Der Ungarländischer Deutscher Volksbildungsverein* (Cultural Association of the German People in Hungary), which received government approval in 1924. The goal of Bleyer and others in the 1920s was to promote a sense of loyalty to both the Hungarian nation and to the German Volk.

Bleyer and his colleagues tried, via the *Volksbildungsverein* and *Das Sonntagsblatt*, to promote what today would be considered a very mild, conciliatory minority policy: one that accepted membership in the Hungarian fatherland, with loyalty to a sense of Germandom as well. Unfortunately, in the interwar years, the majority of the Hungarians, who considered treacherous any deviation from Magyardom, did not welcome this. The fiercest opposition to the Hungarian Germans usually came from petty officials in the counties or the villages.[10]

Jakob Bleyer, Gustav Gratz, and others could be considered the old guard, and as times changed in Hungary and Europe, a new cadre developed. Many, even some of the older generation grew tired of the slow pace of change and the continual opposition to any improvements in the field of minority, especially language, rights. One of Bleyer's students, Franz Basch (1901–1946),[11] began to demand more rights for the Germans. The developing clash intensified after Bleyer's death in 1933.[12]

In November 1938 Basch founded the *Volksbund der Deutschen in Ungarn*[13] (Volksbund of Germans in Hungary) as an opposing organization to the *Volksbildungsverein*, then run by Gratz and Franz Kussbach—Bleyer's actual successor. In all practical purposes the *Volksbildungsverein* ended in 1933 upon Bleyer's death, even though it would continue to exist for seven more years.[14] Because of changes in

Nazi-dominated Europe and Hungary's association with Nazi Germany, the German government convinced Hungary to recognized the German *Volksgruppe* as a national community, as separate from the Magyars, accept Basch as the leader of the German *Volksgruppe*, and grant the *Volksbund* the right to decide who belonged to the German Volk. The protocol also granted the right to members of the German minority to express freely their belief in National Socialism.[15]

The emphasis here on the leadership of the German-speaking minority does not always make clear how far the academic, political, or even cultural goals were the desires of the majority of the Germans, who were peasants. It is possible to point out that in 1930 the *Volksbildungsverein*, the moderate organization of Bleyer, had 10,280 members and was present in 179 villages. Since membership in this organization covered a whole family, there were approximately 60,000 members.[16] Unfortunately, it is not possible to provide exact membership details for the *Volksbund* at its height in 1944, since most of those documents perished during the final phase of the war. Basch, however, asserted in 1941 that there were over 50,000 members. The historian G.C. Paikert argues that if one includes the hangers-on and family members of the *Volksbündler*, 150,000–200,000 would be a conservative estimate for the membership in the *Volksbund*.[17]

In most of Eastern Europe by the late 1930s the new guard—a more "German conscious" group—had come to control the German minority. In cooperation with Nazi Germany Basch and the *Volksbund* would assist in Waffen SS recruitment drives, even before they were authorized by the Hungarian government.[18] Beginning in 1940, before the Germans were desperate for recruits, Swabian youngsters participating in sport programs in the Reich were convinced of the honor of joining the Waffen SS. By early 1942, however, these clandestine attempts were not enough,[19] and Germany concluded an agreement with Hungary to allow, and even coerce, Swabian youth into joining the Waffen SS. There were a number of recruitment drives under modifying conditions. For the poorer Swabians who joined the SS they faced many problems, including being ostracized by their supposed German brethren.[20] The exact number of recruits is questionable, yet one can estimate that by 1943 there were approximately 23,000, and by war's end over 120,000.[21]

As in all parts of Eastern Europe, the German minority drifted into the national socialist camp and participated in Nazi Germany's war, often as "Germans." Yet, as among all these minority groups, this picture is much more complicated. The Hungarian-German Swabians were usually more interested in their rural lives than they were in the rhetoric of the Great Powers or even of their leaders. According to Anthony Komjathy, "the great majority of ethnic Germans still remained apolitical or neutral."[22]

Even though the German movement shifted from the cultural organization of the *Volksbildungsverein* and Jakob Bleyer to the more political *Volksbund* and Franz

Basch, there were other German speakers who chose a different path. In January 1942 an anti-*Volksbund* organization, Loyalty Movement (*Die Treuebewegung or Hűség Mozgalom*), was formed, with support from Franz Kussbach.[23] Despite its difficulties, it possessed 2,000 members in the county of Tolna and 8,500 members in the county of Baranya.[24] It tried to uphold the ideals of a dual loyalty to both the German Volk and the Hungarian nation.

## Saxons and Swabians of Romania

In 1920 the German population of Romania numbered 715,900: 4.5 percent of the population.[25] Most of these German speakers were in territories annexed after the dissolution of Austria-Hungary and the Russian Empire. (Romania in 1912 only possessed 29,400 German speakers.) Even though Romania labeled all German speakers as "Germans," this group was very heterogeneous.[26] Saxons had been in Transylvania since the twelfth century and had enjoyed a privileged status, which allowed them to preserve their language, culture, and many of their customs. The Swabians of the Banat journeyed to this part of Europe after the treaty of Passarovitz in 1718. There were also smaller groups of German speakers in various places, such as those in Bukovina and Moldavia, some of whom had been in that part of Europe since the thirteenth century.[27]

The Saxons and the Swabians, as well as other German speakers scattered throughout Transylvania and the Banat suffered in the nineteenth century because of the Hungarian policy of Magyarization—forced assimilation. This Hungarian chauvinism led the leaders of the Saxons and Swabians to sign the Karlsburg Declaration in 1918 and profess their desire to join Romania, not remain in Hungary. In exchange the Romanian authorities granted a great deal of freedom to the German speakers, especially in the realm of assembly and forming organizations. Of all the Eastern European Germans, the ones in Romania were the best organized and the best administered. Already in 1919 they produced five daily newspapers in German and twenty-seven periodicals, calendars, and other publications. (In 1933 this number increased to around 20 daily newspapers and more than 100 other publications.)[28]

The *Deutsche Partei* (German Party) was formed in 1920 by German members of the Romanian parliament (led by Rudolf Brandsch [1880–1953] and Hans Otto Roth [1890–1953]), and the umbrella organization, the *Verband der Deutschen in Rumänien* (Association of the Germans in Romania) was created in September 1921.[29] The goal of the latter was to maintain the cultural interests of the Germans in Romania and support solidarity among the varied German-speaking groups.

As elsewhere, the advent of National Socialism in Germany led to a rift in the German leadership in Romania—a division that could be described as a struggle between the old and new. The old guard had reservations concerning drifting too far in the direction of Nazi ideology, and in Romania this group was represented by

Hans Otto Roth, a Saxon, who in the early1930s led the *Verband der Deutschen in Rumänien*. The migration towards Nazi ideology began with a "self-help" movement in Romania, led by Friedrich (Fritz) Fabritius (1883–1957), who in 1934 transformed the "self-help" movement into the *Nationalsozialistische Erneuerungsbewegung der Deutschen in Rumänien* (National Socialist Revitalization Movement of the Germans in Romania). And in 1935 Fabritius took over the umbrella organization of the *Verband der Deutschen in Rumänien*.[30]

Fabritius proved too liberal, however, for the Reich German organizations that were trying to control and influence *Volksdeutsche* activity, and in June 1935 there was another split between the supporters of Fabritius and the admirers of Alfred Bonfert (1904–1993) and Waldemar Gust, who went another step closer to Nazi ideology. By 1940 at the helm of the Romanian *Volksdeutsche* appeared the 28-year old Andreas Schmidt (1912–1948), who had been trained by the SS and who diligently followed the lead of the Third Reich. The Germans were then to be represented by the newly formed *NSDAP der Deutschen Volksgruppe in Rumänien* (National Socialist German Workers' Party of the German Volk in Romania). As among other ethnic German communities in Eastern Europe, the subordination to Berlin "confused the simple ethnic German about where his loyalty should be directed: toward Romania or, through the ethnic leaders, toward Germany."[31]

The main work of the National Socialist leadership in Romania was to fulfill the needs of the Reich, which by the early 1940s meant recruiting soldiers for the SS and the German Wehrmacht. As in other parts of Eastern Europe, recruitment drives in 1940 were carried out in secret as young men were shipped off to Germany under the guise of participating in sport programs. The Romanians permitted, according to an agreement with the German government in April 1943, recruitment drives in Romania for the Waffen SS and the German armed forces, and by the end of 1943 more than 60,000 *Volksdeutsche* had enlisted in the Waffen SS and over 15,000 in the Wehrmacht and other German units.[32]

Of course, the question remains as to what was the reaction of the ethnic Germans outside the leadership positions. The number of German-speaking recruits by 1943 is telling: ten percent of the total German population in Romania. Yet the shift toward Nazi ideology in ethnic German organizations was not always welcomed. At times there were counter-forces, usually from the Catholic Swabians in the Banat, against a more intense National Socialist direction.[33] The Swabians of the Banat, as well, "deserted the SS in greater numbers than any other ethnic German group."[34]

# Germans of Yugoslavia

Similar to the majority of the Germans in Romania, those in Yugoslavia had been subjects of the Habsburgs before 1918. In 1921, however, there were 505,790 German speakers in the mostly Slavic state of the Kingdom of Serbs, Croats, and Slovenes.[35]

(The Serbs, Croats, Slovenes, and Macedonians comprised 82.9 percent of the population.)[36] The Germans, who slightly outnumbered the Hungarians, in the new successor state were located mainly in the Banat, Bascka, and Baranja regions (23.8 percent of the total), followed by the provinces of Croatia and Slovenia (3.8 percent).

The majority of these German speakers were peasants: 80 percent lived in agricultural communities. Various co-operatives, financial institutions, and flourmills in these areas were run by Swabians, sometimes with financial subsidies from Germany. Two-thirds of these ethnic Germans were Roman Catholic, and approximately one-third was Lutheran.

Shortly after the proclamation of the southern Slavic state, the German speakers founded the *Schwäbisch-Deutscher Kulturbund* (Swabian-German Cultural Union) on 20 June 1920, with its offices in Novi Sad. Originally it was to be the cultural organization of the ethnic Germans, but it soon became the minority's main organization, and with the advent of Nazism, the *Kulturbund* became an outpost of National Socialist propaganda.

Before the creation of the dictatorship of King Alexander II in 1929 and the dissolution of all political parties, there was a German Party, *Partei der Deutschen im Königreich der Serben, Kroaten und Slowenteten* (Party of the Germans in the Kingdom of the Serbs, Croats, and Slovenes), which was able to send delegates to the Yugoslav parliament during the early 1920s. In the changed circumstances under King Alexander II's dictatorship, the Germans, however, gained definite advantages, thanks to the help of certain members of their leadership who were able to negotiate pro-German minority policies. Part of the reason for these concessions to the Germans was Belgrade's fear of Hungarian irredentism in the border regions inhabited by both Germans and Hungarians.

The increase in Nazi influence among the German speakers of Yugoslavia followed the general pattern of a struggle between the old and new leadership. Those who opposed the moderate Stefan Kraft composed a group that called itself the *Erneuerer* (the revitalizers), which was led by Sepp (Joseph) Janko. The *Erneuerer* were not able to make headway until 1939, when Nazi Germany had made its move in Central Europe and after various Reich organizations poured large amounts of funds into Nazi-leaning activities.

Unfortunately, as in other parts of Eastern Europe the ethnic Germans became pawns in Hitler's wartime plans. When the pro-Axis government of Dragisa Cvetković (1893–1969) was overthrown in March 1941 by the Allied-leaning General Dusan T. Simović (1882–1962), the Swabians became the objects of anti-Nazi sentiment in Yugoslavia. And according to Nazi propaganda, these activities led Hitler to invade Yugoslavia in April 1941, even though Nazi Germany at the time felt obligated to bail out its Axis ally—Italy—in the Balkans.

What was of more interest for the German war effort was to prevent ethnic Germans from joining the Yugoslav military as Germany prepared its attack in 1941. In March 1941 the Supreme Command of the German Armed Forces issued a "Führer's Directive" to the Swabian leadership instructing the youth to „play truant in face of mobilization."[37] Others were informed of how to sabotage the Yugoslav war effort.

Swabian demands, especially for annexation to the Reich or autonomy, were not heeded when Yugoslavia was partitioned after Nazi victory. The northwesternmost part of the Vojvodina was returned to Hungary; the western part of the Banat fell to reduced Serbia, which was under the control of the German military. And the rest of the territory inhabited by Swabians was annexed by the new independent state of Croatia. Germany did make sure that certain rights were guaranteed to their ethnic brethren in these alien states, and German speakers in German-occupied territories, such as the Banat, did gain a certian amount of authority, despite their lack of experience in administration. Often this newly acquired power was used to oppress the local Serbian population, creating thereby more tension between Germans and Serbs.

With German control of Serbia, and Croatia as a loyal underling of the Reich, the German speakers in these regions now followed directives from Berlin as they created new Nazi organizations. A special police force and armed units, composed of ethnic Germans, were formed to fight the growing guerilla activity against the Nazi presence in the Balkans. As in other parts of Eastern Europe, ethnic German youths were recruited into the German war machine; as early as 1938 Swabians left Yugoslavia to join the Waffen SS, and once Germany became a presence in the former Yugoslavia, recruitment drives for the Waffen SS officially began. The goal of the Reich German Gottlob Berger (1896–1975), who had also been active in recruitment campaigns in Romania, was to establish a separate SS division out of the Yugoslav *Volksdeutsche.* Eventually, after some problems attracting new recruits, male German speakers volunteered, were coerced, or forced into the German military; the majority from this regions served together in the 7th SS Volunteer Mountain Division „Prinz Eugen," which was formed in April 1942. From the Banat 15,000 served in the Prinz Eugen Division and 600 in the German Wehrmacht. From Croatia 17,538 served in the Waffen SS, 1,386 in the Wehrmacht, 2,636 in the Croatian military, 3,488 in the police battalions, 2,200 in the Organisation Todt, and approximately 4,500 in the labor force *Einsatz im Reich.*[38]

The Prinz Eugen Division intensified the ethnic tension in the region, since its activities were aimed mainly at the local Slavic population, especially against Serbian and Greek partisans. Perhaps one of the worst atrocities of the Prinz Eugen Division was the massacre on 27 March 1944 when hundreds of Serbian civilians were murdered in the villages of Ruda, Cornji, Dorfer Otok, and Dalnji in Dalmatia. The Division had been involved in murder in various parts of the Balkans, justified in thier minds as collective punishment against partisan supporters. After May 1944 the Division was led by Friedrich Kruger (1894–1945), who had been responsible for liquidating the ghettos of Poland and the operation of major concentration camps. It is clear that these activities created an anti-German population in south Eastern Europe,[39] which might be able to explain the harsh treatment administered by the post-war parties.

Despite the fact that the majority of the ethnic Germans of the former Yugoslavia sided with Nazi Germany and participated in the atrocities against others, there were those who opposed this route. Some Swabians, especially the Catholic clergy believed that National Socialism was too secular and too nationalistic.[40] They were a small number, but there were ethnic Germans among the partisans. Also, one of the most famous, anti-Nazi activists was the Catholic Priest Adam Berenz who published the newspaper *Die Donau* in the city of Apatin.[41]

## The Expulsions

After the Second World War, more than ten million Germans were expelled from Central and Eastern Europe: three million from Czechoslovakia, seven million from within the new borders of Poland and the Soviet Union,[42] and hundreds of thousands from Hungary, Romania, and Yugoslavia. This process began with fierce brutality,[43] and partly because of this, the Allies reached a consensus at Potsdam in August 1945 for the "orderly and humane" transfer of ethnic Germans out of Eastern Europe.[44] By 1949 a figure closer to twelve million ethnic Germans had been resettled in one of the two Germanys. Two-thirds of the expellees were sent to western zones, primarily the American and British zones; one-third found themselves in the Soviet occupation zone. A small percentage also ended up in Austria. Of those in what would become the German Democratic Republic, forty percent left for the West before 1961.[45]

The expulsions from Hungary, Romania, and Yugoslavia all followed similar, yet different paths. The goal was to rid the so-called nation-states of ethnic Germans, those who had acted supposedly as German agents during the war. Theoretically, members of fascist organizations and those allied with Nazi Germany were to be deported, but in practice decisions were often made at random or for someone else's economic gain. Of the three countries under study, only Hungary fell under the guidelines of the Potsdam agreement.

### Hungary

With the arrival of Soviet troops in Hungary, Swabians, as well as Magyars, were removed to labor camps in the Soviet Union. Of the 600,000 people taken by the Red Army 30,000–35,000 were *Volksdeutsche* civilians and approximately 30,000 were *Volksdeutsche* P.O.W.'s.[46] Many of these Swabians and Magyars would not return.

Not only did German speakers suffer at the hands of the Soviet army, but also the new Hungarian authorities and the general Hungarian public very soon took a negative stance vis-à-vis individuals labeled as "Germans."[47] All Swabians were considered collectively guilty for the war and its destruction, and many Hungarians viewed the Hungarian Germans as Hitler's fifth column.

The Communists, who were not yet the governing force in the country, took an unambiguous anti-German stance after the war. Under their influence, the government issued a decree in June 1945 that specified that Swabians who had been members of, or supported, National Socialist organizations would lose their homes and be resettled. The issue of removing Germans was also crucial for the new land reforms and to free housing for Hungarians being resettled in Hungary from Czechoslovakia and Transylvania.[48]

Each country reacted differently to its "German Problem." Of the three under review only Hungary would have to abide by the agreement of the Big Three (the United States, United Kingdom, and the Soviet Union) at Potsdam in August 1945. Initially the Allies had agreed to the expulsion of Germans from Poland and Czechoslovakia, to which the Soviets proposed adding the Germans of Hungary as well.[49] Much of the pressure to move the Germans out of Hungary also came from the Czechoslovaks' desire to rid Czechoslovakia not only of Germans but of Magyars as well, who would then need homes in Hungary. At Potsdam they stipulated that the number of Germans might be 200,000–250,000, which was approximately half the Germans in Hungary. This number was actually doubled in November 1945 to 500,000, which would have included all German-speaking individuals in Hungary.

The actual expulsions from Hungary took place in two separate phases. Throughout the year 1946 approximately 170,000 Swabians were taken to the American zone in Germany. Their arrival with few material goods and little money forced the Americans to request a stop to the expulsions from Hungary. Therefore the next transport, which took place during the second half of 1947 (with one train load in the summer of 1948), shipped 50,000 individuals to the Soviet zone in Germany. Many of the decisions for deportations were carried out "at random at the whim of the authorities and the political stratum in power."[50] Despite all this, approximately 2000,000–220,000 Swabians remained in Hungary, only to be affected by a more intense Magyarization process.

### Romania: The Saxons and Swabians

The coup against Marshal Victor Antonescu (1882–1946) on 23 August 1944 brought to power an anti-German government in Romania that ordered a cease-fire on all fronts. Some of the German speakers, approximately 1,000 were carried away with the retreating German military, as a new line of defense was created on the Romanian-Hungarian border against the advancing Soviet forces. During the last months of 1944 approximately 100,000 Swabians fled Romania; the majority of the Transylvanian Saxons and Banat Swabians, however, remained.[51]

After the advance of the Soviet troops, around 75,000 Swabians were taken as forced laborers to the Soviet Union in 1945. Unlike Hungary, Romania did not resort to official expulsions, yet many Swabians fled to one of the two Germanys,[52] and at various times, some returned. Yet it is well known that during and after the communist period in Romania, many Saxons left for Germany.

### Yugoslavia

The situation in Yugoslavia was different, especially as compared to that in Romania, which was never occupied by Reich Germans. After the dismemberment of Yugoslavia, the German authorities and the German military were very much a part of Croatia and Serbia. And when times turned for the worse for the German military at the end of 1943, preparations commenced for the evacuation of *Volksdeutsche*. By the end of October 1944, all German speakers from west Slavonia and Syrmia had been evacuated, and during October Swabians from the Bacska and Baranja were transported to the Reich. The Swabians of the Banat remained until the last minute, and many were then not able to flee. Paikert points out that according to German estimates, sixty percent (300,000 out of 500,000) of the *Volksdeutsche* left Yugoslavia; and according to Yugoslav sources, over eighty percent fled.

The German speakers who did not flee lost many of their rights. Tito's partisans passed a resolution in November 1944 stripping *Volksdeutsche* of citizenship and the protection of Yugoslav laws. (At this time, however, the real power in the country, at least theoretically, rested with the exiled Royal Yugoslav Government in London.) During the period immediately following the cessation of hostilities, the German speakers fell victim to the general feeling of revenge that permeated the populace. In October and November 1944 communist partisans massacred, often in a very horrific manner, many ethnic Germans, as well as Hungarians, in Bacska and the Vojvodina. Many German speakers were interred in labor camps, in which close to one-third (10,000) died between October 1945 and March 1948. From December 1944 to January 1945 some 27,000 to 37,000, mostly women between 18 and 40, were taken to the Soviet Union, and those who survived were not sent back to Yugoslavia, but rather to East Germany in 1949. These actions left very few German speakers in Yugoslavia; according to the Yugoslav census in 1953, there were 62,000 *Volksdeutsche* in the country.[53]

## Conclusion

German speakers are often considered "German," even though their sense of ethnic belonging may have subtle differences. In the years after the Great War many German-speaking organizations in the East were led by individuals whose actions strengthened the idea that German speakers are German, but they could also be members of other nations and states. For example, a Hungarian German could be loyal to both the Hungarian nation and the German *Volk*. However, influenced by the propaganda of Nazi Germany and an intensifying chauvinism of many of the interwar Eastern European governments (a topic that was not included in this paper) the younger leadership of Eastern European Germans became more and more German. They aligned themselves and their organizations with the country that stood for Germans: National Socialist Germany. This new guard in Hungary, Romania, and Yugoslavia worked toward intensifying a much more "German" and usually National Socialist sense of identity among the Germans in the East.

This static view of what "German" means is very apparent in the ideas and actions of the leaders of the *Volksdeutsche*, as well in the ideology of National Socialism. Unfortunately, this simplified understanding would remain after the war, when most of the new governments of Eastern Europe began expelling the German speakers as "Germans."

The shift in the late 1930s in the direction of National Socialism and the rhetoric that supported the expulsions after the war are based on the same logic: German speakers are German. It has been pointed out that there were German-speaking individuals in all three countries who tried to oppose this direction, but usually with little success. Another topic, one that needs to receive more attention, is how the mass of the German speakers, usually the German-speaking peasants, defined their sense of Germanness. This article on the perspective of the German minorities' leadership should help set the stage for more in-depth studies of the mass of the minorities.

## Notes

1.  The border changes after World War I left approximately five million Germans in countries outside of Germany and Austria. This number does not include the two million German speakers in the newly created Soviet Union. Stefan Wolff, *The German Question since 1919: An Analysis with Key Documents* (London and Westport: Praeger, 2003).

2.  For a more detailed discussion concerning these various levels of understanding, see John C. Swanson, "Minority Building in the German Diaspora: The Hungarian-Germans," *Austrian History Yearbook* 36 (2005), 148–66.

3.  In addition, some of the best studies on Germans in Czechoslovakia are Ronald M. Smelser, *The Sudeten Problem, 1933–1938: Volkstumspolitik and the Formation of Nazi Foreign Policy* (Middletown: Wesleyan University Press, 1975); and Rudolf Jaworski, *Vorposten oder Minderheit? Der sudentendeutsche Volkstumskampf in den Beziehungen zwischen der Weimarer Republik und der CSR* (Stuttgart: Deutsche Verlags-Anstalt, 1977). For a thorough discussion of Germans in Poland, see Richard Blanke, *Orphans of Versailles: The Germans in Western Poland 1918–1939* (Lexington: University Press of Kentucky, 1993). See also Kai Struve and Philipp Ther, eds., *Die Grenzen der Nationen: Identitätenwandel in Oberschlesien in der Neuzeit* (Marburg: Verlag Herder-Institut, 2002).

4.  The Reich organizations and the forms of assistance they offered the ethnic Germans is itself a fairly long and interesting story. Because of space, this article will not focus on this relationship. For more information, see Anthony Komjathy and Rebecca Stockwell, *German Minorities and the Third Reich* (New York and London: Holmes & Meier Publishers, Inc., 1980); and Valdis O. Lumans, *Himmler's Auxiliaries: The Volksdeutsche Mittelstelle*

*and the German National Minorities of Europe, 1933–1945* (Chapel Hill: University of North Carolina Press, 1993).

5. In this paper I will use the expressions German speakers, Swabians, Hungarian Germans and Germans somewhat interchangeably. Officially they are now referred to as Hungarian Germans (*Ungarndeutsche* or *magyarországi németek*). Since the Second World War they also have been lumped into the category of Danubian Swabians, which has become popular in Germany to refer to ethnic Germans expelled from Hungary and Yugoslavia. See Gerhard Seewann, "Siebenbürger Sachse, Ungarndeutscher, Donauschwabe? Überlegungen zur Identitätsproblematik des Deutschtums in Süsosteuropa," in *Ungarndeutsche und Ethnopolitik*, ed. Gerhard Seewann (Budapest: Osiris—MTA Kisebbségkutató Mühely, 2000).

6. The most infamous example is minister-president Gyula Gömbös, whose original family name was Knöpfle. See Paul Lendvai, *The Hungarians: A Thousand Years of Victory in Defeat* (Princeton: Princeton University Press, 2003), 354.

7. For more information about Bleyer, see Hedwig Schwind, *Jakob Bleyer: Ein Vorkämpfer und Erwecker des ungarländischen Deutschtums* (Munich: Verlag des Südostdeutschen Kulturwerks, 1960); and Márta Fata, "Minderheitenkonzeption und -politik Jakob Bleyers," in *Jakob Bleyer: Ein Leben für das Ungarndeutschtum*, ed. Wendelin Hambuch (Budapest: St. Gerhards-Werk Ungarn, 1994).

8. Gustav Gratz, who served as foreign minister for a short time in 1921, often is portrayed as too "Magyar" for most of the German speakers, but one should not forget that he often acted out of what he believed was in the best interest of all Hungarian Germans.

9. According to C. A. Macartney, "Magyar opinion, conscious and unconscious, underwent a violent and perhaps a natural reaction to the old ideas and practices. It felt that concessions to the nationalities were not only futile but wrong in principle. . . . If the nationalities had only been Magyarized they would never have been lost. The fault had thus lain, not in too much Magyarization, but in too little." C. A. Macartney, *Hungary and Her Successors: The Treaty of Trianon and Its Consequences, 1919–1937* (London: Oxford University Press, 1937), 447.

10. G. C. Paikert, *The Danube Swabians: German Populations in Hungary, Rumania and Yugoslavia and Hitler's Impact on Their Patterns* (The Hague: Martinus Nijhoff, 1967), 92.

11. He was executed on 26 April 1946 by the People's Tribunal in Budapest. For more concerning this trial and a detailed picture of Basch, see Gerhard Seewann and Norbert Spannenberger, *Akten des Volksgerichtshofs gegen Franz Basch* (Munich: Oldenburg, 1999).

12. Even before his untimely death, Bleyer had begun to search for alternative avenues of assistance. In May 1933, Bleyer journeyed to Munich, where he met with Rudolf Hess, deputy leader of the Nazi Party, regarding how much pressure the German government was willing to place on its Hungarian counterpart. See György Ránki et al., eds., *A Wilhelmstrasse és Magyarország: német diplomáciai iratok Magyarországról, 1933–1944* (Budapest: Kossuth Könyvkiadó, 1968), 55 ff.

13. A more detailed discussion of the *Volksbund* can be found in Norbert Spannenberger, "A Volksbund: Egy népcsoport nemzetiszocialista szervezete vagy emancipációs kisebbségi egyesület?" *AETAS* 4 (2000), 50–63; and Norbert Spannenberger. *Der Volksbund der Deutschen in Ungarn 1938–1944 unter Horthy und Hitler* (Munich: Oldenburg, 2002).

14. It also received money from Germany during this period, since it was Nazi policy to support a moderate German organization as well as one more in line with Nazi ideals. This is based on Hitler's address to representatives of societies concerning *Auslandsdeutschtum* in 1934. C. A. Macartney, *October Fifteenth: A History of Modern Hungary, 1929–1945*, 2nd ed., volume 1 (Edinburgh: Edinburgh University Press, 1961), 169–170.

15. This was part of a protocol signed by Joachim von Ribbentrop (1893–1946) and Count István Csáky (1894–1941) for Hungary, which was associated with the Second Vienna Accord, on 30 August 1940, when Hungary received territory from Romania.

16. Paikert, *The Danube Swabians*, 91. According to Hedwig Schwind, in 1925 there were 8,000 members in 200 communities. Schwind, *Jakob Bleyer*, 102.

17. Paikert, *The Danube Swabians*, 127.

18. The best literature on this subject is by Loránt Tilkovszky. See Loránt Tilkovszky, "Die Werbeaktionen der Waffen-SS in Ungarn," *Acta Historica* 20 (1974).

19. Many of these early recruits were from the re-annexed territories, especially the Bacska. See Tilkovszky, "Die Werbeaktionen"; and J. Mirnics, "Die Batschkadeutschen zur Zeit der ungarischen Besetzung (1941–1944), *Acta Historica Academiae Scientarum Hungaricae* 18 (1972), 319–351.

20. The Hungarian Germans in the SS usually spoke Hungarian among themselves, since their command of German was more broken German than real fluency. Because of this, German Germans often called the Swabians "Hungarian pigs." Tilkovszky, "Die Werbeaktionen," 152.

21. Paikert, *The Danube Swabians*, 147.

22. Komjathy, *German Minorities*, 63.

23. For a more thorough and balanced view of the Loyalty Movement, see Norbert Spannenberger, "Die "Treuebewegung." Mythos und Wirklichkeit einer "ungarndeutschen" Untergrundbewegung," *Südostdeutsches Archiv* 40/41 (1997/1998), 107–132.

24. Paikert, *The Danube Swabians*, 128–129.

25. Georges Castellan, "Nationalism and Separatism," *Journal of Contemporary History* 6, no. 1 (1971), 52–75.

26. For a discussion of various forms of German-Jewish relations in Romania, see Hildrun Glass, *Zerbrochene Nachbarschaft: Das deutsch-juedische Verhaeltnis in Rumaenien (1918–1938)* (Munich: Oldenbourg, 1996).

27. For a very good analysis of the multicultural society in Bukovina, see Mariana Hausleitner, *Die Rumänisierung der Bukowina: Die Durchsetzung des nationalstaatlichen Anspruchs Grossrumäniens 1918–1944* (Munich: R. Oldenbourg, 2001).

28. Paikert, *The Danube Swabians*, 250–251.

29. For a discussion of the German organizations in Romania during the interwar period, see Harald Roth, *Politische Strukturen und Strömungen bei den Siebenbürger Sachsen 1919–1933* (Cologne: Böhlau Verlag, 1994).

30. Komjathy, *German Minorities*, 112.

31. Komjathy, *German Minorities*, 121.

32. Paikert, *The Danube Swabians*, 254. Komjathy points out that these figures are somewhat controversial. Komjathy, *German Minorities*, 123.

33. Paikert, *The Danube Swabians*, 252.

34. Komjathy, *German Minorities*, 123.

35. Many argue that the results of the 1921 and the 1931 censuses were inaccurate. Representatives of ethnic German organizations did not recognize these results. See D. Biber, *Nacizem in Nemci v Jugoslaviji 1933–1941* (Ljubljana, 1966), 16–17. As cited on http://www.hic.hr/books/seeurope/016e-geiger.htm.

36. For a general discussion of Germans in interwar Yugoslavia, see P. Mentzel, "The German Minority in Inter-War Yugoslavia," *Nationalities Papers* 21, no. 2 (1993).

37. Paikert, *The Danube Swabians*, 276.

38. Paikert, *The Danube Swabians*, 280–281. Paikert notes that the fate of the Prinz Eugen Division is not known in detail.

39. Komjathy, *German Minorities*, 145.

40. Paikert, *The Danube Swabians*, 269.

41. Adam Berenz, *Weitblick eines Donauschwaben* (Dieterskirch: Kreis von Donauschwaben, 1968).

42. See Detlef Brandes, *Der Weg zur Vertreibung 1938–1945: Pläne und Entscheidungen zum "Transfer" der Deutschen aus der Tschechoslowakei und aus Polen* (Munich: Oldenbourg, 2001); Richard G. Plaschka, ed. *Nationale Frage und Vertreibung in der Tschechoslowakei und Ungarn 1938–1948: Aktuelle Forschungen* (Vienna: Verlag der österreichischen Akademie der Wissenschaften, 1997); Bernadetta Nitschke, *Vertreibung und Aussiedlung der deutschen Bevölkerung aus Polen 1945 bis 1949*, trans. Stephan Niedermeier (Munich: Oldenbourg, 2003). Philipp Ther, *Deutsche und polnische Vertriebene. Gesellschaft und Vertriebenenpolitik in der SBZ/DDR und in Polen, 1945–1956* (Göttingen: Vandenhoeck & Ruprecht, 1998).

43. See Alfred-Maurice de Zayas, *A Terrible Revenge: The Ethnic Cleansing of the East European Germans, 1944–1950* (New York: St. Martin's Press, 1994).

44. "All the Allies did in Potsdam was to give formal consent to the 'orderly and humane transfer' of ethnic Germans." Wolff, *The German Question*, 55.

45. Wolff, *The German Question*, 67–69.

46. Theodor Schieder, *Dokumentation der Vertreibung der Deutschen aus Ost-Mitteleuropa*, vol. E (Bonn, 1956–1958), 44. As cited in Paikert, *The Danube Swabians*, 195.

47. Members of the Volksbund were, of course, considered German, but so were all who had listed "German" as their nationality in the 1941 census, which was the first time in Hungary that membership in a nationality was asked in addition to native tongue.

48. To the extent that many of these questions were settled based on economic interests instead of ethnic ones, see Agnes Tóth, *Migrationen in Ungarn 1945–1948. Vertreibung der Ungarndeutschen, Binnenwanderungen und slowakisch-ungarischer Bevölkerungsaustausch*, trans. Rita Fejer (Munich: Oldenbourg, 2001).

49. Stephen Kertész, *Minority Population Exchanges: Czechoslovakia and Hungary* (New Haven, 1948), 179–208. As cited in Paikert, *The Danube Swabians*, 204.

50. Paikert, *The Danube Swabians*, 208. See also Tóth, *Migrationen in Ungarn.*

51. Schieder, *Dokumentation*, vol. E, 75. As cited in Paikert, *The Danube Swabians*, 258.

52. Joseph Mileck, *Zum Exodus der Rumäniendeutschen. Banater Sanktmartiner in Deutschland, Österreich und Übersee* (New York: Peter Lang, 1999).

53. Schieder, *Dokumentation*, vol. E, 117. As cited in Paikert, *The Danube Swabians*, 290.

# The Era of European Integration

## Günter Bischof

In an insightful essay published in the inaugural volume of *Contemporary Austrian Studies*, Charles Maier dissected the intellectual *Mitteleuropa* discourse so prevalent in the late 1980s early 1990s. He contrasted Austrian and German ideas of *Mitteleuropa* with those emanating from Central European intellectuals behind the iron curtain like Hungary's Georgi Konrad, Czechoslovakia's Vaclav Havel, and Poland's Adam Michnik, as well as exiles such as the Czech Milan Kundera. On the Austrian side the "heirs of Musil's Count Leinsdorf" aligned around Minister of Science Erhard Busek proffered an idealistic multicultural *Mitteleuropa*—a roseate "neo-Habsburg revery" of tolerance and liberalism. "In terms of religion, it was a community of Catholic humanists and dead Jews," notes Maier acerbically. It was an Austrian revery that never existed in reality, one that was "long on culture and sentiment, short on funds."

Maier compared the Austrian vision with the economically "well-heeled" German *Mitteleuropa* represented in Musil's vulgar Arnheim. It expressed itself through intellectuals, commerce and conquering soldiers. In Maier's words, "Germany's Central Europe is Protestant and Hanseatic, active and present-minded, endowed with a deep purse and for now a benevolent capitalist vision." He adds: "Where the Viennese spin a network of memories, the Germans press a policy of economic assistance." He concludes that "Mitteleuropa is not a viable enough concept to support Austria's mission [of being a bridge-builder]; focusing attention on German influence will ultimately undermine Austria not reinforce it."

Meanwhile the *Mitteleuropa*-intellectuals behind the Iron Curtain blamed the West for selling their region out to the Soviets and communist oppression at Yalta. They claimed "autonomy of the lands between the Germans and the Soviets against the Brezhnev doctrine." Their vision of *Mitteleuropa* that had been democratic and liberal in the interwar years (at least Czechoslovakia) represented, according to Maier, "a spiritual *maquis* under late communism" that assaulted a spiritually and intellectually decaying state ideology. Their Central Europe was a myth, albeit a useful one, as one of the most astute observers of this region during its era of decaying communism Timothy Garton Ash observed.[1]

Maier's conclusion was a prescient one in 1992 when he wrote the essay. He asserted that "the appropriate construct for these lands of the center must ultimately be an enlarged European Community."[2] Indeed, on May 1, 2004, after a long and complex and controversial accession process, most these lands of East Central Europe did join the European Union. They now resume their drive westward economically, politically, and mentally that had been stopped in its tracks first by Hitler's war of aggression and extermination and then by the heavy-handed Soviet occupation after World War II. Both totalitarianisms cast long shadows into the present. Coming to terms with both those pasts is a challenge that the nations of Central Europe will be facing for a long time. Yet Eva Hahn's essay also raises a cautionary note—there are plenty of skeptics in East Central Europe about the benefits of the "new internationalism" of European unification.

The point Maier is making implicitly is that the interaction between Germans and Austrians and their neighbors in Eastern Europe is a complex one. It needs to be understood from the perspectives and discourses and mental maps of all sides. Historians of this region know all too well that the narratives told in the region are vastly different. All three essays in this section focus on clashing historical narratives between Germans and Austrians and their neighbors to the East. Central to these discourses is the locus of the ravages National Socialism brought to the area during World War II. To Czechs and Poles Hitler's aggressive interwar diplomacy (the 1938 "Munich Agreement") and subsequent invasion and destruction of their state represents their nation's crucial turning point. Millions of people were egregiously victimized—uprooted, killed, or shipped to the Third Reich (Germany and the *Ostmark*) as slave laborers in the war economy. Hungarians and Croats, among others, have to come to terms with their collaboration with the Nazis.

Eva Hahn reminds us that the arrogant German paradigm of bringing civilization and modernization to the backward Slavs is largely rejected by most intellectuals in the region. This narrative of "German exceptionalism" is highly contested by the Eastern European natives, just like American exceptionalism is viewed as a brazen and self-serving ideology of conquest by native Americans.

The expulsion of the Germans from Eastern Europe in the wake of the Soviet liberation and conquest of this region from Hitler's destructive conquest and exploitative occupation left an explosive legacy that still affects bilateral relations with the countries of Eastern Europe, especially Poland and the Czech Republic. William Gray's essay dissects the German revisionist historical narrative of the expellee organizations and their postwar demands for the non-recognition of borders and return (or, more recently, compensation) for the lost property. More recently the historical "guilt" narrative sparked by Willy Brandt's *Ostpolitik* has prevailed, admitting to

German original culpability. The symbolic language of Brandt's *Kniefall* in Warsaw is representative of this narrative.[3]

The Austrian journalist Barbara Coudenhove-Kalergi has written that the expulsions of Sudeten Germans from Czechoslovakia in 1945 has produced two radically different historical narratives among Czechs and Sudeten Germans—with Austrians largely adopting the expellees' version of history.[4]

Meanwhile, the Austrian postwar narrative on relations with East Central Europe allowed the "victim's myth" of Austria as Hitler's first victim to suppress and ignore its own culpability. 1.3 million Austrians served in the Wehrmacht units that invaded, occupied and brutalized Czechoslovakia, Poland, Yugoslavia, and the Soviet Union, and fought in the destructive defense of Budapest in the spring of 1945—events that eventually led to the expulsion of the ethnic Germans of Eastern Europe, who at the end of the war were all seen as "Nazi collaborators." Austrian careerists starting with Eichmann and his team were overrepresented in the machinery of death and destruction producing the Holocaust. Numerous people from Eastern Europe suffered and died in the Austrian concentration camp system of Mauthausen and POW-camps such as Krems-Gneixendorf. Tens of thousands of slave- and forced laborers toiled in the *Hermann Göring Werke* and numerous other industrial establishment as well as on farms in the "*Donau- und Alpengaue.*"[5] Only recently has the Austrian government—following in the wake of a German restitution settlement—agreed to begin facing up to this ugly past and share responsibility for this slave labor exploitation by paying restitution to the aggrieved.[6]

Unlike West Germany, Austria regained her statehood and elected a government by the end of 1945 and reestablished diplomatic relations with its neighbors to the East in 1946. The expulsion of the Germans deeply affected Austria's relations with its neighbors too.[7] As the essay by Günter Bischof and Martin David argues, the traditionally strong trading relationship with Czechoslovakia collapsed amid years of mutual recriminations over the expulsions and unresolved territorial and property claims. The same could also be argued with Yugoslavia and Hungary. Moreover, relations with Hungary were affected deeply by the aftershocks of the Hungarian Revolution of 1956 and the tens of thousands of refugees who fled to Austria.[8] Every Cold War and post-Cold War crisis on Austria's borders sparked similar refugee crises—Czechoslovakia in 1968, Poland in 1981, and the collapse of Yugoslavia in the early 1990s. In each case Austria sheltered and supported thousands of refugees until they found a permanent home further west.

Each of these refugee crises also unleashed old *Feindbilder* and ancient xenophobia about Slavs and "barbarians in the East" on the mental map of the Austrian population.[9] This is, indeed, a reminder that Austria's historical relationship with Eastern Europe is not all multiculturalism and Baroque and Schönbrunn-yellow with its afterglow of roseate memories. There is also the subtext of wars and battles and conquest from the Battle of White Mountain to the suppression of numerous Hungarian rebellions. Eva Hahn rightly points a finger at a similar interaction throughout history between Germans and their neighbors to the East.

During the Cold War Austria's favorite image of its role vis-à-vis its Eastern European neighbors was that of a bridge-builder between the ideological antagonists. Chancellor Leopold Figl invoked this image during his inaugural address to the newly elected parliament on 20 December 1945 when he mentioned the "Austrian spirit" that for centuries had mediated European conflicts and would continue to do so.[10] In 1955 Austria was fortunate to regain full sovereignty and end the four-power occupation regime by pledging "eternal neutrality" as part of the deal that produced the State Treaty. Scholars have argued that Austrian neutrality became a "model" for east European neighbors like Hungary as a means of ending Soviet occupation.[11] Fanciful or not, it indicates that there are many forms of intellectual constructs of Austrian "bridge-building" extant in the postwar era from Figl to Busek. Its historic mission as bridge builder in the Danubian region has been both part of postwar Austrian identity construction and Austrian exceptionalism.

Bruno Kreisky's was the most effective strategy for penetrating the Iron Curtain—that Cold War construct that deeply divided regions which had closely interacted across the centuries.[12] Austria's most gifted postwar political leader initiated an Austrian *Ostpolitik* ten years before his friend Willy Brandt by injecting his activist neutrality policy to bring about détente between the Cold War power blocs.[13] Kreisky's aggressive neutralism made Vienna a favorite site for East-West high-level summitry and arms control negotiations. Kreisky pushed the Helsinki process early on and, thus, can be considered one of the godfathers of the short-lived Cold War period of détente. Helsinki produced the dissident movements that played a crucial subterranean role in bringing down the Iron Curtain and ending the Cold War.[14] Kreisky, first as foreign minister and then as chancellor, also began initiating regular diplomatic visits with Austria's communists neighbors that helped normalize strained bilateral relationships.[15] Clearly, Kreisky's *Ostpolitik* played a role similar to the one Willy Brandt performed for the two Germanies, albeit without a spectacular *Kniefall*. It is still puzzling, but Kreisky's politics of history fully adhered to Austria's postwar victim's myth, which prohibited such symbolic gestures.

Vienna itself played a bridge-building role between East and West. Only Berlin played a more active role as a playground for the Cold War's secret services.[16] Allowing windows to open into the shadowy world behind the Iron Curtain and "knowing your enemy" presumably also served as a form of meditation in the East-West antagonism. As it had for centuries under the Habsburgs, the city's rich cultural scene offered ample opportunities for Czech, Polish and Hungarian cultural elites to interact with the West. Its stages regularly featured Eastern European talent in opera, drama, and classical symphonic music. Refugees such as the journalist Paul Lendvai made spectacular careers—in his case in interpreting events in Eastern Europe from Vienna to the West—just as the expellee Countess Marion Dönhoff wrote for West German audiences with great sensitivity about her former homeland in the East. At the same time, Austria's most discrete bridge-builder surely was the long-time archbishop of Vienna and "Catholic humanist" *par excellence,* Cardinal Franz König. The gentle and modest König was a crucial religious and intellectual bridge-builder, who crossed the Iron Curtain on numerous visits to bring comfort and relief to embattled Catholic communities from Poland to Croatia. He kept the hope alive among Catholic leaders in the East that the Vatican and the West had not forgotten their plight. On one of these visits he met the young bishop of Cracow, Karol Wojtyla, whose election as Pope John Paul II he helped engineer,[17] Theerby, he also indirectly contributed to bringing down the Iron Curtain in the person of the fiercely anti-communist Polish Pope. In West Germany, too, the Protestant churches were precursors for improving relations with Eastern Europe.

This became the basis not only for a revival of the church in Eastern Europe, but for the revival of democracy and civil society after the collapse of the Soviet Empire in Eastern Europe. In other words, there were more subtle and deeper subterranean forces involved in bringing down communism beyond the celebrated actions of Ronald Reagan and Mikhail Gorbachev. Overcoming the East-West divide and the bringing about the demise of communism was the crucial element that eventually allowed Europe—East and West—to grow together again with the EU's historic Eastern Enlargement on 1 May 2004.

As a result of Hitler's racist war of extermination in Eastern Europe, the trajectory of Germany's relations with its Eastern European neighbors was very different from the neutralized "victim" Austria. The destructive war brought two Germanies into existence. The German Democratic Republic was part of the Eastern bloc and Warsaw Pact, while the Federal Republic became part of NATO and the West. The FRG refused to acknowledge the existence of the GDR until the early 1972 by practicing a militant form of global diplomacy with its "Hallstein Doctrine."[18] To the great relief of the Western powers, Konrad Adenauer rejected Josef Stalin's siren call of a neutralized but unified Germany in 1952.[19] But even at the early stage of the Cold War, perceptive operators like Shepard Stone tried to undermine the Iron Curtain and communist control of Eastern Europe by bringing intellectuals together from East and West.[20]

Axel Schild has reminded us that West Germany's fierce anti-communism viewed Eastern Europe monolithically. In Bonn's view Eastern European countries did not play an independent role: "They did not appear to be state protagonists, but were perceived as spineless satellites of the Soviet Union." The expellees, who exerted enormous political influence in postwar West Germany, constituting one fifth of the population of the FRG. While Adenauer's FRG "easternized" demographically, it "westernized" and Americanized politically and culturally. Willy Brandt's courageous *Ostpolitik* began to assuage some of the harsher and doctrinaire policies of Adenauer's early Cold War anti-communist legacies (the "Hallstein Doctrine" being one of them). Brandt normalized diplomatic relations. Eastern Europe and its individual nations began registering once more on the mental map of West Germans as trade, intellectual and tourist exchanges increased.[21] German unification, of course, brought back a pattern of even deeper interaction.

While the GDR became something of an economic power house in the Soviet bloc, Germany's formerly thriving trade with Eastern Europe declined and was only slowly rebuilt as a result of Brandt's *Ostpolitik*.[22] After the end of the Cold War, a united Germany has resumed its traditional role as an economic hub for Eastern Europe through investment and trade. After 1990 the influence of Siemens and the Deutsche Bank once again began make itself felt throughout the region. Clearly German economic power and investment capital will be crucial for building prosperity in the new EU-Europe of 26. Nor should Austria's investments, particularly in the Czech Republic, Slovakia and Hungary be discounted. In the new EU-Europe of 26, the transfer of German and Austrian funds will increasingly come also in the form of EU structural aid programs. People will migrate and look for work and opportunities throughout this newly enlarged EU-Europe as if the Iron Curtain never existed.

Austria's and Germany's relationship with Eastern Europe is a complex and conflicted one in this most recent past, as it has been in the other periods covered in this book. While *Mitteleuropa* and bridge-building are part of the repertoire of intellectual discourses, the subtexts of actual postwar interaction is one full of mutual mistrust and recrimination based on the violent legacies of World War II and the Kremlin's forty years of hegemony. control. It will take generations of peaceful intercourse to rebuild trust and overcome those ghosts of the past. It will be, above all, the younger generation who will exorcize those ghosts by taking advantage of this new Europe being welded ever more closely together across the old fault lines of Germans and Slavs. National identities will coexist while a broader European identity emerges.

# Notes

1. Charles Maier, "Whose Mitteleuropa? Central Europe between Memory and Obsolescence," in Günter Bischof and Anton Pelinka, eds., *Austria in the New Europe* (Contemporary Austrian Studies [CAS] 1) (New Brunswick, NJ: Transaction, 1993), 8–18. For a useful historical introduction to this region, see Lonnie Johnson, *Central Europe: Enemies, Neighbors, Friends,* 2nd ed. (New York: Oxford, 2002).
2. Maier, "Whose Mitteleuropa?" 16.
3. A picture of Brandt on his knees is on the front cover of a collection of essays dealing with this relationship; see Eduard Mühle, ed., *Germany and the European East in the Twentieth Century* (German Historical Perspectives 17) (Oxford: Berg, 2003).
4. Barbara Coudenhove-Kalergi, "Die Wiederkehr des Vergangenen: Zwei Völker, zwei Geschichten," in Barbara Coudenhove-Kalergi and Oliver Rathkolb, eds., *Die Beneš-Dekrete* (Vienna: Czernin, 2002).
5. Austrians' *"Verstrickung"* in all aspects of National Socialism and ordinary Austrians as "willing executioners" of Hitler's murderous policies is exhaustively documented in the

essays of Emmerich Tálos, Ernst Hanisch, Wolfgang Neugebauer, and Reinhard Sieder, eds., *NS-Herrschaft in Österreich: Ein Handbuch* (Vienna: öbv & hpt, 2000); see also the excellent local/regional microstudies in Fritz Mayerhofer and Walter Schuster, eds., *Nationalsozialismus in Linz*, 2 vols. (Linz: Archiv der Stadt Linz, 2000); see also Evan Burr Bukey, *Hitler's Austria: Popular Sentiment in the Nazi Era, 1938–1945* (Chapel Hill: University of North Carolina Press, 2000).

6. The best introduction to the diplomacy of restitution vis-à-vis the governments of Poland, Belarus, Ukraine, Russian Federation, Hungary and the Czech Republic to compensate their former slave- and forced laborers is Martin Eichtinger, "Der Versöhnungfonds. Österreichs Leistungen an ehemalige Sklaven- und Zwangsarbeiter des NS-Regimes," *Österreichs Jahrbuch für Politik* (2000), 195ff.

7. Richard G. Plaschka, Horst Haselsteiner, Arnold Suppan, and Anna M. Drabek, eds., *Nationale Frage und Vertreibung in der Tschechoslowakei und Ungarn 1938–1948* (Vienna: Akademie der Wissenschaften, 1997).

8. See the essays in the excellent volume by Erwin A. Schmidl, ed., *Die Ungarnkrise 1956 und Österreich* (Vienna: Böhlau, 2003).

9. Gernot Heiss and Oliver Rathkolb, eds., *Asylland Wider Willen: Flüchtlinge in Österreich im europäischen Kontext seit 1914* (Vienna: Jugend & Volk, 1995).

10. *Regierungserklärung* of 20 December, 1945, repr. in Eva-Marie Csáky, ed., *Der Weg zu Freiheit und Neutralität: Dokumentation zur österreichischen Außenpolitik 1945–1955* (Vienna, 1980), 60f, and numerous other statements by Austrian politicians in this era calling for Austria's traditional role as "bridge" between East and West.

11. Michael Gehler, "The Hungarian Crisis and Austria 1953–1958: A Foiled Model Case?" in Günter Bischof, Anton Pelinka, and Ruth Wodak, eds., *Neutrality in Austria* (CAS 9) (New Brunswick, NJ: Transaction, 2001), 160–213.

12. Andrea Komlosy makes this point forcefully in "The Marshall Plan and the Making of the 'Iron Curtain' in Austria," in Günter Bischof, Anton Pelinka, and Dieter Stiefel, eds., *The Marshal Plan in Austria* (CAS 8) (New Brunswick, NJ: Transaction, 2000), 98–137.

13. Oliver Rathkolb, "Austria's 'Ostpolitik' in the 1950s and 1960s: Honest Broker or Double Agent?" *Austrian History Yearbook* 26 (1995): 129–46.

14. Matthew Evangelista, *Unarmed Forces: The Transnational Movement to End the Cold War* (Ithaca, NY: Cornell University Press, 1999).

15. Otmas Hőll, "The Foreign Policy of the Kreisky Era," in Günter Bischof, Anton Pelinka, and Oliver Rathkolb, eds., *The Kreisky Era in Austria* (CAS 2) (New Brunswick, NJ: Transaction, 1994), 32–77.

16. Otto Klambauer, *Der Kalte Krieg in Österreich: Vom Dritten Mann zum Fall des Eisernen Vorhangs* (Vienna: Ueberreuter, 2000), 75–81, 124–32.

17. Ibid., 114–23.

18. William Glenn Gray, *Germany's Cold War: The Global Campaign to Isolate East Germany, 1949–1969* (Chapel Hill: University of North Carolina Press, 2003); for the larger international dimensions, see Wilfried Loth, ed., *Die deutsche Frage in der Nachkriegszeit* (Berlin: Akademie Verlag, 1994). Relations with the Soviet Union are exhaustively covered by the essays in Hans-Adolf Jacobson, Jochen Lőser, Daniel Proektor, and Sergej Slutsch, eds., *Deutsch-russische Zeitenwende: Krieg und Frieden 1941–1995* (Baden-Baden: Nomos, 1995).

19. Rolf Steininger, *The German Question: The Stalin Note of 1952 and the Problem of Reunification,* trans. Jane T. Hedges (New York: Columbia University Press, 1990).

20. Volker R. Berghahn, *America and the Intellectual Cold Wars in Europe* (Princeton: Princeton University Press, 2001).

21. Axel Schildt, "Mending Fences: The Federal Republic of Germany and Eastern Europe," in Mühle, ed., *Germany and the European East*, 153–179 (quotation p. 158); this essay features a good introductory bibliography.

22. On trade see the voluminous monograph by Robert Mark Spaulding, *Osthandel und Ostpolitik: German Foreign Trade Policies in Eastern Europe from Bismarck to Adenauer* (Providence: Berghahn, 1997).

# Austrian and Czech Historical Memory of World War II, National Identity, and European Integration

### ◆ Günter Bischof and Martin David ◆

> "I saw no use in the past: only a scene
> Of degradation, ugliness and tears
> The record of disgraces best forgotten
> A sullen page in human chronicles
> Fit to erase."[1]

## Introduction

The historical memory of and the *Vergangenheitspolitik* about World War are part and parcel of past and present European identity constructions. In his celebrated essay "The Past is Another Country: Myth and Memory in Postwar Europe" Tony Judt defines the construction of false memory and myth-making about the World War II past in much of Europe a bit more specifically than the poet Browning: "[The] special character of the wartime experience in continental Europe, and the ways in which the memory of that experience was distorted, sublimated, and appropriated, bequeathed to the postwar era an identity that was fundamentally false, dependent upon the erection of an unnatural and unsustainable frontier between past and present in European public memory."[2] In Judt's analysis postwar Europe's lack of mastering its World War II past—its *Geschichtspolitik* of creating "mismemories and myths"—created a false identity.[3]

Anton Pelinka's analysis goes in the same direction of "identity politics." Pelinka argues that the rejection of National Socialism and the Holocaust after World War II was a "crucial European characteristic" and distinguished postwar Europe from its previous ethno-nationalism. Pelinka argues that the anti-fascist consensus has become a crucial element in postwar European identity. He goes on to say that in the current and future "politics of the past," National Socialism is and will continue to be the antithesis to European democracy.[4]

Austrian political scientist Anton Pelinka has argued that the anti-fascist consensus has become implicitly a basic constituent element of a democratic polity in the fully integrated Europe in the twenty-first century. It is a hypothesis of this essay that Austria squarely needed to face its World War II history and its skeletons-in-the-closet—most notably Austrians' ready collaboration with National Socialism—before it joined the European Union in 1995. Does it follow from the Austrian precedent that the Czech Republic needs to confront its own World War II skeletons—the Beneš Decrees[5] and the tragedy and excesses of the Sudeten German evacuations/expulsions—before it enters the European Union? Could it be that an unwritten rule of the *acquis communautaire* (entering the complex European legal framework) and EU accession is the confrontation with the sordid chapters of a nation's history and their inclusion in the national historical narrative? Is full acknowledgement of a seedy past part and parcel of a new European democratic consensus? Will Croatia have to face the ghosts of its past and Turkey finally confront the Armenian genocide before they will be admitted into the Europen Union?

In this essay we will address these issues in more detail by first setting the context by summarizing the basic framework of Austro-Czech(oslovak) relations. Then we will try to derive possible lessons from Austria's accession to the European Union in 1995, which was preceded by a long-drawn-out controversy over Austria's "unmastered" World War II past and the role of its "Nazi perpetrators." This may help us understand how the current controversy over Czech *Geschichtspolitik* and handling of the Beneš Decrees presented a "moral" problem for the EU accession process. The case study of Austria's postwar politics of history may provide a valuable case study for the Czechs.

## The Context: A Brief Overview of Austro-Czech Relations after 1945

It may come as surprise to an uninitiated observer of the Austrian media that bilateral relations between Vienna and Prague have not always been ridden with tensions.[6] Such a negative perspective of bilateral relations has a long historical tradition. Ever since the final decades of the Austro-Hungarian Empire, radical Czech nationalists have been seen as the "grave-diggers" of the Habsburg Monarchy, particularly by Vienna's German-oriented, liberal bourgeoisie. This fierce German-Czech ethnic rivalry in the waning days of the Monarchy may also have been a symptom of economic and cultural competition between Vienna on the one side and Prague and Brno on the other. The historic province of Bohemia (the region around Prague), which together forms a big part of today's Czech Republic, was highly industrialized and constituted an essential part of the Habsburg Monarchy's economy.[7]

After the breakup of the Dual Monarchy, Austria and Czechoslovakia parted ways and became separate states. During the interwar period (1918–1938), competing and clashing foreign (economic) policies further aggravated the severe and mutual alienation resulting form the ethno-nationalist clashes of the late Habsburg Monarchy and World War I. Both domestic and foreign observers regarded Austria to be economically and politically non-viable while Czechoslovakia was thriving as one of Europe's strongest democracies built on a solid industrial economy. Czechoslovak foreign policy was "Western oriented." Prague concentrated on its alliance with France and its solid relations with Great Britain and ignored neighbors such as Austria and Hungary.[8] While political relations with Vienna were contentions, trade relations remained solid.

Caught in its imperial Habsburg past, Austria, on the other hand, failed to develop a settled national identity. Austria was struggling for economic survival and was torn apart politically by growing tensions between its contentious and armed political camps, which eventually led to a civil war and the demise of parliament and democratic rule. The strategy of resisting Germany dominated by the National Socialists after 1933 by the authoritarian Dollfuss and Schuschnigg regimes failed in the end, leading to the invasion and *Anschluss* of Austria with Hitler's Third *Reich*.[9] Along the lines of long-range Nazi planning for European expansion, the incorporation of Austria also "cleared the flanks" and set the stage for the dismemberment of Czechoslovakia. The fascist movement within the Sudeten German minority played a fateful role as "fifth columnists" for Hitler's diplomatic pressure vis-à-vis Prague that culminated with the Munich Agreement and the breakup of Czechoslovakia. Since those fateful days "Munich" has come to stand for appeasement of aggressors.

Ironically, during the fateful years of World War II, "bilateral" relations were actually better than before. Many of Czechoslovakia's and Austria's postwar leaders got to know each other in Hitler's concentration camps, such as the second Austrian post-war chancellor Leopold Figl and the first postwar Czechoslovak representative in Austria, František Bořek-Dohalský. On the Austrian side also the head of the Austrian mission in Prague, Ferdinand Marek, and his successor Alois Vollgruber, were well-known anti-Nazis. Vollgruber was even imprisoned in a concentration camp.[10] This contributed to a degree of mutual sympathy and understanding. Most members of the Czechoslovak government were returning from exile and recognized that most of the members of the first Austrian postwar cabinet had also suffered from the Nazi regime.[11]

During the war Czechoslovakia experienced much less war-related destruction and dislocation than Austria. When Austria and Vienna needed food and coal to survive the difficult winter of 1945, Czechoslovakia provided its neighbor with the essential goods. The first official state visit of the Austrian Foreign Minister Karl Gruber late in 1945 led him to Prague, where he negotiated and concluded a trade treaty. This visit was economically important. It was even more significant for the fact that Gruber was treated like the minister of a sovereign state. At the time Austria was under the total control of the four great powers occupying the country. Until the signing of the second control agreement in June 1946, the powers did not permit Austria to establish formal diplomatic relations with other states. Gruber's treatment in Prague can be regarded as an implicit Czechoslovak acknowledgement of Austrian sovereignty. As such it was the first state to do so.[12]

There were some close personal ties between Czechs and Austrians in the diplomatic arena. Most members of the Austrian Foreign Service were well acquainted with František Bořek-Dohalský, the first postwar Czechoslovak representative in Vienna. They had gone to school together with him as he had received his diplomatic training at Vienna's Diplomatic Academy. The Nazis had imprisoned him in the Dachau concentration camp along with Austria's first elected postwar Chancellor Leopold Figl. Given these personal ties, Bořek-Dohalský had very good connections with the Austrian political elite. His dispatches and reports from Vienna featured an unusually close and authoritative knowledge of Austrian politics.[13]

Ferdinand Marek, the first postwar Austrian diplomatic representative in Prague, enjoyed similar respect. He acted as Austrian minister in Prague already before the war and was one of the few Austrian diplomats who openly opposed the *Anschluss*. In March 1938, when Austria disappeared from the map, he was the doyen of Prague's *corps diplomatique* and had established excellent personal relations with some of the most important Czechoslovak politicians represented in the postwar government. Given his reputation among Prague's power elite, Marek was able to establish a fledgling Austrian diplomatic representation even before Karl Renner's provisional government was formed in Vienna in the waning days of World War II. The Czechoslovak ministry of foreign affairs and President Edvard Beneš recognized this Austrian diplomatic mission in May 1945 due to Marek's personal efforts.[14]

During the crisis over the expulsion of the Sudeten Germans, Marek played a courageous role and is therefore sometimes described as the "Austrian Wallenberg." When the forced Sudeten German exodus began soon after the end of the war, Marek demanded that Austrian citizens living in Czechoslovakia not be treated as "Germans." With the legal incorporation of Austria in the Third Reich after the *Anschluss*, Austrian citizenship lapsed and all Austrian citizens became Germans, unless they escaped from Nazi Germany by seeking asylum abroad. In May 1945 it was indeed difficult to establish in Czechoslovakia whether a German citizen in 1944 had been an Austrian citizen in 1937.[15]

In May and June hundreds of Austrians camped out on the Austrian Embassy grounds in Prague. In the late spring and summer of 1945 Marek and his staff did not rely on the specific Austrian version of the German language alone to establish a person's citizenship. They designed a test and asked questions about regional specifics to verify the information proffered. Interestingly, these "exams" were acknowledged by Czechoslovak officials. Marek organized a number of transports of Austrians back to their homeland. In the process he saved some lives which may have been lost during the "wild expulsions" of the Sudeten Germans in the initial phase. Marek's unusually creative diplomatic activities during these unsettled time eventually landed him in a Soviet prison. Red Army officers abducted him and brought him to Moscow where he died in jail some years later. Only a few days after his death, the trial was scheduled.[16]

Austrian diplomats managed to get better treatment for Austrian citizens. But they failed to prevent the confiscation of Austrian property as a result of the respective Beneš decrees. Although the National Committee in Prague promised to respect the difference, regional authorities did not care whether they confiscated Sudeten German, German or Austrian property. This summary confiscation of all "German" property became one of the major obstacles in poisoned postwar Austro-Czech relations. From today's perspective it is surprising, however, that the expulsion and evacuation of Sudeten Germans did not appear to be a major problem affecting bilateral relations. Austrian authorities tended to agree with the callous Czechoslovak interpretation that all Sudeten Germans had been National Socialists. This view can be traced back to leading postwar Austrian politicians such as President Karl Renner, who was born in Moravia, Chancellor Figl, and Foreign Minister Gruber.[17]

Czechoslovak diplomats suspected Sudeten German native Cardinal Innitzer and some Social Democrats like Vice Chancellor Adolf Schärf and, later, Minister for the Interior Oskar Helmer, of exercising harmful influence on Austrian policy towards Czechoslovakia. But the actual record does not bear this out. When the Sudeten Germans organized an ethnic lobby (*Landsmannschaft*), Austria's political parties needed to heed their demands if they wanted to get their votes. Each party appointed some of its senior politicians as contact persons with the Sudeten German lobby to listen to their demands. Yet their actual political influence usually was restricted to some shrill rhetoric that did not significantly influence Austria's actual foreign policy vis-à-vis Czechoslovakia. If one reads through the entire record of Austrian diplomatic dispatches from Prague to the Foreign Ministry for the period 1945–1968, Sudeten Germans are referred to as "Germans."[18]

While official Austro-Czech relations remained friendly after the Iron Curtain came down in 1948, economic ties declined with the coming of the Cold War. With its participation in the Marshall Plan, Austria was integrated into the Organization of European Economic Cooperation and the fledgling Western economic integration movement.[19] Czechoslovakia was not so lucky. Stalin prohibited Prague's participation in the Marshall Plan and forced its Eastern integration in the Council of Mutual Economic Assistance (COMECON). The initial Austrian perception did not see the Communist *Putsch* of February 1948 as a turning point. The economic consequences, however, became starkly clear in the years afterward when Czechoslovakia was excluded from American beneficence in the European Recovery Program.[20]

Czechoslovakia had been an industrial powerhouse in Central Europe before

World War II. After the war it lost this position as a result of the expulsion of the Sudeten Germans, its failure to participate in the Marshall Plan, and the economic stagnation in the Soviet trading bloc resulting mainly from one-sided investment in heavy industry and lack of technological innovation. With the expulsion of some 2,500,000 Sudeten Germans after World War II, Czechoslovakia got rid of one of the best-trained and productive segments of its population. In the long term this affected economic productivity enormously.[21] Czechoslovakia wanted to maintain the Austrian export market for its goods. But Czech imports lost their appeal in the course of the 1950s once Western goods and consumer products began flooding into Austria. A modernized Austrian industrial and consumer economy began to flourish as a result of the postwar economic reconstruction driven by Marshall Plan. Meanwhile Czechoslovakia's economic production began to languish as a result of communist reforms.[22]

While the Sudeten German lobby affected bilateral Austro-Czech political relations remarkably little, postwar Czech territorial demands on Austria brought some deterioration. During the negotiations of the Austrian State Treaty, Czechoslovakia demanded minor border corrections in its favor along the rivers Thaya/Dye and March/Morava. Prague declared its readiness to construct of hydroelectric power plants on these rivers and also demanded land nearby the small village of Hardegg. For the future construction of a projected canal between the Danube and the Oder rivers, Prague wanted a region along the river March's mouth near Bratislava and more land on the Western side of the March in the vicinity of Bratislava to ensure the future growth of the Slovak capital. As this demand included two small hills, it had also strategic reasons.[23] In exchange, Czechoslovakia promised the delivery of essential goods and foodstuffs for the Austrian economy in its hard-pressed pre-Marshall Plan days. As has been pointed out, Austrian foreign minister Karl Gruber wanted to establish good relations with Czechoslovakia and therefore contemplated negotiating at least some of these demands. Yet the Czech territorial demands were forwarded at the same time in 1947 when Yugoslavia claimed major territorial concession in southern Carinthia and Styria. In order to maintain its borders of 1937 Austria needed to reject all territorial demands on its borders. Since the Soviets backed Yugoslavia, the Western powers backed Austria in maintaining the inviolability of its 1937 borders.[24]

The confiscation of Austrian property in Czechoslovakia was the other significant issue to affect Austro-Czech bilateral relations in the postwar period. When most assets of the Czechoslovak economy were nationalized in 1945, the confiscation of Austrian property was mainly based on Beneš Decree § 45 and § 108, which treated it the same as Sudeten German property. The Austrian government considered the confiscation of the property of Austrian citizens to be illegal. Negotiations concerning confiscated property only began after the conclusion of the Austrian State Treaty in 1955. While treaties over confiscated property were signed between Austria and other socialist countries (Poland, Hungary, and Rumania) during the later 1950s, there was no progress on such an Austro-Czechoslovak agreement. In 1960 the Austrian government calculated the value of the confiscated property at 12 billion Austrian Schillings (almost $400 million) for which it demanded compensation for its citizens. The feeble Czechoslovak economy could never assume such a financial burden. One of the principal points of contention in these long drawn-out negotiations was the Czech refusal to compensate the "class enemies" (large industrialists or land holders). Prague only wanted to compensate small property holders. Of course, the issue of defining pre- and post-*Anschluss* "Austrian" and "German" citizenship also played a crucial element in these negotiations.[25]

Prague aimed at achieving a "political solution," while quietly burying the property issue. But the Ballhausplatz kept insisting on the nexus between the normalization of bilateral relations and a solution of the property issue. The 1968 Soviet invasion and resulting disruption of Czechoslovak foreign policy delayed the conclusion of the property treaty until 1974. The agreement foresaw a lump sum payment of 1 billion Austrian Schillings. Although the Austrian parliament was not satisfied with the total amount, it declared that this was still better than nothing. Bilateral relations were normalized at last and the diplomatic representation in Prague and Vienna was upgraded from minister to ambassador.[26]

After the "velvet revolution" of 1989, the end of the Cold War in 1990/91, and the peaceful breakup of Czechoslovakia in 1993, new tensions erupted between Austria and the Czech Republic in the late 1990s. Populist politicians such as Jörg Haider riled the Austrian public with his demands that Prague revoke the "unjust and criminal" Beneš Decrees and close down the unsafe Czech nuclear power plant Temelín, without which Haider proposed to block Czech accession to the European Union.

Moreover, the Czech Republic's adoption of the fourteen EU member states' "sanction measures" against Chancellor Wolfgang Schüssel's bourgeois ÖVP/FPÖ coalition government in February 2000 further worsened bilateral relations. Austrian public opinion was greatly upset with the facile Czech compliance of EU-European demands. The political turmoil did not, however, affect improving economic ties. Mutual trade has trebled since 1993 and Austrian entrepreneurs are amongst the most important investors in the Czech Republic today.[27]

## Austrian World War II Historical Memory and *Geschichtspolitik*

When it comes to World War II, Austria has been called the "punching bag (*Watschenmann*) of European memory."[28] The record of both official Austria and many individual Austrians hiding behind the "victim's doctrine" is a long one. Confronting the dark chapters of their World War II history is indeed one of endless delay and procrastination. Only in the 1980s did Austria's long hibernating memory of a complex past peopled with both victims and perpetrators of Nazi war crimes wake up. Ironically, the Waldheim debacle of 1986 heated up the discourse about Austrians' role in World War II. During the 1986 presidential campaign Waldheim's facile explanation of "just having done his duty" as a *Wehrmacht* soldier during the war sounded hollow and no longer credible. After 1986 a new Austrian *Vergangenheitspolitik* was unleashed that began to acknowledge the role of Austrian perpetrators in World War II and most recently engaged in new rounds of paying restitution to the victims of World War II. This coincided with Austria joining the European Union in 1995 and facing enormous pressure from the EU "sanction measures" in 2000 after the formation of the ÖVP/FPÖ coalition government.[29]

The Allied "Moscow Declaration" of November 1, 1943, helped postwar Austria build the doctrine (myth) of Austria being "Hitler's first victim." This notion was built on the March 1938 military invasion and incorporation of Austria into Hitler's Third Reich. This "victim's doctrine" eagerly embraced by the postwar Austrian government served the country fairly well, by protecting it both from paying reparations individually and collectively, and from granting restitution to the true victims of National Socialism. For Cold War reasons the Western occupation powers aided and abetted the postwar Austrian grand coalition governments' efforts to "sell" the "victim's doctrine" to the world. The politics of anti-communism gained priority over the politics of denazification.[30]

Domestically, the ÖVP and SPÖ, the two main parties in the grand coalition, agreed not to touch in their respective politics of history the unseemly Austro-fascist and National Socialist pasts. The participation and complicity of numerous Austrians in Nazi war crimes and the Holocaust was quietly committed to oblivion—or at least a lengthy period of hibernation. This was really a conspiracy of silence. Instead, celebrating and commemorating Austrian resistance and the victims of the resistance against the Nazis became the central part of Austria's narrative of its World War II history. Here a national myth—in Tony Judt's terms a "mismemory" was created—of Austrians as victims, while the history of collaboration and support of Nazi German aggression and extermination policies was forgotten or suppressed.[31]

Also in the domestic arena, a few high-level Foreign and Education Ministry officials set out to construct a new Austrian identity to set it off against its "German" identity of the interwar period. The crimes of National Socialism were all exported ("externalized" )to West Germany; the myth of significant Austrian resistance during World War II served to obliterate the memory of the perpetrators. Austrians this time around were not the "better Germans" (the 1930s construction), but the *non-Germans* who bore no responsibility whatsoever for the massive World War II Nazi criminal record.[32]

During the initial postwar period (1945–48), the worst Nazi criminals were vigorously prosecuted by special "people's courts" (*Volksgerichte*). Forty-two Austrian war criminals were executed and hundreds received long jail sentences. But as a result of the Cold War and domestic politics, the denazification effort waned after 1948 and the justice system's prosecution of Nazi war criminals dried up in the early 1950s. When compared with West Germany, few trials against Nazi war criminals were staged in the 1960s or 1970s and most ended in "not guilty" verdicts.[33]

By the time the Austrian State Treaty was signed in 1955, which ended the four-power occupation and returned full sovereignty to the country, the myth of Austrian victimhood was well established. Austria's "co-responsibility" for Nazi war crimes, cited in the third paragraph of the 1943 Moscow Declaration, was scratched from the preamble of the treaty and eventually also from the memory of both the international community and most Austrians. The long "hibernation" of the memory of Austria's complex World War II past ensued.[34]

This spell was finally broken in the late 1960s as a new generation of the children of the World War II generation finally began the process of "decoding the past."[35] Yet one of the big riddles of Austria's postwar *Vergangenheitspolitik* was the failure to sustain the process of recognition in the 1970s under Chancellor Kreisky, a Jew who had lost many family members in the Holocaust. As late as the mid-1980s it was still impolitic to rock the boat by questioning Austria's "victim's status," which had become part of Austrian identity. By then, however, a new generation of contemporary historians and political scientists began to unearth Austria's wartime record even more vigorously than the New Left "1968er" had done.[36]

The silence was shattered during the Waldheim election campaign in 1986 and the *Gedenkjahr* 1988 commemoration of the fiftieth anniversary of the *Anschluss*. The former *Wehrmacht* lieutenant Waldheim's stonewalling about his wartime service in the Balkans, professed ignorance of Nazi war crimes committed there, and assertion that he had simply "done his duty" as a soldier were so lacking in credibility that he suddenly became a symbol of Austria's unmastered past. Once exposed, the painfully transparent myth of Austrian victimhood and its status as an "island of the blessed" quickly began to unravel.[37]

In the 1990s a new paradigm finally emerged of Austrians as "both victims and perpetrators." The reluctant acceptance of both the good and bad chapters of its wartime experience ushered forth a new historical narrative on the highest official level. Waldheim himself had already introduced the new formulation in a speech during the *Anschluss* commemorations in March 1988. Chancellor Franz Vranitzky further legitimized Austria's ambiguous wartime record in speeches of both victims and perpetrators to the Austrian Parliament in 1991 and to a university audience in Jerusalem one year later. President Thomas Klestil made the same *Canossa Gang* to Israel and spoke of the dark chapters of Austria's wartime history, acknowledging that some of the "worst butchers [*Schergen*] of the NS-dictatorship" had been Austrians. In 1995 the Austrian Parliament even established a national fund (*Nationalfonds*) to support victims of National Socialism.[38]

Austria's acknowledgment was part of a global post-Cold War trend of facing up to the past and accepting responsibility for past misdeeds, attaining historical justice, apologizing for them, and paying restitution.[39] "The demand that nations act morally and acknowledge their own gross historical injustices is a novel phenomenon," notes Elazar Barkan in his brilliant book *The Guilt of Nations*. He adds that the "interaction between perpetrator and victim is a new form of political negotiations that enables the rewriting of memory and historical identity in ways both can share."[40]

Austrian World War II historical memory was, then, reconstructed and rewritten in the course of the 1990s. Why? First, it had been long overdue. During the Waldheim fiasco in 1986 Austria's international reputation had suffered from his and Austria's stubborn defense of the victim's myth. Austria as victim had, indeed, become the laughing stock of the informed international community. Second, Austrian national identity had gelled sufficiently half a century after the war not to be shaken by an admission of guilt. Third, and this is more a hunch and an hypothesis than a firm thesis based on documentation, Austria's accession to the European Union tacitly required a clear confrontation with its complex World War II past. In other words, the politics of history by the Vranitzky government and Klestil's signal speeches in the early to mid-1990s coincided and was in part driven by Austria's access to the European Union. On the one hand, the Austrians had to accept the strict legal and administrative requirement of the *acquis communautaire*. On the other hand, they felt what may be called the "moral pressure" of the European community of coming clean with their past. Here Pelinka's notion that in the "politics of the past" the rejection of National Socialism—including a nation's record of collaboration with and support of the Nazi war of aggression and extermination—are now amounting to constituent part of a new European democracy. This may be more of a gentle and implicit accession condition than a firm explicit and contractual one such as the alignment with the body of European law. If Austria wanted to become a full-fledged member of the European democratic polity it had to master the seedy chapters of its World War II history.

Whether the pressures on Chancellor Vranitzky to rethink and reformulate Austria's wartime role was domestic or international remains to be seen. By the year 2000 the new paradigm of "both victims and perpetrators" in Austria's World War II memory had so acceptable that it even found entry into the preamble of the embattled Schüssel/Riess-Passer government program: "*Unser Land nimbi die hellen und die dunklen Seiten seiner Vergangenheit und die Taten aller Österreicher, gute und böse, als seine Verantwortung an.*" (Our country takes responsibility for both the bright and dark sides of its past and the actions of all Austrians, good and bad.) In Austria, whenever a policy is written down in a coalition agreement, it is here to stay. Given the international pressure on the ÖVP-FPÖ coalition and a more aggressive "theory of restitution" that posited a "new guilt of nations" (Barkan), the Schüssel government embarked on a "hyperactive politics of history" that belatedly addressed the need to compensate the victims of fascism. Arguably and ironically, the ÖVP/FPÖ Schüssel coalition government has done more to atone for Austria's past through restitution settlements for forced laborers and Jewish victims than any previous postwar government.[41]

Clearly, Schüssel's bold politics of history came as a result of pressure from the international pressure and American mediation just as the Austrian political elite had abandoned the "victim's doctrine" in the wake of Waldheim's election. The outcome of this painful confrontation with the past is not the infamous *Schlussstrich* so often demanded by the old and neo-Nazis, but still a sort of moral closure. Gitta Serenyi, a noted authority on Nazi Germany, has observed in the London *Times* that Austria no longer is the "black sheep" of Europe when it comes to mastering its World War II past.[42]

The lesson from this Austrian case study seems to be a formula for the politics of history, a *Vergangenheitsbewältigung* that amounts to an entire process of atonement.

First, it is necessary to confront the past, preferably through a large-scale historical commission establishing the objective facts and, thereby, pointing towards an acceptable historical narrative.[43] In Austria such a commission was set up in late 1998 and completed its work in January 2003. Second, the political elite have to admit to a complex past including the dark chapters in one's national history and, then, apologize to the victims. Third, the nation's leaders must make pilgrimage—a *Canossa Gang*—to Israel in the case of West Germany and Austria, in which they publicly acknowledge responsibility and apologize. Fourth, history books must be rewritten so that school children will absorb the revised historical narrative of a complex past of victims and perpetrators. Fifth, adequate restitution must be paid—symbolically or in hard cash—to the surviving victims.

## Lessons in the Politics of History for the Czech Republic from the Austrian Case Study?

Czechoslovakia shook off its Communist regime in the "velvet revolution" in late 1989. The new democratic government soon faced the demand to face the dark chapters of its past. In the early 1990s this meant above all mastering the dark chapters of postwar communist history. "Lustration" tried to uncover the history of collaboration with and support of the Communist regime, including secret service persecution and the hounding of dissidents.[44] Such a wholesale Czech confrontation with its recent history inevitably encouraged the Sudeten German lobbies (*Sudetendeutsche Landsmannschaften*) in the newly reunified Germany and Austria to reassert their old demands vis-à-vis the government in Prague, namely to face the historical injustice of the expulsion of 2.5 million Sudeten Germans and the wholesale seizure of their property after World War II. Their demands were usually supported by the

Bavarian CSU and Minister President Edmund Stoiber during the annual ritual of the *Sudetendeutscher Tag*.[45] At this time the demand to revoke the Beneš Decrees had not yet appeared on the agenda of Austria's "defiant populist," Jörg Haider.[46]

In the early days of the new democratic regime in Czechoslovakia, elite political voices like that of President Vaclav Havel even gingerly suggested in speeches that historical injustice had been done and that amends needed to be made to the expellees, if only symbolically.[47] But the international context in which the Sudeten German lobbies vociferously raised their old demands was changing radically. The breakup of Yugoslavia produced the revival of a murderous ethno-nationalism in the Balkans. A shocked western Europe watched the horrific Serbian and Croatian "ethnic cleansing" campaigns and massive human rights abuses in Croatia, Bosnia-Herzegovina and Kosovo.[48] In some quarters it became fashionable to appropriate this language and condemn all "ethnic cleansing" and human rights abuses, past and present. Austrian foreign minister Alois Mock noted in the late 1980s and early 1990s that "*Vergangenheitsbewältigung* must never be one-sided, a crime is a crime wherever is committed."[49]

In the mid-1990s Haider jumped on the bandwagon, demanding a revocation of the Beneš Decrees, although not yet explicitly demanding an outright restitution of property. Haider began to make this connection with the global trend toward demanding historical justice and restitution unleashed in the late 1990s on behalf of victims of World War II and other historic victims. Once Switzerland, Germany, and Austria established their historical commissions and made restitution settlements with World War II victims (forced laborers and Jews), the Sudeten German *Landsmannschaft* and their protectors in Germany and Austria were emboldened to demand not only historical justice but also material restitution.[50] The day came in 1998 when Haider upped the ante by directly comparing the Jewish and Sudeten German cases, thereby equalizing their demands for *Wiedergutmachung*. Haider argued that the Jewish émigrés could not endlessly demand restitution while Sudeten Germans were expected to end their demands vis-à-vis the Czech Republic, thereby reviving the famous *Schlussstrich* appeal for closure to the historical injustice committed against them.[51]

The moral issue of correcting a serious historical injustice committed against the Sudeten Germans was now plainly on the table. By 2002 the Beneš Decrees and how to respond to the demands of the Sudeten Germans and their backers in Austria and Bavaria became one of the most contentious issues in Czech domestic politics. Haider added fuel to the fire by demanding revocation of the Beneš Decrees and linking such a revocation with the Czech Republic's accession to the European Union. Haider cynically instrumentalized the new "moral politics" of righting historical injustice by way of restitution. As the vocal opposition leader Haider had opposed Austrian accession to the EU during the 1994 Austrian EU-accession plebiscite. Now from his perch as governor of Carinthia he was trying to make hay out of Czech accession. In his inimitable populist fashion he was both fishing for cheap votes in Austria by stirring up anti-immigrant sentiment (the fear of hordes of Czechs and Eastern Europeans flooding the Austrian labor markets after accession) and continuing his traditional anti-EU stance (even though his party was represented in the pro-EU Schüssel government).

Both Czechs and Germans—and here Haider's old nationalist pedigree kicks in again—dig back into their rich historical repertoire of paranoid misperceptions about each other to feed their respective populist politics. It is indeed the falling back to the atavism of nationalism with its perennial enemy images, which has made the Austro-Czech controversy over the Beneš Decrees so arid and seemingly irresolvable. The cultural philosopher Wolfgang Müller-Funk has put his finger on Haider's shameless instrumentalization of this issue: "the very people, who do not like to talk about their own [historical] crimes, blatantly demand from their neighbors that they do so."[52]

Czech politicians used the controversy around the Beneš Decrees to advance some populism of their own. During the 2002 election campaign in the Czech Republic the whole parliament stonewalled behind a stern defense of the Decrees. The EU-skeptic Vaclav Klaus—Havel's successor as president of the Czech Republic since March 2003—demanded that the EU guarantee the inviolability of the Beneš Decrees. Observing the Czech election campaign of 2002, German journalist Christian Schmidt-Häuer observed in the weekly *Die Zeit* that the Czech Republic was the first country in Europe where all parties were engaging in the politics of populism. The long shadow of Western appeasement at Munich (1938) was regularly invoked with the charge that "the naughty Europeans [were] one again feeding the Czechs to the Sudeten German wolves."[53]

By instrumentalizing the past some Czech and Austrian politicians have been digging themselves ever deeper into the trenches of mutual recrimination. In June 2002 the new Czech Premier Vladimír Špidla noted in an interview with the Austrian news magazine *Format* that the Beneš Decrees cannot be revoked because they "represent a constituent element in the founding of the Czech Republic. Without them it is impossible to exist legally."[54] Some days later, Austrian Foreign Minister Benita Ferrero-Waldner from the conservative ÖVP shot back at the *Europa Forum* in the monastery of Göttweig. Using language originally introduced by the Czech ambassador to Austria, she demanded that the Beneš Decrees be declared "legally extinct" (*totes Unrecht*) before the Czech Republic joined the EU. Since the Decrees were based on an assumption of collective guilt, she explained, they were incompatible with European law. Nor did Ferrero-Waldner stop there. She also asked the Czech Republic to say that they were sorry for this historic injustice, proposing that it make "a symbolic material gesture" on behalf of the expellees.[55]

Some Czech intellectuals have also been openly critical of the Beneš Decrees. Martin Jan Stransky argued in the liberal intellectual magazine *The New Presence* (eited by associates of former President Vaclav Havel) that the "Beneš Decrees remain a symbol of false victory and serve only as a catalyst for further trouble." He criticized the Czech Parliament's resolution, declaring the Beneš Decrees "untouchable . . . an action of grave significance, in that it confirms that democracy is in trouble in the Czech Republic." He called upon the Czech political parties and the "chest-beating boys in parliament" not to create false enemies in the accession debate but rather engage in dialogue with Europe, reminding them that the pan-European structures were not only strategic and economic, but also social and moral. In a way Stransky was making Pelinka's connection that democracy will suffer if you do not squarely face your troubled past.[56]

In the same magazine, Radko Kubicko called a symbolic gesture from Czechs and Slovaks with "the courage to admit to the injustices committed against Germans and Hungarians" just as the German president had apologized to the Poles and Jews. Nor did Jiří Pehe find anything wrong with reviewing the Beneš Decrees for their compatibility with EU law if the Czech Republic and Slovakia wanted to join the European Union. He bemoaned the fact that "a moribund and, to some extent reactionary, political culture that Bavaria and Austria inherited from World War II from the old *Mitteleuropa* has, after the fall of communism, quickly spread to the post-communist countries of the region."[57]

The well-known Austrian journalist Barbara Coudenhove Kalergi noted that the problem was rooted in two opposing national historical narratives of the region's nineteenth- and twentieth-century histories all the way up to the *odsun* (evacuation/expulsion) of the Sudeten Germans. As long as no middle ground for a common narrative is found, Czech and German populists can try to instrumentalize the respective anti-Czech and anti-German *ressentiments* in the region to block Czech EU accession.[58] A ray of light is the work of a younger generation of Czech historians who no longer just speak of Czech victims but also Czech perpetrators. As we have seen, the critical work of young historians was a crucial part of the paradigm change of Austrian memory of World War II.[59]

The European Union has not made the renunciation of the Beneš Decrees a condition for Czech accession. However, the Austrian chairperson of the Joint Committee of the EU and Czech parliament, Ursula Stenzel, did initiate a study of the Beneš Decrees' legal compatibility with European Union law. The study prepared by the noted international lawyers Jochen A. Frowein, Lord Kingsland and Ulf Bernitz came to the final conclusion that "the Czech accession to the European Union does not require the repeal of the Beneš Decrees or other legislation mentioned in that context." But Frowein did note in his report that the Czech Republic ought to express its regrets about Law No. 115 as it had explicitly done in the German-Czech Declaration of 1997.[60] Law No. 115—arguably the most offensive of the Beneš Decrees—formally excluded from criminal sanctions the acts of "just reprisals for actions of the occupation forces and their accomplices" committed in 1945/46. In his conclusion, Frowein tried to combine both memories (mentioned by Barbara

Coudenhove-Kalergi above): "Although most of the victims [of the expulsions] were innocent, it cannot be overlooked that the violence committed against the Germans at that time was in particular a reaction to what happened during the German occupation." Frowein's promotion of such a gesture of Czech regret could constitute a form of moral closure and mastering the past: "It would seem appropriate that a confirmation of that attitude is shown during the accession procedure."[61]

## Conclusion

Though divided in their perceptions of the past, the Czechs now face the same process in overcoming their collective amnesia. Like the Austrians, the Czechs had seen themselves as victims of National Socialism right up until the fall of communism. Their memory of the *odsun* was frozen like Austrian memory of the Holocaust. Now the Czech Republic appears to have entered the very painful process that Austria began in the early 1990s, when mastering its sordid past seemingly became at least an informal part of the EU-accession process. They, too, have found it difficult to face their role as perpetrators of an historical injustice vis-à-vis the Sudeten Germans, when these same people had acted as grave-diggers of Czech democracy before 1938. Even though the European Union has not demanded an outright revocation of the Beneš Decrees as a condition for EU accession, the international community will be watching the Czech Republic and whether it will formally articulate its regrets about past injustices and excesses "contrary to elementary humanitarian principles." In the end, both sides—Sudeten Germans and Czechs—will have to confront their "mismemories" of a painful past in order to build a future acceptable to both sides.

## Notes

This article was completed before the historic accession of the Czech Republic to the European Union on May 1, 2004. It was jointly penned during the academic year 2002/3, when Martin David was the first junior fellow at CenterAustria at the University of New Orleans, generously financed by the Austrian Ministry of Science and Education. We are much indebted to Charlie Ingrao for his numerous useful suggestions to improve the contents and the style of this essay.

1.  From Robert Browning, *Paracelsus* (1835), quoted in David Lowenthal, *The Past Is a Foreign Country* (Cambridge, 1985), 64.

2.  Tony Judt, "The Past Is Another Country: Myth and Memory in Postwar Europe," in István Deák/Jan T. Gross/Tony Judt, eds., *The Politics of Retribution in Europe: World War II and Its Aftermath* (Princeton, 2000), 293.

3.  Ibid., 294. Now with much more detail on postwar European *"Gechichtspolitik,"* see also Tony Judt, *Postwar: A History of Europe since 1945* (New York: Penguin, 2005).

4.  Anton Pelinka, "Die geänderte Funktionalität von Vergangenheit und Vergangenheitspolitik: Das Ende der Konkordanzdemokratie und die Verschiebung der Feindbilder," *Österreichische Zeitschrift für Politikwissenschaft* [hereafter cited as *ÖZP*] 30 (2000), 35–47 (citations 44f) (this signal special issue of the *ÖZP* is dedicated to "Geschichts- und Vergangenheitspolitik in Österreich).

5.   Before the liberation of Czechoslovakia after World War II, the president of the govern-
     ment-in-exile, Edvard Beneš, ruled the country by presidential decrees. "Beneš decrees"
     is a formally incorrect term but has become their publically acceptable expression. These
     decrees are akin to emergency legislation for a transition period concerning multiple is-
     sues, including setting the legal framework for the confiscation of German and Hungar-
     ian property. After the war, the decrees were approved by the Czechoslovak parliament
     and thus promoted to Czech law.
6.   Martin David, "Austro-Czech Relations 2000–2002," in Günter Bischof/Michael Ge-
     hler/Anton Pelinka, eds., *Österreich in der Europäischen Union: Bilanz seiner Mitgliedschaft*
     (Vienna, 2003), 411–427.
7.   Věra Olivová, *Dějiny první republiky* (Prague 2000), 163–166.
8.   Ibid., 125; for an overview cf. Zdeněk Sladek, *Malá dohoda 1919–1938. Její hospodářské,
     politické a vojenské komponenty* (Prague, 2000).
9.   Günter Bischof/Anton Pelinka/Alexander Lassner, eds., *The Dollfuss/Schuschnigg Era in
     Austria: A Reassessment* (Contemporary Austrian Studies XI) (New Brunswick, 2003).
10.  Oliver Rathkolb, "The Austrian Foreign Service and the Anschluss in 1938," *German
     Studies Review* 13 (1990): 68f.
11.  Martin David, "Österreichisch-tschechoslowakische Beziehungen 1945 bis 1974 unter
     besonderer Berücksichtigung aktueller Themen" (University of Vienna PhD thesis, 2002),
     102–105, 111–122.
12.  Klaus Fiesinger, *Ballhausplatz-Diplomatie 1945–1949. Reetablierung der Nachbarschafts-
     beziehungen und Reorganisation des Auswärtigen Dienstes als Formen aussenpolitischer Re-
     emanzipation* Österreichs (Vienna, 1993), 258.
13.  David, "Österreichisch-tschechoslowakische Beziehungen," 113, and Bořek-Dohalský's
     reports, quoted in ibid., 113, 115–122. For the ties between the Austrian and the Czecho-
     slovak Social Democrats, see Oliver Rathkolb, "Ein schwieriges Verhältnis," in Thomas
     Winkelbauer, ed., *Kontakte und Konflikte. Böhmen, Mähren und Österreich: Aspekte eines
     Jahrtausends gemeinsamer Geschichte* (Horn, 1993), 488.
14.  Herbert Steiner, *Der erste Österreichische Gesandte in Prag Ferdinand Marek: Sein Schicksal
     in den Jahren 1938–1947* (Prague, 1995).
15.  David, "Österreichisch-tschechoslowakische Beziehungen," 105ff.
16.  Steiner, *Der erste Österreichische Gesandte*, 88–101.
17.  David, "Österreichisch-tschechoslowakische Beziehungen," 113–118; Oliver Rathkolb,
     "Verdrängung und Instrumentalisierung. Die Vertreibung der Sudetendeutschen und ihre
     verspätete Rezeption in Österreich," in Barbara Coudenhove-Kalergi/Oliver Rathkolb,
     eds., *Die Beneš-Dekrete* (Vienna, 1986), 139ff; see also Emilia Hrabovec's essay in this
     volume.
18.  Rathkolb, "Verdrängung," 144f.
19.  Günter Bischof/Anton Pelinka/Dieter Stiefel, eds., *The Marshall Plan in Austria* (Con-
     temporary Austrian Studies VIII) (New Brunswick, 2000).
20.  David, "Österreichisch-tschechoslowakische Beziehungen," 118–121.
21.  Jan Michal, "Die wirtschaftliche Entwicklung der Nachkriegszeit," in Victor Mamatey/
     Radomír Luža, eds., *Geschichte der Tschechoslowakischen Republik 1918–1948* (Vienna,
     1980), 458, 460.
22.  For the development in Austria, see the essays in Bischof/Pelinka/Stiefel, eds., *The Marshall
     Plan in Austria;* for Czechoslovakia, see Karel Kaplan, *Československo v RVHP 1949–1956*
     (Prague, 1995).
23.  Eventually, the Austrian military established an intelligence center on one of the hills;
     from here much e Warsaw Pact communication was intercepted.
24.  The problems and the negotiations are described in Renate Tuma, "Gebietsansprüche der

Tschechoslowakei gegenüber Österreich," in Lothar Höbelt and Othmar Huber, eds., *Karl Gruber: Landeshauptmann und Aussenminister 1945–1953* (Innsbruck, 1991), 120–135.

25. For the details, see David, "Österreichisch-tschechoslowakische Beziehungen," 214–232, 251–263.

26. Ibid., 256–263.

27. David, "Austro-Czech Relations," 425f.

28. Dan Diner quoted in Christian Thonke, "Der Watschenmann der europäischen Erinnerung," *Kurier*, 22. June 2001.

29. Günter Bischof, "'Watschenmann der europäischen Erinnrung?'": Internationales Image und Vergangenheitspolitik der Schüssel/Riess-Passer ÖVP/FPÖ Koalitionsregierung," in Gehler/Pelinka/Bischof, eds., *Österreich in der Europäischen Union*, 445–78.

30. Günter Bischof, *Austria in the First Cold War, 1945–55: The Leverage of the Weak* (Basingstoke, 1999), 20–29; Robert H. Keyserlingk, *Austria in World War II: An Anglo-American Dilemma* (Kingston-Montreal, 1988); Gerald Stourzh, *Um Einheit und Freiheit: Staatsvertrag, Neutralität und das Ende der Ost-West-Besetzung Österreichs 1945–1955* (Vienna, 1998), 11–28.

31. Bischof, *Austria in the First Cold War*, 52–67; Heidemarie Uhl, "Das 'erste Opfer': Der österreichische Opfermythos und seine Transformation in der Zweiten Republik, *ÖZP* 30 (2001): 19–34; Andreas Maislinger, "'Den Nationalsozialisten in die Hände getrieben'": Zur Geschichtspolitik der SPÖ von 1970 bis 2000," *Europäische Rundschau* (Summer 2001), 81–95.

32. Peter Thaler, *The Ambivalence of Identity: The Austrian Experience of Nation-Building in a Modern Society* (West Lafayette, 2001).

33. Claudia Kuretsidis-Haider and Winfried R. Garscha, eds., *Keine "Abrechunung" NS-Verbrechen, Justiz und Gesellschaft in Europa nach 1945* (Leipzig/Vienna, 1998).

34. Günter Bischof, "Founding Myths and Compartmentalized Past: New Literature on the Construction, Hibernation, and Deconstruction of World War II Memory in Postwar Austria," in Günter Bischof/Anton Pelinka, eds., *Austrian Historical Memory & National Identity* (Contemporary Austrian Studies V) (New Brunswick, 1997), 392–41; see also idem, "Victims? Perpetrators? 'Punching Bags' of European Historical Memory? The Austrians and Their World War II Legacies," *German Studies Review* 27 (February 2004): 17–32.

35. "Decoding of the past" as a psychoanalytical means of unraveling the individual perceptions of the past and the symbolic use of the past is used by Pelinka as an analytical category; "Die geänderte Funktionalität von Vergangenheit und Vergangenheitspolitik," 46. Pelinka bases his use on Peter Loewenberg, *Decoding the Past: The Psychoanalytical Approach* (New York 1983).

36. Maislinger, "Zur Geschichtspolitik der SPÖ," 84f; Günter Bischof, "Der unerwartete Triumph der 'gnadenlos Guten'," *Zeitgeschichte* 28 (November/December 2001), 331–41; Anton Pelinka/Erika Weinzierl, eds., *Das grosse Tabu: Österreichs Umgang mit seiner Vergangenheit* (Vienna, 1987).

37. Heidemarie Uhl, "'Nur jener, der mit seiner Vergangenheit im Reinen ist, hat die Hände frei für die Zukunft': Zur Frage der Instrumentalisierung von 'Vergangenheitsbewältigung'," in Lutz Musner, Gotthart Wunberg, and Eva Cescutti, eds., *Gestörte Identitäten? Eine Zwischenbilanz der Zweiten Republik* (Innsbruck, 2002), 10–26 (here 11–15); Richard Mitten, "Bitburg, Waldheim, and the Politics of Remembering and Forgetting," in David F. Good and Ruth Wodak, eds., *From World War to Waldheim: Culture and Politics in Austria and the United States* (New York-Oxford, 1999), 51–84; Michel Gehler, "Die Affäre Waldheim: Eine Fallstudie zum Umgang mit der NS-Vergangenheit in den späten achtziger Jahren," in Rolf Steininger and Michael Gehler, eds., *Österreich im 20.*

*Jahrhundert,* vol. 2: *Vom Zweiten Weltkrieg bis zur Gegenwart* (Vienna, 1997), 355–414; Uhl, "Das 'erste Opfer'," 26–30.

38. These statements by prominent politicians are conveniently cited and referenced in Uhl, "Das 'erste Opfer'," 27–30; on the politics of establishing the *Nationalfonds,* see Helmut Wohnout, "Eine 'Geste' gegenüber den Opfern? Der Nationalfonds für Opfer des Nationalsozialismus und der schwierige Umgang Österreichs mit den Überlebenden nationalsozialistischer Verfolgung," in Thomas Angerer, Brigitte Baader-Zaar and Margarete Grandner, eds., *Geschichte und Recht: Festschrift für Gerald Stourzh zum 70. Geburtstag* (Vienna, 1999), 247–278.

39. For a summary of Austrian restitution efforts, see David Forster, *"Wiedergutmachung" in Österreich und der BRD im Vergleich* (Innsbruck, 2001).

40. Elazar Barkan, *The Guilt of Nations: Restitution and Negotiating Historical Injustices* (Baltimore, 2000), xvi, xviii.

41 Bischof, "Watschenmann der europäischen Erinnerung"; for a more skeptical account of Schüssel's and Riess-Passer's *Vergangenheitspolitik,* see Uhl, "'Nur jener, der mit seiner Vergangenheit im Reinen ist'," 23–26.

42. Gitta Sereny, London *Times,* May 25, 2001.

43. The final report of the Austrian historians' commission was completed in January 2003 and became public with its acceptance by high governmental leaders. The final report can be downloaded from the commission's website www.historikerkommission.gv.at. Meanwhile private Austrian corporations commissioned their own historical inquiries into World War II-related injustices; see the essays by Brigitte Bailer-Galanda, Eva Blimlinger, Martin Eichtinger, Dieter Stiefel, Oliver Rathkolb, and Margit Reiter in the section "Commissioning History: Austria and World War II Restitution and Reconciliation," in Günter Bischof, Anton Pelinka and Alexander Lassner, eds., *The Dollfuss/Schuschnigg Era in Austria: A Reassessment* (New Brunswick, 2003), 212–266. Political parties have also begun the process. The conservative People Party (ÖVP) has looked at aryanized properties in its possession; see Martin David, Hannes Schönner, Doris SottopietraHelmut Wohnout, "'Wiedergutmachung' und Restitution im Bereich der Parteien am Beispiel der ÖVP," in Helmut Wohnout, ed., *Demokratie und Geschichte* 5 (2001): 188–224.

44. Tina Rosenberg, *The Haunted Land: Facing Europe's Ghosts after Communism* (New York, 1996).

45. Cf. for instance Stoiber's speeches at the Sudetendeutscher Tag 2002 http://www.csu.de/home/UploadedFiles/Reden/020519_Rede_Stoiber_Sudetendt.pdf, and the press releases of the CSU http://www.csu.de/home/Display/disp_Suchergebnis?suche=normal.

46. The most informative biography in English is now Lothar Höbelt, *Defiant Populist: Jörg Haider and the Politics of Austria* (West Lafayette, 2003); for a critical view of Haider see the essays in Anton Pelinka and Ruth Wodak, eds., *The Haider Phenomenon in Austria* (New Brunswick: Transaction, 2002).

47. See his speeches on the homepage of the Czech president: http://www.hrad.cz/president/Havel/nemci/index_uk.html.

48. Misha Glenny, *The Fall of Yugoslavia: The Third Balkan War,* 3rd rev. ed. (Harmondsworth, 1996); Michael Ignatieff, *Blood and Belonging: Journeys into the New Nationalis*m (New York, 1993); David Rieff, *Slaughterhouse: Bosnia and the Failure of the West* (New York, 1996).

49. Rathkolb, "Verdrängung und Instrumentalisierung," 147f.

50. Barkan describes the rippling effects and overlaps of the important international trend of the "politics of restitution" in the 1990s and also dedicates a chapter to the Sudeten German demands; see *Guilt of Nations.*

51. Rathkolb, "Verdrängung und Instrumentalisierung," 148.

52. Wolfgang Müller-Funk, "Streitobjekt Beneš-Dekrete: Vom Elend der Siegergeschichten," *Der Standard*, 15/16 July 2002, 47.

53. Christian Schmidt-Häuer, "Die Geister, die sie rufen," *Die Zeit*, June 13, 2002, 3.

54. Interview with Vladimír Špidla, "Keine Verhandlungen zu Temelin und Beneš," *Format*, 27 June 2002.

55. Benita Ferrero-Waldner, "Regionale Zusammenarbeit—Baustein eines vereinten Europas," lecture delivered at "Europa Forum Wachau," Göttweig, June 29, 2002: http://www.bmaa.gv.at/presseservice/index.html.de.

56. Martin Jan Stransky, "The Beneš Decrees and the Usurpation of Power in the Czech Republic," *The New Presence*, September 6, 2002.

57. Radko Kubičko, "The Smoldering Beneš Decrees," *The New Presence*, September 6, 2002; Jiří Pehe, "Back to Instability," ibid.

58. Barbara Coudenhove-Kalergi, "Die Wiederkehr des Vergangenen; Zwei Vlker, zwei Geschichten," in: Coudenhove-Kalergi/Rathkolb, eds., *Beneš-Dekrete*, 7–14.

59. Bischof, "Der unerwartete Triumph."

60. The exact wording of Czech regrets in the German-Czech Declaration of 1997 was as follows: "The Czech side regrets that, by the forcible expulsion and forced resettlement of Sudeten Germans from the former Czechoslovakia after the war as well as by the expropriation and deprivation of citizenship, much suffering and injustice was inflicted upon innocent people, also in view of the fact that guilt was attributed collectively. *It particularly regrets the excesses which were contrary to elementary humanitarian principles* as well as legal norms existing at that time, and it furthermore regrets that Law No. 115 of 8 May 1946 made it possible to regard theses excesses as not being illegal and that in consequence these acts were not punished" [emphasis added]. See Jochen A. Frowein, "Legal Opinion concerning Beneš-Decrees and Related Issues," September 12, 2002, 27.

61. Ibid., 21–28 (citations 23, 26, 28, 32).

# Austro-Czechoslovak Relations and the Expulsion of the Germans

### ❖ Emilia Hrabovec ❖

Czechoslovakia was the first and until 1946 the only country in which the newly restored Austrian Republic mantained at least a *de facto* diplomatic mission. This relationship however could not conceal the considerable tension between the two partners that continues to influence bi-lateral relations to this day. Much of that tension can be traced to the traumatic Munich Crisis, the decline of the Czechoslovak state perceived by the Czechs as the Czech national state, and six years of Nazi occupation. These experences gave rise to a broadly shared political consensus in the Czech society that stability and security of the renewed Czechoslovakia required the creation of a homogeneous nation-state cleansed of its German minority considered disloyal and responsible for the fall of the first republic. To a certain extent the Allies shared this view, for which reason their own planners and policy makers had begun considering a population transfer as early as 1940/1942.[1] With the end of war and the restoration of the Czechoslovak republic in its pre-Munich borders in May 1945, the Czech leadership herded its German citizens into camps, coerced them into forced labor, placed their property under national administration and, wherever possible, drove them to the nearest German or Austrian border for immediate expulsion.[2]

The first round of deportations from southern Bohemia and Moravia involved sending about 150,000 people over the nearby Austrian frontier. The Soviet-backed provisional government of Karl Renner that had been established on 27 April 1945 acted with surprising pragmatism. In order to hasten the end of Allied occupation and the restoration of full sovereignty, the new regime in Vienna readily embraced the notion that Austria had been the "first victim" of Hitler's Germany. The return to the *Kleinösterreich* option would effectively dissociate Austria from Germany, both historically and legally, including any responsibility for Czechoslovakia's large Sudeten German minority. The Austrian government's Undersecretary for Foreign Affairs, Karl Gruber, officially declared that their future disposition was now a matter for Czechoslovakia to handle, either as a domestic issue or in conjunction with Germany and the Allies.[3] As early as 12 June 1945, Leopold Figl had informed the Cabinet Council that "since all German speakers in Czechoslovakia have opted for Germany, they should all go to Germany and not to Austria."[4]

Austrian pragmatism toward the expulsion also stemmed from the hard political and economic realities that the country faced under military occupation. Not only was the country divided, with a provisional government that was not even recognized by the Western Allies until October 1945, but it lacked sufficient economic resources to secure basic food supplies for its own population. Hence the top priority that the Renner government gave to ending its diplomatic isolation as a defeated belligerent and restoring full state sovereignty.[5] Toward this end, Vienna worked assiduously to maintain correct relations with its neighbors, especially with a Czechoslovak state that was considered politically and economically superior. Clearly, the key to achieving this goal was to collaborate with the Prague regime in resolving any problems stemming from the ongoing expulsions. As Hugo Hantsch from the State Office of the Interior put it: "We are a small, weak state. We shall need Czechoslovakia more than it will need us and we cannot provoke its enmity by forceful measures."[6]

Of decisive significance was the awareness of Austria's dependence on Czechoslovakia for essential coal and food supplies. The future Austrian Ambassador in Prague, Rudolf Seemann—at that time responsible for economic affairs in the State Office for Foreign Affairs—argued against any confrontation with Czechoslovakia "particularly with regard to negotiations about coal deliveries."[7] Karl Renner was less diplomatic and more to the point, explaining to Czechoslovak Prime Minister Zdeněk Fierlinger, "Coal is friendship, no coal is tension!"[8]

There were also political reasons for avoiding any deterioration in diplomatic relations. Czechoslovakia was the only state that *de facto* recognized an Austrian diplomatic mission, thereby strengthening the position of the internationally isolated Renner government whose range of action did not otherwise extended beyond the Soviet zone of occupation. Moreover, the Soviet military forces wished good relations between Vienna and Prague and fostered the idea of a population exchange involving Sudeten Germans of "Austrian origin" in exchange for the Czechs from Vienna.[9]

Yet another factor that influenced the decision making was the presence of Communist politicians in the Renner cabinet who were ostensibly patriotic but also radically anti-Sudeten-German. Thus, the Interior Minister Franz Honner considered the Sudeten Germans "fascist elements almost without exception"[10] while his State Office was of the opinion that "it was necessary to inform the Viennese population through the press about the real state of affairs concerning the refugees in order to prevent them from having a misplaced compassion for them. They are mainly Henlein followers and [Nazi] party members."[11] To a certain extent even non-Communists distrusted the Sudeten Germans, while the bulk of Austria's war-weary and starving population often viewed the expellees as intruders who simultaneously lived off the critically scarce supply of food and medicine, put pressure on the labor market, and posed a security risk.[12] Some even charged them with the responsibility for the war and, therefore, the blame for the whole current misery.

The first official Austrian reactions to the "involuntary invasion of more than one hundred thousand foreign citizens who have turned into beggars" were very cautious. Chancellor Renner supported the remonstrances of the Austrian's plenipotentiary in Prague, Alois Vollgruber, by addressing several private letters to his fellow Social Democrat, Prime Minister Fierlinger, in which he stressed the catastrophic scarcity of food and coal and called for an immediate stop to the transports. Remarkably, Renner did not speak out against the principle of expulsion as such, but only tried to keep the expellees away from Austria or to divert them to Germany.[13] The Czechoslovak side responded by dismissing the expulsions as "impositions by local authorities" that had been effected without their knowledge and promising that they would cease.[14] But the expulsions continued and on 2 July, after his return from Moscow, Prime Minister Fierlinger pronounced himself publicly in favour of resettling "the Germans from southern Bohemia and Moravia who are of Austrian origin and have close family and economic relations with Austria."[15] As a sop he offered to resettle the Czech minority in Vienna to Czechoslovakia. A few hours later in the Council of Ministers he assured his colleagues that "Stalin has reacted positively to our claims concerning the transfer" and that "we are allowed to carry out transfers to Germany, Hungary and, partially, to Austria."[16]

Meanwhile, the Soviets had encouraged the Austrians to enter into negotiations, for which they prepared by sending a memorandum to the Czechoslovak regime that remains to this day the most extensive and sharply worded ever written on this issue. In conformity with the victim thesis, it started from the fundamental assumption that the mutual relationship had to be settled on the principle of the restoration of the *status quo ante* 1938. The memorandum rejected the "forced naturalization of foreigners" as well as the reference to a possible "historic or racial relationship between the Austrian people with the refugees from the frontier zone" because this had been rendered irrelevant by the treaty of St. Germain. The memorandum also questioned the validity under international law of revoking *en masse* the citizenship of people who spoke a different language when they had been ensured "total equality of rights" since 1918. The memorandum asserted that "the national chauvinism of the past decades [was] more or less dead" in Austria and "as far as it had existed, it had not been aimed against the Czechoslovaks, but only the Jews!" The memorandum offered not to hinder the voluntary emigration of the non-German-speaking citizens, but expected appropriate compensation in the matter of the Austrian citizens willing to leave Czechoslovakia. Finally it repeated the fundamental Austrian claim that Czechoslovakia should replace the food and medicine *in natura* and pay compensation for all damages. The sharp tone culminated in the statement that, under the existing conditions, Austria saw itself obliged to expel all foreign citizens within the very near future.[17]

International law and the loyalty of the Czech minority were the most frequent official arguments advanced by the Austrian side to back up its rejection of a population exchange. Yet internal discussions show that other factors were also in play. Within the Cabinet Council, Renner pointed out that the Viennese Czechs were mainly trained craftsmen who were needed in Austria and would, therefore, be difficult to replace. Another consideration was the disparity in the property and material conditions of those involved in the prospective population exchange.[18] Even more important for Renner was the unspoken fact that the majority of the Viennese Czechs were Social Democrats and, as such, voters of his own party. Yet another major foreseeable problem was the lack of clear criteria for defining "persons of Austrian origin" which, it was feared, would lead to inequitable enforcement by the Czechs and a huge numerical imbalance in the number of people exchanged, particularly since voluntary repatriation and assimilation had already considerably reduced the number of Austria's Czech minority.

There was also a pragmatic, tactical argument against entering into negotiations at all. According to one "strictly confidential" internal document of the State Office for Foreign Affairs, "As soon as we begin to get involved in a discussion because of these Sudeten Germans of Austrian origin, we weaken our basis for negotiations right from the beginning." The document expressed the hope that the decisive word in the whole resettlement problem had not been spoken yet, since the Western Allies would not sanction the measures of Czechoslovakia until they could be sure of Austrian acceptance. Therefore, for the time being, Austria had to play for time and try to prove to the soon-to-be-created Allied Control Commission that it was unable to admit foreigners:

> In the course of further negotiations, but not earlier we could finally declare that we would make the sacrifice and accept the category of the Sudeten Germans mentioned by Fierlinger—but only this category—into Austria, but only under the condition that we would also be granted the necessary territory, for example a part of southern Moravia, since Austria within the borders of 1938 would not be able to provide supplies for such a considerable increase in population.[19]

As Renner informed the Czechoslovak Plenipotentiary František Bořek-Dohalský, "Austria is prepared to maintain these Sudeten Germans if they will be left to us with all of their belongings."[20]

These documents suggest two things: *Firstly,* that Vienna had still not forgotten the involuntary cession of the predominantly German-settled southern Moravia in 1919 and that there was a kind of split between her pragmatic outward insistence on the return to the *status quo ante* on the basis of the St. Germain border and the lack of interest in the German speaking population of southern Moravia on the one side and her inward convictions on the other. "The Germans in Southern Moravia put us into an embarrassing position," Chancellor Renner admitted in a Cabinet meeting. "We ought to punish them according to the Prohibition Law, but we cannot ignore the fact that a large number of them were and remain Austrians."[21] And *secondly*, that a population exchange was not considered an ideal, but nevertheless a conceivable option, perhaps as a threatening gesture that had already been articulated by the *Ballhausplatz* after the so-called Brno Death March at the beginning of June.[22]

While the State Office for Foreign Relations discussed the possibilities of diplomatic maneuver, Austria's domestic institutions had to cope with the problem of accommodating the expellees already present on Austrian soil. Their main objective was to provide the refugees with basic foodstuffs and temporary housing, without taking any steps to integrate them into Austrian society so as not to impede their quick removal from Austria. In accordance with the new law on citizenship, neither citizenship nor a residence permit was to be granted to Sudeten Germans—although the law and government officials permitted exceptions, above all for substantial numbers of medical professionals and other qualified employees.[23]

A 4 July meeting of the State Office of the Interior was so emotionally charged that measures were proposed which were so draconian that they could not even be quoted in the minutes; in the end, only the calm and collected attitude of a representative of the ever-cautious State Office for Foreign Affairs prevented their adoption. Nonetheless, all participants agreed that "there was only one solution, namely, to remove the refugees from Austria and not to let any others to enter." Alas, nobody knew how to achieve this. Some officials, including members of the Communist-administered State Office of the Interior and the Police, hoped for help and support from the Soviet military authorities, who might seal the borders and/or enforce reciprocal measures. Indeed, the deputy of the Police Administration observed that "at the moment 400,000 Czechs live in Vienna. If similar legal measures were taken against them, Czechoslovakia would give in." The alarmed diplomat Seemann brought to their attention that "from a Foreign Affairs perspective, an action against the Czechs living in Vienna is undesirable [since] in this case the Austrians living in Czechoslovakia would also be expelled, and that would negatively affect foreign trade." Other participants suggested that Vienna should ask the Americans and the British for help. The idea was rejected because the Austrian Government could not yet communicate with the Western Allies, who were still withholding recognition. Finally all agreed that, without the support from the outside, Austria alone would not be able to solve the problem, so that it would be necessary to wait for a decision from the Allies and the establishing of the Allied Control Commission for Austria. Until then, Vienna should limit its action to appeals to Prague and to the Soviet headquarters, as well as to the concentration and accurate registration of the expellees in camps. This would prevent them both from eluding police control and from privately acquiring supplies which would "rob" the country of scarce supplies, while making it easier to remove them from Austria and to calculate subsequent compensation claims against the Czechoslovak regime.[24]

Regardless of how much Renner and his ministers debated and strategized, the fact remained that they had precious little leverage. The Czechoslovak government ignored the memorandum that they dispatched on 14 July, and the deliberated expulsion of all foreigners from Austria—for which they had support from the Soviet City Commandant—was never put into effect since Vienna was unwilling to face the consequences of losing foreign professionals or incurring reprisals for expelling Allied citizens.[25] When, on 10 August 1945 yet another 2,000 people were expelled to Austria, Vollgruber felt obliged to reopen the question of the expulsions. Since the Renner government could not communicate officially with the Allied Control Commission, he urged the Prague regime to meet with the Commission in Berlin in order to transfer the expellees to Germany and to reimburse Vienna for all of the costs related to their stay in Austria.[26]

The Czechoslovak Foreign Office replied on 27 August by explaining that, since the expelled Germans were citizens of the German Reich, their expulsion to its territory conformed with international law. This assertion assumed that there was still no difference between Austria and Germany. In any event, the note stated that the majority of the Sudeten Germans had fled to Austria voluntarily because of their bad conscience. At the same time Prague insisted that Austrians should share the responsibility for the war and the misdeeds commited in the Czech lands.[27]

The State Office for Foreign Affairs rejected the Czechoslovak position arguing, in conformity with the thesis of the legal continuity, that Austria had never ceased to exist and had only been occupied by the German troops and robbed of the ability to act. The expellees were, therefore, not Austrian citizens and, according to the rules of international law, should have never been expelled to Austrian territory.[28]

However, both sides knew that the question of citizenship was much more problematic. Czechoslovak legal experts had to reconcile the retrospective recognition of the German naturalization acts with the Czechoslovak theory of continuity,[29] while their Austrian counterparts had to clarify the possible legal consequences of at least the *de facto* acceptance of the *Anschluss* of 1938.[30] Indeed, contrary to official statements, Austrian Foreign Office experts conceded Prague's right to reject the citizenship rights of its German-speaking citizens who had subsequently accepted German naturalization, even if it had no right to insist that they were now German citizens. Later on, on this basis, Austrian officials came to regard the Sudeten German expellees as stateless persons, whereas the Federal Republic of Germany accepted them as German citizens since 1938.[31]

Vienna never responded officially to the Czechoslovak note of 27 August. Nonetheless, the expulsions gradually petered to a halt during the autumn. Prague did not want to undermine its international position and endanger the Allied Control Commission's anticipated decision on the general transfer plan for Germany. Moreover, the Soviet High Command in Germany under Marshal Žukov, who had supported the mass expulsion of Germans before Potsdam in order to influence Allied decision making by creating a *fait accompli*, now rejected any further transfers in its overcrowded zone of occupation.[32] The Vienna government understood that the fulfilment of its fundamental claim—the removal of the Sudeten Germans from Austria—depended solely on the Allies and could probably be achieved only by transfers to Germany. Under these circumstances a diplomatic discussion with Prague on historical and legal topics seemed a futile academic debate without practical relevance. From his perch in Prague, Vollgruber also strongly advised against continued diplomatic polemics, which he regarded as inopportune at a time when the Czechoslovak regime was expected to be making important political decisions about the treatment of Austrians in Czechoslovakia.[33] Indeed, the Foreign Ministry in Prague had clearly signalled that it preferred a silent closure of the diplomatic debate and the concentration on the future economic cooperation at a time when it was preparing for comprehensive expulsions to Germany.

Instead of pointless protests in Prague, the new Undersecretary of State for Foreign Affairs, Karl Gruber, was more inclined to use the diplomatic leeway opened with the establishment of the Allied Control Commission in September. In a memorandum addressed to the highest allied authority, he requested the closure of Austrian borders and a quick removal of the expellees from Austria, while shunting responsibility for the Sudeten Germans on the occupation Powers.[34] In its reply of 11 November the Allied Council conceded that "an influx of Germanic peoples from neighboring countries took place some months ago" and assured Vienna that it "will...do everything...to arrange for the eventual removal of these non-Austrian elements." At the same time, however, it disappointed the silent expectations of the Renner government by stating that "no guarantee can be given that it is possible to return these peoples to their countries of origin...as this course of action would not be acceptable to the Governments of the countries concerned" and pointing to the concurrent obligation of the Austrian government to "take urgent measures to gather and employ the expelled Germans for useful public projects."[35]

After this reaction of the Allied Council, Gruber refrained from further diplomatic initiatives, instructing his officials to ignore remonstrances by the expelled Sudeten Germans, above all the southern Moravians who saw the *Ballhausplatz* as a protector of their interests and called for the reopening of the question of border adjustments and the incorporation of their home regions in Austria.[36] To the Czechoslovak Plenipotentiary Bořek-Dohalský, Gruber explained that his government dissociated itself from the anti-Czechoslovak activities of the expellee organizations.[37]

Gruber's foreign policy efforts, completely devoted to the reattainment of national sovereignty, concentrated henceforth on establishing economic relations with Austria's northern neighbour. In December 1945 his efforts were crowned by the successful conclusion of a barter trade agreement. A foreign policy discussion with Prague on the case of the expelled Sudeten Germans was, at least for the time being, put *ad acta.*

The anti-German measures of Czechoslovakia after the end of the war also opened the problem of the treatment of Austrians in the ČSR. Since the decrees of President Beneš were based on the principle of ethnicity rather than on that of citizenship,[38] the anti-German measures were basically applicable also to Austrians. Their legal position reflected the ambivalence with which the Great Powers treated the Austrian question in the Moscow Declaration and in the Yalta Declaration, oscillating between the poles of war guilt and victimhood. Czechoslovakia was willing to grant the Austrians certain concessions, most notably the exemption from restrictions concerning personal freedom. It did not exempt them from the decrees themselves, but was willing to apply to them the general exceptions foreseen in the decrees. Any other "special treatment" of Austrians reflected greater political goals, such as keeping Austria and Germany divided, dissuading Austria from pursuing a pro-Western course, forestalling Austrian countermeasures against the Czech minority, and fulfilling Moscow's desire to maintain essential economic ties between Prague and Vienna. For these reasons it was the Ministry for Foreign Affairs that was most inclined to meet Austrian interests. There was a silent agreement between the ministries that special regulations concerning the Austrians had to be effected by individual arrangements, rather than by an overall public decree. Nevertheless, the nationalistic propaganda machine made little or no distinction between Germans and Austrians, with the result that being Austrian acquired the same, negative connotation as being German. The remarks of the exiled politician Prokop Drtina (known under the radio-name Pavel Svatý) illustrate this clearly. During a mass rally of his National Socialist Party in Brno in September 1945 he told an audience numbering 30,000 that "We do not ask who is an Austrian, a Styrian, a Bavarian, but we do ask if this German has sinned or not, and as long as he does not prove the opposite, we have to assume that he did sin, whether he is now a German or an Austrian. Hitler was also an Austrian. We have to take care and not let happen that, in villages and towns where Konrad Henlein obtained an absolute majority or all of the votes in 1938, you find today only legitimized German anti-fascists."[39]

The first steps toward the protection of the interests of Austrians in Czechoslovakia were a result of a private initiative of the former Austrian Minister Plenipotentiary Ferdinand Marek. On the basis of an agreement with the Czech National Council, he revived the Austrian Legation and began to issue provisional certificates of Austrian citizenship to numerous candidates for repatriation. On 23 May Marek was arrested by the Soviet military forces and deported to the Soviet Union, where he died several years later. The current state of the research does not give definite evidence of whether Marek's arrest was due to his limited wartime collaboration with the Gestapo, his profound knowledge of the diplomatic and political circles which could have been either valuable or embarrassing to someone else, or the liberal practice of the first repatriation actions and the fear of some nationalists that his activities could endanger the overall application of the anti-German measures.[40] It is certain, however, that Chancellor Renner was not inclined to become committed in the matter and quickly entrusted Marek's colleague Vollgruber with running the provisional mission. Perhaps Renner contemplated some kind of barter arrangement when, after giving up Marek, he addressed the same letter to Fierlinger, pleading for the "special treatment" of Austrians in Czechoslovakia.[41]

Vollgruber quickly obtained not only the recognition of *de facto* diplomatic status, but also the reopening of the Austrian repatriation transports, albeit at the price: Prospective repatriates were to be screened for their political views by a newly established Austrian Repatriation Committee, some of whose members were in the service of the Ministry of the Interior and the Police, and maintained contacts with the Communist Party.[42] In the following weeks Vollgruber succeeded in getting Austrians exempted from having to wear the German identification insignia or from the reduced food rations that had been meted out to the Sudeten Germans. They were also permitted to retain the use of their flats and were allowed to use public facilities that had been denied to the Germans. Nevertheless, friction remained over the continued detention in camps or outright expulsion of many Austrians. Despite assurances of Czech officials, reports continued to arrive throughout the summer that Austrians were still included in expulsion transports, ending only with the completion of the systematic expulsions in autumn 1945.

Vollgruber played his part by keeping an awkward distance from everything German, and speaking with authorities about "the German National Socialism." At the beginning of July he celebrated his greatest success when the Ministry of the Interior issued a general decree stating that, since "Austria is a free and independent state which was only a victim...of an attack of the National Socialist German Reich, and expressed the wish to shape the relationship between ČSR and Austria in a friendly manner," Austrian citizens were not to be treated as Germans, but as citizens of the Allied states. Those wanting to leave the ČSR, could do so and could sell or, transportation permitting, take with them all of their own property, except gold.[43] By autumn instructions had been issued that Austrian prisoners of war were to be separated from the Germans and be permitted to return to Austria, and that forced labour was not to be applied to Austrians.[44]

The end of 1945 brought a total reversal in Prague's policies, both because of disputes over property rights and because of political developments in Austria, most notably the total defeat of the communists in the November elections. As a result the Czechoslovak Ministry of Interior revoked its recent decrees that had favoured the Austrians.[45] The government in Vienna tried to preempt this development by designing an "Austrian nationality," a term that Plenipotentiary Vollgruber used for the first time on 10 December in a note to the Prague Foreign Ministry. In consideration of the unclear situation of the regulations of some departments and in fear

398 ◆ EMILIA HRABOVEC

of possible reciprocal measures in Austria, the Prague Foreign Ministry started an inter-ministry survey and proposed a limited acceptance of the Austrian claims. The Ministries of Justice, Agriculture, of Internal Trade and, above all, of the Interior rejected the proposal. They referred to the different meaning of the term nationality in the Czechoslovak legislation and to the fact that "during the war Austria was neither an Allied nor a neutral state but a state in which the majority of the population was unfavourably disposed toward the Czechs, for which reason it is not possible to put its population on the same level as the Allies." The Ministry of the Interior pointed out that the Austrian state had recognised the validity of the ethno-linguistic definition of nationality until 1938 and, during the census of 1934, had defined "linguistic affiliation [as] very close to a profession in favor of nationality." Moreover, the majority of Austrians had been inclined towards Germany due to a German national conciousness, while nobody had professed Austrian nationality before 1945.[46]

Finally, on 8 March 1946 the long overdue decision was made at the highest level. The Presidium of the Council of Ministers decided that Austrian citizens leaving Czechoslovakia would be afforded the same preferential treatment as had German anti-fascists in the disposition of movable belongings. Confiscated unmovable property would, however, not be restored. The Ministry of the Interior inserted an additional qualification that stemmed from its fear that Germans from the Sudetenland or Germany proper or individuals charged with political crimes would benefit from the privilege being granted to Austrian citizens: Only persons who had never been members of the NSDAP or other Nazi-organisations would be eligible. The Austrian Plenipotentiary was, therefore, invited to present a new list of all Austrian citizens in the ČSR, whose political reliability would then be examined by Czechoslovak officials.[47]

The definitive solution of the financial and legal questions of Austrian citizens in Czechoslovakia took much longer. Only with the period of détente was an Austro-Czechoslovak treaty signed in 1975 that granted compensation for losses suffered from confiscation, nationalization, or similar measures. It referred, of course, only to persons who were in possession of Austrian citizenship at the time of these measures, not to those who acquired it later on.[48]

The most important objectives of Austrian foreign policy right after the war were the speedy political consolidation of the restored republic and an escape from its existentially dangerous economic plight. In the interest of this overriding goal it strove very pragmatically to free itself from the shadow of Germany, to end its international isolation, and to resolve the explosive problem of the expulsions of the Germans from neighbouring countries, among them Czechoslovakia. By no means did Austria want to risk a conflict with the Allies or even with Czechoslovakia, which it regarded as politically and economically superior—and a country that Austria needed politically and economically. This strategy of survival, sometimes together with individual political convictions of some politicians (e.g. the communists), fomented a certain lack of interest or mistrust toward the Sudeten Germans. As a result there was little or no solidarity with the expellees and not rarely a conviction that the expellees had to bear their part of political blame that stemmed from their association with the Third Reich. The untenability of a general political accusation, natural national sympathy for the Sudeten German neighbors and many Austrians' intuitive, subliminal feeling that they were being treated unjustly compared to the Czechs, produced some internal tension in Austrian political behavior. The statements of the State Chancellor illustrate this clearly. Renner, a southern Moravian himself, made contradictory statements about the German southern Moravian rural population on two different occasions in the same period of time: Whereas he told the Cabinet Council that the southern Moravians were mainly of Fascist persuasion and should be punished according to the *Verbotsgesetz*,[49] he wrote in a letter to Fierlinger that they were totally apolitical, with only a minute minority having occupied itself with NS-activities.[50] A similar disparity between personal conviction and pragmatic judgment was evident in the classification of the southern Moravians first as Austrians, then as foreigners. Only with the changing constellation of international politics that followed the end of the cold war could the long-suppressed subject of the expulsions be brought into the open.

## Notes

1. Detlef Brandes, *Der Weg zur Vertreibung 1938–1945: Pläne und Entscheidungen zum "Transfer" der Deutschen aus der Tschechoslowakei und aus Polen* (Munich, 2001).

2. Emilia Hrabovec, *Vertreibung und Abschub. Deutsche in Mähren 1945–1947* (Frankfurt am Main, 1996), 61–140.

3. Plenipotentiary in Vienna Bořek-Dohalský to the Ministry of Foreign Affairs in Prague, 2 February 1946, report on a conversation with the Undersecretary Gruber, in Václav Král, ed., *Die Deutschen in der Tschechoslowakei 1933–1947: Acta Occupationis Bohemiae et Moraviae* (Prague, 1964), 585.

4. Robert Knight, ed., "Ich bin dafür, die Sache in die Länge zu ziehen," *Die Wortprotokolle der österreichischen Bundesregierung von 1945 bis 1952 über die Entschädigung der Juden* (Vienna, 2000), Document no. 3, Kabinettsrat (KR) session 12, 12 June 1945, 68.

5. Cf. Robert Knight, "Die Regierung Renner und die österreichische Souveränität," in Gernot Heiss, Alena Míšková, Jiří Pešek, Oliver Rathkolb, eds., *An der Bruchlinie: Österreich und die Tschechoslowakei nach 1945* (Innsbruck & Vienna, 1998), 125–38; Oliver Rathkolb, "Zentrale Trends in der österreichischen Außenpolitik nach 1945," in ibid., 155–74; Günter Josef Bischof, *Between Responsiblity and Rehabilitation: Austria in International Politics, 1940–1950* (Ann Arbor, 1990), xiv–xviii, 101–115, 361–367; Klaus Fiesinger, *Ballhausplatz-Diplomatie 1945–1949: Reetablierung der Nachbarschaftsbeziehungen und Reorganisation des Auswärtigen Dienstes als Formen außenpolitischer Reemanzipation Österreichs* (Munich, 1993).

6. Österreichisches Staatsarchiv (ÖSA), Archiv der Republik (AdR), Karton 2, GZ 461-pol/45, *Amtsvermerk* on a meeting in the State Office of the Interior, 4 July 1945.

7. ÖSA, AdR, AA, Karton 2, GZ 461-pol/45, *Amtsvermerk* on a meeting in the State Office

of the Interior, 4 July 1945. In one of the first conversations of the Austrian Plenipotentiary Vollgruber with the Ministry of Foreign Trade Ripka on 12 July 1945, after having closed the Sudeten question in a few words, Minister Ripka went over to the question of the conclusion of a barter trade agreement, which would effect the exchange Czech coal for Austrian ore. See AdR, Karton 2, GZ 516-pol/45, report Vollgruber to Renner, 12 July 1945.

8. ÖSA, AdR, AA, Karton 1, GZ 65-pol/45, *Aktennotiz*, 17 May 1945.

9. ÖSA, AdR, AA, Karton 2, GZ 258-pol/45 and 493-pol/45.

10. Knight, ed., *Wortprotokolle*, Document No 3, KR session 12, 12 June 1945, pp. 71–72.

11. ÖSA, AdR, AA, Karton 2, GZ 332-pol/45, *Amtsvermerk* about a meeting on the refugee problem, 15th June 1945.

12. Cf. also Bischof, *Between Responsibility and Rehabilitation*, 378–80.

13. ÖSA, AdR, AA, II-pol/1945, Karton 2, GZ 113-po./45, Renner to Fierlinger, 29 May 1945; GZ 279-pol/45, Renner to Fierlinger, 27 June 1945.

14. ÖSA, AA, II-pol./1945, Karton 1, GZ 237-pol./45; Karton 2, GZ 421-pol/45 (conversation between Vollgruber and the political director in the Ministry for Foreign Affairs, Heidrich) and 516-pol/45 (conversation between Vollgruber and the Minister for Foreign Trade Ripka).

15. ÖSA, AA, II-pol./1945, Karton 2, radio speech of Fierlinger, 2 July 1945.

16. Státní ústřední archiv Praha (SÚA), ÚPV, minutes of the 36th session of the 1st Government, 2 July 1945; Hrabovec, *Vertreibung und Abschub*, 107.

17. ÖSA, AdR, AA, Karton 2, GZ 493-pol./45, Memorandum, 14 July 1945. Cf. also Hrabovec, *Vertreibung und Abschub*, 151–52; Oliver Rathkolb, "Ein schwieriges Verhältnis— Österreich und die ČSR 1945–1950," in Thomas Winkelbauer, ed., *Kontakte und Konflikte: Böhmen, Mähren und Österreich: Aspekte eines Jahrtausends gemeinsamer Geschichte* (Waidhofen an der Thaya, 1993), 479–80.

18. ÖSA, AdR, AA, GZ 1524-pol./45, and 138-pol./45, Renner to fellow Social Democrats in Podmokly, Northern Bohemia, 1 October 1945. Renner wrote: "The Czechs simply expel the Germans and send them to us like beggars, they have to abandon their houses without clothes and food. We, however, are expected to allow the local Czechs to abandon our country together with all their property. The Allies do not grant us the right to rob them of their property."

19. ÖSA, AdR, AA, Karton 2, GZ 420-pol/45.

20. ÖSA, AdR, AA, Karton 2, GZ 645-po./45, record of the conversation of the Czechoslovak Plenipotentiary Bořek-Dohalský with Renner, 28th July 1945.

21. Knight, ed., *Wortprotokolle*, Document No 3, KR session 12, 12 June 1945, p. 65.

22. SÚA, ÚPV, 25th session of the 1st Government, 2nd June 1945; Moravský zemský archiv Brno (MZA), fond B-280, karton 65, minutes of the 9th session of the Council of the Moravian National Committee, 5 June 1945.

23. ÖSA, AdR, AA, Karton 2, GZ 332-pol./45, *Amtsvermerk* on the meeting in the Staatsamt für Inneres, 15 June 1945. Cf. Knight, ed., *Wortprotokolle*, Document No 3, KR session 12, 12 June 1945, 64–73.

24. ÖSA, AdR, AA, Karton 2, GZ 461-pol./45, *Aktennotiz* on the meeting in the State Office of the Interior, 4 July 1945; GZ 420-pol./45, report on the same meeting sent to the Plenipotentiary Vollgruber.

25. ÖSA, AdR, AA, Karton 2, GZ 493-pol./45, *Aktennotiz*, 14 July 1945.

26. ÖSA, AdR, AA, Karton 68, GZ 138-pol./45, Vollgruber note to the Czechoslovak Ministry of Foreign Affairs, 20 August 1945.

27. ÖSA, AdR, AA, Karton 68, GZ 138-pol./45, and Karton 2, GZ 493-pol./45. The Czechoslovak note was also published in Král, ed., *Die Deutschen in der Tschechoslowakei*, 564–65;

see also Hrabovec, *Vertreibung und Abschub*, 152–53; Rathkolb, "Ein schwieriges Verhältnis," 480–81.

28. ÖSA, AdR, AA, Karton 68, GZ 138-pol./45, *Aktennotiz*, 26 November 1945, and GZ 111.917-pol./48, *Aktenvermerk*, 11 December 1945.

29. Hrabovec, *Vertreibung und Abschub*, 159–60.

30. Knight, *Die Regierung Renner und die österreichische Souveränität*, 135–36.

31. See Helmut Slapnicka, "Die rechtlichen Grundlagen für die Behandlung der Deutschen und Magyaren in der Tschechoslowakei," in Richard G. Plaschka, Horst Haselsteiner, Arnold Suppan, Anna M. Drabek, eds., *Nationale Frage und Vertreibung in der Tschechoslowakei und Ungarn 1938–1948* (Vienna, 1997), 168.

32. Hrabovec, *Vertreibung und Abschub*, 117, 148, 287.

33. ÖSA, AdR, AA, Karton 68, GZ 1066-pol./45 und 138-pol/45, Vollgruber to Secretary General Wildner, 26 October 1945.

34. ÖSA, AdR, AA, Karton 2, GZ 1523-pol./45, Memorandum to the Allied Control Council for Austria, 19 October 1945. See also Bischof, *Between Responsibility and Rehabilitation*, 381–82.

35. ÖSA, AdR, AA, Karton 2, GZ 1848-pol./45, answer of the Allied Control Council.

36. ÖSA, AdR, AA, Karton 3 and Karton 5.

37. Report of the Czechoslovak Plenipotentiary in Vienna Bořek-Dohalský to the Ministry of Foreign Affairs in Prague, 2 February 1946, in: Král, ed., *Die Deutschen in der Tschechoslowakei*, 584–85.

38. Some lawyers, mainly from the Ministry of Justice, criticized the omission of a precise definition of the relationship between nationality and citizenship, particularly with regard to the implications that could have resulted from the general formulations for German-speaking people from neutral states who resided in Czechoslovakia or owned property there. The Ministry of Foreign Affairs as well as the Ministry of Justice assumed that the legislature did not bear in mind this category of ethnic Germans.

39. Svobodné slovo, 25 September 1945. Cf. ÖSA, AdR, AA, Karton 1, GZ 141-pol./45.

40. See Herbert Steiner, *Der erste österreichische Gesandte in Prag Ferdinand Marek: Sein Schicksal in den Jahren 1938–1947* (Prague, 1995). See also the correspondence between Marek and the State Office for Foreign Affairs in Vienna from May 1945, in: ÖSA, AdR, AA, II-pol/1945, Karton 1.

41. ÖSA, AdR, AA, Karton 2, GZ 201-pol./45, Renner to Fierlinger, 29 May 1945.

42. ÖSA, AdR. AA, GZ 161-pol./45, report Vollgruber to Renner, 3 June 1945. For the political profile of the Committee see *ibidem*, GZ 1532-pol./45, private letter of Vollgruber to the Secretary General Wildner, 29 September 1945.

43. MZA, fond B-280, karton 787, GZ 215/45-dÛv.-ZOB.

44. SÚA, MV-NR, karton 8150, III-2, 146.

45. The Ministry of the Interior considered the confiscation decree No 108 of 28 October 1945, which contained no special provisions concerning Austrians, as an *ex lege* revocation of its previous enactment, and in February 1946 it instructed the authorities to regard Austrians as persons of German nationality. See SÚA, MV-NR, karton 1421, A 5510, Ministry of the Interior, memo, 10 July 1946.

46. SÚA, MV-NR, karton 1421, A 5510.

47. Ibid., resolution of the Presidium of the Government, 8 March 1946.

48. *Österreichisches Bundesgesetzblatt*, 1975, No 451.

49. Knight, ed., *Wortprotokolle*, Document No 3, KR session 12, 12 June 1945, 65.

50. ÖSA, AdR, AA, Karton 1, GZ 65-pol/45, *Notiz* on a verbal message of Renner to Fierlinger, 17 May 1945.

# West Germany and the Lost German East

## Two Narratives

### ◆ William Glenn Gray ◆

After 1945, the *Deutscher Osten* was no more. Not only did the victorious allied powers place the eastern quarter of the German Reich under Polish and Soviet administration; the "German cultural space" in East Central Europe and the Balkans all but evaporated under the impact of the expulsions from points as distant as the Ural Mountains.[1] To be sure, Hitler's own policies of ethnic consolidation had initiated the retreat of German communities "home to the Reich"; and the genocidal onslaught against Jews, Romany, and Slavs had torn asunder the demographic map of Europe's East.[2] But the scale of Germany's cultural—and corporeal—expulsion from the East in the mid-1940s marked one further element in the radical reshaping of the Continent.

Europe's new political geography made the East seem all the more irretrievable, for the establishment of "people's democracies" under Soviet hegemony rendered West German travel to these regions exceedingly difficult. A tone of unrelenting hostility from the Soviet bloc only added to the alienation: not only the Nazi past, but the present reality of the Federal Republic was stigmatized as "fascist, revanchist, militarist." Naturally, West Germans repaid such compliments with vivid condemnations of the soul-less, inhumane Stalinist dictatorships. "*Weit ist der Weg nach Osten*," read one book title by Countess Marion Dönhoff, editor of the influential weekly *Die Zeit* and herself a prominent expellee: "it's a long journey to the East."[3]

The tremendous mental and political distance between the Federal Republic and Eastern Europe would in turn foster two simplistic and diametrically opposed narratives that interpreted the loss of the German East.[4] The first, harbored above all by the expellees themselves, focused on Germany's victim status. The second, developed in response to the expellees' intransigence, dwelt instead on German guilt. Political controversies in the Federal Republic did not always turn on such fundamental categories; but assumptions about guilt and victimization helped to bring a rancorous emotional intensity to the debates about *Ostpolitik*. Ultimately, neither of these extreme positions offered a viable model for constructive West German engagement in Eastern Europe. Only the end of the Cold War has narrowed the gap between East and West, creating the potential for more balanced assessments of the legacy of the German East.

## The "Victim Narrative" and the Era of Revisionism

Fixating on Germany's "victim" status was common currency during the first two decades after 1945. The Allied bombing campaigns; the systematic rape of women in eastern Germany; the plight of POWs in Soviet hands; the westward trek of the expellees—all reinforced the idea that the German people had suffered uniquely in the final phases of World War II. Robert Moeller's *War Stories* describes a concerted government-financed effort in the early 1950s to gather oral testimonies from thousands of expellees, resulting in a series of dense volumes documenting abuses against ethnic Germans in the East. The geographic scope was wide, ranging from Yugoslavia and Romania to largely German regions such as Silesia, East Prussia, and the Sudetenland. The manner of ethnic cleansing varied, from "wild" expulsions in the spring and summer of 1945 to systematically administered evacuation orders in the winter of 1945/46. One thing bound all of the stories together in retrospect: they all played out behind the "Iron Curtain," in the Soviet sphere of influence. The narrative of German suffering would unfold along Cold War lines.[5]

By the turn of the 1950s, the 7.5 million expellees in the western zones of Germany had begun to organize politically. The new expellee lobbies agitated for concrete social goals, above all an "equalization of burdens" between the western Germans and the less fortunate easterners, who had lost their property without compensation.[6] However, for the lobbies, organized as "Homeland Societies," no payment could compensate for the lost *Heimat*. They sought to express their demands in universal terms, postulating a "right to one's homeland," analogous to the catalog of human rights then being elaborated by the United Nations.[7] Granted the right of return, the expellees would, presumably, overwhelm the Slav populations thinly settled on former German lands; and they would then exercise their "right of self-determination" by voting for a return of those lands to German sovereignty. Even while renouncing any military ambitions, the Homeland Societies thus held open the prospect of a peaceful restoration of borders.[8]

Like the expellees, Konrad Adenauer's fledgling government in Bonn framed its arguments in legal terms. Rather than stressing universal rights, however, Adenauer's version of the "victim narrative" revolved around the status of Germany as defined by the victorious Allied powers. Acutely aware of the Federal Republic's lack of sovereignty, the Chancellor's main concern was to entrench his administration as the sole legitimate voice of all Germans—a claim also asserted by the rival government in East Berlin.[9] At the same time, West German leaders were careful to define their state as a *provisorium*, a polity that could not make decisions on behalf of a future united Germany. Only a completely whole, democratically elected German government could negotiate a peace treaty with the Allies—a treaty that would, among other things, determine the permanent extent of Germany's frontiers. Until that time, asserted Adenauer, the German *Reich* still existed within the borders of 1937. Maps printed in West Germany duly marked the Oder-Neisse frontiers with dotted lines and the caption "under Polish administration."

It is doubtful that Adenauer ever expected a restoration of the complete 1937 frontiers. Even if Poland were somehow forced to disgorge all of its newly won territory, was it realistic to expect the Soviet Union to abandon northern East Prussia—now russified as the Kaliningradskaya Oblast? Faced with political pressure from West German expellees, Adenauer did at times identify the goal of his government as the "restoration of the complete unity of Germany: unity with Berlin and the Soviet Zone and the entire east of Germany."[10] But in practice, Adenauer's main concern was to preserve as much maneuvering room as possible by deferring difficult questions about the border to some future date. In September 1955, the chancellor pragmatically chose to establish diplomatic relations with the Soviet Union in spite of the open territorial questions. Only a feeble reservation, couched in a German letter sent to Soviet premier Nikolai Bulganin, upheld Bonn's thesis about the legal status of the 1937 boundaries.

Adenauer's decision in Moscow immediately raised the question as to whether the Federal Republic might follow suit and open formal ties with the other East European governments. Bonn's Foreign Office advised against, warning that this might lead outside observers to conclude that the West Germans now accepted the territorial status quo in Europe. This, in turn, would redound to the benefit of the rival government in East Berlin, which desperately sought to prove its viability as an independent state.[11] The chancellor's own motives were more political in nature. Were the expellees—prominently represented in all the major West German parties—prepared to see the Federal Republic enter into cordial relations with the very governments that had directed the expulsion? Before the 1957 elections, Adenauer was not about to take that chance.[12]

Relations with Yugoslavia provided one early indication of the challenges Bonn would face in trying to normalize relations with Eastern Europe. As a maverick communist state, Yugoslavia enjoyed a special status within Cold War Europe; Bonn and Belgrade exchanged diplomatic representatives in 1951. From the mid-1950s, as Yugoslavia drew closer to the Soviet orbit, Marshall Tito began to express concrete demands for German restitution for the ravages of the Second World War. To avoid setting a precedent for the other East European states, Bonn packaged its compensation as a 99-year loan to the government of Yugoslavia.[13] Even under this guise, the treaty aroused significant opposition within Adenauer's own party, and the CDU/CSU parliamentary group moved to postpone ratification in the summer of 1956. Expellee leaders complained that the treaty made no reference to the expulsion, and insisted that the Bonn government issue a statement avowing that the treaty would not prejudice future material claims by expellees against Belgrade.[14] More quixotically, they tried the patience of their colleagues in the Bundestag's foreign affairs committee by insisting on a lengthy examination of the human rights situation of any remaining ethnic Germans in Yugoslavia.[15]

For ideological reasons, Bonn's Social Democrats evinced considerably more sympathy for East European regimes in the 1950s. SPD leaders maintained ties with the League of Yugoslav Communists and discussed in Belgrade such problems as German unity and Cold War disengagement.[16] De-Stalinization in Poland further excited the left in Bonn, for it stimulated the hope that—despite the crackdown in Budapest—Soviet control over Eastern Europe was starting to ease. At this point, the SPD had still not accepted the permanence of the military blocs in Europe; thus Social Democrats showed keen interest in proposals by the new Polish foreign minister, Adam Rapacki, about a nuclear-free zone in the center of Europe.[17] In retrospect, the SPD's sentimental re-discovery of Poland in the years 1956–58 appears remarkably ahistorical. Carlo Schmid's contacts with intellectuals in Warsaw impressed him unduly, reinforcing the Social Democratic tendency to overestimate the ease with which German ties with the "Polish cultural nation" could be revived.[18] Reform communists would, it seemed, automatically recognize the "good" West Germans as reliable partners in European security. Bonn's Social Democrats also assumed, rather optimistically, that the border question could be left to one side while establishing a working relationship with Warsaw.[19]

Similar optimism spread also among a small group of West German diplomats—invariably those whose careers predated the Cold War. They argued that a softening of German policy toward Eastern Europe might reap substantial returns: the support of Poland (and Yugoslavia) for German unification; a lessening of military tensions in Europe; and in the long run, a restoration of Germany's good name and influence in the East.[20] Like the Social Democrats, these diplomatic proponents of an active *Ostpolitik* were not prepared to write off the Oder-Neisse territories entirely. Albrecht von Kessel, Bonn's chargé in Washington, bemoaned the "all-or-nothing" attitude so common in Bonn and Warsaw. He discreetly sounded out his Polish counterparts in the United States, hinting at a possible border compromise by using the German names for certain locations—including his native Breslau—while in other cases making use of the new Polish place names.[21]

As it happened, Kessel's initiative corresponded very closely with American thinking on the Oder-Neisse problem. Anxious to see a reduction of tensions between

Poland and the Federal Republic, State Department officials earnestly hoped that the two sides would reach some preliminary agreement on the future disposition of the border—one that involved mild revisions to the frontier on Oder and Neisse.[22] George Kennan, after visiting Poland's "recovered territories" in the west in July 1958, concluded that "the depressed state of this region is a serious argument against the perpetuation of the present arrangement."[23] Whether the Poles were open to conversation remains a matter of speculation, though Polish historians have argued that Gomulka's position did not harden until 1959.[24] What is clear is that Adenauer's government and the Homeland Societies showed little interest in such a bargain. For the chancellor and his ministers, the niceties of Germany's legal position made it difficult to conceptualize negotiations on just one aspect of the broader "German problem."[25] Perhaps more surprisingly, the expellee lobbies showed little appetite for securing a piecemeal return of former German lands. Concrete discussions about territorial arrangements would, in all likelihood, pit the interests of Silesians and Pomeranians against East Prussians and Germans from the Sudetenland. The Homeland Societies preferred to stand by their declamatory goal—the peaceful restoration of Germany's 1937 borders.[26] The "victim narrative," that undifferentiated tale of German suffering, did not prepare West German expellees for the prospect of real-world bargaining.

Khrushchev's Berlin ultimatum of November 1958, a menacing threat to resolve the anomalous status of West Berlin by force if necessary, put an abrupt end to any talk of border revisions. Polish representatives became more tight-lipped in their interactions with Westerners; and their remarks on Germany increasingly echoed Khrushchev's tirades against German revanchism and militarism.[27] For their part, the Western Allies—facing the specter of nuclear war over Berlin—had an obvious interest in quelling other points of disagreement with the Soviet Union. In March 1959, France let it be known that it considered the Oder-Neisse line to be the definitive eastern border of any united German state. The Eisenhower administration stood by its standard line—namely, that the question of borders could only be settled in a peace treaty. But in conversation with Gomulka in August 1959, Vice President Nixon acknowledged that the demographic situation in western Poland would strongly sway American judgment on the fate of the Oder-Neisse territories. Seven million Poles now lived there, as opposed to a few thousand Germans.[28] Pragmatic considerations no longer spoke in favor of some territorial compromise between Germany and Poland. "The fact of the matter was that the borders could be changed only by war," Eisenhower remarked to the British prime minister seven months later. With the stakes so high, the U.S. "could not really afford to stand on a dime for the next fifty years. He believed the time would come when we should make a statement on the border."[29]

Under the circumstances, the expellees' revisionism was beginning to cost West Germany sympathy among the allies. Eisenhower commented unfavorably on "the many placards he had seen during his recent visit to Germany demanding the return of the lost East German provinces."[30] Later American observers were even more put off. Dean Rusk, Secretary of State under Kennedy and Johnson, developed something of "a fixation about Germany's eastern frontiers."[31] George McGhee, ambassador to West Germany in the mid-1960s, reported bluntly that "there are no Germans east of the Oder-Neisse line. Germany does not need *Lebensraum*—it has a deficit in workers."[32] Given this turn in Allied sentiments, the border question was effectively closed down. Of the four powers responsible for Germany as a whole, all of them agreed that there would be no change in the borders of a future unified Germany. Legally, East and West Germany had no say in the matter. The tyranny of the majority—the weight of international opinion—stood squarely behind the status quo.

## The "Guilt Narrative" and the Era of *Ostpolitik*

The guiding assumption of most West German commentators in the 1950s—whether or not they consciously embraced the "victim narrative"—was that Germany did not *deserve* to lose the Eastern territories. The "guilt narrative" that emerged during the course of 1960s reversed this premise by relating the territorial losses to Germany's own aggressive behavior. From the outset, this counter-narrative had high-carat intellectual credibility: historians and novelists and the authors of *feuilleton* articles first articulated this standpoint, which was later snapped up by politicians in the Free and Social Democratic Parties. Over time, however, the tenor of the "guilt narrative" shifted. What began as a fairly perceptive response to the political realities of détente evolved into an abject dismissal of German national interests in Eastern Europe.

Scholars have typically pointed to the Berlin Wall as a catalyst of the "new Eastern policy." In standard accounts, Berlin mayor Willy Brandt and his foreign policy advisor, Egon Bahr, figure among the first to grasp that human contacts across the Wall—and across divided Germany—were a prerequisite for maintaining some semblance of unity among Germans. Thus, as Bahr suggested in his famous Tutzing speech of July 1963, West Germans had no choice but to win the trust of the East German leadership and that of the Soviet Union as well.[33] Bahr's thinking remained very much goal-oriented throughout the decade: the point of *Ostpolitik* was to secure concrete advantages for the Federal Republic. Reaching some kind of border agreement with the Eastern powers was simply the price Bonn must pay in order to develop a working relationship with the Warsaw Pact members.[34]

This pragmatic strain showed up often among early promoters of a "new Eastern policy." They observed, quite rightly, that West Germany was unnerving East Europeans and its own allies as well by refusing to accept the existing frontiers in Europe. Carl Friedrich von Weizsäcker, a nuclear physicist turned peace activist, argued that the Federal Republic's only chance at reunification would come if the outside world ceased to fear the potential power of this unified state. Bonn must reassure its neighbors that no third "grasp at power" (*Griff nach der Macht*) would be forthcoming.[35] As this wording suggests, the works of Fritz Fischer had a seminal impact outside scholarly circles in the mid-1960s, reminding publicists of the long, unfortunate history of German revisionism. Rudolf Augstein, publisher of *Der Spiegel*, followed Fischer in tracing a line of continuity from Hitler back to the Wilhelmine era. Persuaded anew of Germany's "explosive force" in international politics, Augstein insisted that Bonn must reassess its foreign policy. "For example, I don't think that we can and should afford our present position on the Oder-Neisse border," he wrote to Bundestag President Eugen Gerstenmaier in September 1964.[36]

The builders of this narrative liked to present themselves as sober realists. Golo Mann, son of the Nobel Prize laureate, complained that it was a fantasy to pretend that the borders of 1937 still existed, or could be somehow bargained away for other concessions at the negotiating table. All that remained for Germany was to recognize the "outcome of the Second World War."[37] As self-evident as it may have sounded, though, the formula "accepting the outcome" of the war proved remarkably hard to pin down. What *was* the outcome of World War II, exactly? Read broadly, this might be taken to include —in the words of one conservative—"the loss of the German eastern territories, the division of Germany and Berlin, the existence of a dictatorship over 17 million of our compatriots, and the wall in Berlin." This commentator contended that it did not make sense to view all of these circumstances as logical outcomes of Hitler's war: they resulted instead from a "rapacious policy on the part of one of the four victors."[38] According to this line of reasoning, the Soviet Union was responsible for the present shape of Europe, and Germans had no particular obligation to come to terms with it.

Precisely here, the "guilt narrative" took an opposing tack, emphasizing Germany's fundamental historical responsibility for the war and its unpleasant after-effects. In this respect, the Evangelical Church in Germany pushed the debate forward with the publication of its "Memorandum on the Situation of the Expellees" in October 1965. "The German people has accumulated a heavy political and moral guilt with respect to its neighbors," read the introduction. "The injustices committed against Germans cannot be removed from the context of political and moral error into which the German people let itself be led by National Socialism."[39] By later standards, the memorandum was cautious in its language and in its recommendations. But it helped to separate discussion of the border issue from the context of the "German Question."[40] The Evangelical Church hinted at a new kind of moral reckoning: the loss of the German East was, in effect, a repayment for the Germans' own rapaciousness under the Nazi regime.

Such reasoning provoked a vicious reaction from the Homeland Societies, which complained that the theologians had strayed into the fundamental error of "collective guilt": all the Germans living in the East had suffered a punishment that should rightfully have been meted out only against the Nazi criminals.[41] However, the unmeasured language employed by the expellee leaders tended to alienate a West German public that was increasingly prone to question the relevance of the 1937 borders. Those who had fled the German East at a young age, and even more so the children of expellees, had no interest in returning to some distant "homeland."[42] More and more Germans appeared willing to accept the moral balance-sheet implicit in the Evangelical Church's memorandum. Novelist Günter Grass, writing to one of the more respected expellee leaders in 1970, offered the following perspective: "We are the ones who originated the injustice—an injustice that produced manifold injustices. There's no point in complaining that the final result of this chain reaction has been booked against us Germans by history."[43] For Grass, a native of Danzig/Gdansk, it was only natural to view the loss of homelands as a loss for all Germans—a collective punishment that did not just apply to the expellees. His solution was to preserve the "cultural substance" of the lost Eastern provinces, perhaps through a deliberate cultivation of the major dialects once spoken there.[44]

A growing sense of responsibility—of German obligation vis-à-vis Eastern Europe—made the absence of formal relations between Bonn and the Warsaw Pact capitals a source of embarrassment in the mid-1960s. The words *Versöhnung* or *Aussöhnung*, implying rueful reconciliation, replaced the more neutral term *Verständigung* (understanding or arrangement) as the conceptual goal of German policy in Eastern Europe.[45] All the same, governing coalitions in Bonn remained slow to confront the problem of historical guilt. "The federal government is pursuing neither revenge nor restoration. Its horizons are directed forward, not backward," affirmed Chancellor Ludwig Erhard in his "peace note" of March 25, 1966. While underlining Bonn's abhorrence of war, the note had little to say about prior German aggression, and it implied that the Warsaw Pact governments were to blame for the miserable state of German relations with Eastern Europe.[46] Nine months later, Erhard's successor Kurt-Georg Kiesinger sounded a more conciliatory note: "we haven't forgotten Poland's history of suffering and we understand Poland's desire to finally live in a state territory with secure frontiers."[47] Apparently the Poles would have to wait, though, because Kiesinger proved no more willing than Erhard to resolve the Oder-Neisse controversy once and for all. The 1937 borders remained valid under international law until a freely elected, unified German government declared otherwise.

Kiesinger's government, a coalition of Social and Christian Democrats, did score some initial successes in the East during the winter of 1966–67. Romania, then behaving as a maverick member of the Warsaw Pact, exchanged ambassadors with Bonn in January 1967 without insisting upon any prerequisites. However, Poland, East Germany, and the USSR moved to block any further West German gains until the Bonn government appeared ready to accept *their* definition of the outcome of the war.[48] Bonn must recognize the GDR and the Oder-Neisse border; sign the nuclear non-proliferation treaty; and accept that the Munich Agreement of 1938 had been invalid *ab initio*, from the moment it was signed.[49] This last demand, though obviously of greatest practical significance to the Czechs, underscored that the Soviet bloc had a historical as well as a political agenda. The West Germans were, in effect, being asked to acknowledge that Hitler and his country had single-handedly violated the peace of Europe and thus originated all the European calamities that followed.

Increasingly, Social Democrats—then sharing in government under the "grand coalition"—were prepared to accept this proposition. "The starting point for any consideration [of the border question] is the not gladly heard, but indisputable fact that we unleashed the last war and lost it," argued State Secretary Duckwitz of the foreign ministry, an official with strong SPD ties. "As history teaches, this has got to be paid for." In a memorandum to Willy Brandt, then serving as foreign minister, Duckwitz insisted that there was no point in keeping the border question open until a peace treaty; such a treaty would only serve to confirm the present distribution of territory. A unilateral West German move to recognize the Oder-Neisse frontier would at least win the Federal Republic a modicum of international good will.[50] Brandt was not prepared to go quite this far, but at the SPD Party Congress in March 1968 the foreign minister did stress the need to "respect and recognize" the fact that Poland's border now ran along Oder and Neisse.

Christian Democrats continued to resist a one-sided emphasis on German guilt. Soviet repression in Czechoslovakia revived the German conservatives' distrust of Moscow and reinforced their emphasis on Soviet depredations—in 1945 as well as 1968. Electoral opportunism also dictated a swing to the right: the CDU/CSU was eager to absorb votes from the upstart National Democratic Party, so it gave free rein to the resentment of the Homeland Societies during the 1969 election season.[51] On the center-left, the Social Democrats raced to keep up with the Free Democrats, who advertised their relevance in the late 1960s by making iconoclastic, self-important pronouncements. "Why reunification at all?" asked Hans Rubin in the FDP's leading theoretical journal. "There won't be a reactionary *Anschluss*-reunification. The German national state is no longer a realizable goal. The time for such a construct is past."[52] FDP chairman Walter Scheel endorsed this sentiment in more dignified terms, suggesting that "the future lies only in the political integration of Europe." In a united Europe, border questions would scarcely matter; Cold War problems such as the Oder-Neisse frontier and the recognition of the GDR would simply disappear.[53]

By 1970, many in the SPD had also reached the point of challenging national identity as such. "We know that there is no legal action that can rectify the injustice of the Second World War, foisted upon Poland by National Socialist Germany, or the injustice of the expulsion from the German eastern territories," wrote one Social Democratic parliamentarian. "However, we know that this *Unheil* had its roots in nationalist thinking, and that therefore a lasting peace can only be built upon the final overcoming of nationalistic categories of thought."[54] The moral implications of this argument were clear: those who could not distance themselves from "nationalistic categories of thought" were a menace to the present peace of Europe, and the intellectual heirs of the Nazi crimes to boot. In some cases, this was undoubtedly apt; prominent expellee leaders had "brown" pasts, and so did the rising stars of the

National Democratic Party. But a blanket condemnation of all forms of nationalism was nevertheless a highly aggressive posture. The "guilt narrative" no longer represented a sober judgment about the constraints on German power; it now postulated its own highly particular understanding of an appropriate German identity.

It would be a mistake to confuse these extreme sentiments with the position of the Brandt government. In the years 1969–74, the Social-Liberal coalition under Willy Brandt negotiated its *modus vivendi* with the East on the basis of West German interests. The Moscow Treaty of August 1970 was not a "second capitulation" to Soviet power, whatever the CDU/CSU opposition might claim. In arduous negotiations with the Soviets, Egon Bahr reaffirmed Bonn's intention to pursue a peaceful unification of Germany. Even the Oder-Neisse question was handled circumspectly: in describing the present border as "inviolable," Brandt's government neither explicitly recognized it under international law nor tied the hands of a future united Germany.[55] In sum, the Federal Republic continued to resist certain Soviet interpretations of the status quo in postwar Europe.

All the same, Brandt's symbolic language—most famously his "knee-fall" at the Warsaw Ghetto monument in December 1970—tended to project a highly moral posture. Internationally, this was a tremendous boon to West German credibility, underlined by Brandt's receipt of the Nobel Peace Prize in 1971. Domestically, the chancellor's political foes managed to find insult in Brandt's displays of humility. Those who nursed the old "victim" identity took umbrage at the chancellor's ready acknowledgment of German sins. Consider, for example, the following remark: "Dear fellow citizens, nothing is lost with this [Moscow] treaty that was not gambled away long ago."[56] This admirably succinct expression of German responsibility could have little meaning to died-in-the-wool expellee revisionists, who failed to appreciate why *they* had been dealt the losing hand.

At its root, then, the ugly, polarizing clash over *Ostpolitik* in the early 1970s can be understood as a showdown between adherents of two mutually contradictory versions of history. Neither Brandt nor his principal rival, Rainer Barzel, sympathized fully with the "guilt" or "victim" narratives; indeed, Barzel's prescriptions for Eastern policy scarcely different from those of the governing coalition.[57] Emotions ran high because partisans on each side felt the other was betraying core values. Foes of Brandt's Eastern Treaties feared that German interests were being sold out to Moscow, the very source of Germany's travails; the chancellor's supporters worried that the nationalist, backward-looking obstructionism of the Christian Democrats would provoke Soviet wrath and unravel the course of détente. In the end, the elections of November 1972 proved just how marginalized the national values of the CDU/CSU had become. The Homeland Societies could scarcely have done more to discredit the memory of the lost German East. A generation turned away from these aging "eternal-yesteryear" expellees in disgust.

## Conclusion: Toward a Post-Cold War Synthesis

What would a synthesis of the two narratives look like? How might one seek to construct a more balanced interpretation of the loss of the German East? In the abstract, one can imagine a history emphasizing both German responsibility (the invasions of 1939 and 1941; the pursuit of race warfare) and Soviet decisions (seizing eastern Poland; instigating the ethnic cleansing of Germans). It will never be possible to add and subtract these crimes with cool, arithmetic precision; there is no genuine symmetry among these various examples of inhumanity. At any rate, the very concept of "master narratives" is suspect to the present generation.[58] But whether one describes it as a narrative or merely a discourse, the passing of the Cold War presents opportunities for a new conversation about the German East.

Such a conversation could never really take root in the 1980s. Lingering remnants of the "victim narrative" yielded intense reactions from West German intellectuals and the press.[59] When Chancellor Helmut Kohl ventured to speak at an expellee conference in 1985, the conference theme—"Silesia Remains Ours"—provoked indignation throughout the spectrum of published opinion. What might today be registered as a statement of cultural identity appeared at the time an expression of revisionism—one that in some ways became more menacing when, under the force of public pressure, the expellees modified the slogan to read "Silesia Remains Our Future."[60] On balance, fears of a *Wende* or cultural "turn" toward conservative, even nationalist agendas proved exaggerated. The "reluctant realists" in the CDU leadership had long since adjusted to the loss of territory beyond Oder and Neisse.[61] Mainstream politicians and journalists in the 1980s no longer cast doubt on Germany's historical responsibility for the destruction of war and the division of the continent. Anniversaries and official commemorations for the victims of Nazism offered a constant reminder of the crimes of the past. A post-national Federal Republic was emerging, one that derived its identity from European integration and a distinct de-emphasis on German culture as such.[62]

Consciousness of guilt did not, of itself, offer a consistent rationale for a "normalization" of relations between Germany and its eastern neighbors. For one thing, German attention in the 1970s and 1980s tended to focus specifically on the Holocaust while devoting rather less consideration to the Third Reich's barbarous treatment of Poles, Russians, and other Slavic peoples.[63] At any rate, heightened awareness of German crimes in the East could be taken as an argument *against* West German engagement beyond Oder and Neisse, lest this merely replicate the earlier colonial *Drang nach Osten*. A new form of travel literature emerged stressing the complete transformation of the former German landscapes in the East; this, too, tended to make these regions appear remote and disconnected from the everyday reality of Western Europe.[64] Nor did the growth in trade with the East signal deeper involvement in that region. Although eager recipients of German exports (and credits), Poland and even the Soviet Union remained marginal to the Federal Republic's economy except as conduits for energy and raw materials. At a time of forward momentum in Franco-German relations and West European unity more generally, West German horizons scarcely extended past the Elbe, let alone the Polish border. Tellingly, the German left, which had once followed Yugoslav, Polish, and later Czech revisionism with such hope, took little heed of the dissident movements of the late 1970s and 1980s.[65]

The one-sidedness of the German "guilt narrative" also proved an obstacle. For their part, the Warsaw Pact states were congenitally incapable of acknowledging historical misdeeds. Until the late 1980s, the Molotov-Ribbentrop Pact, the Soviet murders at Katyn, and the expulsion of Poles from the great eastern cities of Vilna and Lvov remained off-limits as topics of conversation. It was little wonder that a joint Polish-West German textbook committee advanced a tepid catalog of recommendations in 1976, paying scant attention to the circumstances of the expulsions from the German East.[66] In the 1980s, some West Germans tried to adapt to the contortions of Poland's martial-law press—suggesting, for example, that Germans themselves were to blame for the deaths of more than a million expellees during the chaos at the close of World War II.[67] But in the end, there was little hope of a genuine reconciliation between a free West Germany and the dictatorships to the east. Governments in the Soviet bloc found it more convenient to keep blasting the "revanchism" of Kohl's Germany in a feeble attempt to mobilize popular support for the stepped-up Cold War.[68]

Just as the advent of détente in the 1960s helped to force the pace of discussion within West Germany and render the "victim narrative" untenable, so the collapse of the Soviet empire in the late 1980s rocked the post-national complacency of West German elites. Quite suddenly, the history of the German East became topical again—precisely because remnants of that history were arriving in the Federal Republic en masse. Pockets of ethnically ambiguous Upper Silesians now claimed German citizenship and emigrated from Poland by the hundreds of thousands—with 250,000 arriving in 1989 alone.[69] Ethnic Germans in Romania rushed to dissolve their historic communities in Transylvania and seek their fortune in West Germany. On the horizon was an indeterminate reservoir of "Russian Germans." Kohl's government gladly welcomed "resettlers" from the East, arguing that these robust workers would fuel the Federal Republic's growth just as the expellees had done in the 1950s.[70] The parliamentary opposition—Social Democrats and Greens—proved unable to formulate any coherent objections. In part they were disarmed by the humanitarian vocabulary that cloaked this wave of immigration: who could rightly object to "bringing families together" [*Familienzusammenführung*]?[71] Having sought for decades to deny the continuing persistence of German culture in small East European enclaves, the left was hard pressed to endorse the most obvious solution—a concerted effort to support the cultural and economic life of those tiny islands of Germandom.[72] The post-national

Federal Republic was poorly equipped to navigate the re-nationalized politics of the 1990s. As a result, the newly unified Germany experienced an influx of more than two million ethnic Germans with minimal language skills and little preparation for the German job market.

Aside from liberating these streams of migrants, the fall of communism in Eastern Europe has provided a more solid basis for addressing the clashing versions of history surrounding the lost German East. Without returning to the thoroughly discredited "victim narrative" of the 1950s, scholars are able to address some of the weaknesses of the "guilt narrative" as articulated from the 1960s onward. Historians from the former Warsaw Pact are free to acknowledge the arbitrariness of the postwar territorial settlements; German historians recognize that the forced resettlement of Slavs into the "areas of expulsion" in the late 1940s occasioned considerable hardships for the families in question.[73] Across the board, moral criteria have less relevance now: in a Europe of consensual boundaries, there is no need to assign blame for the present state of territorial distribution. The "spatial" paradigm is particularly useful in focusing attention on the concrete, physical reality of the former German cities in the East—built environments fashioned both by ethnic Germans and the populations that have replaced them. Not coincidentally, the foremost practitioner of this methodology is Karl Schlögel at the German-Polish Viadriana University in Frankfurt an der Oder.[74]

On a practical level, too, the opening of borders has defused a great many tensions. Surviving German expellees now routinely visit their places of birth, albeit without the right to reclaim or repurchase former property: they can look, but not touch. In the early 1990s, the Polish government even responded calmly to the creation of "German friendship circles" in Upper Silesia and the election of ethnic German representatives to the Sejm.[75] Controversies still flare, of course; proposals for a "center against expulsions" in Berlin have raised hackles in Warsaw. The Homeland Societies remain suspect to Polish populists.[76] On balance, though, the following prediction has proved remarkably accurate: "we are certain that a free Poland and a freely unified Germany will find their way to one another on the basis of European cooperation."[77] The League of Expellees, when drafting this proclamation in 1965, adamantly opposed the prospect of abandoning territorial claims in the course of seeking German unification. But now that unification has come, that no longer matters, even to most expellees. Refreshingly, the problematic term "German East" has given way to a more accurate rendering: "German history in Europe's East."[78]

## Notes

Thanks to Pertti Ahonen and Gregor Thum for helpful comments on a draft version; and to Ingrid Fry and Charles Grair for organizing the colloquium at Texas Tech University where I first had an opportunity to present these observations.

1.    On the origins of the geographic concept "German cultural space," see Guntram Henrik

Herb, *Under the Map of Germany: Nationalism and Propaganda 1918–1945* (New York: Routledge, 1997), 55–60. Surprisingly, there is still no satisfactory book-length overview of the course of the expulsions. For recent article-length case studies, see Philipp Ther and Ana Siljak, eds., *Redrawing Nations: Ethnic Cleansing in East-Central Europe, 1944–1948* (Lanham, Md.: Rowman & Littlefield, 2001); also Steven Béla Várdy and T. Hunt Tooley, eds., *Ethnic Cleansing in Twentieth-Century Europe* (Boulder: East European Monographs, 2003).

2. Götz Aly, *"Endlösung": Völkerverschiebung und der Mord an den europäischen Juden* (Frankfurt: S. Fischer, 1995); Doris Bergen, "The Volksdeutsche of Eastern Europe and the Collapsing Nazi Empire, 1944–45," in Alan Steinweis and Daniel E. Rogers, eds., *The Impact of Nazism: New Perspectives on the Third Reich and Its Legacy* (Lincoln: University of Nebraska Press, 2003), 101–28.

3. I am referring to the second, expanded edition of Dönhoff's essay collection, published in Munich by dtv in 1988.

4. These narratives should not be confused with public opinion or the views of "ordinary Germans." I am referring here to standard interpretations implicit in the writings of German publicists, novelists, and political activists. How individuals used these narratives in making sense of their own individual experiences is another subject altogether, one that would require other methodologies.

5. Robert Moeller, *War Stories: The Search for a Usable Past in the Federal Republic of Germany* (Berkeley: University of California Press, 2001), 51–87; Mathias Beer, "Im Spannungsfeld von Politik und Zeitgeschichte. Das Großforschungsprojekt 'Dokumentation der Vertreibung der Deutschen aus Ost-Mitteleuropa,'" *Vierteljahrshefte für Zeitgeschichte* [*VfZ*] 46, 3 (1998): 345–89.

6. On the general topic of "equalization of burdens," see Michael L. Hughes, *Shouldering the Burdens of Defeat: West Germany and the Reconstruction of Social Justice* (Chapel Hill: University of North Carolina Press, 1999).

7. This right was proclaimed with great fanfare in the "Charter of the German Expellees," dated Aug. 5, 1950. For the next forty years, this document would be cited ad nauseam by expellee leaders. *Dokumente zur Deutschlandpolitik* [*DzD*] II/3 (Munich: Oldenbourg, 1997), 272–73.

8. This dynamic is explained in Pertti Ahonen, *After the Expulsion: West Germany and Eastern Europe, 1945–1990* (Oxford: Oxford University Press, 2004), 42–48.

9. William Glenn Gray, *Germany's Cold War: The Global Campaign to Isolate East Germany, 1949–1969* (Chapel Hill: University of North Carolina Press, 2003), 10–13.

10. Adenauer in Berlin, Oct. 6, 1951, quoted in Axel Frohn, "Adenauer und die deutschen Ostgebiete in den fünfziger Jahren," *VfZ* 44, 4 (1996): 485–525; here 503.

11. Gray, *Germany's Cold War*, 37–39.

12. See Adenauer's remarks to the cabinet on June 25, 1956, in *Die Kabinettsprotokolle der Bundesregierung*, vol. 9 (Munich: Oldenbourg, 1998), 449.

13. Hans Günter Hockerts, in a very useful survey of "Wiedergutmachung," observes that in the 1970s Poland and Yugoslavia demanded credits from Bonn as a kind of "indirect restitution" for the ravages of the Second World War. Hockerts does not, however, mention the 1956 credit treaty with Belgrade in this context, suggesting that its implications for the history of West German reconciliation with Eastern Europe have not yet been recognized. "Wiedergutmachung in Deutschland. Eine historische Bilanz 1945–2000," *VfZ* 49, 2 (2001): 167–214; here 196–97. On the terms of the relatively modest credit (240 million marks), see the cabinet meeting of March 5, 1956: *Kabinettsprotokolle*, vol. 9, 230.

14. For insight on expellee concerns, see the densely detailed tactics discussed in the CDU's Arbeitskreis V, July 3, 1956: Archiv für christlich-demokratische Politik [ACDP], VIII-006-1/1.

15. Note the exasperation expressed openly by Kurt-Georg Kiesinger, then chair of the foreign affairs committee, in the meeting of the Auswärtiger Ausschuß on June 6, 1956, p. 91: Parlamentarisches Archiv des Deutschen Bundestages, Ausw. Aussch., 2. WP, 59. Sitzung. The expellees did eventually get what they wanted: a lengthy report by Wilhelm Grewe of the Auswärtiges Amt on the situation in Yugoslavia.

16. For reports following visits to Yugoslavia, see Herbert Wehner in the SPD-Parteivorstand, June 1, 1956: Archiv der sozialen Demokratie, Bestand SPD-PV; also Fritz Erler in the SPD-Fraktion, April 10, 1959: *Die SPD-Fraktion im Deutschen Bundestag: Sitzungsprotokolle 1957–1961* (Düsseldorf: Droste, 1993), 267–68.

17. Dietrich Orlow, *Common Destiny: A Comparative History of the Dutch, French, and German Social Democratic Parties, 1945–1969* (New York: Berghahn, 2000), 220–21.

18. Petra Weber, *Carlo Schmid 1896–1979. Eine Biographie* (Munich: Beck, 1996), 598–603.

19. This is implicit in two SPD platforms in the second half of the 1950s: chairman Erich Ollenhauer advocated the establishment of diplomatic relations with Warsaw, but refused to consider abandoning Bonn's claim to the borders of 1937.

20. See "Neugestaltung der deutschen Ostpolitik," a draft memo by Karl-Georg Pfleiderer, ambassador to Belgrade, Oct. 8, 1957: Stiftung Bundeskanzler-Adenauer-Haus, Bd. A40. Herbert Blankenhorn, once Adenauer's closest political associate, strongly supported Pfleiderer's agenda, as did Bundestag President Eugen Gerstenmaier.

21. Kessel to Brentano, Jan. 23, 1957, pp. 2–3: Bundesarchiv Koblenz [BAK], NL Brentano, Bd. 165, Bl. 166ff.

22. DG Washington (Kessel), Sept. 19, 1957: Politisches Archiv des Auswärtiges Amts [PA/AA], NL Kessel, Bd. 8.

23. Kennan, "Impressions of Poland, July 1958," *Foreign Relations of the United States* [FRUS] 1958–60, X/2, 129–33; here 131–32.

24. Dieter Bingen and Janusz Josef Wec, *Die Deutschlandpolitik Polens 1945–1991: Von der Status-quo-Orientierung bis zum Paragmawechsel* (Krakow: Jagellonian University, 1993), 62–65.

25 To understand why, one has to think like a German legal scholar. See Dieter Blumenwitz, *What Is Germany? Exploring Germany's Status after World War II* (Bonn: Kulturstiftung der deutschen Vertriebenen, 1989), 28–42.

26. Ahonen notes that the expellees agreed amongst themselves early on not to engage in special pleading for specific territories; the "borders of 1937" represented a suitably vague formula. *After the Expulsion*, 40–42. As late as 1964, expellees within the CDU/CSU argued that they needed pledges from the Erhard government to "fight for every square foot of German territory." Carstens, Aufz., "Gespräch mit dem Arbeitskreis Oder-Neiße am 13. November 1964": PA/AA, B 2, Bd. 142.

27. Tellingly, the staff of the Polish military mission in Berlin all but stopped their low-level contacts with Westerners after the ultimatum of Nov. 10, 1958. See US Berlin (Anderson) Air Pouch 103, Aug. 6, 1959: National Archives and Record Administration [NARA], RG 59, CDF, 648.62A/8-659. For an example of the fairly direct conversations held in Berlin before this time, see Baron Guttenberg and Berthold Martin to Kurt-Georg Kiesinger, Oct. 8, 1958: PA/AA, B 1, Bd. 128.

28. Nixon/Gomulka conversation, Aug. 3, 1959: *FRUS* 1958–60, X/2: 200–1.

29. Eisenhower/Macmillan conversation at Camp David (as recorded by an American participant, Foy Kohler), March 28, 1960: *FRUS* 1958–60, IX: 258–59.

30. Ibid.

31. Comments by Dick Finn, Deputy Director at State's Office of German Affairs, cited in UK Washington (Whitehead), Jan. 15, 1965: Public Record Office, FO 371, 183052. See also Rusk's message to Ambassador McGhee, conveyed in DepSta to US Bonn 1978, Jan. 14, 1965: *FRUS* 1964–68, XV: doc. 84.

32. McGhee to Rusk, Aug. 25, 1966: *FRUS* 1964–68, XV: doc. 163. Interestingly, even at this late date McGhee spoke of "minor modifications" to the current Oder-Neisse boundary—presumably a suggestion designed to save face for whichever German government signed on to this agreement.

33. Heinrich Potthoff, *Im Schatten der Mauer: Deutschlandpolitik 1961 bis 1990* (Berlin: Propyläen, 1999), 20–40; Peter Bender, *Die "Neue Ostpolitik" und ihre Folgen: Vom Mauerbau bis zur Vereinigung*, 3rd ed. (Munich: dtv, 1995), 126–32.

34. For a perceptive study of Bahr's foreign policy conceptions, see Andreas Vogtmeier, *Egon Bahr und die deutsche Frage* (Bonn: Dietz, 1996).

35. C. F. von Weizsäcker writing in *Die Zeit*, Jan. 21, 1966; reprinted in *DzD* IV/12 (Frankfurt: Metzner, 1981), 122–27; here esp. 126.

36. Augstein to Eugen Gerstenmaier, Sept. 11, 1964: ACDP, NL Gerstenmaier, I-210-017/1. This letter forms part of an interesting exchange between Gerstenmaier and Augstein on questions of *Zeitgeschichte* and German guilt.

37. "Deutsche Ostpolitik, als wären wir im Jahre 1937," *Handelsblatt*, March 7, 1966; reprinted in *DzD* IV/12, 300–1. See also Mann's letter to Karl Carstens, May 13, 1966: BAK, NL Carstens, Bd. 556.

38. M. Walden, "Bleibt uns nur noch eine 'zweite Kapitulation'?", *Die Welt*, Nov. 20, 1967; reprinted in *DzD* V/1 (Frankfurt: Metzner, 1984), 2038–39.

39. "Die Lage der Vertriebenen und das Verhältnis des deutschen Volks zu seinen östlichen Nachbarn," Oct. 1965, published in Reinhard Henkys, ed., *Deutschland und die östlichen Nachbarn: Beiträge zu einer evangelischen Denkschrift* (Stuttgart: Kreuz-Verlag, 1966), 176–217; here p. 178.

40. This was precisely the objection offered by State Secretary Karl Carstens of the foreign ministry (a later president of West Germany); see his letter to Bishop Kunst, Oct. 27, 1965: BAK, NL Carstens, Bd. 554.

41. "Es ist von deutscher Seite politischer Selbstmord, eine Kollektivschuld aller Deutschen anzuerkennen und zu verkünden," wrote the League of Expellees in a statement published Oct. 22, 1965. For a tendentious but detailed account of the debate in the winter of 1965/66, see Henkys, *Deutschland und die östlichen Nachbarn*, 33–91; quote from 37. On the origins of German polemicizing against collective guilt, see Jan Friedrich and Jörg Später, "Britische und deutsche Kollektivschuld-Debatte," in Ulrich Herbert, ed., *Wandlungsprozesse in Westdeutschland: Belastung, Integration, Liberalisierung 1945–1980* (Göttingen: Wallstein Verlag, 2002), 53–90.

42. Ahonen, *After the Expulsion*, 222–27.

43. Grass to Hans-Joachim Merkatz, head of the Ostdeutscher Kulturrat, June 25, 1970: Willy-Brandt-Archiv [WBA], Bundeskanzler, Bd. 6, Bl. 135–37.

44. Grass to Brandt, Feb. 12, 1970: WBA, Bundeskanzler, Bd. 6, Bl. 95–9. For Brandt's own notes on a fascinating conversation on Sept. 30, 1970 with Grass, Böll, and others on concepts like "Heimat," "Vaterland," "Nation," and "Staat," see WBA, Bundeskanzler, Bd. 166.

45. The ever-perceptive Timothy Garton Ash suggests that these terms were used interchangeably; see *In Europe's Name: Germany and the Divided Continent* (New York: Random House, 1993), 299–30. That may have been the case in the 1980s, but my own reading of the relevant documents suggests that the term *"Verständigung"* predominated in the 1950s, while *"Versöhnung"* played a greater role in the 1960s.

46. Printed in Boris Meissner, ed., *Die deutsche Ostpolitik 1961–1970: Kontinuität und Wandel* (Köln: Verlag Wissenschaft und Politik, 1970), 120–24; quote from 121.

47. Deutscher Bundestag, 5. Wahlperiode, 80. Sitzung (Dec. 13, 1966): *Verhandlungen des Deutschen Bundestages, Stenographische Berichte*, 3662C.

48. Douglas Selvage, "The Treaty of Warsaw: The Warsaw Pact Context," in David Geyer and Bernd Schaefer, eds., *American Détente and German Ostpolitik, 1969–1972* (Washington, DC: German Historical Institute, 2004), 67–79; here 69–70.

49. Admittedly, the precise content of these demands varied slightly through the course of the late 1960s. At times another prerequisite, the recognition of West Berlin as an independent political unit, was raised by Soviet bloc leaders.

50. Duckwitz, Aufzeichnung, March 6, 1968: *Akten zur Auswärtigen Politik der Bundesrepublik Deutschland* 1968 (Munich: Oldenbourg, 1999), 328–29.

51. Ahonen, *After the Expulsion*, 234–42.

52. Rubin, "Warum überhaupt Wiedervereinigung?", *liberal*, Aug. 1967, reprinted in *DzD* V/1, 1489–96; here esp. 1491–92.

53. Scheel to the FDP-Parteitag in Freiburg im Breisgau, Jan. 31, 1968, excerpted in Meissner, ed., *Ostpolitik*, 241–42.

54. Karl-Hans Kern, "Nicht nur durch leidvolle Geschichte verbunden. Versöhnung zwischen Deutschen und Polen eine geschichtliche Aufgabe," *SPD-Pressedienst*, July 13, 1970, pp. 3–4.

55. For analyses of the treaty negotiations in Moscow, see Vogtmeier, *Bahr*, 121–40, and Werner Link, "Die Entstehung des Moskauer Vertrages im Lichte neuer Archivalien," *VfZ* 49, 2 (2001): 295–315.

56. Cited in Hans Edgar Jahn, *Die deutsche Frage von 1945 bis heute: Der Weg der Parteien und Regierungen* (Mainz: Hase und Koehler, 1985), 458.

57. After years of thundering against the treaties, Barzel famously refused to risk their rejection by the Bundestag during the decisive vote in May 1972; he even recommended that the CDU/CSU vote in favor, though instead the party opted to abstain (with the exception of a few "no" votes). The most vivid account of this frantic period remains Arnulf Baring, *Machtwechsel: Die Ära Brandt-Scheel* (Berlin: Ullstein, 1998), 514–17, 527–35.

58. Konrad Jarausch and Michael Geyer, *Shattered Past: Reconstructing German Identity* (Princeton: Princeton University Press, 2003).

59. Robert Moeller offers some evidence of a persistent "victim" identity into the 1980s: a TV miniseries called *Flucht und Vertreibung* reminded Germans in 1981 of the horrors of the expulsion; and the *Historikerstreit* of 1986–87 involved an effort to draw moral equivalency between the Holocaust and German suffering. *War Stories*, 182–83, 188–94. However, neither served to keep alive a sense of immediate attachment to lost homelands.

60. "Kapitulation," *Die Zeit*, Jan. 25, 1985, p. 1.

61. Clay Clemens, *Reluctant Realists: The Christian Democrats and West German Ostpolitik* (Durham: Duke University Press, 1989). After outlining the CDU/CSU's painful adjustment to the Eastern Treaties, Clemens does nevertheless suggest that Kohl very nearly lost control of "sentiment he himself had promoted and tolerated" (305)—due to the chancellor's reluctance to alienate fundamentalists in the party.

62. Obviously this is a subjective determination, but the "post-national" mood of the 1980s has been widely diagnosed. See Jan-Werner Müller, *Another Country: German Intellectuals, Unification and National Identity* (New Haven: Yale University Press, 2000). Stefan Berger appears to disagree, however; see *The Search for Normality: National Identity and Historical Consciousness in Germany since 1800* (New York: Berghahn, 2003), which savagely indicts efforts to "re-nationalize" German historiography in the 1990s.

63. As late as 1994, when asked to commemorate the Warsaw Uprising of 1944, Federal President Roman Herzog managed to confuse this with the Warsaw Ghetto Uprising of 1943. As Krzysztof Ruchniewicz points out, Poles could not help but be insulted by German ignorance about the razing of Warsaw in 1944. "Die historische Erinnerung in Polen," *Aus Politik und Zeitgeschichte* 5–6/2005, 23.

64. See, for example, Christian Graf von Krockow, *Die Reise nach Pommern: Bericht aus einen verschwiegenen Land* (Stuttgart: DVA, 1984).

65. Garton Ash, *In Europe's Name*, 279–98.

66. This, in turn, provoked considerable discussion in West Germany. See Wolfgang Jacobmeyer, ed., *Die deutsch-polnischen Schulbuchempfehlungen in der öffentlichen Diskussion der Bundesrepublik Deutschland* (Braunschweig, Georg-Eckert-Institut für internationale Schulbuchforschung, 1979). For a more positive evaluation of the commission's activities, see Michael G. Müller, "The Joint Polish-German Commission for the Revision of School Textbooks and Polish Views of German History," *German History* 22, 3 (2004): 433–47.

67. Horst Sielaff, "Wie Deutsche die Deutschen vertrieben. Die Nazi-Führung trägt die Verantwortung für die Opfer," *SPD-Pressedienst*, May 21, 1985, pp. 3–5. Here Sielaff repeats polemical assertions from *Trybuna Ludu*. There is some logic to these assertions—Nazi leaders did, after all, discourage evacuation until the last moment—but in the end it is surely the advance of the Red Army that is most directly responsible for the tragedies surrounding "Flucht und Vertreibung."

68. Garton Ash makes a persuasive case about the impossibility of reconciliation before the collapse of communism; see *In Europe's Name*, 310–11. See also Andreas Timmerman-Levanas, *Die politischen Beziehungen zwischen der Bundesrepublik Deutschland und der Republik Polen von 1970 bis 1991* (Saarbrücken: Verlag Rita Dadder, 1992), 98–100, 119–21.

69. For a useful breakdown by country of origin from 1950–2003, see Bundesverwaltungsamt Köln, "Jahresstatistik Aussiedler 2003," p. 4; available at http://www.bva.bund.de/aufgaben/aussiedleraufnahme/statistik/jahr/index.html.

70. See Kohl's remarks to the Bundestag, Sept. 5, 1989: *Sten. Ber.*, 11. WP, 11746B–C.

71. This was particularly true because in 1975 it had been a Social Democratic chancellor, Helmut Schmidt, who defined Poland's permissive attitude toward the emigration of ethnic Germans as a yardstick for measuring that country's cooperative behavior. Bogdan Koszel, "Die Außenpolitik der Volksrepublik Polen gegenüber der Bundesrepublik Deutschland 1949–1989," in Jan-Pieter Barbian and Marek Zybura, eds., *Erlebte Nachbarschaft: Aspekte der deutsch-polnischen Beziehungen im 20. Jahrhundert* (Wiesbaden: Harrassowitz, 1999), 57–75; here 66–68.

72. Instead, the SPD's first reaction was to criticize the preferential treatment of ethnic German resettlers over refugees from Africa; see the Bundestag debate of Dec. 2, 1988: *Sten. Ber.*, 11. WP, 8290–95. The Kohl government consistently claimed that its primary goal was to create more amenable circumstances in the countries of origin so that ethnic Germans wouldn't need to migrate. The sums involved were hardly serious, though: DM 55 million in aid to Kazakhstan did nothing to dissuade two-thirds of the (million-strong) ethnic German community from leaving by 1997. "To the fatherland," *The Economist*, June 28, 1997, 47–8.

73. See remarks by Jan Joszef Lipski cited in Ruchniewicz, "Die historische Erinnerung in Polen," 22. A useful overview of recent Polish scholarship appears in Klaus Zernack and Karin Friedrich, "Developments in Polish Scholarship on German History, 1945–2000," *German History* 22, 3 (2004): 309–22.

74. Karl Schlögel, *Im Raume lessen wir die Zeit. Ueber Zivilisationsgeschichte und Geopolitik*

(München: Carl Hanser, 2003). For an outstanding example of this methodology in practice, see Gregor Thum, *Die fremde Stadt: Breslau 1945* (Berlin: Siedler, 2003).

75. Thomas Urban, *Deutsche in Polen: Geschichte und Gegenwart einer Minderheit*, 3rd ed. (Munich: Beck, 1994), 102–31. Charles Ingrao observes that the Vojvodina Assembly in Serbia invited ethnic German families for an exchange in 2002.

76. Pawel Lutomski, "The Debate about a Center against Expulsions: An Unexpected Crisis in German-Polish Relations?" *German Studies Review* 27, 3 (October 2004); also the contributions by Dieter Bingen and Thomas Urban to *Aus Politik und Zeitgeschichte*, 5–6/2005.

77. Henkys, *Deutschland und die östlichen Nachbarn*, 37.

78. See the contribution by Klaus Zernack in this volume.

# The "Germans and the East"

## Back to Normality—But What Is Normal?

## ◆ Eva Hahn and Hans Henning Hahn ◆

> *"In my view, humanizing and balancing these desires is preferable to trying to abolish the one in favour of the other or to denying both in the name of some abstract cosmopolitan ideal."*[1]

In his book on Anglomania in Europe, Ian Buruma tells a story about his visit to Walhalla, the large temple on the banks of Danube near Regensburg; it was built in 1807 in the classical Greek style, and inside, along the walls, as the author put it "ranked like soldiers, are marble busts of great German personalities." To his surprise, he did not find Shakespeare among the many marble busts of gods in toga—"Gods of the German tongue," as he put it—exhibited there. But why should he expect to find Shakespeare there? This is his answer: "For, by the time Walhalla was built, Shakespeare had become a German playwright."[2]

Ian Buruma describes the period of Shakespearomania in Germany around 1800 and how it happened that Shakespeare's universal appeal was ascribed to the *Geist* of the German language. He reminds us that Schlegel's famous translation of Shakespeare has been hailed not just as a translation, but as a transmutation; with this linguistic metamorphosis, a new German creation was born out of Shakespeare's words that proved to some Germans the superiority of their language. They claimed that Shakespeare's genius had been rediscovered in German, that he really should have been German and, indeed, *was* German. In contrast to the English language, Buruma believes, the German language became the object of a nativist cult in the early nineteenth century.[3]

Ian Buruma's Walhalla story reminds us of one of the most troublesome problems in modern German history: attitudes towards the eastern part of the European

421

continent. While many Germans believed that their culture flourished wherever the German language was spoken, the concept of the "German East" similarly inspired the hearts and minds of many Germans very much like the Shakespearomania some decades earlier. Therefore, the idea of Christianization, medieval colonization, Enlightenment, or industrialization was viewed as a way in which the Germans supposedly brought the superior Western culture and civilization to the less "civilized and cultured" neighbors in the "East."

The German nativist cult of language has not been shared by all Europeans, and this is why when, say, Czechs visit Walhalla or read German history books, they are often surprised to find a great number of personalities there whom they usually consider Czech "Gods," in very much the same way as Shakespeare is generally viewed as being an English—and not a German—playwright. Some Czechs dislike the Germans' exhibiting Czech-born "Gods" in their history books as if they had been Germans, such as Emperor Charles IV, the great general Albrecht Waldstein (Wallenstein), the famous botanist Gregor Mendel, or the technician Josef Ressel. Many Czechs do not like Germans talking about the University of Prague as the "oldest German university" or the history of the Bohemian lands as a part of "German history."

Although Czechs no longer worry too much about the Walhalla, their dislike for German attitudes towards Czech history has been growing in the past few years. This has come as a surprise to many, who point to the widely spread acknowledgement in Germany in recent years, that the "German East" has been lost due to the two great wars of the twentieth century. Czech anxieties focus instead on the fact that German minds still do not seem to be troubled by how "German" the "German East" had become. Hans-Ulrich Wehler expressed this attitude in a *SPIEGEL* interview, stressing that no one lays claim to the former eastern territories any longer: "These territories which had been inhabited by Germans for centuries are lost to us."[4] Like many others, not even the historian Wehler raised the question why territories such as the so-called Sudetenland should have been considered as "ours" in the first place; his somewhat threatening worries that, in the view of the EU-Enlargement, the Germans might ask themselves why they should be accepting the "children of the perpetrators" in the EU did little to contribute to the dissipation of the Czech anxieties.

Such anxieties cannot be overlooked. Even some of the leading Czech historians have repeatedly voiced their worries with respect to what they consider "endangerment of the Czech historical consciousness," emerging from the "German" or "Sudeten German" interpretations of the Czech past;[5] Jaroslav Pánek, the director of the Historical Institute of the Academy of Science in Prague, or Jan Křen, the most prominent expert in the field of the history of the Czech-German relations, voiced repeatedly their criticism of "distorted historical reflection" and "mistakes and deformations" being spread around in the Czech media about interpretations of the Czech past, calling for "deeds" challenging "German attitudes of superiority and Czech complexes of inferiority."[6] As opposed to Anglo-German relations, the disputes about what is to be viewed in the history books as "Czech" and "German" are still far from over.

Yet there are also other examples of the ongoing disputes between the Germans and their eastern neighbors about the present forms of collective memory, like the recent German and Polish controversies about the planned new memorial in Berlin. According to large sections of the German political public, a "Center against Expulsions" (*Zentrum gegen Vertreibungen*) should be created next along the lines of the recently erected Holocaust-Memorial. Prominent German politicians like Erika Steinbach and Peter Glotz strongly support the idea of a memorial of the postwar expulsions of the Germans and argue that the future *Zentrum gegen Vertreibungen* should be created and run by the *Vertriebenenverbände* whom they consider to be the representatives of the victims;[7] in Poland, this project has been viewed as highly controversial because of its clear implication that, while Poland has hitherto been considered a victim of Nazi Germany, the Germans might now be viewed as victims of Polish "crimes." And indeed, similar criticism has been voiced in Germany, emphasizing the dangerous political consequences arising from new constructions of collective memory.[8] Only a few Polish intellectuals, like Adam Michnik and Andrzej Kaminski, joined the German politician Markus Meckel in advocating such an alternative project as an international memorial in Wrocław.[9]

Controversies over contested spaces in the historic memory of the "German relationship with its Eastern neighbors" are thus still raging with great vehemence, not only between German politicians, but also among German historians and their eastern colleagues, in spite of the intensive and friendly international cooperation, which has been taking place since the fall of the Iron Curtain. Obviously, the well-known long-term issues centering on historic identities still trouble people's minds along the eastern border of Germany. The German-speaking population was expelled from East Central Europe more than half a century ago, and, yet, not only does this topic—*die Vertreibung*—continue to be an object of political conflict, even moreso, it continues to function as a battlefield for disputes about historic and national identities.

This state of affairs does not, however, necessarily need to raise fears and anxieties. Rather, it can be viewed as a "normal" state of affairs within an international neighborhood. If we recall Anthony D. Smith's reminder that "the importance of symbolic and cultural issues in ethnic conflicts and national aspirations is one that requires as much attention as the material and political aspects,"[10] we could turn our attention to a detached study and discussion of the contemporary controversies without any unnecessary worries. They will then appear as "normal" controversies about contested spaces of memory and collective identities in very much the same way as Ian Buruma's book on Anglomania provides us with a fascinating variety of examples, in which the idea of England and Englishness has been constructed during the last two hundred years by all kinds of Europeans. Moreover, against this background, the ongoing disputes about national identities in Central Europe appear ever so familiar: There is not so much difference there, Buruma indicates, between Western and Central Europe after all.

Against this background, "Germany's relationship with its Eastern neighbors" looks far less "unique" and "special" than many Germans and their eastern neighbors still tend to think. Moreover, it is a relationship that is impossible to pin down, to describe once and for all in fixed, immutable terms, in order to grasp its essence, its spirit or character. Like any other "neighborhood," it offers a complex, fragmented and fluid texture for all kinds of historical narrative, and the worst service that historians can offer to the public would be to reduce its complex, fragmented and fluid history into politically correct slogans and, by so doing, to produce new obscuring smokescreens between the present and the past.

Yet the above mentioned controversies are often seen as troublesome on both sides of Germany's eastern border. Many Poles or Czechs are worried so much that even the old slogan about the German *Drang nach Osten* appears now and again, suggesting that the eastern neighbors of Germany might still be objects of ancient German expansive ambitions in the East of the European continent.[11] The central problem today of the "German relationship with its eastern neighbors" is certainly not open political conflict. There are no serious political issues between Germany and its Eastern neighbors now like those of the early twentieth century, even though serious observers continue to be troubled by the continuing political and financial support on behalf of the so-called Expellees-Organizations-Networks and their claims to recover the collective rights in their so-called homelands in Eastern Europe.[12] Yet because there are no political parties in Germany that openly back the demands of these organisations, the policies of the *Vertriebenenverbände* are generally not presently viewed as constituting an immediate political issue. Long-term cultural issues remain more troublesome, for it is not the everyday "normality" that people experience in the contemporary world along the eastern border that has caused conflicts thus far, but rather the images of what has or has not been "normal" in the long history of this relationship.

Nowadays, the unresolved conflicts are most obvious in the field of the Czech-German relations. Since 2000, the German demands—recently echoed by the right-wing Austrian government—that the Czech Republic should abolish the so-called *Beneš-Dekrete* have repeatedly figured prominently on the front pages of the Czech and German media. Even though this is a clear-cut political issue,[13] it has been contributing to the reawakening of ancient stereotypes along the common border. Particularly in Germany, the Czechs are increasingly seen as intransigently anti-German because of their unwillingness to fulfil the wishes of their western neighbors. A Hungarian historian summed up in one question what many Germans have been thinking recently: Are the Czechs unwilling to learn or are they incapable of understanding? The times of hostility between the Germans and their eastern neighbors have passed, he explained, so what is all this Czech-German arguing about? We cannot go on as if World War II has only just ended. Even the Communist regimes now belong to the past, so we need to get back to normality, he argued. A Czech historian sighed and remarked: It is easy for *you* to get along with the Germans since 1) you are not a Slav, so they do not despise you; 2) you do not share a common border with them, so they do not demand any *Heimat* in your country; and last but not least, 3) they beat *you* already in A.D. 955, but we Czechs dare never surrender since they would just swallow us . . . . He did not spell out his position in a seriously presented argument because he was responding emotionally rather than rationally, and because, as he reminded us, the contemporary discursive fashion does not allow for bringing up these kind of emotions: "Today, only stories about the peaceful past of the Germans in the East are 'in,'" he said. "You must not mention the longterm conflicting issues between the Germans and their eastern neighbors nowadays, if you want to look up-to-date."

Neither of the two historians has ever shown any signs of national chauvinism; both are old liberal erstwhile dissidents, fluent in several foreign languages, and also well-read in contemporary western historiography. However, they both use two different, currently popular ways of conceptualizing the German relationships with East Europeans in the past. The Hungarian is one of those historians who embraced wholeheartedly the presently most popular view of "Germany's relationship with its eastern neighbors," what he himself has called the "Back-to-Normality" model, whereas his Czech colleague belongs to those who are less happy with the present fashion.

As the dialogue shows, the visions of "Germany's relationship with its eastern neighbors" vary from "neighbor" to "neighbor," which is true not only with respect to various nations, but also within each country as well in various historical circumstances. The need to differentiate in this way does not have to be stressed among historians, but careful reflection about the legitimacy of a generalization certainly does belong to this profession. The following deliberations are not an attempt to introduce a generalizing view of the "German relationship with its eastern neighbors." Instead, attention should be drawn to the most interesting aspects of the contemporary discourse about the past between many "Germans [and Austrians] and their eastern neighbors." The above-mentioned dispute between a Hungarian and Czech historian is a suitable example to indicate the core of present controversies, underlying the fact that the issue dealt with here is an intellectual problem concerning discourses and must not been linked to any kind of allegedly primordial problem of what "Germany's relationship with its eastern neighbors" really might have been like.

Within the framework of the "Back-to-Normality" model, the "normality" of the German-Eastern neighborhood is said to have been much more peaceful and cooperative before the late nineteenth and century the first half of the twentieth and, therefore, it is widely believed that all we need in order to restore a harmonious relationship between the Germans and their eastern neighbors is to overcome the mental, political and cultural distortions of the last one hundred years or so. The protagonists of this idea tend to construe images of Central Europe along the lines of what Anthony D. Smith calls the "modernist orthodoxy" of nationalist theories, echoing the tradition of contempt for the "history-less peoples" between Germany and Russia, with their "small-scale, fissiparous, ethnolinguistic nationalisms."[14] These approaches towards the history of "Germany's Eastern neighbors," which have become fashionable far beyond Germany itself, focus on general aspects of nationalism and tend to underscore national chauvinism, stereotypes, and ethnic animosities as ingredients in a so-called exaggerated nationalism that suggests that Central and Eastern Europe have been more impacted by this ideology than other parts of the continent. Accordingly, the inspiration for overcoming these problems should be imported from the West, and Franco-German reconciliation is often held up as a preferred model for normalizing the "German relationship with its eastern neighbors."

Specifically, the narrative of the history of the "German relationship with its eastern neighbors" according to this "Back-to-Normality" model offers the following scenario in five acts:

1. During the process of Christianization, the Germans are said to have made the decisive move in the process of bringing the ancient Slavic pagans into the orbit of European culture and civilization

2. Thanks to medieval colonization, Germany's Eastern neighbors had the opportunity to catch up in terms of modernization

3. A multicultural East Central Europe then emerged as a kind of natural order, represented by the idea of multicultural empires ruled by nationally neutral dynasties

4. The destruction of this Central European *Arcadia* came about as a consequence of the generally popular forms of modern nationalism, that is, the emergence of ethnic nationalism at the political level in the nineteenth century, which took place in three steps through

   a) the establishment of the new order in Central Europe in the wake of World War I,

   b) the NS-Regime and in particular the Holocaust, and finally

   c) the postwar expulsion of the Germans from Central and Eastern Europe

5. The last chapter of this scenario could be called the period of "post-Communist internationalism," which was expected to bring about a general overcoming of "nationalism" in representations of the past and, accordingly, in national identities generally.[15]

The critics of this model tend to question above all two major components of this concept: the notions that the "German relationship with its eastern neighbors" is "normal" like any other relationship between nations, and that history can teach us what "normality" looks like.[16] They consider the history of the "German relationship with its eastern neighbors" as incomparable with the history of relationships among other East European nations themselves, and with the history of the "German relationship with its western neighbors." The "German relationship with its eastern neighbors" is looked upon as special, because its "normality" is supposed to have been governed by a long-term German preponderance over and arrogance towards their eastern neighbors. The critics surely tend to admit that national chauvinism, stereotypes and prejudices are a burden for the relationships among all other nations in general, but that none of that has caused as great a problem as the German versions of it. National chauvinism is bad, these critics usually say, but German national chauvinism toward their Eastern neighbors is worse than any other form of chauvinism in Europe (with the possible exception of anti-Semitism and Russian arrogance towards other nations). The "normality" of the "German relationship with its eastern neighbors" is, then, viewed as determined by its "abnormality."

This kind of criticism has not been very popular in recent years, and it is not difficult to understand why: The exponents of this notion of a *deutscher Sonderweg* for the "German relationship with its eastern neighbors" usually do not offer more than two kinds of recipe for a better future: They tend either to limit themselves to expressing the desire that German society should "at last overcome" the sins of its centuries-old past, or they readily accept a kind of cultural primordialism by maintaining that *Jak świat światem, Niemec nigdy nie był Polakowi bratem* (As long as the world exists, a German has never been a brother to a Pole.) As we know, however, the lack of rational arguments only exacerbates underlying emotions, so that the significance of so called "nationalistic" voices among Germany's eastern neighbors should not be downplayed even if they sound somewhat old fashioned and do not produce any impressive scholarly output.

Summing up, the mental anxieties accompanying the contemporary images of the history of the Germans' relationship towards their eastern neighbors concentrate on questions surrounding the slogan "let history teach us what is normal." In this concept, the history of the German relationship towards the eastern neighbors as experienced by the last few generations is viewed as exceptional, and those few still remaining among us who had lived through World War II are often looked upon as kind of "mentally incapacitated" by their experience. It is rather the younger generation that is looked upon as the hope of a better future, and expected to find the way "back to normality" by searching for inspiration in the more distant, allegedly better past. The protagonists of this scenario usually emphasize the so-called positive aspects of the more distant past by stressing the significance of communication and cooperation, and they tend to emphasise the testimonies about amicable relations between the Germans and their eastern neighbors, avoiding the discussion of conflicting issues. The discovery of a kind of "ancient internationalism" has been accompanied by the promotion of a "new internationalism" among historians, using references to European unification as a kind of re-creation of premodern or medieval Europe.

The critics of these hopes for "a better future" tend above all to hint at the fact that we can hardly learn useful lessons from the past because the history of the "German relationship with its eastern neighbors" has never been as peaceful as the protagonists of the "back-to-normality" model will have it. To start with, the critics would hint at the fact expressed by Norman Davies recently pointedly in a few words: already "Charlemagne ravaged the Slavs on at least four fronts. He reduced the Abodrites and Sorbs, to the east of the Elbe, in 789. He forced the Czechs of Bohemia to pay tribute in 805–6, and the Carinthian Slavs of the Sava and Drava likewise."[17]

Or, as Christian Lübke reminds us, "the beginning of a real, planned 'Eastern policy' [*Ostpolitik*] by Germany's rulers toward their Slavonic neighbors becomes evident during the reign of King Henry I, 'The Fowler' (919–936)" and, by that, the interaction of the German- and Slavic-speaking peoples during the high and late-medieval colonization period resulted in the Germanification and, in some sense, the Europeanization of lands that had been inhabited by Slavs for centuries before.[18] Therefore, the critics of the "Back-to-Normality" paradigm say that it has never been very peaceful to live along Germany's borders, and that it is hardly surprising to find ancient references to German arrogance (*die den Deutschen angeborene Arroganz*) and haughtiness toward the Slavs and their language (*hochnäsige Ablehnung der Slawen und ihrer Sprache*) at such an early date.[19]

Such words from the first chronicle of the Bohemian Lands, the Cosmas chronical of the early twelfth century, are well known in the Czech public, but hardly ever mentioned nowadays. Only the critics of the "Back-to-Normality" model tend to point to these aspects of what others might cite as examples of the Germans' useful contribution to the Christianization and civilization of their eastern neighbors. Our inattention to these aspects of the past amounts to the surviving of the impression that a kind of primordial German hegemonic attitude towards eastern neighbors would be unavoidable. Rudolf Jaworski surely deserves attention far beyond the field of German-Polish relations when he states "that it is fashionable today even in scholarly discourse to play down German-Polish points of conflict in the past and present, including attempts on all sides to achieve harmony by no means marks a turning point in the direction of greater objectivity."[20] If we are not to leave new "fashions" in interpreting the past of peoples and in constructing their collective identities to unarticulated emotions, then we should include the "old-fashioned" attitudes as a legitimate component of public discourse.

The other major criticism of the "Back-to-Normality" model concerns the currently popular mantra about "multicultural societies" that, if only people of various nationalities live together, get to know each other and cooperate with each other, they will also start tolerating and even *liking* each other. This concept does not sound convincing to those of us who have studied nationalism and ethnocentrism in the Habsburg Empire, Czechoslovakia or modern Yugoslavia as examples of how friendly neighborhoods, cultural communication or economic cooperation can inoculate people against the emergence of explosive ethnic and national conflicts. The critics argue that we are unduly ignoring the Moravian-born Viennese Sigmund Freud's observation as far back as 1917 that "the closer the relations between human groups, the more hostile they were likely to be toward each other."[21] Therefore, as the critics say, it is hardly surprising that the recent promotion of scholarly and personal communication and cooperation among German historians and their eastern neighbors has not brought the results that many historians expected in the early 1990s, and it would be naïve to expect such an easy solution to outstanding disputes over historic identity and legitimacy. They argue that neither personal contacts and academic cooperation, nor any political unification of Europe (or even globalization) will *necessarily* bring about a "peaceful normalization" in the "German relationship with its eastern neighbors." Indeed, Michael Ignatieff suggests in his book on the recent ethnic wars that the contrary might happen since "the less substantial the differences between two groups, the more they both struggle to portray those differences as absolute."[22]

And yet, we need not view with anxiety the present controversies about new forms of collective memory in Central Europe, about historic identities and legitimacy. In fact, they are hardly surprising. The devastation which has ravaged Central and Eastern Europe for most of the twentieth century has been unprecedented in modern times. Consequently, it is easy to get caught in the fallacy of finding indications of a putative not only economic, but also moral and cultural superiority of contemporary Western nations. It is easy then to forget that neither an agreeable landscape, nor a stable political system, nor an efficient economy should allow for generalizations in the field of ethical judgments or cultural history. There are surely differences between the western and the eastern parts of the European continent, but they will need careful reconsideration before historians will be able to liberate themselves from the centuries-old stereotypes about the alleged East-West dichotomy, and genuinely understand the implications of those stereotypes for the above-mentioned controversies over the "German relationship with its eastern neighbors."

Such a liberation seems urgent. For example, some historians still believe that it is sufficient to exchange the word "German" for "European" when speaking about the "German relationship with its eastern neighbors," and that the infamous attitudes of Germans as *Kulturträger* among their eastern neighbors will be overcome. What used to be seen as the medieval "German colonization" has therefore often in recent years been presented as a medieval "European colonization." But the change in terminology has only obscured the reality that the contested space of memory has not always been filled in by any new topics. The memory of a "medieval colonization" of new rural and urban settlements and a large-scale social and cultural transformation needs to be balanced by the memory of the hardships caused by and reactions to this conquest, without which we cannot acknowledge the equal importance of all the symbolic and cultural issues involved in current discourses.

Robert Bartlett's *The Making of Europe: Conquest, Colonisation and Cultural Change, 950–1350,*[23] offers a fine example of a different and carefully reconsidered approach to the topic. His study of the medieval process of cultural homogenization as social, political and cultural interaction does not neglect or even denounce the various forms of response to colonization: expressions of grief, polarization, conflicts between languages, cultures and, sometimes, religions. Bartlett does not portray the medieval Central and East European countries as areas in need of colonization as a process of delayed civilization, but rather as equal subjects in an interaction, in which "the mental habits and institution of European racism and colonialism were born in the medieval world."[24] Moreover, he reminds us that "The cultural identity and political fortunes of the inhabitants of the Celtic lands or Eastern Europe have been irrevocably shaped by that expansionary movement," and "the direct historical consequences of high medieval migration and ethnic mingling are with us to the present day." And this is, of course, also the reason for why it matters so much how we remember and why we need to pay utmost attention to the ongoing controversies about the ways in which we still remember even such a distant past like the age of medieval colonization.

Nowadays, no one seems to doubt that the relationship between the Germans and their eastern neighbors has always been in part an extremely close and enriching relationship. Yet, the history of this relationship also abounds in blood and unresolved cultural tensions. Conquest, colonization, struggles against political hegemony and cultural domination are constitutive elements in the history of the "German relationship with its eastern neighbors" as is economic cooperation and cultural diffusion, exchange and assimilation. Recent controversies are not about the question of whether "eternal struggle" or "peaceful cooperation" have dominated the history of "Germany's relationship with its eastern neighbors," but about the space in memory shared between them. They can be resolved neither by political means or governmental commissions, nor by disputes about political, economic or social facts. They can only reasonably be approached as a problem of cultural studies.

Culture is a contested category. The concept of culture as "the signifying system through which necessarily (though among other means) a social order is communicated, reproduced, experienced and explored,"[25] used by contemporary cultural studies, offers itself as an extremely useful concept also for the present controversies concerning our topic. Culture in this sense of the word does not allow us to use the idea of one-way cultural transfer any longer and should, therefore, prevent historians from filling in the contested space of memory by repetitive references to German (or

Western) contributions to the development of their eastern neighbors. Moreover, this concept of culture allows us to understand to what a large extent human beings not only create culture but also how culture creates them and significantly impacts their subjectivity.

Historians' repeated emphasis on the Christianization, medieval colonization and subsequent modernization that the Germans brought to the societies of Eastern Europe over the centuries seem plausible to many, because German expertise did indeed play a significant role in those societies. Yet we also need to understand to what a significant extent these stories cast the members of the receiving nations in the role of "passive recipients," as backward, culturally inferior pupils of their "better" others. Historians have often contributed to the perpetuation of an unequal relationship between the Germans and their eastern neighbors by representing the past and its unequal relationship in images that suggest a kind of permanence.

Because we still often witness the transference of past German dominance into the present in this way—despite the fact that the neighboring countries of Germany act in the diplomatic arena as equal partners of Germany—we do need to pay great attention to the problem if we are to avoid growing anxieties. The great differences in economic and political power between Germany and its neighbors along the eastern border need to be openly acknowledged, rather than quietly projected into the past, thereby exaggerating their emotional significance. The diplomatic arena is not an adequate platform to provide nations with self-confident identities and a sense of their own dignity. The images of the past have always carried much greater weight than diplomacy.

Any serious consideration of the history of the "Germany's relationship with its eastern neighbors" needs to take some inspiration from Edward Said's concept of Orientalism. If we substitute the words "Germany" and "Eastern Europe" for "the West" and "the Orient," we can find valuable ideas concerning our topic in Said's texts: Germany has had a long tradition of what we could term "East-Europeanism"—a way of coming to terms with the East of Europe that is based on the special place of that area in German experience. The East of Europe is not only adjacent to Germany; it is also the place of Germany's greatest and oldest colonies, its widespread diaspora, its cultural contestant, and one of its deepest and most recurring images of the Other. In addition, the East of Europe has helped to define Germany by providing its contrasting image, idea, personality, and experience. Yet none of this East is merely an intellectual construct. The East is an integral part of German material civilization and culture, so that the ongoing discourses about the German relationship with its eastern neighbors are carried out within the framework of real supporting institutions, vocabulary, scholarship, imagery, doctrines, etc.[26]

This paraphrase of Said's concept of Orientalism suggests that we need very profound studies of the cultural interdependencies between the Germans and their eastern neighbors if we want to understand the present controversies. The interaction between the Germans and their eastern neighbors has always been much closer and deeper than political, economic and social history have been able to encompass. We need to study the intertwined identities of the Germans and their eastern neighbors, and to induce the public to see the "German relationship with its eastern neighbors" in more subtle ways than just in the traditional answers to the question "What did the Germans bring to the civilization and modernization of their eastern neighbors?" The most urgent question to ask nowadays seems to turn the story upside down by asking "What did the eastern neighbors mean to the Germans through the centuries?"

The Czech president Václav Havel made himself popular in present-day Germany by recalling the significance of the Germans for the Czechs. The Germans are our destiny, he said in one of his speeches[27], but we still have not heard any kind of similar statement made by a German statesman. Nor have historians dedicated much space in the shared Central European memory to discussions about the role which Eastern European neighbors have played and continue to play in the long-term continuities of the German identity. Moreover, as Anthony Smith has reminded us repeatedly in the recent years, "It is . . . a great error to commence analysis of nations and nationalism from the nineteenth century or later."[28]

Very much as is the case with studying the history of Czech attitudes towards their German neighbors, we also have to turn our attention to the ancient chronicles if we want to study German attitudes towards their eastern neighbors. Already in the first detailed "German study" about the Eastern neighbors in Helmold von Bosau's *Chronik der Slawen* from the late twefth century, we can find numerous striking indications about the role that the expansion in the East played for the German identity: "Peace and security prevailed throughout the whole Empire, because the courageous Emperor Heinrich subdued the Hungarians, the Czechs, the Slavs and all neighboring lands with his forceful arm."[29] This sentence alone hints at the implication of these words for the identity of the author, as if the eastern neighbors of the Germans had controlled events in the *Reich*—and as if the suitable form of relationship was "subduing with an iron hand." Obviously, we need to get to know these long-term aspects of German identity better if we are to understand why they became a constituent element of the "German East" so popular in Germany during the nineteenth century and, indeed, why it had become a core element of the modern German national identity itself. Without understanding how important the "East" has been throughout the centuries, we cannot understand why the special academic discipline of *Ostforschung* enflamed the minds of German historians and politicians during early the twentieth century, and later led to the excessive obsession of the National Socialist regime with the "East." Can we discuss reasonably Hitler's expansion in the East or even Brandt's *Ostpolitik* without understanding the importance of symbolic and cultural issues in ethnic conflicts and national aspirations and their long-term implications for German identity?

However, it is not sufficient to conceptualize the interdependencies between the Germans and their eastern neighbors as just one facet of the general problem of national identity. "Germany's relationship with its eastern neighbors" demands a discussion of questions related to intertwined identities among *unequal* partners. The distinction between the so-called "historic" and "history-less" nations dominated the nineteenth-century debates on nationalism. It was generally assumed that the established powers—France, Britain, Prussia, Austria, and Russia—possessed a historic destiny to rule the "history-less" nations, for which reason the legitimacy of their claim to rule "Germany's eastern neighbors" has been widely accepted. This is a heritage that badly needs to be drawn into the focus of our discussions, the moreso because of the twentieth-century experience so brutally confirmed the worst ancient stereotypes about the Germans as oppressors.

Victor Kiernan reminds us that "there has been more than one parallel in Europe" to the English experience, meaning the "situation of a stronger people learning to be a 'nation' by dominating weaker, more 'backward' ones; the closest is the rise of Austria through subjugation of Slav territories on its mountains south and southeast, and then of the Slav kingdom of Bohemia. Nationalism in Europe owes to a background of this kind a great deal of its domineering temper; it helped to mould the modern militarist state, ambitious of triumphs as England sought in the Hundred Years' War, and in later times in imperialist expansion outside Europe."[30] Surely one could add to this litany Germany's relationship with its eastern neighbors. Power, influence and hegemonialism are categories that urgently need to be addressed in any future discussion of the "German relationship with its eastern neighbors." The often nostalgic visions of the past that inform the "Back-to-Normality" model obscure this most significant issue, which just may be the most serious problem involved in recent controversies. As Anthony D. Smith reminds us, humanizing and balancing national desires is preferable to trying to abolish the one in favor of the other or to denying both in the name of some abstract cosmopolitan ideal.[31]

Summing up, we might understand better why the search for "normality" in the German relationship towards Eastern Europe cannot be understood as an attempt at "overcoming" the tragedies of the twentieth century by looking for "normality" in the allegedly more peaceful, more distant past. That would once again amount to little more than subjugating history writing to political wishful thinking. The history of the relationship between Germans and their eastern neighbors has its rich and complex cultural traditions, the continuity of which has not been interrupted or even destroyed by wars, by the most terrible crimes or even by the mass expulsions of the Germans from Eastern Europe. Neither can the best intentions of historians interrupt this continuity, because—as Neal Ascherson puts it—to demonstrate that any tradition is wrong or invented does not put an end to the story.[32]

Historians should not try to influence reality by suggesting which parts of our past are "normal." By doing so, they might put their work once again at the service of politicians. "Normality" cannot be created or found in the past and copied. What is "normal" in the German relationship with its eastern neighbors cannot be decided by the subjective value judgments of politicians or historians; indeed, the present controversies between Germans and their eastern neighbors concerning the contested space of collective memory are as normal as any other human discourse. If we begin by seeing them in this way, we shall be able to recognize that the difference between the above-mentioned Hungarian historian and his Czech colleague is not in their liking or disliking of their German neighbors, but only in their focus on different aspects of the past.

Obviously, they both need a new framework for their discussion, one which would accommodate all arguments brought forward and would not disqualify any kind of collective memory as "abnormal," wrong, sick, or old-fashioned. We should not disqualify any voices as *Deutschenhass*, if they plead for remembering also those aspects of the past that have been forgotten in Germany, and vice versa. The Czechs are neither more nor less "anti-German" than other nations; it is only an ancient German stereotype that suggests that the Czechs cannot but hate the Germans.[33] If we understand that the contested space of memory is a central platform on which not only subjectivity bases its cultural expression and that culture also creates subjectivity, we can free ourselves from viewing the present controversies as ethnic, national or political conflicts, and begin to understand that acknowledging the legitimacy of all forms of collective memory is a necessary precondition for any relationship based on cultural equality. The contemporary discussions about the contested space of memory are an indication of the freedom and intellectual dynamic within all societies concerned. Plurality, controversies, and continuous change have always been characteristic of the relationship between Germans and their eastern neighbors, as for any other "living" relationship, and neither the complexity, nor the fluidity of this relationship make it special.

Nor does it differ fundamentally from the German relationship towards its western neighbors, as Ian Buruma has shown in his book on Anglomania. The numerous, fascinating stories of individual Germans and their often irrational relationship to England introduced in his book could well be matched by similarly amusing and often absurd stories about Germans and their relationship with their eastern neighbors and, of course, vice versa. Moreover, these similarities also indicate wide-ranging interdependencies, even where the most serious political consequences of such attitudes are concerned.

Ian Buruma has shown this in a very spectacular way in the case of "The Anglomane Who Hated England," his epithet for Emperor William II, whose relationship toward both the English as well as the Germany's eastern neighbors can hardly be studied in isolation from each other. In Buruma's view, when England and Germany, "largely through the Kaiser's own fault, did grow further and further apart and threatened to destroy not only each other but the whole of Europe, the Kaiser's reaction was rather like Hitler's would be some decades later: a form of ethnic pique." How was it possible, he wrote furiously in the margins of his ambassador's despatch in 1912, that in the "final struggle between the Slavs and the Teutons" the Anglo-Saxons will be on the side of the Slavs and the Gauls"?"[34]

It would be a grave mistake to assume that national identities have been more stable and relations between nations more amicable in Western Europe than in Central Europe. As Norman Davies's book on the history of the British "Isles" has recently shown, not even on the (British) Isles has there ever existed a clear-cut nation-state because the "nation is a body with a fluid membership," and because "all states and empires are ephemeral."[35] This is the conclusion of the author who not only acknowledges the previously neglected cultural equality of the Irish, Scottish or Welsh nations with the English, but has also admitted that "until I started writing, I myself did not realize just how many different states the Isles have supported over the centuries," which he tabulated at sixteen, and did his best to undermine any residual belief in the unbroken continuity of so-called English or British history.

Yet one important difference still seems to remain between the British Isles and Central Europe, and it concerns the discourse about the past or, more precisely, the attitudes towards unequal relationships. It was the reevaluation of just these attitudes in the past which enabled historians like Norman Davies to find a new understanding of British history, accommodating the memory of a much larger number of states, societies, groups and nations than had his predecessors. Dealing with unequal relationships is an old problem, represented in Central European history most clearly by the example of the German ways of dealing with the mixture of economic and political superiority, accompanied by the mental habit of the traditional contempt for the Slavs (and Germany's other eastern neighbors). As opposed to the British Isles, this issue of *inequality* has not yet received the sufficient space in the present discussions about the contested space of shared memory between the Germans and their eastern neighbors; the use and misuse of power and cultural influence, dominance, political hegemony and imperialism are not concepts presently employed in discussions about the history of the German relationship with its eastern neighbors.

As already indicated above, this is the most serious aspect of the present problems surrounding the relations between the Germans and their eastern neighbors, because any means of perpetuating inequality through historic images has direct consequences for political identity. Any kind of misuse of political and economic supremacy to support or delegitimize certain elements of collectively shared memory can only weaken democratic political identities. And, to recall Ian Buruma once again, one particular West European experience tells us that wherever political identities have been weakened, historical and cultural romance take over. Buruma was, in this case, pointing to the situation in eighteenth-century Scotland, where Macpherson's collection of Ossianic verse appeared and one of the first modern mythological traditions was born, namely, the tradition of drawing on history while encountering political misery.[36] Yet, as is well known, this tradition has also enjoyed great popularity among both the Germans and their eastern neighbors. And it is precisely for this is reason that we should pay particular attention to this issue.

Disputes about the past cannot be separated from politics, nor do historians construct their visions of the past in a political vacuum. Politics is very much about contested spaces of memory, and the best historians can do is not to follow the emotional calls made by politicians demanding their help in resolving conflicts between states in overcoming the past (*Vergangenheitsbewältigung*), but rather to continue with their job of critically reexamining the existing visions of the past and correcting the obvious errors. These visions are constitutive elements of the political visions of the future. Timothy Garton Ash was one of the first observers to stress the necessity of watching carefully the developments discussed here, pointing out already in the summer 1989 that

> one of the greatest questions of the moment is whether German hopes for a new Central Europe can be reconciled with those of their immediate neighbors to the east. Of course, there are many German visions of Central Europe, just as there are many Czech, Polish, and Hungarian ones. But there is also a hard reality of West German policy in this region: *Ostpolitik*. Now more than ever we need to look carefully at both, the visions and the reality.[37]

The notion that human conflicts can be resolved or even future conflicts prevented by popularizing harmonious visions of the past is too simple-minded; too well-known are the sad practical consequences of all visions suggesting that any conflicting issues can be definitively resolved once for all.

Walhalla, the large temple of the "marble Gods of the German tongue" on the banks of Danube near Regensburg attracts tourists without worrying anyone unduly. The voices of anxiety among Germany's eastern neighbors are not so much worried about Walhalla nowadays as they point to the living memory of the so-called German East. And they need to be heard and accepted as legitimate in order to get the chance to be articulated rationally. Only intellectual controversies can inspire a continuous critical reexamination of both our visions and the reality that they create for us. Therefore, we should fear the current controversies if too many historians subscribe too willingly to the presently fashionable, politically correct interpretations of the past that uncritically embrace the "Back-to-Normality" paradigm. Unfortunately, as we know, not even this attitude among historians would be abnormal in the history of "Germany's relationship with its eastern neighbors."

## Notes

1.  Anthony D. Smith, *The Nation in History: Historiographical Debates about Ethnicity and Nationalism* (Cambridge, 2000), 26.
2.  Ian Buruma, *Voltaire's Coconut or Anglomania in Europe* (London, 2000), 52.
3.  Ibid., 53.

4. Hans-Ulrich Wehler in "Die Debatte wirkt befreiend": Der Historiker Hans-Ulrich Wehler über die verspätete Aufarbeitung von Leid und Elend der Vertriebenen," *Der Spiegel* 13 (2002), 61–64.

5. Historikové proti znásilňování dějin. Stanovisko Sdružení historiků České republiky (ed. Jiří Kocian), Příloha ke *Zpravodaji Historického klubu* 12 (2001), No. 2 (Praha 2002).

6. Jaroslav Pánek, "Česká historická věda a české historické vědomí (Několik námětů do diskuse)," *Český časopis historický*, 97 (1999), 311–20; Jan Křen, "Česká a německá historická paměť—včerejšek a dnešek," *Český časopis historický*, 97 (1999), 321–51, here 351.

7. Zentrum gegen Vertreibungen. Stiftung der deutschen Heimatvertriebenen, DOD-Sonderdruck 16 June 2000, ed., *Deutscher Ostdienst, Informationsdienst des Bundes der Vertriebenen—Vereinigte Landsmannschaften und Landesverbände.* For the ongoing discussions compare "Deutsche Unfähigkeit zum besonnenen Diskurs über Geschichte. Kritische Anmerkungen zur Diskussion um das 'Zentrum gegen Vertreibungen,'" *Frankfurter Rundschau,* 4 July 2002; and "Flucht und Vertreibung in europäischer Perspektive," *Zeitschrift für Geschichtswissenschaft,* 51 (2003), 2: 1–104.

8. Samuel Salzborn, "Kollektive Unschuld. Deutsche als Opfer. Anmerkungen zu Funktion und Intention der neuen Debatte um Flucht und Vertreibung," *Freitag 18,* 26 April 2002.

9. Adam Krzeminski and Adam Michnik, "Wo Geschichte europäisch wird: Das 'Zentrum gegen Vertreibungen' gehört nach Breslau," *Die Zeit,* 20 June 2002.

10. Smith, *The Nation in History,* 76.

11. See, for example, the Polish magazine *Wprost,* 10 November 2002, which carried the slogan in German, *Drang nach Osten,* on its front page.

12. Samuel Salzborn, *Heimatrecht und Volkstumskampf: Außenpolitische Konzepte der Vertriebenenverbände und ihre praktische Umsetzung* (Hannover, 2001); Samuel Salzborn, *Grenzlose Heimat—Geschichte, Gegenwart und Zukunf der Vertriebenenverbände* (Berlin, 2000).

13. The conflict had been resolved by the EU in the fall of 2002, leaving Germany and Austria isolated, without however deterring them from pursuing relentlessly this agenda. For information on this issue see http://www.europarl.eu.int/studies/benesdecrees/pdf/opinions_cs.pdf.

14. Smith, *The Nation in History,* 32.

15. An excellent example of this interpretative scheme is presented by the series Deutsche Geschichte im Osten Europas, which was published in 10 volumes by the Siedler Verlag in Berlin 1992–1999; for the popular usage of the scheme, see *Studienhandbuch Östliches Europa,* 1: Harald Roth, ed., *Geschichte Ostmittel- und Südosteuropas* (Weimar-Vienna, 1999), particularly Joachim Bahlcke's general survey "Ostmitteleuropa," 59–72, which relies heavily on the influential book by Werner Conze, *Ostmitteleuropa. Von der Spätantike bis zum 18. Jahrhundert* (Munich, 1992). To see how this interpretative model constructs the presently popular vision of the so-called German history in the East, see the catalogue of the politically influential exhibition *Deutsche im Osten. Geschichte—Kultur—Erinnerungen. Deutsches Historisches Museum Berlin* (Berlin 1994).

16. For critical voices compare the Czech journal *Spory o dějiny* [Disputes about the Past] and a survey by Eva Hahn, "La place des Allemands dans la recherche de nouvelles représentation historiques aujourd'hui chez les Tschèques," in Marie-Elizabeth Ducrex and Antoine Marès, eds., *Enjeux de l'histoire en Europe Centrale* (Paris-Budapest-Turin, 2002), 161–98. For divergent and conflicting views of Polish and German historiography that were the subject of a profound discussion at a recent symposium organized by the German Historical Institute in Warsaw, see Claudia Kraft, "Landes- und Regionalgeschichteim

deutsch-polnischen Kontaktbereich—verbindend oder trennend?" in Deutsches Historisches Institut Warschau, *Bulletin*, 10 (2003), 68–72.

17. Norman Davies, *Europe: A History* (Oxford-New York, 1996), 307.

18. See Christian Lübke's contribution to this collection, 18.

19. Cosmas von Prag, in Alexander Heine, ed., *Chronik Böhmens,* 1 (Essen-Stuttgart, 1987), 122.

20. Rudolf Jaworski, "Deutsche Ostforschung und polnische Westforschung in ihren histo-
risch-politischen Bezügen," *Deutsche Ostforschung und polnische Westforschung im Spannungsfeld von Wissenschaft und Politik: Disziplinen im Vergleich* (Osnabrück-Poznań, 2002), 11–23, here 21.

21. Michael Ignatieff, *The Warriors's Honour: Ethnic War and the Modern Conscience* (London, 1998), 49.

22. Ibid., 51.

23. Robert Bartlett: *The Making of Europe: Conquest, Colonisation and Cultural Change* (London, 1993) 950–1350.

24. Ibid., here cited from the Penguin Books edition (1994), 313.

25. Glenn Jordan and Chris Weedon, *Cultural Politics: Class, Gernder, Race and the Postmodern World* (Oxford, 1995), 8.

26. Paraphrase of Edward W. Said, *Orientalism: Western Conceptions of the Orient* (Harmondsworth, 1991), 1–2.

27. "Our relationship to Germany and the Germans has been more than merely one of
the many themes of our diplomacy. It has been a part of our destiny, even a part of our
identity. Germany has been our inspiration as well as our pain; a source of understandable traumas, of many prejudices and misconceptions, as well as of standards to which
we turn; some regard Germany as our greatest hope, others as our greatest peril. It can
be said that the attitude they take toward Germany and the Germans has been a factor
through which the Czechs define themselves, both politically and philosophically, and
that it is through the type of that attitude that they determine not only their relationship
to their own history but also the type of their conception of themselves as a nation and a
state." "Czechs and Germans on the Way to a Good Neighbourship," Prague, February
17, 1995 (http://www.vaclavhavel.cz/index.php?sec=7&id=11&setln=2).

28. Smith, *The Nation in History*, 75.

29. Helmold, *Chronik der Slaven* (Alexander Heine, ed.) (Stuttgart, 1990), 86.

30. Victor Kiernan, "The British Isles: Celt and Saxon," in Mikuláš Teich and Roy Potter,
eds., *The National Question in Europe in Historical Context* (Cambridge, 1994), 1–34, here
1–2.

31. Smith, *The Nation in History*, 26.

32. Neal Ascherson, *Black Sea: The Birthplace of Civilisation and Barbarism*, 1st ed. (London, 1996), 274.

33. Walter Brand, *Die geistigen Grundlagen unserer Bewegung* (Carlsbad, 1935), 17–18; Rudolf
Lochner, *Sudetendeutschland: Ein Beitrag zur Grenzlanderziehung im ostmitteldeutschen
Raum* (Berlin-Leipzig, 1937), 28–35; Georg Stadtmüller, *Geschichte Südosteuropas* (Mu-
nich, 1950), 234.

34. Buruma, *Voltaire's Coconut*, 234–35.

35. Norman Davies, *The Isles: A History* (Basingstoke-Oxford 1999), 1039–40, 1053.

36. Buruma, *Voltaire's Coconut*, 81–82.

37. Timothy Garton Ash, *Mitteleuropa?*, in Stephen R. Graubard, ed. *Eastern Europe . . .
Central Europe . . . Europe* (Boulder-San Francisco-Oxford, 1991), 1–21, here 1.

# Contributors

**Günter Bischof** is the Marshall Plan Professor, the Chair of History Department, and the Director of the Center for Austrian Culture and Commerce at the University of New Orleans. He is the author of *Austria in the First Cold War, 1945-55: The Leverage of the Weak* (1999) and the co-editor of 15 volumes in the *Contemporary Austrian Studies* series and the co-editor of *Transatlantic Relations: Austria and Latin America in the 19th and 20th Centuries* (2006).

**James Bjork** is a Lecturer in Modern European History at King's College, London. His current research explores the relationship between national exceptionalism and the idea of the "Christian West" in shaping the religious revival in Poland during the 1960s and 1970s. His book, *Neither German nor Pole: Catholicism and National Indifference in a Central European Borderland, 1890-1922* is forthcoming.

**Peter Black** is Senior Historian at the United States Holocaust Memorial Museum. Before joining the staff at the United States Holocaust Memorial Museum in 1997, Black was the Chief Historian for the Office of Special Investigations (OSI), Criminal Division of the United States Department of Justice. Black is the author of *Ernst Kaltenbrunner: Ideological Soldier of the Third Reich* (1984).

**Richard Blanke** is Professor of History at the University of Maine. He has published several books on aspects of German-Polish relations, including *Prussian Poland in the German Empire* (1981), *Orphans of Versailles: Germans in Western Poland, 1918-1939* (1993), and *"Polish-speaking Germans?"–Language and Nationality among the Masurians* (2001). He is currently investigating the ethnic cleansing of Germans from east-central Europe after World War II.

**Béla Bodó**, independent scholar, has previously taught at the University of Oklahoma and the University of South Florida. His publications include *Tiszazug: A Social History of a Murder Epidemic (2003)* and *The White Terror: History of Paramilitary, State and Mob Violence in Hungary, 1919-1923 (forthcoming)*.

**Martin David** holds a Dr. Phil. in history from the University of Vienna, where he wrote a dissertation on Austro-Czechoslovak relations after World War II. He was a Ministry of Science fellow at the Center for Austrian Culture and Commerce at the University of New Orleans and is now working at the Austrian Ministry of the Interior.

**Elizabeth A. Drummond** is Assistant Professor of History at Loyola Marymount University in Los Angeles. She earned her doctorate from Georgetown University with a dissertation entitled "Protecting Poznania: Germans, Poles and the Conflict over National Identity, 1886 - 1914." She has published articles on nationalist discourse, the role of women and the "Jewish question" in the Polish-German national conflict in the Prussian borderlands.

**Robert Forrest** is Associate Professor and Head of the History Department at McNeese State University. He has published several articles on the history of Transylvania and the Danubian principalities during the eighteenth century and on Romania's Ceauşescu era.

**Eagle Glassheim** teaches Central European History at the University of British Columbia. He is author of *Noble Nationalists: The Transformation of the Bohemian Aristocracy* (2005) and is currently researching a book on the post-war history of the "Black Triangle," an industrial and coal mining region spanning Poland, the Czech Republic and eastern Germany.

**William Glenn Gray** is Assistant Professor of History at Purdue University specializing in transnational German history. He is the author of *Germany's Cold War* (2003). Articles from his current book project, *After Adenauer* have appeared in *Central European History* and *Diplomatic History.*

**Eva Hahn** was a research fellow at the Institute for Czech and Sudeten German History Collegium Carolinum in Munich until 1999 when she began working as an independent historian in Oldenburg. She is the author of numerous studies on the intellectual history of Central Europe in the nineteenth and twentieth centuries, in particular on Czech-German relations.

**Lothar Höbelt** is Associate Professor of Modern History at the University of Vienna and Lecturer at the Theresian Military Academy. Among his numerous books are *1848: Österreich und die deutsche Revolution* (1998), *Von der Vierten Partei zur Dritten Kraft: Die Geschichte des VdU* (1999), and *Jörg Haider and the Politics of Austria* (2003).

**Emilia Hrabovec** is Professor of History at the University in Trnava, Slovakia. Her most recent publications include *Vertreibung und Abschub: Deutsche in Mähren 1945-1947* (1995) and *Der Heilige Stuhl und die Slowakei 1918 -1922 im Kontext internationaler Beziehungen* (2002).

**Charles Ingrao** is Professor of History at Purdue University. His books include *The Hessian Mercenary State* (1987) and *The Habsburg Monarchy, 1618-1815* (2000). He has served as editor of *The Austrian History Yearbook* (1997-2006) and currently directs the Scholars' Initiative and international consortium dedicated to resolving the controversies arising from the Yugoslav conflicts.

**Pieter M. Judson** is Professor of History at Swarthmore College and editor of the *Austrian History Yearbook.* His most recent book, *Guardians of the Nation: Activists on the Language Frontiers of Imperial Austria* (2006), challenges standard accounts of the rise of nationalism in imperial Austria.

**Paul W. Knoll** is Professor of History and former three-time Chair of the Department of History at the University of Southern California. He is the co-translator of *Chronicles and Deeds of the Dukes or Princes of the Poles* by Gallus Anonymus (2002) and the author of *The Rise of the Polish Monarchy: Piast Poland in East Central Europe 1320-1370* (1972).

**Vejas Gabriel Liulevicius** is Associate Professor of History at the University of Tennessee. He is the author of *War Land on the Eastern Front: Culture, National Identity and German Occupation* *in World War I* (2000). He is currently completing his next book, a survey of German views and stereotypes of Eastern Europe from 1800 to 2000.

**Christian Lübke** is Professor and Chair of East European History at the University of Greifswald. Germany. His recent publications include *Fremde im östlichen Europa. Von Gesellschaften ohne Staat zu verstaatlichten Gesellschaften (9.-11. Jahrhundert)* (2001) and *Das östliche Europa (Die Deutschen und das europäische Mittelalter)* (2004).

**Rasa Mazeika** is an independent scholar and the former curator of the Lithuanian Museum and Archives in Toronto. She is the author of numerous articles on medieval Baltic history.

**Geoffrey Megargee** is the author of *Inside Hitler's High Command* (2000) and *War of Annihilation: Combat and Genocide on the Eastern Front, 1941* (2006). He currently holds the position of Applied Research Scholar at the Center for Advanced Holocaust Studies, United States Holocaust Memorial Museum, where he is editing a multi-volume encyclopedia on detention, forced labor, and extermination sites run by Nazi Germany and its European allies and satellites.

**Michael G. Müller** is Professor for East European History at Martin-Luther-University Halle-Wittenberg. He is the author of *Rozbiory Polski. Historia Polski i Europy XVIII wieku* (2005) and co-author of *Eine kleine Geschichte Polens* (2000).

**David Pickus** is a senior lecturer at the Barrett Honors College, Arizona State University. He is the author of *Dying with an Enlightening Fall: Poland in the Eyes of German Interllectuals 1764-1800* (2000). His current research focuses on German-Jewish intellectual refugees in America.

**Jan M. Piskorski** is a professor of Comparative History of Europe at the University of Szczecin (Poland), chair of the Advisory Board of the Humanity in Action Foundation (Warsaw), and member of several research institute boards and editorial boards, including, the editorial board of *German History,* the journal of the German History Society.

**Karl A. Roider** is the Thomas and Lillian Landrum Alumni Professor of History at Louisiana State University. He is the author of *The Reluctant Ally: Austria's Policy in the Austro-Turkish War, 1737-1739* (1972), *Austria's Eastern Question, 1700-1790* (1982), and *Baron Thugut and Austria's Response to the French Revolution* (1987).

**Drago Roksandić** is Professor of Early Modern History at the University of Zagreb, Head of the Center for Comparative Historical and Intercultural Researches, and the Project Director of the Triplex Confinium: Croatian Multiple Borderlands in Euro-Mediterranean Context. He is the author of *Vojna Hrvatska - La Croatie militaire* (1988), *Srbi u hrvatskoj: od 15. stoljeca do nasih dana* (1991), and *Triplex confinium, ili, O granicama i regijama hrvatske povijesti 1500-1800* (2003).

**Dennis Showalter** is a Professor of History at Colorado College and Past President of the Society for Military History. Joint Editor of *War in History,* he specializes in comparative military history. His recent works include *Tannenberg: Clash of Empires* (revised edition, 2004), *Patton and Rommel: Men of War in the Twentieth Century* (2005.); and *Soldiers' Lives through History: The Early Modern World* (with William Astore, 2007).

**Ronald Smelser** is the James Clayton Distinguished Research Professor in the History Department at the University of Utah. His most recent publication is *The Myth of the Eastern Front: The Nazi-Soviet War in American Popular Culture* (with Edward J. Davies II, 2007). He has also been president of the German Studies Association and the American Historical Association's Conference Group on Central European History.

**Arnold Suppan** is the Professor of East European History at the University of Vienna and the Chairman of the Historical Commission at the Austrian Academy of Sciences. He is the author of *Die österreichischen Volksgruppen : Tendenzen ihrer gesellschaftlichen Entwicklung im 20. Jahrhundert* (1983), *Zwischen Adria und Karawanken* (1998) and *Aussenpolitische Dokumente der Republik Österreich, 1918-1938* (1993).

**John C. Swanson** is an Associate Professor of History at Utica College of Syracuse University. His publications include *The Remnants of the Habsburg Monarchy: The Shaping of Modern Austria and Hungary, 1918-1922* (2001) and articles concerning the German minority in Hungary.

**Klaus Zernack** is one of Germany's leading professors of east European history, who was instrumental in deconstructing traditional German "Ostforschung" and replacing it with a less Germanocentric approach. His most important works include *Osteuropa. Eine Einführung in seine Geschichte* (1977) and *Polen und Russland. Zwei Wege in der europäischen Geschichte* (1994). He was also co-editor and co-author of the multi-volume *Handbuch der Geschichte Russlands* (1986–2004).

# Index